raga

Bragança

● Viseu

● Guarda

CENTRAL
PORTUGAL

oimbra

| 0 kilometres | 50 |
| 0 miles | 25 |

Castelo
● Branco

Portalegre ●

● Évora

SOUTHERN
PORTUGAL

● Beja

Faro

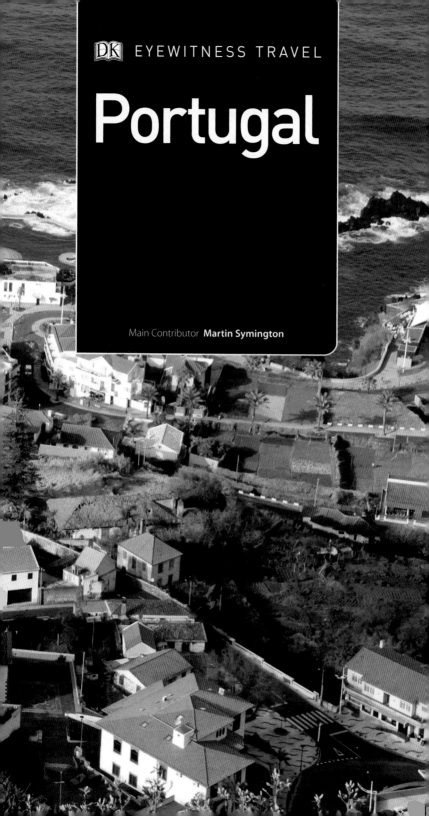

DK EYEWITNESS TRAVEL

Portugal

Main Contributor **Martin Symington**

Penguin
Random
House

Project Editor Ferdie McDonald
Art Editor Vanessa Hamilton
Editors Caroline Ball, Francesca Machiavelli
Designers Anthea Forlee, Carolyn Hewitson,
Nicola Rodway, Dutjapun Williams

Main Contributors Susie Boulton,
Christopher Catling, Clive Gilbert, Marion
Kaplan, Sarah McAlister, Alice Peebles, Carol
Rankin, Norman Renouf, Joe Staines, Robert
Strauss, Martin Symington, Nigel Tisdall,
Tomas Tranæus, Edite Vieira

Photographers Joe Cornish, Paul Harris,
Robert Reichenfeld, Linda Whitwam, Peter
Wilson, Francesca Yorke

Illustrators Richard Draper, Paul Guest,
Stephen Gyapay, Claire Littlejohn, Maltings
Partnership, Isidoro González-Adalid Cabezas/
Acanto Arquitectura y Urbanismo S.L.,Paul
Weston, John Woodcock, Martin Woodward

Printed and bound in China

First published in the UK in 1997 by Dorling
Kindersley Limited
80 Strand, London WC2R 0RL

18 19 20 21 10 9 8 7 6 5 4 3 2 1

Reprinted with revisions
1999, 2000, 2001, 2002, 2003, 2004,
2006, 2008, 2010, 2012, 2014, 2016,
2018

Copyright 1997, 2018 © Dorling Kindersley
Limited, London
A Penguin Random House Company

ISBN 978-0-24130-931-5

MIX
Paper from
responsible sources
FSC
www.fsc.org FSC™ C018179

Portuguese water jug,
Museu Guerra Junqueiro

Lisbon's skyline as seen from across the Tagus, in Almada

◀ **Title page** View of Porto Moniz, with its natural rock pools, Madeira   **Front cover image** A boat sails past the beautiful Ponta de
Piedade near the town of Lagos, the Algarve   **Back cover image** The Alfama district of Lisbon

Contents

A traditional tram transports passengers around Porto

Mosteiro dos Jerónimos, Lisbon

HOW TO USE THIS GUIDE

This guide helps you get the most from a visit to Portugal, providing expert recommendations as well as detailed practical information. The opening chapter, *Introducing Portugal*, maps the country and sets it in its historical and cultural context. Each of the nine regional chapters, plus *Lisbon Area by Area*, describe important sights, using maps, pictures and illustrations. Features cover topics ranging from architecture and festivals to beaches and food. Hotel and restaurant recommendations can be found in *Travellers' Needs*. The *Survival Guide* contains practical information on everything from transport to personal safety.

Lisbon

Lisbon has been divided into five main sightseeing areas. Each of these areas has its own chapter, which opens with a list of the major sights described. All sights are numbered and plotted on an *Area Map*. Information on the sights is easy to locate as the order in which they appear in the chapter follows the numerical order used on the map.

1 Area Map
For easy reference, the sights covered in the chapter are numbered and located on a map. The sights are also marked on the Street Finder maps on pages 132–45.

A locator map shows clearly where the area is in relation to other parts of the city.

All the pages relating to Lisbon have pink thumb tabs.

Sights at a Glance lists the chapter's sights by category: Churches, Museums and Galleries, Historic Buildings, Parks and Gardens.

2 Street-by-Street Map
This gives a bird's-eye view of the heart of each of the sightseeing areas.

A suggested route for a walk is shown in red.

Stars indicate the sights that no visitor should miss.

3 Detailed Information
All the sights in Lisbon are described individually. Addresses and practical information are provided. The key to the symbols used in the information block is shown on the back flap.

THE LISBON COAST

Within an hour's drive northwest of Lisbon you can reach the rocky Atlantic coast, the wooded slopes of Sintra or countryside dotted with villas and royal palaces. South of Lisbon you can enjoy the sandy beaches and fishing towns along the coast or explore the lagoons of the Tagus and Sado river estuaries.

1 Introduction

A general account of the landscape, history and character of each region is given here, explaining both how the area has developed over the centuries and what attractions it has to offer the visitor today.

Portugal Region By Region

Outside Lisbon, the rest of Portugal has been divided into nine regions, each of which has a separate chapter. The most interesting cities, towns and sights to visit are located and numbered on a *Regional Map*.

Exploring the Lisbon Coast

Sights at a Glance

2 Regional Map

This shows the main road network and gives an illustrated overview of the region. All entries are numbered and there are also useful tips on getting around the region.

Each area of Portugal can be identified quickly by its colour coding, shown on the inside front cover.

3 Detailed Information

All the important towns and other places to visit are described individually. They are listed in order, following the numbering given on the Regional Map. Within each entry, there is further detailed information on important buildings and other sights.

Story boxes explore specific subjects further.

For all the top sights, a Visitors' Checklist provides the practical information you need to plan your visit.

Palácio Nacional de Sintra

4 The Top Sights

These are given two or more full pages. Historic buildings are dissected to reveal their interiors; museums and galleries have colour-coded floorplans to help you locate the most interesting exhibits.

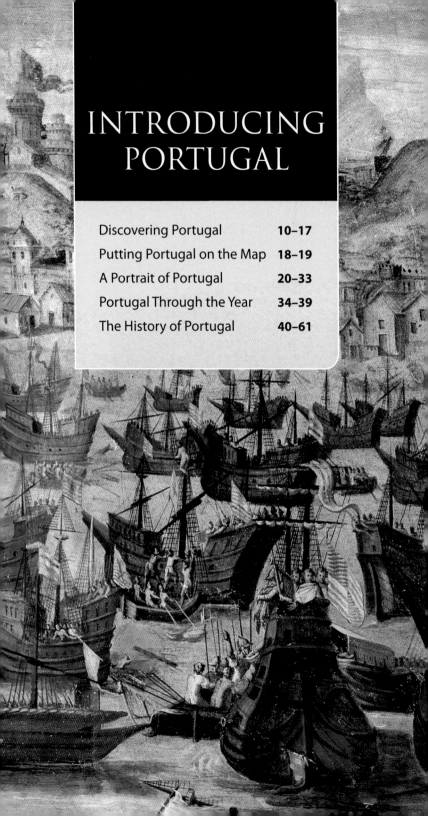

INTRODUCING PORTUGAL

DISCOVERING PORTUGAL

The following itineraries have been designed to take in as many of Portugal's highlights as possible, while keeping long-distance travel to a minimum. First come three two-day tours of, respectively, the vibrant capital Lisbon, the fascinating city of Porto and the beautiful island of Madeira. A one-week itinerary of northern Portugal and a themed one-week tour of the Atlantic coastline are next. These can easily be combined into a two-week tour. Finally, there are two more themed one-week itineraries, designed to showcase the Alentejo's medieval heritage and the resort region of the Algarve, in southern Portugal. Travelled together, they provide a memorable 14-day jaunt. Pick, combine and follow your favourite tours, or simply dip in and out and be inspired.

View of Castro Laboreiro
Famous for a breed of sheepdog, this village lies in the Peneda range, in northern Portugal, close to the border with Spain.

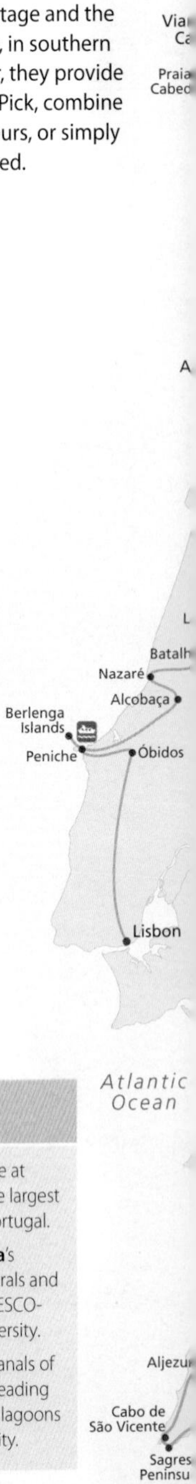

One Week in Northern Portugal

- Get to know Portugal's second-largest city, **Porto**.
- Explore the rugged beauty of the **Parque Nacional de Peneda-Gerês**.
- Visit **Braga** and admire its churches, 18th-century mansions and the sanctuary of **Bom Jesus do Monte**.
- Immerse yourself in **Guimarães**, the birthplace of the nation.
- Stand in front of **Casa de Mateus**, the manor house depicted on the labels of Mateus Rosé.
- Take the **Port Country Tour** through the stunning Douro Valley, a UNESCO World Heritage site.

Key

— Northern Portugal tour
— Atlantic Coastline tour
— Medieval Portugal tour
— Southern Portugal tour

A Tour of the Atlantic Coastline

- Visit **Lisbon**, Portugal's cosmopolitan capital.
- Explore fairy-tale **Óbidos**, a wedding present from a king to his queen.
- Discover the reefs and grottoes around the **Berlenga Islands**.
- Marvel at **Batalha** abbey, a masterpiece of Portuguese Gothic.
- Step back in time at **Conímbriga**, the largest Roman site in Portugal.
- Admire **Coimbra**'s beautiful cathedrals and its hallowed UNESCO-recognized university.
- Walk the briny canals of **Aveiro** before heading for the river and lagoons that fringe the city.

(Map labels: Via... Ca... , Praia... Cabec..., A..., L..., Batalh..., Nazaré, Alcobaça, Berlenga Islands, Peniche, Óbidos, Lisbon, Atlantic Ocean, Aljezu..., Cabo de São Vicente, Sagres Peninsu...)

◀ Detail of a fresco depicting the Spanish conquest of Lisbon in 1580

The unspoilt Pinhão Beach in Lagos, Algarve
Fringed by rocky cliffs, secluded Pinhão Beach is in a small bay near Lagos harbour.

A Tour of Medieval Portugal

- Explore the splendid city of **Évora**, a UNESCO World Heritage site.

- Visit the stunning medieval hamlet of **Marvão**, in the Serra de São Mamede range.

- Walk the lofty battlements surrounding **Elvas**, located near the Spanish border.

- Take a guided tour of the ducal palace at **Vila Viçosa** and then visit the castle.

- Try the ewe's milk cheese in charming **Serpa**.

- Discover Roman and Islamic art in **Mértola** and stroll along the River Guadiana.

- Climb to the top of **Beja**'s landmark castle keep.

0 kilometres 50

0 miles 50

A Week in Southern Portugal

- Combine **Faro**, the Algarve's capital, with the **Parque Natural da Ria Formosa**.

- Visit attractive **Tavira**, then head offshore to sandy **Ilha de Tavira**.

- Discover the lively resort of **Lagos**, with its wide bay and picture-postcard beaches.

- Explore the remote **Sagres** peninsula and the **Cabo de São Vicente** promontory.

- Travel to the **Serra de Monchique** and relax at the Caldas de Monchique spa resort.

- Walk the red sandstone battlements of **Silves**'s Moorish castle.

Two Days in Lisbon

Portugal's cosmopolitan capital melds the past with the present to offer a rich diversity of visitor attractions.

- **Arriving** Lisbon Airport is 7 km (4 miles) northeast of the city. Taxis take about 20 minutes to get to the city centre; the Aerobus slightly longer. The Metro is inexpensive and efficient.

Day 1

Morning Start the day by taking the Metro to Oriente Station for **Parque das Nações** *(p123)*. From here, it's a short walk to the **Oceanário de Lisboa** *(p123)*, home to hundreds of aquatic species. Look out for the bizarre sunfish, the beautiful and delicate sea dragon and, uniquely in Europe, sea otters. Afterwards, enjoy the views from the cable car that takes visitors from one end of the park to the other. Stop to admire the striking Torre Vasco da Gama – Lisbon's tallest building – then break for lunch at any one of the promenade restaurants that overlook the River Tagus.

Afternoon Allow a good hour to absorb the priceless collection of art in the **Museu Calouste Gulbenkian** *(pp118–21)*. Exhibits include works by Rubens, Rembrandt and René Lalique. Don't miss the marble statue of *Diana* by the French sculptor Jean-Antoine Houdon. Afterwards, take a leisurely downhill stroll towards the city centre through **Parque Eduardo VII** *(p117)* and along fashionable **Avenida da Liberdade** *(p86)*. For impressive city views, take a ride on the **Elevador de Santa Justa** *(p88)*, a Neo-Gothic lift that links the Baixa (downtown) area of Lisbon with the elegant Chiado neighbourhood. Take a moment to contemplate the evocative ruins of the nearby 14th-century **Igreja do Carmo** *(p94)*, badly damaged by the great earthquake of 1755. In the evening, soak up the bohemian vibe of **Bairro Alto** *(pp92–3)*.

Day 2

Morning Take the number 15 tram at **Praça da Figueira** *(p87)* or the train at Cais do Sodré and travel to Belém and the architecturally stunning **Mosteiro dos Jerónimos** *(pp108–9)*. Linger in the richly decorated cloisters before exploring the church of Santa Maria, where the tombs of Vasco da Gama and Luís de Camões lie. Next, head for the equally exuberant **Torre de Belém** *(p112)*. The tower's Renaissance loggia affords fine views across the River Tagus. For a truly outstanding panorama of the area, however, head back along the esplanade and climb to the top of the 52-m (170-ft) **Monument to the Discoveries** *(pp110–11)*. Stop for a bite to eat at the **Antiga Confeitaria de Belém** *(p105)*, where they serve *pastéis de Belém* – deliciously rich custard tarts.

Afternoon Head back to the city centre and **Praça do Comércio** *(p89)*, Lisbon's huge landmark square. From here, walk up to the **Castelo de São Jorge** *(pp80–81)* and climb the towers or stroll the shady terrace for spectacular views over the city. Afterwards, amble down to **Largo das Portas do Sol** *(p72)* and pause for refreshments at the outdoor café before venturing into **Alfama** *(pp72–3)*. Lose yourself in the maze of narrow streets and winding alleys typical of this ancient quarter. Return after dark and seek out one of the many traditional *fado* restaurants hidden away in this captivating neighbourhood.

Two Days in Porto

Porto is Portugal's second-largest city. The historical centre is compact and easily explored on foot, and the area is famous all over the world for its port wine.

- **Arriving** Porto Airport is 20 km (12 miles) north of the city. Taxis take around 30 minutes to reach the city centre. The Metro provides an efficient and cheaper alternative, as do shuttle buses.

- **Booking ahead** The Palácio da Bolsa.

Day 1

Morning Start with a visit to the **Sé** *(p246)*. The cathedral's Gothic 14th-century cloisters are particularly striking. The **Casa-Museu Guerra Junqueiro** *(p246)* is located next door. Among the collections of religious art, rare ceramics and antique furniture is a colourful parade of Chinese dogs. Afterwards, explore the traditional shops clustered around Avenida Dom Afonso Henriques before taking time to marvel at the *azulejos* that decorate the interior of **São Bento Station** *(p245)*. Next, climb the steps of the

Shoals of fish at the impressive Oceanário de Lisboa

View of the Castelo de São Jorge and the Baixa neighbourhood in Lisbon

18th-century **Torre dos Clérigos** (p247) for a dizzy perspective of the city and the distant Douro Valley. The nearby **Cordoaria** gardens (p242) are an ideal picnic spot; alternatively, there are plenty of cafés in the area.

Afternoon Join a pre-booked guided tour of the **Palácio da Bolsa** (p246) and be dazzled by the magnificently gilded Arabian Room. Follow up with a visit to the nearby church of **São Francisco** (p247). Don't miss the extraordinary Tree of Jesse or the spooky catacombs. Next, head down to the river and the **Casa do Infante** (p246), the house where Prince Henry the Navigator was supposedly born in 1394. Spend the evening exploring the **Ribeira** (p242), an area with a large number of excellent restaurants.

Day 2
Morning Devote at least an hour musing over the modern art collection in the **Fundação de Serralves Museu de Arte Contemporânea** (p252). For a calm, scenic interlude, head to Foz do Douro, where the river meets the ocean. Explore **Forte de São João Baptista da Foz** (p252), a mighty sea fort dating from the 16th century. Stop for lunch at a beachfront café.

Afternoon Take a tram back to the Ribeira, then stroll across the impressive **Ponte Luís I** (pp248–9), built in 1886 by an assistant of Gustave Eiffel. This landmark bridge links the city with **Vila Nova de Gaia** (p253), the centre of port wine production. Join a pre-booked tour of one of the wine lodges and enjoy tasting some of the many wine varieties on offer. End the day by walking up to the esplanade in front of the **Mosteiro da Serra do Pilar** (p252) for majestic views of the city and the river.

Two Days in Madeira

- **Arriving** Cristiano Ronaldo International Airport is 18 km (11 miles) east of Funchal. Taxis charge a fixed fare into the city centre, and the journey takes around 30 minutes. A shuttle bus service runs throughout the day.

- **Transport** A car is essential for this trip. Taxis can be hired to follow the same route but will be expensive.

- **Booking ahead** The Old Blandy Wine Lodge.

Day 1: Funchal
Morning Start the day early to experience the **Mercado dos Lavradores** (p353) at its liveliest. Afterwards, take the scenic cable car up to the **Jardim Botânico** (p352) and admire the astonishing display of colourful subtropical flora. On the return to Funchal, board the cable car to **Monte** (p354) and complete the descent by toboggan. Walk back to the city centre for lunch at one of the restaurants near Avenida Arriaga.

Afternoon While in the area, visit the **Sé** (p352), the 16th-century cathedral noted for its intricately patterned ceiling and beautifully carved choir stalls. The island's history is embodied in **Quinta das Cruzes** (p352), a mansion-museum built on a spot where João Gonçalves Zarco, the man who claimed Madeira for Portugal in 1418, is said to have lived. Spend some time here before taking in the nearby **Convento de Santa Clara** (p352), where Zarco is buried under the high altar. The convent walls feature some fabulous 17th-century azulejos. End the day with a pre-booked tour of **Blandy's Wine Lodge** (p353), where fine vintage Madeira wines can be tasted. The restaurants and bars in the Zona Velha (Old Quarter) offer plenty of evening entertainment.

Day 2: A Tour of the Island
Morning Head to the other side of the island and the coastal village of **São Vicente** (p362). Join a guided tour of the eerie underground caves and lava channels at the Grutas e Centro do Vulcanismo, then browse the centre's fascinating exhibition. The route east to **Santana** (p357) skirts the northern coast and takes in some stunning seascapes before turning inland to follow a steeper, hairpin course. Look out for the quirky A-framed houses and the family-friendly Parque Temático da Madeira.

Afternoon Incredible mountain scenery provides the backdrop for the drive to the pretty hamlet of **Ribeiro Frio** (p357). Here you can park the car and follow a 30-minute levada walk signposted "Balcões" (Balconies) to reach a viewpoint that affords breathtaking views across the laurel forest. Return to the car park and drive to the summit of **Pico do Arieiro** (p357), Madeira's third-highest mountain. The mesmerizing view takes in a landscape of volcanic peaks and spectacular mountain ridges poking through the clouds and is especially dramatic at sunset.

One Week in Northern Portugal

- **Airports** Arrive and depart from Porto Airport.
- **Transport** A car is essential for this trip.
- **Booking ahead** The Casa de Mateus.

Day 1: Porto
Pick a day from the city itinerary on pages 12–13.

Day 2: Viana do Castelo
Head north to the 13th-century town of **Viana do Castelo** (pp280–81). From Praça da República, the historic quarter is easily explored on foot. Admire the Gothic arches of the restored Paços do Concelho, formerly the town hall, before taking in the imposing Igreja Matriz, the 15th-century parish church. Shop for handicrafts, then pack a picnic and head to the beach of **Praia do Cabedelo** (p281). To reach it, cross the river by ferry or via the road. Round off the day by visiting the basilica of **Monte de Santa Luzia** (p281), 5 km (3 miles) north of the town centre. From here, you can enjoy views of Viana and the coast.

Day 3: Ponte de Lima to Parque Nacional de Peneda-Gerês
Head east out of Viana do Castelo towards **Ponte de Lima** (p278), a picturesque town on the banks of the River Lima. Wander the narrow streets and look out for the medieval forti- fications of the 15th-century Palácio dos Marqueses de Ponte de Lima. Amble across the Roman

The Neo-Classical basilica of Bom Jesus do Monte, near Braga

bridge to the 15th-century church of Santo António and return later to browse the tradi- tional open-air market for souvenirs. Drive on to **Ponte da Barca** (p273) for a restaurant lunch or consider a picnic in the tranquil Jardim dos Poetas (Poets' Garden). Carry on to explore the **Parque Nacional de Peneda- Gerês** (pp276–7), one of Portugal's greatest natural attractions. If you have time, visit the traditional villages of Soajo and Lindoso.

Day 4: Braga
The drive south brings you to **Braga** (pp282–3). Begin by visiting the Sé, the city's cathedral, which is noted for its ornate chapel and Baroque organ. Pause for coffee in the delightful 19th-century salon- style Café Brasileira, then look out for the impressive 14th- century Torre de Menagem as you head for Praça da República, the central square. Devote the afternoon to exploring the sanctuary of **Bom Jesus do Monte** (pp284–5). Climb the enormous Baroque Escadaria (stairway) or ride the vintage

funicular that leads to the church of Bom Jesus. Return to Braga for dinner.

Day 5: Guimarães and Citânia de Briteiros
It's a short drive to **Guimarães** (pp286–7), the birthplace of the nation. Acquaint yourself with the brooding Castelo de Guimarães before walking through the Paço dos Duques, the 15th-century palace built by Dom Afonso, Portugal's first king. Nearby, the former monastery of Nossa Senhora da Oliveira features a beautiful Romanesque cloister and overlooks Largo da Oliveira, where lunch can be enjoyed alfresco. Use the afternoon to visit **Citânia de Briteiros** (p287), an Iron Age settlement of impressive dimensions.

Day 6: Amarante to Alijó
Head south out of Guimarães to explore **Amarante** (pp254–5). A walk along the pretty river- front will lead to the Ponte de São Gonçalo and the 16th-century Igreja de São Gonçalo. Continue east to **Vila Real** (p261) for lunch, before heading to Mateus and the magnificent **Casa de Mateus** (pp260–61). This 18th-century manor house is famously depicted on the labels of Mateus Rosé wine. Book ahead for a tour of the ornate interior and the beautiful landscaped gardens. The route to **Alijó** (p259) takes you deep into port wine country.

Day 7: The Douro Valley
Start early and head for **Sabrosa**, another village on the **Port Country Tour** route (pp258–9), set above the River Pinhão. Continue south through countryside combed with vineyards until you reach **Pinhão**. Stop here and admire the fabulous azulejo panels decorating the railway station. Next, follow the River Douro west past numerous wineries, many of which offer tours and port-wine tasting, to reach **Peso da Régua**. A leisurely drive along the banks of the Douro takes you back to Porto.

The Ponte de São Gonçalo, leading to the Igreja de São Gonçalo in Amarante

For practical information on travelling around Portugal, see pp440–49

The picturesque, flower-filled cobbled streets of Óbidos

A Tour of the Atlantic Coastline

Explore Estremadura and the Beiras regions for their historic cities, impressive monuments and lively coastal resorts.

- **Airports** Arrive at Lisbon Airport and depart from Porto Airport, or vice versa if you reverse the itinerary.

- **Transport** A car is essential for this trip.

Day 1: Lisbon
Pick a day from the city itinerary on page 12.

Day 2: Óbidos to Peniche
Begin your day with a visit to the enchanting medieval hilltown of **Óbidos** (pp180–81). Walk the sentry path along the castle battlements for fine views of the town centre and surrounding countryside. Next, call in at **Peniche** (p180). A visit to the Museu de Peniche includes access to the prison cells inside the 16th-century Fortaleza. Later, pack a picnic lunch and take the ferry to the **Berlenga Islands** (p180). Spend the afternoon on this isolated archipelago, then head back for dinner in one of Peniche's famed seafood restaurants.

Day 3: Alcobaça to Nazaré
First stop is **Alcobaça** (pp184–5), for the hallowed 12th-century Mosteiro de Santa Maria de Alcobaça, Portugal's largest church. Spend time wandering the beautiful and serene Cloister of Dom Dinis, then admire the intricately carved tombs of Pedro I and Inês de Castro. Next, travel to the lively coastal town of **Nazaré** (p186). Take the funicular to Sítio, a tiny village set on a cliff high above the town. Visit the pocket-sized chapel of Ermida da Memória and the 17th-century church of Nossa Senhora da Nazaré. Spend the evening soaking in the nightlife near the beach.

Day 4: Batalha to Leiria
Drive to **Batalha** (pp188–9) and devote a good hour to the magnificent abbey of Santa Maria da Vitória. Marvel at the Royal Cloister and the Unfinished Chapels. Afterwards, linger in the Founder's Chapel, where Henry the Navigator is buried. The next stop is the attractive town of **Leiria** (p187). Work up an appetite by beating a path up to the splendid castle. Admire the views from the loggia before descending back into town. After lunch, take a walk in the Pinhal de Leiria, a pine forest, then relax on the beach. End the day with dinner in Leiria's charming old quarter.

Day 5: Coimbra
Start off early to explore **Conímbriga** (p214), the largest and most extensively excavated Roman site in Portugal, then carry on to **Coimbra** (pp208–11). Begin your visit in the scholarly environs of the **University** (pp212–13), with the richly

View of Coimbra and the River Mondego at sunset

decorated Biblioteca Joanina and the exuberant Capela de São Miguel. Other attractions are the nearby cathedrals: Sé Velha, one of the finest Romanesque buildings in Portugal, and Sé Nova, noted for its elaborate façade. Browse the Museu Nacional Machado de Castro, a highlight of which is the collection of medieval sculpture. Later, walk across the Ponte de Santa Clara and admire the city from the other side of the River Mondego. Spend the evening in the Arco de Almedina area, where there are excellent restaurants.

Day 6: Aveiro
Aveiro (pp206–7) offers a complete change of scenery. Follow the Canal Central, where colourful seaweed-collecting *moliceiros* are moored. The Museu de Aveiro features an absorbing collection of 15th-century Portuguese primitive paintings, among other rare exhibits. Amble over to the old quarter to explore the Canal das Pirâmides and the Canal de São Roque before heading for the busy Praça Humberto Delgado for lunch. In the afternoon, explore the **Ria de Aveiro** (p207) and the picturesque fishing villages of Torreira and São Jacinto. Leave time at the end of the day to tour the Museu da Vista Alegre, where you can purchase fine porcelain.

Day 7: Porto
Pick a day from the city itinerary on pages 12–13.

A Tour of Medieval Portugal

Delve into the Alentejo and discover a region of vast rolling plains peppered with whitewashed villages and hilltop hamlets crowned by ancient castles.

- **Airports** Arrive and depart from Lisbon Airport, or combine this itinerary with the tour of southern Portugal and depart from Faro Airport, or vice versa.
- **Transport** A car is essential for this trip.
- **Booking ahead** Vila Viçosa.

Day 1: Évora

It's a 90-minute drive from Lisbon to **Évora** (pp308–11). Start with a visit to the Sé, the city's 13th-century cathedral. The upper level of the Gothic cloisters offers a view across the rooftops. Around the corner is the Museu de Évora, home to a dazzling Flemish polyptych in 13 panels. Next, walk over to the ruins of the Roman Temple, then admire the 18th-century *azulejos* that decorate the church of São João Evangelista, part of the Convento dos Lóios. End the day at the Capela dos Ossos, the macabre chapel of bones inside the church of São Francisco.

Day 2: Serra de São Mamede

Drive north to the **Serra de São Mamede** (p300) to visit the spa town of **Castelo de Vide** (p301). Amble through the maze-like Judiaria before venturing up to the ruins of the 14th-century castle. Next, drive to idyllic **Marvão** (p300). The castle, hewn out of granite, dates from the late 13th century. Continue to **Portalegre** (pp300–301) and admire the valuable collection of tapestries in the Museu da Tapeçaria de Portalegre.

Day 3: Elvas

Drive south to the frontier town of **Elvas** (pp302–3). Walk along the massive fortifications around the old town, then visit the early 13th-century castle. Afterwards, walk down to the cathedral of Nossa Senhora da Assunção. In the afternoon, meander around the arches of the enormous 17th-century Aqueduto da Amoreira. Round off the day by exploring the nearby Forte de Santa Luzia.

Day 4: Estremoz and Vila Viçosa

A leisurely drive west leads to **Estremoz** (pp306–7). Explore the medieval upper town, dominated by a 13th-century marble keep. For a glimpse of the castle and palace, visit the nearby *pousada* (p393). Double back to **Vila Viçosa** (p305), where you can take a pre-booked guided tour of the splendid Paço Ducal. After lunch, amble up to the medieval castle for fine town and countryside views, then take a leisurely walk through the town's narrow cobbled lanes.

Day 5: Monsaraz to Serpa

Head south to whitewashed **Monsaraz** (p313). Peer inside the Igreja Matriz, then work your way past the rows of ancient cottages to the medieval castle. Clamber to the top of the keep for uninterrupted views in every direction. Continue to the marina at **Amieira** (p313); if there's time, indulge in some kayaking on Lake Alqueva. Next, drive through countryside peppered with cork oak and olive trees to reach **Serpa** (p316). Walk under the monumental Porta de Beja and explore the castle, but be sure to leave time to visit the quirky Watch Museum. In the evening, sample the local ewe's milk cheese during dinner.

Praça do Giraldo, Évora's main square, with its remarkable mosaic paving

Day 6: Mértola

Set high above the River Guadiana, the *vila museu* of **Mértola** (p319) is a melting pot of archaeological treasures. Tour the castle and its grounds, then admire the collection of Portuguese Islamic art in the Núcleo Islâmico or catch up on the Roman period at the Núcleo Romano. For an interesting diversion, head to the old copper mines at Minas de São Domingos.

Day 7: Beja and Viana do Alentejo

Drive to the regional capital of **Beja** (p317). The Museu Regional Rainha Dona Leonor, in a former convent, is worth visiting for its remarkable blend of architectural styles. For an overview of the old town, climb the Torre de Menagem. After lunch, head to **Viana do Alentejo** (p313). Explore the 14th-century castle and the impressive church of Nossa Senhora de Aires before heading back to Lisbon.

The medieval castle of Marvão, perched on a dramatic escarpment in the Alentejo

For practical information on travelling around Portugal, *see pp440–49*

One Week in Southern Portugal

- **Airports** Arrive and depart at Faro Airport.
- **Transport** A car is essential for this trip.

The golden sands and clear waters of Dona Ana beach in Lagos, Algarve

Day 1: Faro and Parque Natural da Ria Formosa

Start the day in the historic centre of **Faro** (pp332–4). The engaging Museu Municipal rewards the visitor with exhibits such as an impressive Roman floor mosaic and a collection of Moorish oil lamps. Admire the Sé, then climb the cathedral's belltower for lovely views across the lagoon. In the afternoon, join a sightseeing cruise around the protected nature reserve of **Parque Natural da Ria Formosa** (p335). The city's nightlife is at its liveliest around the harbour.

Day 2: Tavira

Head east out of Faro on the N125 to **Tavira** (p336). Clamber the ancient walls of the Moorish castle for wonderful town views before walking up to the former convent of Nossa Senhora da Graça, now a pousada. Non-guests can visit the bar, where it is possible to see the Moorish street foundations unearthed during the refurbishment. Look out for the tombs of Dom Paio Peres Correia and his seven knights in the church of Santa Maria do Castelo. Later, catch the ferry from Quatro Águas to the offshore Ilha de Tavira.

Day 3: Lagos

Take the A22 to go directly to **Lagos** (pp326–7). Ponder the astonishing collection of artifacts and curios in the Museu Municipal Dr José Formosinho. Admission includes a visit to the 18th-century church of Santo António, with a fabulous gilded interior. Next, take to the water for a sightseeing tour of the spectacular sea caves along the coast, or relax on pretty Dona Ana beach. End the day at Ponta da Piedade. Lagos nightlife is some of the best in the region, particularly in the summer.

Day 4: The Sagres Peninsula

Follow the N125 all the way to **Sagres** (p326). Visit the fort and stand over the mysterious pebble wind compass, the Rosa dos Ventos, reputedly used by Henry the Navigator. The windblown **Cabo de São Vicente** (p325) is equally evocative. Roam the isolated headland and gaze across the Atlantic Ocean before admiring the landmark lighthouse. Back in Sagres, take a dip in the warm, shallow waters off Martinhal beach. The restaurants lining the sheltered bay offer mouthwatering seafood menus.

Day 5: Serra de Monchique

Travel along the west coast as far as **Aljezur** (p324). The ruins of the village's Moorish castle are worth a look before turning inland towards the dramatic **Serra de Monchique** (p324).

The clock tower of the church of Santa Maria do Castelo, in Tavira

Pause at the spa village of **Caldas de Monchique** (p325), then continue to the rural market town of **Monchique** (p324). Later, carry on up to Fóia, the highest point of the range, for a jaw-dropping panorama of the entire western Algarve.

Day 6: Portimão and Silves

Head south to **Portimão** (p328) and visit the award-winning Museu de Portimão, set in a former fish-canning factory. Afterwards, drive over to the nearby resort of Praia da Rocha, with its scenic beach. Mingle with sightseers at the Fortaleza de Santa Catarina, which overlooks the marina and the mouth of the River Arade. Travel inland to **Silves** (pp328–9) and roam the Moorish castle, one of the region's greatest monuments. Catch up on the town's history in the engaging Museu Arqueológico, where a large 12th-century Arab well-cistern is the star exhibit.

Day 7: Rural Algarve

The road to **Alte** (p329) meanders through an idyllic, pastoral landscape. One of the prettiest villages in the region, Alte warrants a pit stop. Continue to **Loulé** (pp330–31) and visit the bustling market for jams, cheeses and other home-made goodies. Admission to the castle includes access to the ethnographic museum and the battlements. Leave time to visit **Estoi** (p331) to investigate Milreu, the ruins of a 3rd-century Roman villa. Faro is 15 minutes away.

Putting Portugal on the Map

Situated in the extreme southwest corner of Europe, Portugal occupies roughly one-sixth of the Iberian Peninsula with a population of just over 10 million. To the north and east, a border measuring approximately 1,300 km (800 miles) separates Portugal from its only neighbouring country, Spain, and to the south and west, 830 km (500 miles) of coastline meets the Atlantic Ocean. The Atlantic archipelagos of Madeira and the Azores are included in Portugal's territory.

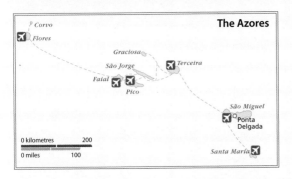

The Azores

Madeira

See inset map right

Atlantic Ocean

Key

- ═══ Motorway
- ═══ Major road
- ⋯⋯ Minor road
- —— Main railway line
- ▬▬ International boundary
- – – Ferry route

For keys to symbols *see back flap*

Sarria

Ponferrada

SPAIN

Bragança

Chaves

N122

Miranda
do Douro

Sendim

Duero

Torre de
Moncorvo

Freixo de Espada
à Cinta

Penedono

N102

Pinhel

Trancoso

A25

Ciudad Rodrigo

Guarda

Sabugal

Sortelha

Penamacor

GAL

Castelo
Branco

Plasencia

Portalegre

Campo Maior

Mérida

Badajoz

Zafra

Moura

Aracena

N433

Huelva

Almonte

Europe

NORWAY

ESTONIA

LATVIA

SWEDEN

LITHUANIA

DENMARK

UNITED
KINGDOM

REPUBLIC
OF
IRELAND

NETHERLANDS

BELGIUM

LUXEMBOURG

POLAND

GERMANY

CZECH
REPUBLIC

SLOVAKIA

AUSTRIA

HUNGARY

SLOVENIA

SWITZERLAND

FRANCE

ITALY

PORTUGAL

SPAIN

Lisbon

Azores

TUNISIA

Madeira

MOROCCO

ALGERIA

LIBYA

Ávila

Madrid

SPAIN

Greater Lisbon

Odivelas

Sacavém

Queluz

Amadora

LISBON

Belém

Cacilhas

Montijo

Trafaria

Almada

Barreiro

Moita

Costa da
Caparica

Seixal

Coina

0 kilometres   10

0 miles   5

Córdoba

Sevilla

Estepa

Genil

Granada

Málaga

Motril

Jerez de
la Frontera

A PORTRAIT OF PORTUGAL

Most visitors to Portugal head for the sandy coves, rocky coastline and manicured golf links of the Algarve. But beyond the south coast resorts lies the least explored corner of Western Europe: a country of rugged landscapes, sophisticated cities, rural backwaters and sharply contrasting traditions.

Portugal appears to have no obvious geographical claim to nationhood, yet this western extremity of the Iberian Peninsula has existed within borders virtually unchanged for nearly 800 years. Its ten million people speak their own language, follow their own unique cultural traditions, and have a centuries-old history of proud independence from Spain, although their Iberian neighbour is Portugal's biggest trading parrtner.

For a small country, the regions of Portugal are immensely varied. The rural Minho and Trás-os-Montes in the north are the most traditional. Over the last few decades many inhabitants of these neglected regions have been forced to emigrate in search of work.

The south of the country could not be more different. The Algarve, blessed with beautiful sandy beaches and a wonderful, warm Mediterranean climate all year round, has been transformed into a holiday playground for North Europeans.

Two great rivers, the Tagus (or Tejo) and the Douro, rise in Spain and then flow westwards across Portugal to the Atlantic Ocean. From the wild upper reaches of the Douro valley, comes Portugal's most famous product – port wine, from steeply terraced vineyards hewn out of the mountainsides. The Tagus, by contrast, is wide and languid, often spilling out over the flat, fertile, Ribatejo flood plain where fine horsesand fighting bulls graze.

At the mouths of the Tagus and Douro stand Portugal's two major cities, Lisbon and Porto respectively. Lisbon, the capital, is a cosmopolitan metropolis with a rich cultural life and many national museums and art galleries, but this is not the be all and end all.

The beautiful coast of Albufeira, a major tourist attraction in the Algarve

◀ Detail of *azulejo* tiles on the wall of the Igreja do Carmo, Porto

The breathtaking Monte Palace Tropical Garden in Funchal, on Madeira

Porto is a serious rival to Lisbon in history, food and culture, and visitors can access the Douro Valley by river cruise boat from Porto. Most of the country's centres of population, however, are smaller: from the fishing communities on the Atlantic coast to the tiny medieval villages in the vast sun-baked plains of the Alentejo and the mountainous interior of the Beiras. Providing a natural link between the cool, green pastures of the north and the hot, dry expanses of the south, the picturesque Beiras region also encompasses the enchanting city of Coimbra, home to one of the oldest universities in the world.

Far out in the Atlantic Ocean lie two remote archipelagos that are self-governing regions of the Portuguese state – Madeira and the Azores. Warm and luxuriant Madeira is off the coast of Morocco, with its sister island Porto Santo boasting a long, sandy beach. Then there are the nine rainy, green, volcano tips that make up the Azores, about one third of the way across the Atlantic between Lisbon and New York. Here visitors can climb Portugal's highest peak and hike along Europe's most westerly coast.

Politics and Economics

In the final quarter of the 20th century, a new era of Portuguese history began. From the late 1920s, under the long dictatorship of António Salazar, the country was a virtual recluse in the world community. The principal concern of foreign policy was the ultimately futile defence of Portugal's African and Asian colonies. Domestic industry and commerce were dominated by a few wealthy families, in an economic framework of extreme fiscal tightness.

The Carnation Revolution of 1974 brought this era to an end. At first the re-establishment of democracy was a painful process, but since the 1980s Portugal has assumed an increasingly

Colourful buildings in Porto, the second-largest city in Portugal

confident Western European demeanour. Entry into the European Community in 1986 was welcomed at all levels of society, and led to an explosion of new construction, the like of which Portugal had never seen. Traditional exports, such as cork, resin, textiles, tinned sardines and wine, have been joined by new, heavier industries such as vehicle construction and cement manufacturing.

Luxury yachts in the harbour at Vilamoura in the Algarve

Grants and loans from the EU have funded the building of roads, bridges and hospitals, and brought significant improvements in agriculture. Porto was the European Capital of Culture in 2001 and in January 2002 the euro became Portugal's currency. Like other European countries, Portugal experienced an economic slump around 2008 that led to austerity, which in turn prompted strikes and social discontent.

The Portuguese Way of Life

A mild-mannered and easy-going people, the Portuguese have an innate sense of politeness, a quality they also respect in others. They tend to use formal modes of address, calling new acquaintances by their Christian names, prefixed by Senhor, Senhora or Dona. In spite of this, they are gregarious folk, often to be seen eating, drinking and making merry in large groups – at a *festa*, or in a restaurant celebrating a birthday or a first communion. Except for the older sectors of the population, most Portuguese have good knowledge of English and will be eager to speak it. There is a special weakness for children, who are cherished, indulged and welcomed everywhere. Visitors who bring their youngsters with them will discover an immediate point of contact with their hosts. Nevertheless, behind the smiles and the good humour, there is a deep-rooted aspect of the national psyche which the Portuguese themselves call *saudade*, a sort of ethereal, aching melancholy that seems to yearn for something lost or unattainable.

Rossio Square, in downtown Lisbon, is a popular place to relax and socialize

An icon of Our Lady of Fátima is carried to the sanctuary of Fátima as pilgrims observe in silence

gradually changing, especially in the cities, it is quite common for three generations to live under one roof. One thing that has changed dramatically is family size. A generation ago, families of ten or more children were commonplace – especially in remote, rural areas. Nowadays, one or two children constitute an average-sized family, often looked after by a grandmother while both parents go out to work.

Visitors to Portugal should not interpret lack of punctuality as a personal slight. However, in the major cities this is certainly a dated custom. An hour for lunch, 1–2pm usually, and then back to work. Some Portuguese tend to discard their native courtesy completely when they are behind the wheel of a car, although fatalities caused by reckless driving have decreased in recent years.

The family is the bosom of Portuguese daily life. Although old customs are

Catholicism is at the heart of Portuguese life, especially in the north, where you will see a crucifix

Tiled housefront in Alcochete, a small town on the Tagus estuary

or the image of a saint watching over most homes, cafés and barbers' shops. Weddings and first communion services are deeply religious occasions. Although church attendance is in decline, particularly in cities, national devotion to Our Lady of Fátima remains steadfast, as does delight in festivals *(romarias)* honouring local saints, another tradition that is strongest in the north.

Language and Culture

There are few faux pas more injurious to national esteem, than to suggest that Portuguese is a mere dialect of Spanish. Great pride is taken in the language and literature. *Os Lusíadas*, the national epic by 16th-century poet Camões, is studied reverentially, while many Portuguese also delight in the

Town gate of Óbidos with shrine of Nossa Senhora da Piedade, lined with 18th-century tiles

Vibrant and surreal street on a tiled wall in Alfama, Lisbon

detached, ironic portrait of themselves in the 19th-century novels of Eça de Queirós. Pride too, is taken in *fado*, the native musical tradition which expresses the notion of *saudade*. In rural areas, especially the Minho, there is still an enthusiastic following for folk dancing.

There are several excellent newspapers, but the country's best-selling daily is *A Bola*, which is devoted exclusively to sport, football being a national obsession. Bullfighting too has its adherents, although with nothing like the passion found in Spain.

The Portuguese have long been avid watchers of television and produce many home-grown soap operas, films and documentaries.

The country has become more forward-looking, but most aspects of heritage hark back to the Discoveries. The best-loved monuments are those built in the one uniquely Portuguese style of architecture, the Manueline, which dates from the early 16th century. Many *azulejo* tile paintings, another cherished tradition, also glory in Portugal's great maritime past.

When the Portuguese joined the European Community in 1986, Commission President Jacques Delors solemnly warned them that they should think of themselves as "Portuguese first, and European second". Typically, the Portuguese were too polite to laugh out loud. How could anyone have imagined that this little country was in danger of suddenly throwing overboard centuries of rich culture and history nurtured in staunch independence?

Tourists exploring a market in Sintra, a popular destination in Portugal

Vernacular Architecture

Traditionally, Portugal's rural architecture varied with climatic conditions and locally available building materials. Although lightweight bricks are now ubiquitous, many older houses still stand. There are the thick-walled granite houses of the north designed to keep out the cold and rain. The Beiras' milder climate means their houses are made of brick or limestone. In the Alentejo and the Ribatejo, the clay houses are long and low, to suit hot summers and chilly winters. The Algarve's gentler Mediterranean climate has led to houses of clay or stone.

Yellow-trimmed houses below walls of Óbidos *(see pp180–81)*

Chimneys are small or non-existent. Instead, smoke escapes through openings in the roof.

Roofs are constructed of slate or schist tiles, or occasionally thatch.

Village houses in the Minho *(see p269)* and Trás-os-Montes regions *(see p239)* are two-storeyed and usually built with the staircase on the outside. The veranda is used for extra living space.

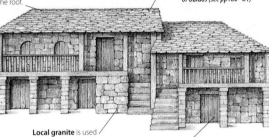

Local granite is used for rustic stonework.

The ground floor is used to keep animals and for storage.

Fishermen's houses foun in the Costa Nova region south of Aveiro *(see p207)* painted in brightly coloure stripes. Forests planted to prevent the sand dunes fr encroaching on the land provide the raw materia

Raised platforms guard against flooding.

Modern examples use tiles or painted façades to continue the tradition of striped houses.

Different coloured stripes painted onto the wood allowed the fishermen to identify their houses through the region's frequent mists.

Rooftops of Castelo de Vide in the Alentejo *(see p301)*

Tiled Roofs

Throughout Portugal, red clay roof tiles give towns and villages a memor-able skyline. The most traditional and widely used type of roof tile is the *telha de canudo* or tubular tile. Originating

Telhados de quatro águas, the distinctive tiled roofs found in Tavira, the Algarve *(see p336)*

from the Moors, these half-cylindrical tiles are placed in two layers: the first is placed with the concave side facing up and the second with the concave side facing down, covering the joints of the first.

Telhas de canudo are used to cover the roof.

Verandas are glassed in and so can be used all year round.

Limestone used for the walls is usually stuccoed and whitewashed.

...ouses in the Beiras *(see pp200–27)* ...ten have verandas, usually on the ...st floor. These are built to face the sun, ...the same time affording protection ...om the cold north winds.

Portugal's Windmills

Windmills are thought to have existed in Portugal since the 11th century. Many pristine examples still dot the hillsides, particularly in coastal regions.

Most windmills have a cylindrical brick or stone base. The upper section revolves to catch the wind in its canvas sails. Estremadura *(see pp176–99)* has good examples.

...atched houses in the Sado ...tuary *(see p175)* are now ...re. Surviving examples ...ve walls that consist ...a wooden ...me supporting ...oven sections ...ade of straw and ...ed. The simple ...uses use only ...cal materials.

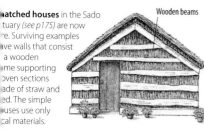

Wooden beams

Azorean windmills, such as this example on Faial *(see p376)*, are fairly similar to the Portuguese model, but show the clear influence of early Dutch and Flemish settlers in their sail design.

Some roof tiles can be removed in summer for more light.

Wooden windows have a painted surround.

Huge chimneys provide spaces for smoking hams and sausages.

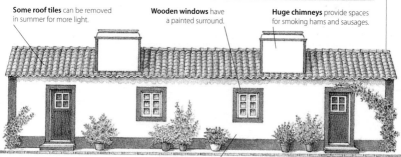

Colour-trimmed houses of the Alentejo and Ribatejo regions are mainly constructed of clay. Long and oblong in shape, they have few openings, to ensure that the heat is trapped in winter and kept out in summer.

Whitewashing protects the walls, deflects the hot summer sun and acts as a deterrent for pests and vermin. Many householders consider it a point of honour ro renew their whitewash each year.

Chimneys of the Algarve

These are an important decorative feature of houses in the Algarve *(see pp320–37)*. The Moorish influence can be seen in their cylindrical or prismatic shapes and the geometric designs perforating the clay. The chimneys are whitewashed and many have details picked out in colour to accentuate their ornamentation.

Manueline Architecture

The style of architecture that flourished in the reign of Manuel I (*see pp50–53*) and continued after his death is essentially a Portuguese variant of Late Gothic. It is typified by maritime motifs inspired by Portugal's Age of Discovery, and by elaborate "all-over" decoration. The artists behind it include João de Castilho and Diogo Boitac, renowned for the cloister of the Mosteiro dos Jerónimos (*see pp108–9*), and Francisco and Diogo de Arruda, designers of the Torre de Belém (*see p112*).

Twisted Manueline pillory in Chaves (*see pp262–3*)

The portal of the church of Conceição Velha in Lisbon (*see p89*) was commissioned by Manuel in the early 16th century. The king himself appears in the carved relief in the tympanum.

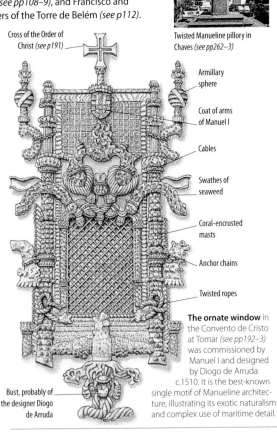

Cross of the Order of Christ (*see p191*)

Armillary sphere

Coat of arms of Manuel I

Cables

Swathes of seaweed

Coral-encrusted masts

Anchor chains

Twisted ropes

Bust, probably of the designer Diogo de Arruda

The ornate window in the Convento de Cristo at Tomar (*see pp192–3*) was commissioned by Manuel I and designed by Diogo de Arruda c.1510. It is the best-known single motif of Manueline architecture, illustrating its exotic naturalism and complex use of maritime detail.

Gil Vicente created the Belém Monstrance (1506) from the first gold brought back from India. Made for Santa Maria de Belém (*see p109*), its superstructure echoes the south portal.

Decorative Details

The most important motifs in Manueline architecture are the armillary sphere, the Cross of the Order of Christ and twisted rope. Naturalistic and fantastic forms are often used, as well as flatter, finely crafted designs similar to those found on contemporary Spanish silverware. Later Manueline schemes sometimes incorporate Italian Renaissance ornamentation.

The armillary sphere wa a navigational device th became the emblem o Manuel I himself.

The Cross of the Order of Christ was the emblem of a military order that helped to finance early voyages. It also emblazoned sails and flags.

Rebuilding the Manueline Portal of Madre de Deus

The Manueline portal of the church of Madre de Deus in Lisbon *(see p125)* was destroyed in the 1755 earthquake, but it was not until 1872 that João Maria Nepomuceno was commissioned to rebuild it. For accuracy, he referred to an early 16th-century painting by an unknown artist, *The Arrival of the Relics of Santa Auta at the Church of Madre de Deus*, now in the Museu Nacional de Arte Antiga *(see pp98–101)*. The splendid procession in the picture is shown heading towards the Manueline portal of the church, which is clearly depicted. Like others of that period, it stands proud of the building and dominates the façade. The Manueline style favoured rounded rather than pointed arches and this one has an interesting trefoil shape.

Portal of Madre de Deus church today

The painting of *The Arrival of the Relics* showing the original 16th-century portal

Curving branches and crinkled exotic foliage recall Indian sculptural motifs.

In the Royal Cloister of Batalha *(see pp188–9)*, early 15th-century pointed Gothic arches incorporate exquisite Manueline screens on colonnettes, probably by Diogo Boitac, whose two designs alternate.

Soft limestone allowed complex patterns to be carved in the tracery.

Cross of the Order of Christ

Armillary sphere

The colonnettes have all-over ornamentation, with repeated patterns of pearls, shells and coil motifs.

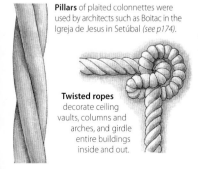

Pillars of plaited colonnettes were used by architects such as Boitac in the Igreja de Jesus in Setúbal *(see p174)*.

Twisted ropes decorate ceiling vaults, columns and arches, and girdle entire buildings inside and out.

Bussaco Palace, today a luxury hotel *(see p216)*, was originally built as a royal hunting lodge about the end of the 19th century. An extraordinary building, the palace incorporates every conceivable element of Manueline architecture and decoration, illustrating the persistence of the style in Portuguese design, which continues to this day.

Azulejos – Painted Ceramic Tiles

The idea of covering walls, floors and even ceilings with tiles was introduced to Spain and Portugal by the Moors. From the 16th century onwards, Portugal started producing its own decorative tiles. By the 18th century, no other European country was producing as many tiles, for such a variety of purposes and in so many different designs; the blue and white tiles of the Baroque era are considered by many to be the finest. *Azulejos* became and remain an important addition to the interior and exterior of Portuguese buildings.

1716 Detail from *Panel of Christ Teaching in the Temple*
Around 1690 blue and white story-telling tiles began to be produced. These figures are from a typical scheme by António de Oliveira Bernardes (c.1660–1732), the greatest master of the genre. The central panels are surrounded by a complex architectural border (*Igreja da Misericórdia, Évora, see p309*).

c.1520 Frieze of Spanish-made Tiles
These Moorish-style tiles were produced by compartmental techniques using raised and depressed areas to prevent the tin-glaze colours from running (*Palácio Nacional de Sintra, see pp164–5*).

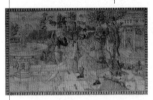

c.1680 Hunting Cat
Naturalistic panels of this period were often naively drawn, but used a wide range of colours (*Museu Nacional do Azulejo, see pp124–5*).

1500	1600	1700
Renaissance	Mannerist	Baroque
1500	1600	1700

c.1650 Carpet Tiles
So-called because they imitated the patterns of Moorish rugs, these were produced mainly in blue, yellow and white. They often covered whole walls (*Museu Nacional do Azulejo, see pp124–5*).

1565 Susannah and the Elders
The mid-16th century saw the introduction of the majolica technique. This allowed artists to paint directly onto prepared flat tiles using several colours, as these did not run in the firing process. This panel of a biblical episode is one of the earliest produced in Portugal. The decorative details are typical of the Renaissance (*Quinta da Bacalhoa, see p173*).

1736 Capela de São Filipe
The small chapel inside Setúbal's castle is a fine example of a complete decorative scheme using blue and white tiles. The panels, illustrating the life of St Philip, are signed by Policarpo de Oliveira Bernardes, son of the great António (*Castelo de São Filipe, see p174*).

c.1670 Tiled Altar Frontal
The exuberant scheme incorporates Hindu motifs and other exotic themes inspired by the printed calicoes and chintzes brought back from India (*Museu Nacional do Azulejo, see pp124–5*).

1865 Viúva Lamego Tile Factory, Lisbon
For the first half of the 19th century, relatively few tiles were produced. The fashion then returned for covering whole surfaces with tiles, and simple stylized designs were used to decorate shop fronts and residential areas. This naive, chinoiserie figure is part of a scheme dating from 1865 that covers the entire façade of the factory.

c.1970 Tile Pattern
The original design for this strikingly modern scheme by architect Raúl Lino dates from about 1910. Many of Portugal's leading modern artists have worked with *azulejos* (*Museu Nacional do Azulejo, see pp124–5*).

c.1770–84 Corredor das Mangas
The Rococo period saw the reintroduction of polychromatic *azulejos*. This antechamber in the royal palace at Queluz has tiled panels showing hunting scenes, the seasons and the continents (*Palácio de Queluz, see pp170–71*).

1927 *Battle of Ourique*
The early years of the 20th century saw a revival of large-scale historical scenes in traditional blue and white. This panel is by Jorge Colaço (*Carlos Lopes Pavilion, Parque Eduardo VII, Lisbon, see p117*).

1800	1900	
Neo-Classical	Art Nouveau	Modern
1800	1900	

c.1800 *The Story of António Joaquim Carneiro, Hatmaker*
Delicate Neo-Classical ornamentation surrounds the blue and white central subject matter in this charming tale of a shepherd boy who makes his fortune as a hatmaker in the big city. Sophisticated designs of this kind disappeared during the upheavals of the Peninsular War (*see p58*) at the beginning of the 19th century (*Museu Nacional do Azulejo, see pp124–5*).

c.1770 *Gatekeeper*
"Cut out" figures like this musketeer are an amusing feature of tile schemes in many palaces and mansions from the 18th century onwards. They stand guard at the entrance, on landings or on staircases (*Museu Nacional do Azulejo, see pp124–5*).

Tiles in Domestic Architecture

Art Nouveau friezes and decorations in deep colours enliven the façade of this early 20th-century house in Aveiro. To this day, tiles cover the façades of houses. They are relatively cheap to produce, long-lasting and need little maintenance. Tiled houses brighten up many Portuguese towns and villages. The town of Ovar (*see pp204–5*) is particularly striking.

Vila Africana, Aveiro (*see p206*)

The Wines of Portugal

Although still overshadowed by the excellence and fame of port, Portuguese table wine deserves to be taken seriously. After years of investment in the industry, many of the reds, such as the full-bodied wines from the Douro (made with some of the same grapes as port), have established an attractive style all of their own. Great whites are fewer, but most regions have some. And of course there is *vinho verde*, the usually white, light, slightly carbonated wine from the north.

Sparkling rosés, such as Mateus and Lancers, have been Portugal's great export success. But the country also has many other excellent wines.

Wine Regions

Many of Portugal's wine regions maintain their individual style by specializing in particular Portuguese grape varieties. The introduction of modern wine-making techniques has improved overall quality, and as yet the increasing use of imported grape varieties seems no threat to Portuguese individuality.

Viana do Castelo · Bragança · Braga · Chaves · Porto · Vila Real · Penedono · Aveiro · Viseu · Guarda · Figueira da Foz · Coimbra · Castelo Branco · Leiria · Peniche · Santarém · Portalegre · Lisbon (Lisboa) · Évora · Setúbal · Moura · Sines · Vila Nova de Milfontes · Castro Verde · Aljezur · Almodôvar · Alte · Portimão · Faro

0 km 50
0 miles 50

Key

- Vinhos Verdes
- Douro
- Dão
- Bairrada
- Lisboa
- Tejo
- Setúbal
- Alentejo
- Algarve

Vinho verde vineyards in the village of Lapela, near Monção in the Minho

Cellar of the Bussaco Palace Hotel, *(see p217)*, famous for its red wine

How to Read a Wine Label

Tinto is red, *branco* is white, *seco* is dry and *doce* is sweet. Other essential information is the name of the producer, the region and the year. Wines made to at least 80 per cent from a single grape variety may give the name of that grape on the label. *Denominação de Origem Controlada* (DOC) indicates that the wine has been made according to the strictest regulations of a given region, but, as elsewhere, this need not mean higher quality than the nominally simpler *Vinho Regional* appellation. The back label often describes grape varieties and wine-making techniques used.

This wine is from the Douro and is made according to DOC regulations for the region.

The name of this wine means "banks of the River Tua", further specifying its geographical origin.

Reserva means that the wine has been aged, probably in oak casks. It also implies that the wine is of higher quality than non-reserva wine from the same producer.

The Sociedade Agricola e Comercial dos Vinhos Vale da Corça, Lda, produced and bottled this wine.

DOURO
ENCOSTAS DO TUA
Reserva de 2000

Minho produces *vinho verde*, a "green wine" that can be either red or white, but the fizzy, dry reds are generally consumed locally. Typical white *vinho verde* is bone dry, slightly fizzy, low in alcohol and high in acidity. A weightier style of white *vinho verde* is made from the Alvarinho grape, near the Spanish border. Among the best brands are Soalheiro and Palácio da Brejoeira.

Bairrada is a region where the small and thick-skinned Baga grape dominates. It makes big, tannic wines, sometimes with smoky or pine-needle overtones and, like the older Dão wines, they need time to soften. Modern winemaking and occasional disregard for regional regulations have meant more approachable reds (often classified as Vinho Regional das Beiras) and crisper whites. Quality producers include Luís Pato and Caves Aliança.

Setúbal, south of Lisbon, is best known for its sweet, fortified Muscat wine, Moscatel de Setúbal. It also produces excellent, mostly red, table wine. Two big quality producers dominate: José Maria da Fonseca *(see p173)* and J P Vinhos. The co-operative at Santo Isidro de Pegões makes good-value wines, while interesting smaller producers include Freitas, Venâncio Costa Lima, Hero do Castanheiro and Ermelinda.

The Douro region is best known as the source of port wine, but in most years about half of the wine produced is fermented dry to make table wine, and these wines are now at the forefront of Portuguese wine-making. The pioneer, Barca Velha, was launched in 1952 and is both highly regarded and among the most expensive. Other producers include Calheiros Cruz, Domingos Alves de Sousa, Quinta do Crasto, Niepoort and Ramos-Pinto.

Estremadura is Portugal's westernmost wine area and has only recently emerged as a region in its own right. Several producers now make modern *Vinho Regional* wines with character; look for wines by DFJ, Casa Santos Lima, Quinta de Pancas and Quinta do Monte d'Oiro. The most interesting DOC is Alenquer. Bucelas, to the south of the region, produces characterful white wines.

Alentejo produced wine is world-class and has won numerous awards. Long dismissed by experts as a region of easy-drinking house reds for restaurants, this area now produces some of Portugal's most serious red wines and a surprising number of excellent whites. Among the top producers are Herdade do Esporão, Herdade dos Coelheiros, Cortes de Cima and João Portugal Ramos.

The Dão region now offers some of Portugal's best wines. Leading the pack are smaller producers, such as Quinta dos Roques, Quinta da Pellada and Quinta de Cabriz, and the large Sogrape company. They are known for fruity reds; fresh, dry whites; and deeper, richer reds that retain their fruit with age – a far cry from the heavy, hard-edged, and often oxidized wines of the past.

Ribatejo is the fertile valley of the Tagus to the north and east of Lisbon. After Estremadura, it is Portugal's biggest wine region measured by volume, but its potential for quality wines has only just begun to be realized. As in Estremadura, *Vinho Regional* bottlings are frequently better than DOC ones. Producers to look for include Quinta da Alorna, Casa Branco and Fiuza & Bright.

Algarve is Portugal's southernmost wine region. Portimão, Lagos and Lagoa in the west and Tavira in the east are the four main wine-producing areas here, notable for their fruity reds (Touriga Nacional, Cabernet Sauvignon and Negra Mole) and dry, crisp whites (Arinto, Verdelho and Castelão). Top producers include Quinta do Barranco Longo, Quinta da Penina, Quinta do Francês, Quinta dos Vales and Quinta do Morgado da Torre.

PORTUGAL THROUGH THE YEAR

While July and August are the most popular months for visiting, spring and autumn can be more rewarding if you want to tour and experience local culture. Free of excessive heat and crowds, the country is more relaxed. There is deep-rooted respect throughout the nation for ancient traditions, which are most often reflected in religious festivals. *Festas* are held throughout the year, most frequently celebrating saints' days, but also marking the end of the harvest, or gastronomic and even sporting events. *Festas* call for prayers, processions, fireworks, eating and drinking, traditional folk dances and general merrymaking.

Spring

From the Algarve to Trás-os-Montes, the country erupts in wild flowers as warmer days set in. This is the time to see the countryside at its most beautiful, although rain can be expected until the end of May.

Easter is a time of great religious celebration, with Holy Week processions taking place all over the country.

March
International Chocolate Festival *(Mar/Apr)*, Óbidos. This event attracts people from all over the world. The date changes from year to year.
Madeira Islands Golf Open *(Mar)*. Venue and date change each year.

Costume at the Funchal Flower Festival

April
Holy Week *(week before Easter)*, Braga. Events in the country's religious capital are particularly traditional. Torchlit processions are led by church authorities.

Easter Sunday is also the beginning of the bullfighting season throughout Portugal.

Fátima on 13 May, when 100,000 pilgrims gather every year

Mãe Soberana *(second Sun after Easter)*, Loulé, Algarve. Pilgrimage to Nossa Senhora da Piedade *(see p331)*.
FIAPE *(end Apr/early May)*, Estremoz. An international agricultural, cattle and handicrafts fair.
Algarve Nature Week *(5–14 May)*, Algarve. Several outdoor activities are held to promote nature, including walks, birdwatching and dolphin- and whale-watching trips.

May
Flower Festival *(late Apr/ early May)*, Funchal, Madeira. Shops and houses are decorated with flowers. Ends with a parade of floats.
Festas das Cruzes *(early May)*, Barcelos. The Festival of the Crosses celebrates the day the shape of a cross appeared in the earth in 1504.
Pilgrimage to Fátima *(12–13 May)*. Huge crowds make the pilgrimage to the place where the Virgin appeared to three children in 1917 *(see p190)*.

Queima das Fitas *(mid-May)*, Coimbra. Lively celebrations mark the end of the university's academic year *(see p213)*.
Festa do Senhor Santo Cristo dos Milagres *(fifth Sun after Easter)*, Ponta Delgada, São Miguel, Azores. The largest religious festival in the Azores.
Festa do Espírito Santo *(Pentecost)*, Azores. Climax of the festival of the Holy Spirit *(see p372)*.
Pilgrimage to Bom Jesus *(Pentecost)*, Braga. Penitents climb the spectacular staircase on their knees *(see pp284–5)*.

Children carrying a cross at the Festas das Cruzes, Barcelos (May)

Summer

Most visitors choose the summer months to visit Portugal. Since many businesses shut down in August, it is holiday time for locals too. Many families spend the entire summer by the seaside.

Summer is a good time to visit the cooler Minho, when the north is busy with saints' day festivals (see pp232–3).

The famed horsemen of the Ribatejo, Vila Franca de Xira (July)

Historic parade at the Madeira Wine Festival in Funchal

June

Festa de São Gonçalo (first weekend), Amarante. Young, unmarried men and women in the town swap phallus-shaped cakes as tokens of love.
Feira Nacional da Agricultura (early Jun), Santarém. A combination of agricultural fairs, bullfighting and displays of folk dancing.
Sintra Festival (Jun–Jul), Sintra. Classical music concerts and ballet programme.
Santo António (12–13 Jun), Lisbon. Celebrated in the Alfama district with singing and dancing, food and drink. Locals put up lanterns and streamers and bring out chairs for the thousands who arrive.
Festa da Coca (Thu after Trinity Sun), Monção. Part of the Corpus Christi Day celebrations, the festival features scenes of St George in comic battle with the dragon.
São João (23–24 Jun), Porto. Mid-summer festivities include making wishes while jumping over small fires, and the barcos rabelos boat race (see pp232–3).
São Pedro (29 Jun), Lisbon. More street celebrations with eating, dancing and singing.

July

Festa do Colete Encarnado (first weekend), Vila Franca de Xira. Named after the red waistcoats of the Ribatejo horsemen, the festival consists of bullfights and bull running.
Festa dos Tabuleiros (every four years, next in 2019), Tomar. Music, dancing, fireworks and a bullfight (see pp190–91). Four hundred women carry trays of decorated loaves on their heads.
Festa da Ria (mid–late Jul), Aveiro. Folk dances, boat races and a best-decorated boat competition (see p207).

August

Feira Medieval de Silves (early to mid-Aug), Silves. The city centre is turned into a medieval marketplace, with barbecues and street entertainers.
Festas Gualterianas (first weekend), Guimarães. Three-day festival dating back to 1452. Torchlight procession, dancing, and medieval parade.
Madeira Wine Rally (first weekend), Funchal, Madeira. Car enthusiasts flock to this challenging car rally, one of the stages of the European championships.
Festa da Nossa Senhora da Boa Viagem (early Aug), Peniche. A crowd gathers at the harbour with lighted candles to greet a statue of the Virgin that arrives by boat. Fireworks and dancing in the evening.
Jazz em Agosto (early Aug), Lisbon. Popular jazz festival with music in the gardens of the Gulbenkian Centre.
Semana do Mar (1 week in Aug), Horta, Faial, Azores. Food, music, crafts, water sports and lively competitions in this sea festival.
Festival do Marisco (mid-Aug), Olhão. A seafood festival, hosted by one of the big fishing ports in the Algarve.
Romaria de Nossa Senhora da Agonia (weekend nearest to 20 Aug), Viana do Castelo. Religious procession, followed by display of floats, drinking, folk dancing, fireworks and bands. There is also a Saturday afternoon bullfight, and a ceremonial blessing of the town's fishing boats.

The sun-drenched Algarve, a major attraction for summer visitors

Procession at the Romaria de Nossa Senhora da Nazaré

Autumn

In many ways, this is the best season for touring and sightseeing. From mid-September temperatures cool sharply, and autumn is usually drier than spring. This is a mellow, fruitful time of year with the countryside a collage of brown, gold and red.

September is also the start of the *vindima* (the harvest) season. Grapes are harvested and crushed to wine in a spirit of festivity, especially in the port-growing Douro region.

September

Avante! (early Sep), Seixal. A three-day festival of folk music. There are also film screenings, a book fair and food stalls.

Festa das Vindimas (early Sep), Palmela. A festival to celebrate the grape harvest.

Wine Festival (early Sep), Funchal and Estreito de Câmara de Lobos, Madeira. The Funchal festival is a lively, popular event, but the one in Estreito de Câmara de Lobos is more authentic.

Romaria da Nossa Senhora dos Remédios (6–9 Sep), Lamego. The annual pilgrimage to this famous Baroque shrine is the main feature of three days of celebration. Activities include a torchlit procession and live bands.

Romaria da Nossa Senhora da Nazaré (8 Sep and following weekend), Nazaré. Includes processions, folk dancing, and bullfights.

Feiras Novas (mid-Sep), Ponte de Lima. A huge market with fairground, fireworks, carnival costumes and a brass band competition.

Festa da Senhora da Consolação (throughout Sep), Sintra. A celebration of one of Portugal's patron saints, the Lady of Consolation, with a month of parties, music and food in the Assafora area.

Feira de São Mateus (last week), Elvas. Festival offering a mixture of religious, cultural and agricultural events.

Pilgrims on the massive esplanade in front of the basilica at Fátima

October

Feira de Outubro (first or second week), Vila Franca de Xira. Bulls are run through the streets and bullfights staged.

Playing out of a fairway bunker during the Portugal Masters

Portugal Masters (Oct), Oceânico Victoria golf course, Vilamoura.

Pilgrimage to Fátima (12–13 Oct). The final pilgrimage of the year coincides with the date of the Virgin's last appearance in 1917.

Festa das Latas (late Oct), Coimbra. A celebration to welcome new students.

Festival de Gastronomia (late Oct–early Nov), Santarém. Sample the best of regional cooking at this food festival.

November

All Saints' Day (1 Nov). Candles are lit in churches and homes, and flowers placed on graves to honour the dead.

Feira Nacional do Cavalo (first 2 weeks), Golegã. Horse parades and races. The celebrations for St Martin's Day (11 Nov), with a grand parade and running of bulls, also take place during this time.

Casinos do Algarve Rally (mid-Nov), Algarve. Car rally.

Horsemen at the Feira Nacional do Cavalo, Golegã

Lisbon's impressive Praça do Comércio decorated for Christmas

Winter

Seekers of mild, sunny climes fly south to the Algarve where many of the resorts remain alive in winter. For golfers too, the coolest months of the year are the most appealing. January and February also see the spectacular blossoming of almond trees right across southern Portugal.

Other visitors migrate even further south to subtropical Madeira where winter, in particular Christmas and the New Year, is high season.

December

Christmas *(25 Dec)*. Churches and shops everywhere display cribs. On Christmas Eve *bacalhau* (salted

dried cod) is eaten. Presents are opened, and people go to midnight mass. In Madeira traditional *bolo de mel* (honey cake) is made, and children plant wheat, maize or barley in pots. The pots are placed around the crib to symbolize renewal and plenty.

January

New Year. Celebrations all over Portugal with spectacular firework displays welcoming in the New Year.
Festa dos Rapazes *(25 Dec–6 Jan)*, around Bragança. Boys dress up in masks and rampage through their villages in an ancient pagan rite of passage. *(see p233)*.
Epiphany *(6 Jan)*. The traditional crown-shaped cake for Epiphany, *bolo rei* (king's cake), is made with a lucky charm and a bean inside. The person who gets the bean must buy the next cake. *Bolo rei* is also made at Christmas.

Festa de São Gonçalinho
(2nd week), Aveiro. Festival in which loaves of bread are thrown to the crowds from the top of a chapel in thanks for the safe return of a fisherman, or for finding a husband.

February

Fantasporto *(mid-Feb/mid-Mar)*, Porto. An important international film festival, showing many films by new directors, including science fiction films.
Carnaval *(varies according to Easter)*. Celebrated all over Portugal with spectacular costumes and floats; particularly colourful parades take place in Ovar, Sesimbra, Torres Vedras, Funchal and Loulé. Loulé's festivities are connected with the annual Almond Gatherers' Fair.

Public Holidays

New Year's Day (1 Jan)
Carnaval (Feb)
Good Friday (Mar or Apr)
Dia 25 de Abril, *commemorating 1974 Revolution* (25 Apr)
Dia do Trabalhador, *Labour Day* (1 May)
Corpus Christi (15 Jun)
Camões Day (10 Jun)
Assumption Day (15 Aug)
Republic Day (5 Oct)
All Saints' Day (1 Nov)
Dia da Restauracção, *commemorating independence from Spain, 1640* (1 Dec)
Immaculate Conception (8 Dec)
Christmas Day (25 Dec)

Participants of the Carnaval Parade in Loule

The Climate of Portugal

Mainland Portugal has a pleasant climate, with long, hot summers and mild winters. In the north winters are cool and wet; heading further south temperatures increase and rainfall decreases all the way down to the Algarve, where the climate is Mediterranean. Further inland a more Continental climate prevails, with hotter summers and colder winters than on the coast. Madeira is rainy in the north, warmer and drier in the south, and the Azores are mild with year-round rainfall and strong winds.

MINHO

°C		28/82		
	19/66		21/70	
	15/59			12/54
	8/46		10/50	
				4/39

	6 hrs	8.5 hrs	5 hrs	3 hrs
	77 mm	20 mm	109 mm	113 mm
month	Apr	Jul	Oct	Jan

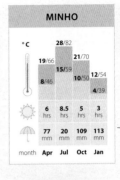

Viana do Castelo

Po

The Azores

Corvo
Flores
Graciosa
São Jorge
Faial
Pico
Terceira
São Miguel
Santa Maria

0 kilometres 200
0 miles 100

ESTREMADURA AND RIBATEJO

°C		21/70	20/68	
	17/63	16/61	15/59	14/57
	12/54			9/48

	8 hrs	11 hrs	6.5 hrs	4.5 hrs
	55 mm	2.5 mm	60 mm	92.5 mm
month	Apr	Jul	Oct	Jan

Ave
Beira L

L

Santaré

LISBON

Setúbal

THE AZORES

°C		25/77	23/73	
	19/66	17/63	16/61	17/63
	12/54			12/54

	4.5 hrs	6 hrs	4.5 hrs	2.5 hrs
	67 mm	27 mm	103 mm	120 mm
month	Apr	Jul	Oct	Jan

THE LISBON COAST

°C		28/82		
	20/68		23/73	
	12/54	17/63	14/57	14/57
				8/46

	9 hrs	12.5 hrs	7.5 hrs	5 hrs
	47.5 mm	0 mm	65 mm	95 mm
month	Apr	Jul	Oct	Jan

Madeira

Porto Santo

Madeira

0 kilometres 20
0 miles 10

Funchal

MADEIRA

°C		25/77	24/75	
	19/66	18/64		19/66
	14/57		18/64	13/55

	6 hrs	7.5 hrs	6 hrs	4.5 hrs
	39 mm	2.5 mm	75 mm	103 mm
month	Apr	Jul	Oct	Jan

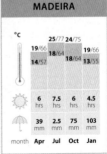

L

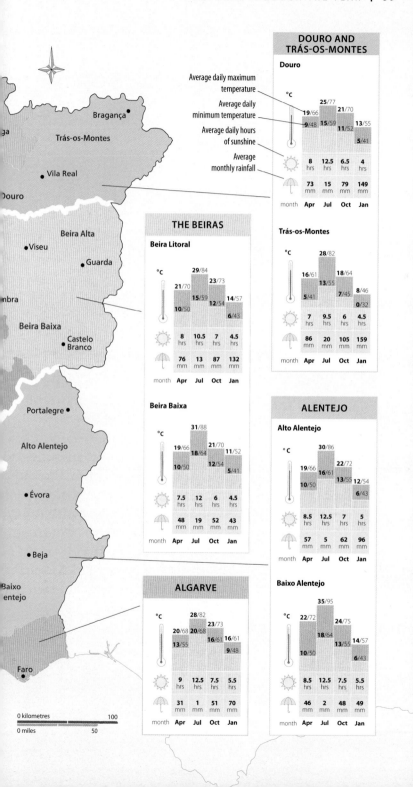

DOURO AND TRÁS-OS-MONTES

Douro

Average daily maximum temperature
Average daily minimum temperature
Average daily hours of sunshine
Average monthly rainfall

°C	Apr	Jul	Oct	Jan
max	19/66	25/77	21/70	13/55
min	9/48	15/59	11/52	5/41
hrs	8 hrs	12.5 hrs	6.5 hrs	4 hrs
mm	73 mm	15 mm	79 mm	149 mm
month	Apr	Jul	Oct	Jan

Trás-os-Montes

°C	Apr	Jul	Oct	Jan
max	16/61	28/82	18/64	8/46
min	5/41	13/55	7/45	0/32
hrs	7 hrs	9.5 hrs	6 hrs	4.5 hrs
mm	86 mm	20 mm	105 mm	159 mm
month	Apr	Jul	Oct	Jan

THE BEIRAS

Beira Litoral

°C	Apr	Jul	Oct	Jan
max	21/70	29/84	23/73	14/57
min	10/50	15/59	12/54	6/43
hrs	8 hrs	10.5 hrs	7 hrs	4.5 hrs
mm	76 mm	13 mm	87 mm	132 mm
month	Apr	Jul	Oct	Jan

Beira Baixa

°C	Apr	Jul	Oct	Jan
max	19/66	31/88	21/70	11/52
min	10/50	18/64	12/54	5/41
hrs	7.5 hrs	12 hrs	6 hrs	4.5 hrs
mm	48 mm	19 mm	52 mm	43 mm
month	Apr	Jul	Oct	Jan

ALENTEJO

Alto Alentejo

°C	Apr	Jul	Oct	Jan
max	19/66	30/86	22/72	12/54
min	10/50	16/61	13/55	6/43
hrs	8.5 hrs	12.5 hrs	7 hrs	5 hrs
mm	57 mm	5 mm	62 mm	96 mm
month	Apr	Jul	Oct	Jan

Baixo Alentejo

°C	Apr	Jul	Oct	Jan
max	22/72	35/95	24/75	14/57
min	10/50	18/64	13/55	6/43
hrs	8.5 hrs	12.5 hrs	7.5 hrs	5.5 hrs
mm	46 mm	2 mm	48 mm	49 mm
month	Apr	Jul	Oct	Jan

ALGARVE

°C	Apr	Jul	Oct	Jan
max	20/68	28/82	23/73	16/61
min	13/55	20/68	16/61	9/48
hrs	9 hrs	12.5 hrs	7.5 hrs	5.5 hrs
mm	31 mm	1 mm	51 mm	70 mm
month	Apr	Jul	Oct	Jan

Bragança
Trás-os-Montes
Vila Real
Douro
Beira Alta
Viseu
Guarda
Beira Baixa
Castelo Branco
Portalegre
Alto Alentejo
Évora
Beja
Baixo Alentejo
Faro

0 kilometres 100
0 miles 50

OM MANUEL

per graça de d̃s. Rey de portugall
τ dos algarues daquem τ dale m
em africa, senñor de guinee τ da conquista nauegaçam τ
merçio dethiopia arabia persia. τ da jndia τc. J
quantos, esto aperpetua memoria feito buem fazer
saber que assi como oproprio τ prñcipall cuydado dos
tem alguñ cargo deue ser trabalhar como as cousas
lhes sam encarregadas seiam postas no mais, prosꝑ
τ melhorado estado que ser possa. assy tanto mais a
sto nos, Reis, τ prñceꝑe. fazello. quanto com mais e
cellente preminençia sam per d̃s postos. na terra pe
bem della τ de seus bassallos. τ pa toda excelam τc
plo de virtudes. E por que esta obrigaçam tam deui

THE HISTORY OF PORTUGAL

Portugal is one of the oldest nation states in Europe: there is evidence that there was human life in Portugal during the Ice Age, and the country's foundation in 1139 pre-dates that of its Iberian neighbour, Spain, by nearly 350 years. Perhaps most famously, Portugal's Age of Discovery in the 15th and 16th centuries saw the country firmly plant itself on the map.

The Romans, who arrived in 218 BC, called the Iberian Peninsula "Hispania." When the Roman Empire collapsed in the 5th century, Hispania was overrun first by Germanic tribes, then by Moors from North Africa. Reconquest by the Christian kingdoms of the north began in earnest in the 11th century and it was during this process that Portucale, a county of the kingdom of León and Castile, was declared independent by its first king, Afonso Henriques.

The kingdom expanded southwards to the Algarve and Portuguese sailors began to explore the African coast and Atlantic Ocean. Portugal's Golden Age reached its zenith during the reign of Manuel I, with Vasco da Gama's voyage to India in 1498 and the discovery of Brazil two years later. Eastern trade brought incredible wealth to the Portuguese coffers, but military defeat in Morocco meant that the country's prosperity was short-lived. Spain invaded in 1580 and ruled Portugal for the next 60 years.

After Portugal regained independence, her fortunes were restored by the discovery of gold in Brazil and, in the 18th century, the Marquês de Pombal, began to modernize the country. However, Napoleon's invasion in 1807, and the loss of Brazil in 1825, left Portugal impoverished and divided. Power struggles between Absolutists and Constitutionalists further weakened the country, and the debt crisis worsened. In 1910, a republican revolution overthrew the monarchy.

The economy continued to deteriorate until a military coup led to the dictatorship of António Salazar, who held power from 1928 to 1968. Although Salazar died in 1970, the right-wing authoritarian regime he had established continued until the Carnation Revolution of 1974; democracy was restored in 1976.

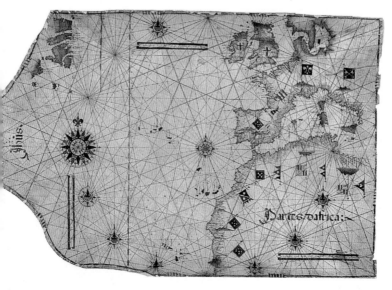

Portuguese mariners' chart of the North Atlantic drawn on parchment (c.1550)

◀ Illuminated frontispiece of the *Leitura Nova*, showing Portugal's coat of arms and portrait of Manuel I (c.1520)

The Rulers of Portugal

Afonso Henriques declared himself Portugal's first king in 1139, but his descendants' ties of marriage to various Spanish kingdoms led to dynastic disputes. João I's defeat of the Castilians in 1385 established the House of Avis which presided over the golden age of Portuguese imperialism. In 1580, in the absence of a direct heir, Portugal was ruled by Spanish kings for 60 years before the Duke of Bragança became João IV. A Republican uprising ended the monarchy in 1910. However, in the first 16 years of the Republic there were 40 different governments, and in 1926 Portugal became a dictatorship under the eventual leadership of Salazar. Democracy was restored by the "Carnation" Revolution of 1974.

1656–83 Afon

1481–95 João II

1557–78 Sebastião

1580–98 Felipe I (Philip II of Spain)

1248–79 Afonso III

1211–23 Afonso II

1185–1211 Sancho I

1279–1325 Dinis

1438–81 Afonso V

1100	1220	1340	1460	
House of Burgundy		Avis		Hapsburg
1100	1220	1340	1460	

1325–57 Afonso IV

1357–67 Pedro I

1223–48 Sancho II

1367–83 Fernando I

1433–8 Duarte

1578–80 Henrique

1139–85 Afonso Henriques (Afonso I)

1521–57 João III

1598–162 Felipe II (Phili III of Spair

1385–1433 João I

1495–1521 Manuel I

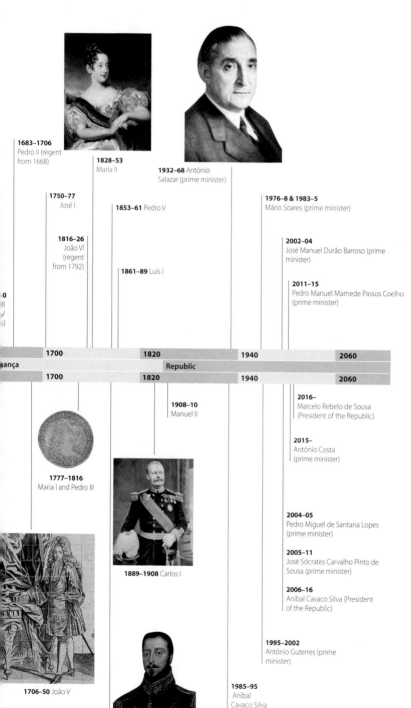

1683–1706
Pedro II (regent from 1668)

1828–53
Maria II

1932–68 António Salazar (prime minister)

1750–77
José I

1853–61 Pedro V

1976–8 & 1983–5
Mário Soares (prime minister)

1816–26
João VI (regent from 1792)

2002–04
José Manuel Durão Barroso (prime minister)

1861–89 Luís I

2011–15
Pedro Manuel Mamede Passos Coelho (prime minister)

0
||
||
|)

1700 **1820** **1940** **2060**

ança   Republic

1700 **1820** **1940** **2060**

1908–10
Manuel II

2016–
Marcelo Rebelo de Sousa (President of the Republic)

2015–
António Costa (prime minister)

1777–1816
Maria I and Pedro III

2004–05
Pedro Miguel de Santana Lopes (prime minister)

2005–11
José Sócrates Carvalho Pinto de Sousa (prime minister)

1889–1908 Carlos I

2006–16
Aníbal Cavaco Silva (President of the Republic)

1995–2002
António Guterres (prime minister)

1985–95
Aníbal Cavaco Silva (prime minister)

1706–50 João V

0–56 João IV

1826–28 Pedro IV

Prehistoric and Roman Portugal

From about 2000 BC Portugal's Stone Age communities were supplanted by foreign invaders, most notably the Iberians and the Celts. When Rome defeated the Carthaginians in 216 BC and took over all their territories in eastern Spain, she still had to subdue Celtiberian tribes living in the west. One of these, the Lusitani, put up fierce resistance. After their defeat in 139 BC, their name was preserved in Lusitania, a province of Roman Hispania, corresponding roughly to present-day Portugal. Romanization led to four centuries of stability and prosperity, but as the Roman Empire collapsed, Lusitania was overrun by Germanic tribes, first the Suevi and then the Visigoths.

Iberian Peninsula in 27 BC
▨ Roman Provinces

The amphitheatre probably dated from the building boom of the 1st century AD.

The forum and principal temple

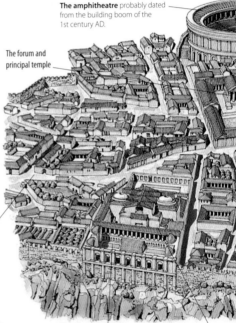

Dolmen of Comenda
Dolmens such as this one near Évora were communal burial chambers. Many were built by the Neolithic peoples who lived in the Iberian Peninsula in the third millennium BC.

The main road led north to Aeminium (Coimbra).

Porca of Murça
Trás-os-Montes has preserved 16 statues of animals like this granite pig *(see p263)*, probably used in Celtic fertility rituals.

Palestra (exercise area of the baths)

The Baths of Trajan had a spectacular view of the ravine below the city walls.

c.2000 BC Iberian tribes arrive in the peninsula, probably from Africa

Iberian Gold gorget

139 BC Celtiber⸙ resistance to Rom⸙ rule ends with t⸙ death of Viriatus, lead⸙ of the Lusitani tr⸙

3000 BC	2000 BC	1000 BC

2500 BC Portugal inhabited by late Stone Age people. Many megalithic tombs date from this time

Celtic stone warrior, 1st millennium BC

1000 BC Phoenicians set up trading stations and settlements along the southern coast

c.700 BC Celtic invaders settle in Portugal

218 BC The⸙ Romans⸙ invade the⸙ Iberian⸙ Peninsula⸙

Floor Mosaic
Under Roman rule, the wealthy built lavishly decorated villas. This mosaic of a triton (1st century AD) comes from the House of the Fountains just outside the walls of Conímbriga.

Where to See Prehistoric and Roman Portugal

The Alentejo is rich in Stone Age megaliths (see p312), while the north has the two best examples of Celtiberian settlements at Sanfins (p254) and Briteiros. Many traces of the Roman period, including roads and bridges, are found throughout Portugal. Apart from Conímbriga, major sites, such as the villas at Pisões (p317) and Milreu (p331), are mainly in the south. Faro's Museu Municipal (p333) has a good collection of local finds.

Roman Amphora
Garum, a popular, spiced sauce made of fermented fish, was manufactured at Tróia (see p175) and exported in 27-litre (6-gal) amphorae like this one.

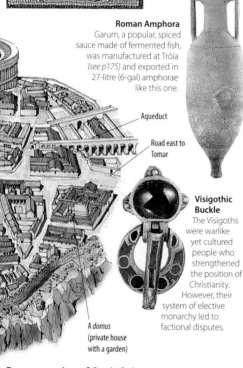

Aqueduct

Road east to Tomar

Visigothic Buckle
The Visigoths were warlike yet cultured people who strengthened the position of Christianity. However, their system of elective monarchy led to factional disputes.

A *domus* (private house with a garden)

Citânia de Briteiros, a hilltop settlement founded around the 5th century AD, survived until well into the Roman period. It was discovered in 1874 (p287).

Reconstruction of Conímbriga

The extensive remains of Conímbriga (see p214) give a vivid picture of how thoroughly Romanized Portugal became under the empire. The town expanded rapidly in the 1st century AD, when it achieved the self-governing status of a municipium. It fell to the Suevi in AD 468.

Évora's temple dates from the 2nd century AD (see p308). It is almost all that remains of an important Roman city.

AD 73 Emperor Vespasian grants towns in the Iberian Peninsula same rights as Latin towns in Italy	**415** Visigoths invade the peninsula and drive out the Vandals and the Alani	**585** Visigoths take over the Suevian kingdom, fixing their capital at Toledo in Spain
	AD 200 Christianity becomes established in the peninsula	
AD 1	**AD 200** ⎪ **AD 400**	**AD 600**
During the rule of the Emperor [Augu]stus the Iberian Peninsula is [divid]ed into three; Lusitania is the [nam]e given to the central province [south] of the River Douro	**409** Invasion by "barbarian" tribes from central Europe: the Vandals, the Alani and the Suevi

411 Suevian kingdom established in Galicia and northern Portugal | *Visigothic chapel at São Frutuoso (see p283)* |

Moorish Domination and Christian Reconquest

When Muslims from North Africa defeated the Visigoths in 711, the Iberian Peninsula became a province of the Caliphate of Damascus. Then, in 756, Abd al Rahman established the independent kingdom of Al Andalus, his capital Córdoba becoming one of the world's great centres of culture. Moorish control of the peninsula remained virtually undisputed for the next 300 years until the small Christian kingdoms in the north began the Reconquest. In the 11th century, as Moorish power waned, "Portucale" was just a small county of the Kingdom of León and Castile, centred on the Douro. It became independent after Afonso Henriques defeated the Moors at Ourique in 1139.

Iberian Peninsula in 1100
- Country of Portucale
- Kingdom of León and Castile
- Moorish kingdoms

Without the Virgin to watch over them, the Faro fishermen's nets are empty.

Moorish Plate
Vivid depictions of a hunting dog, a falcon and a gazelle decorate this 11th-century plate found at Mértola, a river port on the Guadiana used by eastern traders.

The fishermen set off with new hope.

Coexistence
Under Moorish rule, co-operation between the faiths was common. This miniature from the 13th century shows the friendly meeting of two knights, one a Christian, the other a Moor.

711 Large Muslim army of Berbers and Arabs (the Moors) conquers Iberian Peninsula following dispute over Visigothic succession

722 Christian victory at Covadonga in Asturias marks start of gradual reconquest

868 Vimara Peres takes Porto from the Moors

878 Christian forces recapture Coimbra

10th-century Hispano-Moorish ivory casket

AD 700 **AD 800** **AD 900** **AD 100**

756 Battle of Al Musara; Abd al Rahman defeats governor of Córdoba and founds kingdom of Al Andalus
Nora, a bucket wheel for raising water introduced by the Moors

955 Moorish leader Al Mansur retakes Coimbra, then forces Christian frontier back to the River Douro

1008–31 Civil war; Al Andalus divided into small kingdoms known as *taifas*

Stone Relief of São Tiago

In wars against the Moors, the apostle St James (São Tiago) assumed a special role. At Ourique in 1139, soldiers claimed to have seen him leading the Christian forces into battle.

12th-century Silver Dirham
This coin was minted at Beja by the Almohads, a Muslim sect even stricter than their forerunners, the Almoravids.

Where to See Moorish Portugal

The influence of the Moors is strongest in the south, in towns like Lagos (see p326), Faro (p332) and Silves, where they ruled for longer and the architecture (p27) retains many Arab features. In Mértola (p319), the church preserves much of the old mosque. Further north, the Castelo dos Mouros, in Sintra (p163), and many other fortresses were taken over and rebuilt by the Christians.

This cistern well was found on the site of the archaeological museum at Silves, a Moorish centre in the Algarve (p329).

The lost statue of the Virgin is recovered from the sea and restored to its rightful place on the walls.

Out at sea the fishermen's nets are full once more.

Capture of Lisbon
The Reconquest was given the status of a crusade by the pope. Lisbon was taken in 1147 with the aid of English troops bound for the Holy Land.

Faro Under Moorish Rule
Christians who lived under Moorish rule were called Mozarabs. At Faro they placed a statue of the Virgin on the walls of the city, but resentful Muslims took the statue down. These four scenes from the Cantigas de Santa Maria tell the story of the miracle that followed.

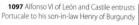

1097 Alfonso VI of León and Castile entrusts Portucale to his son-in-law Henry of Burgundy

1086 Invasion of the Almoravids

1139 Battle of Ourique; Afonso Henriques declares himself King of Portugal

1143 Treaty of Zamora establishes Portugal's independence

1165–9 Geraldo sem Pavor captures a number of cities from the Almohads, including Évora and Badajoz

1050

1064 Christians regain Coimbra

Henry of Burgundy

1100

1128 Battle of São Mamede; Afonso Henriques defeats his mother Teresa to win control of county of Portucale

1150

1153 Founding of Cistercian Abbey at Alcobaça

1147 Fall of Lisbon to Crusader army; Almoravid empire falls to the Almohads

The New Kingdom

The Portuguese Reconquest was completed in 1249 when Afonso III captured Faro in the Algarve. His successor, King Dinis, encouraged agriculture and commerce, earning the nickname of the "farmer king". He also built castles to defend the border from Castilian attack and expanded the navy. Territorial disputes with Castile came to a head in 1383 when King Fernando died and his son-in-law, Juan I of Castile, claimed the Portuguese throne for his wife Beatriz. Juan's opponents favoured Pedro I's illegitimate son, João of Avis, elected king by the *cortes* (parliament) in Coimbra in 1385.

Iberian Peninsula in 1200
- Kingdom of Portugal
- Spanish kingdoms
- Territory under Moorish rule

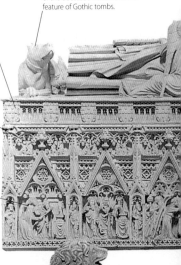

The faithful dog at the feet of the deceased was a common feature of Gothic tombs.

Coat of arms of Portugal

The frieze shows scenes from the life of Pedro and Inês.

Cancioneiro da Ajuda
King Dinis was a fine musician and poet. This illumination is from a collection of troubadour songs, many by the king himself.

The aedicules contain finely carved scenes from the life of St Bartholomew, Dom Pedro's patron saint.

Fortifications of Serpa
King Dinis had a chain of fortified towns and castles built along the borders with Castile and Moorish Spain. This 16th-century drawing shows the medieval walls and towers of Serpa (*see p316*).

1185 Sancho I becomes king; his victories in the Algarve are reversed by Al-Mansur, the Almohad caliph

1211 First *cortes* (parliament) held at Coimbra

Leiria Castle

1254 The *cortes* held at Leiria includes representatives of the towns

1200

1250

1173 Remains of St Vincent brought from Cabo de São Vicente to Lisbon

1179 Portugal recognized as kingdom by the pope

Afonso III

1248 Anarchic reign of Sancho II ends in his deposition by his brother Afonso III

1249 Afonso III completes reconquest of the Algarve, but his claim to sovereignty is challenged by Castile

1256 Lisbon becomes capital of Portugal in place of Coimbra

St Isabel (1271–1336)
King Dinis did not approve of his wife's acts of charity. A legend tells how the bread Queen Isabel was about to distribute to the poor turned into roses when she was challenged by her husband.

Six angels support the recumbent king.

Cross of Sancho I
Sancho's reign (1185–1211) saw royal power and wealth increase despite disputes between the king and his bishops over papal authority.

St Bartholomew is martyred by being flayed alive.

Tomb of Pedro I
The Gothic carvings on the royal tomb at Alcobaça (see pp184–5) are the finest of their kind in Portugal. The forthright Pedro, who ruled from 1357–67, is remembered chiefly for the tragic tale of his murdered mistress, Inês de Castro, whose matching tomb stands facing Pedro's.

Where to See Medieval Portugal
Of the many castles built or rebuilt in this period, the most picturesque are at Almourol *(see p195)* and Óbidos. In the citadel of Bragança *(pp264–5)* stands the Domus Municipalis, a medieval meeting hall. Most surviving Romanesque buildings, however, are religious: the cathedrals in Porto, Lisbon *(p76)* and Coimbra *(p208)* and many smaller churches in the north, such as those at Rates *(p278)*, Roriz *(p254)* and Bravães *(p273)*.

Óbidos Castle, now a *pousada*, was rebuilt by King Dinis when he gave this fairy-tale town to his wife Isabel as a wedding present in 1282 *(p180)*.

Porto's Sé *(p246)* has been much altered, but the twin-towered west front retains its original 13th-century character.

79–1325 King Dinis consolidates rtugal's independence

1288 Portugal's first university founded in Lisbon

1297 Castile recognizes Portugal's sovereignty over the Algarve

1300

Knight of the Order of Christ

1319 Foundation of the Order of Christ *(see p191)*

1336 Death of St Isabel of Portugal

1349 Following Black Death, a law is passed enforcing compulsory rural labour

1355 After murder of Inês de Castro, Pedro takes up arms against his father Afonso IV

1350

1357 Accession of Pedro I, who has murderers of Inês de Castro brutally executed

1372 Fernando I's unpopular marriage to Leonor Teles leads to riots

1383 João of Avis ends regency of Leonor Teles and proclaims himself defender of the realm

1384 Juan I of Castile invades Portugal

The House of Avis

After João of Avis had defeated the Castilians in 1385 to become
João I of Portugal, he strengthened his position through an
important alliance with England. His long reign saw the start of
Portuguese imperialism and the beginning of maritime expeditions
promoted by his son, Henry the Navigator (see pp52–3). Further
voyages of discovery in the reign of Manuel I "the Fortunate", led to
trade with India and the East and, following Afonso de Albuquerque's
capture of Goa, initially brought great wealth. So, too, did the
colonization of Brazil. However, the lure of overseas adventure
weakened mainland Portugal, which suffered serious depopulation.
The age of expansion ended when a foolhardy military expedition
to Morocco, led by King Sebastião, was soundly defeated in 1578.

Iberian Peninsula in 1500

🔲 Portugal

🔲 Spain (Castile and Aragon)

16th-century Porcelain Plate
In 1557 the Portuguese were
granted Macao as a trading
post in China. This Chinese plate
bears the arms of Matias de
Albuquerque, a descendant of
the great Afonso, conqueror of Goa.

**Arms of English
royal family**

John of Gaunt used the
alliance with Portugal to
pursue his own claim
to the throne of Castile.

Troops Landing at Arzila
The kings of the Avis dynasty
constantly sought to extend their
domains to Morocco, where they
established a small colony around
Tangier. This Flemish tapestry
celebrates Afonso V's capture
of Arzila in 1471.

Luís de Camões
After serving in India and
Morocco, where he lost
an eye, the poet wrote
Os Lusíadas (see p194),
an epic on the Discoveries.

1385 João I defeats Castilian army at Battle of Aljubarrota	**c.1425** Leal Conselheiro, a treatise on courtly behaviour written by King Duarte		**1496** Jews expelled from the country or forcibly converted
1415 Capture of Ceuta in Morocco		**1441** Lagos is site of first slave market in modern Europe	**1495–1521** Reign of Manuel I and great period of discoveries
1400	**1425**	**1450**	**1475**
1386 Alliance with England formalized by Treaty of Windsor	**1418** Henry the Navigator made governor of the Algarve	**1471** Conquest of Moroccan fortresses of Arzila and Tangier • King Duarte • **1482–3** João II successfully resists the Conspiracy of the Nobles	**1494** Spain and Portugal divide the Atlantic region by Treaty of Tordesillas

Wedding of Manuel I

Manuel's reign marked the highest point in Portugal's golden age of discovery and conquest. His marriages were made to reinforce ties with Spain. Shown here is his third: to Leonor, sister of Carlos I of Spain, in 1518.

João I drew support from the merchants of Lisbon and Porto rather than the nobles, many of whom sided with Castile.

Where to See Gothic Portugal

Many churches include Gothic elements, such as the cloister of the Sé in Porto (see p246) and the richly sculpted portal of the Sé in Évora (p310). Tomar's Convento de Cristo (pp192–3) is predominantly Gothic, as is the church at Alcobaça (pp184–5). The finest church, however, is at Batalha, built in thanks for João I's victory at the Battle of Aljubarrota. It also contains major examples of Manueline architecture (see pp28–9).

Batalha (pp188–9) incorporates a wide range of Gothic styles. The plain, lofty nave contrasts with the ornamented exterior.

Archbishop of Braga

Portugal's bishops took João's side after the pope had refused to legitimize the children of Inês de Castro (see pp48–9).

João I and the English

João's alliance with England against Castile led to his marriage in 1387 to Philippa of Lancaster, daughter of John of Gaunt, son of Edward III. This illustration from the chronicle of Jean de Wavrin shows the new king entertaining his father-in-law.

Battle of Alcácer-Quibir (1578)
King Sebastião saw his African expedition as a crusade against Islam. After Alcácer-Quibir, he and 8,000 of his troops lay dead, 15,000 captives were sold into slavery and the House of Avis dynasty was doomed.

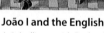

Belém Monstrance (see p28)

1510 Beginning of Portuguese empire in Asia; Goa conquered by Afonso de Albuquerque

1531 Inquisition introduced into Portugal

1536 Death of Gil Vicente, Portugal's greatest dramatist

1572 Publication of *Os Lusíadas*, a verse epic celebrating Portugal's history by Luís de Camões

1500   **1525**   **1550**   **1575**

c.1502 Work starts on the Jerónimos monastery in Belém (see pp108–9)

Vasco da Gama es India

1521–57 Reign of João III, known as "the Pious"

Gil Vicente

1559 Jesuit University established at Évora (see p310)

1578 King Sebastião's expedition to Morocco ends in his death and total defeat at the Battle of Alcácer-Quibir

The Age of Discovery

Portugal's astonishing period of conquest and exploration began in 1415 with the capture of the North African city of Ceuta. Maritime expeditions into the Atlantic and along the West African coast followed, motivated by traditional Christian hostility towards Islam and desire for commercial gain. Great riches were made from the gold and slaves taken from the Guinea coast, but the real breakthrough for Portuguese imperialism occurred in 1498 when Vasco da Gama (see p110) reached India. Portugal soon controlled the Indian Ocean and the spice trade, and established an eastern capital at Goa. With Pedro Álvares Cabral's "discovery" of Brazil, Portugal became a mercantile super-power rivalled only by Spain.

Armillary Sphere
This celestial globe with the earth in its centre was used by navigators for measuring the positions of the stars. It became the personal emblem of Manuel I.

Magellan (c.1480–1521)
With Spanish funding, Portuguese sailor Fernão de Magalhães, known as Magellan, led the first circumnavigation of the globe (1519–22). He was killed in the Philippines before the voyage's end.

1500–1501 Gaspar Corte Real reaches Newfoundland.

1427 Diogo de Silves discovers the Azores.

1434 Gil Eanes rounds Cape Bojador (Western Sahara).

1460 Diogo Gomes discovers the Cape Verde archipelago.

1470s Discovery of island of São Tomé.

1482 Diogo Cão reaches the mouth of the Congo.

1500 Pedro Álvares Cabral reaches Brazil.

1485 On his third voyage Diogo Cão reaches Cape Cross (Namibia).

1488 Bartolo[meu] Dias rounds C[ape] of Good H[ope]

The Adoration of the Magi
Painted for Viseu Cathedral shortly after Cabral returned from Brazil in 1500, this panel is attributed to Grão Vasco (see p219). The second king, Baltazar, is depicted as a Tupi Indian.

African Ivory Salt Cellar
This 16th-century ivory carving shows Portuguese warriors supporting a globe and a ship. A sailor peers out from the crow's nest at the top.

Japanese Screen (c.1600)
This screen shows traders unloading a *nau*, or great ship. Between 1575 and their expulsion in 1638, the Portuguese monopolized the carrying trade between China and Japan.

Henry the Navigator

Although he did not sail himself, Henry (1394–1460), the third son of João I, laid the foundations for Portugal's maritime expansion that were later built upon by João II and consolidated by Manuel I. As Master of the wealthy Order of Christ and Governor of the Algarve, Henry was able to finance expeditions along the African coast. By the time he died he had a monopoly on all trade south of Cape Bojador. Legend tells that he founded a great school of navigation either at Sagres *(see p326)* or Lagos.

Key

— Discoverers' routes

1543 Portuguese arrive in Japan.

1513 Trading posts set up in China at Macau and Canton.

1510 Capture of Goa.

1498 Vasco da Gama reaches Calicut in India.

1518 Fortress built in Colombo (Sri Lanka).

1512 Portuguese reach Ternate in the Moluccas (Spice Islands).

Cloves

Pepper

Nutmeg

Cinnamon

The Spice Trade
Exotic spices were a great source of wealth for Portugal. The much-disputed Moluccas, or Spice Islands, were purchased from Spain in 1528.

Portuguese Discoveries

The systematic attempt to find a sea route to India, which led to a monopoly of the spice trade, began in 1482 with the first voyage of Diogo Cão, who planted a padrão *(stone cross) on the shores where he landed.*

Crow's nest

Square sail on foremast

Cross of the Order of Christ (see p191)

Lateen-rigged Caravel
These ships with three triangular sails were favoured by the first Portuguese explorers who sailed close to the African coast. For later journeys across the open ocean, square sails were found more effective.

Spanish Rule

When Henrique, the Cardinal-King, died without an heir in 1580, Philip II of Spain successfully claimed the Portuguese throne through his mother, a daughter of Manuel I. Under Spanish rule, influential positions were held by Portuguese nobles, but a common foreign policy led to a steady loss of colonies to the Dutch. In 1640 a Portuguese revolt took place in Lisbon and the Duke of Bragança was chosen to become King João IV. Spain retaliated and the ensuing war continued until 1668. Meanwhile Portugal was forced to rely economically on her overseas territories.

Restoration of João IV
Two weeks after his supporters had ousted the Spanish in 1640, João was crowned on a platform outside the Royal Palace in Lisbon.

Spanish Armada
In 1588 Philip II of Spain hoped to invade England with his great fleet. It sailed from Lisbon where it had been equipped and provisioned.

The Graça fort was held by the Spanish.

War of Restoration
Portugal's long war against Spain (1640–68) was fought mostly in the Alentejo. This azulejo panel from Palácio Fronteira in Lisbon (see p127) shows the Battle of Linhas de Elvas (1658). A Portuguese army besieged in Elvas (see pp302–3) was relieved by fresh troops from Estremoz, who soundly defeated the Spanish.

António Vieira
Vieira (1606–97) was a Jesuit priest, writer and orator. He was sent on many diplomatic missions and clashed with the Inquisition over his support for Christianized Jews.

1580 Battle of Alcântara; Spanish invade and Philip II of Spain becomes King of Portugal

1588 Spanish Armada sets sail from Lisbon to invade England

1614 Publication of the *Peregrinação* by Fernão Mendes Pinto, an account of his travels in Asia in the mid-16th century

1624 Dutch capture Portuguese colony of Bahia in Brazil

1631 Birth of painter Josefa d... Óbidos

1580

1600

1620

1583 Philip returns to Spain leaving his nephew, Cardinal-Archduke Albert of Austria, as viceroy

1581 The king invites Italian architect Filippo Terzi to Lisbon to remodel the Royal Palace and to build many churches

Church of São Vicente de Fora (see p74) by Filippo Terzi and Baltasar Álvares, completed in 1627

1626 Jesuit missionary António de Andrade cross... the Himalayas into Tibet

Indo-Portuguese Contador

Luxury cabinets, known as *contadores*, were made from teak and ebony in Portugal's overseas colonies. Many came from Goa. This fine 17th-century example is from the Museu Nacional de Arte Antiga *(see pp98–101).*

The besieged Portuguese army at Elvas was retreating from a previous unsuccessful campaign in Spain.

Stout bastions deflected the attackers' cannon fire.

The relieving army from Estremoz surprised and routed the Spanish.

Josefa de Óbidos

Born in Spain, Josefa (1631–84) came to Óbidos *(see pp180–81)* when young. Trained by her father, she painted religious subjects and realistic still lifes.

Where to See 17th-Century Portugal

Under Spanish rule an austere style of architecture prevailed, typified by São Vicente de Fora *(see p74)* in Lisbon, the Sé Nova in Coimbra *(p210)* and Santarém's Jesuit church *(p197).* At Vila Viçosa the style is evident in the long, plain façade of the palace of the dukes of Bragança *(pp304–5).* Colourful *azulejos* from the period can be seen at Palácio Fronteira *(p127)* and the Museu Nacional do Azulejo *(pp124–5).*

Museu dos Biscainhos in Braga *(p283)* was built by rich emigrants returning from Brazil. Enlarged in later centuries, it retains its 17th-century core.

The Inquisition

In the 16th and 17th centuries, the Inquisition, set up by the Catholic church, burned heretics in Lisbon's Terreiro do Paço to ensure religious conformity.

1639 Portuguese vessels barred from Japanese ports

1654 Fall of Pernambuco; Dutch driven from Brazil

1656 Death of João IV; his widow, Luisa de Guzmán, is regent for young King Afonso VI

1665 Spanish defeated at Battle of Montes Claros

1668 Spain recognizes Portuguese independence

Pedro II

1683 Pedro II becomes King

1640 The Restoration: 4th Duke of Bragança crowned King João IV after uprising against Spanish rule

Catherine of Bragança

1662 Catherine of Bragança marries Charles II of England

1667 Degenerate Afonso VI is deposed by his brother Pedro, who marries Afonso's French wife and becomes regent

1697 Gold discovered in Minas Gerais region of Brazil

1698 Last meeting of Portuguese *cortes*

1640   **1660**   **1680**

The Age of Absolutism

The 18th century was a period of mixed fortune for Portugal. Despite vast revenues from Brazilian gold and diamonds, João V almost bankrupted the country with his extravagance. In contrast, Pombal, chief minister of João's successor José I, applied the ideas of the Enlightenment, reforming government, commerce and education. When Maria I succeeded in 1777, she reversed many of Pombal's decrees. The French invasion of 1807 forced Maria, by then mad, and the royal family into exile in Brazil.

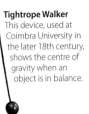

Tightrope Walker
This device, used at Coimbra University in the later 18th century, shows the centre of gravity when an object is in balance.

The library contains richly carved Baroque bookcases and more than 40,000 volumes.

Marquês de Pombal (1699–1782)
After the 1755 earthquake *(see pp66–7)*, Pombal insisted that Lisbon be rebuilt on strictly rational lines. Here he proudly presents the new city.

Queen's apartments

João V
This miniature (1720) by Castriotto shows João V drinking chocolate, a fashionable drink of the nobility, served to him by the Infante Miguel.

The basilica contains many marble statues made by Italian masters set amid a stunning scheme of yellow, pink, red and blue marble.

1703 Methuen Treaty with Britain secures market for Portuguese wines in Britain, and for British woollen goods in Portugal

1723 Building of Baroque staircase of Bom Jesus near Braga *(see pp284–5)*

1755 Earthquake devasta[tes] Lisbon and much [of] southern Port[ugal]

1730 Consecration of basilica at monastery-palace at Mafra

Bom Jesus do Monte

1700	1720	1740

1706–50 Reign of João V "the Magnanimous", a period of great artistic extravagance

1733 First Portuguese opera, *The Patience of Socrates* by António de Almeida, performed at Royal Palace in Lisbon

1748 First water flows along Águas Livres aqueduct in Lisbon

1750 José I succeeds João V

Águas Livres Aqueduct

Opened in 1748, the aqueduct was paid for by the citizens of Lisbon. João V had it built across the Alcântara valley against the advice of his engineers.

Where to See 18th-Century Portugal

Baroque churches are found throughout Portugal, many with ornate interiors of gilded wood (talha dourada) such as São Francisco (see p247) and Santa Clara (p245) in Porto. Tiled interiors are also very common (pp26–7). Coimbra University houses the glittering Capela de São Miguel and a fine Baroque library. As well as the palaces at Mafra and Queluz, many elegant country houses, notably the Casa de Mateus, date from this era (pp260–61).

18th-Century Dressing Chair
This richly gilded walnut chair has sturdy cabriole legs, showing the influence of the English Queen Anne style.

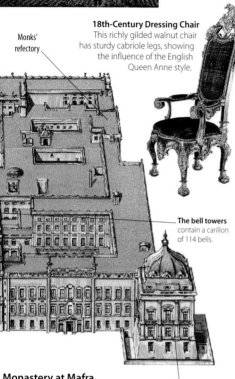

Monks' refectory

The bell towers contain a carillon of 114 bells.

Queluz Palace (pp170–71), residence of Maria I, was begun in 1747. It is the finest example of Rococo architecture in Portugal.

Monastery at Mafra

Begun in 1717, this vast monument to João V incorporates a royal palace, a church and a monastery (see p158). It took 38 years to complete and contains some 880 rooms and 300 monks' cells.

The King's apartments are separated from the Queen's by a long gallery.

The Capela de São Miguel at Coimbra University (pp212–13) was redecorated in Baroque style in the reign of João V.

1756 Douro valley becomes world's first demarcated wine region

1759 Pombal expels Jesuits from Portugal

1760

1762 Spain declares war on Portugal

Statue of José I

1772 Pombal reorganizes Coimbra University, adding mathematics and natural sciences to the syllabus

1777 Accession of Maria I, who dismisses Pombal

1780

1775 Machado de Castro's statue of José I unveiled as centrepiece of reconstructed Lisbon

1789 Portuguese suppress Brazilian independence movement in Minas Gerais

Maria I

1808 French forced to retreat by Anglo-Portuguese force under Sir Arthur Wellesley; Treaty of Sintra

1800

1792 Maria I's son João named regent

1807 The French, under Junot, invade Portugal; royal family flees to Brazil

Reform and Revolution

Portugal suffered many depredations during the upheavals of the Peninsular War, and after the loss of Brazil. A period of chaos culminated, in 1832, in civil war between the Liberal Pedro IV and the Absolutist Miguel: the War of the Two Brothers. Though the Liberals won, later governments were often reactionary. The second half of the century saw a period of stability and industrial growth, but attempts at expansion in Africa failed. By 1910, discontent with the constitutional monarchy was such that a Republican uprising forced King Manuel II into exile.

1820 Revolution
The revolution led to the royal family's return from Brazil and a new Liberal constitution. This proved unworkable and was revoked following an army coup in 1823.

Republican ships shell the king's palace in Lisbon.

Personification of Portuguese Republic

Zé Povinho
This long-suffering, Everyman figure first appeared in 1875, created by artist and potter Rafael Bordalo Pinheiro. He expressed the concerns of the average Portuguese working man.

Priests are led away by Republican soldiers.

Peninsular War (1808–14)
Napoleon tried twice to invade Portugal but was repulsed by an Anglo-Portuguese force led by Wellington. A key victory for the allies came at Buçaco (see pp216–17) in 1810.

The Birth of the Republic

Republicanism spread among the middle classes and the army via a secret society called the Carbonária. The revolution took place in Lisbon in October 1910 and lasted less than five days. This contemporary poster celebrates the main events.

1809–20 Regency dominated by Charles Stuart, British minister at Lisbon

1822 Radical new constitution. Brazil becomes independent under João VI's son Pedro

Teatro Nacional Dona Maria II

1853 First Portuguese postage stamps issued

1856 Opening of first railway from Lisbon to Carregad

1810

1826 Moderate charter introduced by Pedro IV, who then abdicates in favour of his young daughter Maria

1810 Battle of Buçaco

1828 Miguel, who is betrothed to his niece Maria, is crowned king

1830

1842 Founding of National Theatre

1834 Monasteries dissolved

1832–4 War of the Two Brothers; defeat of Absolutist Miguel

1851–80 The Regeneration: period of industrial development

1850

5 Reis stamp

The Drunkards by José Malhôa
Malhôa (1855–1933) created a virtual social history of the period in genre paintings like this one, showing a group of peasants sampling new wine.

Where to See 19th-Century Portugal

Neo-Classicism, which dominated the early part of the century, can be seen in Lisbon's Palácio da Ajuda (see p113). More Romantic historical styles emerged later in the century, ranging from the fantastical Neo-Gothic of the Palácio da Pena (pp166–7) in Sintra to the subtle Orientalism of Monserrate (p161). Notable stations associated with the spread of Portugal's railways include Lisbon's Rossio and São Bento in Porto (p245).

King Manuel II flees to England from Ericeira aboard the royal yacht.

Portugal and Africa
Captain Serpa Pinto's crossing of southern Africa in 1879 led to a plan to form a Portuguese colony from coast to coast.

Rossio station (p84) in Lisbon has a striking façade in Neo-Manueline style by José Luís Monteiro. Completed in 1887, the station contains one of the first iron vaults in Portugal.

Republican troops set up barricades at key points in Lisbon. They meet with little opposition.

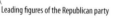

Leading figures of the Republican party

Ponte de Dom Luís I (p248) in Porto dates from 1886. Its two-tier design by Teófilo Seyrig was inspired by the nearby railway bridge built by Gustave Eiffel.

Eça de Queirós
The great novelist (1845–1900) painted a scathing picture of the Portuguese bourgeoisie. He spent many years abroad as a diplomat.

1865–8 Coalition of two main parties

1869 Slave trade abolished in all Portuguese territories

1888 Publication of *Os Maias* by Eça de Queirós, a satirical examination of Portuguese lethargy

Manuel II

1910 Revolution: Manuel II abdicates and flees into exile

1870

1890

1910

1861–89 Reign of moderate Luís I

1877 Serpa Pinto sets out from Benguela in Angola to cross southern Africa

1886 Building of Ponte de Dom Luís I in Porto

1908 Carlos I and his heir, Luís, assassinated by Republicans

1890 Plan to link African colonies of Mozambique and Angola is thwarted by ultimatum from the British

Modern Portugal

The early years of the new Republic were marked by political and economic crisis, until a military coup in 1926 paved the way for the New State of 1933. Under the oppressive regime of prime minister António Salazar, the country was freed of its debts, but suffered poverty and unemployment. Portugal's reliance on its African colonies led to costly wars, unrest in the army and the overthrow of the government in 1974. The painful return to democracy was rewarded by admission to the European Community in 1986.

1949 Portugal signs the North Atlantic Treaty and becomes a founder member of NATO

1966 Opening of Ponte Sala (now Ponte 25 de Abril) acr the Tagus *(see p1*

1966 National football team wit brilliant Eusébio *(centre, kneeling* reach quarter-finals of World Cu

1933 Founding of the *Estado Novo* (New State), harsh dictatorship led by Salazar. Government bans all strikes and censors the press, crushing opposition through brutal secret police force, the PIDE

1935 Death of poet Fernando Pessoa who wrote under four different names, in four distinct styles. This portrait by José de Almada Negreiros is in Lisbon's Centro de Arte Moderna *(see p122)*

1955 Armenian oil magnate Calouste Gulbenkian dies leaving 2,355 million escudos (£55 million) to set up a foundation for the arts and education

1922 First flight across the South Atlantic by Gago Coutinho and Sacadura Cabral

1911 Women given the vote

1910	1920	1930	1940	1950	1960
1910	1920	1930	1940	1950	1960

1916 Portugal enters World War I on side of the British and French

1918 Assassination of President Sidónio Pais; post-war years are period of social unrest with frequent strikes and changes of government

1928 António Salazar made finance minister; he imposes austerity measures, balancing the budget by 1929. In 1932 he becomes prime minister

1949 Neurosurgeon António Egas Moniz wins Nobel Prize for Medicine for his work developing the prefrontal lobotomy

1958 In the pre-sidential elections, the opposition candidate General Delgado wins so much support that the result is rigged against him. He is later assassinated

1917 Three peasant children in Fátima claim to see Virgin Mary; site of vision becomes focus of major pilgrimage

1942 Salazar meets Spanish dictator Franco to confirm mutual policy of non-aggression

1961 India annexes Portuguese colonies of Goa, Damão and Diu

1926 Coup puts military in charge of Republic; General Carmona is new president, holding office until his death in 1951

1939–45 In World War II Portugal is theoretically neutral but, after threats to her shipping, is forced to sell minerals to Germany. From 1943 Portugal permits British and American bases in the Azores. Here Salazar *(centre)* talks to troops stationed there

1986 Portugal joins European Community. Soares becomes the first civilian president of Portugal in 60 years

1985 Social Democrats, under Aníbal Cavaco Silva, come to power

1998 Lisbon hosts Expo '98; the mascot Gil embodies the theme of water and the oceans

1974 Carnation Revolution: in a near-bloodless coup, Marcelo Caetano's regime is overthrown by the MFA (Armed Forces Movement), a group of discontented left-wing army officers

2004 Portugal hosts the Euro 2004 football tournament

1995 António Guterres of the Socialist Party elected prime minister

2011 Prime Minister José Socrates steps down after two terms; he is replaced by Pedro Passos Coelho

| 70 | 1980 | 1990 | 2000 | 2010 | 2020 |

| 70 | 1980 | 1990 | 2000 | 2010 | 2020 |

1976 In the first free elections for nearly 50 years, the Socialist Mário Soares becomes prime minister

1988 Rosa Mota *(centre)* wins women's marathon at the Olympic Games in Seoul

2016 Portugal wins UEFA Euro 2016 under Captain Cristiano Ronaldo. Former Prime Minister, and United Nations High Commissioner for Refugees, António Guterres is elected United Nations Secretary-General

1975 All of Portugal's remaining colonies except Macao are granted independence, putting an end to long, unwinnable wars in Africa. Troops, such as these on patrol in the Angolan bush, are hastily brought home

The Carnation Revolution

The revolution of 25 April 1974 gained its popular name when people began placing red carnations in the barrels of soldiers' guns. Led by army officers disaffected by the colonial wars in Africa, the revolution heralded a period of great celebration, as Portugal emerged from decades of insularity. The political situation, however, was chaotic: the new government pushed through a controversial programme of nationalization and land reform in favour of the peasants, but in November 1975 the left-wing radicals were ousted by a short-lived counter-coup.

GOLPE MILITAR
"MOVIMENTO DAS FORÇAS ARMADAS" DESENCADEIA ACÇÃO DE MADRUGADA

Newspaper headline announcing revolution

LISBON AREA BY AREA

Lisbon at a Glance

Portugal's capital sits on the north bank of the Tagus estuary, 17 km (11 miles) from the Atlantic. The city has a population of about 550,000, but the conurbation of "Grande Lisboa", which has engulfed many surrounding villages, has nearly two million people. Razed to the ground by the earthquake of 1755 *(see pp66–7)*, the city centre is essentially 18th century, with carefully planned, elegant streets in the Baixa. On the hills on either side of the centre, the narrow streets of the Alfama and Bairro Alto make it a personal, approachable city. Since its days of glory during the Age of Discovery, when the city was at the forefront of world trade, Lisbon has been an important port. Today the docks have moved; however, the great monuments in Belém still bear witness to the city's maritime past.

The Museu Nacional de Arte Antiga houses paintings, decorative art and sculpture. Of particular interest are the Flemish-influenced Portuguese paintings such as this *Apparition of Christ to the Virgin* by Jorge Afonso *(see pp98–9)*.

The Mosteiro dos Jerónimos is a magnificent 16th-century monastery. Commissioned by Manuel I, much of it is built in the peculiarly Portuguese style of architecture, known as Manueline. The extravagantly sculpted south portal of the church, designed by João de Castilho in 1516, is one of the finest expressions of the style *(see pp108–9)*.

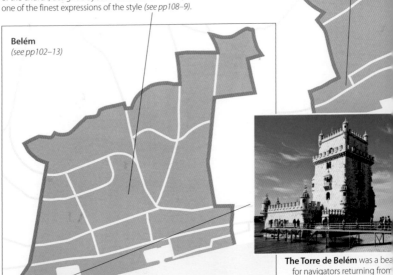

Belém
(see pp102–13)

| 0 metres | 500 |
| 0 yards | 500 |

The Torre de Belém was a bea[con] for navigators returning from [the] Indies and the New World, [and] a symbol of Portuguese [naval] power *(see p[...])*

◀ The splendid Baroque fountain in Lisbon's Rossio square

The Elevador de Santa Justa, built at the turn of the 20th century, is a wrought-iron lift decorated with filigree that links the Baixa quarter with the Largo do Carmo *(see p88)*.

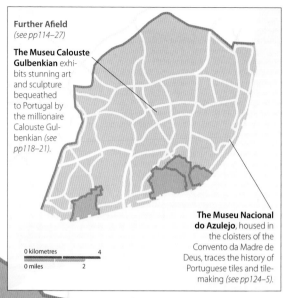

Further Afield
(see pp114–27)

The Museu Calouste Gulbenkian exhibits stunning art and sculpture bequeathed to Portugal by the millionaire Calouste Gulbenkian *(see pp118–21)*.

The Museu Nacional do Azulejo, housed in the cloisters of the Convento da Madre de Deus, traces the history of Portuguese tiles and tile-making *(see pp124–5)*.

0 kilometres   4
0 miles   2

Baixa and Avenida
(see pp82–89)

Bairro Alto and Estrela
(see pp90–101)

Alfama
(see pp70–81)

The Castelo de São Jorge, once a Moorish castle and then the abode of the Portuguese kings, was transformed in the 1930s into tranquil public gardens. The battlements afford spectacular views of the city *(see pp80–81)*.

The Sé, Lisbon's greatly restored cathedral, is a sturdy Romanesque building noted for its beautiful rose window. Ecclesiastical robes and silver are among the many religious objects on display in the treasury *(see p76)*.

0 metres   500
0 yards   500

The 1755 Lisbon Earthquake

The first tremor of the devastating earthquake was felt at 9:30am on 1 November. A few minutes later there was a second, far more violent shock, reducing over half the city to rubble. Although the epicentre was close to the Algarve, Lisbon, as the most populated area, bore the worst. Over 20 churches collapsed, crushing the crowds who had assembled for All Saints' Day. A third shock was followed by fires which quickly spread. An hour later, huge waves came rolling in from the Tagus and flooded the lower part of the city. Most of Portugal suffered damage and the shock was felt as far away as Italy. It is estimated that 15,000 people lost their lives in Lisbon alone.

This anonymous painting of the arrival of a papal ambassador at court in 1693 shows how Terreiro do Paço looked before the earthquake.

Some buildings that might have survived an earthquake alone were destroyed by the fire that followed.

The old royal palace, the 16th-century Paço da Ribeira, was utterly ruined by the earthquake and ensuing flood.

The royal family was staying at the palace in Belém, a place far less affected than Lisbon, and survived the disaster unscathed. Here the king surveys the city's devastation.

Ships crammed full of people fleeing the fire were wrecked and anchors thrown up to water level.

This detail is from an ex-voto painting dedicated to Nossa Senhora da Estrela, given by a grateful father in thanks for the sparing of his daughter's life in the earthquake. The girl was found miraculously alive after being buried under rubble for seven hours.

Marquês de Pombal (1699–1782)

The Reconstruction of Lisbon

No sooner had the tremors abated than Sebastião José de Carvalho e Melo, chief minister to José I and later to become Marquês de Pombal, was outlining ideas for rebuilding the city. While philosophers moralized, Pombal's initial response is said to have been, "bury the dead and feed the living". He restored order, then began a progressive town-planning scheme. His efficient handling of the crisis gained him almost total political control.

Reactions to the Disaster

The earthquake had a profound effect on European thought. Eyewitness accounts appeared in the papers, many written by foreigners living in Lisbon. A heated debate arose as to whether the earthquake was a natural phenomenon or an act of divine wrath. Lisbon had been a flourishing city, famed for its wealth – also for its Inquisition and idolatry. Interpreting the quake as punishment, many preachers prophesied further catastrophes. Leading literary figures debated the significance of the event, among them Voltaire, who wrote a poem about the disaster, propounding his views that evil exists and man is weak and powerless, doomed to an unhappy fate on earth.

French author, Voltaire

The ancient castle walls succumbed to the reverberating shock waves.

Flames erupted as the candles lit for All Saints' Day ignited the city's churches. The fire raged for seven days.

Some of Lisbon's finest buildings were destroyed, along with gold, jewellery, priceless furniture, archives, books and paintings.

At 11am, tidal waves rolled into Terreiro do Paço. The Alcântara docks, to the west, bore the brunt of the impact.

Churches, homes and public buildings all suffered in the disaster. The Royal Opera House, here shown in ruins, was only completed in March the same year.

A Depiction of the Earthquake

This anonymous German engraving of 1775 gives a vivid picture of the scale of the disaster. Many who fled the flames made for the Tagus, but were washed away in the huge waves which struck the Terreiro do Paço. The human and material losses were incalculable.

The reconstruction of the centre of Lisbon took place rapidly. By the end of November the Marquês de Pombal had devised a strikingly modern scheme for a grid of parallel streets running from the waterfront to Rossio. The new buildings are shown in yellow.

Modern-day Lisbon holds many reminders of the earthquake. Pombal's innovative grid system is clearly visible in this aerial view of the Baixa (see pp82–9). The scheme took many years to complete, and the triumphal arch spanning Rua Augusta was not finished until over a century later, in 1873.

Fado: the Music of Lisbon

Like blues music, *fado* is an expression of longing and sorrow. Literally meaning "fate", the term may be applied to an individual song as well as the genre itself. The music owes much to the concept known as *saudade*, meaning a longing both for what has been lost, and for what has never been attained, which perhaps accounts for its emotional power. The people of Lisbon have nurtured this poignant music in backstreet cafés and restaurants for over 150 years, and it has altered little in that time. It is sung as often by women as men, always accompanied by the *guitarra* and viola (acoustic Spanish guitar). *Fado* from Coimbra has developed its own lighter-hearted style.

A depiction of the music's bohemian associations from the 1920s

Female *fadistas* traditionally wear a black shawl in memory of Maria Severa.

The *guitarrista* plays the melody and will occasionally perform a solo instrumental piece.

Maria Severa (1810–36) was the first great *fadista* and the subject of the first Portuguese sound film in 1931. Her scandalous life and early death are pivotal to *fado* history, and her spiritual influence has been enormous, inspiring *fados*, poems, novels and plays.

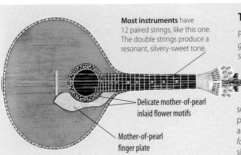

Most instruments have 12 paired strings, like this one. The double strings produce a resonant, silvery-sweet tone.

Delicate mother-of-pearl inlaid flower motifs

Mother-of-pearl finger plate

The Guitarra

Peculiar to Portuguese culture, the *guitarra* is a flat-backed instrument shaped like a mandolin, with eight, ten or twelve strings, arranged in pairs. It has evolved from a simple 19th-century design into a finely decorated piece, sometimes inlaid with mother-of-pearl. The sound of the *guitarra* is an essential ingredient of a good *fado*, echoing and enhancing the singer's melody line.

All kinds of themes may occur in *fado*. This song of 1910, for example, celebrates the dawning of the liberal republic. Such songsheets remained a favoured means of dissemination, even after the first records were made in 1904.

Alfredo Duarte (1891–1982) was a renowned writer of *fado* lyrics dealing with love, death, longing, tragedy and triumph. Affectionately known as *O Marceneiro* (the master carpenter) because of his skill as a joiner, he is still revered and his work widely performed.

A cultural icon for the Portuguese, Amália Rodrigues (1921–99) was the leading exponent of *fado* for over 50 years. She crystallized the music's style in the post-war years, and made it known around the world.

The *viola* provides rhythm accompaniment, but the player will never take a solo.

The music has long inspired great writers and painters. *O Fado* (1910) by José Malhôa *(see p59)* shows it in an intimate setting with the *fadista* captivating his listener. The air of abandonment underlines the earthiness of many of the songs.

The Fado House

Lisbon's best fado *houses are those run by* fadistas *themselves. Based on a love of the music and on relationships with other performers, such houses usually offer a truer to experience than the larger, tourist-oriented houses. A good example is the* **Parreirinha de Alfama***, owned by Argentina Santos (centre left). Less slick, but more emotionally charged, are performances of fado vadio, "itinerant" fado, in humbler restaurants and bars such as* Tasca do Chico *in Bairro Alto.*

Where to Enjoy Fado in Lisbon

Any of these *fado* houses will offer you good food, wine and music – or visit the Museu do Fado *(see p75)* for a fascinating exhibition on the history of *fado*.

Café Luso
Travessa da Queimada 10.
Map 7 A3.
Tel 213 422 281.

Casa de Linhares
Beco dos Armazéns do Linho 2.
Map 8 D4. **Tel** 910 188 118.

Clube de Fado
Rua S João de
Praça 92. **Map** 8 D4.
Tel 218 852 704.

O Faia
Rua da Barroca 54–6.
Map 4 F2.
Tel 213 426 742.

Parreirinha de Alfama
Beco do Espírito Santo 1.
Map 8 E4.
Tel 218 868 209.

Senhor Vinho
Rua do Meio à Lapa 18.
Map 4 D3. **Tel** 213 972 681.

ALFAMA

It is difficult to believe that this humble neighbourhood was once the most desirable quarter of Lisbon. For the Moors, the tightly packed alleyways around the fortified castle comprised the whole city. The seeds of decline were sown in the Middle Ages when wealthy residents moved west for fear of earthquakes, leaving the quarter to fishermen and paupers. The buildings survived the 1755 earthquake *(see pp66–7)* and, although there are no Moorish houses still standing, the quarter retains its kasbah-like layout. Compact houses line steep streets and stairways, their façades strung with washing.

Restoration work on some buildings is under way in the most dilapidated areas, but daily life still revolves around local grocery stores and small, cellar-like tavernas.

Above the Alfama, the imposing Castelo de São Jorge crowns Lisbon's eastern hill. This natural vantage point was a defensive stronghold and royal palace until the 16th century; today it is a popular promenade, with spectacular views of the city and the river from its reconstructed ramparts.

West of the Alfama stand the proud twin towers of the Sé. To the northeast, the domed church of Santa Engrácia and the white façade of São Vicente de Fora dominate the skyline.

Sights at a Glance

Museums and Galleries
2 Museu de Artes Decorativas Portuguesas
6 Museu Militar
7 Museu do Fado

Churches
3 São Vicente de Fora
5 Santa Engrácia
9 Sé
10 Santo António à Sé

Historic Buildings
8 Casa dos Bicos
11 *Castelo de São Jorge pp80–81*

Belvederes
1 Miradouro de Santa Luzia
12 Miradouro da Graça

Markets
4 Feira da Ladra

See also Street Finder pp132–45

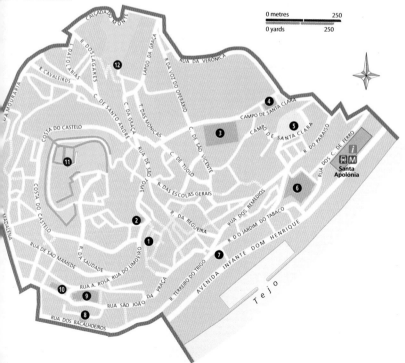

0 metres 250
0 yards 250

◀ An antique tram passing through one of Alfama's picturesque streets

For keys to symbols *see back flap*

Street-by-Street: Alfama

A fascinating quarter at any time of day, the Alfama comes to life in the late afternoon and early evening when the locals emerge at their doorways and the small tavernas start to fill. A new generation of younger residents has resulted in a small number of design-led shops and bars. Given the steep streets and steps of the quarter, the least strenuous approach is to start at the top and work your way down. A walk around the maze of winding alleyways will reveal picturesque corners and crumbling churches as well as panoramic views from the shady terraces, such as the Miradouro de Santa Luzia.

On Largo das Portas do Sol, café tables look out over the Alfama towards the Tagus estuary. Portas do Sol was one of the entrance gates to the old city.

The church of Santa Luzia has 18th-century blue and white *azulejo* panels on its south wall.

Statue of St Vincent

Largo das Portas do Sol has its own terrace viewpoint on a converted rooftop on the east side of the Santa Luzia church.

Castelo de São Jorge

❷ ★ Museu de Artes Decorativas
Set up as a museum by the banker Ricardo do Espírito Santo Silva, the 17th-century Palácio Azurara houses fine 17th- and 18th-century Portuguese furniture and decorative arts.

Key

— Suggested route

| 0 metres | 25 |
| 0 yards | 25 |

❶ ★ Miradouro de Santa Luzia
The view from this bougainvillea-clad terrace spans the tiled roofs of the Alfama toward the Tagus. This is a pleasant place to rest after a walk around the area's steep streets.

Beco das Cruzes, like most of the alleyways *(becos)* that snake their way through the Alfama, is a steep cobbled street. Locals often hang washing between the tightly packed houses.

Locator Map
See Lisbon Street Finder map 8

Rua de São Pedro is the scene of a lively early-morning fish market where the *varinas* sell the catch of the day. *Peixe espada* (scabbard fish) is one of the fish sold here.

Largo do Chafariz de Dentro is named after the 17th-century fountain *(chafariz)* that was originally placed within *(dentro)* rather than outside the 14th-century walls.

BECO DAS CRUZES

BECO DA CARDOSA

RUA DE SÃO MIGUEL

BECO DO MEXIAS

LARGO DO CHAFARIZ DE DENTRO

BECO DO POCINHO

RUA DE SÃO PEDRO

The church of Nossa Senhora dos Remédios was rebuilt after the 1755 earthquake *(see pp66–7)*. The pinnacled Manueline portal is all that remains of the original building.

São Miguel was rebuilt after it was damaged in the 1755 earthquake. It retains a few earlier features, including a fine ceiling of Brazilian jacaranda wood.

Popular restaurants hidden in the labyrinth of alleyways spill out onto open-air patios.

Tile panel showing pre-earthquake Praça do Comércio, Santa Luzia

❶ Miradouro de Santa Luzia

Rua do Limoeiro. **Map** 8 D4. 🚌 28.

The terrace by the church of Santa Luzia provides a sweeping view over the Alfama and the River Tagus. Distinctive landmarks, from left to right, are the cupola of Santa Engrácia, the church of Santo Estêvão and the two startling white towers of São Miguel. While tourists admire the views, old men play cards under the bougainvillea-clad pergola. The south wall of Santa Luzia has two modern tiled panels, one of Praça do Comércio before it was flattened by the earthquake, the other showing the Christians attacking the Castelo de São Jorge (see pp80–81) in 1147.

❷ Museu de Artes Decorativas Portuguesas

Largo Portas do Sol 2. **Map** 8 D3.
Tel 218 814 600. 🚌 737. 🚋 12, 28.
Open 10am–5pm Wed–Mon.
📷 11am & 3pm Mon & Wed, 3pm Thu. **Closed** 1 Jan, 1 May, 25 Dec.
♿ **W** fress.pt

Also known as the Ricardo do Espírito Santo Silva Foundation, the museum was set up in 1953 to preserve the traditions and increase public awareness of the Portuguese decorative arts. The foundation was named after a banker who bought the 17th-century Palácio Azurara in 1947 to house his fine collection of furniture, textiles, silver and ceramics. Among the 17th- and 18th-century antiques displayed in this handsome mansion are many fine pieces in exotic woods, including an 18th-century rosewood backgammon and chess table. Also of note are the collections of 18th-century silver and Chinese porcelain, and the Arraiolos carpets (see p307). The spacious rooms still retain some original ceilings and azulejo panels.

In the adjoining building are workshops where artisans preserve the techniques of cabinet-making, bookbinding, gilding and other traditional crafts. Temporary exhibitions, lectures and concerts are also held in the palace.

18th-century china cutlery case, Museu de Artes Decorativas

❸ São Vicente de Fora

Largo de São Vicente. **Map** 8 E3.
Tel 218 810 500. 🚌 712, 734. 🚋 28.
Church: **Open** 9am–1pm, 2:30–5pm Tue–Sat. Monastery: (incl cloisters).
Open 10am–6pm Tue–Sun. ✝
♿ to museum.

St Vincent was proclaimed Lisbon's patron saint in 1173, when his relics were transferred from the Algarve (see p325) to a church on this site outside (fora) the city walls. Designed by Italian architect Filippo Terzi, and completed in 1627, the sober, off-white façade is in Italian Renaissance style, with statues of saints Vincent, Augustine and Sebastian over the entrance. Inside, one is drawn immediately into Machado de Castro's Baroque canopy over the altar, flanked by life-size wooden statues.

The adjoining former Augustinian monastery, with its 16th-century cistern and vestiges of the former cloister, is famous for its 18th-century azulejos. Among the panels in the entrance hall off the first cloister there are lively, though historically inaccurate, tile scenes of Afonso Henriques attacking Lisbon and Santarém. Around the cloisters the tiled rural scenes, surrounded by floral designs and cherubs, illustrate the fables of La Fontaine. A passageway leads to the old refectory, transformed into the Bragança Pantheon in 1885. Except for Maria I and Pedro IV, every king and queen is here, from João IV, who died in 1656, to Manuel II, last king of Portugal. A stone mourner kneels at the tomb of Carlos I and his son Luís Felipe, assassinated in Praça do Comércio in 1908.

The small Museu do Patriarcado displays sacred art, some from as far back as the 16th century.

Stone figure of a woman praying by the tomb of Carlos I in São Vicente de Fora

❹ Feira da Ladra

Campo de Santa Clara. **Map** 8 E2. **Open** 9am–6pm Tue & Sat. 712. 28.

The stalls of the so-called "Thieves' Market" have occupied this site for over a century. As the fame of this market has grown, bargains are increasingly hard to find amongst the mass of bric-a-brac, but a few of the vendors have interesting wrought-iron work, prints and tiles, as well as second-hand clothes. Evidence of Portugal's colonial past is reflected in the stalls selling African statuary, masks and jewellery. Fish, vegetables and herbs are sold in the central wrought-iron marketplace.

The multicoloured marble interior beneath Santa Engrácia's dome

❺ Santa Engrácia

Campo de Santa Clara. **Map** 8 F2. **Tel** 218 854 820. 28. **Open** 10am–5pm Tue–Sun (Apr–Sep: to 6pm). **Closed** 1 Jan, Easter, 1 May, 25 Dec.

One of Lisbon's most striking landmarks, the soaring dome of Santa Engrácia punctuates the skyline in the east of the city. The original church collapsed in a storm in 1681. The first stone of the Baroque monument, laid in 1682, marked the beginning of a 284-year saga which led to the invention of a saying that a Santa Engrácia job was never done. The church was not completed until 1966.

The interior is paved with coloured marble and crowned by a giant cupola. As the National Pantheon, it houses cenotaphs of Portuguese heroes, such as Vasco da Gama (see p110) and Afonso de Albuquerque, Viceroy of India (1502–15) on the left, and

on the right Henry the Navigator (see p53). The fadista Amália Rodrigues (see p69) is also buried here. A lift up to the dome offers 360-degree views of the city.

❻ Museu Militar

Largo do Museu de Artilharia. **Map** 8 F3. **Tel** 218 842 567. 712, 728, 757. 28. Santa Apolónia. **Open** 10am–5pm Tue–Fri, 10am–12:30pm & 1:30–5pm Sat & Sun. **Closed** 1 Jan, Easter, 1 May, 25 Dec. (free Sun am). **exercito.pt**

Located on the site of a 16th-century cannon foundry and arms depot, this museum contains an extensive display of arms, uniforms and historical documents. Visits begin in the Vasco da Gama Room with a collection of cannons and modern murals depicting the discovery of the sea route to India. The Salas da Grande Guerra display exhibits related to World War I. Other rooms focus on the evolution of weapons, from flints to spears to rifles. The large courtyard, flanked by cannons, tells the story of Portugal in tiled panels, from the Christian Reconquest to World War I. The Portuguese artillery section displays the wagon used to transport the triumphal arch to Rua Augusta (see p88).

❼ Museu do Fado

Largo do Chafariz de Dentro 1. **Map** 8 E4. **Tel** 218 823 470. 728, 735, 745, 759, 794. **Open** 10am–6pm Tue–Sun. **museudofado.pt**

Alfama is considered the true home of fado and this museum

portrays the influence that this ever-popular and intensely heartfelt genre of music has had on the city over the past two centuries. A permanent display traces the genre's history from its origins in the early 19th century to the present day, from Maria Severa, the first fado diva, to more contemporary singers like Amália Rodrigues and Mariza. Regular temporary exhibitions take place throughout the year on a range of musical themes, along with the occasional live fado concert.

❽ Casa dos Bicos

Rua dos Bacalhoeiros. **Map** 8 D4. **Tel** 218 802 040. 728, 746, 759. 18, 25. **Open** 10am–6pm Mon–Sat.

This conspicuous house, faced with diamond-shaped stones (bicos), was built in 1523 for Brás de Albuquerque, illegitimate son of Afonso, Viceroy of India and conqueror of Goa and Malacca. The façade is an adaptation of a style popular in Europe during the 16th century. The two top storeys, ruined in the earthquake of 1755, were restored in the 1980s, recreating the original from old views of Lisbon in tile panels and engravings. In the interim the building was used for salting fish (Rua dos Bacalhoeiros means street of the cod fishermen). Nowadays it houses the headquarters of the José Saramago Foundation. In addition to a permanent exhibition dedicated to this Nobel Prize-winning author, there are often concerts and debates taking place here.

The curiously faceted Casa dos Bicos, and surrounding buildings

The façade of the Sé, the city's cathedral

❾ Sé

Largo da Sé. **Map** 8 D4. **Tel** 218 866 752. 🚌 737. 🚊 12, 28. Sé: **Open** 9am–7pm daily. Church, Cloister & Treasury: 10am–6.30pm Mon–Sat. ✝ 🚫 to Gothic cloister and treasury.

In 1150, three years after Afonso Henriques recaptured Lisbon from the Moors, he built a cathedral for the first bishop of Lisbon, the English crusader Gilbert of Hastings, on the site of the old mosque. Sé is short for Sedes Episcopalis, the seat (or see) of a bishop. Devastated by three earth tremors in the 14th century, as well as the earthquake of 1755, and renovated over the centuries, the cathedral

you see today blends a variety of architectural styles. The façade, with twin castellated bell towers and a splendid rose window, retains its solid Romanesque aspect. The gloomy interior, for the most part, is simple and austere, and hardly anything remains of the embellishment lavished upon it by King João V in the first half of the 18th century. Beyond the renovated Romanesque nave the ambulatory has nine Gothic chapels. The Capela de Santo Ildefonso contains the 14th-century sarcophagi of Lopo Fernandes Pacheco, companion in arms to King Afonso IV, and his wife, Maria Vilalobos. The bearded figure of the nobleman, sword in hand, and his wife, clutching a prayer book, are carved onto the tombs with their

Carved tomb of the 14th-century nobleman Lopo Fernandes Pacheco in chapel in the ambulatory

Detail of the Baroque nativity scene by Joaquim Machado de Castro

dogs sitting faithfully at their feet. In the adjacent chancel are the tombs of Afonso IV and his wife Dona Beatriz.

The Gothic cloister, reached via the third chapel in the ambulatory, has elegant double arches with some finely carved capitals. One of the chapels is still fitted with its 13th-century wrought-iron gate. Archaeological excavations in the cloister have unearthed various Roman and other remains.

To the left of the cathedral entrance the Franciscan chapel contains the font where the saint was baptized in 1195 and is decorated with a charming tiled scene of St Antony preaching to the fishes. The adjacent chapel contains a Baroque nativity scene made of cork, wood and terracotta by the celebrated sculptor Joaquim Machado de Castro (1766).

The treasury is at the top of the staircase on the right. It houses silver, ecclesiastical robes, statuary, illustrated manuscripts and a few relics associated with St Vincent, which were transferred to Lisbon from Cabo de São Vicente in 1173 (see p325). Legend has it that two sacred ravens kept a permanent vigil over the boat that transported the relics. The ravens and the boat became a symbol of the city of Lisbon, still very much in use today. It is also said that the descendants of the two ravens used to live in the cloisters of the cathedral.

Santo António (c.1195–1231)

The best-loved saint of the Lisboetas is St Antony of Padua. Although born and brought up in Lisbon, he spent the last months of his life in Padua, Italy. St Antony joined the Franciscan Order in 1220, impressed by some crusading friars he had met at Coimbra, where he was studying. The friar was a learned and passionate preacher, renowned for his devotion to the poor and his ability to convert heretics. Many statues and paintings of St Antony depict him carrying the Infant Jesus on a book, while others show him preaching to the fishes, as St Francis preached to the birds.

In 1934 Pope Pius XI declared St Antony a patron saint of Portugal. The year 1995 saw the 800th anniversary of his birth – a cause for major celebrations throughout the city. Lisbon celebrates St Antony on 13 June, the day of the saint's death (see p35).

➓ Santo António à Sé

Largo Santo António à Sé 24. **Map** 7 C4. **Tel** 218 869 145. 🚌 737. 🚋 12, 28. **Open** 8am–7pm daily (to 8pm Sat & Sun). 🚹 Museu Antoniano: **Tel** 218 860 447. **Open** 10am–6pm Tue–Sun. 🚫

The popular little church of Santo António allegedly stands on the site of the house in which St Antony was born. The crypt, reached via the tiled sacristy on the left of the church, is all that remains of the original church destroyed by the earthquake of 1755. Work began on the new church in 1757 headed by Mateus Vicente, architect of the Basílica da Estrela *(see p97)* and was partially funded by donations collected by local children with the cry "a small coin for St Antony". Even today the floor of the tiny chapel in the crypt is strewn with coins and the walls are scrawled with devotional messages from worshippers.

The church's façade blends the undulating curves of the Baroque style with Neo-Classical Ionic columns on either side of the main portal. Inside, on the way down to the crypt, a modern *azulejo* panel commemorates the visit of Pope John Paul II in 1982. In 1995 the church was given a face-lift for the saint's eighth centenary. It is traditional for young couples to visit the church on their wedding day

and leave flowers for St Antony who is believed to bring good luck to new marriages.

Next door the small Museu Antoniano houses artifacts, relating to St Antony, as well as gold and silverware which used to decorate the church. The most charming exhibit is a 17th-century tiled panel of St Antony preaching to the fishes.

➓ Castelo de São Jorge

See pp80–81.

Tiled panel recording Pope John Paul II's visit to Santo António à Sé

The Miradouro and Igreja da Graça seen from the Castelo de São Jorge

➓ Miradouro da Graça

Map 8 D2. 🚌 737. 🚋 12, 28.

The working-class quarter of Graça developed at the end of the 19th century. Today, it is visited chiefly for the views from its *miradouro* (belvedere). The panorama of rooftops and skyscrapers is less spectacular than the view from the castle, but it is a popular spot, particularly in the early evenings when couples sit at café tables under the pines. Behind the *miradouro* stands an Augustinian monastery, founded in 1271 and rebuilt after the earthquake. Once a flourishing complex, the huge building is now used as barracks but the church, the Igreja da Graça, can still be visited. Inside, in the right transept, is the *Senhor dos Passos,* a representation of Christ carrying the cross on the way to Calvary. This figure, clad in brilliant purple clothes, is carried on a procession through Graça on the second Sunday in Lent. The *azulejos* on the altar front, dating from the 17th century, imitate the brocaded textiles usually draped over the altar.

⑪ Castelo de São Jorge

Following the recapture of Lisbon from the Moors in 1147, King Afonso Henriques transformed their hilltop citadel into the residence of the Portuguese kings. In 1511 Manuel I built a more lavish palace in what is now the Praça do Comércio and the castle was used as a theatre, prison and arms depot. After the 1755 earthquake the ramparts remained in ruins until 1938 when Salazar *(see pp60–61)* began a complete renovation, rebuilding the "medieval" walls and adding gardens and wildfowl. The castle may not be authentic but the gardens and the narrow streets of the Santa Cruz district within the walls make a pleasant stroll and the views are the finest in Lisbon.

Torre de Ulisses has a camera obscura that projects views of Lisbon onto the inside walls of the tower.

RUA DAS COZINHAS

★ **Battlements**
Visitors can climb the towers and walk along the reconstructed ramparts of the castle walls.

Casa do Leão Restaurant
Part of the former royal residence, this restaurant can be booked for meals and parties *(see p398)*.

Museu do Castelo
has archaeological artifacts illustrating lifestyle and culture through the ages.

★ **Observation Terrace**
This large shaded square affords spectacular views over Lisbon and the Tagus. Local men play backgammon and cards under the trees.

Key

— Suggested route

◀ The crenellated walls of the Castelo de São Jorge

Porta de Martim Moniz is named after a knight who gave his life to keep the gate open for Afonso Henriques's troops in 1147. His bust is in a niche by the gate.

This important archaeological site, the location of the city's first known settlement (7th century BC), reveals much about Lisbon's history.

Porta de Santo André opens out into Largo Rodrigues de Freitas.

VISITORS' CHECKLIST

Practical Information
Porta de S Jorge, Rua do Chão da Feira (entrance on Rua de Santa Cruz do Castelo). **Map** 8 D3. **Tel** 218 800 620. **W** castelodesaojorge.pt **Open** 9am–9pm daily (Nov–Feb: to 6pm), (last adm: 30 mins before closing). Camera Obscura: **Open** 10am–5pm daily. every 20 mins, with a maximum of 20 people. Museu do Castelo: **Open** 9am–9pm daily (Nov–Feb: to 6pm). **Closed** 1 Jan, 1 May, 24 & 25 Dec.

Transport
737. 28.

Inside the 12th-century church of Santa Cruz do Castelo is a 17th-century statue of St George.

Santa Cruz square is a pleasant open space surrounded by the area's elegantly restored buildings.

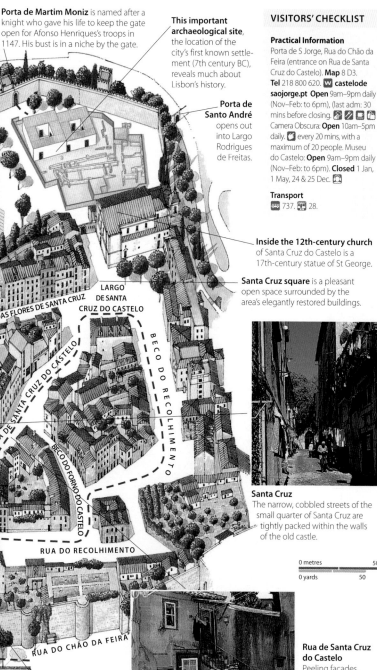

DAS FLORES DE SANTA CRUZ

LARGO DE SANTA CRUZ DO CASTELO

BECO DO RECOLHIMENTO

BECO DE SANTA CRUZ DO CASTELO

BECO DO FORNO DO CASTELO

RUA DE SANTA CRUZ DO CASTELO

RUA DO RECOLHIMENTO

RUA DO CHÃO DA FEIRA

Porta de São Jorge

Santa Cruz
The narrow, cobbled streets of the small quarter of Santa Cruz are tightly packed within the walls of the old castle.

0 metres 50
0 yards 50

Rua de Santa Cruz do Castelo
Peeling façades, potted plants and washing strung between windowsills characterize the pretty streets south of the Castelo de São Jorge.

For hotels and restaurants in this area see pp386–7 and pp398–401

BAIXA AND AVENIDA

From the ruins of Lisbon, devastated by the earthquake of 1755 *(see pp66–7)*, the Marquês de Pombal created an entirely new centre. Using a grid layout of streets, he linked the stately, arcaded Praça do Comércio beside the Tagus with the busy central square of Rossio. The streets were flanked by uniform, Neo-Classical buildings and named according to the shopkeepers and craftsmen who traded there. The Baixa (lower town) is still the commercial hub of the capital, housing banks, offices and shops. At its centre, Rossio is a popular meeting point with cafés, theatres and restaurants. The geometric layout of the area has been retained, but most of the buildings constructed since the mid-18th century have not adhered to Pombaline formality. The streets are crowded by day, particularly the lively Rua Augusta, but after dark the quarter is almost deserted.

Sights at a Glance

Museums and Galleries
❹ Museu da Sociedade de Geografia

Churches
❾ Nossa Senhora da Conceição
    Velha

Parks and Gardens
❶ Jardim Botânico

Lifts
❼ Elevador de Santa Justa

Historic Streets and Squares
❷ Avenida da Liberdade
❸ Praça dos Restauradores
❺ Rossio
❻ Praça da Figueira
❽ Rua Augusta
❿ Praça do Comércio

0 metres — 250
0 yards — 250

See also Street Finder
pp132–45

◀ Street view of the Elevador de Santa Justa

For keys to symbols *see back flap*

Street-by-Street: Restauradores

This is the busiest part of the city, especially the central squares of Rossio and Praça da Figueira. Totally rebuilt after the earthquake of 1755 *(see pp66–7)*, the area was one of Europe's first examples of town planning. Today, the large Neo-Classical buildings on the wide streets and squares house business offices. The atmosphere and surroundings are best absorbed from one of the busy pavement cafés. Rua das Portas de Santo Antão, a pedestrianized street where restaurants display tanks of live lobsters, is more relaxing for a stroll.

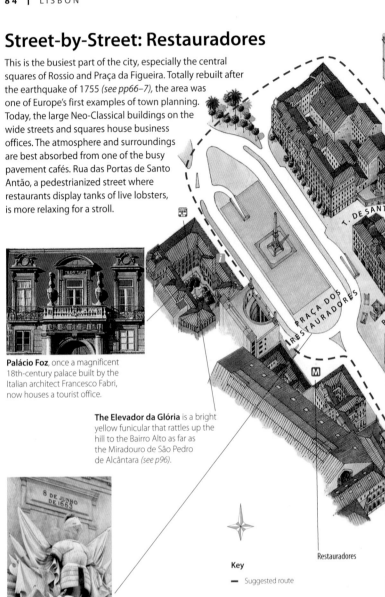

Palácio Foz, once a magnificent 18th-century palace built by the Italian architect Francesco Fabri, now houses a tourist office.

The Elevador da Glória is a bright yellow funicular that rattles up the hill to the Bairro Alto as far as the Miradouro de São Pedro de Alcântara *(see p96)*.

Restauradores

Key

— Suggested route

❸ **Praça dos Restauradores**
This large tree-lined square, named after the men who fought during the 1640 War of Restoration, is dominated by a tall obelisk with an ornate pedestal. There are café terraces on the square's patterned pavements.

Rossio station, designed by José Luìs Monteiro, is an eye-catching late 19th-century Neo-Manueline building with two Moorish-style horseshoe arches.

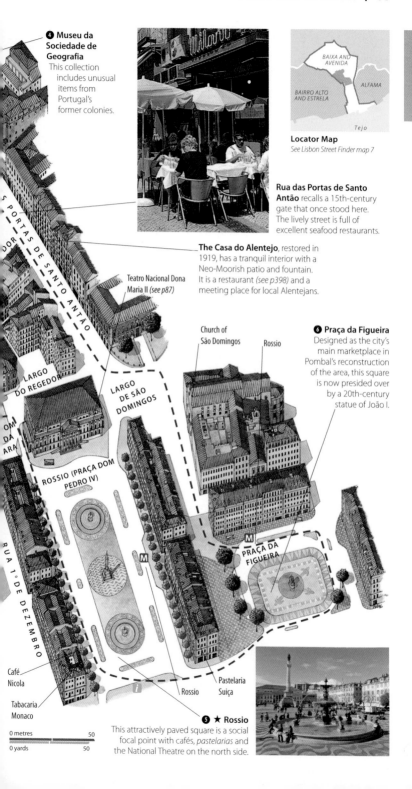

❹ Museu da Sociedade de Geografia
This collection includes unusual items from Portugal's former colonies.

Locator Map
See Lisbon Street Finder map 7

Rua das Portas de Santo Antão recalls a 15th-century gate that once stood here. The lively street is full of excellent seafood restaurants.

The Casa do Alentejo, restored in 1919, has a tranquil interior with a Neo-Moorish patio and fountain. It is a restaurant *(see p398)* and a meeting place for local Alentejans.

Teatro Nacional Dona Maria II *(see p87)*

Church of São Domingos

Rossio

❻ Praça da Figueira
Designed as the city's main marketplace in Pombal's reconstruction of the area, this square is now presided over by a 20th-century statue of João I.

LARGO DO REGEDOR

LARGO DE SÃO DOMINGOS

ROSSIO (PRAÇA DOM PEDRO IV)

PRAÇA DA FIGUEIRA

RUA 1º DE DEZEMBRO

Café Nicola

Tabacaria Monaco

0 metres 50
0 yards 50

Rossio

Pastelaria Suiça

❺ ★ Rossio
This attractively paved square is a social focal point with cafés, *pastelarias* and the National Theatre on the north side.

Bridge and pond shaded by trees in the Jardim Botânico

❶ Jardim Botânico

Rua da Escola Politécnica 58. **Map** 4 F1. **Tel** 213 921 800. 🚌 758. Ⓜ Rato. Gardens: **Open** Apr–Sep: 9am–8pm daily (Oct–Mar: to 6pm). **Closed** 1 Jan, 25 Dec. 🅰️ ♿ Ⓦ jb.ul.pt Museu Nacional de História Natural e da Ciência: **Tel** 213 921 808. **Open** 10am–5pm Tue–Fri, 11am–6pm Sat & Sun. 🅰️ (free until 2pm Sun). Ⓦ **museus.ulisboa.pt**

The complex, owned by the University of Lisbon, comprises 2 museums and 4 hectares (10 acres) of gardens. The botanical gardens have a distinct air of neglect. However, it is worth paying the entrance fee to wander among the exotic trees and dense paths of the gardens as they descend from the main entrance towards Rua da Alegria. A magnificent avenue of lofty palms connects the two levels.

The Museu Nacional de História Natural e da Ciência (Natural History and Science Museum) houses a number of permanent exhibitions. Some of them, like Plants in the Age of Dinosaurs and Mathematical Games Through the Ages, are very popular with school children.

❷ Avenida da Liberdade

Map 7 A2. 🚌 709, 711, 736 & many other routes. Ⓜ Restauradores, Avenida.

Following the earthquake of 1755 (see pp66–7), the Marquês de Pombal created the Passeio Público (public promenade) in the area now occupied by the lower part of Avenida da Liberdade and Praça dos Restauradores. Despite its name,

enjoyment of the park was restricted to Lisbon's high society and walls and gates ensured the exclusion of the lower classes. In 1821, when the Liberals came to power, the barriers were pulled down and the Avenida and square became open to all.

The boulevard you see today was built in 1879–82 in the style of the Champs-Elysées in Paris. The wide tree-lined avenue became a focus for pageants, festivities and demonstrations. A war memorial stands as a tribute to those who died in World War I. The avenue retains a certain elegance with fountains and café tables shaded by trees, but it no longer makes for a peaceful stroll. The once majestic thoroughfare, 90 m (295 ft) wide and decorated with abstract pavement patterns, is divided by seven lanes of traffic linking Praça dos Restauradores and Praça Marquês de Pombal to the north. Some original mansions are preserved, including the Neo-Classical Tivoli cinema at No. 188, with an original 1920s kiosk outside, and Casa Lambertini with its colourful mosaic decoration at No. 166. However, many Art Nouveau façades have unfortunately given way to newer ones occupied by offices, hotels or shopping complexes.

Detail from the memorial to the dead of World War I in Avenida da Liberdade

19th-century monument in honour of the Restoration in Praça dos Restauradores

❸ Praça dos Restauradores

Map 7 A2. 🚌 709, 711, 736 & many other routes. Ⓜ Restauradores.

The square, distinguished by its soaring obelisk, erected in 1886, commemorates the country's liberation from the Spanish yoke in 1640 (see pp54–5). The bronze figures on the pedestal depict Victory, holding a palm and a crown, and Freedom. The names and dates inscribed on the obelisk are those of the battles of the War of Restoration.

On the west side, the Palácio Foz houses a tourist office and work premises. It was built by Francesco Savario Fabri in 1755–77 for the Marquês de Castelo-Melhor, and was renamed after the Marquês de Foz, who lived here in the 19th century. The smart Avenida Palace Hotel on the southwest side of the square, was designed by José Lúis Monteiro (1849–1942), who also built Rossio railway station (see p87).

❹ Museu da Sociedade de Geografia

Rua das Portas de Santo Antão 100.
Map 7 A2. **Tel** 213 425 401.
🚌 709, 711, 736. Ⓜ Restauradores.
Open 3pm 1st Tue of month. 🎫 compulsory. 🖥 ♿

Located in the Geographical Society building, the museum houses an idiosyncratic ethno-graphical collection brought back from Portugal's former colonies. On display are circumcision masks from Guinea Bissau, musical instruments and snake spears. From Angola there are neck rests to sustain coiffures and the original *padrão* – the stone pillar erected by the Portuguese in 1482 to mark their sovereignty over the colony. Most of the exhibits are arranged along the splendid Sala Portugal.

❺ Rossio

Map 7 B3. 🚌 709, 711, 736 & many other routes. Ⓜ Rossio.

Formally called Praça de Dom Pedro IV, this large square has been Lisbon's nerve centre for six centuries. During its history it has been the stage of bull-fights, festivals, military parades and gruesome *autos da fé (see p55)*. However, today there is little more than an occasional political rally. The square has mostly been restored to its

Teatro Nacional Dona Maria II in Rossio illuminated by night

former glory, and the sober Pombaline buildings, disfigured on the upper level by the remains of neon signs, are occupied at street level by souvenir shops, jewellers and cafés. Centre stage is a statue of Dom Pedro IV, the first emperor of independent Brazil *(see p58)*. At the foot of the statue, the four female figures are allegories of Justice, Wisdom, Strength and Moderation.

In the mid-19th century the square was paved with wave-patterned mosaics which gave it the nickname of "Rolling Motion Square". The hand-cut grey and white stone cubes were the first such designs to decorate the city's pavements.

On the north side of Rossio is the Teatro Nacional Dona Maria II, named after Dom

Pedro's daughter. The Neo-Classical structure was built in the 1840s by the Italian archi-tect Fortunato Lodi. The interior was destroyed by fire in 1964 and reconstructed in the 1970s. On top of the pediment is Gil Vicente (1465–1536), the founder of Portuguese theatre.

Café Nicola on the west side of the square was a favourite meeting place among writers, including the poet Manuel du Bocage (1765–1805), who was notorious for his satires. Pastelaria Suiça, on the opposite side, is a café popular with tourists for its sunlit terrace.

❻ Praça da Figueira

Map 7 B3. 🚌 714, 759, 760 & many other routes. 🚊 15. Ⓜ Rossio.

Before the 1755 earthquake *(see pp66–7)* the square next to Rossio was the site of the Hospital de Todos-os-Santos (All Saints). In Pombal's design for the Baixa, the square took on the role of the city's central marketplace. In 1885 a covered market was introduced, but this was pulled down in the 1950s. Today, the four-storey buildings are given over to hotels, shops and cafés and the square is no longer a marketplace. Perhaps its most eye-catching feature is the multitude of pigeons that perch on the pedestal supporting Leopoldo de Almeida's bronze equestrian statue of João I, erected in 1971.

Bronze statue of King Joao I in Praça da Figueira

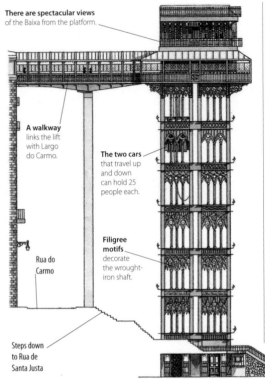

There are spectacular views of the Baixa from the platform.

A walkway links the lift with Largo do Carmo.

The two cars that travel up and down can hold 25 people each.

Rua do Carmo

Filigree motifs decorate the wrought-iron shaft.

Steps down to Rua de Santa Justa

❼ Elevador de Santa Justa

Rua de Santa Justa & Largo do Carmo. **Map** 7 B3. **Tel** 213 613 000. **Open** Jun–Sep: 7am–11pm daily; Oct–May: 7am–10pm daily.

Also known as the Elevador do Carmo, this Neo-Gothic lift was built at the turn of the 20th century by the French

Views from the top platform of the Elevador de Santa Justa

architect Raoul Mesnier du Ponsard, an apprentice of Alexandre Gustave Eiffel. Made of iron and embellished with filigree, it is one of the more eccentric features of the Baixa. Tickets can be purchased at the foot of the lift.

Passengers can travel up and down inside the tower in one of two smart wood-panelled cabins with brass fittings; they can also brave the walkway linking the lift to the Largo do Carmo in the Bairro Alto, 32 m (105 ft) above.

The very top of the tower, reached via a tight spiral stair-way, is given over to a viewing gallery. This high vantage point commands splendid views of the whole of downtown Lisbon, including Rossio, the grid pattern of the Baixa, the castle on the opposite hill, the river and the nearby ruins of the Carmo church. The fire that gutted the Chiado district in 1988 (see p94) was extinguished very close to the lift.

❽ Rua Augusta

Map 7 B3. Ⓜ Rossio. 🚌 714, 736, 759, 760 & many other routes. MUDE: Rua Augusta 24. **Tel** 218 886 117. **Open** 10am–6pm Tue–Sun.

A lively pedestrianized street decorated with mosaic pavements and lined with boutiques and cafés, Rua Augusta is the main tourist thoroughfare and the smartest in the Baixa. Street performers provide entertainment, while vendors sell lottery tickets, street art, books and souvenirs. The triumphal Arco da Rua Augusta, built to commemorate the city's recovery from the earthquake (see pp66–7), was completed only in 1873. There are great views from the top of the arch, which is accessed by elevator. A former bank on Rua Augusta now houses MUDE, a dynamic design and fashion museum.

The other main thoroughfares of the Baixa are Rua da Prata (silversmiths' street) and Rua do Ouro or Rua Aurea (goldsmiths' street). Cutting across these main streets are smaller streets that give glimpses up to the Bairro Alto to the west and the Castelo de São Jorge (see pp80–81) to the east. Many of the streets retain shops that gave them their name: there are jewellers in Rua da Prata and Rua do Ouro, shoemakers in Rua dos Sapateiros and banks in Rua do Comércio.

The most incongruous sight in the Baixa is a small section of the Roman baths within the Millennium BCP bank in Rua dos Correeiros. The ruins and mosaics can be seen from the window at the back of the bank; if you wish to visit the "museum", call ahead on 211 131 681.

Shoppers and strollers in the pedestrianized Rua Augusta

❾ Nossa Senhora da Conceição Velha

Rua da Alfândega. **Map** 7 C4. **Tel** 218 870 202. 🚌 759, 794. 🚊 15, 18. **Open** 9am–6pm daily. ✝ ♿

The elaborate Manueline doorway of the church is the only feature that survived from the original 16th-century Nossa Senhora da Misericórdia, which stood here until the 1755 earthquake. The portal is decorated with a profusion of Manueline detail including angels, beasts, flowers, armillary spheres and the cross of the Order of Christ (see p28). In the tympanum, the Virgin Mary spreads her protective mantle over various contemporary figures. These include Pope Leo X, Manuel I (see pp50–51) and his sister, Queen Leonor, widow of João II. It was Leonor who founded the original Misericórdia (almshouse) on the site of a former synagogue.

Unfortunately, enjoyment of the portal is hampered by the stream of traffic hurtling along Rua da Alfândega and the cars that park right in front of the church. The gloomy interior has an unusual stucco ceiling; in the second chapel on the right is a statue of Our Lady of Restelo. This came from the Belém chapel where navigators prayed before embarking on their historic voyages east.

Detail from portal of Conceição Velha

❿ Praça do Comércio

Map 7 B5. 🚌 711, 714, 732, 759, 794 & many other routes. 🚊 15, 18, 25. Arco da Rua Augusta: Rua Augusta 2–10. **Open** 9am–7pm (Jun–Sep: to 9pm) daily. 🚻 Lisboa Story Centre: Praça do Comércio, Ala Nascente 78–81. **Tel** 211 941 099. **Open** 10am–8pm daily. 🚻

More commonly known by the locals as Terreiro do Paço (Palace Square), this huge open space was the site of the royal palace for 400 years. Manuel I moved the royal residence from Castelo de São Jorge to this more convenient location by the river in 1511. The first palace, along with its library and 70,000 books, was destroyed in the earthquake of 1755. In the rebuilding of the city, the square became the *pièce de résistance* of Pombal's Baixa design. The new palace occupied spacious arcaded buildings that extended around three sides of the square. After the revolution of 1910 (see pp58–9) these were converted into government administrative offices and painted Republican pink. However, they have since been repainted royal yellow.

The south side, graced by two square towers, looks across the Tagus. This has always been the finest gateway to Lisbon, where royalty and ambassadors would alight and take the marble steps up from the river. You can still experience the dramatic approach by taking a ferry across from Cacilhas on the southern bank. The busy Avenida Infante Dom Henrique, which runs along the waterfront, is lined by trendy bars and restaurants. In the centre of the square is the equestrian statue of King José I erected in 1775 by Machado de Castro, the leading Portuguese sculptor of the 18th century. The bronze horse earned the square its third name of "Black Horse Square", used by English travellers and merchants. Over the years, however, the horse has acquired a green patina.

Shaded arcades along the north side of Praça do Comércio

Arco da Rua Augusta, the impressive triumphal arch on the north side of the square, leads into Rua Augusta and is the gateway to the Baixa. An elevator ride to the top affords unparalleled views of the Tagus river basin. In the northwest of the square is the Lisboa Welcome Center, while in the opposite corner stands Lisbon's oldest café, the Martinho da Arcada, formerly a haunt of the city's literati. Also on the square is the Lisboa Story Centre, an attraction that takes visitors on an interactive journey through the events that have shaped Lisbon, including the earthquake of 1755 (see pp66–7).

On 1 February 1908, King Carlos and his son, Luís Felipe, were assassinated as they were passing through the square (see p59). In 1974 the square saw the first uprising of the Armed Forces Movement which overthrew the Caetano regime in a bloodless revolution (see p61).

Arco da Rua Augusta and the statue of King José I in Praça do Comércio

BAIRRO ALTO AND ESTRELA

Laid out in a grid pattern in the late 16th century, the hilltop Bairro Alto is one of the most picturesque districts of the city. First settled by rich citizens who moved out of the disreputable Alfama, by the 19th century it had become a run-down area frequented by prostitutes. Today, its small workshops and family-run *tascas* (cheap restaurants) exist alongside a thriving nightlife. Very different in character to the heart of the Bairro Alto is the elegant commercial district known as the Chiado, where affluent Lisboetas do their shopping. To the northwest, the Estrela quarter is centred on the huge domed basilica and popular gardens. The mid-18th century district of Lapa, to the southwest, is home to foreign embassies and large, smart residences.

Sights at a Glance

Museums and Galleries
5 Museu Nacional de Arte Contemporânea – Museu do Chiado
6 Museu da Marioneta
11 *Museu Nacional de Arte Antiga pp98–101*

Churches
1 São Roque
2 Igreja do Carmo
13 Basílica da Estrela

Historic Buildings and Districts
3 Chiado
4 Teatro Nacional de São Carlos
7 Solar do Vinho do Porto
10 Palácio de São Bento

Gardens and Belvederes
8 Miradouro de São Pedro de Alcântara
9 Praça do Príncipe Real
12 Jardim da Estrela

See also Street Finder pp132–45

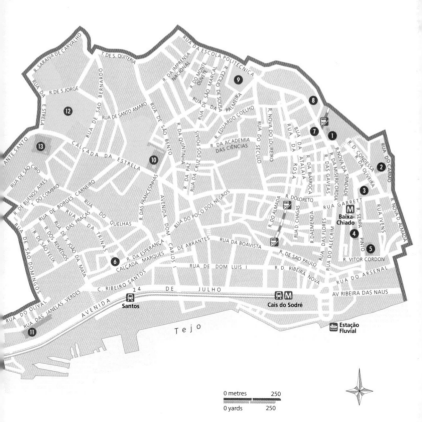

◄ The ruins of the 14th-century Igreja do Carmo, destroyed by the 1755 earthquake

For keys to symbols *see back flap*

Street-by-Street: Bairro Alto and Chiado

The Bairro Alto (high quarter) is a fascinating area of cobbled streets, adjacent to the Carmo and Chiado areas. Since the 1980s, this has been Lisbon's best-known nightlife zone, with countless small bars and restaurants alongside the older *casas de fado*. Much restoration work is continuing to take place around this area, and many modern buildings stand side by side with old, peeling houses and tiny grocery shops. In contrast, the Chiado is an area of elegant shops and old-style cafés that extends down from Praça Luís de Camões towards Rua do Carmo and the Baixa. Major renovation work has taken place since a fire in 1988 *(see p94)* destroyed many of the buildings.

Once a haunt of writers and intellectuals, Chiado is now an elegant shopping district. The Brasileira café, on Largo do Chiado, is adorned with gilded mirrors.

Praça Luís de Camões

RUA DO NORTE

RUA DAS GÁVEAS

RUA DO ALECRIM

L. DO CHIADO

Largo do Chiado is flanked by the churches of Loreto and Nossa Senhora da Encarnação.

Baixa/Chiado

RUA GARR

Rua Garrett is the main shopping street of the Chiado.

The statue of Eça de Queirós (1845–1900), by Teixeira Lopes, was erected in 1903. The great novelist takes inspiration from a scantily veiled muse.

0 metres		50
0 yards		50

Key

━ Suggested route

Tavares, at No. 37 Rua da Misericórdia, first opened as a café in 1784. Today it is an elegant restaurant decorated at the turn of the 20th century with mirrors and elaborate stucco designs.

Elevador da
Glória

The Museu de São Roque
has an interesting exhibition of
religious artifacts and explains
the history of the treasures in the
church of São Roque next door.

Locator Map
See Lisbon Street Finder map 7

BAIXA AND
AVENIDA

BAIRRO ALTO
AND ESTRELA

Tejo

**Cervejaria
Trindade**
is a popular
beer hall and
restaurant
decorated with
azulejo panels.

❶ ★ São Roque
Opulent mosaics
and semiprecious
stones adorn the
Baroque Capela de
São João inside the
16th-century church
of São Roque.

Teatro da
Trindade

The tile decoration on
the façade of this house,
erected in 1864 on Largo
Rafael Bordalo Pinheiro,
features allegorical figures
of Science, Agriculture
Industry and Commerce.

❷ ★ Igreja do Carmo
The graceful skeletal arches of this Carmelite
church, once the largest in Lisbon, stand as
a reminder of the earthquake of 1755. The
chancel and main body of the church
house an archaeological museum.

The Elevador de Santa Justa
has a walkway that links the
Baixa with Largo do Carmo.

The shops in Rua do Carmo have
been completely restored after the
devastating fire in 1988 *(see p94)*.

Ruins of the 14th-century Igreja do Carmo seen from the Baixa

❶ São Roque

Largo Trindade Coelho. **Map** 7 A3.
Tel 213 235 380. 758 & Glória lift.
Open Apr–Sep: 9am–7pm (from 2pm
Mon, to 8pm Thu); Oct–Mar: 9am–
6pm (from 2pm Mon). **Closed** 1 Jan,
Easter Sun, 1 May, 25 Dec. Museu
de São Roque: **Tel** 213 235 380.
Open Apr–Sep: 10am–7pm (from
2pm Mon, to 8pm Thu); Oct–Mar:
10am–6pm (from 2pm Mon).
Closed 1 Jan, Easter Sun, 1 May, 25 Dec.
(free until 2pm Sun).

São Roque's plain
façade belies a
remarkably rich
interior. The church
was founded at
the end of the 16th
century by the Jesuit
Order, then at the peak
of its power. In 1742
the Chapel of St John
the Baptist was
commissioned by the

Tile detail, Chapel
of São Roque

prodigal João V from the Italian
architects Luigi Vanvitelli and
Nicola Salvi. Constructed in
Rome and embellished with
lapis lazuli, agate, alabaster,
amethyst, precious marbles,
gold, silver and mosaics, the
chapel was given the Pope's
blessing in the church of
Sant'Antonio dei Portoghesi
in Rome, dismantled and sent
to Lisbon in three ships.

Among the many tiles in the
church, the oldest and most
interesting are those in the
third chapel on the right, dating
from the mid-16th century
and dedicated to São Roque
(St Roch), protector against
the plague. Other features
of the church are the scenes of
the Apocalypse painted on the
ceiling, and the sacristy, with its
coffered ceiling and painted
panels of the life of St Francis
Xavier, the 16th-century
missionary. Treasures from the
Chapel of St John, including the
silver and lapis lazuli altar front,
are in the adjoining Museu de
São Roque.

❷ Igreja do Carmo

Largo do Carmo. **Map** 7 B3.
Tel 213 460 473. 28 &
Santa Justa lift. 758.
Open Jun–Sep: 10am–
7pm Mon–Sat; Oct–May:
10am–6pm Mon–Sat.
Closed Sun.

The Gothic ruins of
this Carmelite church
on a slope overlooking
the Baixa, are evoc-
ative reminders of the
devastation left by
the earthquake of 1755. The
church collapsed during mass,
depositing tons of masonry on
to the people below. Founded
in the late 14th century by
Nuno Álvares Pereira, the
commander who became a
member of the Carmelite Order,
the church was at one time the
biggest in the city of Lisbon.

Nowadays the main body
of the church and the chancel,
whose roof withstood the
violent shock waves, house an
archaeological museum with
a small, heterogeneous collection of sarcophagi, statuary,
ceramics and mosaics.

Among the more ancient
finds from Europe are a remnant
from a Visigothic pillar and a
Roman tomb carved with
reliefs depicting the Muses.
There are also finds from
Mexico and South America,
including ancient mummies.

Outside the ruins, in the Largo
do Carmo, stands the Chafariz do
Carmo, an 18th-century fountain designed by Ângelo Belasco,
elaborately decorated with
four dolphins.

❸ Chiado

Map 7 A4. 1, 758. 28.
Baixa-Chiado.

Hypotheses abound for the
origin of the word Chiado, in
use since 1567. One of the most
interesting recalls the creak
(chiar) of the wheels of the carts
as they negotiated the area's
steep slopes. A second theory
refers to the nickname given to

The Chiado Fire

On 25 August 1988 a disastrous
fire began in a store in Rua do
Carmo, the street that links the
Baixa with the Bairro Alto. Fire
engines were unable to enter
this pedestrianized street and
the fire spread into Rua Garrett.
Along with shops and offices,
many important 18th-century
buildings were destroyed, the
worst damage being in Rua do
Carmo. The renovation project,
which is now complete, has
preserved many original façades,
and was headed by Portuguese
architect Álvaro Siza Vieira.

Firemen attending the raging fire in
Rua do Carmo

Stalls and circle of the 18th-century Teatro Nacional de São Carlos

the 16th-century poet António Ribeiro, "O Chiado". Various statues of literary figures can be found in this area, known for its intellectual associations. Fernando Pessoa, Portugal's most famous 20th-century poet, is seated at a table outside the Café Brasileira, once a favourite rendezvous of intellectuals.

The name Chiado is often used to mean just Rua Garrett, the main shopping street of the area, named after the author and poet João Almeida Garrett (1799– 1854). This elegant street, which descends from Largo do Chiado towards the Baixa, is known for its clothes shops, cafés and bookshops. Devastated by fire in 1988, the former elegance of this quarter has now been restored.

On Largo do Chiado stand two Baroque churches: the Italian church, Igreja do Loreto, on the north side and opposite, Nossa Senhora da Encarnação, whose exterior walls are partly decorated with *azulejos*.

Art Nouveau façade of the popular Café Brasileira in the Chiado

❹ Teatro Nacional de São Carlos

Rua Serpa Pinto 9. **Map** 7 A4. **Tel** 213 253 045. 758, 790. 28. Baixa-Chiado. **Open** Mon–Fri 1–7pm. **tnsc.pt**

Replacing a former opera house which was ruined by the earth-quake of 1755, the Teatro de São Carlos was built in 1792–5 by José da Costa e Silva. Designed on the lines of La Scala in Milan and the San Carlo in Naples, the building has a beautifully proportioned façade and an enchanting Rococo interior. Views of the exterior, however, are spoiled by the car park that occupies the square in front. The opera season lasts from September to June, but concerts and ballets are also staged here at other times of the year.

❺ Museu Nacional de Arte Contemporânea – Museu do Chiado

Rua Serpa Pinto 4–6. **Map** 7 A5. **Tel** 213 432 148. 758, 790. 28. Baixa-Chiado. **Open** 10am–6pm Tue–Sun. **Closed** 1 Jan, Easter, 1 May, 25 Dec. (free first Sun of month). **museuarte contemporanea.pt**

The National Museum of Contemporary Art occupies a stylishly restored warehouse. The paintings and sculpture are arranged over three floors in 12 rooms. Each room has a different theme illustrating the develop-ment from Romanticism to Modernism. The majority are

works by Portuguese, often showing the marked influence from other European countries. This is particularly noticeable in the 19th-century landscape painters who had contact with artists from the French Barbizon School. The few international works of art on display include a collection of drawings by Rodin (1840–1917) and some French sculpture from the late 19th century. There are also temporary exhibitions which are held for "very new artists, preferably inspired by the permanent collection".

Grotesque puppet in Museu da Marioneta

❻ Museu da Marioneta

Convento das Bernardas, Rua da Esperança 146. **Map** 4 E3. **Tel** 213 942 810. 713, 727, 760. 25. Cais do Sodré. Santos. **Open** 10am–6pm Tue–Sun. **Closed** 1 Jan, 1 May, 24 & 25 Dec. (free 10am–1pm Sun). **museudamarioneta.pt**

This small puppet museum, housed in an elegantly refurbished convent building, includes characters dating from 17th- and 18th-century theatre and opera, among them devils, knights, jesters and satirical figures. Many of the puppets possess gruesome, contorted features that are unlikely to appeal to small children. The museum explains the history of the art form and runs videos of puppet shows. Call ahead to see if a live performance is being held on the small stage. There is also a space for children's entertainment and pedagogical activities.

The wide selection of port at the Solar do Vinho do Porto

❼ Solar do Vinho do Porto

Rua de São Pedro de Alcântara 45. **Map** 4 F2. **Tel** 213 475 707. 758. 28, Elevador da Glória. **Open** 11am–midnight Mon–Fri, 3pm–midnight Sat. **Closed** public hols.

The Portuguese word *solar* means mansion or manor house and the Solar do Vinho do Porto occupies the ground floor of an 18th-century mansion. The building was once owned by the German architect, Johann Friedrich Ludwig (Ludovice), who built the monastery at Mafra (see p158). The port wine institute of Porto runs a pleasant if dated bar here for the promotion of port. Nearly 200 types of port are listed in the lengthy drinks menu, with every producer represented and including some rarities. Unfortunately, many of the listed wines are often unavailable. All but the vintage ports are sold by the glass, with prices ranging from €1 for the simplest ruby to €70 for a glass of 40-year-old tawny.

❽ Miradouro de São Pedro de Alcântara

Rua de São Pedro de Alcântara. **Map** 7 A2. 758. 28, Elevador da Glória.

The Belvedere (*miradouro*) commands a sweeping view of eastern Lisbon, seen across the Baixa. A tiled map placed against the balustrade helps you locate the landmarks in the city below. The panorama extends from the battlements of the Castelo de São Jorge (see pp80–81), clearly seen surrounded by trees on the hill to the southeast, to the 18th-century church of Penha da França in the northwest. The large monastery complex of the Igreja da Graça (see p77) is also visible on the hill, and in the distance São Vicente de Fora (see p75) is recognizable by the symmetrical towers that flank its white façade.

Benches and ample shade from the trees make this terrace a pleasant stop after the steep walk up Calçada da Glória from the Baixa. Alternatively, the yellow funicular, Elevador da Glória, will drop you off nearby.

The memorial in the garden, erected in 1904, depicts Eduardo Coelho (1835–89), founder of the newspaper *Diário de Notícias*, and below him a ragged paper boy running with copies of the famous

daily. This area was once the centre of the newspaper industry, however the modern printing presses have now moved to more spacious premises west of the city.

The view is most attractive at sunset and by night when the castle is floodlit and the terrace becomes a popular meeting point for young Lisboetas.

Playing cards in Praça do Príncipe Real

❾ Praça do Príncipe Real

Map 4 F1. 758.

Laid out in 1860 as a prime residential quarter, the square still retains an air of affluence. Smartly painted mansions surround a particularly pleasant park with an open-air café, statuary and some splendid robinia, magnolia and Judas trees. The branches of a huge cedar tree have been trained on a trellis, creating a wide shady spot for the locals who play cards beneath it. On the large square, at No. 26, the eye-catching pink and white Neo-Moorish building with domes and pinnacles is part of Lisbon university.

View across the city to Castelo de São Jorge from Miradouro de São Pedro de Alcântara

For hotels and restaurants in this area see pp386–7 and pp398–401

Attractive wrought-iron music pavilion in Jardim da Estrela

⑩ Palácio de São Bento

Largo das Cortes. **Map** 4 E2. **Tel** 213 919 000. 🚌 758. 🚊 28. **Open** by appt. 📷 last Sat of month, 3pm & 4pm, 213 919 625. 🖥 **parlamento.pt**

Also known as the Assembleia da República, this massive white Neo-Classical building is the seat of the Portuguese Parliament. It started life in the late 1500s as the Benedictine monastery of São Bento. After the dissolution of the religious orders in 1834, the building became the seat of Parliament, known as the Palácio das Cortes. The interior is suitably grandiose with marble pillars and Neo-Classical statues.

Neo-Classical façade and stairway of Palácio de São Bento

⑪ Museu Nacional de Arte Antiga

See pp98–101.

⑫ Jardim da Estrela

Praça da Estrela. **Map** 4 D2. 🚌 720, 738. 🚊 25, 28. **Open** 7am–midnight daily.

Laid out in the middle of the 19th century, opposite the Basilica da Estrela, the popular gardens are a focal part of the Estrela quarter. Local families congregate here at weekends to feed the ducks and carp in the lake, sit at the waterside café or wander among the flower beds, plants and trees. The formal gardens are planted with herbaceous borders and shrubs surrounding plane trees and elms. The central feature of the park is a green wrought-iron bandstand, decorated with elegant filigree, where musicians strike up in the summer months. This was built in 1884 and originally stood on the Passeio Público, before the creation of Avenida da Liberdade (see p86).

The English Cemetery to the north of the gardens is best known as the burial place of Henry Fielding (1707–54), the English novelist and playwright who died in Lisbon at the age of 47. The *Journal of a Voyage to Lisbon*, published posthumously in 1775, recounts his last voyage to Portugal made in a fruitless attempt to recover his failing health.

The tomb of the pious Maria I in the Basílica da Estrela

⑬ Basílica da Estrela

Praça da Estrela. **Map** 4 D2. **Tel** 213 960 915. 🚌 738. 🚊 25, 28. **Open** 7:45am–8pm daily. Large groups by appt only. 🚻

In the second half of the 18th century Maria I (see p171), daughter of José I, vowed she would build a church if she bore a son and heir to the throne. Her wish was granted and construction of the basilica began in 1779. Her son José, however, died of smallpox two years before the completion of the church in 1790. The huge domed basilica, set on a hill in the west of the city, is one of Lisbon's great landmarks. A simpler version of the basilica at Mafra (see p158), the church was built by architects from the Mafra School in late Baroque and Neo-Classical style. The façade is flanked by twin bell towers and decorated with an array of statues of saints and allegorical figures.

The spacious interior, where light streams down from the pierced dome, is clad in grey, pink and yellow marble. The elaborate Empire-style tomb of Queen Maria I, who died in Brazil, lies in the right transept. Locked in a room nearby is Machado de Castro's extraordinary Nativity scene, composed of over 500 cork and terracotta figures. (To see it, ask the sacristan.)

⑪ Museu Nacional de Arte Antiga

Portugal's national art collection is housed in a 17th-century palace that was built for the counts of Alvor. In 1770 it was acquired by the Marquês de Pombal and remained in the possession of his family for over a century. Inaugurated in 1884, the museum is known to locals as the Museu das Janelas Verdes, referring to the former green windows of the palace. In 1940 a modern annexe (including the main façade) was added. This was built on the site of the St Albert Carmelite monastery, which was partially demolished between 1910 and 1920. The only surviving feature is the chapel, now integrated into the museum.

★ St Jerome
This masterly portrayal of old age by Albrecht Dürer expresses one of the central dilemmas of Renaissance humanism: the ephemeral nature of man (1521).

St Augustine by Piero della Francesca

Stairs down to

The Temptations of St Anthony by Hieronymus Bosch

The Mystic Marriage of St Catherine
Hans Holbein the Elder's balanced composition of the *Mystic Marriage of St Catherine* (1519) is set among majestic Renaissance architecture, with saints in detailed contemporary costumes sewing or reading.

St Leonard
This sculpture of the saint was made by Florentine sculptor Andrea della Robbia (1435–1525), the nephew of Luca della Robbia.

Key to Floorplan

- ☐ European painting
- ☐ Portuguese painting and sculpture
- ☐ Portuguese and Chinese ceramics
- ☐ Oriental and African art
- ☐ Silver, gold and jewellery
- ☐ European Decorative arts
- ☐ Chapel of St Albert
- ☐ Portuguese Furniture
- ☐ Cribs
- ☐ Non-exhibition space

Gallery Guide

The ground floor (not shown) houses research facilities and a gallery for temporary exhibitions. The first level contains 14th–19th-century European paintings, decorative arts and furniture. Jewellery, Oriental and African art, and Chinese and Portuguese ceramics are on the second floor. The top floor is dedicated to local art and sculpture.

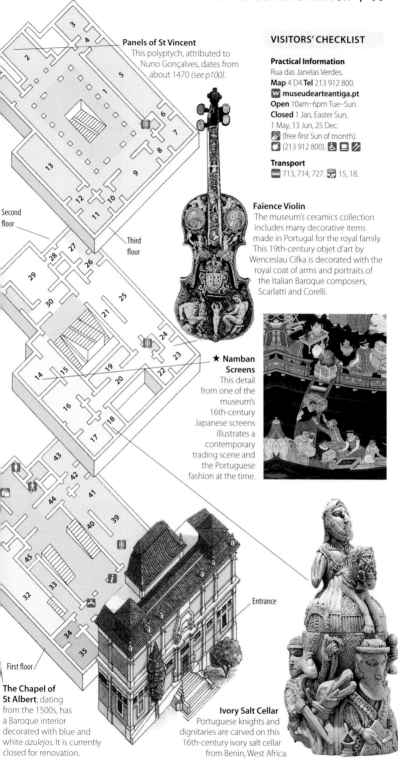

Panels of St Vincent
This polyptych, attributed to Nuno Gonçalves, dates from about 1470 *(see p100)*.

Second floor

Third floor

Faïence Violin
The museum's ceramics collection includes many decorative items made in Portugal for the royal family. This 19th-century objet d'art by Wenceslau Cifka is decorated with the royal coat of arms and portraits of the Italian Baroque composers, Scarlatti and Corelli.

★ Namban Screens
This detail from one of the museum's 16th-century Japanese screens illustrates a contemporary trading scene and the Portuguese fashion at the time.

Entrance

Ivory Salt Cellar
Portuguese knights and dignitaries are carved on this 16th-century ivory salt cellar from Benin, West Africa.

First floor

The Chapel of St Albert, dating from the 1500s, has a Baroque interior decorated with blue and white *azulejos*. It is currently closed for renovation.

Exploring the Collections of the Museu Nacional de Arte Antiga

The museum has the largest collection of paintings in Portugal and is particularly strong on early religious works by Portuguese artists. The majority of exhibits came from convents and monasteries following the suppression of religious orders in 1834. There are also extensive displays of sculpture, silverware, porcelain and applied arts giving an overview of Portuguese art from the Middle Ages to the 19th century, complemented by many fine European and Oriental pieces. The theme of the discoveries is ever-present, illustrating Portugal's links with Brazil, Africa, India, China and Japan.

Panels of St Vincent

Cistercian monks from Alcobaça (*see pp184–5*)

Friar

Fisherman

Painted around 1470–80 and believed to be by Nuno Gonçalves, the altarpiece portrays the *Panels of St Vincent*, patron saint of Lisbon, surrounded by dignitaries, knights, monks, fishermen and beggars. Though the identification of these characters isn't historically factual, the painting is an invaluable historical and social document.

Later works include a 16th-century portrait of the young Dom Sebastião (*see pp50–51*) by Cristóvão de Morais and paintings by Neo-Classical artist Domingos António de Sequeira.

The museum's sculpture collection has many Gothic polychrome stone and wood statues of Christ, the Virgin and saints. There are also statues from the 17th century and a nativity scene in the Chapel of St Albert painted by Barros Laborão between 1796 and 1807.

European Art

Paintings by European artists, dating from the 14th to the 19th century, are arranged chronologically on the ground floor. Unlike the Portuguese art, most of these works were donated from private collections, contributing to the great diversity of works on display. The first rooms, dedicated to the 14th and 15th centuries, trace the transition from medieval Gothic taste to the aesthetic of the Renaissance.

The painters best represented in the European Art section are 16th-century German and Flemish artists. Notable works here include *St Jerome* by Albrecht Dürer (1471–1528), *Salomé* by Lucas Cranach the Elder (1472–1553), *Virgin and Child* by Hans Memling (c.1430–94) and *The Temptations of St Anthony* by the great Flemish master of fantasy, Hieronymus Bosch (1450–1516). Of the small number of Italian works here, the finest pieces are *St Augustine* by the Renaissance painter Piero della Francesca (c.1420–92) and a graceful early altar panel representing the Resurrection by Raphael (1483–1520).

Portuguese Painting and Sculpture

Many of the earliest works are by the Portuguese primitive painters, such as Josefa de Óbidos (*see p55*), who were influenced by the realistic detail of Flemish artists. There had always been strong trading links between Portugal and Flanders, and in the 15th and 16th centuries several painters of Flemish origin, for example Frey Carlos of Évora, set up workshops in Portugal.

Also in this section is the São Vicente de Fora polyptych, the main painting of 15th-century Portuguese art and one that has become a symbol of national pride in the Age of Discovery.

Portuguese and Chinese Ceramics

The extensive collection of ceramics enables visitors to trace the evolution of Chinese porcelain and Portuguese faïence and to see the influence of oriental designs on Portuguese pieces,

Central panel of The *Temptations of St Antony* by Hieronymus Bosch

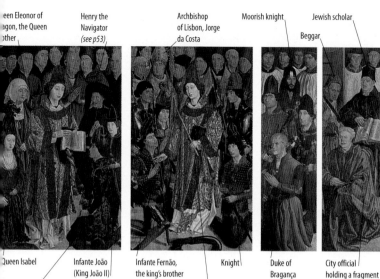

Queen Eleonor of Aragon, the Queen Mother

Henry the Navigator *(see p53)*

Archbishop of Lisbon, Jorge da Costa

Moorish knight

Jewish scholar

Beggar

Queen Isabel

Infante João (King João II)

Infante Fernão, the king's brother

Knight

Duke of Bragança

City official holding a fragment of St Vincent's skull

King Afonso V

St Vincent

---

and vice versa. From the 16th century Portuguese ceramics show a marked influence of Ming, and conversely the Chinese pieces bear Portuguese motifs such as coats of arms. By the mid-18th century individual potters had begun to develop an increasingly personalized, European style, with popular, rustic designs. The collection also includes ceramics from Italy, Spain and the Netherlands.

Chinese porcelain vase, 18th century

Oriental and African Art

The collection of ivories and furniture, with their European motifs, further illustrates the reciprocal influences of Portugal and her colonies. The 16th-century predilection for the exotic gave rise to a huge demand for items such as carved ivory hunting horns from Africa. The fascinating 16th-century Japanese Namban screens show the Portuguese trading in Japan. *Namban-jin* (barbarians from the south) is the name the Japanese gave to the Portuguese.

Silver, Gold and Jewellery

The collection of ecclesiastical treasures includes King Sancho I's gold cross (1214) and the Belém monstrance (1506) *(see p28)*. Also on display is the 16th-century Madre de Deus reliquary, which allegedly holds a thorn from the crown of Christ. Highlight of the foreign collection is a sumptuous set of rare 18th-century silver tableware. Commissioned by José I from the Paris workshop of François-Thomas Germain, the 1,200 pieces include intricately decorated tureens, sauce boats and salt cellars. The rich collection of jewels came from the convents, originally donated by members of the nobility and wealthy bourgeoisie on entering the religious orders.

Decorative Arts

Furniture, tapestries and textiles, liturgical vestments and bishops' mitres are among the wide range of objects on display. The furniture collection includes many Medieval and Renaissance pieces, as well as Baroque and Neo-Classical items from the reigns of King João V, King José and Queen Maria I. Of the foreign furniture, French pieces from the 18th century are prominent.

The textiles include 17th-century bedspreads, tapestries, many of Flemish origin, such as the *Baptism of Christ* (16th century), embroidered rugs and Arraiolos carpets *(see p307)*.

Holy relics of Queen Leonor (c.1458–1525), Museu Nacional de Arte Antiga

BELÉM

At the mouth of the River Tagus, where the caravels set sail on their voyages of discovery, Belém is inextricably linked with Portugal's Golden Age *(see pp50–53)*. When Manuel I came to power in 1495 he reaped the profits of those heady days of expansion, building grandiose monuments and churches that mirrored the spirit of the time. Two of the finest examples of the exuberant and exotic Manueline style of architecture *(see pp28–9)* are the Mosteiro dos Jerónimos and the Torre de Belém. Today Belém is a spacious,

relatively green suburb with many museums, parks and gardens, as well as an attractive riverside setting with cafés and a promenade. On sunny days there is a distinct seaside feel to the embankment.

Before the Tagus receded, the monks in the monastery used to look out onto the river and watch the boats set forth. In contrast, today several lanes of traffic along the busy Avenida da Índia cut central Belém off from the picturesque waterfront, and silver and yellow trains rattle past regularly.

Sights at a Glance

Museums and Galleries
- **2** Museu Nacional dos Coches
- **5** Museu Nacional de Arqueologia
- **6** Planetário Calouste Gulbenkian
- **7** Museu de Marinha
- **10** Museu de Arte Popular

Parks and Gardens
- **3** Jardim Botânico Tropical
- **14** Jardim Botânico da Ajuda

Churches and Monasteries
- **4** *Mosteiro dos Jerónimos pp108–9*
- **12** Ermida de São Jerónimo
- **13** Igreja da Memória

Historic Buildings
- **1** Palácio de Belém
- **11** *Torre de Belém p112*
- **15** Palácio Nacional da Ajuda

Monuments
- **9** Monument to the Discoveries

Cultural Centres
- **8** Centro Cultural de Belém

See also Street Finder pp132–45

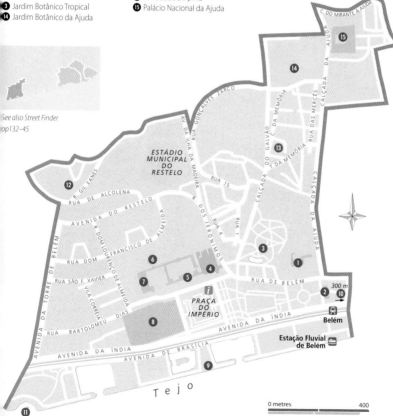

◄ Manueline arches in the cloister of Mosteiro dos Jerónimos

For keys to symbols *see back flap*

Street-by-Street: Belém

Portugal's former maritime glory is evident
across Belém, specifically expressed in the
imposing buildings such as the Jerónimos
monastery. In an attempt to revive and celebrate
Portugal's Golden Age, Salazar ordered the area
along the waterfront, which had silted up since
the days of the caravels, was restructured to
celebrate the former greatness of the nation.
Praça do Império was laid out for the Exhibition
of the Portuguese World in 1940 and Praça
Afonso de Albuquerque was dedicated to
Portugal's first viceroy of India. The royal
Palácio de Belém, restored with gardens and
a riding school by João V in the 18th century,
briefly housed the royal family after the
1755 earthquake.

❹ ★ Mosteiro dos Jerónimos
Vaulted arcades and richly carved columns
adorned with foliage, exotic animals and
navigational instruments decorate the Manuel
cloister of the Jerónimos monastery.

**Antiga Confeitaria de
Belém**, a 19th-century café, sells
pastéis de Belém, rich custard in
a flaky pastry cup.

❺ Museu Nacional de Arqueologia
Archaeological finds ranging from an
Iron Age gold bracelet to Moorish
artifacts are among the interesting
exhibits on display.

TRAVESSA DOS FER

LARGO

DOS

JERÓNIMOS

PRAÇA DO IMPÉRIO

RUA VI

Torre
de Belém
(see p112)

Rua Vieira Portuense runs
along a small park. Its colourfu
16th- and 17th-century houses
contrast with the typically
imposing buildings in Belém.

Key

— Suggested route

Praça do Império, an impressive
square that opens out in front of
the monastery, is lit up on special
occasions with a colourful light
display in the central fountain.

Locator Map
See Lisbon Street Finder maps 1 & 2

❸ Jardim Botânico Tropical
Exotic plants and trees gathered from Portugal's former colonies fill these peaceful gardens that were once part of the Palácio de Belém.

0 metres 50
0 yards 50

→
Central
Lisbon

RUA DE BELÉM

❷ ★ Museu Nacional dos Coches
This 18th-century coach used by the ambassador to Pope Clement XI is part of the museum's collection. The museum was moved to the east side of Praça Afonso de Albuquerque in 2016.

❶ Palácio de Belém
Also known as the Palácio Cor de Rosa (pink palace) because of its faded pink façade, the former royal palace is the residence of the Portuguese president. It also houses the Museu da Presidência da República.

Praça Afonso de Albuquerque
is named after the first Portuguese viceroy of India. A Neo-Manueline column in the centre bears his statue, with scenes from his life carved on the base.

❶ Palácio de Belém

Praça Afonso de Albuquerque.
Map 1 C4. **Tel** 213 614 600. 🚌 714,
727, 728, 729, 751. 🚋 15. 🚊 Belém.
Belém Palace: Open 10am–4:30pm
Sat. 🎫 compulsory for large groups
(book ahead: 213 614 980). 🏛 Museu
da Presidencia: **Open** 10am–6pm Tue–
Fri, 10am–6pm & 2–6pm Sat & Sun.
🏛 (free until 1pm Sun).
🌐 **museu.presidencia.pt**

Pink façade of the Palácio de Belém, the official residence of the President of Portugal

Built by the Conde de Aveiras
in 1559, this palace once had
gardens bordering the river. In
the 18th century it was bought
by João V, who radically altered
it, rendering the interior suitably
lavish for his amorous liaisons.

When the 1755 earthquake
(*see pp66–7*) struck, the king,
José I, and his family were
staying here. Fearing another
earth tremor, they set up camp
in tents in the palace grounds
and the building was used as
a hospital. Today the elegant
palace is the official residence of
the President of Portugal. The
Presidential Museum contains
personal items and state gifts
of former presidents, as well
as the official portrait gallery.

❷ Museu Nacional dos Coches

Praça Afonso de Albuquerque. **Map** 2
D4. **Tel** 210 732 319. 🚌 714, 727, 728,
729, 751. 🚋15. 🚊 Belém. **Open**
10am–6pm Tue–Sun. **Closed** 1 Jan,
Easter, 1 May, 25 Dec. 🏛 (free first Sun
of month). 🎫 available for groups. ♿
🌐 **museudoscoches.pt**

The museum's collection of
coaches is arguably the finest in
Europe and takes the accolade
of the world's original coach
museum. First occupying the old
Royal Riding School, the building was adapted to showcase a
unique and opulent collection
of coaches, carriages, and sedan
chairs dating from the 17th,
18th and 19th centuries. By
contrast, the collection was
moved to a new, modern building by the Brazilian architect
Paulo Mendes da Rocha,
winner of the 2006 Pritzker
Prize, in 2015.

Made in Portugal, Italy,
France, Austria and Spain, the
coaches range from the plain
to the preposterous. The main
gallery, in Louis XVI style with
splendid painted ceiling, is the
setting for two rows of coaches
created for Portuguese royalty.

The collection starts with the
comparatively simple 17th-
century red leather and wood
coach of Philip II of Spain (*see
pp54–5*). The coaches become
increasingly sumptuous,
interiors lined with red velvet
and gold, exteriors carved and
decorated with allegories
and royal coats of arms.

The rows end with three
huge Baroque coaches made
in Rome for the Portuguese
ambassador to the Vatican,
Dom Rodrigo Almeida e Menezes,
the Marquês de Abrantes.
The epitome of pomp and
extravagance, these 5-tonne
carriages are embellished
with a plush interior and
life-size gilded statues.

The neighbouring gallery
has further examples of royal
carriages, including two-
wheeled cabriolets, landaus
and pony-drawn chaises
used by young members of
the royal family. There is also
a 19th-century Lisbon cab,
painted black and green, a
colour scheme that was abandoned in the 1990s in favour
of beige but that is now making
a comeback. The 18th-century

Rear view of a coach built in 1716 for the Marquês de Abrantes,
the Portuguese ambassador to Pope Clement XI

Eyeglass Chaise, whose black leather hood is pierced by sinister eye-like windows, was made during the era of Pombal *(see pp56–7)* when lavish decoration was discouraged. The upper gallery has a collection of harnesses, court costumes and portraits of members of the royal family.

In late 2016, the museum will move to a new building on the eastern side of the square.

❸ Jardim Botânico Tropical

Largo do Jerónimos. **Map** 1 C4. **Tel** 213 921 850/1. 🚌 727, 728, 729, 751. 🚊 15. **Open** Feb, Mar & Oct: 10am–6pm daily; Apr & Sep: 10am–7pm daily; May–Aug: 10am– 8pm daily; Nov–Jan: 10am–5pm daily. **Closed** public hols. 🎫 ♿

Also known as the Jardim do Ultramar, this peaceful park with ponds, waterfowl and peacocks attracts surprisingly few visitors. Laid out at the start of the 20th century as the research centre of the Institute for Tropical Sciences, it is more of an arboretum than a flower garden. The emphasis is on rare and endangered tropical and subtropical trees and plants. Among the most striking are dragon trees, native to the Canary Islands and Madeira, monkey puzzle trees from South America and a handsome avenue of Washington palms. The oriental garden, with its streams, bridges and hibiscus, is heralded by a large Chinese-style gateway that represented Macau in the Exhibition of the Portuguese World in 1940 *(see p104)*.

The research buildings are located in the Palácio dos Condes da Calheta, whose interior walls are covered with *azulejos*. The palace is open to the public only for temporary exhibitions.

❹ Mosteiro dos Jerónimos

See pp108–9.

Washington palms in the Jardim Botânico Tropical

❺ Museu Nacional de Arqueologia

Praça do Império. **Map** 1 B4. **Tel** 213 620 000. 🚌 714, 727, 728, 729, 751. 🚊 15. 🚉 Belém. **Open** 10am–6pm Tue–Sun. **Closed** 1 Jan, Easter, 1 May, 25 Dec. 🎫 (free first Sun of month). ♿ 🌐 museuarqueologia.pt

The long west wing of the Mosteiro dos Jerónimos *(see pp108–9)*, formerly the monks' dormitory, has been a museum since 1893. Reconstructed in the middle of the 19th century, the building is a poor imitation of the Manueline original. The museum houses Portugal's main archaeological research centre and the exhibits, from

Visigothic gold buckle, Museu de Arqueologia

sites all over the country, include a gold Iron Age bracelet found in the Alentejo and Visigothic jewellery from Beja *(see p317)*, Roman ornaments and early 8th-century Moorish artifacts. The main Egyptian and Greco-Roman section is strong on funerary art, featuring figurines, tombstones, masks, terracotta amulets and funeral cones inscribed with hieroglyphics alluding to the solar system. The dimly lit Room of Treasures has an exquisite collection of coins, necklaces, bracelets and other jewellery dating from 1800–500 BC. This room has been refurbished to allow more of the magnificent jewellery, unseen by the public for decades, to be shown.

❻ Planetário Calouste Gulbenkian

Praça do Império. **Map** 1 B4. **Tel** 213 620 002. 🚌 727, 728, 751. 🚊 15. **Open** times vary so check website for details. 🎫 ♿ 🌐 ccm.marinha.pt

Financed by the Gulbenkian Foundation *(see p121)*, this modern building sits incongruously beside the Jerónimos monastery. Inside, the Planetarium reveals the mysteries of the cosmos. There are shows in Portuguese, Spanish, English and French explaining the movement of the stars and our solar system, as well as presentations on more specialist themes, such as the constellations or the Star of Bethlehem (Belém).

The dome of the Planetário Calouste Gulbenkian

❹ Mosteiro dos Jerónimos

A monument to the wealth of the Age of Discovery *(see pp52–3)*, the monastery is the culmination of Manueline architecture *(see pp28–9)*. Commissioned by Manuel I in around 1501, after Vasco da Gama's return from his historic voyage, it was financed largely by "pepper money", a tax levied on spices, precious stones and gold. Various master builders worked on the building, the most notable of whom was Diogo Boitac, replaced by João de Castilho in 1517. The monastery was cared for by the Order of St Jerome (Hieronymites) until 1834, when all religious orders were disbanded.

Tomb of Vasco da Gama
The 19th-century tomb of the navigator *(see p110)* is carved with ropes, spheres and other seafaring symbols.

Refectory
The walls of the refectory are tiled with 18th-century *azulejos*. The panel at the northern end depicts the Feeding of the Five Thousand.

KEY

① **Gallery**

② **The west portal** was designed by the French sculptor Nicolau Chanterène.

③ **The modern wing**, built in 1850 in Neo-Manueline style, houses the Museu Nacional de Arqueologia *(see p107)*.

④ **The fountain** is in the shape of a lion, the heraldic animal of St Jerome.

⑤ **The chapterhouse** holds the tomb of Alexandre Herculano (1810–77), historian and first mayor of Belém.

⑥ **The chancel** was commissioned in 1572 by Dona Catarina, wife of João III.

⑦ **The tombs** of Manuel I, his wife Dona Maria, João III and Catarina are supported by elephants.

Entrance to church and cloister

View of the Monastery
This 17th-century scene by Felipe Lobo shows women at a fountain in front of the Mosteiro dos Jerónimos.

★ Cloister
João de Castilho's pure Manueline creation was completed in 1544. Delicate tracery and richly carved images decorate the arches and balustrades.

VISITORS' CHECKLIST

Practical Information
Praça do Império. **Map** 1 C4. **Tel** 213 620 034. **Open** 10am–6:30pm (Oct–Apr: to 5:30pm). **Closed** 1 Jan, Easter, 1 May, 13 Jun, 25 Dec.
🏛 🚫 (free first Sun of month).
♿ 🌐 mosteirojeronimos.pt

Transport
🚌 714, 727, 728, 729, 751. 🚊 15.
🚉 Belém.

Nave
The spectacular vaulting in the church of Santa Maria is held aloft by slender octagonal pillars. These rise like palm trees to the roof creating a feeling of space and harmony.

★ South Portal
The strict geometrical architecture of the portal is almost obscured by the exuberant decoration. João de Castilho unites religious themes, such as this image of St Jerome, with the secular, exalting the kings of Portugal.

Tomb of King Sebastião
The tomb of the "longed for" Dom Sebastião stands empty. The young king never returned from battle in 1578 (see p51).

Façade of the Museu de Marinha

🕖 Museu de Marinha

Praça do Império. **Map** 1 B4. **Tel** 213 620 019. 🚌 727, 728, 729, 751. 🚋 15. 🚆 Belém. **Open** 10am–6pm Tue–Sun (18 Apr–1 Oct: to 5pm). **Closed** 1 Jan, Easter, 1 May, 25 Dec. 🎫 (free first Sun of month). ♿ 🇼 ccm.marinha.pt

The Maritime Museum was inaugurated in 1962 in the west wing of the Jerónimos monastery *(see pp108–9)*. It was here, in the chapel built by Henry the Navigator *(see p53)*, that mariners took mass before embarking on their voyages. A hall about the Discoveries illustrates the progress in shipbuilding from the mid-15th century, capitalizing on the experience of long-distance explorers. Small replicas show the transition from the bark to the lateen-rigged caravel, through the faster square-rigged caravel, to the Portuguese *nau*. Also here are navigational instruments, astrolabes and replicas of 16th-century maps showing the world as it was known then. The stone pillars, carved with the Cross of the Knights of Christ, are replicas of the types of *padrão* set up as monuments to Portuguese sovereignty on the lands discovered.

A series of rooms displaying models of modern Portuguese ships leads on to the Royal Quarters, where you can see the exquisitely furnished wood-panelled cabin of King Carlos and Queen Amélia from the royal yacht *Amélia*, built in Scotland in 1900.

The modern, incongruous pavilion opposite houses original royal barges, the most extravagant of which is the royal brig built in 1780 for Maria I. The collection ends with a display of seaplanes, including the *Santa Clara* which made the first crossing of the South Atlantic in 1922.

🕗 Centro Cultural de Belém

Praça do Império. **Map** 1 B5. **Tel** 213 612 400. 🚌 727, 728, 729, 751. 🚋 15. 🚆 Belém. Berardo Collection Museum: **Tel** 213 612 878. **Open** 10am–7pm daily. ♿ 🎫 🇼 ccb.pt 🇼 museuberardo.pt

Standing between the Tagus and the Jerónimos monastery, this stark, modern building was erected as the headquarters of the Portuguese presidency of the European Community. In 1993 it opened as a cultural centre offering performing arts, music and photography. The centre houses the Berardo Collection Museum, which has contemporary art by the likes of Francis Bacon, Willem de Kooning and Michel Basquiat.

Both the café and restaurant spill out onto the ramparts of the building, whose peaceful gardens of olive trees and geometric lawns look out over the quay and river.

The modern complex of the Centro Cultural de Belém

🕘 Monument to the Discoveries

Padrão dos Descobrimentos, Avenida de Brasília. **Map** 1 C5. **Tel** 213 031 950. 🚌 727, 728. 🚋 15. 🚆 Belém. **Open** Oct–Feb: 10am–6pm Tue–Sun; Mar–Sep: 10am–7pm daily. **Closed** 1 Jan, 1 May, 25 Dec. 🎫 for lift. 🇼 padraodosdescobrimentos.pt

Standing prominently on the Belém waterfront, this massive angular monument, the Padrão dos Descobrimentos, was built in 1960 to mark the 500th anniversary of the death of Henry the Navigator *(see p53)*. The 52-m (170-ft) high monument, commis-sioned by the Salazar regime, com-memorates the mariners,

Vasco da Gama (c.1460–1524)

In 1498 Vasco da Gama sailed around the Cape of Good Hope and opened the sea route to India *(see pp52–3)*. Although the Hindu ruler of Calicut, who received him wearing diamond and ruby rings, was not impressed by his humble offerings of cloth and wash basins, da Gama returned to Portugal with a cargo of spices. In 1502 he sailed again to India, establishing Portuguese trade routes in the Indian Ocean. João III nominated him Viceroy of India in 1524, but he died of a fever soon after.

16th-century painting of Vasco da Gama in Goa

The huge pavement compass in front of the Monument to the Discoveries

royal patrons and all those who took part in the development of the Portuguese Age of Discovery. The monument is designed in the shape of a caravel, with Portugal's coat of arms on the sides and the sword of the Royal House of Avis rising above the entrance. Henry the Navigator stands at the prow with a caravel in hand. In two sloping lines either side of the monument are stone statues of Portuguese heroes linked with the Age of Discovery, such as Dom Manuel I holding an armillary sphere, the poet Camões with a copy of *Os Lusíadas* and the painter Nuno Gonçalves, as well as famous navigators, cartographers and kings. On the monument's

north side, the huge mariner's compass cut into the paving stone was a gift from South Africa in 1960. The central map, dotted with mermaids and galleons, shows the routes of the discoverers in the 15th and 16th centuries. Inside the monument a lift whisks you up to the sixth floor where steps then lead to the top for a splendid panorama of Belém. The basement level is used for temporary exhibitions, but not necessarily related to the Discoveries.

The rather ostentatious Padrão is not to everyone's taste but the setting is undeniably splendid and the caravel design is imaginative. The monument looks particularly dramatic when viewed from the west in the light of the late afternoon sun.

⑩ MAAT – Museu de Arte, Arquitetura e Tecnologia

Av. Brasília, Central Tejo, 1300-598. **Map** 2 D5. **Tel** 210 028 130. 🚌 727, 728, 729. 🚋 15. 🚉 Belém. **Open** 12–8pm Wed–Mon. **Closed** 1 Jan, 1 May & 25 Dec. 🚻 **w** maat.pt;

With a spectacular riverside view, the stylish Museu de Arte, Arquitetura e Tecnologia is operated by the EDP Foundation, and is dedicated to contemporary art, primarily Portuguese, along with modern architecture and technology. Popularly known as MAAT, the exhibits are housed in an award-winning building designed by the London-based architect Amanda Levete. Its structure is a sharp contrast to the well-known Lisbon power station, which stands next door, and forms an integral part of this building complex. Visits to the MAAT include a tour of the iconic power station, not forgetting the pedestrian roof from which visitors can gain stunning views of Lisbon and the Tagus river.

Aside from unique temporary exhibitions, the museum also features the Pedro Cabrita Reis Collection, which consists of some 400 works by over 70 artists from the end of the 20th century.

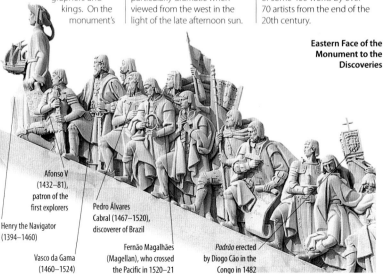

Eastern Face of the Monument to the Discoveries

Afonso V (1432–81), patron of the first explorers

Pedro Álvares Cabral (1467–1520), discoverer of Brazil

Henry the Navigator (1394–1460)

Vasco da Gama (1460–1524)

Fernão Magalhães (Magellan), who crossed the Pacific in 1520–21

Padrão erected by Diogo Cão in the Congo in 1482

⑪ Torre de Belém

Commissioned by Manuel I, the tower was built as a fortress in the middle of the Tagus in 1515–21. The starting point for the navigators who set out to discover the trade routes, this Manueline gem became a symbol of Portugal's great era of expansion. The real beauty of the tower lies in the decoration of the exterior. Adorned with rope carved in stone, it has openwork balconies, Moorish-style watchtowers and distinctive battlements in the shape of shields. The Gothic interior below the terrace, which served as a storeroom for arms and a prison, is very austere but the tower's private quarters are worth visiting for the loggia and the panorama.

VISITORS' CHECKLIST

Practical Information
Av Brasília. **Map** 1 A5. **Tel** 213 620 034. **Open** 10am–6:30pm Tue–Sun (Oct–Apr: to 5:30pm). **Closed** 1 Jan, Easter Sun, 1 May, 13 Jun, 25 Dec. 🖼 (free first Sun of month & public hols). ♿ ground floor only.

Transport
🚌 729. 🚊 15. 🚆 Belém.

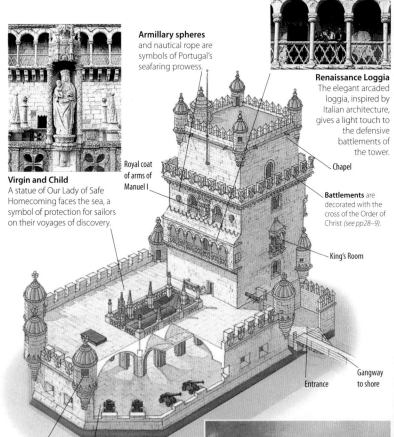

Armillary spheres
and nautical rope are symbols of Portugal's seafaring prowess.

Renaissance Loggia
The elegant arcaded loggia, inspired by Italian architecture, gives a light touch to the defensive battlements of the tower.

Virgin and Child
A statue of Our Lady of Safe Homecoming faces the sea, a symbol of protection for sailors on their voyages of discovery.

Royal coat of arms of Manuel I

Chapel

Battlements are decorated with the cross of the Order of Christ (see pp28–9).

King's Room

Entrance

Gangway to shore

The vaulted dungeon
was used as a prison until the 19th century.

Sentry posts

The Torre de Belém in 1811
This painting of a British ship navigating the Tagus, by J T Serres, shows the tower much further from the shore than it is today. In the 19th century land on the north bank was reclaimed, making the river narrower.

The simple Manueline chapel, Ermida de São Jerónimo

⑫ Ermida de São Jerónimo

Praça de Itália. **Map** 1 A3.
Tel 210 966 989. 🚌 714, 728, 729, 751. **Open** Mon–Sat (by appt).

Also known as the Capela de São Jerónimo, this elegant little chapel was constructed in 1514 when Diogo Boitac was working on the Jerónimos monastery (see pp108–9). Although a far simpler building, it is also Manueline in style and may have been built to a design by Boitac. The only decorative elements on the monolithic chapel are the four pinnacles, corner gargoyles and Manueline portal. Perched on a quiet hill above Belém, the chapel has fine views. A path from the terrace winds down the hill towards the Torre de Belém.

⑬ Igreja da Memória

Calçada do Galvão, Ajuda. **Map** 1 C3. **Tel** 213 635 295. 🚌 714, 727, 728, 732. 🚋 18. **Open** for mass 6pm Mon–Sat, 10am Sun. ✝ ♿

Built in 1760, the church was founded by King José I in gratitude for his escape from an assassination plot on this site in 1758. The king was returning from a secret liaison with a lady of the noble Távora family when his carriage was attacked and a bullet hit him in the arm. Pombal (see pp56–7), whose power had become absolute, used this as an excuse to get rid of his enemies in the Távora family, accusing them of conspiracy. In 1759 they were savagely

tortured and executed. Their deaths are commemorated by a pillar in Beco do Chão Salgado, off Rua de Belém.

The Neo-Classical domed church has a marble-clad interior and a small chapel containing the tomb of Pombal, who died a year after being banished from Lisbon.

⑭ Jardim Botânico da Ajuda

Calçada da Ajuda. **Map** 1 C2. **Tel** & **Fax**: 213 622 503. 🚌 714, 727, 728, 729, 732. 🚋 18. **Open** Nov–Mar: 10am–5pm daily; Apr & Oct: 10am–5pm Mon–Fri,10am–6pm Sat & Sun; May–Sep: 10am–6pm Mon–Fri, 9am–8pm Sat & Sun. **Closed** 1 Jan, 25 Dec. ♿ 📷

Laid out by Pombal (see p56) in 1768, these Italian-style gardens provide a pleasant respite from Belém's noisy suburbs. The entrance on Calçada da Ajuda (wrought-iron gates in a pink wall) is easy to miss. The park has 5,000 plant species from Africa, Asia and America. Notable features are the 400-year-old dragon tree, native of Madeira, and the flamboyant 18th-century fountain decorated with serpents, winged fish, sea horses and mythical creatures. A majestic terrace looks out over the lower level of the gardens.

⑮ Palácio Nacional da Ajuda

Calçada da Ajuda. **Map** 2 D2. **Tel** 213 620 264. 🚌 714, 732, 742, 760. 🚋 18. **Open** 10am–6pm Thu–Tue (last entry 5pm). **Closed** 1 Jan, Easter Sun, 1 May, 25 Dec. 📷 (free first Sun of month). ♿ 📷 🌐 palacioajuda.pt

The royal palace, destroyed by fire in 1795, was replaced in the early 19th century by this Neo-Classical building. Left incomplete when the royal family was forced into exile in Brazil in 1807 (see pp56–7), the palace only became a permanent residence of the royal family when Luís I became king in 1861 and married an Italian Princess, Maria Pia di Savoia. No expense was spared in furnishing the apartments, which are decorated with silk wallpaper, Sèvres porcelain and crystal chandeliers. A prime example of regal excess is the extraordinary Saxe Room, a wedding present to Maria Pia from the King of Saxony, in which every piece of furniture is decorated with Meissen porcelain. On the first floor the huge Banqueting Hall, with crystal

19th-century throne from the Palácio Nacional da Ajuda

chandeliers, silk-covered chairs and an allegory of the birth of João VI on the frescoed ceiling, is truly impressive. At the other end of the palace, Luís I's Neo-Gothic painting studio is a more intimate display of intricately carved furniture.

Manicured formal gardens of the Jardim Botânico da Ajuda

FURTHER AFIELD

Most of the outlying sights, which include some of Lisbon's finest museums, are easily accessible by bus or metro from the city centre. A ten-minute walk north from the gardens of the Parque Eduardo VII brings you to Portugal's great cultural complex, the Calouste Gulbenkian Foundation, set in a pleasant park. Few tourists go further north than the Gulbenkian, but the Museu de Lisboa on Campo Grande is worth a detour for its fascinating overview of Lisbon's history.

The charming Palácio Fronteira, decorated with splendid tiles, is one of the many villas built for the aristocracy. Those interested in tiles will also enjoy the Museu Nacional do Azulejo in the cloisters of the Madre de Deus convent.

Visitors with a spare half-day can cross the Tagus to the Cristo Rei monument. Northeast of Lisbon is the vast oceanarium, Oceanário de Lisboa, in the Parque das Nações, which includes other family-oriented attractions, hotels and shops.

Sights at a Glance

Museums and Galleries

3 Fundação Oriente Museu
7 *Museu Calouste Gulbenkian – Coleção do Fundador pp118–21*
8 Museu Calouste Gulbenkian – Coleção Moderna
10 Museu da Água
11 *Museu Nacional do Azulejo pp124–5*
14 Museu de Lisboa

Modern Architecture

1 Cristo Rei
2 Ponte 25 de Abril
4 Centro Colombo
12 Parque das Nações

Historic Architecture

5 Praça Marquês de Pombal
9 Campo Pequeno
16 Aqueduto das Águas Livres
17 Palácio Fronteira

Parks and Gardens

6 Parque Eduardo VII
18 Parque do Monteiro-Mor

Zoos

13 Oceanário de Lisboa
15 Jardim Zoológico

Key

▨ Main sightseeing areas
▭ Motorway
▬ Major road
▭ Minor road

0 kilometres   4
0 miles   2

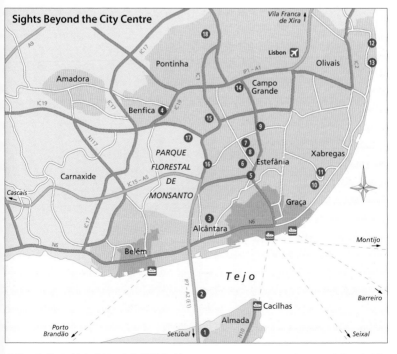

Sights Beyond the City Centre

◀ Decorative tiles *(azulejos)* and statuary in the Palácio Fronteira   **For keys to symbols** *see back flap*

❶ Cristo Rei

Santuário Nacional do Cristo Rei, Alto do Pragal, Almada. **Tel** 212 751 000. 🚢 Transtejo Cacilhas ferry from Cais do Sodré to Cacilhas, then 🚌 101. Lift: **Open** 1 Jul–20 Sep: 9:30am–6:45pm daily; 21 Sep–30 Jun: 9:30am–6pm daily. 🅿 🅦 **cristorei.pt**

Modelled on the more famous Cristo Redentor in Rio de Janeiro, this giant statue stands with arms outstretched on the south bank of the Tagus. The 28-m-(92-ft-) tall figure of Christ, mounted on an 82-m (269-ft) pedestal, was built by Francisco Franco in 1949–59 at the instigation of Prime Minister Salazar.

You can see the monument from various viewpoints in the city, but it is fun to take a ferry to Margem Sul, also known as Outra Banda (the other bank), then a bus or taxi to the monument. A lift, plus some steps, takes you to the top of the pedestal, affording fine views of the city.

❷ Ponte 25 de Abril

Map 3 A5. 🚌 753.

Originally called the Ponte Salazar after the dictator who had it built in 1966, Lisbon's suspension bridge was renamed (like many other monuments) to commemorate the revolution of 25 April 1974 which restored democracy to Portugal (see p61).

Inspired by San Francisco's Golden Gate Bridge, this steel construction stretches for 2 km (1 mile). The lower tier was

The top of the towering monument of Cristo Rei overlooking the Tagus

modified in 1999 to accommodate the Fertagus, a much-needed railway across the Tagus.

The bridge's notorious traffic congestion has been partly resolved by the opening of the 11-km (7-mile) Vasco da Gama bridge. Spanning the river from Montijo to Sacavém, north of the Parque das Nações, this bridge was completed in 1998.

❸ Fundação Oriente Museu

Avenida Brasília, Doca de Alcântara Norte. **Map** 3 B4. **Tel** 213 585 200. 🚌 712, 714, 728, 738, 742. **Open** 10am–6pm Tue–Sun (to 10pm Fri). **Closed** 1 Jan, 25 Dec. 🅿 🅰 🅦 🖥 🅦 **museudooriente.pt**

Opened in 2008, this museum and cultural centre belonging to Portugal's Orient Foundation is

dedicated to showing the historical and cultural links between Portugal and its former colonies in the East.

The core of the permanent exhibition is split into two main collections. The Portuguese Presence in Asia section has a wide selection of exhibits, ranging from furniture and jewellery to porcelain, paintings and textiles. Highlights include 17th- and 18th-century Chinese and Japanese folding screens and some rare examples of Namban art – Portuguese-influenced Japanese art of the 16th and 17th centuries. A room dedicated to Portugal's days as the world's mercantile power when it dominated the spice routes contains Catholic Asian exhibits and pieces representative of multicultural Asian society, including crucifixes, ornaments and antiques. There are also maps and charts from early colonial times.

The second permanent exhibition is the Kwok On Collection, which features over 13,000 exhibits on the performing arts of a vast geographic area extending from Turkey all the way to Japan. It includes a fine collection of masks from all over Asia and a section exploring shadow and puppet theatre traditions from India, China and Indonesia. The Gods of Asia exhibit has fascinating Buddhist and Hindu artifacts.

The cultural centre organizes Asian cooking, theatre, dance and music activities.

Ponte 25 de Abril linking central Lisbon with Margem Sul, the south bank of the Tagus

For hotels and restaurants in this area see pp386–7 and pp398–401

❻ Parque Eduardo VII

Praça Marquês de Pombal. **Map** 5 B4.
Ⓜ Marquês de Pombal. 🚌 711, 712, 736. Estufa Fria: **Tel** 213 882 278. **Open** 10am–7pm daily (Nov–Mar: 9am–5pm). **Closed** 1 Jan, 1 May, 25 Dec. 🅿

Beautifully landscaped grounds of Parque Eduardo VII in central Lisbon

The largest park in central Lisbon was named in honour of King Edward VII of England who came to Lisbon in 1902 to reaffirm the Anglo-Portuguese alliance. The wide grassy slope that extends for 25 ha (62 acres) was laid out as Parque de Liberdade, a continuation of Avenida da Liberdade *(see p86)* in the late 19th century. Neatly clipped box hedging, flanked by mosaic patterned walk-ways, stretches uphill from the Praça Marquês de Pombal to a belvedere at the top. Here, in the flower-filled landscaped garden dedicated to Amália Rodrigues *(see p69),* you will find the *Fat Mama* sculpture by Botero. From here there are fine views of the city. On clear days it is possible to see as far as the Serra da Arrábida *(see p173).*

Located at the northwest corner, the most inspiring feature of this park is the jungle-like Estufa Fria, or greenhouse, where exotic plants, streams and waterfalls provide an oasis from the city streets.

There are in fact two green-houses: in the Estufa Fria (cold greenhouse), palms push through the slatted bamboo roof and paths wind through a forest of ferns, fuchsias, flowering shrubs and banana trees; the Estufa Quente, or hot-house, is a glassed-over garden with lush plants, water-lily ponds and cacti, as well as tropical birds in cages.

Near the *estufas* a pond with large carp and a play area in the shape of a galleon are popular with children. On the east side, the Pavilhão Carlos Lopes, named after the 1984 Olympic marathon winner, is now a venue for concerts and conferences. The façade is decorated with a series of modern tiled scenes.

❹ Centro Colombo

Avenida Lusíada. **Tel** 217 113 636.
Ⓜ Colégio Militar. 🚌 703, 729, 764, 765, 799. **Open** 10am–midnight daily. 🅿 🚻 colombo.pt

The huge Centro Colombo in Benfica is the biggest shopping centre in the Iberian Peninsula, almost matching the adjacent Estádio da Luz football stadium in size. With over 360 shops, 60 restaurants and 10 cinemas, this mall provides the ultimate everything-under-one-roof shopping experience. Other amenities include a well-equipped health club.

❺ Praça Marquês de Pombal

Map 5 B5. Ⓜ Marquês de Pombal. 🚌 711, 712, 720, 723, 727, 732, 736, 738 & many other routes.

At the top of the Avenida da Liberdade *(see p86),* traffic thunders round the "Rotunda"

Detail representing agricultural toil on the base of the monument in Praça Marquês de Pombal

(roundabout), as the *praça* is also known. At the centre is a 1934 monument to Pombal. The despotic statesman, who virtually ruled Portugal from 1750–77, stands on the top of the column, his hand on a lion (symbol of power) and his eyes directed down to the Baixa, whose creation he masterminded *(see pp66–7).* Allegorical images depicting Pombal's political, educational and agricultural reforms dec-orate the base of the monument. Standing figures represent Coimbra University, where he introduced a new Faculty of Science. Broken blocks of stone at the foot of the monu-ment and tidal waves flooding the city are an allegory of the destruction caused by the 1755 earthquake.

An underpass, which is not always open, leads to the centre of the square where the sculptures on the pedestal and the inscriptions relating to Pombal's achievements can be seen. Nearby, the well-tended Parque Eduardo VII extends northwards behind the square. The paving stones around the Rotunda are decorated with a mosaic of Lisbon's coat of arms. Similar patterns decorate many of the city's streets and squares.

❼ Museu Calouste Gulbenkian – Coleção do Fundador

Thanks to the wealthy Armenian oil magnate Calouste Gulbenkian (see p121), this museum has one of the finest collections of art in Europe. The purpose-built museum was inaugurated in 1969 and created as part of the charitable institution bequeathed to Portugal by Gulbenkian. The building was designed to best display the founder's collection, with a spacious park allowing for as much natural light as possible.

Mustard Pot
This 18th-century silver mustard pot was made in France by Antoine-Sébastien Durand.

Lalique Corsage Ornament
The sinuous curves of the gold and enamel snakes are typical of René Lalique's Art Nouveau jewellery.

14
13
15
17
16

★ Diana
This fine marble statue (1780) by the French sculptor Jean-Antoine Houdon, was once owned by Catherine the Great of Russia. The graceful Diana, goddess of the hunt, is portrayed in motion, with a bow and arrow in hand.

Entrance

Stairs to

★ Bust of St Catherine (?)
This serene bust, thought to be of St Catherine, was painted by the Flemish artist Rogier Van der Weyden (1400–64). The thin strip of landscape on the left of the wooden panel brings light and depth to the still portrait.

★ Portrait of an Old Man
Rembrandt was a master
of light and shade. In this
expressive portrait, dated
1645, the fragile
countenance of the old
man is contrasted with the
strong and dramatic lighting.

VISITORS' CHECKLIST

Practical Information
Avenida de Berna 45. **Map** 5 B2.
Tel 217 823 000. **Open** 10am–
6pm Wed–Mon. **Closed** 1 Jan,
Easter Sun, 1 May, 25 Dec.
(free Sun after 2pm).
w gulbenkian.pt/museu

Transport
M Praça de Espanha or
São Sebastião. 713, 716,
726, 742, 756.

Renaissance art

Vase of a Hundred Birds
The enamel decoration that
adorns this Chinese porcelain
vase is known as Famille Verte.
This type of elaborate design is
characteristic of the Ch'ing
dynasty during the reign of the
Emperor K'ang Hsi (1662–1722).

Gallery Guide

*The galleries are laid out both
chronologically and geographically, the first section (rooms
1–6) dedicated to Classical and
Oriental art, the second section
(rooms 7–17) housing the
European collection of paintings,
sculpture, furniture, silverware
and jewellery.*

Armenian art

Egyptian Bronze Cat
This bronze of a cat feeding and playing with her kittens
dates from the Saite Period (664–525 BC). Other stunning
Egyptian pieces include a gilded mask of a mummy.

Persian
faïence

Turkish Faïence Plate
The factories at Iznik
in Turkey produced
some of the most
beautiful jugs, plates
and vases of the
Islamic world,
including this
17th-century deep
plate decorated with
stylized animal forms.

Key to Floorplan

- Egyptian, Classical and Mesopotamian art
- Oriental Islamic art
- Far Eastern art
- European art (14th–17th centuries)
- French 18th-century decorative arts
- European art (18th–19th centuries)
- Lalique collection
- Non-exhibition space

Exploring the Gulbenkian Collection

Housing Calouste Gulbenkian's unique collection of art, the museum ranks with the Museu de Arte Antiga *(see pp98–101)* as the finest in Lisbon. The exhibits, which span over 4,000 years from ancient Egyptian statuettes, through translucent Islamic glassware, to Art Nouveau brooches, are displayed in spacious and well-lit galleries, many overlooking the gardens or courtyards. The museum is quite small, however each individual work of art, from the magnificent pieces that make up the rich display of Oriental and Islamic art, to the selection of European paintings and furniture, is worthy of attention.

Early 17th-century Persian faïence tile from the School of Isfahan

Egyptian, Classical and Mesopotamian Art

Priceless treasures chart the evolution of Egyptian art from the Old Kingdom (c.2700 BC) to the Roman Period (1st century BC). The exhibits range from an alabaster bowl of the 3rd Dynasty to a surprisingly modern-looking blue terracotta torso of a statuette of *Venus Anadyomene* from the Roman period.

Outstanding pieces in the Classical art section are a magnificent red-figure Greek vase and 11 Roman medallions, found in Egypt. These are believed to have been struck to mark a series of festivals held at Beroia (Macedonia) in honour of Alexander the Great. In the Mesopotamian art section the large Assyrian alabaster bas-relief

5th-century BC Greek vase

represents the winged genie of Spring, carrying a container of holy water (9th century BC).

Oriental Islamic Art

Being Armenian, Calouste Gulbenkian had a keen interest in art from the Near and Middle East. The Oriental Islamic gallery has a fine collection of Persian and Turkish carpets, textiles, costumes and ceramics. In the section overlooking the courtyard, the Syrian mosque lamps and bottles commissioned by princes and sultans, are beautifully decorated with coloured enamel on glass. The Armenian section has some exquisite illustrated manuscripts from the 16th to 18th centuries, produced by Armenian refugees in Istanbul, Persia and the Crimea.

Far Eastern Art

Calouste Gulbenkian acquired a large collection of Chinese porcelain between 1907 and 1947. One of the rarest pieces is the small blue-glazed bowl from the Yüan dynasty (1279–1368), on the right as you go into the gallery. The majority of exhibits, however, are the later, more exuberantly decorated *famille verte* porcelain and the K'ang Hsi biscuitware of the 17th and 18th centuries. Further exhibits from the Far East are translucent Chinese jades and other semi-precious stones, Japanese prints, brocaded silk hangings and bound books, and lacquerwork.

European Art (14th–17th Centuries)

Illuminated manuscripts, rare printed books and medieval ivories introduce the section on Western art. The delicately sculpted 14th-century ivory diptychs and triptychs, made in France, show scenes from the lives of Christ and the Virgin.

The collection of early European paintings starts with panels of *St Joseph* and *St Catherine* by Rogier van der Weyden, leading painter of the mid-15th century in Flanders. Italian Renaissance painting is represented by Cima da Conegliano's *Sacra Conversazione* from the late 15th century and Domenico Ghirlandaio's *Portrait of a Young Woman* (c.1490).

The collection progresses to Flemish and Dutch works of the 17th century, including two works by Rembrandt: *Portrait of an Old Man* (1645), a

French ivory triptych of *Scenes from the Life of the Virgin* (14th century)

masterpiece of psychological penetration, and *Pallas Athena* (c.1655–59), said to have been modelled on Rembrandt's son, Titus, and previously thought to have portrayed Alexander the Great. Rubens is represented by three paintings, the most remarkable of which is the *Portrait of Hélène Fourment* (c.1630), the artist's second wife.

The gallery beyond the Dutch and Flemish paintings has tapestries and textiles from Italy and Flanders, Italian ceramics, rare 15th-century medallions and sculpture.

French 18th-Century Decorative Arts

Some remarkably elaborate Louis XV and Louis XVI pieces, many commissioned by royalty, feature in the collection of French 18th-century furniture. The exhibits, many of them embellished with lacquer panels, ebony and bronze, are grouped together according to historical style with Beauvais and chinoiserie Aubusson tapestries decorating the walls.

The French silverware from the same period, much of which once adorned Russian palaces' dining tables, includes lavishly decorated soup tureens, salt-cellars and platters.

Louis XV chest of drawers inlaid with ebony and bronze

European Art (18th–19th Centuries)

The art of the 18th century is dominated by French painters, including Watteau (1684–1721), Fragonard (1732–1806) and Boucher (1703–70). The most celebrated piece of sculpture is a statue of *Diana* by Jean-Antoine Houdon. Commissioned in 1780 by the Duke of Saxe-Gotha for

View of the Molo with the Ducal Palace (c.1790) by Francesco Guardi

his gardens, it was purchased by Catherine the Great and became one of the main exhibits in the Hermitage in Russia during the 19th and early 20th centuries.

One whole room is devoted to views of Venice by the 18th-century Venetian painter Francesco Guardi, and a small collection of British art includes works by leading 18th-century portraitists, such as Gainsborough's *Portrait of Mrs Lowndes-Stone* (c.1775) and Romney's *Portrait of Mrs Constable* (1787). There are also two stormy seascapes by J M W Turner (1775–1851). French 19th-century landscape painting is well represented here, reflecting Gulbenkian's preference for naturalism, with works by the Barbizon school, the Realists and the Impressionists. The best-known paintings in the section, however, are probably Manet's *Boy with Cherries*, painted in about 1858 at the beginning

of the artist's career, and *Boy Blowing Bubbles*, painted about 1867. Renoir's *Portrait of Madame Claude Monet* was painted in about 1872 when the artist was staying with Monet at his country home in Argenteuil, in the outskirts of Paris.

Lalique Collection

The tour of the museum ends with an entire room filled with the flamboyant creations of French Art Nouveau jeweller, René Lalique (1860–1945). Gulbenkian was a close friend of Lalique's and he acquired many of the pieces of jewellery, glassware and ivory on display here directly from the artist. Inlaid with semi-precious stones and covered with gold leaf or enamel, the brooches, necklaces, vases and combs are decorated with the dragonfly, peacock or sensual female nude motifs characteristic of Art Nouveau.

Calouste Gulbenkian

Born in Scutari (Turkey) in 1869, Gulbenkian started his art collection at the age of 14 when he bought some ancient coins in a bazaar. In 1928 he was granted a 5 per cent stake in four major oil companies, including BP and Shell, in thanks for his part in the transfer of the assets of the Turkish Petroleum Company to those four companies. He thereby earned himself the nickname of "Mr Five Percent". With the wealth he accumulated, Gulbenkian was able to indulge his passion for fine works of art. During World War II, he went to live in neutral Portugal and, on his death in 1955, bequeathed his estate to establish a foundation in his name based in Portugal. The Foundation supports many cultural activities and has its own orchestra, art library, concert halls and a modern art collection.

A light-filled gallery at the Museu Calouste Gulbenkian – Coleção Moderna

❽ Museu Calouste Gulbenkian – Coleção Moderna

Rua Dr Nicolau de Bettencourt.
Map 5 B3. **Tel** 217 823 000. Ⓜ São Sebastião. 🚌 716, 726, 742, 746, 756.
Open 10am–6pm Wed–Mon. **Closed** 1 Jan, Easter, 1 May, 25 Dec. 🖼 (free Sun after 2pm). 🖥 **gulbenkian.pt/cam/colecao-moderna**

The Museu Calouste Gulbenkian – Coleção Moderna lies across the gardens from the Calouste Gulbenkian Coleção do Fundador and is part of the same cultural foundation (see p121).

The permanent collection features paintings and sculpture by Portuguese artists from the turn of the 20th century to the present day. One of the most famous paintings is the striking portrait of poet Fernando Pessoa in the Café Irmãos Unidos (1964) by José de Almada Negreiros (1893– 1970), a main exponent of Portuguese Modernism. Also of interest are paintings by Eduardo Viana (1881–1967), Amadeo de Souza-Cardoso (1887–1918), as well as contemporary artists such as Paula Rego, Rui Sanches, Graça Morais and Teresa Magalhães.

The Coleção Moderna's building is light and spacious, with pleasant gardens and a busy cafeteria.

❾ Campo Pequeno

Map 5 C1. Ⓜ Campo Pequeno. 🚌 727, 736. Bullring: **Tel** 217 998 450.
Open Easter–Oct: for bullfights. 🖼 🚻

This square is dominated by the red-brick Neo-Moorish bullring built in the late 19th century. A full renovation added a roof, a shopping and leisure centre and an underground car park. Much of the bullring's distinctive architecture, such as keyhole-shaped windows and double cupolas was retained. Call the tourist office or the number listed above for information on this and other bullfight venues.

Renovated 19th-century steam pump in the Museu da Água

❿ Museu da Água

Rua do Alviela 12. **Tel** 218 100 215.
🚌 735, 794. **Open** 10am–5:30pm Tue–Sat. **Closed** public hols. 🖼

Dedicated to the history of Lisbon's water supply, this small but informative museum was imaginatively created around the city's first steam pumping station. It commemorates Manuel da Maia, the 18th-century engineer who masterminded the Águas Livres aqueduct (see p126). The excellent layout of the museum earned it the Council of Europe Museum Prize in 1990.

Pride of place goes to four lovingly preserved steam engines, one of which still functions (by electricity) and can be switched on for visitors. The development of technology relating to the city's water supply is documented with photographs. Particularly interesting are the sections on the Águas Livres aqueduct and the Alfama's 17th-century Chafariz d'El Rei, one of Lisbon's first fountains. Locals used to queue at one of six founts, depending on their social status.

⓫ Museu Nacional do Azulejo

See pp124–5.

Neo-Moorish façade of the bullring in Campo Pequeno

The impressive Oriente Station, located next to Parque das Nações

⓬ Parque das Nações

Avenida Dom João II. **Tel** 218 919 133.
Ⓜ Oriente. 🚌 705, 725, 728, 744, 750, 782. 🚉 Gare do Oriente. **Open** daily.
♿ 🚻 Pavilhão do Conhecimento
– Ciência Viva: **Tel** 218 917 100. **Open** 10am–6pm Tue–Fri, 11am–7pm Sat & Sun. **Closed** 1 Jan, 24, 25 & 31 Dec.
🅿 Casino Lisboa: **Tel** 218 929 000.
Open 3pm–3am Sun–Thu, 4pm–4am Fri & Sat. **Closed** 24 Dec.
🌐 **portaldasnacoes.pt**

Originally the site of Expo '98, Parque das Nações has renewed the eastern waterfront, formerly an industrial wasteland, with its contemporary architecture and family-oriented attractions.
The soaring geometry of the platform canopies over Santiago Calatrava's Oriente Station set the architectural tone for the development. The impressive Portugal Pavillion, designed by the Portuguese architect Álvaro Siza Vieira has a reinforced-concrete roof suspended like a sailcloth above its forecourt.

The Pavilhão do Conhecimento – Ciencia Viva (Knowledge and Science Pavilion) is a modern museum of science and technology that houses several interactive exhibitions. Also in the park is the Casino Lisboa, located in the space formerly occupied by the Pavilion of the Future.

Views can be had from the cable car that lifts visitors from one end of the park to the other or the Torre Vasco da Gama, Lisbon's tallest building which is now a hotel. The promenade along the river, which offers delightful views of the Tagus, is not to be missed.

The 17-km (11-mile) long Vasco da Gama bridge is the longest in Europe and was completed in 1998. Also in the area is the Pavilhão Atlantico, which hosts concerts and sporting events.

⓭ Oceanário de Lisboa

Esplanada D Carlos 1, Parque das Nações. **Tel** 218 917 000. Ⓜ Oriente. 🚌 705, 728, 744, 750. 🚉 Gare do Oriente. **Open** Apr–Oct: 10am–8pm daily; Nov–Mar: 10am–7pm daily (last adm: 1 hr before closing). 🅿 ♿
🌐 **oceanario.pt**

The main attraction at Parque das Nações, the oceanarium was designed by American architect Peter Chermayeff. Resembling an aircraft carrier, it is perched on the end of a pier, surrounded by water. It is one of the largest aquariums in the world, and holds an impressive array of species – as well as fish and other underwater dwellers, there are birds and, uniquely in Europe, sea otters.

18th-century Indian toy, Museu da Cidade

Four separate sea- and landscapes represent the habitats of the Atlantic, Pacific, Indian and Antarctic oceans, with suitable fauna and flora. The main attraction for most visitors, though, is the vast central tank with a dazzling variety of fish, large and small. Sharks coexist peaceably with bream, barracudas with rays.

⓮ Museu de Lisboa

Campo Grande 245. **Tel** 217 513 200. Ⓜ Campo Grande. 🚌 701, 736, 750. **Open** 10am–6pm Tue–Sun. **Closed** public hols. 🅿 (free until 1pm Sun). ♿

Palácio Pimenta was allegedly commissioned by João V *(see pp56–7)* for his mistress Madre Paula, a nun from the nearby convent at Odivelas. When the mansion was built, in the middle of the 18th century, it occupied a peaceful site outside the capital. Nowadays it has to contend with the teeming traffic of Campo Grande. The house itself, however, retains its period charm and the city museum is one of the most interesting in Lisbon.

The displays follow the development of the city, from prehistoric times, through the Romans, Visigoths and Moors, traced by means of tiles, drawings, paintings, models and historical documents.

Visits also take you through the former living quarters of the mansion, including the kitchen, decorated with blue and white tile panels of fish, flowers and hanging game.

Some of the most fascinating exhibits are those depicting the city before the earthquake of 1755, including a highly detailed model made in the 1950s and an impressive 17th-century oil painting by Dirk Stoop (1610–86) of *Terreiro do Paço* (Praça do Comércio, *see p89*). One room is devoted to the Águas Livres aqueduct *(see p126)* with detailed architectural plans for its construction as well as prints and watercolours of the completed aqueduct.

The earthquake theme is resumed with pictures of the city amid the devastation and various plans for its reconstruction. The museum brings you into the 20th century with a large colour poster celebrating the Revolution of 1910 and the proclamation of the new republic *(see pp58–9)*.

⓫ Museu Nacional do Azulejo

Dona Leonor, widow of King João II, founded the Convento da Madre de Deus in 1509. Originally built in Manueline style, the church was restored under João III using simple Renaissance designs, and the striking Baroque decoration was added by João V. The convent cloisters provide a stunning setting for the National Tile Museum. Decorative panels, individual tiles and photographs trace the evolution of tile-making from its introduction by the Moors, through Spanish influence and the development of Portugal's own style *(see pp30–31)*, up to the present day.

Hunting Scene
Artisans rather than artists began to decorate tiles in the 17th century. This detail shows a naive representation of a hunt.

Level 2

Kitchen Tiles
The walls of the restaurant are lined with 19th-century tiles showing hanging game, including wild boar and pheasant.

Level 1

Gallery Guide

The rooms around the central cloister are arranged chronologically with the oldest tiles on the ground floor. Access to the Madre de Deus is via level 1 of the museum. The front entrance of the church is used only during religious services.

★ **Nossa Senhora da Vida**
This detail showing St John is part of a fine 16th-century majolica altarpiece. The central panel of the huge work depicts The Adoration of the Shepherds.

Key to Floorplan

☐ Moorish tiles
☐ 16th-century tiles
☐ 17th-century tiles
☐ 18th-century tiles
☐ 19th-century tiles
☐ 20th-century tiles
☐ Temporary exhibition space
☐ Non-exhibition space

Tiles from the 17th century with oriental influences are displayed here.

Moorish Tiles
Decorated with a stylized animal motif, this 15th-century tile is typical of Moorish *azulejo* patterns.

Level 3

VISITORS' CHECKLIST

Practical Information
Rua da Madre de Deus 4. **Tel** 218 100 340. **W** museudoazulejo.pt
Open 10am–6pm Tue–Sun (last adm: 30 mins before closing).
Closed 1 Jan, Easter, 1 May, 25 Dec. (free first Sun of month).

Transport
718, 728, 742, 759, 794.

Panorama of Lisbon
A striking 18th-century panel on the top floor depicts Lisbon before the 1755 earthquake *(see pp66–7)*. This detail shows the royal palace on Terreiro do Paço.

Entrance

The Renaissance cloister is the work of Diogo de Torralva (1500–66).

★ Madre de Deus
Completed in the mid-16th century, it was not until two centuries later, under João V, that the church of Madre de Deus acquired its ornate decoration. The sumptuous Rococo altarpiece was added after the earthquake of 1755.

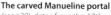

The carved Manueline portal
(see p29), dates from the 19th century but was recreated from a 16th-century painting.

★ Manueline Cloister
An important surviving feature of the original convent is the graceful Manueline cloister. Fine geometrical patterned tiles were added to the cloister walls in the 19th century.

⑮ Jardim Zoológico

Praça Marechal Humberto Delgado.
Tel 217 232 900. Ⓜ Jardim Zoológico.
🚌 716, 754, 768 & other routes. 🚉
Sete-Rios. **Open** 10am–6pm daily (21
Mar–20 Sep: to 8pm). 🅿️ 🅆 zoo.pt

The gardens here are as much
a feature as the actual zoo.
Opened in 1905, the zoo has
been revamped since, and most
of its aviaries and cages provide
more comfortable conditions
for the specimens. The most
bizarre feature is the dogs'
cemetery, complete with
tombstones and flowers. Other
attractions include a cable
car touring the park, a reptile
house, dolphin shows and an
amusement park. The area is
divided into four zones, all
included in the admission ticket.

⑯ Aqueduto das Águas Livres

Best seen from Calçada da Quintinha.
Tel 213 251 652. 🚌 774, 783. **Open**
10am–5:30pm Tue–Sat. **Closed** public
hols. Mãe d'Água das Amoreiras:
Praça das Amoreiras. **Tel** 218 100 215.
Open 10am–12:30pm & 1:30–5:30
Tue–Sat. ♿

Considered the most beautiful
sight in Lisbon at the turn of
the century, the impressive
structure of the Aqueduto
das Águas Livres looms over
the Alcântara valley to the
northwest of the city. The
construction of an aqueduct
to bring fresh water to the city
gave João V *(see pp56–7)* an
ideal opportunity to indulge his
passion for grandiose building

A flamboyance of flamingos at the Jardim Zoológico

schemes, as the only area of
Lisbon with fresh drinking
water was the Alfama. A tax on
meat, wine, olive oil and other
comestibles funded the project,
and although not complete
until the 19th century, it was
already supplying the city
with water by 1748. The main
pipeline measures 19 km
(12 miles), but the total length,
including all the secondary
channels, is 58 km (36 miles).
The most visible part of this
imposing structure are
the 35 arches that cross the
Alcântara valley, the tallest of
which rise to a spectacular
65 m (213 ft) above the city.

The public walkway along
the aqueduct, once a pleasant
promenade, has been closed
since 1853. This is partly due
to Diogo Alves, a robber who
threw his victims over the edge.
Today, visitors may take an

informative guided tour over
the Alcântara arches. There are
also tours of the Mãe d'Água
reservoir and trips to the Mãe
d'Água springs, the source of the
water supply. These tours can be
irregular, so it is best to contact
the Museu da Água *(see p122)*
for details of the trip on offer.

At the end of the aqueduct,
the Mãe d'Água das Amoreiras is
a castle-like building which
once served as a reservoir for
the water supplied from the
aqueduct. The original design
of 1745 was by the Hungarian
architect, Carlos Mardel, who
worked under Pombal *(see
pp66–7)* in the rebuilding of
the Baixa. Completed in 1834,
it became a popular meeting
place and acquired a reputation
as the rendezvous for kings and
their mistresses. Today the space
is used for art exhibitions,
fashion shows and other events.

Imposing arches of the Aqueduto das Águas Livres spanning the Alcântara valley

For hotels and restaurants in this area see pp386–7 and pp398–401

⏱ Palácio Fronteira

Largo São Domingos de Benfica 1.
Tel 217 782 023. Ⓜ Jardim Zoológico.
🚌 770. 🚉 Benfica. **Open** Mon–Sat.
🎫 compulsory. Jun–Sep: 10:30, 11 &
11:30am & noon Mon–Sat; Oct–May:
11am & noon Mon–Sat. **Closed** Sun,
public hols. ♿

Tiled terrace leading to the chapel of the Palácio Fronteira

This delightful country manor house was built as a hunting pavilion for João de Mascarenhas, the first Marquês de Fronteira, in 1640. Although skyscrapers are visible in the distance, it still occupies a quiet spot, by the Parque Florestal de Monsanto. Both house and garden have *azulejo* decoration whose subjects include battle scenes and trumpet-blowing monkeys.

Although the palace is still occupied by the 12th Marquis, some of the living rooms and the library, as well as the formal gardens, are included in the tour. The Battles Room has lively tiled panels depicting scenes of the War of Restoration (see pp54–5), with a detail showing João de Fronteira fighting a Spanish general. It was his loyalty to Pedro II during this war that earned him the title of Marquis. Interesting comparisons can be made between these naive 17th-century Portuguese tiles and the Delft ones from the same period in the dining room, depicting naturalistic scenes. The dining room is also decorated with frescoed panels and portraits of Portuguese nobility.

The late 16th-century chapel is the oldest part of the house. The façade is adorned with stones, shells, broken glass and bits of china. These fragments of crockery are believed to have been used at the feast inaugurating the palace and then smashed to ensure no one else could sup off the same set. Visits to the garden start at the chapel terrace, where tiled niches are decorated with figures personifying the arts

Bust of João I in gardens of Palácio Fronteira

and mythological creatures. In the formal Italian garden the immaculate box hedges are cut into shapes to represent the seasons of the year. To one end, tiled scenes of dashing knights on horseback, representing ancestors of the Fronteira family, are reflected in the waters of a large tank. On either side of the water, a grand staircase leads to a terrace above. Here, decorative niches contain the busts of Portuguese kings and colourful majolica reliefs adorn the arcades. More blue and white tiled scenes, realistic and allegorical, decorate the wall at the far end of the garden.

Entrance to the theatre museum in Parque do Monteiro-Mor

⏱ Parque do Monteiro-Mor

Largo Júlio Castilho. **Tel** 217 567 620.
🚌 703, 736. Ⓜ Lumiar. Park: **Open**
2–6pm Tue, 10am–6pm Wed–Sun.
Closed 1 Jan, Easter, 1 May, 13 Jun,
25 Dec. Museu Nacional do Traje:
Tel 217 567 620. **Open** 2–6pm
Tue, 10am–6pm Wed–Sun. Museu
Nacional do Teatro: Estrada de Lumiar
10. **Tel** 217 567 418. **Open** 10am–6pm
Tue–Sun. 🎫 combined ticket for park
& museums; free first Sun of month.
♿ 🖥 museudotraje.pt;
🖥 museudoteatro.pt

Monteiro-Mor Park was sold to the state in 1975 and the 18th-century palace buildings were converted to museums. The gardens are attractive and romantic; much of the land is wooded, though the area around the museums has gardens with flowering shrubs, duck ponds and tropical trees.

The rather old-fashioned Museu Nacional do Traje (costume museum) has a vast collection of textiles, accessories and costumes worn by musicians, politicians, poets, aristocrats and soldiers.

The Museu Nacional do Teatro has two buildings, one devoted to temporary exhibitions, the other containing a small permanent collection. Photographs, posters and cartoons feature famous 20th-century Portuguese actors and one section is devoted to Amália Rodrigues, the famous *fado* singer (see pp68–9).

SHOPPING IN LISBON

With recognised high street names, large and modern shopping centres, charming markets and unique gift shops, Lisbon has an eclectic range of shopping opportunities. The cobbled and idyllic streets of the Baixa and the chic Chiado district are the city's traditional shopping areas, and the wine merchants here are the best in the country. The more exclusive designer shops are found around the Avenida da Liberdade, which is based on Paris's Champs-Elysees in design and character. If you are looking for something typically Portuguese, such as hand-woven tapestries, ceramics or clothes, there are countless gift shops and markets around the city where you will unearth charming souvenirs.

Beautiful Lello Library is one of of the oldest bookstores in Portugal

Opening Hours

Traditional shopping hours are Monday to Friday 9am to 1pm and 3pm to 7pm, and Saturday 9am to 1pm. However, in order to satisfy growing consumer demand, many shops, especially those in the Baixa, open during the lunch hour and on Saturday afternoons. Shopping centres are open daily from 10am to midnight.

How to Pay

Most shops in Lisbon accept Visa and other credit cards, plus it is also possible to obtain euros from one of the many ATMs located around the centre of town.

Tax Free Goods

Many shops are affiliated to the Global Blue Tax Free system and are identified by the logo of the same name. The shop assistant will issue a tax exemption form *(isencão na exportação)* which should be presented to customs on your departure from Portugal in order to obtain a rebate.

Shopping Centres

Shopping centres have had a dramatic impact on shopping in Lisbon, combining vast supermarkets and restaurants with shops, cinemas and banks. Well-known centres include **Amoreiras**, **Vasco da Gama**, **Centro Colombo** and **El Corte Inglés**.

Food and Markets

There are markets of every variety in Lisbon, from municipal markets selling fresh produce to the famous Feira da Ladra *(see p75)*. Bargains can be found among the bric-a-brac, second-hand clothes and general arts and crafts. Coin collectors head for the Feira Numismática in Praça do Comércio *(see p89)*. Other good spots are the **Feira de Antiguidades, Velharias e Artesanato** for antiques and **Feira dos Alfarrabistas** for old books.

Gourmets will find Lisbon's delicatessens *(charcutarias)* irresistible. They are lined with superb cheeses, tasty smoked meats and wild game, delicious sweets *(ovos moles)* and an assortment of dried and crystallized fruits. **Mercearia dos Açores**, **Manuel Tavares**, which has a fine selection of port and madeira, and **Celeiro Dieta**, known for organic foods, are popular.

Wines and Spirits

Portugal's large variety of wines and spirits is well represented in Lisbon's specialist shops. **Napoleão**, the city's best-known wine merchants, has a number of outlets, with its oldest in the Baixa. For port specifically, visit Solar do Vinho do Porto *(see p96)* where it is possible to sample before deciding what to buy.

Books and Music

The music scene in Portugal is a lively mix of traditions and the very latest. *Fado* music is hugely popular, while dance music has a dedicated following. **FNAC** is Lisbon's best music retailer. **Discoteca**

Bric-a-brac on display at the popular Feira da Ladra market

Brightly painted ceramic plates

Amália specializes in *fado*. Portugal also boasts a great literary tradition, with a range of authors including Luís de Camões, Fernando Pessoa, Eça de Queiróz and José Saramago. Translations of their works are found in most bookshops. **Aillaud & Lellos** and **Livraria Bertrand** are among Lisbon's oldest bookshops.

Clothes

Most of the large chain stores have outlets in Lisbon, particularly in the shopping centres.

The Spanish **Zara** chain sell affordable clothes for everyone. More exclusive shops, including designer outlets, can be found on and around Avenida de Liberdade. **Rosa & Teixeira** is one of an increasing number of known Portuguese designers.

Regional Crafts

Portugal has a rich history of fine craftwork *(artesanato)*, notably embroidery, fine lace, hand-knitted woollens and delicate gold and silver thread jewellery. Head for the gift shops in the Restauradores and Rossio areas of Lisbon and **Arte Rústica** in the Baixa. Portugal's ceramics are renowned for their quality and variety, and in Lisbon you can find everything from delicate porcelain to rustic terracotta, and from tiles to tableware. Fine porcelain tableware from **Vista Alegre Atlantis** makes for an excellent souvenir.

Antiques

The majority of Lisbon's antique shops are located either on Rua Dom Pedro V or Rua São Bento. There are numerous religious artifacts to be found in the area and **Solar** specializes in antique tiles *(azulejos)*. Beautiful prints sold at second-hand bookshops in the Bairro Alto are good value for money. **Livraria Olisipo** stocks books and also old prints of landscapes, fauna and maps. Look for shops that are members of APA *(Associação Portuguesa de Antiquário)*, often indicated by a sign in the window.

DIRECTORY

Shopping Centres

Amoreiras
Avenida Engenheiro Duarte Pacheco, Amoreiras. **Map** 5 A5. **Tel** 213 810 200. w amoreiras.com

Centro Colombo
Avenida Lusíada. **Tel** 217 113 636. w colombo.pt

El Corte Inglés
Avenida António Augusto Aguiar 31. **Map** 5 B3. **Tel** 707 211 711. w elcorteingles.pt

Vasco da Gama
Avenida Dom João II, Parque das Nações. **Tel** 218 930 600. w centrovasco dagama.pt

Food and Markets

Celeiro Dieta
Avenida António Augusto de Aguiar 130, Saldanha. **Map** 5 B3. **Tel** 213 558 164.

Feira dos Alfarrabistas
Rua Anchieta. **Open** Sat.

Feira de Antiguidades, Velharias e Artesanato
Príncipe Real. **Map** 4 F1. **Open** Last Sat of every month.

Mercearia dos Açores
Rua da Madalena 115. **Map** 7 C4. **Tel** 218 880 070.

Manuel Tavares
Rua da Betesga 1. **Map** 7 B3. **Tel** 213 424 209.

Wines and Spirits

Napoleão
Rua dos Fanqueiros 70. **Map** 7 C4. **Tel** 218 872 042.

Books and Music

Aillaud & Lellos
Rua do Carmo 82, Chiado. **Map** 7 B4. **Tel** 213 424 450.

Discoteca Amália
Rua do Ouro 272, Baixa. **Map** 7 B4. **Tel** 213 420 939.

FNAC
Armazéns do Chaido, Rua do Carmo 2, Loja 407. **Map** 7 B4 **Tel** 707 313 435.

Livraria Bertrand
Rua Garrett 73, Chiado. **Map** 7 A4. **Tel** 213 476 122.

Clothes

Rosa & Teixeira
Avenida da Liberdade 204, Avenida. **Map** 5 C5. **Tel** 213 110 350.

Zara
Rua Garrett 1, Chiado. **Map** 7 B4. **Tel** 213 243 710.

Regional Crafts

Arte Rústica
Rua Augusta 193, First Floor, Baixa. **Map** 7 B4. **Tel** 213 461 004.

Vista Alegre Atlantis
Largo do Chiado 20–23, Chiado. **Map** 7 A4. **Tel** 213 461 401.

Antiques

Livraria Olisipo
Largo Trindade Coelho 7–8, Bairro Alto. **Map** 7 A3. **Tel** 213 462 771.

Solar
Rua Dom Pedro V 70, Bairro Alto. **Map** 4 F2. **Tel** 213 465 522.

ENTERTAINMENT IN LISBON

For a smallish European capital, Lisbon has a great, varied cultural calendar. Musical events range from classical and opera performances to intimate *fado* evenings, and large rock concerts. Dance, both classical and modern, is well represented in Lisbon. The Gulbenkian Foundation, long the only major arts patron, has been joined by other private funds as well as state institutions.

Football is a consuming passion of the Portuguese, and Lisbon's Sporting and Benfica teams play regularly at home. Lisbon out-parties many larger capitals, with a nightlife known for its liveliness.

Booking Tickets

Tickets can be reserved by phoning the Agência de Bilhetes para Espectáculos Públicos (**ABEP**). Pay in cash when you collect them from the kiosk. Tickets are also sold at **FNAC**. Not all cinemas and theatres accept credit card bookings – check first.

ABEP kiosk selling tickets on Praça dos Restauradores

Listings Magazines

Previews of forthcoming cultural events plus listings and reviews of the city's latest bars and clubs appear each week in major newspapers. English-language publications on offer include the monthly *Follow Me Lisboa*, which can be obtained free from tourist offices. The monthly *Agenda Cultural* is in Portuguese.

Cinema and Theatre

Movie-goers are very well served in Lisbon. Films are shown in their original language with Portuguese subtitles, and tickets are inexpensive. On Mondays most cinemas offer reductions. The city's older cinemas have now largely given way to modern multiplexes, usually located in shopping centres such as Amoreiras, Centro Colombo or El Corte Inglés. While these screen mainstream Hollywood fare, cinemas such as **São Jorge Cinema** show more European films. For classics and retrospectives, head to the **Cinemateca Portuguesa**; a programme is available at tourist offices. Theatre performances are most often in Portuguese, but large institutions such as the **Teatro Nacional Dona Maria II** and the **Teatro da Trindade** occasionally stage guest performances by visiting companies. Less formally, **Chapitô** sometimes has open-air shows.

Classical Music, Opera and Dance

Lisbon's top cultural centres are the modern **Centro Cultural de Belém** (*see p110*) and the **Fundação Calouste Gulbenkian** (*see pp118–21*). They host national and international events such as ballet and concerts. Ballet is also the focus of the **Teatro Camões**. The **Teatro Nacional de São Carlos** is Portugal's national opera, with a varied season that mixes its own productions with guest performances. The **Coliseu dos Recreios** has no institution attached and so offers a variety of events.

Live rock performance at the Hard Rock Café, Lisbon

World Music, Jazz, Pop and Rock

Lisbon's musical soul may be *fado* (*see pp68–9*), but the city is no stranger to other forms of musical expression. African music, particularly that of former Portuguese colony Cape Verde, plays a big part in Lisbon's music scene. Venues such as **Bartô** and **B.Leza** have frequent live performances.

The **Hot Clube** has been Lisbon's foremost jazz venue for as long as anyone can remember, and has the right intimate atmosphere.

The modern Centro Cultural de Belém in Lisbon

Teatro Nacional Dona Maria II

Hard Rock Café is younger, slightly bigger, and varies live jazz with up-tempo blues, particularly at weekends.

Large rock and pop concerts are held at outdoor venues such as **Parque da Bela Vista** and football stadiums, or indoors at **MEO Arena** or **Coliseu dos Recreios**.

Nightclubs

Bairro Alto remains a lively area for Lisbon nightlife, although its mostly small bars don't usually have dance floors or keep very late hours. There are exceptions, including **Incógnito**, popular for its alternative sounds.

Among the larger and more mainstream dance venues are **Station** and **Main**; the first a nearly historic house club, the second a very middle-of-the-road disco.

Bar Lounge, located in Lisbon's Cais do Sodré district, has live bands and regular DJ sessions until late from Tuesday to Sunday. **K Urban Beach** in Santos and **Silk Club** in Chiado also draw a fun-loving crowd, while eastwards, along the river near Santa Apolónia station, is **Lux**, the cream of Lisbon's current club scene.

Spectator Sports

Portugal hosted the 2004 European Football Championship, and Lisbon's two main teams, Sporting and Benfica, built new stadiums for the event, the **Estádio José Alvalade** and the **Estádio da Luz** respectively. Portuguese football cup finals, as well as other events such as the Estoril Open tennis tournament, are held at the **Estádio Nacional-Jamor**. The MEO Arena is also used for indoor events such as tennis, volleyball and basketball. The **Autódromo do Estoril** is a motor-racing venue.

DIRECTORY

Booking Tickets

ABEP
Praça dos Restauradores.
Map 7 A2.
Tel 213 470 768.

FNAC
Armazéns do Chiado, Rua do Carmo 2, Loja 407.
Map 7 B4. **Tel** 707 313 435.

Cinema and Theatre

Chapitô
Costa do Castelo 7.
Map 7 C3.
Tel 218 855 550.

Cinemateca Portuguesa
Rua Barata Salgueiro 39.
Map 5 C5.
Tel 213 596 200.

São Jorge Cinema
Avenida da Liberdade 175.
Map 5 C5.
Tel 213 103 400.

Teatro Nacional Dona Maria II
Praça Dom Pedro IV.
Map 7 B3.
Tel 213 250 800.

Teatro da Trindade
Largo da Trindade 7A.
Map 7 A3.
Tel 213 423 200.

Classical Music, Opera and Dance

Centro Cultural de Belém
Praça do Império.
Map 1 B5.
Tel 213 612 400.

Coliseu dos Recreios
Rua das Portas de Santo Antão 96.
Map 7 A2.
Tel 213 240 580.

Fundação Calouste Gulbenkian
Avenida de Berna 45.
Map 5 B2.
Tel 217 823 000.

Teatro Camões
Parque das Nações, Passeio de Neptuno.
Tel 218 923 470.

Teatro Nacional de São Carlos
Rua Serpa Pinto 9.
Map 7 A4.
Tel 213 253 000.

World Music, Jazz, Pop and Rock

B.Leza
Rua Cintura do Porto de Lisboa 16, Armazem B, Cais da Ribeira Nova.
Tel 210 106 837.

Bartô
Costa do Castelo 1.
Map 7 C3.
Tel 218 855 550.

Hot Clube
Praça da Alegria 48.
Map 4 F1.
Tel 213 460 305.

MEO Arena
Parque das Nações.
Tel 218 918 409.

Parque da Bela Vista
Avenida Arlindo Vicente.
Tel 808 203 232.

Hard Rock Café
Av. da Liberdade 2.
Map 4 F1.
Tel 213 245 280.

Nightclubs

Bar Lounge
Rua da Moeda 1.
Map 4 F3.
Tel 213 973 730.

Incógnito
Rua dos Poiais de São Bento 37, 1200-349 Lisbon.
Map 4 E3.
Tel 213 908 755.

K Urban Beach
Cais da Viscondessa, Rua da Cintura, Santos.
Map 4 E4.
Tel 213 932 930.

Lux
Avenida Infante Dom Henrique. **Map** 8 D5.
Tel 218 820 890.

Main
Avenida 24 de Julho 68.
Map 4 E3.
Tel 961 553 745.

Silk Club
Rua da Misericórdia 14, 6th Floor.
Map 7 A4.
Tel 913 009 193.

Station
Cais do Gás, Armazém A, Porta 7, 1200-109 Lisbon (Cais do Sodré).
Map 4 F4.
Tel 210 116 546.

Sports

Autódromo do Estoril
Tel 214 609 500.

Estádio José Alvalade
Rua Pr Fernando da Fonseca 1600.
Tel 707 204 444.

Estádio da Luz
Avenida Gen Norton Matos 1500.
Tel 707 200 100.

Estádio Nacional-Jamor
Cruz Quebrada.
Tel 214 146 030.

LISBON STREET FINDER

Map references given in this guide for sights and entertainment venues in Lisbon refer to the Street Finder maps on the following pages. Map references are also given for Lisbon's hotels *(see pp386–7)* and restaurants *(see pp398–401)*. The first figure in the map reference indicates which Street Finder map to turn to, and the letter and number that follow refer to the grid reference on that map. The map below shows the area of Lisbon covered by the eight Street Finder maps. Symbols used for sights and useful information are displayed in the key below. An index of street names and all the places of interest marked on the maps can be found on the following pages.

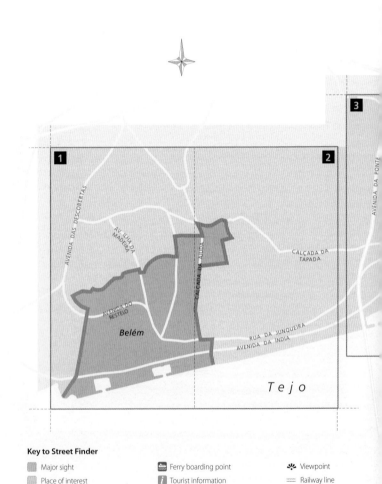

Key to Street Finder

Major sight	Ferry boarding point	Viewpoint
Place of interest	Tourist information	Railway line
Railway station	Hospital with casualty unit	Motorway
Metro station	Police station	Pedestrianized street
Main coach stop	Church	
Tram stop	Synagogue	
Funicular	Mosque	

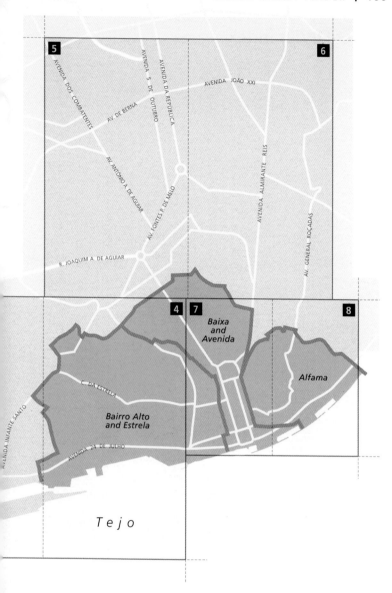

5

AVENIDA DOS COMBATENTES

AVENIDA 5 DE OUTUBRO

AVENIDA DA REPÚBLICA

AV. DE BERNA

AVENIDA JOÃO XXI

6

AV ANTONIO A. DE AGUIAR

AV. FONTES P. DE MELO

AVENIDA ALMIRANTE REIS

AV. GENERAL ROÇADAS

R. JOAQUIM A. DE AGUIAR

4 **7**

*Baixa
and
Avenida*

8

C. DA ESTRELA

Alfama

AVENIDA INFANTE SANTO

*Bairro Alto
and Estrela*

AVENIDA 24 DE JULHO

Tejo

Scale of Map Pages 1–6

| 0 metres | 250 |
| 0 yards | 250 |

Scale of Map Pages 7–8

| 0 metres | 200 |
| 0 yards | 200 |

| 0 kilometres | 1 |
| 0 miles | 0.5 |

Street Finder Index

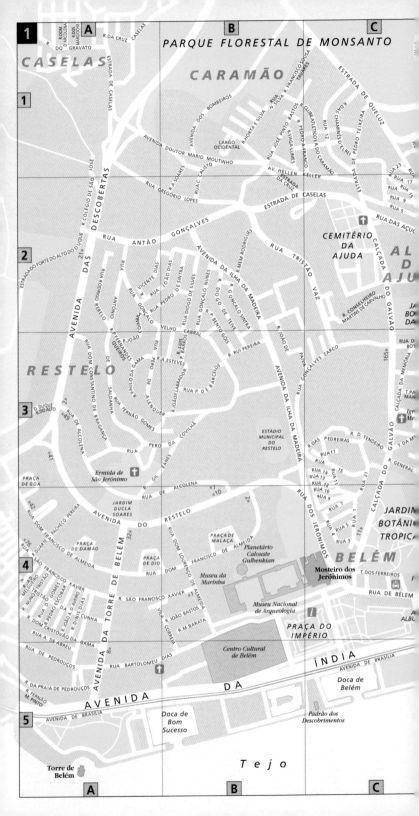

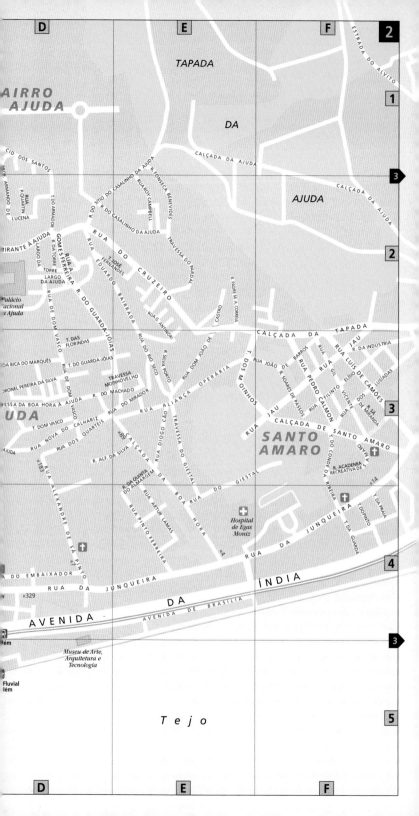

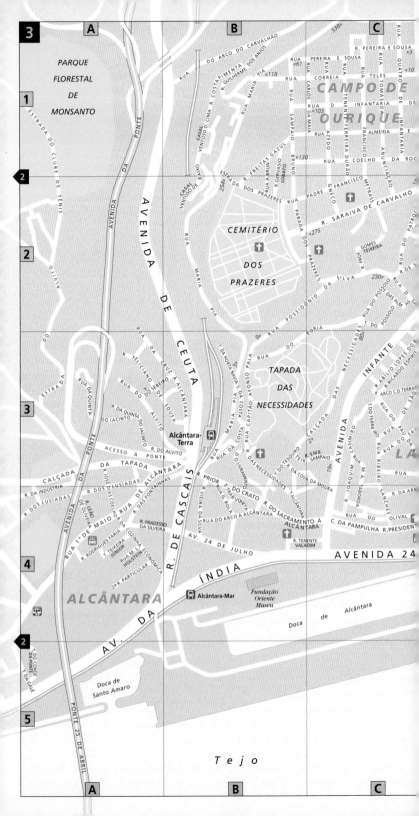

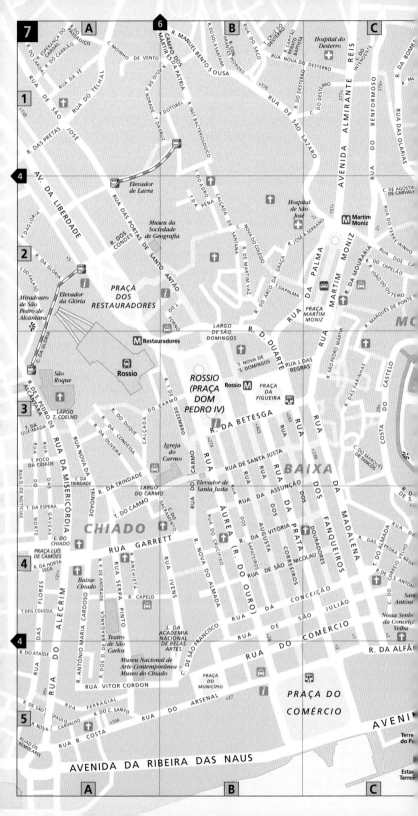

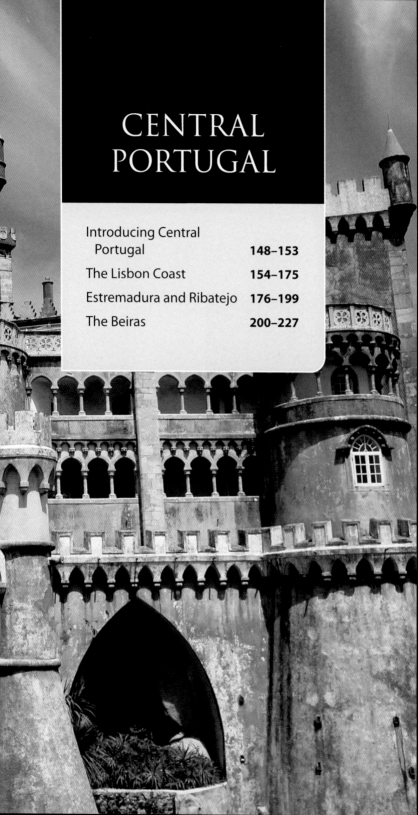

CENTRAL PORTUGAL

Central Portugal at a Glance

Between Portugal's capital and its second city, Porto, you can find some of the country's most impressive architecture and important historical sights. Near Lisbon are the stunning palaces of Sintra and Queluz, and several of Portugal's foremost religious sites in Estremadura. Estremadura and Beira Litoral mix empty beaches with quaint fishing villages and smart resorts, while the lush country stretching inland to the banks of the Tagus supports livestock and crops from rice to grapes and other fruits. Further north, the Beiras are more varied, with the historic university town of Coimbra, the vine-clad valleys of the Dão wine region and the bleak highlands and fortress towns of Beira Alta and Beira Baixa. Dominating this remote region is the granite range of the Serra da Estrela.

Batalha means "battle" and the monastery of Santa Maria da Vitória at Batalha was built to give thanks for victory over the Spanish at the Battle of Aljubarrota in 1385. Its delicate style makes it one of Portugal's finest Gothic buildings (see pp188–9).

Alcobaça is principally known for its abbey, founded in the 12th century by Portugal's first king, Afonso Henriques. The graceful, contemplative air of this great Cistercian house (see pp184–5) is exemplified by its huge vaulted dormitory.

Sintra, just west of Lisbon, is a cool wooded retreat from the heat of the capital. This is where the Portuguese monarchs chose to spend their summers. The Palácio Nacional is full of remarkable decorative effects, such as this painted "magpie" ceiling (see pp164–5).

The Palácio de Queluz, a masterpiece of Rococo architecture (see pp170–71), lies just outside Lisbon. The Lion Staircase leads up to the colonnaded pavilion named after its architect, Jean-Baptiste Robillion.

Praia de M
Figueira da Foz
Mo Vel
Conín
São Pedro de Muel
Le
Batalha
Nazaré
Fátima
Alcobaça
Caldas da Rainha
São Martinho do Porto
Peniche
Óbidos
ESTREMADU AND THE RIBA (see pp176–19
Lourinhã
Alpiarç
Santarém
Aln
Torres Vedras
Alenquer
Ericeira
Mafra
Vila Franca de Xira
Co
Alverca
Colares
Sintra
Lisbon
Alcochete
THE LISBON COAST (see pp154–175)
Costa da Caparica
Palmela
Setúbal
Tróia
Sesimbra
Alc d

0 kilometres
0 miles 50

◀ The colourful and unusual 18th-century Palácio da Pena, in Sintra

Buçaco's walled forest is an arboretum and a religious retreat. A Via Sacra winds among mossy trunks to stunning views from the hilltop Calvary *(see pp216–17).*

The Serra da Estrela, the highest mountain range in mainland Portugal, offers startling contrasts of scenery, from bare ice-eroded peaks to green pastures dotted with shepherds' huts *(see pp224–5).*

Coimbra University is the oldest and most prestigious in Portugal *(see pp212–13).* Long ago it expanded beyond the royal palace which became its home in 1537, but the old palace, with its gilded Capela de São Miguel and spectacular library, are still at the heart of the campus.

THE BEIRAS
(see pp200–227)

Castro Daire
Sernancelhe
Trancoso
Pinhel
Almeida
Viseu
Celorico da Beira
Vilar Formoso
Tondela
Guarda
Gouveia
Sabugueiro
Manteigas
Sabugal
Avô
Covilhã
Arganil
Penamacor
Fundão
Monsanto
Idanha-a-Velha
Castelo Branco

Abrantes

Tomar was founded by the Knights Templar in the 12th century, when these warrior monks played a leading role in the campaigns to win back Portugal from the Moors. The Templars' fortress survives, as does the drum-shaped bulk of their Rotunda, or oratory. This forms the core of the Convento de Cristo which over the centuries was built up around the original church *(see pp190–93).*

Horsemanship and Bullfighting

Classical dressage and *bravura* bullfighting in Portugal are linked to the Marquês de Marialva, the King's Master of the Horse from 1770 to 1799. He made famous the most advanced and difficult dressage techniques, including some in which the horse lifts itself off the ground like a ballet dancer. The Art of Marialva, as it is called, is of great use to horsemen in the bullring, and they will usually demonstrate some dressage movements for the entertainment of the crowd. In Portugal, the bull is never killed in the arena. The Ribatejo is the traditional centre of bullfighting, and it is also seen in the Alentejo, but it courts controversy; though seen by many as part of their culture, the younger generation, and tourists, generally don't approve.

Advertising a summer bullfight in Santarém

Ribatejan herdsmen or *campinos*, who round up the fighting bulls, here demonstrate their skills.

Leading bullfighter João Moura salutes the crowd at a *tourada*.

The mane is plaited with ribbons for a beautifully groomed effect.

The Cavaleiro

The bullfighter or *cavaleiro* wears traditional 18th-century costume, including the satin coat of a grandee, and rides an elaborately adorned horse. He has to plant a number of darts *(farpas)* in the bull's shoulders, and his performance is judged on style and courage.

The costly saddle cloth is embroidered with João Moura's initials.

Box stirrups are traditional, stylish and secure.

Tail tidying and decoration go back to the ornate French style of Louis XV.

Traditional Equestrian Skills

Lisbon's Escola Portuguesa de Arte Equestre, and equestrian centres in the Ribatejo, today maintain the standards set by Marialva. The Lisbon school performs several times a year around the country. On Lusitanian horses of Alter Real stock (*see p302*), riders in 18th-century costume give superb dressage displays. Their movements resemble these illustrations of 1790 from a book on equestrianism, dedicated to Dom João (later João VI), himself a keen horseman.

Plaque of Lezíria Grande Equestrian Centre (*see p198*)

The Marquês de Marialva trains his horse in the *croupade*, its hind legs tucked up beneath it, as it springs into the air.

Partnership between man and horse is paramount in a bullfighting ring. Most *cavaleiros* ride a Lusitanian, the world's oldest saddle horse and a classic warrior steed, famed for its courage, grace and strength. Its agility and speed are essential in the ring, and defenders of bullfighting believe the spectacle has helped preserve the breed.

At this opening ceremony in Montijo, the two *cavaleiros* line up with the *forcados* on either side.

The cape is used to both distract and provoke the bull.

The bull charges, its horns blunted and sheathed in leather, a cause of controversy.

The Bullfight

The *corrida* or *tourada* combines drama and daring. First, a team of bullfighters on foot (*peões de brega*) distracts the bull with capes, preparing it for the *cavaleiro*. He is followed by eight volunteer *forcados*, who aim to overcome the bull with their bare hands in what is known as the *pega*.

After a bullfight on Graciosa, in the Azores, the matador accepts gifts of flowers and waves to the crowd.

The bullfight ends with the *pega*. The leader of the *forcados* challenges the bull to charge, then launches himself over its head. The others try to hold him in place and use their combined weight to bring the bull to a standstill, with one of the men holding onto its tail. Eight times out of ten the *forcados* get tossed in all directions, then re-form to repeat the challenge. Finally the bull is herded from the ring among a group of farm oxen.

The main bullfighters at a Portuguese *tourada* wear elaborate costume with intricate gold stitching, a symbol of their status.

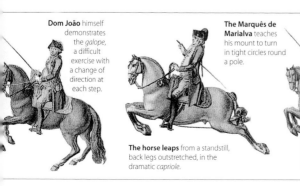

Dom João himself demonstrates the *galope*, a difficult exercise with a change of direction at each step.

The Marquês de Marialva teaches his mount to turn in tight circles round a pole.

The horse leaps from a standstill, back legs outstretched, in the dramatic *capriole*.

The Flavours of Central Portugal

The geography of central Portugal ranges from a lagoon-dotted Atlantic coastline and a vast flood plain to a hilly, then rocky, interior crowned by Portugal's highest mountains. The food here is equally varied, with roast suckling pig in the north, a rich choice of fish and seafood from the ports, unique cheeses and hearty stews from the mountains. One popular dish reflecting this diversity is *porco à alentejana*, a mixture of pork and clams. Cuisines old and new, exotic and familiar, rub along together in Lisbon, where cosmopolitanism has quietly thrived for half a millennium.

Sardines

Lisbon's famed lettuces take pride of place on a vegetable stall

Lisbon

The capital is not just the place where all the flavours of Portugal come together, but also where the influences of Portugal's 16th-century overseas expansion get their strongest expression. This applies equally to older influences, long since assimilated into the local cuisine, and to newer phenomena, from Cape Verdean restaurants to sushi bars. One old favourite,

barbecued chicken with chilli (*frango à piri-piri*), originated in former colonies in Africa. The Lisbon speciality *peixinhos da horta* (runner beans coated in batter and deep fried) provides an interesting insight into influences going the other way. Japanese tempura is said to have developed from this Portuguese dish, introduced to Japan in the 16th century. The

nickname *alfacinhas* for natives of Lisbon may have a connection with *alface* (lettuce) – the city is famous for an especially delicious variety.

The Bairrada and Sierra da Estrela

The town of Mealhada, in the Bairrada region to the north, is known throughout Portugal for

Fine ewe's and goat's milk cheeses from central Portugal

(Labels: Saloio, Serra da Estrela, Palhais, Queijo fresco, Alavão)

Regional Dishes and Specialities

Feijoada is a paprika-spiced stew of beans, vegetables and cured meat (usually pork), with many local variations.

Chanfana is a speciality of Beira Litoral in which goat's meat is cooked slowly with wine and spices in an earthenware pot known as a *caçoilo*. *Cabrito à padeiro* is a similar dish using kid that, after a wine marinade, is roasted and continually basted with the marinade.

Paprika

Traditionally, this would be done in the local baker's large wood-fired oven, and the best restaurants to eat it in are the ones with such ovens. *Caldeirada de peixe* is cooked all over Portugal but does not get any better than in Nazaré or Peniche, preferably eaten outdoors within sight of the sea. *Feijoada* is one of Portugal's most versatile dishes, mixing beans with a wide range of ingredients, including cuttlefish and snails. The latter is a speciality of Tomar. *Favas à Portuguesa* is a Lisbon favourite.

Meats, cheeses and sausages on sale at a market in Sintra

ts *leitão*, spit-roasted suckling pig. The local custom is to drink red sparkling wine, unique to this area, with the crisp-skinned but mild-tasting pig. Nearby Luso is the source of one of Portugal's finest mineral waters. The granite Serra da Estrela mountain range is home to Portugal's most famous cheese, the distinctive and buttery Serra. It is made from ewe's milk, and the rounds are wrapped in muslin to maintain their shape. Bay leaves are often used in Portuguese cooking, and the black-barked bay tree is common in these parts – though the scent in the air is not of bay but of eucalyptus. Bean stews are another common feature of the local cuisine, particularly *feijoada*, of which every town and village seems to have its own version.

Estremadura and Ribatejo

Further south, in Estremadura, the fishing ports of Nazaré and Peniche boast a smaller catch than they once did, but the local sardines in particular are well worth sampling. The rolling hills of Estremadura give way, as you cross the Tejo eastwards,

Traditional Lisbon egg tarts, known as *Pasteis de Belém*

to the fertile Lezíria flood plain of Ribatejo, land of bulls, horses and juicy melons. Vila Franca de Xira, back on the west bank of the river, is a good place to try the local bull meat. For the most part, the regional cuisine of Ribatejo is frugal and thrifty. A classic example is *magusto*, a thick purée of dry maize (corn) and white bread blended with water, olive oil, and boiled kale served with oven-baked *bacalhau* (salt cod).

REGIONAL WINES

The Dão wine region now produces some of Portugal's finest red wines, often distinguishable from the wines of the Douro to the north by their greater elegance. The Bairrada region borders Dão but has only one authorized grape variety for making reds: Baga. There are some great examples of traditional style, with deep tannins and hints of pine and bonfire, but modernity features too, with fruitier, more approachable reds and fresh, light whites. Estremadura and Ribatejo once produced vast amounts of fairly unpalatable wine for mass consumption or distillation. Now they shine, with wines often made from foreign grape varieties. Of Lisbon's own appellations – Colares, Carcavelos and Bucelas – only the last remains commercially viable, making some of the country's most distinctive whites.

Caldeirada de peixe, a fish stew, uses a selection of seafood along with potatoes, tomatoes and peppers.

Favas à Portuguesa combines broad (fava) beans with *morcela* (blood sausage) and chopped pork ribs.

Arroz doce is a delicious dessert of lemon-zest scented rice pudding topped with a decoration of cinnamon.

THE LISBON COAST

Within an hour's drive northwest of Lisbon you can reach the rocky Atlantic coast, the wooded slopes of Sintra or countryside dotted with villas and royal palaces. South of Lisbon you can enjoy the sandy beaches and fishing towns along the coast or explore the lagoons of the Tagus and Sado river estuaries.

From the Phoenicians to the Spanish, traders and invaders have left their mark on this region, such as the forts and castles of the Moors, rebuilt many times over the centuries, which can be found all along this coast. After Lisbon became the capital in 1256, Portuguese kings and nobles built summer palaces and villas in the countryside west of the city, particularly on the cool, green heights of the Serra de Sintra.

Across the Tagus, the southern shore (Margem Sul) could be reached only by ferry, until the suspension bridge was built in 1966. Now, the long sandy beaches of the Costa da Caparica, the coast around the fishing town of Sesimbra and even the remote Tróia peninsula have become popular resorts during the summer months. Fortunately, large stretches of coast and unspoilt countryside are being protected as conservation areas and nature reserves. Despite the region's rapid urbanization, small fishing and farming communities still remain. Lively fish markets offer a huge variety of fresh fish and seafood; Palmela and the Sado region are noted for their wine; sheep still roam the unspoilt Serra da Arrábida, providing milk for Azeitão cheese; and rice is the main crop in the Sado estuary. Traditional industries also survive, such as salt panning near Alcochete and marble quarries at Pero Pinheiro.

Though the sea is cold and often rough, especially on west-facing coasts, the beaches are among the cleanest in Europe. As well as surfing, fishing and scuba diving, the region provides splendid golf courses, horse riding facilities and a motor-racing track. Arts and entertainment range from music and cinema festivals to bullfights and country fairs where regional crafts, such as hand-painted pottery, lace and baskets, are on display.

Palácio de Mafra *(see p158)*, an 18th-century Baroque palace and monastery on the Lisbon coast

◀ A stretch of stunning coastline in Cascais, near Lisbon

Exploring the Lisbon Coast

North of the Tagus, the beautiful hilltown of Sintra is dotted with historic palaces and surrounded by wooded hills, at times enveloped in an eerie sea mist. On the coast, cosmopolitan Cascais and the traditional fishing town of Ericeira are both excellent bases from which to explore the rocky coastline and surrounding countryside. South of the Tagus, the Serra da Arrábida and the rugged coast around Cabo Espichel can be visited from the small port of Sesimbra. Inland, the nature reserves of the Tagus and Sado estuaries offer a quiet retreat.

Sights at a Glance

1. Palácio de Mafra
2. Ericeira
3. Colares
5. Monserrate
6. Sintra pp162–7
7. Cascais
8. Estoril
9. Palácio de Queluz pp170–71
10. Alcochete
11. Costa da Caparica
12. Cabo Espichel
13. Sesimbra
14. Palmela
15. Serra da Arrábida
16. Setúbal
17. Península de Tróia
18. Alcácer do Sal

Tours

4. Serra de Sintra

0 kilometres 10
0 miles 5

Key

═══ Motorway

── Secondary road

═══ Minor road

── Scenic route

╍╍ Main railway

── Minor railway

═══ Regional border

Cabo da Roca on the western edge of Serra de Sintra

Getting Around

Motorways give quick access from Lisbon to Sintra, Estoril, Palmela and Setúbal. Main roads are generally well-signposted and surfaced, though traffic congestion can be a problem, particularly at weekends and holidays. Watch out for potholes on smaller roads. Fast, frequent trains run from Lisbon: from Cais do Sodré station to Estoril and Cascais, from Roma-Areeiro and Entrecampos stations to Queluz and Sintra and from Rossio station to Queluz and Sintra. Crossing the April 25 bridge, trains south to Setúbal leave from Roma-Areeiro station, and high-speed Alfa Pendular services south to Évora and the Algarve depart from Oriente station. There are good bus services to all parts of the region, most of which leave from Sete Rios.

Convento da Arrábida in the hills of the Serra da Arrábida

Fishing boats in the harbour at Sesimbra

The stunning library in the Palácio de Mafra, paved with chequered marble

❶ Palácio de Mafra

Road Map B5. Terreiro de Dom João V, Mafra. **Tel** 261 817 550. 🚌 Ericeira bus from Lisbon. Ⓜ Campo Grande, then 🚌 Ericeira. **Open** 9:30am–5:30pm Wed–Mon (last entry 4:30pm). **Closed** 1 Jan, Easter, 1 May, 24 & 25 Dec. ✝ 🏛 (free first Sun of month). 📷 🌐 palaciomafra.pt

The massive Baroque palace and monastery (see pp56–7), which dwarfs the small town of Mafra, was built during the reign of Portugal's most extravagant monarch, João V. It began with a vow by the young king to build a new monastery and basilica, supposedly in return for an heir (but more likely, to atone for his sexual excesses). Work began in 1717 on a modest project to house 13 Franciscan friars but, as wealth began to pour into the royal coffers from Brazil, the king and his Italian-trained architect, Johann Friedrich Ludwig (1670–1752), made ever more

extravagant plans. No expense was spared: 52,000 men were employed and the finished project housed not 13, but 330 friars, a royal palace and one of the finest libraries in Europe, decorated with precious marble, exotic wood and countless works of art. The magnificent basilica was consecrated on the king's 41st birthday, 22 October 1730, with festivities lasting for eight days.

The palace was only popular with those members of the royal family who enjoyed hunting deer and wild boar. Today, a wolf conservation project runs here. Most of the finest furniture and art works were taken to Brazil when the royal family escaped from the French invasion in 1807. The monastery was abandoned in 1834 following the dissolution of all religious orders, and the palace itself was abandoned in 1910, when the last Portuguese king, Manuel II, escaped from here to the Royal Yacht anchored off Ericeira.

Allow at least an hour for the tour, which starts in the rooms of the monastery, through the pharmacy, with fine old medicine jars

and some alarming medical instruments, to the infirmary, where patients could see and hear mass in the adjoining chapel without leaving their beds.

Upstairs, the sumptuous palace state rooms extend across the whole of the monumental west façade, with the King's apartments at one end and the Queen's apartments at the other. Halfway between the two, the long, imposing façade is relieved by the twin towers of the domed basilica. The interior of the church is decorated in contrasting colours of marble and furnished with six early 19th-century organs. Fine Baroque sculptures, executed by members of the Mafra School of Sculpture, adorn the atrium of the basilica. Begun by José I in 1754, many renowned Portuguese and foreign artists trained in the school under the directorship of the Italian sculptor Alessandro Giusti (1715–99). Further on, the Sala da Caça has a grotesque collection of hunting trophies and boars' heads. Mafra's greatest treasure, however, is its magnificent library, with a patterned marble floor, Rococo-style wooden bookcases, and a collection of over 40,000 books in gold embossed leather bindings, including a prized first edition of Os Lusíadas (1572) by the Portuguese poet Luís de Camões (see p50).

Statue of St Bruno in the atrium of Mafra's basilica

Environs

Once a week, on Thursday mornings, the small country town of Malveira, 10 km (6 miles) east of Mafra, has the region's biggest market, selling clothes and household goods as well as food.

At the village of Sobreiro, 6 km (4 miles) west of Mafra, Zé Franco's model village is complete with houses, farms, a waterfall and working windmill, all in minute detail.

The king's bedroom in the Royal Palace

Tractor pulling a fishing boat out of the sea at Ericeira

❷ Ericeira

Road Map B5. 🚗 7,500. 🚌
🛈 Praça da República 17 (261 863
122). 🗓 Jun–Sep: daily; Oct–May:
closed Mon.

Ericeira is an old fishing village
which keeps its traditions despite
an ever-increasing influx of
summer visitors who enjoy
the bracing climate, clean,
sandy beaches and fresh
seafood. In July and August,
when the population leaps
to 30,000, pavement cafés,
restaurants and bars around the
tree-lined Praça da República
are buzzing late into the night.
Red flags warn when swimming
is dangerous: alternative attractions include crazy golf in Santa
Marta park and an interesting
museum of local history, the
Museu da Ericeira, exhibiting
models of traditional regional
boats and fishing equipment.

The unspoilt old town, a maze
of whitewashed houses and
narrow, cobbled streets, is
perched high above the ocean.
From Largo das Ribas, at the top
of a 30-m (100-ft) stone-faced
cliff, there is a bird's-eye view
over the busy fishing harbour
below, where tractors have
replaced the oxen that once
hauled the boats out of reach
of the tide. On 16 August, the
annual fishermen's festival is
celebrated with a candlelit
procession to the harbour at
the foot of the cliffs for the
blessing of the boats.

On 5 October 1910, Manuel II,
the last king of Portugal *(see
pp58–9)*, sailed into exile from
Ericeira as the Republic was
declared in Lisbon; a tiled panel

in the fishermen's chapel
of Santo António above the
harbour records the event.
The banished king settled
in Twickenham, southwest
London, where he died in 1932.

🏛 Museu da Ericeira
Largo da Misericórdia. **Tel** 261 862
536. **Open** 10:30am–12:30pm,
2:30–5pm Wed. 🎟 donation.

❸ Colares

Road Map B5. 🚗 7,500. 🚌
🛈 Cabo da Roca (219 280 081).

On the lower slopes of the
Serra de Sintra, this lovely
village faces the sea over a
green valley, the Várzea de
Colares. A leafy avenue winds
its way up to the village. Small
quantities of the famous
Colares wine are still made,
but current vintages lack the
character and ageing potential

of classic Colares and growers
face a financial struggle to
survive. Their hardy old vines
grow in sandy soil, with their
roots set deep below in
clay; these were the only
vines in Europe to survive the
disastrous phylloxera epidemic
brought from America in the
late 19th century with the first
viticultural exchanges. The insect,
which destroyed vineyards
all over Europe by eating the
vines, could not penetrate
the dense sandy soil of the
Atlantic coast. Wine can be
sampled at the Adega Regional
de Colares on Alameda de
Coronel Linhares de Lima.

Environs
There are several popular beach
resorts west of Colares. Just
north of Praia das Maçãs is the
picturesque village of Azenhas
do Mar, clinging to the cliffs; just
to the south is the larger resort
of Praia Grande. Both have
natural pools in the rocks, which
are filled by seawater at high
tide. The unspoilt Praia da Adraga,
1 km (half a mile) further south,
has a delightful beach café and
restaurant. In the evenings
and off-season, fishermen set up
their lines to catch bass, bream
and flat fish that swim in on
the high tide. A tramway that
opened in 1910 links the district
of Estefânia, in Sintra, to the
Ribeira de Sintra; it then
continues on to Praia das Maçãs,
which runs daily all year round.

Natural rock pool at Azenhas do Mar, near Colares

❹ Serra de Sintra Tour

This round trip from Sintra follows a dramatic route over the top of the wooded Serra. The first part is a challenging drive with hazardous hairpin bends on steep, narrow roads that are at times poorly surfaced. It passes through dense forest and a surreal landscape of giant moss-covered boulders, with breathtaking views over the Atlantic coast, the Tagus estuary and beyond. After dropping down to the rugged, windswept coast, the route returns along small country roads passing through hill villages and large estates on the cool, green northern slopes of the Serra de Sintra.

Atlantic coastline seen from Peninha

⑥ Colares
The village of Colares rests on the lower slopes of the wooded Serra, surrounded by gardens and vineyards (see p159).

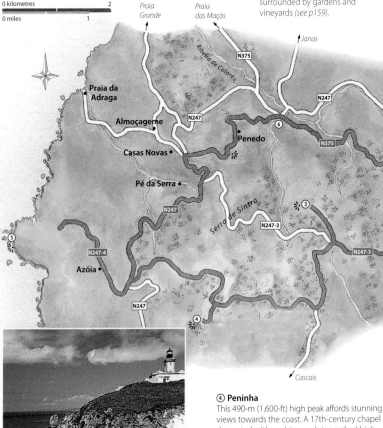

0 kilometres 2

0 miles 1

④ Peninha
This 490-m (1,600-ft) high peak affords stunning views towards the coast. A 17th-century chapel decorated with *azulejo* panels is perched high on the grey rocks.

⑤ Cabo da Roca
A lighthouse at the top of an impressive cliff, 140 m (459 ft) high, marks the most westerly point of the European mainland.

Key

━━ Tour route

═══ Other roads

✷ Viewpoint

For keys to symbols *see back flap*

⑧ Seteais
The elegant palace, now a luxury hotel and restaurant *(see p388 & p403)*, was built in the 18th century for the Dutch Consul, Daniel Gildemeester.

⑦ Monserrate
The cool forest park and elaborate 19th-century palace epitomize the romanticism of Sintra.

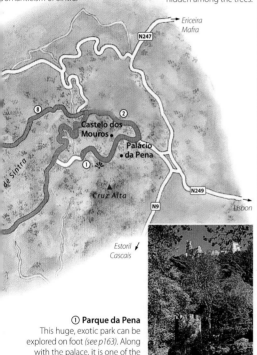

Tips for Drivers

Length: 36 km (22 miles).
Stopping-off points: At Cabo da Roca you will find a café, restaurant, tourist office and souvenir shops; at Colares there are several delightful restaurants and bars. Due to fire risks, picnicking is not allowed in the Sintra woods and Parque da Pena.

② Sintra
From the centre of the old town the road winds steeply upwards past magnificent *quintas* (country estates) hidden among the trees.

Ericeira
Mafra
N247

⑧

②

Castelo dos Mouros

Palácio da Pena

①

Cruz Alta

N249

N9

Lisboa

de Sintra

Estoril
Cascais

① **Parque da Pena**
This huge, exotic park can be explored on foot *(see p163)*. Along with the palace, it is one of the best examples of 19th-century romanticism in Portugal.

③ **Convento dos Capuchos**
Two huge boulders guard the entrance to this remote Franciscan monastery, founded in 1560, where the monks lived in tiny rock-hewn cells lined with cork. There are stunning views of the coast from the hill above this austere, rocky hideaway.

Palace of Monserrate

❺ Monserrate

Road map: B5. Estrada de Monserrate. **Tel** 219 237 300. 🚌 to Sintra then bus 435 or taxi. **Open** Palace: 9:30am–8pm daily (29 Oct–25 Mar: 10am–6pm); gardens: 9:30am–8pm daily (29 Oct–25 Mar: 10am–6pm). Last adm: 1 hr before closing time. **Closed** 1 Jan, 25 Dec. 🖥 🌐 parquesdesintra.pt

The wild, romantic garden of this estate is a jungle of exotic trees and flowering shrubs. Among the subtropical foliage and valley of tree ferns are a waterfall, a small lake and a chapel, built as a ruin, tangled in the roots of a giant *Ficus* tree. Its history dates back to the Moors, but it takes its name from a small 16th-century chapel dedicated to Our Lady of Montserrat in Catalonia, Spain. The gardens were land-scaped in the late 18th century by a wealthy young Englishman, William Beckford. They were later immortalized by Lord Byron in *Childe Harold's Pilgrimage* (1812).

In 1856, the abandoned estate was bought by another Englishman, Sir Francis Cook, who built a fantastic Moorish-style palace and transformed the gardens with a large sweeping lawn, camellias and subtropical trees from all over the world. These include the giant *Metrosideros* (Australian Christmas tree, covered in a blaze of red flowers in July); the native *Arbutus* (known as the strawberry tree because ofs its juicy red berries), from which the *medronho* firewater drink is distilled; cork oak, with small ferns growing on its bark, and Chinese weeping cyprus.

The house and gardens have now been restored to their former glory.

⑥ Sintra

Sintra's stunning setting on the north slopes of the granite Serra, among wooded ravines and fresh water springs, made it a favourite summer retreat for the kings of Portugal. The tall conical chimneys of the Palácio Nacional de Sintra *(see pp164–5)* and the Palácio da Pena *(see pp166–7)* are landmarks, and eerily impressive on its peak when the Serra is blanketed in mist.

Today, the town (recognized as a UNESCO World Heritage cultural landscape in 1995) draws thousands of visitors all through the year. Even so, there are many quiet walks in the wooded hills around the town, especially beautiful in the long, cool evenings of the summer months.

Exploring Sintra

Present-day Sintra is in three parts, Sintra Vila, Estefânia and São Pedro, joined by a confusing maze of winding roads scattered over the surrounding hills. In the pretty cobbled streets of the old town, Sintra Vila, which is centred on the Palácio Nacional de Sintra, are the museums and beautifully tiled post office. The curving Volta do Duche leads from the old town, past the lush Parque da Liberdade, north to the Estefânia district and the striking Neo-Gothic Câmara Municipal (town hall). To the south and east, the hilly village of São Pedro spreads over the slopes of the Serra. The fortnightly Sunday market here extends across the broad market square.

Fonte Mourisca on Volta do Duche

Exploring Sintra on foot involves a lot of walking and climbing up and down its steep hills. For a more leisurely tour, take one of the horse and carriage rides around the town. The Miradouro da Vigia in São Pedro offers impressive views, as does the cosy Casa de Sapa café, where you can also sample *queijadas*, the local sweet speciality.

The many fountains around the town are used by locals for their fresh spring drinking water. Two of the most striking are the tiled Fonte Mourisca (Arab Fountain), named for its Neo-Moorish decoration, and Fonte da Sabuga, where the water spouts from a pair of breasts.

🏛 Centro Cultural Olga Cadaval

Praça Dr Francisco Sá Carneiro. **Tel** 219 107 118. **Open** 9am–5pm Mon–Fri, & 1 hour before performances. **Closed** public hols. 🇼 ccolgacadaval.pt

Named after the aristocratic lady and dedicated patron of arts who once lived here, the Centro Cultural Olga Cadaval is a major venue for music, film, theatre and dance performances held throughout the year. The building itself dates back to World War II and was carefully restored after a fire destroyed a large part of it in 1985. Every year in May and June, it becomes one of the hubs of the region's annual cultural showcase, the Sintra Festival, which Olga Cadaval herself founded over fifty years ago.

🏛 Museu das Artes de Sintra

Av Heliodoro Salgado. **Tel** 219 107 110. **Open** 10am–8pm Tue–Fri, 2–8pm Sat & Sun.

This arts centre features an interesting permanent collection and several rare landscapes of Sintra dating from the mid-18th century. It is located in the old Casino de Sintra building, a place full of local history, with an ornate façade dating from 1924.

🏛 Quinta da Regaleira

Rua Barbosa do Bocage. **Tel** 219 106 650. 🚌 405. **Open** Apr–Sep: 9:30am–8pm; Oct–Mar: 9:30am–6pm; (last adm: 1 hour before closing). **Closed** 24 & 25 Dec. 📷 call to book. 🅿 ♿ 📱 🇼 regaleira.pt

Built between 1904 and 1910, this palace and its extensive gardens are a feast of historical and religious references, occult symbols and mystery. The obsession of the eccentric millionaire António Augusto Carvalho Monteiro, they are a must for anyone interested in esoterica.

Chimneys of the Palácio Nacional de Sintra above the old town

Castelo dos Mouros

Estrada da Pena. **Tel** 219 237 300. 434. **Open** daily. **Closed** 1 Jan, 25 Dec.

Standing above the old town, the ramparts of the 10th-century Moorish castle, conquered by Afonso Henriques in 1147, snake over the top of the Serra. On a fine day, there are breathtaking views from the castle walls over the old town to Palácio da Pena, on a neighbouring peak, and far along the coast. Outside the walls, a former church (the first Christian church in Sintra) now houses an interpretation centre on the history of the castle.

A steep footpath threads up through wooded slopes from the 12th-century church of Santa Maria. Follow the signs to a dark green swing gate where the footpath begins. The monogram "DFII" carved on the gateway is a reminder that the castle walls were restored by Fernando II *(see p167)* in the 19th century.

Parque da Pena

Estrada da Pena. **Tel** 219 237 300. 434. **Open** daily. **Closed** 1 Jan, 25 Dec. **w** parquesdesintra.pt

In the huge park surrounding the Palácio da Pena, footpaths wind among a lush vegetation of exotic trees and shrubs. Hidden among the foliage are gazebos, follies and fountains, and a Romantic chalet built by Fernando II for his second wife, the Countess of Edla, in 1869. Cruz Alta, the highest point of the Serra at 529 m (1,736 ft), commands spectacular views. On a nearby crag stands a statue thought to represent the king, dressed in medieval military garb, admiring his life's work.

VISITORS' CHECKLIST

Practical Information
Road map: B5. 25,000.
Praça da República 23 (219 231 157); train station (211 932 545). 2nd & 4th Sun of month. May–Jun: Festival de Sintra.

Transport
Avda Dr Miguel Bombarda.

Battlements of the Castelo dos Mouros perched on the slopes of the Serra

Sintra Town Centre

① Museu das Artes de Sintra
② Centro Cultural
   Olga Cadaval
③ Câmara Municipal
④ Casa de Sapa
⑤ *Palácio Nacional de Sintra*
   pp164–5
⑥ Post office
⑦ Fonte Mourisca
⑧ Quinta da Regaleira
⑨ Fonte da Sabuga
⑩ Santa Maria
⑪ Castelo dos Mouros
⑫ Parque da Pena

Palácio Nacional de Sintra

At the heart of the old town of Sintra (Sintra Vila), a pair of unusual conical chimneys rises high above the Royal Palace. The main part of the palace, including the central block with its plain Gothic façade and the large kitchens beneath the chimneys, was built by João I in the late 14th century, on a site once occupied by the Moorish rulers. The Paço Real, as it is also known, became the favourite summer retreat for the court, and continued as a residence for Portuguese royalty until the 1880s. Additions to the building by the wealthy Manuel I, in the early 16th century, echo the Moorish style. Gradual rebuilding of the palace has resulted in a fascinating amalgamation of various different styles.

★ Sala das Pegas
The ceiling shows 136 magpies (*pegas*) holding ribbons with João I's motto *Por bem* (for good) and roses to signify the House of Lancaster, to which Queen Filipa belonged.

★ Sala dos Brasões
The domed ceiling of this majestic room is decorated with stags holding the coats of arms (*brasões*) of 72 noble Portuguese families. The lower walls are lined with 18th-century Delft-like tiled panels.

KEY

① **Jardim da Preta**, a walled garden

② **Quarto de Dom Sebastião**, the bedroom

③ **The Sala das Galés** (galleons)

④ **The Torre dos Brasões** has dovecotes below the cornice decorated with armillary spheres and nautical rope.

⑤ **The Sala dos Árabes** is decorated with fine *azulejos*.

⑥ **The kitchens**, beneath the huge conical chimneys, have spits and utensils once used for preparing royal banquets.

⑦ **Sala dos Archeiros**, the entrance hall

⑧ **Manuel I** added the *ajimene* windows, a distinctive Moorish design with a slender column dividing two arches.

Chapel
Symmetrical Moorish patterns decorate the original 15th-century chestnut and oak ceiling and the mosaic floor of the private chapel.

For hotels and restaurants in this area see pp388–9 and pp401–2

★ **Sala dos Cisnes**
The magnificent ceiling of the former banqueting hall, painted in the 16th century, is divided into octagonal panels decorated with swans (cisnes).

VISITORS' CHECKLIST

Practical Information
Largo Rainha Dona Amélia.
Tel 219 237 300.
Ⓦ **parquesdesintra.pt**
Open 9:30am–6pm daily
(29 Mar–24 Oct: to 7pm).
Closed 1 Jan, 25 Dec. 🎫 📷

Sala das Sereias
Intricate Arabesque designs on 16th-century tiles frame this door in the Room of the Sirens.

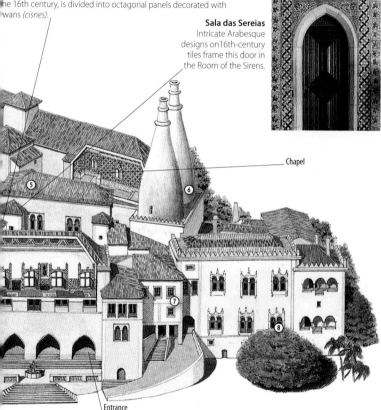

Chapel

Entrance

10th century First reference to the palace, as residence of Moorish governor	**1281** King Dinis orders restoration of palace; work is carried out by Moors living in Colares	**1495–1521** Reign of Manuel I; major restoration and Manueline additions	**1683** Afonso VI dies after being imprisoned here for nine years by brother Pedro II		**1755** Parts of palace damaged in great earthquake (see pp66–7)

800	1000	1200	1400	1600	1800

1147 Christian reconquest; Afonso Henriques takes over palace

1385 João I orders complete rebuilding of central buildings and kitchens

1880s Maria Pia (grandmother of Manuel II) is last royal resident

8th century Start of Moorish occupation of the region

Siren, Sala das Sereias (c.1660)

1910 Palace becomes a national monument

Sintra: Palácio da Pena

On the highest peaks of the Serra de Sintra stands the spectacular palace of Pena, an eclectic medley of architectural styles built in the 19th century by the husband of the young Queen Maria II, Ferdinand Saxe-Coburg and Gotha, who personally designed many of its elements. It stands over the ruins of a Hieronymite monastery founded here in the 16th century on the site of the chapel of Nossa Senhora da Pena. Ferdinand appointed a German architect, Baron von Eschwege, to build his summer palace filled with oddities from all over the world and surrounded by a park. With the declaration of the Republic in 1910, the palace became a museum, preserved as it was when the royal family lived here. Allow at least an hour and a half to visit this enchanting place.

Entrance Arch
A studded archway with crenellated turrets greets the visitor at the entrance to the palace. The palace buildings are painted the original daffodil yellow and strawberry pink.

Manuel II's Bedroom
The oval-shaped room is decorated with green walls and stuccoed ceiling. A portrait of Manuel II, the last king of Portugal, hangs above the fireplace.

★ Hall
The spacious hall is sumptuously furnished with German stained-glass windows, precious Oriental porcelain and four life-size turbaned torch-bearers holding giant candelabra.

KEY

① **In the kitchen**, the copper pots and utensils still hang around the iron stove. The dinner service bears the coat of arms of Ferdinand II.

② **The Triton Arch** is encrusted with Neo-Manueline decoration and is guarded by a fierce sea monster.

③ **The cloister**, decorated with colourful patterned tiles, is part of the original monastery buildings.

★ Arab Room
Marvellous trompe-l'oeil frescoes cover the walls and ceiling of the Arab Room, one of the loveliest in the palace. The Orient was a great inspiration to Romanticism.

VISITORS' CHECKLIST

Practical Information
Estrada da Pena, 5 km (3 mile) S of Sintra. **Tel** 219 237 300.
🅦 **parquesdesintra.pt**
Open 9:30am–7pm daily (25 Oct–28 Mar: 10am–6pm).
Closed 1 Jan, 25 Dec. 🖼

Transport
🚌 434 from Avenida Dr Miguel Bombarda, Sintra.

★ Chapel Altarpiece
The impressive 16th-century alabaster and marble retable was sculpted by Nicolau Chanterène. Each niche portrays a scene of the life of Christ, from the manger to the Ascension.

Ferdinand: King Consort

Ferdinand was known in Portugal as Dom Fernando II, the "artist" king. Like his cousin Prince Albert, who married the English Queen Victoria, he loved art, nature and the new inventions of the time. He was himself a watercolour painter. Ferdinand enthusiastically adopted his new country and devoted his life to patronizing the arts. In 1869, 16 years after the death of Maria II, Ferdinand married an opera singer, Elise, Countess of Edla. His lifelong dream of building the extravagant palace at Pena was completed in 1885, the year he died.

Entrance

Outdoor café in the popular holiday resort of Cascais

➐ Cascais

Road map B5. 🚄 33,000. 🚆 🚌
🛈 Largo Cidade Vitória (912 034 214).
🛒 Wed & Sat.

Having been a holiday resort for well over a century, Cascais possesses a certain illustriousness that younger resorts lack. Its history is most clearly visible in the villas along the coast, built as summer residences by wealthy *Lisboetas* during the late 19th century, after King Luís I had moved his summer activities to the 17th-century fortress here. The military importance of Cascais, now waned, is much older as it sits on the north bank of the mouth of the Tagus.

The sandy, sheltered bay around which the modern suburb has sprawled was a fishing harbour in prehistoric times. Fishing still goes on, and it was given a municipal boost with the decision to build a

quay for the landing and initial auctioning of the fishermen's catch. But Cascais today is first of all a favoured suburb of Lisbon, a place of apartments with a sea view and pine-studded plots by golf courses. It may sometimes seem more defined by its ceaseless construction boom than by any historic or even touristic qualities, but the beautiful, windswept coastline beyond the town has been left relatively undeveloped.

The Museu do Conde de Castro Guimaraes is perhaps the best place to get a taste of Cascais as it was just over a century ago. A castle-like villa on a small creek by a headland, its grounds are today part of a park. The house and its contents were bequeathed to the municipality.

Across the road from the museum is the marina, one of the most emblematic developments in Cascais. With its small shopping centre, restaurants and cafés it is becoming a weekend magnet for today's car-borne Cascais residents and tourists.

🏛 **Museu do Conde de Castro Guimarães**
Avenida Rei Humberto II de Itália.
Tel 214 815 308. **Open** 10am–5pm Tue–Sun (excl 1–2pm Sat & Sun).
📷 **Closed** public hols.

Environs

At Boca do Inferno (Mouth of Hell) about 3 km (2 miles) west on the coast road, the sea rushes into clefts and caves in the rocks, making a booming sound and sending up spectacular spray.

The magnificent sandy beach of Guincho, located 10 km (6 miles) further west, has Atlantic breakers that make this a paradise for experienced windsurfers and surfers, though beware of the strong currents.

The **Casa das Histórias Paula Rego** is a museum dedicated to the work of the painter, illustrator and printmaker.

🏛 **Casa das Histórias Paula Rego**
Avenida da República 300, Cascais.
Tel 214 826 970. **Open** 10am–6pm Tue–Sun (Apr–Oct: to 7pm). 📷

Spectacular view of the weather-beaten coastline at Boca do Inferno, near Cascais

➒ Estoril

Road map B5. 🚄 24,000. 🚆 🚌
🛈 Largo Cidade Vitória, Cascais (912 034 214).

Despite once being the haunt of exiled royalty and nobility fleeing European republicanism, the lovely resort town of Estoril is a thriving place. Today, it is a tourist and business resort, and a place for comfortable retirement. As such, it relies equally on its historical reputation and on the natural attractiveness it has always possessed. There are also a number of good golf courses.

What separates Estoril from Cascais, besides a pleasant beach promenade of 3 km (2 miles) and a mansion-covered ridge known as Monte Estoril, is its sense of place. The heart of Estoril is immediately accessible from the train station. On one side of the tracks, the riviera-like

Sandy beach and promenade along the bay of Estoril

beach, on the other, a palm-lined park flanked by grand buildings, stretches up past fountains to what is said to be Europe's biggest casino. Dwarfing the casino is the Estoril Congress Centre, a vast multipurpose edifice that speaks confidently of Estoril's contemporary role.

❾ Palácio de Queluz

See pp170–71.

❿ Alcochete

Road map C5. 🚗 9,000. 🚌
ℹ️ Largo da Misericórdia (212 348 655).

This delightful old town overlooks the wide Tagus estuary from the southern shore. Salt has long been one of the main industries here, and saltpans can still be seen to the north and south of the town, while in the town centre a large statue of a muscular salt worker has the inscription: "Do Sal a Revolta e a Esperança" (From salt to Rebellion and Hope). On the outskirts of town, is a statue of Manuel I (see pp50–51), who was born here on 1 June 1469 and granted the town a Royal Charter in 1515.

Statue of a salt worker in Alcochete (1985)

Environs

The **Reserva Natural do Estuário do Tejo** covers a vast area of estuary water, salt marshes and small islands around Alcochete and is a very important breeding ground for water birds. Particularly interesting are the flocks of flamingos that gather here during the autumn and spring migration, en route from colonies such as the Camargue in France and Fuente de Piedra in Spain. Ask at the tourist office about boat trips to see the wildlife of the estuary, which includes wild bulls and horses.

⌖ Reserva Natural do Estuário do Tejo
Avenida dos Combatentes da Grande Guerra 1. **Tel** 212 348 021.

Pilgrims' lodgings, Cabo Espichel

⓫ Costa da Caparica

Road map B5. 🚗 12,000. 🚉 to Pragal, then 194 bus. ℹ️ Frente Urbana de Praias (212 900 071).

Long sandy beaches, backed by sand dunes, have made this a popular holiday resort for Lisboetas who come here to swim, sunbathe and enjoy the seafood restaurants and beach cafés. A railway, with open carriages, runs for 10 km (6 miles) along the coast during the summer months. The first beaches reached from the town are popular with families with children, while the furthest beaches suit those seeking quiet isolation. Further south, sheltered by pine forests, Lagoa de Albufeira offers a peaceful windsurfing centre and camp site.

⓬ Cabo Espichel

Road map B5. 🚌 from Sesimbra.

Sheer cliffs drop straight into the sea at this windswept promontory where the land ends dramatically. The Romans named it Promontorium Barbaricum, alluding to its dangerous location, and a lighthouse warns sailors of the treacherous rocks below. Stunning views of the ocean and the coast can be enjoyed from this bleak outcrop of land but beware of the strong gusts of wind on the cliff edge.

In this desolate setting stands the impressive Santuário de Nossa Senhora do Cabo, a late 17th-century church with its back to the sea. On either side of the church a long line of pilgrims' lodgings facing inwards form an open courtyard. Baroque paintings, ex votos and a frescoed ceiling decorate the interior of the church. A domed chapel, tiled with blue and white azulejo panels, is located nearby.

The site became a popular place of pilgrimage in the 13th century when a local man had a vision of the Madonna rising from the sea on a mule. Legend has it that the tracks of the mule can be seen embedded in the rock. The large footprints, on Praia dos Lagosteiros below the church, are actually believed to be fossilized dinosaur tracks.

The façade of Câmara Municipal de Alcochete, the town hall of Alcochete

❾ Palácio de Queluz

In 1747, Pedro, younger son of João V, commissioned Mateus Vicente to transform his 17th-century hunting lodge into a Rococo summer palace. The central section, which includes a music room and chapel, was built and the palace was further extended after Pedro's marriage to the future Maria I, in 1760. French architect Jean-Baptiste Robillion then added the sumptuous Robillion Pavilion and gardens, cleared space for the Throne Room and redesigned the Music Room. During Maria's reign, the royal family kept a menagerie and went boating on the *azulejo*-lined canal.

Corridor of the Tiles
Painted *azulejo* panels (1784) representing the continents and the seasons, as well as hunting scenes, line the walls of this bright corridor.

★ Sala dos Embaixadores
Built by Robillion, this stately room was used for diplomatic audiences as well as concerts. The *trompe l'oeil* ceiling shows the royal family attending a concert.

To canal

Don Quixote Chamber
The royal bedroom, where Pedro IV (*see p58*) was born and died, has a domed ceiling and magnificent floor decoration in exotic woods, giving the square room a circular appearance. Painted scenes by Manuel de Costa (1784) tell the story of *Don Quixote*.

KEY

① **The Robillion Pavilion** displays the flamboyance of the French architect's Rococo style.

② **Shell Waterfall**

③ **The Lion Staircase** is an impressive and graceful link from the lower gardens to the palace.

④ **Neptune's Fountain**

⑤ **The royal family's living rooms** and bedrooms opened out onto the Malta Gardens.

⑥ **Chapel**

⑦ **Malta Gardens**

⑧ **The Hanging Gardens**, designed by Robillion, were built over arches, raising the ground in front of the palace above the surrounding gardens.

Music Room
Operas and concerts were performed here by Maria I's orchestra, "the best in Europe" according to English traveller William Beckford. A portrait of the queen hangs above the forte piano.

VISITORS' CHECKLIST

Practical Information
Road Map B5. Largo do Palácio. **Tel** 214 343 860. **Open** 9am–5:30pm daily (late Mar–Oct: to 7pm). **Closed** 1 Jan, 25 Dec.

Transport
🚉 Queluz–Belas or Queluz–Massama. 🚌 from Lisbon (Colégio Militar).

★ Throne Room
The elegant state room (1770) was the scene of splendid balls and banquets. The gilded statues of Atlas are by Silvestre Faria Lobo.

Entrance

Maria I (1734–1816)

Maria, the eldest daughter of José I, lived at the palace in Queluz after her marriage to her uncle, Pedro, in 1760. Serious and devout, she conscientiously filled her role as queen, but suffered increasingly from bouts of melancholia. When her son José died from smallpox in 1788, she went hopelessly mad. Visitors to Queluz were dismayed by her agonizing shrieks as she suffered visions and hallucinations. After the French invasion of 1807, her younger son João (declared regent in 1792) took his mad mother to Brazil.

★ Palace Gardens
The formal gardens, adorned with statues, fountains and topiary, were often used for entertaining. Concerts performed in the Music Room would spill out into the Malta Gardens.

⑬ Sesimbra

Road map C5. 🚹 42,000. 🚌
ℹ️ Rua da Fortaleza de Santiago (212 288 540). 🛒 2nd & 4th Sat of month.

A steep narrow road leads down to this busy fishing village in a sheltered south-facing bay. Protected from north winds by the slopes of the Serra da Arrábida, the town has become a popular holiday resort with Lisboetas. It was occupied by the Romans and later the Moors until King Sancho II *(see pp46–7)* conquered its heavily defended forts in 1236. The old town is a maze of steep narrow streets, with the Santiago Fort (now a customs post) in the centre overlooking the sea. From the terrace, which is open to the public during the day, there are views over the town, the Atlantic and the wide sandy beach that stretches out on either side. Sesimbra is fast developing as a resort, with holiday flats mushrooming on the surrounding hillsides and plentiful pavement cafés and bars that are always busy on sunny days, even in winter.

The fishing fleet of brightly painted boats is moored in the Porto do Abrigo to the west of the main town. The harbour is reached by taking Avenida dos Náufragos, a sweeping

Colourful fishing boats in the harbour at Sesimbra

promenade that follows the beach out of town. On the large trawlers *(traineiras)*, the catch is mainly sardines, sea bream, whiting and swordfish; on the smaller boats, octopus and squid. In the late afternoon, when the fishing boats return from a day at sea, a colourful, noisy fish auction takes place on the quayside. The day's catch can be tasted in the town's excellent fish restaurants along the shore.

High above the town is the Moorish castle, greatly restored in the 18th century when a church and small flower-filled cemetery were added inside the walls. There are wonderful views from the ramparts, especially at sunset.

⑭ Palmela

Road map C5. 🚹 57,000. 🚌 🚉
ℹ️ Castelo de Palmela (212 332 122).

The formidable castle at Palmela stands over the small hill town, high on a northeastern spur of the wooded Serra da Arrábida. Its strategic position dominates the plain for miles around, especially when floodlit at night. Heavily defended by the Moors, it was eventually conquered in the 12th century and given by Sancho I to the Knights of the Order of Santiago *(see p49)*. In 1423, João I transformed the castle into a monastery for the Order, which has been restored and converted into a splendid *pousada (see p388)*, with a restaurant in the monks' refectory and a swimming pool for residents, hidden inside the castle walls.

From the castle terraces, and especially from the top of the 14th-century keep, there are fantastic views all around, over the Serra da Arrábida to the south and on a clear day across the Tagus to Lisbon. In the town square below, the church of São Pedro contains 8th-century tiles of scenes from the life of St Peter.

The annual wine festival, the Festa das Vindimas, is held on the first weekend of September in front of the 17th-century Paços do Concelho (town hall). Traditionally dressed villagers press the wine barefoot and on the final day of celebrations there is a spectacular firework display from the castle walls.

The castle at Palmela with views over the wooded Serra da Arrábida

🅑 Serra da Arrábida

Road map C5. 🚌 Setúbal.
ℹ️ Parque Natural da Arrábida, Praça da República, Setúbal (265 541 140).

The Parque Natural da Arrábida covers the small range of limestone mountains which stretches east-west along the coast between Sesimbra and Setúbal. It was established to protect the wild, beautiful landscape and rich variety of birds and wildlife, including eagles, wildcats and badgers.

The name Arrábida is from Arabic meaning a place of prayer, and the wooded hillsides are indeed a peaceful, secluded retreat. The sheltered, south-facing slopes are thickly covered with aromatic and evergreen shrubs and trees such as pine and cypress, more typical of the Mediterranean. Vineyards also thrive on the sheltered slopes and the town of Vila Nogueira de Azeitão is known for its wine, especially the Moscatel de Setúbal.

The Estrada de Escarpa (the N379-1) snakes across the top of the ridge and affords astounding views. A narrow road winds down to Portinho da Arrábida, a sheltered cove with a beach of fine white sand and crystal clear sea, popular with underwater fishermen. The sandy beaches of Galapos and Figueirinha are a little further east along the coast road towards Setúbal. Just east of Sesimbra, the Serra da Arrábida

Portinho da Arrábida on the dramatic coastline of the Serra da Arrábida

drops to the sea in the sheer 380-m (1,250-ft) cliffs of Risco, the highest in mainland Portugal.

🏛 Convento da Arrábida

Serra da Arrábida. **Tel** 212 197 620.
🕐 by appt only on Wed, Sat & Sun.
Closed Aug. 🈹

Half-hidden among the trees of the Serra, this 16th-century building was once a Franciscan monastery. The five round towers on the hillside were probably used for meditation. Today, the building houses a cultural centre.

🏛 Museu Oceanográfico

Fortaleza de Santa Maria, Portinho da Arrábida. **Tel** 265 009 982.
Open 10am–4pm Tue–Fri, 3–6pm Sat.
Closed public hols. 🈹

This small fort, just above Portinho da Arrábida, was built by Pedro, the Prince Regent, in 1676 to protect local communities from attacks by Moorish pirates. It now houses a Sea Museum and Marine Biology Centre where visitors can see aquaria containing many local sea creatures, including sea urchins, octopus and starfish.

🍷 José Maria da Fonseca

Rua José Augusto Coelho 11, Vila Nogueira de Azeitão. **Tel** 212 197 500. **Open** Apr–Oct: 10am–7pm; Nov–Mar: 10am–noon & 2:30–5:30pm daily. **Closed** 1 & 2 Jan, 24 & 25 Dec.
🈹 🈹 🈹

The Fonseca winery produces quality table wines and is famous for its fragrant dessert wine, Moscatel de Setúbal (see p33). Tours of the winery explain the process of making moscatel and feature a visit to a series of old cellars containing huge oak and chestnut vats. Tours last about 45 minutes and include a wine tasting.

Lisbon
Palmela
N379
N252
Vila Fresca de Azeitão
Lisbon
N10
Vila Nogueira de Azeitão
Setúbal
N379
N379-1
N379-1
N10-4
Convento da Arrábida
Figueirinha
Galapos
Portinho da Arrábida
tana
imbra
Baía de Setúbal

Key

▬▬	Major road
▭▭	Minor road
▭▭	Other road

0 kilometres — 5
0 miles — 3

Manueline interior of Igreja de Jesus, Setúbal

⓰ Setúbal

Road map C5. 🚫 119,000. 🚌 🚏
🏨 ℹ️ Casa da Baía, Avenida Luísa
Todi 468 (265 545 010 or 915 174 442).

Although this is an important
industrial town, and the third-
largest port in Portugal (after
Lisbon and Porto), Setúbal can
be used to explore the area. To
the south of the central gardens
and fountains are the fishing harbour, marina and ferry port, and
a lively covered market. North of
the gardens is the old town, with
attractive pedestrian streets and
squares full of shops and cafés.

The 16th-century cathedral,
dedicated to Santa Maria da
Graça, has glorious tiled panels
dating from the 18th century,
and gilded altar decoration.
Street names commemorate
two famous Setúbal residents:
Manuel Barbosa du Bocage
(1765–1805), whose satirical
poetry landed him in prison,
and Luísa Todi (1753–1833),
a celebrated opera singer. In
Roman times, fish-salting was
the most important industry

here. Rectangular tanks, carved
from stone, can be seen under
the glass floor of the Regional
Tourist Office at No. 10 Travessa
Frei Gaspar.

🏛 Igreja de Jesus

Largo de Jesus. **Tel** 913 873 015.
Open 9:30am–1pm & 2–6pm Tue–
Sat. ♿ Museum: **Tel** 913 873 015.
Open Tue–Sun. **Closed** public
hols. 📷

To the north of the old town,
this striking Gothic church is
one of Setúbal's architectural
treasures. Designed by the
architect Diogo Boitac in 1494,

the lofty interior is adorned with
twisted columns, carved in
three strands from pinkish
Arrábida limestone, and rope-
like stone ribs decorating the
roof, recognized as the earliest
examples of the distinctive
Manueline style *(see pp28–9)*.

On Rua do Balneário, in
the old monastic quarters, a
museum houses 14 remarkable
paintings of the life of Christ.
The works are attributed to
the followers of Jorge Afonso
(1520–30), influenced by the
Flemish school.

🏛 Museu de Arqueologia e Etnografia

Avenida Luísa Todi 162. **Tel** 265 239
365. **Open** 9am–12:30pm & 2–5:30pm
Tue–Sat. **Closed** public hols.

The archaeological museum
displays a wealth of finds from
digs around Setúbal, including
Bronze Age pots, Roman coins
and amphorae made to carry
wine and *garum*, a sauce made
from fish marinated in salt and
herbs. The ethnography display
shows local arts, crafts and
industries, including the
processing of salt and cork
over the centuries.

🏛 Castelo de São Filipe

Estrada de São Filipe. **Tel** 265 545 010.
Open 10am–midnight Tue–Sun.

The star-shaped fort was built
in 1595 by Philip II of Spain
during the period of Spanish
rule *(see pp54–5)* to keep a wary
eye on pirates, English invaders
and the local population.
A massive gateway and stone
tunnel lead to the sheltered
interior, which houses a bar,
lounge area as well as the
original chapel. A broad terrace
offers marvellous views over
the city and the
Sado estuary.

Environs

Setúbal is an
excellent starting
point for a tour by
car of the unspoilt
**Reserva Natural do
Estuário do Sado**, a
vast stretch of mud
flats, shallow lagoons
and salt marshes
with patches of pine

Fisherman's boat on the shallow mud flats of the Reserva
Natural do Estuário do Sado

forest, which has been explored and inhabited since 3500 BC. Otters, water birds (including storks and herons), oysters and a great variety of fish are found in the reserve. The old tidal water mill at Mouriscas, 5 km (3 miles) to the east of Setúbal, uses the different levels of the tide to turn the grinding stones. Rice-growing and fishing are the main occupations today, and pine trees around the lagoon are tapped for resin.

Reserva Natural do Estuário do Sado
Praça da República, Setúbal (265 541 140).

A boardwalk crosses the sand dunes to the beach of Tróia

Península de Tróia

Road map C5. Tróia. Tróia Resort (265 499 400/421).

High-rise holiday apartments dominate the tip of the Tróia peninsula, easily accessible from Setúbal by ferry. The Atlantic coast, stretching south for 18 km (11 miles) of untouched sandy beach, lined with dunes and pine woods, is now the haunt of sun-seekers in the summer.

Near Tróia, in the sheltered lagoon, the Roman town of **Cetóbriga** was the site of a thriving fish-salting trade, established in the 3rd century. The stone tanks and ruined buildings, which are signposted as Ruinas Romanas, are open to visit. To the south, smart holiday villas and golf clubs are springing up along the lagoon.

Further on, Carrasqueira is an old fishing community where you can still see traditional reed houses. The narrow fishing boats moored along the mud

View over Alcácer do Sal and the River Sado from the castle

flats are reached by walkways raised on stilts. From here to Alcácer do Sal, great stretches of pine forest line the road, and there are the first glimpses of the cork oak countryside typical of the Alentejo.

Cetóbriga
N253-1. **Tel** 265 499 413. **Open** Jun–Sep: 10am–1pm, 2:30–6pm Wed–Sun..

Alcácer do Sal

Road map C6. 14,000. Largo Luís de Camões (265 009 987). 1st Sat of month.

Bypassed by the main road, the ancient town of Alcácer do Sal (al-kasr from the Arabic for castle, and do sal from its trade in salt) sits peacefully on the north bank of the River Sado. The imposing castle was a hillfort as early as the 6th century BC. The Phoenicians established an inland trading port here, and the castle later became a stronghold for the Romans. Rebuilt by the Moors, it was finally conquered by Afonso II in 1217. The restored buildings have taken on a new life as a *pousada* (see p387), with sweeping views over the rooftops and untidy storks' nests. Also here is the **Cripta Arqueológica do Castelo**, an archaeological museum holding locally excavated items. The collections include artifacts from the Iron Age, as well as from the Roman, Moorish and medieval periods.

There are pleasant cafés along the riverside promenade and several historic churches. The bullring is a focus for summer events and hosts the agricultural fair in October.

Cripta Arqueológica do Castelo
Castelo de Alcácer, Piso Inferior Pousada Dom Afonso II. **Tel** 265 612 058. **Open** Tue–Sun.

Birds of the Tagus and Sado Estuaries

Many water birds, including black-winged stilts, avocets, Kentish plovers and pratincoles are found close to areas of open water and mud flats as well as the dried out lagoons of the Tagus and Sado estuaries. Reed-beds also provide shelter for nesting and support good numbers of little bitterns, purple herons and marsh harriers. From September to March, the area around the Tagus estuary is extremely important for wildfowl and wintering waders.

Black-winged stilt, a wader that feeds in the estuaries

ESTREMADURA AND RIBATEJO

Between the Tagus and the coast lies Estremadura, an area of rolling hills that tumble down to rugged cliffs and sandy beaches. In contrast, the Ribatejo is a vast alluvial plain stretching along the banks of the Tagus. Portugal's finest medieval monasteries here bear witness to the illustrious, if turbulent, past of these regions.

The name Estremadura comes from the Latin *Extrema Durii*, "beyond the Douro", once the border of the Christian kingdoms in the north. As Portugal expanded southwards in the 12th century, land taken from the Moors (*see pp46–7*) was given to the religious orders. The Cistercian abbey at Alcobaça celebrates Afonso Henriques's capture of the town of Santarém in 1147, and the Knights Templar began their citadel at Tomar (*see p191*) soon after.

Spanish claims to the Portuguese throne brought more fighting: Batalha's magnificent abbey was built near the site of João I's victory over the Castilians at Aljubarrota in 1385. In 1808–10, Napoleonic forces sacked many towns in the region, but were stopped by Wellington's formidable defences, the Lines of Torres Vedras.

Nowadays, Estremadura is an area of expanding commerce, where vineyards, wheatfields and market gardens flourish. In the Ribatejo (the name means "Banks of the Tagus") the river's vast flood plain provides fertile soil for agriculture and grazing land for Portugal's prized black fighting bulls and fine horses.

The area around Tomar and the river towns along the Tagus have thriving industries, while on the River Zêzere, the dam built at Castelo de Bode in the 1940s heralded a new era of hydroelectric power. The Atlantic coast is a popular holiday destination, especially the fishing village of Nazaré and the sandy beaches along the Pinhal de Leiria forest. Visitors also flock to Portugal's most important religious shrine at Fátima, the scene of celebrated visions of the Virgin Mary in 1917.

The pentagonal Forte de São João Baptista, located on the Berlenga Islands (*see p180*)

◀ Capelas Imperfeitas, in the monastery of Santa Maria da Victória, Batalha

Exploring Estremadura and the Ribatejo

The impressive monuments in Estremadura recall the important role the region has played in Portugal's history. Tomar and Óbidos are convenient bases from which to visit the great abbeys at Batalha and Alcobaça or the modern shrine at Fátima. Leiria's charming old town is also a good place to stay and it is possible to make day trips from Lisbon. Those in search of more leisurely pursuits can enjoy boating on the Castelo de Bode lake or relaxing on the coast's stunning beaches. The fertile Lezíria plain of the Ribatejo is an area famous for bull- and horse-breeding. Here visitors can enjoy lively local festivals at Santarém, the Ribatejo's lively capital.

Sights at a Glance

Key

═══ Motorway
──── Secondary road
∷∷∷∷ Minor road
──── Scenic route
━·━· Main railway
──── Minor railway
═══ Regional border

Colourful beach tents at São Martinho do Porto, near Nazaré

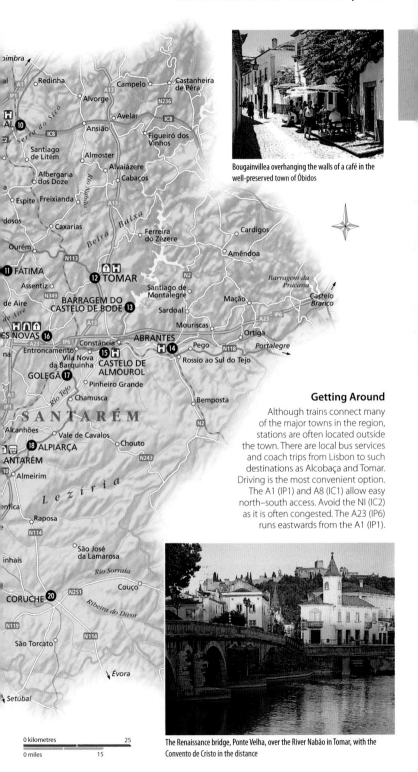

Bougainvillea overhanging the walls of a café in the well-preserved town of Óbidos

Getting Around

Although trains connect many of the major towns in the region, stations are often located outside the town. There are local bus services and coach trips from Lisbon to such destinations as Alcobaça and Tomar. Driving is the most convenient option. The A1 (IP1) and A8 (IC1) allow easy north–south access. Avoid the NI (IC2) as it is often congested. The A23 (IP6) runs eastwards from the A1 (IP1).

The Renaissance bridge, Ponte Velha, over the River Nabão in Tomar, with the Convento de Cristo in the distance

0 kilometres 25

0 miles 15

❶ Berlenga Islands

Road map B4. 🚢 from Peniche.
🅸 Peniche.

Monks, a lighthouse keeper, fishermen and biologists have inhabited this rocky archipelago that juts out from the Atlantic Ocean 12 km (7 miles) from the mainland. Berlenga Grande, the biggest island, can be reached by ferry in about an hour. This island is a nature reserve with nesting sites for sea birds including guillemots and herring gulls.

On the southeast side of the island is the 17th-century pentagonal Forte de São João Baptista. This stark, stone fort suffered repeated assaults from pirates and foreign armies over the years. Today it is a basic hostel. Small boats can be hired from the jetty to explore the reefs and marine grottoes around the island. Furado Grande is the most spectacular of these; a 70-m (230-ft) tunnel, opening into the Covo do Sonho (Dream Cove) framed by imposing red granite cliffs.

❷ Peniche

Road map B4. 🅰 28,000. 🚌 🅸 Rua Alexandre Herculano (262 789 571). 🗓 Last Thu of the month (except Jul & Dec).

Set on a peninsula, this small, pleasant town is partly enclosed by 16th-century walls. Totally dependent on its port, Peniche has good fish restaurants and deep-sea fishing facilities. At the water's edge on the south side

Stone fortress of São João Baptista on Berlenga Grande

of town stands the 16th-century Fortaleza, used as a prison during the Salazar regime *(see pp60–61)*. The fortress was made famous by the escape in 1960 of the communist leader Álvaro Cunhal. Inside, the **Museu de Peniche** offers a tour that includes a look into the prison cells. In Largo 5 de Outubro, the Igreja da Misericórdia has 17th-century painted ceiling panels depicting the *Life of Christ*, and patterned *azulejo* panels from the same period.

🏛 Museu de Peniche
Campo da República. **Tel** 262 780 116.
Open Tue–Sun. **Closed** 1 Jan, Easter, 1 May, 25 Dec. 🅿

Environs

On the peninsula's western headland, 2 km (1 mile) from Peniche, Cabo Carvoeiro affords grand views of the ocean and the strange-shaped rocks along the eroded coastline. Here, the interior of the chapel of Nossa Senhora dos Remédios is faced with 18th-century tiles on the *Life of the Virgin* attributed to the workshop of António de Oliveira Bernardes *(see p30)*.

Along the coast, 2 km (1 mile) east of Peniche, Baleal is a small community with gorgeous beaches and an idyllic fishing cove across a causeway.

❸ Óbidos

Road map B4. 🅰 11,000. 🚉 🚌 🅸 Rua da Porta da Vila (Parque do Estacionamento Grande) (262 959 231). 🗓 First Sun of the month.

This enchanting hill town with whitewashed houses is enclosed within 14th-century walls. When King Dinis *(see pp48–9)* married Isabel of Aragon in 1282, Óbidos was one of his wedding presents to her. At the time Óbidos was an important port, but by the 16th century the river had silted up and its strategic importance declined. It has since been restored and preserved.

Boats anchored in the old harbour at Peniche

The entrance into the town is through the southern gate, Porta da Vila, whose interior is embellished with 18th-century tiles. Rua Direita, the main shopping street, leads to Praça de Santa Maria. Here, a Manueline pelourinho (pillory) is decorated with a fishing net, the emblem of Dona Leonor, wife of João II. She chose this emblem in honour of the fishermen who tried in vain to save her son from drowning.

Opposite the pillory is the church of Santa Maria, with a simple Renaissance portal. The future Afonso V was married to his cousin Isabel here in 1441. He was ten years old, she eight. The interior of the church retains a simple clarity with a painted wooden ceiling and 17th-century tiles. In the chancel, a retable depicting the *Mystic Marriage of St Catherine* (1661) is by Josefa de Óbidos (*see p55*). The artist lived most of her life in Óbidos and is buried in the church of São Pedro on Largo de São Pedro. Her work is also on display in the **Museu Municipal**.

Dominating the town is the castle, rebuilt by Afonso Henriques after he took the

View of the castle over the whitewashed houses of Óbidos

town from the Moors in 1148. Today it is a charming *pousada* (*see p389*). The sentry path along the battlements affords fine views of the rooftops.

Southeast of town is the Baroque Santuário do Senhor da Pedra, begun in 1740 to a hexagonal plan. An early Christian stone crucifix on the altar remains a venerated item.

▥ Museu Municipal
Solar da Praça de Santa Maria, Rua Direita. **Tel** 262 959 299. **Open** Tue–Sun. **Closed** 1 Jan, 25 Dec. ▨

❹ Caldas da Rainha

Road map B4. ⛰ 22,000. 🚊 🚌
🛈 Rua Engenheiro Duarte Pacheco (262 240 000). 🛍 Mon.

The "queen's hot springs", a sprawling spa town, owes its prosperity to three different fields: thermal cures, ceramics and fruit farming. The town is named after Dona Leonor, founder of the Misericórdia hospital on Largo Rainha Dona Leonor. The original hospital chapel later became the impressive Manueline Igreja do Populo, built by Diogo Boitac (*see pp108–9*). Inside is the 15th-century chapel of São Sebastião, faced with 18th-century *azulejos*.

The shops in Rua da Liberdade sell local ceramics, including the local green majolica ware. Examples of the work of the caricaturist and potter Rafael Bordalo Pinheiro (1846–1905) can be seen in the **Museu de Cerâmica**, in the ceramics factory. The Museu José Malhoa is dedicated to the artist known as "the painter of Portuguese sun and light".

▥ Museu de Cerâmica
Rua Dr Ilídio Amado. **Tel** 262 840 280. **Open** 10am–12:30pm & 2–5:30pm Tue–Sun. **Closed** 1 Jan, 25 Dec. ▨ (free first Sun of month).

Environs
Saltwater Lagoa de Óbidos, 15 km (9 miles) west, is a popular lagoon for sailing and fishing.

Pillory in front of the Igreja de Santa Maria in Óbidos

The colourful courtyard of a house in Óbidos ▶

❺ Alcobaça

Portugal's largest church, the Mosteiro de Santa Maria de Alcobaça, is renowned for its simple medieval architecture. Founded in 1153, this UNESCO World Heritage site is closely linked to the arrival of the Cistercian order in Portugal in 1138 as well as the birth of the nation. In March 1147, King Afonso Henriques (see pp46–7) conquered the Moorish stronghold of Santarém. To commemorate the victory, he fulfilled his vow to build a church for the Cistercians, a task completed in 1223. The monastery was further endowed by other monarchs, notably King Dinis who built the main cloister. Among those buried here are the tragic lovers King Pedro and his murdered mistress Inês.

Sacristy Doorway
Exotic foliage and elaborate pinnacles adorn the Manueline doorway, attributed to João de Castilho (see p108).

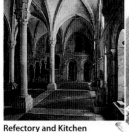

Refectory and Kitchen
Stairs lead up to the pulpit where one of the monks read from the Bible as the others ate in silence. In the vast kitchen next door, oxen could be roasted on the spit inside the chimney and a specially diverted stream provided a constant water supply.

KEY

① **The octagonal lavabo** was where the monks washed their hands.

② **The kitchen's huge chimney**

③ **The chapterhouse** was where the monks met to elect the abbot and discuss issues regarding the monastery.

④ **Dormitory**

⑤ **Tomb of Inês de Castro**

⑥ *Death of St Bernard*, a late 17th-century ceramic sculpture created by the monks.

⑦ **The façade** is a richly decorated 18th-century addition. Marble statues of St Benedict and St Bernard flank the main doorway.

★ **Cloister of Dom Dinis**
Also known as the Cloister of Silence, the exquisite cloister was ordered by King Dinis in 1308. The austere galleries and double arches are in keeping with the Cistercian regard for simplicity.

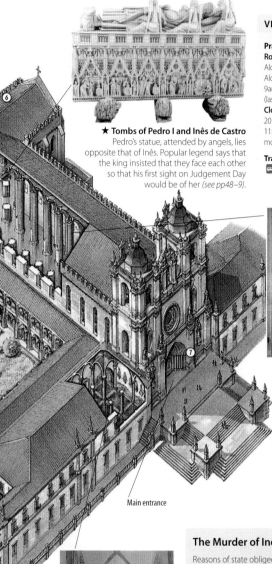

★ **Tombs of Pedro I and Inês de Castro**
Pedro's statue, attended by angels, lies opposite that of Inês. Popular legend says that the king insisted that they face each other so that his first sight on Judgement Day would be of her *(see pp48–9)*.

Main entrance

Central Nave
The vaulted roof and soaring columns of the central nave create an impression of harmony and austere simplicity.

Sala dos Reis
Tiles from the 18th century depict the founding of the abbey and statues of Portuguese kings adorn the walls.

The Murder of Inês de Castro

Reasons of state obliged Pedro, son and heir of Afonso IV *(see pp48–9)*, to marry Costanza, Infanta of Castile. When Costanza died, Pedro went to live with Inês de Castro, a lady at court with whom he had fallen in love, in Coimbra. Persuaded that Inês's family was dangerous, Afonso IV had her murdered on 7 January 1355 *(see p209)*. On Afonso's death, Pedro took revenge on two of the killers by having their hearts torn out. Declaring that he had been married to Inês, Pedro had her corpse exhumed and crowned. In a final gruesome gesture, he compelled his court to kneel before Inês and kiss her decomposed hand.

The beach at Nazaré viewed from Sítio

❻ Nazaré

Road map C4. 🚉 15,000. 🚌
ℹ️ Avenida Vieira Guimarães 54,
Mercado Municipal(262 561 194).
🎪 Fri (closed Aug).

Beside a glorious beach in a sweeping bay backed by steep cliffs, this fishing village is a popular summer resort that has maintained some of its traditional character. Fishermen dressed in checked shirts and black stocking caps and fishwives wearing several layers of petticoats can still be seen mending nets and drying fish on wire racks on the beach. The bright boats with tall prows that once were hauled from the sea by oxen are still used, although now they have a proper anchorage south of the beach. According to legend the name Nazaré comes from a statue of the Virgin Mary brought to the town by a monk from Nazareth in the 4th century.

High on the cliff above the town is Sítio, reached by a funicular that climbs 110 m (360 ft). At the cliff edge stands the tiny Ermida da Memória. This is said to be where the Virgin Mary saved Dom Fuas Roupinho, a local dignitary, and his horse from following a deer that leapt off the cliff in a sea mist in 1182. Across the square, the 17th-century church of Nossa Senhora da Nazaré, with two Baroque belfries and 18th-century tiles inside, contains an anonymous painting of the miraculous rescue. The church also contains the revered image of Our Lady of Nazaré. In September this statue is borne down to the sea in a traditional procession.

Environs
São Martinho do Porto, 13 km (8 miles) south of Nazaré, is a sandy beach on a curving, almost landlocked bay. The safe location makes it popular with families and children. The Visigothic church of São Gião, 5 km (3 miles) further south, has fine sculpting and well-roportioned arches.

❼ Porto de Mós

Road map C4. 🚉 25,000. 🚌 ℹ️
Jardim Municipal (244 491 323). 🎪 Fri.

Originally a Moorish fort, and rebuilt over the centuries by successive Christian kings, the rather fanciful castle perches on a hill above the small town of Porto de Mós. Its present appearance, with green cone-shaped turrets and an exquisite loggia, was the inspired work of King Afonso IV's master builders in 1420.

In the town below, the 13th-century church of São João Baptista retains its original Romanesque portal. In the public gardens is the richly decorated Baroque church of São Pedro. Just off the Praça da República, the **Museu Municipal** displays a varied collection of local finds dating back to Roman remains and dinosaur bones. More modern exhibits include the local *mós* (millstones), as well as present-day ceramics and woven rugs.

🏛️ **Museu Municipal**
Travessa de São Pedro. **Tel** 244 499 652.
Open Tue–Sat. **Closed** public hols.

Donkey in the Serra de Aire nature reserve, south of Porto de Mós

Environs
South of the town, the 390-sq-km (150-sq- mile) Parque Natural das Serras de Aire e Candeeiros covers a limestone landscape of pastures, olive groves and stone walls and is a nesting place for the red-beaked chough.

The area is also dotted with vast and spectacular underground caverns with odd rock formations and festoons of stalactites and stalagmites. The **Grutas de Mira de Aire**, 17 km (11 miles) southeast of Porto de Mós, are the biggest, descending 110 m (360 ft) into tunnels and walkways around subterranean lakes. A tour through caverns with names such as the "Jewel Room", past bizarre rocks dubbed "Chinese Hat" or "Jellyfish", ends in a theatrical light and water show.

🎇 **Grutas de Mira de Aire**
Av Dr Luciano Justo Ramos.
Tel 244 440 322. **Open** daily. 🐾

❽ Batalha

See pp188–9.

Baroque church of Nossa Senhora da Nazaré in Sítio

⑨ Leiria

Road map C4. 🚏 123,000. 🚌
🚂 ℹ️ Jardim Luís de Camões
244 848 770). 🛒 Tue & Sat.
🌐 **turismodocentro.pt**

Episcopal city since 1545, Leiria is set in attractive countryside on the banks of the River Lis. Originally the Roman town of Collipo, it was recaptured from the Moors by Afonso Henriques (see pp46–7) in the 12th century. In 1254 Afonso III held a *cortes* here, the first parliament attended by common laymen.

The resplendent hilltop **castle** houses a museum and meeting rooms. Along with Pombal, Ourém and Tomar, the Leiria castle was part of the defence system of central Portugal. In the early 1300s, King Dinis turned it into a royal residence for himself and his queen, Isabel of Aragon. Within the castle battlements is the Gothic church of Nossa Senhora da Pena, today little more than a roofless shell of dark granite walls. The view from the castle loggia overlooks the wide expanse of pine forest, the Pinhal de Leiria, and the rooftops of the town below.

The old town below the castle is full of charm, with tiny dwellings over archways, graceful arcades and the small 12th-century church of São Pedro on Largo de São Pedro. The Romanesque portal is all that remains

of the original church. The muted 16th-century Sé above Praça Rodrigues Lobo has an elegant vaulted nave and an altarpiece in the chancel painted in 1605 by Simão Rodrigues. From Avenida Marquês de Pombal, climbing the hill opposite the castle, an 18th-century stairway takes you up to the elaborate 16th-century Santuário de Nossa Senhora da Encarnação. The small Baroque interior is tightly packed with colourful geometric *azulejo* panels and 17th-century paintings of the *Life of the Virgin*.

Exposed and rugged coastline west of Leiria

🏛 Castle
Largo de São Pedro. **Tel** 244 839 670. **Open** Apr–Sep: 10am–6pm; Oct–Mar: 9:30am–5:30pm. **Closed** 1 Jan, Easter, 25 Dec. ♿

Environs

Close to the town centre is the Estádio Dr Magalhães Pessoa, built for the Euro 2004 football championship. West of Leiria is a long coastal pine forest, the Pinhal de Leiria, planted by King Dinis to supply wood for shipbuilding. The forest extends northwards to the beach of Pedrógão. São Pedro de Muel, 22 km (14 miles) to the west of Leiria, is a small resort on a marvellous beach.

⑩ Pombal

Road map C4. 🚏 58,000. 🚌 🚌
ℹ️ Rua do Castelo (236 210 556).
🛒 Mon & Thu.

Closely associated with the Marquês de Pombal (see pp56–7) who retired here in disgrace in 1777, this small town of whitewashed houses is overlooked by the stately and well-preserved castle, founded in 1161 by the Knights Templar (see p191).

In the Praça Marquês de Pombal the old prison and the *celeiro* (granary) are adorned with the Pombal family crest. The **Museu Marquês de Pombal** features a collection of documents and artworks focusing on the Marquis.

🏛 Museu Marquês de Pombal
Praça Marquês de Pombal. **Tel** 236 210 564. **Open** 10am–1pm & 2–6pm Tue–Sun. **Closed** public hols. ♿

Arcaded loggia and castle towers guarding the town of Leiria

❽ Batalha

The Dominican monastery of Santa Maria da Vitória at Batalha, a UNESCO World Heritage site, is a masterpiece of Portuguese Gothic architecture notable for its Manueline elements. The pale limestone monastery celebrates João I's 1385 victory over Castile at Aljubarrota. Today, two unknown soldiers from World War I lie in the chapterhouse. The monastery was begun in 1388 under master builder Afonso Domingues, succeeded in 1406 by David Huguet. Over the next two centuries successive kings left their mark on the monastery: João's son, King Duarte, ordered a royal pantheon behind the apse, and Manueline additions include the Unfinished Chapels and much of the decoration of the monastery buildings.

Chapterhouse
Guards keep watch by the Tomb of Unknown Soldiers beneath Huguet's striking star-vaulted ceiling.

★ Royal Cloister
Gothic arches by Afonso Domingues and Huguet around the cloister are embellished by Manueline tracery *(see pp28–9)* to achieve a harmony of form and decoration.

KEY

① **Refectory**

② **The lavabo**, where friars washed their hands before and after meals, contains a fountain built around 1450.

③ **The stained-glass window** behind the choir dates from 1514.

④ **Lofty nave by Afonso Domingues**

⑤ **The chapel** is topped by an octagonal lantern.

⑥ **João I's motto**, *Por bem* (for good), is inscribed on his tomb.

Main entrance

Portal
The portal was decorated by Huguet with religious motifs and statues of the apostles in intricate late-Gothic style.

★ Unfinished Chapels

Begun under King Duarte, the octagonal mausoleum was abandoned by Manuel I in favour of the Jerónimos monastery in Belém (see pp108–9).

VISITORS' CHECKLIST

Practical Information
Road map C4. Mosteiro de Santa Maria da Vitória, Batalha.
Tel 244 765 497.
Open 9am–6pm (Oct–Mar: to 5:30pm) daily. **Closed** 1 Jan, Easter, 1 May, 24 & 25 Dec. 🌐 (free first Sun of month).

Transport
🚌 from Lisbon, Leiria, Porto de Mós & Fátima.

Manueline Portal
Most of the decoration of the Unfinished Chapels dates from the reign of Manuel I. Designed by architect Mateus Fernandes, this delicate portal was carved in 1509.

★ Founder's Chapel

The tomb of João I and his English wife Philippa of Lancaster, lying hand in hand, was begun in 1426 by Huguet. Their son, Henry the Navigator, is also buried here.

The Battle of Aljubarrota

In 1383 Portugal's direct male line of descent ended with the death of Fernando I (see pp48–9). Dom João, the illegitimate son of Fernando's father, was proclaimed king, but his claim was opposed by Juan of Castile. On 14 August 1385 João I's greatly outnumbered forces, commanded by Nuno Álvares Pereira, faced the Castilians on a small plateau near Aljubarrota, 3 km (2 miles) south of Batalha. João's spectacular victory ensured 200 years of independence from Spain. The monastery now stands as a symbol of Portuguese sovereignty and the power of the house of Avis.

Commander Nuno Álvares Pereira

Curved limestone gallery around the vast esplanade in front of the basilica at Fátima

⑪ Fátima

Road map C4. 🏛 9,000. 🚌
ℹ️ Avenida Dom José Alves Correia da Silva (249 531 139). 🚂 Sat.
🌐 turismodocentro.pt

The sanctuary of Fátima is a devotional shrine on a prodigious scale, a pilgrim destination on a par with Lourdes in France. The Neo-Baroque limestone basilica, flanked by statues of saints, has a 65-m (213-ft) tower and an esplanade twice the size of St Peter's Square in Rome.

On 12 and 13 of May and October, vast crowds of pilgrims arrive to commemorate appearances of the Virgin to three shepherd children (the three *pastorinhos*). On 13 May 1917, 10-year-old Lucia Santos and her young cousins, Jacinta and Francisco Marto, saw a shining figure in a holm oak tree. The apparition ordered the children to return to the tree on the same day for six months and by 13 October 70,000 pilgrims were

with the children by the tree. Only Lucia heard the "Secret of Fátima", spoken on her last appearance. The first part of the secret was a vision of hell; the second was of a war more devastating than World War I. The third part, a vision of papal assassination, was finally revealed by Pope John Paul II on the occasion of the Millennium. The Pope beatified Jacinta and Francisco in 2000. Their tombs can be found inside the basilica. Lucia, who became a nun, died in 2005.

The stained-glass windows show scenes of the sightings. In the esplanade, the Capela das Aparições marks the site of the apparition. Inside, the crown of the Virgin holds the bullet used in the 1981 assassination attempt on Pope John Paul II. East of the sanctuary, the childrens' homes have been preserved in the Casa da Lúcia/Museu de Aljustrela. Waxworks and a multimedia show complete the experience.

For most people, however, the most impressive sight is the intense emotion and faith of the penitents who approach the shrine on their knees. Wax limbs are burned as offerings for miracles performed by the Virgin and thousands of candles light the esplanade in the night-time masses.

🏛 Casa da Lúcia and Museu de Aljustrela
Rua dos Pastorinhos de Aljustrel. **Tel** 249 532 828. **Open** daily. 🚹 ♿

Environs
The medieval town of Ourém, 10 km (6 miles) northeast of Fátima, is a walled citadel, dominated by the 15th-century castle of Ourém built by Afonso, grandson of Nuno Álvares Pereira (see p189). His magnificent tomb is in the 15th-century Igreja Matriz. The town's name is said to derive from Oureana, a Moorish girl who, before she fell in love with a Christian knight and converted, was called Fátima.

Ruined secret passage connecting the towers of the castle in Ourém

⑫ Tomar

Road map C4. 🏛 43,000. 🚉 🚌
ℹ️ Avenida Dr Cândido Madureira (249 329 823). 🚂 Fri.

Founded in 1157 by Gualdim Pais, the first Grand Master of the Order of the Templars in Portugal, the town is dominated by the 12th-century castle containing the Convento de Cristo (see pp192–3). The heart of this charming town is a neat grid of narrow streets. The lively shopping street, Rua Serpa Pinto, leads to the Gothic church of São João Baptista on Praça da República, the town's main square. The late 15th-century church has an elegant Manueline portal and is capped by an octagonal spire. Inside, there is a carved stone pulpit and 16th-century paintings including a *Last Supper* by Gregório Lopes (1490–1550).

Church and clock tower of São João Baptista in Tomar's main square

A particularly gory beheading of John the Baptist is also attributed to Lopes.

The area outside the church is the focus of the spectacular Festa dos Tabuleiros, a festival with pagan origins held in July, every four years, in which girls in white carry towering platters of bread and flowers on their heads. The festival has similar roots to the Festa do Espírito Santo *(see p372)*, popular in the Azores.

Nearby, in Rua Dr Joaquim Jacinto, stands one of the oldest synagogues in Portugal, built in 1430–60 with four tall columns and a vaulted ceiling. The building was last used as a place of worship in 1497 after which Manuel I *(see pp50–51)* banished all Jews who refused to convert to Christianity. It has since been a prison, a hay loft and a warehouse. Today, it holds a small Jewish museum, the **Museu Luso-Hebraico de Abraham Zacuto**, named after a renowned 15th-century astronomer and mathematician.

Further south stands the 17th-century church of São Francisco. Its former cloisters now house the **Museu dos Fósforos**, a match museum proudly boasting the largest collection in Europe – over 43,000 matchboxes from 104 countries of the world.

On the east side of the River Nabão, just off Rua Aquiles da Mota Lima, is the 13th-century church of Santa Maria do Olival, with a distinctive three-storey bell tower. Restored various times over the centuries, the church preserves its Gothic façade and rose window. Inside are the graves of Gualdim Pais (died 1195) and other Templar Masters, and an elegant Renaissance pulpit. The church once had significance far beyond Tomar as the mother church for mariners in the Age of Discovery.

Heading north, Rua Santa Iria takes you to the Capela de Santa Iria, beside the 15th-century bridge, Ponte Velha. This Renaissance chapel is said to have been built where the saint was martyred in the 7th

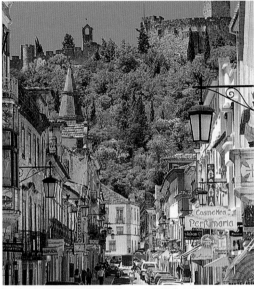

Tomar's main shopping street, Rua Serpa Pinto, overlooked by the castle

century *(see p197)*. A powerful stone retable depicting *Christ on the Cross* (1536) stands above the altar in the Capela dos Vales. On an island in the river, the shaded Parque do Mouchão is a pleasant walk; an allegedly Roman waterwheel turns with the passing water. Continuing northwards, past the octagonal 16th-century Ermida de São Gregório with its wild Manueline doorway, a huge flight of steps leads to a 17th-century chapel, Nossa Senhora da Piedade.

On the slopes of the hill leading up to the Convento do Cristo is the Renaissance basilica, Nossa Senhora da Conceição, built between 1530 and 1550. Its exterior simplicity contrasts with the elegantly proportioned and delicately carved Corinthian columns of the interior. The architect is believed to be Francisco de Holanda (1517–84), who worked for King João III.

🏛 **Museu Hebraico (Synagogue)**
ℹ Rua Joaquim Jacinto. **Tel** 249 329 823 (tourist office). **Open** Tue–Sun. **Closed** public hols.

🏛 **Museu dos Fósforos**
Av General Bernardo Faria. **Tel** 249 329 823 (tourist office). **Open** Tue–Sun. **Closed** public hols. ♿

The Order of Christ

During the 12th and 13th centuries, the crusading Order of the Knights Templar helped the Portuguese in their battle against the Moorish "infidels". In return they were rewarded with extensive lands and political power. Castles, churches and towns sprang up under their protective mantle. In 1314, Pope Clement V was forced to suppress this rich and powerful Order, but in Portugal King Dinis turned it into the Order of Christ, which inherited the property and privileges of the Templars. Ideals of Christian expansion were revived in the 15th century when their Grand Master, Prince Henry the Navigator, invested the order's revenue in exploration. The emblem of the order, the squared cross, adorned the sails of the caravels that crossed the uncharted waters *(see pp52–3)*.

Cross of the Order of Christ

Tomar: Convento de Cristo

Founded in 1160 by the Grand Master of the Templars, the Convent of Christ still retains some reminders of these monk-knights and the inheritors of their mantle, the Order of Christ (see p191). Under Henry the Navigator, the Governor of the Order from 1418, cloisters were built between the Charola and the Templars' fortress, but it was the reign of João III (1521–57) that saw the greatest changes. Architects such as João de Castilho and Diogo de Arruda, engaged to express the Order's power and royal patronage in stone, built the church and cloisters with dazzling Manueline flourishes, which reached a crescendo with the window in the west front of the church.

★ Manueline Window
Marine motifs entwine round this elaborate window. The carving at the base is thought to be either the architect (see p28) or the Old Man of the Sea.

★ Great Cloister
Begun in the 1550s, probably by Diogo de Torralva, this cloister reflects João III's passion for Italian art. Concealed spiral stairways in the corners lead to the Terrace of Wax.

KEY

① **The Terrace of Wax** is where honeycombs were left to dry.

② **Cloister of the Crows,** flanked by an aqueduct

③ **The "Bread" Cloister** was where loaves were handed out to the poor who came to beg at the monastery.

④ **The Manueline Church** by Diogo de Arruda, was begun in the early 16th century and is on two levels. The ornate ribbed vaulting in the upper choir incorporates the insignia and initials of Manuel I.

⑤ **The south portal** is initialled by João de Castilho.

⑥ **Internal octagon of the Charola**

⑦ **The Washing Cloister** was built around a pair of large reservoirs, today planted with flowers.

⑧ **Ruins of the former royal quarters**

⑨ **Castle keep**

The gilded octagon

The Charola

The nucleus of the monastery is the 12th-century Charola, the Templars' oratory. Like many of their temples, its layout is based on the Rotunda of Jerusalem's Holy Sepulchre, with a central octagon of altars. In 1356, Tomar became the headquarters of the Order of Christ in Portugal, and the Charola's decoration reflects the Order's wealth. The paintings and frescoes (mostly 16th-century biblical scenes) and the gilded statuary below the Byzantine cupola have undergone much careful restoration.

When the Manueline church was built, an archway was created in the side of the Charola to link the two, making the Charola the church's main chapel.

★ Charola
The original Templar church, sometimes called the Rotunda, was built in the shape of a 16-sided drum.

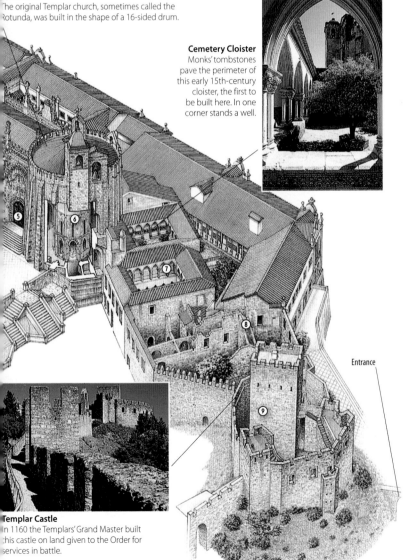

Cemetery Cloister
Monks' tombstones pave the perimeter of this early 15th-century cloister, the first to be built here. In one corner stands a well.

Entrance

Templar Castle
In 1160 the Templars' Grand Master built this castle on land given to the Order for services in battle.

The defensive walls of the early 13th-century fortress at Abrantes

⑬ Barragem do Castelo de Bode

Road map C4. 🚌 to dam. 🚤 from Castanheira. **Open** by appt (249 362 239). 🚩 Tomar (249 329 823).

Perhaps there once was a "Castle of the Billygoat", but today the name refers to a large dam (barragem) that blocks the flow of the River Zêzere 10 km (6 miles) upstream from its confluence with the Tagus. Construction of the dam began in 1946 to serve the first of Portugal's hydroelectric power stations. Above it, a long, sprawling lake nestles between hills covered in pine and eucalyptus forests in which lie small, isolated villages. The valley is a secluded area popular for boating, fishing and water sports and it is possible to hire equipment from centres along the lake shore. Canoes, windsurf boards and water-skis can be found at the Centro Náutico do

Zêzere, in Castanheira on the western side of the lake, and yachting facilities are usually available from the lakeside hotels such as the peaceful Estalagem Lago Azul (see p389). A cruise can also be taken from the hotel, stopping at the sandy beaches and the small islands.

⑭ Abrantes

Road map C4. 🏛 42,000. 🚉 🚌 🚩 Esplanada 1° de Maio (241 330 100). 🛍 Mon.

Grandly situated above the Tagus, the town of Abrantes was once of strategic importance. It had a vital role in the Reconquest (see pp46–7), and during the Peninsular War (see p58) both the French General Junot and the Duke of Wellington made it a base. The ruined fortress that overlooks the town and the surrounding flatlands is a reminder of its status. The 15th-century church of Santa Maria

do Castelo, within the castle walls, is now the small **Museu Dom Lopo de Almeida**. Besides local archaeological finds, it houses the tombs of the Almeida family, counts of Abrantes. On Rua da República, the Misericórdia church, constructed in 1584, has six magnificent religious panels attributed to Gregório Lopes (1490–1550).

🏛 **Museu Dom Lopo de Almeida**
Rua Capitão Correia de Lacerda. **Tel** 241 371 724. **Open** Tue–Sun.

Whitewashed houses in Constância above the banks of the Tagus

Environs

The 16th-century church of São Tiago e São Mateus, in the unspoiled town of Sardoal, 8 km (5 miles) north of Abrantes, holds a compelling thorn-crowned Christ by the 16th-century painter, the Master of Sardoal. An 18th-century tile panel on the façade of the Capela do Espírito Santo, in Praça da República, honours Gil Vicente, the 16th-century playwright born here.

The pretty whitewashed town of **Constância**, 12 km (7 miles) west of Sardoal, nurtures the memory of the poet Luís Vaz de Camões. Sent away from court for misbehaving with a court lady, he lived here briefly after 1546.

🏛 **Centro Ciência Viva de Constância**
Alto de Santa Bárbara. **Tel** 249 739 066. **Open** Tue–Sun. ♿

Luís Vaz de Camões (1524–80)

The author of Portugal's celebrated epic poem, Os Lusíadas, had a passionate nature and was often in trouble. Banished from court, he enlisted in 1547 and set sail for North Africa, where he lost an eye. Imprisoned after another brawl, he agreed to serve his country in India, but his was the only ship from the fleet to survive the stormy seas. This experience gave his subsequent poem its vibrant power. A unique record of the Discoveries, this Classical-style epic charts the voyage of Vasco da Gama to India and recounts events and legends from Portuguese history. There was to be no success for Camões, however, and he passed bleak years in India yearning for Lisbon. His poem was published in 1572, but he died almost unnoticed.

Statue of Camões on the river bank at Constância

ⓑ Castelo de Almourol

Road map C4. 🚌 to Barquinha then taxi then ferry. **Open** Tue–Sun during daylight hours. 🛈 Largo 1 Dezembro, Barquinha (915 081 737).

Dramatically set on a tiny island in the Tagus, this enchanting castle was built over a Roman fortress in 1171 by Gualdim Pais *(see p191)*. Legends of this magical place abound. A 16th-century verse romance called *Palmeirim de Inglaterra* weaves a tale of giants and knights and the fight of the crusader Palmeirim for the lovely Polinarda. Some say the castle is haunted by the ghost of a princess sighing for the love of her Moorish slave.

Over the centuries, the castle, surrounded by ramparts and nine towers, has never been taken by invading forces.

⓰ Torres Novas

Road map C4. 🏘 16,000. 🚌 🛈 Largo dos Combatentes 4–5 (249 813 019). 🛒 Tue.

Animated streets and many fine churches cluster beneath the castle walls of this handsome town. The ruins of the 12th-century fortress, the scene of bitter fighting between the Moors and the Christians during the Reconquest, now enclose a garden. Just below the castle is the 16th-century Misericórdia church with a Renaissance portal and an interior lined

The evocative ruins of the island fortress of Almourol

with colourful "carpet" *azulejos* from 1674. The Igreja de Santiago, on Largo do Paço, was probably built in 1203, although tiles and a gilded retable with a wood carving of the young Jesus assisting Joseph in his carpentry are 17th-century additions.

In the centre of town is the **Museu Municipal de Carlos Reis**, named after the painter Carlos Reis (1863–1940) who was born here. The museum contains paintings by 19th- and early 20th-century artists, a 15th-century Gothic figure of Nossa Senhora do Ó, as well as coins and bronze and ceramic artifacts from the Roman ruins at Vila Cardílio.

🏛 Museu Municipal de Carlos Reis
Rua do Salvador. **Tel** 249 812 535. **Open** Tue–Sun. **Closed** public hols.

Environs
Roman ruins dating from the 4th century AD at **Vila Cardílio**, 3 km (2 miles) southwest of Torres Novas, retain some superb mosaics and baths. On the northeast outskirts of town are the large Neolithic caves of **Grutas das Lapas**. The small wetland Reserva Natural do Paúl de Boquilobo, 8 km (5 miles) south, between the Tagus and Almondo rivers, was declared a nature reserve in 1981. The willow trees and aquatic plants along the river shelter wildfowl in winter, and nesting egrets and herons in spring.

🏛 Vila Cardílio
Estrada Municipal de St António da Caveira. **Tel** 249 839 430 (ext: 3361). **Open** daily. **Closed** public hols. ♿

🏛 Grutas das Lapas
Rua José da Mota e Silva. **Tel** 249 836 709. **Open** daily.

Remains of the hypocaust, the Roman underfloor heating system, at Vila Cardílio outside Torres Novas

Portal of the Igreja Matriz in Golegã

ⓘ Golegã

Road map C4. 👥 9,000. ⛢ ℹ️ Rua de D Afonso Henriques, Largo da Imaculada Conceição (249 979 002). ⛢ Wed.

Usually a quiet town, Golegã is overrun during the first two weeks of November by thousands of horse enthusiasts who throng to the annual Feira Nacional do Cavalo. This horse fair, which attracts Portugal's finest horses, breeders and equestrians, coincides with the tasting of the year's new wine on St Martin's Day (11 November). The atmosphere is enlivened by the consumption of the young wine known as *agua-pé* (literally, "foot water").

In the centre of town, the 16th-century Igreja Matriz, attributed to Diogo Boitac *(see pp108–9)*, has an exquisite Manueline portal and a calm interior. The small **Casa-Estúdio Carlos Relvas** is housed in the elegant Art Nouveau house and studio of the photographer (1838–94). A vivid modern art collection can be seen in the **Museu de Pintura e Escultura Martins Correia** in the old post office.

🏛 Casa-Estúdio Carlos Relvas
Largo Dom Manuel I. **Tel** 249 979 120.
Open 10am–12:30pm & 2–6pm Tue–Sun (Jun–Sep to 7pm). **Closed** public hols. 📷

🏛 Museu de Pintura e Escultura Martins Correia
Rua D João IV. **Tel** 249 979 000. **Open** as above. **Closed** as above. ♿ limited.
📷 Portal of Igreja Matriz in Golegã.

ⓘ Alpiarça

Road map C4. 👥 8,000. ⛢ ℹ️ Praça José Faustino Rodrigues Pinhão (243 556 000). ⛢ Wed.

Set in the vast, fertile plain known as the Lezíria, which stretches east of the Tagus and is famous for horse breeding, Alpiarça is a small, neat town. The fine twin-towered parish church, on Rua José Relvas, is dedicated to Santo Eustáquio, patron saint of the town. Built in the late 19th century, it houses paintings from the 17th century, including a charming *Divine Shepherdess* in the sacristy in which the young Jesus is shown conversing with a sheep. The stone cross in the courtyard is dated 1515.

On the southern outskirts of town is the striking **Casa Museu dos Patudos** surrounded by vineyards. This was the residence of the wealthy and cultivated José Relvas (1858–1929), an art collector and diplomat as well as a politician and – briefly – premier of the Republic. The exterior of this eye-catching country house, built for him by Raúl Lino in 1905–9, has simple whitewashed walls and a green and white striped spire. The colonnaded loggia, reached via an outside staircase, is lined with *azulejo* panels. The museum contains Relvas's personal collection of fine and decorative art. Renaissance paintings include *Virgin with Child and St John* by the school of Leonardo da Vinci and *Christ in the Tomb* by the German school. There

are also paintings by Delacroix and Zurbarán as well as many works by 19th-century Portuguese artists, including 30 by Relvas's friend, José Malhôa *(see p59)*. Relvas also collected exquisite porcelain, bronzes, furniture and Oriental rugs, as well as early Portuguese Arraiolos carpets, including a particularly fine one in silk.

🏛 Casa Museu dos Patudos
2 km (1 mile) S, N118. **Tel** 243 558 321. **Open** Tue–Sun. **Closed** public hols. 📷

Elegant façade of the country manor, Quinta da Alorna, outside Almeirim

Environs
Almeirim, 7 km (4 miles) to the south, was a favourite abode of the House of Avis *(see pp50–51)*. Today little of its royal past remains and most visitors come here to sample the famous *sopa de pedra* (stone soup).

Many large estates and fine stables extend across the vast flat plains of this fertile horse and cattle breeding area. The Quinta da Alorna, a handsome 19th-century manor house within walled gardens and well known for its wines, lies just outside Almeirim.

Tiled loggia of the Casa Museu dos Patudos, Alpiarça

The Tagus seen from the Jardim das Portas do Sol in Santarém

⑲ Santarém

Road map C4. 🏙 30,000. 🚉 🚌
ℹ Rua Capelo Ivens 63 (243 304 437).
🗓 2nd & 4th Sun of month.

The lively district capital of the Ribatejo, overlooking the Tagus, has an illustrious past. To Julius Caesar it was an important bureaucratic centre, Praesidium Iulium. To the Moors it was the stronghold of Xantarim. To the Portuguese kings, who ousted the Moors in 1147, Santarém was a pleasing abode and the site of many gatherings of the *cortes* (parliaments).

The city's name derives from "Santa Iria", the 7th-century martyred nun from Tomar *(see pp190–91)* whose body was thrown into the River Nabão and allegedly reappeared here on the Tagus shore.

At the centre of the old town, in Praça Sá da Bandeira, is the vast Igreja do Seminário, a multi-windowed Baroque edifice built by João IV for the Jesuits in 1640 on the site of a royal palace. The huge interior has a painted wooden ceiling and marble and gilt ornamentation. From here, Rua Serpa Pinto runs southeast past a cluster of older buildings. The lofty Igreja de Marvila, built in the 12th century and later altered, has a Manueline portal and is lined with dazzling early 17th-century diamond-patterned *azulejo* panels. The medieval, although much restored 22-m- (72-ft-) high Torre das Cabaças, was once a clock tower and now houses a small museum of time, Núcleo Museológico do Tempo.

Opposite the tower, the Museu Arqueológico was formerly the Romanesque church of São João de Alporão.

Rua Serpa Pinto leads into Rua 5 de Outubro and up to the Jardim das Portas do Sol, built on the site of a Moorish castle. The gardens are enclosed by the city's medieval walls, and a terrace affords a panorama of the river and its vast meadowlands.

Returning into town, on Largo Pedro Álvares Cabral, the 14th-century Igreja da Graça has a spectacular rose window carved from a single stone. The church contains the tombstone of Pedro Álvares Cabral, the explorer who discovered Brazil *(see p52)*.

Further south, the 14th-century Igreja do Santíssimo Milagre, on Rua Braamcamp Freire, has a Renaissance interior and 16th-century *azulejos (see p30)*. A small crystal flask in the sacristy is said to contain the blood of Christ. The belief stems from a 13th-century legend in which a holy wafer intended to help persuade a husband to stop beating his wife was miraculously transformed into blood.

Santarém is an important bullfighting centre with a modern bullring at the south-west corner of town. During the first ten days of June, the town hosts the Ribatejo Fair, Portugal's largest agricultural fair, in which there are bull-fights and contests between the colourfully dressed herds-men, *campinos*. In the autumn (Oct/Nov) Portugal's biggest gastronomy festival is held here, with lots of informal eating at stands representing the country's regions and types of food.

Tomb of Duarte de Meneses in the Museu Arqueológico, Santarém

Fields and vineyards in the low-lying Lezíria extending beyond Coruche

⑳ Coruche

Road map C5. ☒ 3,500. ☐ ☐
🛈 Galeria do Mercado Municipal
(243 619 072). ☐ last Sat of month.

Coruche is an attractive little town in the heart of the bullfighting country with a riverside location overlooking the Lezíria, the wide open plain that stretches east of the Tagus. The town, inhabited since Palaeolithic times, was razed to the ground in 1180 by the Moors as reprisal against the reconquering Christians.

In the central pedestrian street, Rua de Santarém, the O Coruja café is lined with vivid modern *azulejo* panels showing bulls in the Lezíria, the town's bullring and scenes of local life. A short walk up the street stands the tiny church of São Pedro. Its interior is completely covered with 17th-century blue and yellow carpet tiles. An *azulejo* panel on the altar front shows St Peter surrounded by birds and animals. Above the town stands the simple 12th-century

Chancel in the church of São Pedro covered in *azulejos*, Coruche

blue and white church of Nossa Senhora do Castelo. From here there are excellent views over the fertile agricultural land and cork oaks of the Sorraia valley and the Lezíria.

㉑ Vila Franca de Xira

Road map C5. ☒ 130,600. ☐ ☐
🛈 Rua Alves Redol 5 (263 285 605).
☐ Tue & Fri.

Sitting beside the Tagus, surrounded by the riverside industries that dominate this area, the town has a reputation larger than its modest appearance suggests. Traditionally the area has been the centre for bull-and-horse rearing communities. Twice a year crowds flock here to participate in the bull-running through the streets and watch the *tourada* and traditional horsemanship. The animated and gaudy Festa do Colete Encarnado (named after the red waistcoat worn by *campinos*, the Ribatejo herdsmen) takes place over several days in early July. The festival is a lively occasion with folk dancing, boat races on the Tagus and sardines grilled in the street. A similar festival, the Feira de Outubro, takes place in October.

Archaeological exhibits and artifacts relating to regional

history are on display in the **Museu Municipal**.

The town centre retains an exuberantly tiled covered market dating from the 1920s. Further east, on Largo da Misericórdia, striking 18th-century *azulejos* adorn the chancel of the Misericórdia church. South of town, the Ponte Marechal Carmona, built in 1951, is the only bridge across the River Tagus between Santarém to the north and Lisbon to the south.

🏛 Museu Municipal
Rua Serpa Pinto 65. **Tel** 263 280 350.
Open 9:30am–12:30pm & 2–5:30pm
Tue–Sun. **Closed** public holidays.

Bull-running (*largada*) in Vila Franca de Xira

Environs

At the **Centro Equestre da Lezíria Grande** in Póvos, 3 km (2 miles) south, you can watch stylish dressage displays on Lusitanian horses (*see p302*).

☯ Centro Equestre da Lezíria Grande
N1. **Tel** 263 285 160. **Open** Tue–Sun.
Closed 1 Jan, Easter, Aug, 25 Dec.

㉒ Alenquer

Road map C5. 🅰 42,000. 🚌
ℹ Parque Vaz Monteiro (263 711
133). 🏛 2nd Mon of month.

Vila Alta, the old part of town,
climbs steeply up the slopes
of the hillside, high above the
newer town by the river. In
the central Praça Luís de
Camões, the 15th-century
church of São Pedro contains
the tomb of the humanist
chronicler and native son,
Damião de Góis (1501–74).
Pêro de Alenquer, a navigator
for the explorers Bartolomeu
Dias in 1488 and Vasco da
Gama in 1497 (see pp52–3),
was also born here. Uphill,
near the ruins of a 13th-
century castle, the monastery
church of São Francisco retains
a Manueline cloister and a
13th-century portal. Founded
in 1222, this was Portugal's
first Franciscan monastery.

Environs
At Meca, 5 km (3 miles) northwest, is the huge pilgrimage
church of Santa Quitéria, where
a blessing of animals takes place
each May.

Defensive walls and the castle overlooking Torres Vedras

㉓ Torres Vedras

Road map B5. 🅰 74,800. 🚉 🚌
ℹ Rua 9 de Abril (261 310 483).
🏛 Apr–Oct: 1st Sat of month.

The town is closely linked
with the Lines of Torres Vedras,
fortified defenses built by the
Duke of Wellington to repel
Napoleon's troops during the
Peninsular War (see p58). North
of the town, near the restored
fort of São Vicente, traces of
trenches and bastions are still
visible, but along most of the
lines the forts and earthworks
have gone, buried by time and
rapid change.

Above the town, the restored
walls of the 13th-century castle
embrace a shady garden and
the church of Santa Maria do
Castelo. Down in the town, on
Praça 25 de Abril, a memorial
to those who died in the
Peninsular War stands in front
of the 16th-century Convento
da Graça. Today the monastery
houses the well-lit **Museu
Municipal**. A room devoted
to the Peninsular War displays
a model of the lines; other
interesting exhibits include a
15th-century Flemish School
Retábulo da Vida da Virgem.
Open for mass at weekends,
the monastery church, Igreja
da Graça, has a 17th-century
gilded altarpiece. In a niche in
the chancel is the tomb of São
Gonçalo de Lagos (see p326).

Beyond the pedestrian Rua 9
de Abril, the Manueline church
of São Pedro greets the visitor
with an exotic winged dragon
on the portal. The interior has a
painted wooden ceiling, and
colourful 18th-century azulejo
panels depicting scenes of daily
life adorn the walls. Behind the
church, on Rua Cândido dos Reis,
is a 16th-century water fountain,
the Chafariz dos Canos.

🏛 **Museu Municipal**
Praça 25 de Abril. **Tel** 261 310 484.
Open Tue–Sun. **Closed** 1 Jan, Easter
Sun, 1 May, 25 Dec. 🚫

The Lines of Torres Vedras

In October 1809, to save Lisbon
from Napoleonic invasion, Arthur
Wellesley (later the Duke of
Wellington) ordered an arc of defensive
lines (Linhas de Torres) to be built. When
complete, over 600 guns and 152 redoubts
(masonry forts) lay along two lines
stretching from the sea to the River Tagus.
One was 46 km (29 miles) long, from the
Sizandro river mouth, west of Torres Vedras, to Alhandra, south
of Vila Franca de Xira. The second line, running
behind the first as far as the sea, was 39 km
(24 miles) long. A short third line covered the
possibility of retreat and embarkation.
Construction of the lines took place in extraordinary secrecy: rivers had to be dammed,
earthworks raised, hills shifted and homes
and farms demolished, but within a year
the chain of hilltop fortresses was
complete. On 14 October 1810,
General Masséna, at the head of
65,000 French troops, saw with
astonishment the vastly altered and
fortified landscape and realized it was
impregnable. In November, the invaders
fell back to Santarém (see p197) and
in 1811, suffering hunger and defeat,
withdrew beyond the Spanish border.

**Flintlock
pistol from
Peninsular War**

Portrait of the Duke of
Wellington, 1814

THE BEIRAS

Stretching from the Spanish frontier to the sea, the Beiras are a bulwark between the cool green north and the parched south. This diverse region encompasses the heights of the Serra da Estrela and the salt marshes of the Ria de Aveiro, and its towns vary from lively Figueira da Foz to the stately old university town of Coimbra.

The three provinces of the Beiras, which form a part of the Centro region, may not be a tourist hub, but their past commercial and defensive significance has left its mark. In Beira Litoral, the prows of Aveiro's seaweed boats are a legacy of trade with the Phoenicians. All over Beira Baixa, from Castelo Branco to little granite villages, are relics of foreign occupations, and Viseu, Beira Alta's capital, grew up at a crossroads of Roman trading routes.

The Romans were never as firmly entrenched here as further south, but the ruins of Conímbriga speak eloquently of the elegant city that once stood here, and which gave its name to Coimbra, the principal city of Beira Litoral. Afonso Henriques, as king of the new nation of Portugal (see p46), moved his court to Coimbra, the young country's capital for over a century.

The upheavals of the nation's founding and a hard-won independence have left a rich heritage of castles and fortified towns.

Conscious of Spain's proximity and claim on their land, successive Portuguese kings constructed a great defensive chain of forts along the vulnerable eastern border. The seemingly impregnable walls of Almeida still stand as a reminder of the region's unsettled history. These border fortresses continued to prove vital in the fight for independence from Spain in the 17th century, and again against Napoleon's forces (see p58) . Even Buçaco, revered for the peace and sanctity of its forest, is known also as the site of Wellington's successful stand against Masséna.

Despite the unforgiving terrain, the Beiras are the source of some gastronomic treats: Portugal's favourite cheese is made in the Serra da Estrela, and the lush Bairrada district around Mealhada is renowned for its *leitão*, suckling pig. The region's red wines are among Portugal's best known: elegant Bairradas and powerful Dãos (see pp32–3) are particularly noteworthy.

Distinctive candy-striped beach houses in Costa Nova, between the Ria de Aveiro and the sea

◀ Boats anchored at the Canal de São Roque, Aveiro

Exploring the Beiras

The Beiras, encompassing some of Portugal's finest scenery, comprise three regions. Along the Beira Litoral are the sleepy backwaters of the Ria de Aveiro and, in contrast, the busy seaside resort of Figueira da Foz. The stately old university city of Coimbra repays exploration, and is a convenient base for visiting the historic forest of Buçaco and several of Portugal's spas.

Inland lies Viseu, the charming capital of Beira Alta, on the route to the medieval strongholds of Guarda, Trancoso and the border castles. One of the country's highest mountains, the Serra da Estrela, separate the Beira Alta from the little-visited Beira Baixa, where Monsanto, voted "Most Portuguese Village", and the handsome little city of Castelo Branco are contrasting attractions.

Coimbra's Museu Nacional Machado de Castro, with a fine sculpture collection

Sights at a Glance

1. Arouca
2. Santa Maria da Feira
3. Ovar
4. *Aveiro pp206–7*
5. Praia de Mira
6. Figueira da Foz
7. Montemor-o-Velho
8. *Coimbra pp208–13*
9. Conímbriga
10. Penela
11. Lousã
12. *Buçaco pp216–17*
13. Luso
14. Arganil
15. Piódão
16. Oliveira do Hospital
17. Caramulo
18. Viseu
19. Sernancelhe
20. Trancoso
21. Celorico da Beira
22. Almeida
24. Guarda
25. *Serra da Estrela pp224–5*
26. Belmonte
27. Sabugal
28. Penamacor
29. Monsanto
30. Idanha-a-Velha
31. Castelo Branco

Tours

23. Border Castles Tour

Summer at the seaside in popular Figueira da Foz

| 0 kilometres | 25 |
| 0 miles | 15 |

vineyards between Viseu and Mangualde

Getting Around

A rail network links the principal cities to smaller towns, but stations are often outside the town. Buses run from Coimbra to outlying areas, and local buses link villages and towns throughout the region. The most convenient way to explore the Beiras, however, is by car. The Porto-Lisbon A1 (E2) motorway passes close to Coimbra and Aveiro, while the A25 motorway links Aveiro and the eastern uplands. Long inclines and bad bends make the A25 Portugal's worst road for accidents. All but the major routes are relatively traffic-free and a pleasure to drive, although unpaved surfaces can still be expected.

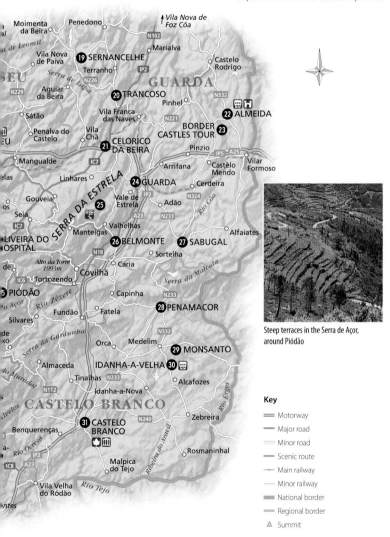

Steep terraces in the Serra de Açor, around Piódão

Key

- ▬▬ Motorway
- ▬ Major road
- ▭ Minor road
- ▬ Scenic route
- ✷ Main railway
- — Minor railway
- ▬▬ National border
- ▬▬ Regional border
- △ Summit

❶ Arouca

Road map C2. 🅰 24,000. 🚌
ℹ Rua Alfredo Vaz Pinto (256 940 258). 🅐 5 & 20 of month.

This small town in a green valley owes its principal attraction, the great **Mosteiro de Arouca**, to its saintly royal benefactor, Mafalda. Princess Mafalda was born in 1195, the daughter of Sancho I. She was betrothed to the teenage Prince Enrique of Castile, but when he died in an accident, Mafalda took the veil in Arouca. Under her, the convent became Cistercian and Mafalda's wealth and dedication made the house highly influential. She died in 1256, and her incorrupt corpse was discovered in 1616, leading to her beatification in 1793.

For over a thousand years the convent has stood beside Arouca's church on the cobbled main square. In the early 18th century the church underwent costly redecoration: 104 carved choir stalls are surmounted by paintings in sumptuous gilded panels, and the organ and chancel retable are also heavily gilded. Honoured with its own altar is a recumbent effigy of Santa Mafalda in a silver and ebony casket; her mummified remains lie below the casket.

Guided tours take visitors round the convent's museum, in which are displayed some exquisite silver monstrances, furniture and religious works

of art, including two paintings by 18th-century artist André Gonçalves, showing Mafalda saving the monastery from fire. The Neo-Classical double cloister, begun in 1781, the large refectory and kitchen and a chapterhouse covered with cheerful Coimbra tiles of rural scenes can also be visited.

🏛 **Mosteiro de Arouca**
Largo de Santa Mafalda. **Tel** 256 943 321. **Open** Tue–Sun. **Closed** public holidays. 🎦 🎫

Silver and ebony casket in the convent church at Arouca, containing the effigy of Santa Mafalda

❷ Santa Maria da Feira

Road map C2. 🅰 140,500. 🚊 🚌
ℹ Rua Dr. Roberto Alves 52 (256 370 802). 🅐 20 of month.

Prosperous from cork and its thriving markets, Santa Maria derives its name from long tradition – a document from 1117 refers to "Terra de Santa Maria, a place people call Feira", after the fairs held here. A large market each month in the broad Rossio upholds the

town's reputation. A double stairway leads from the Rossio to the Igreja dos Lóios, with blue 17th-century tiles decorating the façades of its two symmetrical bell towers. On the opposite side of the Rossio, winding streets of solid merchants' houses from the 18th and 19th centuries lead to a decorative stairway with an ornamental fountain. This rises up to the 18th-century Misericórdia church.

Crowning a wooded hill on the southern edge of the town is the fairy-tale **castle**. Although much is a 20th-century reconstruction, it follows the 15th-century design of a local, Fernão Pereira, and his son. They added crenellations and towers to an 11th-century fort which in turn had been built over a temple to a local god. The title of Conde da Feira was bestowed on Pereira, and the castle remained in his family until 1700. There is not much inside the castle now, but it retains its romantic air.

🏰 **Castle**
Largo do Castelo. **Tel** 256 372 248. **Open** Tue–Sun, including public hols. 🎦

❸ Ovar

Road map C2. 🅰 56,300. 🚊 🚌
ℹ Rua Elias Garcia (256 572 215). 🅐 Tue, Thu & Sat (general), 3rd Sun of month (antiques).

Varinas, the hardworking Portuguese fishwives, take their name from Var, or O Var, this small town which earned its living from the sea and the Ria de Aveiro that spreads out to the south (see p207). Industry has arrived in the shape of foundries and steel mills, but oxen still plod along the roads.

Gleaming tiles cover many of the small houses, as well as the twin-towered 17th-century Igreja Matriz in Avenida do Bom Reitor. In the town centre the Calvary chapel of the 18th-century Capela dos Passos is adorned with woodcarvings carrying a shell motif.

The pinnacled and crenellated castle crowning Santa Maria da Feira

House façades in Ovar with their traditional eye-catching blue tiles

Ovar's Carnaval parade is one of Portugal's most colourful, and its sponge cake, *pão-de-ló*, is highly esteemed. Tableaux in the **Museu de Ovar** recreate the lifestyle of a bygone era, alongside displays of regional costume and dolls. There are also mementoes of *Júlio Dinis*, a popular Portuguese novelist who lived in Ovar in the 1800s.

🏛 Museu de Ovar
Rua Heliodoro Salgado 11.
Tel 256 572 822. **Open** Tue–Sat.
Closed Sun, Mon, public hols. 🖼

❹ Aveiro

See pp206–7.

Fishing boat on the beach at Praia de Mira

❺ Praia de Mira

Road map C3. 🔼 5,000. 🚌 🚏 **ℹ** Av da Barrinha (924 473 751). 🛒 11, 23 & 30 of month.

Tourism is only now making an impact on this stretch of coast backed by a wooded reserve, the Mata Nacional das Dunas de Mira. Praia de Mira, with the dunes and Atlantic on one side and the peaceful lagoon of Barrinha de Mira on the other, is a pretty fishing village developing as a resort. High-prowed fishing boats are still drawn up the

spectacular beach by oxen, but leisure craft now cruise the shore and the inland waterways, and the fishermen's striped *palheiros (see p26)*, popular as seaside cottages, are fast vanishing amid shops, bars and cafés.

❻ Figueira da Foz

Road map C3. 🔼 63,000. 🚉 🚌 **ℹ** Avenida 25 de Abril (233 422 610). 🛒 Closed Sun in winter.

Lively and cosmopolitan, this popular resort has a busy marina, a casino and a wide, curving beach with breakers that attract intrepid surfers.

General jollity is the keynote, but the **Museu Municipal Dr Santos Rocha** has a notable archaeological collection, and an eclectic display extending to Arraiolos carpets *(see p307)*, religious art, Indo-Portuguese furniture, a musical archive, fans and photographs.

The amazing interior of the **Casa do Paço** is lined with 8,000 Delft tiles taken from a shipwreck in the late 1600s. The 16th-century fortress of Santa Catarina stands where the Mondego meets the sea. The Duke of Wellington briefly made this little fort his base when he landed to retake Portugal from Napoleon in 1808 *(see p58)*.

🏛 Museu Municipal Dr Santos Rocha
Rua Calouste Gulbenkian. **Tel** 233 402 840. **Open** 9:30am–5pm Tue–Fri, 2–7pm Sat (Jul & Aug: 9:30am–6pm Tue–Fri, 2–7pm Sat & Sun). **Closed** 1 Jan, Easter, 1 May, 25 Dec.

🏛 Casa do Paço
Largo Professor Vitor Guerra 4 . **Tel** 233 430 103. **Open** call ahead of your visit.

❼ Montemor-o-Velho

Road map C3. 🔼 2,600. 🚌 **ℹ** Castelo de Montemor-o-Velho (239 680 380). 🛒 every other Wed.

This attractive and historic hillside town rises out of fields of rice and maize beside the River Mondego. Its **castle**, which served as a primary defence of the city of Coimbra *(see pp208–13)* is mostly 14th century, but it had previously been a Moorish stronghold, and the keep has fragments of Roman stonework. The church of Santa Maria de Alcaçova within its walls was founded in 1090. Restored in the 15th century, its naves and arches reflect the Manueline style.

Montemor was the birthplace of Fernão Mendes Pinto (1510–83), famous for the colourful accounts of his travels in the east. Another explorer, Diogo de Azambuja (died 1518), is buried here. Columbus is said to have sailed with Azambuja, who intrepidly navigated along the West African coast. His tomb, by the Manueline master Diogo Pires, is in the Convento de Nossa Senhora dos Anjos in the square of the same name (ask at the tourist office for key). Its 17th-century façade hides an earlier, more lavish interior, with Manueline and Renaissance influences.

🏰 Castle
Rua do Castelo. **Open** daily.

Enjoying café life in the spring sunshine of Figueira da Foz

❹ Aveiro

This little city, once a great sea port, has a long history – Aveiro's salt pans were featured in the will of Countess Mumadona in AD 959. By the 16th century it was a considerable town, rich from salt and the *bacalhoeiros* fishing for cod off Newfoundland. When storms silted up the harbour in 1575 this wealth vanished rapidly, and the town languished beside an unhealthy lagoon, the *ria*. Only in the 19th century did Aveiro regain some of its prosperity; it is now ringed with industry and is home to an important university. The *ria* and canals give Aveiro its individual character.

Old Quarter

Tucked in between the Canal das Pirâmides and the Canal de São Roque are the neat, whitewashed houses of Aveiro's fishermen. In the early morning the focus of activity is the Mercado do Peixe, where the fish from the night's catch is auctioned.

Bridge across the Canal de São Roque

Skirting the Canal Central, along Rua João de Mendonça, are Art Nouveau mansions and some of the many *pastelarias* selling Aveiro's speciality: *ovos moles*. Literally "soft eggs", these are a rich confection of sweetened egg yolk in candied casings shaped like fish or barrels. As so often in Portugal, the original recipe is credited to nuns. *Ovos moles* are sold by weight or in little barrels.

Across the Canal Central

South of the Canal Central and the bustling Praça Humberto Delgado are the principal historic buildings of Aveiro. The Misericórdia church in the Praça da República dates from the 16th century, its façade of *azulejos* framing a splendid Mannerist portal. In the same square stands the stately 18th-century Paços do Concelho, or town hall, with its distinctive Tuscan-style pilasters.

Nearby, opposite the museum, is Aveiro's modest 15th-century cathedral of São Domingos. The figures of the Three Graces over the door on the Baroque façade were added in 1719.

A short walk south lies the **Igreja das Carmelitas**, its nave and chancel decorated with paintings of the life of the Carmelite reformer, St Teresa.

🏛 Museu de Aveiro

Ave Santa Joana Princesa. **Tel** 234 423 297. **Open** 10am–12:30pm, 1:30–6pm Tue–Sun. **Closed** 1 Jan, 1 May, 25 Dec. 🅐

The former Mosteiro de Jesus is full of mementoes of Santa Joana, who died here in 1490. The daughter of Afonso V, Joana retreated to the convent in 1472 and spent the rest of her life here. She was beatified in 1693 and her ornamental Baroque marble tomb, completed 20 years later, is in the lower choir. Simpler in style are the 18th-century paintings in the chapel, showing scenes of her life. This was once the needle-work room where Santa Joana died. Among Portuguese primitive paintings is a 15th-century full-face portrait of the princess in court dress.

Also part of the museum are the superb gilded chancel (1725–9), 15th-century cloisters and refectory faced in Coimbra tiles. Between the refectory and chapterhouse lies the Gothic tomb of an armoured knight, Dom João de Albuquerque.

Environs

Lying about 8 km (5 miles) south of Aveiro, at Ílhavo, is the modern block of the **Museu Marítimo de Ílhavo**, where the region's long seafaring history

The Cathedral of Aveiro, also known as the Church of St Dominic, Aveiro

For hotels and restaurants in this area see pp390–91 and pp404–5

Raking the salt as it dries in the pans fringing the Ria de Aveiro

is told through displays of fishing craft and equipment, with maritime memorabilia from shells to model boats.

About 4 km (2 miles) further south a small sign points to the **Museu da Vista Alegre**. A name renowned in the world of porcelain (see p417), the Vista Alegre factory was established in 1824, and samples of its fine porcelain can be bought from the factory shop. The museum traces the history of the factory, and has displays of porcelain (together with some crystal glass) from the 1850s to the present day.

🏛 **Museu Marítimo de Ílhavo**
Avenida Dr Rocha Madahíl. **Tel** 234 329 990. **Open** 10am–6pm Tue–Sat, 2–6pm Sun. **Closed** public hols.

VISITORS' CHECKLIST

Practical Information
Map C3. 🏔 73,500.
ℹ Rua João Mendonça 8 (234 423 680). 🗓 28 of month. 🎉 Jul–Aug: Festa da Ria.

Transport
🚉 Avenida Dr Lourenço Peixinho. 🚌 Avenida Dr Lourenço Peixinho. ⛴ Forte de Barra–São Jacinto: daily.

🏛 **Museu da Vista Alegre**
Tel 234 320 628. **Open** May–Sep: 10am–7:30pm daily; Oct–Apr 10am–7pm daily. **Closed** public hols.

Ria de Aveiro

Old maritime charts show no lagoon here, but in 1575 a terrible storm raised a sand bar that blocked the harbour. Denied access to the sea, Aveiro declined, its population cut down by the fever bred in the stagnant waters. It was not until 1808 that the *barra nova* was created, linking Aveiro once more to the sea.

The lagoon which remains covers some 65 sq km (25 sq miles), and is nearly 50 km (30 miles) long, from Furadouro south past Aveiro's salt pans and the Reserva Natural das Dunas de São Jacinto (Nature Reserve of São Jacinto) to Costa Nova. The reserve includes beaches, dunes and woods as well as the lagoon, and is home to a large and varied bird population, including pintails and goshawks. Of the boats seen here, the most elegant is the *moliceiro*. Despite the bright, often humorous decoration on its high, curving prow, this is a working boat, harvesting *moliço* (seaweed) for fertilizer. Chemical fertilizers have drastically cut demand for *moliço*, but a few of the stately craft survive; the Festa da Ria is a chance to see them in full sail.

Intricately painted prow of a *moliceiro* in the Ria

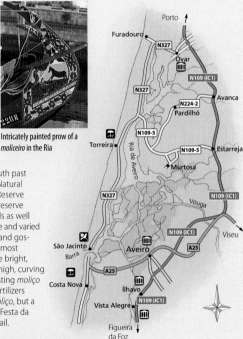

Key
━━ Motorway
━━ Major road
━━ Minor road
── Other road
▢ Salt marsh

The seaward waterfront at the fishing village of Torreira

⑧ Coimbra

The birthplace of six kings and the seat of Portugal's oldest university, Coimbra arouses an affection in the Portuguese shared by no other city. To the Romans the town founded on Alcaçova hill was Aeminium, but as its importance grew it took on the mantle and name of nearby Conímbriga (see p214). Coimbra was wrested from the Moors in AD 878, only to come under their control again a century later, until finally freed by Ferdinand the Great of Castile in 1064. When Afonso Henriques, the first king of Portugal, decided to move his capital south from Guimarães in 1139 (see pp46–7), his choice was Coimbra, an honour it retained until 1256. For the Portuguese, Coimbra carries the roots of nationhood and, for visitors, a wealth of fascinating historic associations.

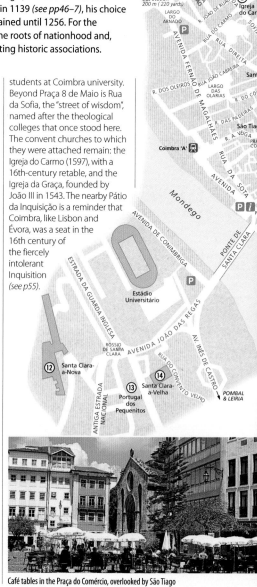

Orientation

In the historic heart of the city, high above the Mondego, lie the cathedrals, university and a fine museum, but a first impression of Coimbra is likely to be of commerce, not culture. Shops, traffic and the railway rule the riverside and around the Praça do Comércio. The Largo da Portagem is a useful starting point, and river trips depart from nearby, alongside the Parque Dr Manuel Braga.

Tomb of Portugal's first king, Afonso Henriques, in Santa Cruz

The Lower Town

From Largo da Portagem, Rua Ferreira Borges leads past shops, lively bars, restaurants and *pastelarias* to the Praça do Comércio. In one corner of this bustling square stands the church of São Tiago. Its plain façade is a restoration of the 12th-century original, but inside is an exuberant Rococo altarpiece in gilded wood.

Running north of the Praça do Comércio, Rua Visconde da Luz leads to the Praça 8 de Maio and the historic church of Santa Cruz (see p211). Portugal's first two kings are buried here, and monks from the adjacent monastery of Santa Cruz tutored the first

students at Coimbra university. Beyond Praça 8 de Maio is Rua da Sofia, the "street of wisdom", named after the theological colleges that once stood here. The convent churches to which they were attached remain: the Igreja do Carmo (1597), with a 16th-century retable, and the Igreja da Graça, founded by João III in 1543. The nearby Pátio da Inquisição is a reminder that Coimbra, like Lisbon and Évora, was a seat in the 16th century of the fiercely intolerant Inquisition (see p55).

Café tables in the Praça do Comércio, overlooked by São Tiago

The stunning garden of Quinta das Lagrimas, in Coimbra

VISITORS' CHECKLIST

Practical Information
Road map C3. 🚗 143,800.
ℹ️ Praça da República (939 010 084); Universidade de Coimbra (239 242 744); Largo da Portagem (239 488 120).
🚌 Mon–Sat. 🎉 May: Queima das Fitas.

Transport
🚉 Coimbra A, Av Emídio Navarro; Coimbra B, N of city, on N11. 🚌 Av Fernão de Magalhães.

The tower now houses an arts and crafts gallery. Among the houses lining the maze of steep alleys that wind up to the top of the hill are a number of *repúblicas*, student lodgings since medieval times.

Coimbra's two cathedrals, Sé Velha and Sé Nova (*see p210*), lie in the shadow of the hilltop university (*see pp212–13*). Beyond is the upper town's main square, Praça da República.

Across the Mondego

It is worth crossing the river just to admire the view of old Coimbra. The two convents of Santa Clara (*see p211*) on the southern bank have close ties with Santa Isabel, and with Inês de Castro, Pedro I's luckless lover, who was stabbed to death here in 1355 (*see p185*). A romantic legend tells how a spring, the Fonte dos Amores, rose on the spot. This can be seen in the garden of the 18th-century Quinta das Lágrimas, now a hotel (*see p390*), just south of Santa Clara-a-Velha.

Coimbra City Centre

0 metres 200
0 yards 200

The Upper Town
The altered and restored 12th-century Arco de Almedina, off the Rua Ferreira Borges, is the gateway to the old city (in Arabic *medina* means town). Steps lead up past the Torre de Anto, whose Renaissance windows and medallions are from the workshop of the 16th-century sculptor Jean de Rouen.

The Arco de Almedina arching over the steps to the upper town

Exploring Coimbra

That the citizens of Coimbra fondly call their river, the Mondego, "O Rio dos Poetas" gives a clue to the affection they have for their vibrant and beautiful city. From the university (see pp212–13) at the top of Alcáçova hill, down the narrow streets and stairways to the lower town, the city is crammed with historic buildings and treasures (and, all too often, slow-moving traffic). Most sights are within walking distance of each other, and despite its steep hill, Coimbra is a city best appreciated on foot. Across the Mondego there are further historic sights and an unusual theme park for children.

Elaborate façade of the Sé Nova

The Sé Velha's gilded altarpiece

🏛 Sé Velha

Largo da Sé Velha. **Tel** 239 825 273. **Open** 10am–6pm Mon–Sat, 11:30am–6pm Sun. 🕭 6pm Mon–Fri, 7pm Sat & 10am Sun. **Closed** Sun & public hols. 🚫 to church and cloister.

The fortress-style Old Cathedral is widely regarded as the finest Romanesque building in Portugal, a celebration in stone of the triumph over the Moors in 1064. The nation's first

king, Afonso Henriques, made the city of Coimbra his capital and his son, Sancho I, was crowned here in 1185, soon after the cathedral was completed.

Inside, square piers lead the eye up the nave to the flamboyant retable over the altar. The work of Flemish woodcarvers in about 1502, this depicts the birth of Christ, the Assumption and many saints. A 16th-century altarpiece in the south transept is also highly decorated, as is the Manueline font, thought to be by Diogo Pires the Younger. In contrast is the quiet restraint of the cloister, built in 1218 but restored in the 18th century.

The tomb of the city's first Christian governor, Sisinando (a Muslim convert who died in 1091), lies in the chapterhouse, and in the north aisle is the tomb of the Byzantine Dona Vetaça (died 1246), tutor to the wife of King Dinis, the saintly Queen Isabel (see p49).

🏛 Sé Nova

Largo da Sé Nova. **Tel** 239 823 138. **Open** 9am–6:30pm daily. 🕭 6pm Mon–Sat, 11am & 7pm Sun. 🚫

New is a relative term, as this church – a short walk from the university – was founded by the Jesuits in 1598. (Their adjacent Colégio das Onze Mil Virgens is today part of the sciences faculty.) The Jesuit Order was banned by the Marquês de Pombal in 1759 (see p56) but their church became the episcopal seat in 1772. Jesuit saints still look out from the façade.

The interior, more spacious than the Sé Velha, is barrel-vaulted, with a dome over the crossing. To the left of the entrance is a Manueline-style octagonal font brought, like the choir stalls, from the Sé Velha. The paintings above the stalls are copies of Italian masters. The altarpiece in the 17th-century chancel, featuring more Jesuit saints, is flanked by a pair of 18th-century organs.

Coimbra seen from the Mondego, with the university's landmark bell tower crowning Alcáçova hill

🏛 Museu Nacional Machado de Castro

Largo Dr José Rodrigues. **Tel** 239 53 070. **Open** 10am–6pm Wed–Sun, 2–6pm Tue. **Closed** 1 Jan, Easter, 1 May, 25 Dec. 🖼 (free first Sun of month).
🌐 **museumachadocastro.pt**

The elegant 16th-century loggias of the former bishop's palace are the setting for the display of some of Portugal's finest sculpture. The museum is named after master sculptor Joaquim Machado de Castro (1731–1822). Among the medieval pieces is an endearing knight holding a mace. Also in the collection, along with furnishings and vestments, are paintings from the 12th to 20th centuries, including the *Assumption of Mary Magdalen* by the Master of Sardoal.

An intriguing feature is the Criptoportico de Aeminium, a maze of underground passages holding a collection of Roman sculpture and stelae and Visigothic artifacts.

Claustro do Silêncio (Cloister of Silence) in the monastery of Santa Cruz

🏛 Santa Cruz

Praça 8 de Maio. **Tel** 239 822 941. **Open** 9am–5pm Mon–Fri, 9am–noon & 2–6pm Sat, 4–5:30pm Sun. 🖼 to cloister.

Founded by the canons of St Augustine in 1131, the church and monastery of Santa Cruz are rich in examples of the city's early 16th-century school of sculpture. Carvings by Nicolau Chanterène and Jean de Rouen adorn the church's Portal da Majestade, designed by Diogo de Castilho in 1523. The chapterhouse by Diogo Boitac is Manueline in style, as are the Claustro do Silêncio and the choir stalls, carved in 1518 with a frieze about exploration. Portugal's first two kings, Afonso Henriques and Sancho I, were reinterred here

in 1520. Their elaborate tombs are thought to be by Chanterène, also buried here.

🌿 Jardim Botânico

Calçada Martim de Freitas. **Tel** 239 855 215. **Open** Oct–Mar: 9am–5:30pm daily; Apr–Sep: 9am–8pm daily.

These, Portugal's largest botanical gardens, were created in 1772 when the Marquês de Pombal introduced the study of natural history at the University of Coimbra.

The entrance, near the 16th-century aqueduct of São Sebastião, leads into 20 ha (50 acres) devoted to a remarkable collection of some 1,200 plants, including many rare and exotic species. The gardens are used for research, but are laid out as pleasure gardens, with greenhouses and a wild area overlooking the Mondego.

🏛 Santa Clara-a-Velha

Santa Clara. **Tel** 239 801 160. **Open** 10am–7pm Tue–Sun (to 6pm in winter). **Closed** 1 Jan, 1 May, 25 Dec. 🖼 (free first Sun of month).

Santa Isabel, the widow of King Dinis, had the convent of Santa Clara rebuilt for her retreat. She died in 1336 in Estremoz (*see p306*) but was buried here. Inês de Castro was also laid to rest here 20 years later, but was re-entombed at Alcobaça (*see pp184–5*).

Almost from the day it was built, Santa Clara suffered from flooding; it was finally abandoned in 1677. In 1696 Santa Isabel's remains were moved to the Convent of Santa Clara-a-Nova. The original Gothic church, in silted ruins since the late 1600s, has at last been restored.

🏛 Santa Clara-a-Nova

Alto de Santa Clara. **Tel** 239 441 674. **Open** 9am–6pm daily (Apr–Sep: to 7pm). 🖼

The vast "new" convent of the Poor Clares was built between 1649 and 1677 to house the nuns from Santa Clara-a-Velha on drier land uphill. The building was designed by a mathematics professor, João Turriano, and although intended as a convent, now serves in part as a barracks for the army. In the richly

Open-air study in the Jardim Botânico

Baroque church, pride of place is given to the silver tomb of Santa Isabel, installed in 1696 and paid for by the people of Coimbra. The saint's original tomb, a single stone, lies in the lower choir and polychrome wooden panels in the aisles tell the story of her life. The convent's large cloister, built by the Hungarian Carlos Mardel, was contributed in 1733 by João V, a generous benefactor who was well-known for his charity to nuns.

🎠 Portugal dos Pequenitos

Santa Clara. **Tel** 239 801 170. **Open** daily. Mid-Oct–Feb: 10am–5pm; Mar–May: 10am–7pm; Jun–mid-Sep: 9am–8pm; mid-Sep–mid-Oct: 10am–7pm. **Closed** 25 Dec. 🖼 ♿
🌐 **portugaldospequenitos.pt**

At this world in miniature, children and adults alike can explore scaled-down versions of Portugal's finest national buildings, whole villages of typical regional architecture, and pagodas and temples representing the far-flung reaches of the former Portuguese empire.

Child-sized model of an Algarve manor house in Portugal dos Pequenitos

Coimbra University

In 1290 King Dinis founded a university in Lisbon, one of the world's oldest and most illustrious. In 1537 it was transferred to Coimbra and located in what used to be King Afonso's palace. Study was mostly of theology, medicine and law until the reforms by the Marquês de Pombal in the 1770s broadened the curriculum. Several 19th-century literary figures, including Eça de Queirós *(see p59)*, were alumni of Coimbra. Many buildings were replaced after the 1940s, but the halls around the Pátio das Escolas echo with 700 years of learning. Coimbra University is a UNESCO World Heritage site.

Museu de Arte Sacra
As well as works of art on religious themes, this museum has vestments, chalices and books of early sacred music. It is currently closed.

★ **Capela de São Miguel**
Although begun in 1517 the chapel's interior is mostly 17th and 18th century. The *azulejos*, ornate walls, even the fine Mannerist altar, are eclipsed by the dazzling organ, with angels trumpeting its Baroque glory.

KEY

① **Portrait of João V (c.1730)**

② **The portal** of Capela de São Miguel is Manueline in style, the work of Marcos Pires before his death in 1521.

③ **The bell tower**, symbol of the university, can be seen from all over the city. The best known of its three bells, called *a cabra*, the goat, has summoned generations of students to lectures since the tower was completed in 1733.

④ **The Via Latina** is a colonnaded walkway added to the original palace in the 18th century. The Portuguese coat of arms above the double staircase is crowned by a statue of Wisdom, while below, figures of Justice and Fortitude flank José I, in whose reign (1750–77) the Marquês de Pombal modernized the university.

★ **Biblioteca Joanina**
Named after its benefactor, João V (whose coat of arms is over the door), the library was built in the early 18th century. Its rooms, rich in gilt and exotic wood, are lined with 300,000 books.

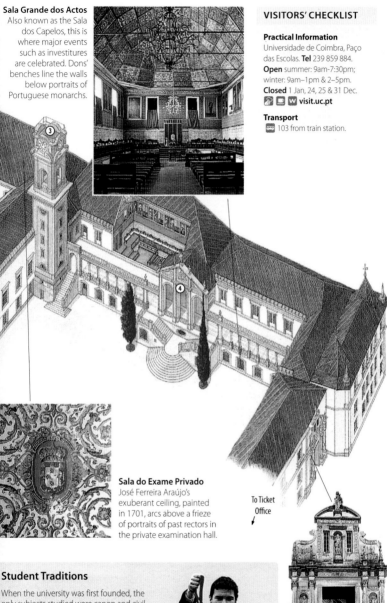

Sala Grande dos Actos
Also known as the Sala dos Capelos, this is where major events such as investitures are celebrated. Dons' benches line the walls below portraits of Portuguese monarchs.

VISITORS' CHECKLIST

Practical Information
Universidade de Coimbra, Paço das Escolas. **Tel** 239 859 884.
Open summer: 9am–7:30pm; winter: 9am–1pm & 2–5pm.
Closed 1 Jan, 24, 25 & 31 Dec.
🖼 💻 🅦 visit.uc.pt

Transport
🚌 103 from train station.

Sala do Exame Privado
José Ferreira Araújo's exuberant ceiling, painted in 1701, arcs above a frieze of portraits of past rectors in the private examination hall.

To Ticket Office ↓

Student Traditions

When the university was first founded, the only subjects studied were canon and civil law, medicine and letters – grammar and philosophy. To indicate which faculty they belonged to, students began to pin coloured ribbons to their gowns: red for law, yellow for medicine, dark blue for letters. Much has changed in 700 years, but students are still initiated in rites whose origins are long forgotten, and in May, as the academic year ends, there is a ceremonial burning of ribbons, the Queima das Fitas.

Burning faculty ribbons in best scholastic tradition

Porta Férrea
Built in 1634, this heavy iron gate to the university *pátio* is flanked by figures representing the original faculties.

❾ Conímbriga

Road map C3. 2 km (1 mile) S of Condeixa-a-Nova. 🚌 from Coimbra. Site: **Open** 10am–7pm daily. **Closed** 1 Jan, 1 May, Easter Sun, 25 Dec. Museum: **Tel** 239 941 177. **Open** 10am–7pm daily. **Closed** 1 Jan, 1 May, Easter Sun, 25 Dec. 🖭 🚻 museum only.

This, the largest and most extensively excavated Roman site in Portugal (see pp44–5), was on the Roman road between Lisbon (Olisipo) and Braga (Bracara Augusta). There is evidence of Roman habitation here as early as the 2nd century BC, but even before this time there was a Celtic settlement here.

Under the Roman emperor Augustus, from about 25 BC, Conímbriga became a substantial town: baths, a forum and the aqueduct have been uncovered from this era. The finest buildings, however, date from the 2nd and 3rd centuries AD, and they provide a vivid image of a prosperous city.

Detail of a bedroom floor in a house near the entrance

The site is approached along a section of Roman road that led into the city from the east. Just to the left cluster the outlines of shops, baths and two once-luxurious houses, both with exquisite mosaic floors.

At Conímbriga is one of the largest houses discovered in the western Roman empire.

This opulent villa, known as the Casa de Cantaber, is built around ornamental pools in colonnaded gardens, with its own bath complex and a sophisticated heating system. Some of the fine mosaics in the museum probably came from this huge residence.

The Casa das Fontes, dating from the early 2nd century, is under a protective cover but walkways provide good views. Its mosaics and fountains, rare survivals, which give the house its name, form a strong image of the Roman taste for good living. The city's pools, and the baths and steam rooms of Trajan's *thermae*, were fed by a spring 3.5 km (2 miles) away via a mostly subterranean aqueduct. Official excavation was begun here in 1912, but a considerable part of the 13-ha (32-acre) site has yet to be explored, including an amphitheatre north of the city. In the 3rd or early 4th century, buildings were plundered for stone as defensive walls were hastily raised against Barbarian hordes. In a successful assault in AD 468, the Suevi burned the city and murdered the inhabitants. Excavated skeletons may date from this episode.

An informative museum explains the history and layout of the site, and has exhibits of Roman busts, mosaics and coins alongside more ancient Celtic artifacts. There is also a restaurant and picnic site.

View of the church of São Miguel within the castle walls at Penela

❿ Penela

Road map C3. 🚹 6,500. 🚌 🚹 Praç do Município (239 560 120). 🗓 Thu.

Penela's thickset castle was buil in 1087 by Sisinando, governor of Coimbra, as part of the line of defences of the Mondego valley. Its squat towers provide wonderful views over the village and, to the east, of the wooded Serra da Lousã. The church within the castle walls, São Miguel, dates back to the 16th century. Below, in Penela itself, Santa Eufémia, dated 1551 above its decorative doorway, has a Roman capital used as a font.

Environs

Among walnut and olive grove 5 km (3 miles) to the west, is the tiny village of Rabaçal, whose tasty cheese, made with a mixture of sheep's and goat's milk, is a regional speciality. Some village women still mature the cheese rounds in darkened rooms in their homes

⓫ Lousã

Road map C3. 🚹 16,700. 🚉 🚌 🚹 Rua João Luso (239 990 040). 🗓 Tue & Sat.

The paper factory at Lousã, on the forested banks of the River Arouce, was opened in 1716 and is still working. Skilled papermakers imported from Italy and Germany by the Marquês de Pombal (see p56) brought prosperity, still evident in the handsome 18th-century

The central garden of the Casa das Fontes in Conímbriga

The castle at Arouce, near Lousã, oddly defenceless in its deep valley

houses. Most elegant of these is the Palácio dos Salazares, a private home in Rua Viscon-dessa do Espinhal. Also notable is the Misericórdia, with a 1568 Renaissance portal, in Rua do Comércio.

Environs

Deep in a valley, 3 km (2 miles) south of Lousã, is the Castelo de Arouce. Legend says it was built in the 11th century by a King Arunce who took refuge in the valley when fleeing from raiders. Permission to visit the castle is available from the town hall. Near the castle are the three shrines of the Santuário de Nossa Senhora da Piedade.

A viewpoint on the tortuous road south towards Castanheira de Pêra gives a splendid view across the valley. A turning east leads up to Alto do Trevim which, at 1,204 m (3,950 ft), is the highest point in the Serra de Lousã.

❷ Buçaco

See pp216–17.

❸ Luso

Road map C3. **⚄** 3,000. **▨** **ℹ** Rua Emídio Navarro 136 (231 939 133). **⊕** daily.

In the 11th century Luso was just a village linked to a monastery at Vacariça, but it developed into a lively spa town in the 18th century as its hot-water springs became a focus for tourism. The thermal waters, which originate from a spring below the Capela de São João, are said to be of therapeutic value in the treatment of a wide range of conditions, from bad circulation and muscle tone to renal problems and rheumatism.

There are a number of grand, if somewhat faded, hotels here, and an elegant Art Nouveau lobby adorns the former casino, but the main reason for visiting the resort is to enjoy its spa facilities. An additional attraction of Luso is the proximity of the treasured national forest of Buçaco, which is a powerful presence above the town.

Environs

Between Luso and Curia, Mealhada is an attractive small town in the heart of a region famous for *leitão*, suckling pig. This enormously popular dish is prominently advertised at numerous hotly competing restaurants in the area.

❹ Arganil

Road map D3. **⚄** 13,300. **▨** **ℹ** Avenida das Forças Armadas (235 200 137). **⊕** Thu.

Tradition says that this was a Roman city called Argos. In the 12th century, Dona Teresa, the mother of Afonso Henriques (*see pp46–7*), gave the town to the bishopric of Coimbra, whose incumbent also acquired the title of Conde de Arganil. Most of the town's architecture is unremarkable, but the church of São Gens, the Igreja Matriz in Rua de Visconde de Frias, dates back perhaps to the 14th century.

Menino Jesus in Mont' Alto sanctuary, Arganil

Environs

One of the most curious local sights is kept in the sanctuary of Mont'Alto, 3 km (2 miles) above the town. Here, the Capela do Senhor da Ladeira harbours the Menino Jesus, a Christ Child figure in a bicorne hat (part of a full wardrobe). He comes out for *festas* but the chapel key is otherwise available from the last house on the right.

Taking the spa waters at the Fonte de São João, Luso

Thermal Spas

In response to the Portuguese enthusiasm for thermal waters and health-orientated holidays, spa resorts have developed across the northern half of the country, with several of them in the Beiras, near Luso. All offer extensive sports facilities and a calm ambience as well as treatments for all the body's major systems. Most spas close for the winter, but Curia, 16 km (10 miles) northwest of Luso, is open all year for relaxation and treatments. Luso itself produces the country's best-known bottled mineral water.

⑫ Buçaco

Part ancient woodland, part arboretum, the National Forest of Buçaco is a magic place. As early as the 6th century it was a monastic retreat, and in 1628 the Carmelites built a monastery here, walling in the forest to keep the world at bay (women had already been banned by the pope in 1622). In their secluded forest the monks established contemplative walks, chapels – and trees. The trees, added to by Portuguese explorers, gained papal protection in 1632, and the 105 ha (260 acres) contain some 700 native and exotic species, including the venerable "Buçaco cedar". The peace of the forest was disturbed in 1810 as British and Portuguese troops fought the French on Buçaco ridge. In 1834 the monastery closed, but the forest endures, with its shady walks, hermits' grottoes and the astonishing Bussaco Palace Hotel at its centre.

★ Fonte Fria
This impressive cascade, fed by the greatest of the forest's six springs, tumbles down to a magnolia-fringed pool.

KEY

① **The Portas de Coimbra** incorporate the papal bulls defending the trees and forbidding entry to women.

② **Porta dos Degraus and steps leading to Luso**

③ **Tasmanian eucalyptus (1876)**

④ **The Porta da Rainha** was made for Catherine of Bragança, but when her visit in 1693 was cancelled the gateway was sealed up for 11 years.

⑤ **The Museu Militar** is devoted to the Peninsular War.

⑥ **The Monument to the Battle of Buçaco** marks Wellington's victory on the ridge of Buçaco on 27 September 1810. As the nearby Museu Militar explains, this decisive battle halted the French march on Coimbra.

⑦ **Porta da Cruz Alta**

⑧ **Cruz Alta**, the forest's highest point, has glorious views as far as the sea.

⑨ **The Buçaco cedar**, now 28 m (92 ft) high, is believed to have been planted in 1644.

Vale dos Fetos
Leading down to a small lake, the Valley of Ferns is lined with luxuriant specimens collected worldwide. The magnificent tree ferns give the valley a tropical air.

Key

— Wall

••• Route of Via Sacra

Monastery

Only the cloisters, chapel and a few monks' cells of the Carmelite monastery remain. A plaque records that Wellington slept in one of the cork-lined cells.

VISITORS' CHECKLIST

Practical Information
Road map C3. 3 km (2 miles) SE of Luso. **i** Luso (231 939 133).**Open** 9am–6pm (last adm: 5pm). Forest: **Open** daily. 🚗 for vehicles all year round. Museu Militar: Almas do Encarnadouro. **Tel** 231 937 000. **Open** Tue–Sun. 🚗 ♿ 📷 27 Sep: Anniversary of Battle of Buçaco.
W fmb.pt

Transport
🚌

0 metres   250
0 yards   250

★ Bussaco Palace Hotel

Completed in 1907, the Neo-Manueline folly of a hunting lodge built by Luigi Manini includes murals and tiles by prominent artists. *Azulejos* in the hall feature scenes of the Battle of Buçaco.

Bussaco Palace Hotel

King Carlos, who commissioned this extravaganza in 1888, never lived to see his creation. His son, Manuel II, visited only briefly before his exile in 1910 *(see p59)* – he is said to have brought the French actress, Gaby Deslys, here for a romantic interlude. Its rebirth as a luxury hotel, serving its own renowned wines, was the inspiration of the royal chef and it became a fashionable rendezvous for socialites; in World War II it was also rumoured to be frequented by spies. It is now one of the great hotels of Portugal *(see p390).*

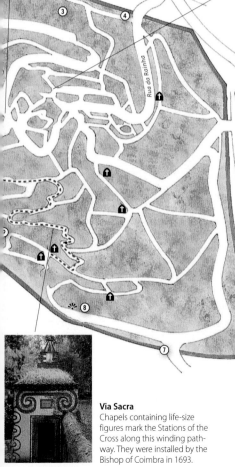

Gaby Deslys, with whom Manuel II reputedly had a brief romance

Via Sacra

Chapels containing life-size figures mark the Stations of the Cross along this winding pathway. They were installed by the Bishop of Coimbra in 1693.

For additonal map symbols *see back flap*

The village of Piódão, blending with the granite of the surrounding Serra de Açor

⑮ Piódão

Road map D3. 🗺 60. 🚌 to Coja 20 km (12 miles) away. 🚹 Largo Cónego Manuel Fernando Nogueira (235 732 787).

The Serra de Açor (Hills of the Goshawk) is a place of bleak beauty, where solitary villages cling to precipitous terraces. Piódão is the most striking of these dark schist and slate hamlets. Seemingly remote, Piódão was, until the late 1800s, on the main commercial route from Coimbra to Covilhã, but with newer roads the village was forgotten. With help from EU funding, it is coming back to life: shops are opening, houses are being repainted with traditional blue trim, and in the main square the bright white Igreja Matriz stands out against the surrounding dark stone. Happily, Piódão retains its old-world charm.

⑯ Oliveira do Hospital

Road map D3. 🗺 22,000. 🚌 🚹 Casa da Cultura, Rua do Colégio (238 605 244). 🛒 2nd Mon & last Sun of month.

These lands once belonged to the Knights Hospitallers, a gift in 1120 from the mother of Afonso Henriques. The 13th-century Igreja Matriz in Largo Ribeira do Amaral houses a magnificent reminder of the era of these warrior monks. One of the founders of the town, Domingues Joanes, lies in a large tomb surmounted by a charming equestrian statue. Today, this lively industrial town is perfectly situated for exploring the valleys of the Mondego and the Alva.

Environs

At Lourosa, 12 km (7 miles) to the southwest, the 10th-century church of São Pedro reflects the changing fate of Portugal over the centuries. A cemetery excavated beneath the church dates from the Roman era; the porch is Visigothic, while inside are ten impressive Roman arches and an *ajimene* (Moorish window).

⑰ Caramulo

Road map C3. 🗺 2,000. 🚌 🚹 Avenida Dr Jerónimo de Lacerda 750 (232 861 437).

In a grassy rolling serra west of Viseu, this small town was once, with its clear mountain air, a centre for sanatoria. It is better

Interior of São Pedro at Lourosa, near Oliveira do Hospital

known today for two very disparate museums in a single institutional block.

In the Museu do Caramulo, the exhibits range from 16th-century Flemish tapestries, sculpture, porcelain, silver and ivory to Egyptian bronzes from 1580 to 900 BC. The paintings are as varied: from Portuguese primitives to the 20th century. Chagall and Dalí are represented, as is the Portuguese Maria Helena Vieira da Silva (1908–92). One of Picasso's still lifes was donated by the artist in 1947.

The collection in the Museu do Automóvel is just as eclectic: a working 1899 Peugeot, Bugattis and Rolls-Royces, and a bulletproof 1938 Mercedes-Benz ordered for Salazar when he was prime minister *(see pp60–61)* but never used.

🏛 **Museu do Caramulo (Fundação Abel e João de Lacerda) and Museu do Automóvel**
Caramulo. **Tel** 232 861 270. **Open** 10am–1pm & 2–6pm Tue–Sun (Oct–Mar: to 5pm). **Closed** Easter Sun, 24 Dec, 25 Dec am. 🅿

Environs

From the museum the road winds southwest up to two viewpoints and picnic spots in the Serra do Caramulo. About 4 km (2 miles) from Caramulo are the wild-flower pastures of Cabeça da Neve, at 970 m (3,200 ft). A little further on, signposted to the West, is the boulder-strewn upland of

aramulinho, rising to 1,074 m
,524 ft). The views from here
e magnificent.

Viseu

ad map D3. 🏔 19,500. 🚌
Casa do Adro, Adro da Sé
32 420 950). 🕎 Tue.

n enthralling old town is at
e heart of this lively regional
apital. Viseu has been a major
orthern crossroads since the
me of the Romans and is
e centre of the Dão wine-
rowing region (see p33).
This was the home town
one of Portugal's great
5th-century artists, Grão Vasco,
hose name graces a hotel, a
useum, even a wine label.
On the western side of the old
wn is the striking 15th-century
orta do Soar de Cima, a
mnant of the original walls.
the Rossio, the main square,
e Igreja dos Terceiros de São
ancisco (1773) has an Italianate
çade and gilded interior.
e 1887 town hall on the west
de has a grand stairway and
zulejos relating the history of
seu and its personalities. Just
orth is Rua Augusto Hilário,
amed after the originator of
oimbra-style fado (see pp68–9)
ho was born here.

e two-towered 17th-century façade of
seu's cathedral

Sé
argo da Sé. **Tel** 232 436 065.
pen 9am–noon & 2–6pm daily.

seu's cathedral still retains a
w Romanesque features, but
has been altered over the
enturies in a variety of styles
hich work together sur-
risingly well. The façade is a
7th-century replacement of

The graceful Rococo façade of the church of the Misericórdia, Viseu

a Manueline frontage that
fell down in 1635. Inside, the
vaulted roof is supported by
16th-century knotted ribs on
13th-century columns. In the
north chapel are fine azulejos
from the 18th century, while
those in the two-storey cloister
date from a century earlier. The
sacristy has a lavishly painted
ceiling and early "carpet" tiles
(see p30). In the chancel, choir
stalls in Brazilian jacaranda
contrast with a startling modern
altar, an inverted pyramid in
polished granite and steel.
The Sé's treasury, housed in
the chapterhouse, includes a
12th-century Gospel and a
13th-century Limoges coffer.
Facing the cathedral is the
Misericórdia church, with its
18th-century Rococo façade. It
houses a permanent exhibition
from the Museu de Grão Vasco.

🏛 Museu de Grão Vasco
Largo da Sé. **Tel** 232 422 049. **Open**
10am–6pm Tue–Sun (from 2pm Tue).
Closed 1 Jan, Easter, 1 May, 25 Dec.
🎟 (free first Sun of month).

In the 16th-century former
bishops' palace abutting the
cathedral is the Museu de Grão
Vasco, Viseu's "great Vasco". The
paintings of Vasco Fernandes
(c.1475–1540) and his fellow
artists of the Viseu School are
highly esteemed for their naturalism, background landscapes,
drapery and attention to detail.
Their treatment of light betrays

the marked influence of Flemish
painters. On the top floor of
the three-storey museum
are the masterpieces that once
adorned the cathedral's chancel
altarpiece, including Grão Vasco's
monumental St Peter and, from
a series of 14 panels on the life
of Christ, The Adoration of the
Magi. Painted around 1503–5,
it is memorable for the inclusion
of a Brazilian Indian among
those paying homage to the
newborn Christ (see p52). Some
of the other panels are thought
to be by fellow artists in the
Viseu School.
Among other masterpieces
here are works by Grão Vasco's
great rival, Gaspar Vaz, including
a Last Supper. On the lower
floors are works by Portuguese
artists from the 19th and 20th
centuries, including Columbano
Bordalo Pinheiro.

St Peter (1530–5) by Vasco Fernandes in
the Museu de Grão Vasco, Viseu

⓳ Sernancelhe

Road map D2. 🚹 6,200. 🚌 ℹ️ Town
Hall (254 598 300). 🛍️ every other Thu.

Small whitewashed houses
cluster around the granite heart
of this modest Beira town which
was established on the banks of
the Távora in the 10th century.
In the central Praça da República
stands the Romanesque Igreja
Matriz. The granite statues in its
façade niches, survivors from
the 12th century, flank a notable
arched portal embellished by a
semicircle of carved angels. The
pillory that stands across the
square is dated 1554.

The grandest house here is
the Baroque Solar dos Carvalhos
behind the church. Long and
low, with carved granite portals
against whitewashed
walls, it is where the
local noble family
lived in the 18th
century. It is still
a private house.

Only a few
stubs of castle
wall remain on
the rocky outcrop
overlooking the square, but a
small battlemented house has
been built into them.

Carved arch over the portal of the
Igreja Matriz, Sernancelhe

Environs
In the Serra da Lapa, which rises
to the south of Sernancelhe,
stands a popular shrine
known as the Santuário da
Nossa Senhora da Lapa.
The story tells of a mute
shepherd girl, Joana,
who found a statue of
the Virgin Mary on a
great boulder and took
it home. Irritated, her
mother threw it on the
fire, at which moment
the child miraculously
spoke: "Don't burn it,"
cried Joana. "It is the
Senhora da Lapa."

A chapel was built to
enshrine the boulder,
and the image, now
with a slightly scorched
face, looks down from
an ornamental recess.
The space below her
niche is packed with
images and offerings left
by pilgrims.

The main gateway into the old walled town of Trancoso

The castle at Penedono is
captivating. Perched on rocks
in the middle of this small town
17 km (11 miles) northeast of
Sernancelhe, it has survived
since at least the 10th century.
The castle is mentioned in the
medieval tale of a knight
known as O Magriço,
who went to
England with
11 other knights
to joust in
honour of 12
English ladies.
There is little to
see inside the
castle – if closed, the key is in
the store beside the *pelourinho*
(pillory), but there are splendid
views from the walls.

🏛️ Santuário da Nossa Senhora da Lapa
Quintela da Lapa, 11 km (7 miles)
SW of Sernancelhe. **Tel** 232 688 993.
Open daily.

The castle of Penedono, near Sernancelhe, with its
imposing medieval battlements

⓴ Trancoso

Road map D2. 🚹 6,000. 🚌
ℹ️ Largo das Portas d'El Rei 2
(271 811 147). 🛍️ Fri.

When King Dinis married Isabel
here in 1283 (*see pp48–9*), he
gave her Trancoso as a wedding
gift. He was also responsible for
the walls that still encircle the
town and, in 1304, established
here the first unrestricted fair in
Portugal. Left in peace after
1385, the town became a lively
commercial centre. Trancoso
once had a large Jewish
population; in the old Judiaria,
houses survive with one broad
and one narrow door, separating
domestic life from commerce.

From the southern gate, Rua da
Corredoura leads to São Pedro,
restored after 1720. A tombstone
in the church commemorates
Gonçalo Anes, a local shoemaker who, in the 1580s, wrote
the celebrated *Trovas* under
the name of Bandarra. These
prophesied the return of the
young King Sebastião (*see p109*).

Environs
Tumbledown ruins above a
humble village are all that
remain of the medieval citadel
of Marialva, 14 km (9 miles) to
the northeast of Trancoso.
Granite walls, fragments of
stone carvings and a striking
15th-century pillory emanate an
aura of lost grandeur. Probably
founded by Ferdinand of León
and Castile early in the 11th
century and fortified by Sancho
Marialva fell into ruin. It is not
known why. No battle destroyed
it; it seems merely to have been
abandoned as townsfolk moved
to more fruitful lands.

Serra Cheese

Serra, made from the milk of ewes grazing in the Serra da Estrela *(see pp224–5)*, is Portugal's finest cheese. It is made in the winter – its success was once governed by the temperature of the women's hands as they worked in their cool granite kitchens – and traditionally the milk is coagulated with *flor do cardo*, thistle. Now the small factories producing the cheese, in rounds of 1.5–2 kg (about 3–5 lb), are certified to ensure quality and authenticity (fakes are not uncommon). At room temperature Serra becomes runny. The cheese is scooped out with a spoon through a hole cut into the top.

A shepherd with his flock on the slopes of the Serra da Estrela

Celorico da Beira

oad map D3. 8,800. ua Sacadura Cabral (271 742 109). cheese festival: Feb & Mar.

the lee of the Serra da Estrela, e pastures around Celorico a Beira have long been a ource of the region's famous erra cheese. From November February a cheese market is eld in the Praça Municipal, nd there is a cheese fair every ebruary. Around Rua Fernão acheco, running from the ain road up to the castle, is e old centre of Celorico,

which is manifested in a cluster of granite houses with Manueline windows and Gothic doors.

Of the 10th-century castle, battered by a long succession of frontier disputes with Spain, only a tower and the outer walls remain. Its stark silhouette is less dramatic at close quarters. The Igreja Matriz, which was restored in the 18th century, has a painted coffered ceiling. During the Peninsular War, the church served briefly as a makeshift hospital for the English forces.

㉒ Almeida

Road map E2. 1,500. Portas de São Francisco (271 570 020). 8th day & last Sat of month.

Formidable defences in the form of a 12-pointed star guard this small, delightfully preserved border town.

Almeida was recognized by Spain as Portuguese territory under the Alcañices Treaty on 12 September 1297, but this did not stop further incursions. The present Vauban-style strong-hold *(see p303)* was designed in 1641 by Antoine Deville after Spain's Philip IV, in post-Restoration rage, destroyed the earlier defences protecting the town and its medieval castle.

From 1742 to 1743 Almeida was in Spanish hands again, and then during the Peninsular War was held in turn by the French under Masséna and the British under the Duke of Wellington. In 1810, a French shell lit a powder trail that destroyed the castle.

To breach the town's fortifi-cations today, it is necessary to cross a bridge and pass through a tunnel. The underground casamatas, soldiers' barracks, can be visited and an armoury in the main gateway, the Portas de São Francisco, holds further mementoes of Almeida's military past. In the town itself are a 17th-century parish church and a Misericórdia church of a similar age, attached to one of Portugal's oldest almshouses. A walk around the grassy walls gives rewarding views of the town.

lmeida's complex fortifications, still discernible despite the incursion of grass and wild flowers

㉓ Border Castles Tour

Defending Portugal's frontiers was a vital priority of the nation's early kings. The greatest period of castle-building was in the reign of King Dinis (1279–1325). All along the shakily held border, Spanish incursions were frequent and loyalties divided. Castles were constantly being assaulted, besieged and rebuilt, and the 20 that survived are a lasting reminder of this long period of dispute. Much of the terrain, especially in the Serra da Marofa, is bleak and rocky, but near Pinhel and beyond Castelo Mendo the scenic valley of the River Côa provides a dramatic backdrop.

② Castelo Rodrigo
This tiny fortified village still has its encircling walls built by King Dinis in 1296. But the fine palace of its lord, the Spanish sympathizer Cristóvão de Moura, was burnt down at the Restoration in 1640 *(see pp54–5)*.

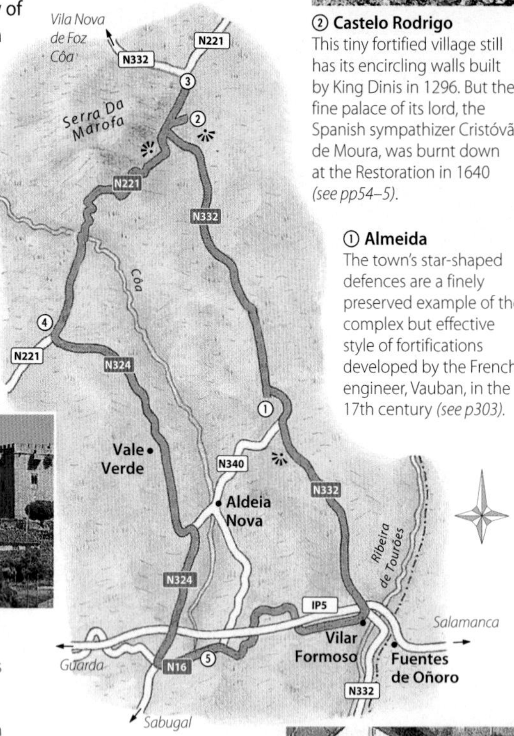

③ Figueira de Castelo Rodrigo
From the 18th century, Castelo Rodrigo was largely abandoned in favour of less isolated Figueira, now a flourishing little town known for its almond blossom. Just to the south, topped by a huge stone Christ the King, is the highest point of the Serra da Marofa, 977 m (3,205 ft).

① Almeida
The town's star-shaped defences are a finely preserved example of the complex but effective style of fortifications developed by the French engineer, Vauban, in the 17th century *(see p303)*.

④ Pinhel
Part of the region's defences since Roman times, Pinhel formed the fulcrum for a network of fortresses, and in the early 14th century King Dinis built it up into an impressive citadel. Much of this ring of walls survives, as do two towers.

Tips for Drivers
Length: 115 km (72 miles).
Stopping-off points: Most villages have cafés, and Pinhel and Almeida have restaurants.
Road conditions: The tour uses well-surfaced roads; short cuts are deceptive and not recommended. *(See also pp444–5.)*

Key
▬ Tour route
═ Other roads
▬ᐧ International boundary

0 kilometres   10

0 miles   5

⑤ Castelo Mendo
Beyond the main gate, guarded by two stone boars, little survives of the castle here, but the distant views make its role as a frontier fort easy to appreciate.

Map labels: Vila Nova de Foz Côa · N221 · N332 · Serra Da Marofa · N221 · N332 · Côa · N221 · N324 · Vale Verde · N340 · N332 · Aldeia Nova · Ribeira de Tourões · N324 · IP5 · Salamanca · Vilar Formoso · Fuentes de Oñoro · Guarda · N16 · N332 · Sabugal

The soaring triple-aisled interior of Guarda's Gothic cathedral

Guarda

Road map D3. 26,000. 🚉 🚌
🚉 Praça Luís de Camões (271 205
30). 🗓️ 1st & 3rd Wed of month.

Spread over a bleak hill on the northeast flank of the Serra da Estrela, Guarda is Portugal's highest city, at 1,056 m (3,465 ft). Founded in 1199 by Sancho I, the city's original role as frontier guard explains its name and its rather forbidding countenance. Some of its arcaded streets and squares are lively and interesting, but the great fortress-like Sé, with its flying buttresses, pinnacles and gargoyles, could never be described as lovely. Master architects who worked on the cathedral, begun in 1390 and completed in 1540, included Diogo Boitac (from 1504 to 1517) and the builders of Batalha (see pp188–9). The interior, by contrast, is light and graceful. The 100 carved figures high on the altarpiece in the chancel were worked by Jean de Rouen in 1552.

On display in the nearby **Museu de Guarda** are two floors of paintings, artifacts, archaeological discoveries and a section on the city's own poet, Augusto Gil (1873–1929).

From the cathedral square, Rua do Comércio leads down to the 17th-century Misericórdia church. Inside the ornamental portal are Baroque altars and pulpits. Just north of the cathedral, in the historic town centre, is the 18th-century

church of São Vicente, which has 16 elaborate *azulejo* panels depicting the life of Christ.

Guarda used to support a thriving Jewish community, which was founded in the beginning of the 13th century. History records that João I, on a visit to Guarda, was smitten by Inês Fernandes, the beautiful daughter of a Jewish shoemaker. From their liaison a son, Afonso, was born. In 1442 the title of first Duke of Bragança was bestowed on Afonso, and 200 years later his descendant would take the throne as João IV, first of the Bragança monarchs (see p305).

Centum Cellas, a curious Roman landmark near Belmonte

🏛️ **Museu de Guarda**
Rua Alves Roçadas 30. **Tel** 271 213
460. **Open** Tue–Sun. **Closed** public
holidays. 🎫 (free first Sun of month).

㉕ Serra da Estrela

See pp224–5.

㉖ Belmonte

Road map D3. 3,500. 🚉 🚌
🗺️ Castelo de Belmonte (275 911
488). 🗓️ 1st & 3rd Mon of month.

Belmonte was for generations the fiefdom of the heroic Cabral family. Pedro Álvares Cabral, the first navigator to land in Brazil, had forebears who fought at Ceuta (see p52) and Aljubarrota (see p189). Fernão, an earlier ancestor, was famed for his feats of strength. The family crest, incorporating a goat (cabra), can be seen in the castle and adjacent chapel. The castle, begun in 1266, retains its keep and a Manueline window added later. The little church of São Tiago nearby has preserved its Romanesque simplicity: the frescoes above the altar and, in a tiny side chapel, a granite pietà date from the 13th century. Beside

Cabral family crest in the chapel, Belmonte

the church is the 15th-century Capela dos Cabrais which holds the Cabral family tombs.

The modern Igreja da Sagrada Família (1940) is the repository for a treasured statue of Nossa Senhora da Esperança said to have accompanied Cabral on his voyage to Brazil. The **Museu Judaico de Belmonte** charts the development of the Jewish community in the region.

🏛️ **Museu Judaico de Belmonte**
Rua da Portela 4. **Tel** 275 088 698.
Open Tue–Sun.

Environs
Northeast of Belmonte is the Roman Centum Cellas, also called Torre de Colmeal. It is not known what the role of this square, three-storeyed structure was – maybe a hostel or military base, a mansion or a temple.

㉕ Serra da Estrela

These "star mountains" are the highest range on mainland Portugal, with much of the Serra over 1,500 m (5,000 ft). The highest point rises to 1,993 m (6,539 ft) but is topped by a small stone tower – the Torre – to "stretch" it to 2,000 m. The exposed granite of the upper slopes is good for little but grazing sheep, and stone shepherds' huts form part of the landscape, their thatched roofs renewed each year after the harsh winter. Sheep have shaped the fortunes of the area, providing wool for a textile industry and supplying milk for Portugal's best-known cheese. A designated nature reserve, the Serra's long-distance paths and stunning flora attract walkers and nature enthusiasts, while a winter snowfall brings skiers to the slopes around Torre.

Cabeça do Velho
The granite of the mountain tops has been eroded into many weird shapes, such as this "old man's head" near Sabugueiro. It is matched by an "old woman's head" south of Seia.

Serra Cheese Shop
The best Serra cheese, prized for its rich flavour *(see p221)*, is still made by hand. Farmers sell their produce at cheese fairs and at stalls or small shops such as this one near the summit of Torre.

Valezim
In Valezim are several old water mills of a type not often found in Portugal. Two of them are still used to grind grain.

KEY

① **Penhas de Saúde**, once a health spa, is now popular with skiers.

② **Seia** is one of the main entry points to the Parque Natural da Serra da Estrela.

③ **Manteigas**, at the heart of the Serra, is a textile centre. Just to the west there is a *pousada (see p390)*.

④ **Covilhã**, the largest town in the area, is known for its fine textiles woven from locally produced wool. The textile museum here deserves a visit.

Map labels: Viseu, Seia, Cabeça do Velho, Sabugueiro, Alva, N339, Cur M, Valezim, Rodeio Grande, N231, Coimbra, Penha dos Abutres, Vide, Muro, Ribeira de Alvoco, Torre, Pen, N231, Unhais da Serra, Alto da Pedrice, N230, N230

Torre
Despite the unpredictability of snow, the slopes below Torre are used for skiing, tobogganing or just fun in the snow.

★ Linhares
Guarded by the towers of its medieval castle, Linhares is like a living museum. The forum, from which medieval justice was dispensed, survives, as do many fine houses from its 15th-century heyday.

VISITORS' CHECKLIST

Practical Information
Road map D3. 🛈 Mercado Municipal, Rua Pinto Lucas Marrão, Seia (238 317 762); Covilhã (275 319 560); Gouveia (238 083 930); Manteigas (275 981 129).
🚌 Sat in most towns. 🎉 Feb: Carnaval & annual cheese fairs; Dec: Santa Luzia.

Transport
🚉 Covilhã, Guarda. 🚌 to Covilhã, Seia & Guarda. Limited local service within park.

Key

═══ Major road

═══ Minor road

★ Zêzere Valley
The Zêzere eventually joins the Tagus, but here, near its source, the young river flows through a classic glacier-cut valley. The golden broom growing here is used to thatch mountain huts.

Poço do Inferno
This cascade in a gorge of the River Leandros is a spectacular sight, especially when it freezes in winter.

Sheepdog of the Serra

Intelligent, loyal and brave, the Serra da Estrela sheepdog embodies all the qualities required in this wild region. Its heavy coat, as shaggy as its charges, helps it survive the bitter high-altitude winters and in the past its strength was called upon to defend the flock from wolves. Pedigree Serra da Estrela dogs (reputedly with some wolf's blood introduced in their breeding) are raised at kennels near Gouveia and west of Manteigas.

㉗ Sabugal

Road map E3. 🏔 3,000. 🚌
ℹ️ inside the castle (271 750 080).
🏛 1st Thu & 3rd Tue of month.

In 1296, when this small town beside the River Côa was confirmed as Portuguese in the Treaty of Alcañices, the castle was refortified by the ever-industrious King Dinis (*see p48*). Its imposing towered walls and unusual five-sided keep survive from this era, although the castle suffered in peacetime from villagers raiding it for building stone.

Peopled since prehistoric times, Sabugal still has part of its medieval walls, reinforced in the 17th century and now ringed by newer houses. In the Praça da República stands a granite clock tower, reconstructed in the 17th century.

Environs
Wrapped in its ring of walls, **Sortelha**, 20 km (12 miles) west, is enchanting. It sits on a granite outcrop and the views from the high keep of its gem of a 13th-century castle are stunning. In front of the arched castle entrance is a 16th-century pillory with an armillary sphere on top. In the tiny citadel are a school and stony lanes of granite houses, some discreetly converted into restaurants (*see p405*).

The local fondness for bull-fights (*see pp150–51*) is reflected in names of nearby villages such as Vila do Touro. In a local

The castle at Sabugal, with its distinctive five-sided keep

variation, the *capeia*, bulls were taunted into charging into a huge fork of branches.

㉘ Penamacor

Road map D3. 🏔 6,200. 🚉 🚌
ℹ️ Rua Tenente Coronel Rodrigues da Silva (277 394 106). 🏛 1st & 3rd Wed of month.

Fought over by successive waves of Romans, Visigoths and Moors, this frontier town was fortified in the 12th century by Gualdim Pais, Master of the Knights Templar (*see pp190–91*). Today the weather-beaten castle walls rise above a quiet town at the heart of hardy, sparsely inhabited country where the main attraction is the hunting of small game.

From the main square, the road up to the old town passes beside the former town hall, built over a medieval archway. Beyond lie the restored castle

keep and the 16th-century Igreja da Misericórdia, with an elegant Manueline portal capped by armillary spheres, the emblem of Manuel I.

Environs
Penamacor is the headquarters of the **Reserva Natural da Serra da Malcata**. These 20 sq km (8 sq miles) of forested wilderness shelter wolves, otters and, most importantly, are one of the last refuges of the Iberian lynx. Visitors should first call at the information centre for advice.

🏞 **Reserva Natural da Serra da Malcata**
🚌 to Penamacor or Sabugal. ℹ️ Rua Ribeiro Sanches 60, Penamacor (277 394 467). 🕒 9am–5:30pm Mon–Fri.

㉙ Monsanto

Road map E3. 🏔 1,500. 🚌 ℹ️ Rua Marquês de Graciosa (277 314 642). 🏛 3rd Sat.

An odd fame hit Monsanto in 1938 when it was voted "most Portuguese village in Portugal". The village is at one with the granite hillside on which it perches: its lanes blend into the grey rock, the houses squeezed between massive boulders. Tiny gardens sprout from the granite and dogs drink from granite bowls.

The ruined castle began as a *castro*, a Lusitanian fortified settlement, and suffered a long history of sieges and battles for its commanding position. It was finally destroyed by a 19th-century gunpowder

Monsanto's houses, dwarfed by immense granite boulders

For hotels and restaurants in this area see pp390–91 and pp404–5

explosion. Cars cannot venture beyond the village centre, but the view alone is worth the walk up to the ruined walls.

A story is told of how a long siege by the Moors drove the hungry villagers to a desperate ploy. They threw their last calf, full of their last grain, over the walls, a show of profligacy that convinced the Moors to give up. Each May there is a mock re-enactment of this victory amid much music and singing.

⑳ Idanha-a-Velha

Road map D3. 90. Rua da Sé (277 914 280).

This modest hamlet among the olive groves encapsulates the history of Portugal. Discreet signposts and explanations in Portuguese, French and English guide visitors round the landmarks of this fascinating living museum.

Idanha-a-Velha was, it is said, the birthplace of the Visigothic King Wamba, and had its own bishop until 1199. The present appearance of the cathedral comes from early 16th-century restoration, but in the echoing interior are stacked inscribed and sculpted Roman stones.

In the middle of the village stand several historic monuments: a 17th-century pillory and the Renaissance Igreja Matriz, while near an early 20th-century olive press is a ruined Torre dos Templários, a relic of the Templars. This order of religious knights held sway in Idanha until the 14th century (see pp192–3).

Statue-lined Stairway of the Apostles in the unusual Jardim Episcopal, Castelo Branco

㉛ Castelo Branco

Road map D4. 32,500. Avenida Nuno Alvares 30 (272 330 339). Mon; antiques: every 3rd Sun.

This handsome, busy old city, overlooked by the vestiges of a Templar castle, is the most important in the Beira Baixa.

Much the greatest attraction is the extraordinary **Jardim Episcopal** beside the former bishops' palace. Created by Bishop João de Mendonça in the 18th century, the garden's layout is conventionally formal; its individuality lies in its dense population of statues. Baroque in style and often bizarre in character, stone saints and apostles line the box-edged paths, lions peer at their reflections in pools and monarchs stand guard along the balustrades – the hated kings of the 60-year Spanish rule (see p54) conspicuously half-size.

The 17th-century Paço Episcopal itself now houses the **Museu Francisco Tavares Proença Júnior**. Its wide-ranging collection includes archaeological finds, displays of 16th-century tapestries and Portuguese primitive art. Castelo Branco is also well known for its fine silk-embroidered bedspreads, called *colchas*, and examples of these are also exhibited in the museum. The popular **Museu Cargaleiro** houses a remarkable collection of rare paintings, tapestries and ceramics, donated by the Manuel Cargaleiro Foundation. Beside the road back to the town centre stands a 15th-century cross known as the Cruzeiro de São João.

🔲 Jardim Episcopal
Rua Bartolomeu da Costa.
Open daily.

🏛 Museu Francisco Tavares Proença Júnior
Largo Doutor José Dias Lopes.
Tel 272 344 277. **Open** 10am–1pm & 2–6pm Tue–Sun. **Closed** pub hols.

🏛 Museu Cargaleiro
Rua dos Cavaleiros 23. **Tel** 272 337 394.
Open 10am–1pm & 2–6pm Tue–Sun.
Closed 1 Jan, Easter, 25 Apr, 1 May, 25 Dec.

The historic little village of Idanha-a-Velha, among its olive groves beside the River Ponsul

NORTHERN PORTUGAL

Northern Portugal at a Glance

Portugal north of the River Douro is rural and unspoilt, yet offers splendid opportunities for cultural sightseeing, walking and water sports. Beyond the cultivated valley of the Douro and the fertile Minho rises the remote and romantically named Trás-os-Montes ("Behind the Mountains"), with its tracts of wilderness and tiny medieval townships. It could be said the nation was conceived between the Minho and the Douro, and historic cities such as Porto, Bragança and Braga give fascinating insights into the country's past.

In the Parque Nacional da Peneda-Gerês scenery ranges from dramatic forested valleys to flowery meadows. Local farmers store their grain in curious stone *espigueiros (see pp276–7).*

Viana do Castelo, at the mouth of the River Lima, is elegant and relaxed *(see pp280–81).* The stately buildings in the Praça da República, including the arcaded *Paços do Concelho* (the old town hall), reflect the town's wealthy past.

Monção

Vila Nova
de Cerveira

Caminha

Arcos de
Valdevez

Vila Praia
de Âncora

Ponte da
Barca

Viana do
Castelo

MINHO
(See pp268–287)

Vieira do
Minho

Esposende

Barcelos

Braga

Guimarãe

Póvoa de Varzim

Vila do Conde

Santo
Tirso

Leça da Palmeira

Amarant

Porto

Penafiel

Douro Litoral

Bom Jesus do Monte, near Braga, attracts worshippers, penitents and tourists, who all come to climb 116 m (380 ft) up the Baroque staircase *(see pp284–5).* This is the Staircase of the Five Senses, with fountains depicting each of the senses.

Porto, set on Penaventosa Hill above the River Douro, is Portugal's second city *(see pp242–9).* Alongside a wealth of historic sights and sophisticated shopping, it offers the charm of its steep medieval alleys tumbling down to the lively riverside quays, and a chance to taste port at its point of origin.

◀ The Douro Valley near Quinta dos Canais, in the Upper Douro

The Casa de Mateus, familiar to many from the Mateus Rosé wine label, lies in the hills above the valley of the Douro. This Baroque *solar*, or manor house, is set in beautifully manicured formal gardens, its distinctive pinnacles rising above the orchards and vineyards that surround it *(see pp260–61).*

Bragança, capital of Trás-os-Montes, gave its name to Portugal's last and longest-ruling royal dynasty. The keep and walls of this remote citadel, founded in the 12th century, look out over the valley of the River Fervença *(see pp264–5).*

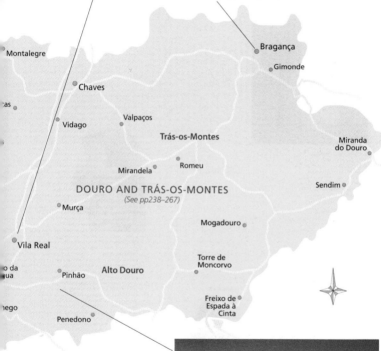

Montalegre

Chaves

...as

Vidago

Valpaços

Trás-os-Montes

Bragança

Gimonde

Miranda do Douro

Mirandela

Romeu

DOURO AND TRÁS-OS-MONTES
(See pp238–267)

Murça

Mogadouro

Sendim

Vila Real

...o da ...ua

Pinhão

Alto Douro

Torre de Moncorvo

...ego

Penedono

Freixo de Espada à Cinta

0 kilometres 25

0 miles 10

Port Country, as the scenic valley of the Upper Douro is commonly called, is the nursery of Portugal's port industry. A tour of a *quinta*, or wine estate, with its steeply terraced riverside vineyards, is highly recommended *(see pp258–9).*

The Festivals of the North

Portuguese cities, towns and villages all have their own particular saints' days. These are primarily religious occasions, particularly in the Minho and across the devout north, but are also a chance to put aside the cares of life for a day or two. It is a popular maxim that a holy day is best celebrated by eating, drinking, dancing and merrymaking, as well as worshipping and giving thanks. The most solemn and spectacular celebrations of Holy Week, Semana Santa, can also be seen in the north, especially in Braga *(see pp282–3)*, Portugal's ecclesiastical capital.

A solemn moment as Easter candles are lit in Braga

Easter

Holy Week, culminating in Easter Sunday, is the major religious festival of the year. In Braga, processions snake round the city walls to the great cathedral, and every village has its own ceremonies.

The start of Holy Week is heralded by Palm Sunday, when locals line the streets and wave palm leaves to commemorate the entry of Christ into Jerusalem. The evening of Good Friday is palpably solemn, as innumerable groups of locals process, following the 14 Stations of the Cross, many believers doing public penance as they recall Christ's suffering. In some villages an effigy of the lifeless and bleeding Christ is carried through the streets.

On Easter Sunday, after an uplifting mass proclaiming the risen Christ, every parish priest processes around his village with a crucifix on a tall staff for parishioners to kiss the feet of Jesus. While the priest takes a customary glass of wine, his entourage ecstatically let off rockets. Families then traditionally lunch on roast kid *(cabrito)*.

After Easter, in early May, the passion of Christ is recalled in Barcelos *(see p279)*. Crosses are erected the length of a petal-strewn route for the **Festa das Cruzes**.

São João

Porto's celebration of São João (23–24 Jun) is one of Portugal's most exuberant festivals. It coincides with the summer solstice. To celebrate, people eat,

Wielding a São João hammer

Street procession during the Festa das Cruzes in Barcelos

drink and dance all night, playfully hitting each other over the head with giant garlic-leek (or, even more strangely, with squeaky plastic hammers).

Bonfires are lit and a spectacular display of fireworks explodes over the Douro. A tradition that has become a part of São João is the annual regatta of the *barcos rabelos*, the boats in which port used to be shipped down the Douro *(see p258)*.

Costume in the Minho

Gold necklets

Embroidered apron pockets

Festivals are vital vehicles for keeping alive tradition, and regional costume in particular echoes the importance of religious festivals across the country. These days, on-trend fashions and designer clothes are as much part of young people's life in Minho villages as elsewhere in western Europe, but traditional dress is worn with pride on days of celebration. The Minho's costume is the most colourful in Portugal, with exquisitely embroidered scarves and aprons in colours denoting village loyalties. Messages of love and friendship are stitched on to pockets, and bodices are half-lost under tiers of gold filigree, meaning there is more to these costumes than meets the eye.

Romarias

Any kind of celebration or party can be described as a *festa*, but one billed as a *romaria* implies a religious dimension. Most *festas* in the north are *romarias;* they begin with a special mass, then saints' statues are brought from the church to be paraded through the streets on litters. Blessings are dispensed in all directions – fire engines and ambulances frequently also getting the treatment followed by a spraying with some Raposeira sparkling wine. Many *romarias* take place in the summer, and in August few days go by without a celebration.

Assumption Day *(15 Aug)* is fêted all over Portugal with dancing and music. *Gigantones,* grotesque carnival giants of pre-Christian origin, join street processions to keep

Stick Dancing

Stick dancers, or *pauliteiros,* can still be seen at village festivals in Trás-os-Montes. The dances are of ancient origin, probably associated with fertility rites, and the sticks may once have been swords. The most famous troupe comes from the village of Duas Igrejas, near Miranda do Douro *(see p266).*

Dancers performing at a *festa*

The Procession to the Sea during the Nossa Senhora da Agonia Festival

the bad spirits away and fireworks light the sky. A few days later, around 20 August, one of the year's most spectacular *romarias* in Northern Portugal takes place in Viana do Castelo *(see pp280–81).* The festivities celebrating **Nossa Senhora da Agonia** include a bullfight and an afternoon devoted to a kaleidoscopic display of regional costume, which may include more than a thousand participants. As a finale, fireworks are let off from the bridge over the River Lima to cascade down into the water as a fiery waterfall.

On the coast just to the west of Braga, villagers in São Bartolomeu do Mar mark the end of their *romaria (22–24 Aug)* by dipping their children in the sea, as a mock sacrifice to the waves.

Outlandish costumes and masks donned for the Dia dos Rapazes

Christmas and Winter

On Christmas Eve, families gather to enjoy enormous quantities of *bacalhau* (salt cod) and mulled port, and to exchange presents, before attending midnight mass.

Between Christmas and Epiphany, Trás-os-Montes village boys dress in crazy, fringed suits to take part in the rite-of-passage **Dia dos Rapazes**.

The Christmas season ends on **Dia de Reis** *(6 Jan),* when the *bolo rei,* or "king cake", rich with crystallized fruit "jewels", is eaten *(see p37).*

Comical giants leading an Assumption Day parade in Peso da Régua

The Story of Port

The "discovery" of port dates from the 17th century when British merchants added brandy to the wine of the northern Douro region to prevent it souring in transit. They found that the stronger and sweeter the wine, the better flavour it acquired. Methods of maturing and blending continue to be refined by the main port producers. Croft was one of the first big shippers, followed by other English and Scottish firms. Despite the consolidation of the global drinks industry, much of the port trade is still in British hands, and some firms are still family-run.

Barco rabelo ferrying port down the Douro river

The Port Region

Port comes only from a demarcated region of the upper Douro valley, stretching 100 km (62 miles) to the Spanish border. Régua and Pinhão are the main centres of production, but most top-quality vineyards lie on estates or *quintas* in the harsh eastern terrain.

Styles of Port

There are essentially two categories of port: red and wood-aged. The former are deeper in colour and will develop after bottling; the latter, which include tawny ports, are ready to drink when they are bottled. White port is in a category of its own.

Vintage, the star of any shipper's range, is made from wines of a single year, from the best vineyards. It is blended and bottled after two years in wood, and may then mature for a very long time in the bottle.

Vintage

Late Bottled Vintage (LBV) is wine of a single year, bottled between four and six years after the harvest. Filtered LBV may have less flavour than unfiltered, "traditional" LBV.

LBV

Aged tawny port is blended from top-quality wines that have been aged in wood for a long time. The age on the label is not precise, but the older it is, the paler, more delicate, less fruity and more expensive the port is likely to be.

Aged Tawny

Tawny port without indication of age may not have been in wood for long enough to develop the complex flavours of aged tawny. It may be a blend of red and white ports, and its price is fairly low.

Tawny

Ruby port is deep red and should be full of lively fruit flavour. It has been aged for two or three years, sometimes in wood, sometimes not. It is less complex than either LBV or Vintage, but costs considerably less.

Ruby

White port is ma[de] from white grape[s] and may be swee[t] or not so sweet. [It is] mainly drunk chi[lled] as an aperitif. Som[e] types of white port have a slightly lower alcohol content than the normal 20 per cent for port.

White

Collecting grapes in tall wicker baskets for transport to the wineries

How Port is Made

The climax of the Douro farmers' year comes in late September when bands of pickers congregate to harvest the grapes. More than 40 varieties are used for making port, but there are five recommended top varieties.

Treading the grapes in stone tanks or *lagares* to extract the juice is a feature of very traditional *quintas*. Some shippers believe it adds a special quality.

Fermentation in cement or steel tanks is a more common method. Carbon dioxide builds up within the tank, forcing the fermenting must (juice from the grapes) up a tube into an open trough at the top. The gas is released and the must sprays back over the pips and skins, in a process similar to treading.

In the fortification process, the semi-fermented must is run into a second vat where brandy – actually grape spirit – is added. This arrests the fermentation, leaving the wine sweet from natural grape sugar.

Thousands of bottles of Graham's vintage port from 1977 await full maturation in the cellars of the Vila Nova de Gaia lodge.

Quality tawny port is matured in oak casks in the port lodges. Once bottled, it is ready for drinking and does not require decanting.

Vintage Port

In the interests of maintaining the highest standards of quality – and of not saturating the market – port producers do not "declare" a vintage every year. Each year, the wine from the best vineyards is closely monitored for 18 months, other producers are consulted about their quality, and then a decision is taken. If a vintage is not declared, the wine may remain in wood to be blended as tawny or LBV in future, or it may be bottled as a "single quinta" port – a kind of second-label vintage. On average, producers declare a vintage three times in a decade, though not always in the same years.

A good vintage needs time in bottle to reveal itself. Fifteen years is seen as a minimum, although many impatient drinkers do not actually wait that long; there is even a fashion for drinking young vintage port. The nature of vintage port's aging process results in a continuously evolving list of great vintages. Most experts agree, however, that no vintage has yet equalled that produced in 1963.

Pre-war vintages

1927, 1931, 1935: All great and now very rare.

Post-war vintages

1945, 1947, 1948, 1955: For the very rich and extremely lucky.
1963 Perhaps the greatest post-war vintage.
1994 A fine vintage, particularly from Dow, Taylor and Quinta do Noval.
1997 Another fine vintage.
2000 A very promising year.
2003 A superb vintage with attractive ripe fruit flavours.

Taylor's 1994 vintage

The Flavours of Northern Portugal

There is a smoky flavour to the rustic food of the north. This seems to come not only from the area's wealth of cured, often smoked, pork products (frequently used to add spice to other dishes), but from the woodsmoke-scented air of the quiet valleys of the interior, too. The cuisine consists of rich stews and thick soups, beans, chestnuts and cabbage, and crusty maize bread. The prized pig does service in everything from the pale, lightly cured hams of Amarante to clove- and cumin-spiced *morcela* (blood sausage). Local beef is renowned, and *cabrito* (kid) is a favourite in roasts and stews.

Maize bread (corn bread)

Sheets of salt cod drying in the sun and coastal breezes

Minho

Northernmost Portugal is a landscape of dense greenery, punctuated with granite and traversed by rivers. Trout, eel and lamprey all still feature prominently on local menus, even if the trout nowadays is mostly farmed and the lamprey often imported. The Minho region is also home to *caldo verde*, the best-known of Portugal's soups. It is made with *couve galega*, the tall-growing, open-leafed kale typical of the Minho. The Portuguese love affair with *bacalhau*, dried salted cod, is as ardent here as it is anywhere in the country, despite the availability of fresh fish throughout the region. Try it com broa – baked with a crust of the rich maize bread *(broa de milho)*, another speciality of the north.

Douro and Trás-os-Montes

These are meatier regions, famed for their *embutidos* or *enchidos* (cured pork products). Vila Real is a centre for the production of spiced, salted, sometimes marinated and smoked meats and sausages, but each area makes its own, often on a small scale. *Presunto* (cured ham) from Chaves,

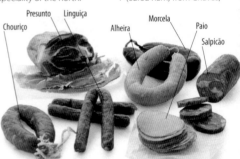

Presunto Linguiça
Chouriço   Morcela Paio
                    Alheira   Salpicão

Some of the cured and smoked pork produce of Northern Portugal

Regional Dishes and Specialities

Caldo verde is by far the best-known dish from the north, and its simple composition and strong flavours, though sometimes diluted by too much potato, are represent-ative of the northern style of cooking. Combinations of fish and meat, in particular cured pork, are another feature, as in *lampreia à moda do Minho* (lamprey cooked in white wine with *chouriço*), *trutas com presunto* (trout with cured ham) and *bacalhau à Transmontana* (salt cod with pork belly). *Cozido* is a pan-Portuguese dish whose origins are thought to be in the north or across the border in Spain. It is a stew of beef, vegetables and sausages, including *morcela*. Traditionally, the meat and vegetables are served separately, with rice and beans respectively, and the stock is served on the side.

Portuguese cabbage

Caldo Verde is a hearty soup of kale or cabbage with spicy *chouriço* sausage. The colour is as vibrant as the flavour.

Weekly regional market at Barcelos in the Minho

traditionally covered in paprika powder after salting and drying, has a long-standing reputation as among the country's best. Serra do Barroso, the mountainous area bordering the Minho, gives its name to the Barrosã breed of cow, made tasty by grazing the high pastures of this wet area.

Extreme Climates

The rows of vines that line the slopes of the upper Douro valley, neatly tracing its con-tours, give this once remote region a tamed appearance that belies its extremes of climate. Cold winters, slow warming in spring, and blistering-hot summers bring out the best in the thick-skinned grape varieties that go into making port. On the valley's northern side are the

olive groves and orchards of the Terra Quente, the "hot lands" of the lower Trás-os-Montes region. Interestingly, the olive oils from here are prized for their mildness of flavour. Farther north, beyond Bragança, lie the drier and colder high plains of the Terra Fria, where some inhabitants still spend the winter indoors, warmed by their animals and living off

The shop window of an Porto *pastelaria* (pastry shop)

their stocks of chestnuts, cabbages and cured meats.

Porto

Modern cooking is largely confined to Porto, which has some of the country's most innovative chefs, but the city also retains culinary traditions such as cooking tripe, which has earned its citizens the nickname *tripeiros* (tripe-eaters). It is also famed for its egg-based pastries.

REGIONAL WINES

Vinho verde, the familiar light white and slightly fizzy wine from the Minho, has made something of a comeback after a period of neglect by producers as well as consumers. Its appeal lies in its acidity (the "crispness" and "freshness" of wine writing), its carbon dioxide sparkle and its relatively low alcohol content – around 10 per cent. There is also a fuller-bodied, more complex style, made from the Alvarinho grape in and around the town of Monção. The red version of *vinho verde* is rarely found outside the region. Port wine *(see pp234–5)* is the other highlight among northern Portuguese drinks, but modern wines from the Douro also merit serious attention. They match the regional cuisine admirably, and their distinctive character includes rare wine flavours such as violets and heather.

Trutas com presunto wraps fat river trout in lean cured ham before they are fried in bacon fat until golden.

Cozido à Portuguesa is a winter stew of beef, sausage and root vegetables, suited to the cold northern plains.

Toucinho do céu translates as "heavenly bacon" but is actually a rich and mouthwatering almond cake.

OURO AND TRÁS-OS-MONTES

n its way to the Atlantic, the Douro or "Golden River" weaves its enic path through deep-cleft gorges, terraced with thousands vineyards, to the historic city of Porto, home of port. To the ortheast, the high plateaus and mountain ranges of Trás-os-ontes, "Behind the Mountains", form Portugal's wildest region.

early as the 9th century BC, Phoenician erchants arrived in the Douro estuary trade. The Romans later developed e settlements of Portus and Cale on ther side of the river, and the names bsequently united, as Portucale, to enote the region between the Minho d Douro rivers. This was the nucleus the kingdom of Portugal (see pp46–7). e estuary and coastal strip, or Douro toral, is now a mix of fishing ports, beach sorts and industrial zones, while Portus, the river's mouth, became Porto, the gional capital and Portugal's second city. Rich from centuries of trade, cosmopolitan orto is at once modern and steeped the past, its waterfront and higgledy-ggledy streets a delight to explore. om its hillside, Oporto looks across the ouro to the lodges that nurture e precious wine to which the city ave its name: port.

The upper reaches of the river are devoted to the cultivation of grapes for port, the landscape shaped by endless vineyards and wine estates (quintas).

In contrast with the thriving Douro valley, Trás-os-Montes is remote and untamed, a refuge in the past of religious and political exiles. The hard life and lack of opportunity to better it have depopulated the land; those who remain till the fields and herd their flocks in the unforgiving climate, according to the rhythm of the seasons.

The rural north clings closely to tradition and local festas are some of the country's most colourful (see pp232–3). Outside influences are beginning to make an impact on Trás-os-Montes, but for the visitor it remains a land of quiet stone villages amid fields of rye and moorland, where the wild Parque Natural de Montesinho stretches from Bragança to the Spanish border.

raced vineyards covering the hillsides between Pinhão and Alijó, in the valley of the Upper Douro

A bridge over the River Sabor in Trás-os-Montes

Exploring the Douro and Trás-os-Montes

Porto itself is so full of interest that many visitors venture
no further. But to follow the Douro upstream is to discover a
world of neat terraced vineyards and prosperous *quintas* all
dedicated to producing wine and port. Porto apart, either
Peso da Régua or the pilgrimage town of Lamego would
make a convenient base from which to explore the area.

Trás-os-Montes is Portugal's poorest and least-known
region. Its isolated capital, Bragança, is full of historic
associations, and lies on the edge of the wild terrain of
the Montesinho reserve. Between here and Chaves is
spectacular country seldom visited by tourists.

Rocky outcrops of the Parque Natural do
Alvão

Sights at a Glance

1. Porto pp242–53
2. Santo Tirso
3. Penafiel
4. Amarante
5. Cinfães
6. Mesão Frio
7. Peso da Régua
8. Lamego
10. Casa de Mateus pp260–61
11. Vila Real
12. Parque Natural do Alvão
13. Serra do Barroso

14. Chaves
15. Murça
16. Mirandela
17. Bragança pp264–5
18. Parque Natural de Montesinho
19. Miranda do Douro
20. Mogadouro
21. Torre de Moncorvo
22. Freixo de Espada à Cinta

Tours

9. Port Country Tour pp258–9

Porto's quayside, the Cais da Ribeira, in the early morning

For keys and symbols *see back flap*

Key

▬▬ Motorway
▬▬ Major road
▭▭▭ Minor road
▬▬ Scenic route
▬ ▪ ▪ Main railway
▬▬ Minor railway
▬▬ National border
▬▬ Regional border

kilometres   25

miles   10

Port country near Pinhão, where vineyards clothe the banks of the Douro

Getting Around

With the frenetic tempo of traffic in Porto, it is best to negotiate the inner city by bus, taxi or on foot. Boat trips from Porto are a good way to see the varied Douro landscape at a relaxed pace. Trains link Porto to the major towns of the north and also run along the Douro valley. Services are less frequent beyond Peso da Régua, but a trip alongside the Douro is highly recommended. In Trás-os-Montes, public transport is minimal and driving is the most convenient way to explore this remote region, especially now the A4 links Vila Real and Bragança. However, the state of repair of many minor roads leaves a lot to be desired.

The Sabor near Bragança, on the southern edge of the Parque Natural de Montesinho

● Porto

Ever since the Romans built a fort here, where their trading route crossed the Douro, Porto has prospered from commerce. Quick to expel the Moors in the 11th century and to profit from provisioning crusaders en route to the Holy Land, Porto took advantage of the wealth generated by Portugal's maritime discoveries in the 15th and 16th centuries. Later, the wine trade with Britain compensated for the loss of the lucrative spice trade. Still a thriving industrial centre and Portugal's second-largest city, Porto, sometimes referred to as Oporto, blends industry with charm. In 2001 the city, the historic centre of which is a UNESCO World Heritage site, was the European Capital of Culture.

A shop specializing in *bacalhau* (dried salted cod)

The Cathedral District

Porto's cathedral (see p246) crowns the city's upper level and in the surrounding streets are a variety of monuments to the city's past. These include the Renaissance church of Santa Clara (see p245) and the turn-of-the-century railway station of São Bento (see p245), which both stand alongside bustling street markets.

Beneath the towering cathedral lies the crowded Barredo, a quarter seemingly unchanged since medieval days, where balconied houses cling to each other and to the vertiginous hillside, forming a maze of ancient alleys; some are no more than outside staircases.

Ribeira

The riverside quarter of Porto, is a warren of narrow, twisting streets and shadowy arcades that perfectly capture the city's rich history. Behind brightly tiled or pastel-painted façades, many in faded glory, a working population earns its living, hangs out the washing, chats and mixes in lively street scenes. A UNESCO neighbourhood, restoration work on many of the old buildings and façades is widely ongoing. There is a growing number of trendy bars and cafés opening in the district, next to traditional grocery stores and family-run restaurants, meaning there are plenty of great places to eat, drink and people-watch in both new and old Ribeira.

It is worth paying a few euros and getting on the Teleférico de Gaia cable car, across the Ponte de Dom Luis I. The journey affords spectacular views of the historic and characterful Ribeira quarter, along with the Duoro, providing plenty of excellent photo opportunities. Ribeira is also home to the Casa do Infante (see p246).

Sights at a Glance

① Sé
② Casa-Museu Guerra Junqueiro
③ Casa do Infante
④ Palácio da Bolsa
⑤ World of Discoveries
⑥ Museu dos Transportes e Comunicações
⑦ Igreja da Misericórdia
⑧ São Francisco
⑨ Igreja dos Congregados
⑩ Igreja dos Clérigos
⑪ Igreja do Carmo
⑫ Museu Soares dos Reis
⑬ Igreja de São Martinho de Cedo
⑭ Museu Romântico da Quinta da Macieirinha
⑮ Jardim do Palácio de Cristal
⑯ Ponte de Dom Luís I

The cathedral (Sé) and statue of Vímara Peres (see p246)

Looking north up the Avenida dos Aliados to the Câmara Municipal

Cordoaria

The Cordoaria gardens are simply referred to as Cordoaria, and lie in the lee of the hilltop landmark of the Torre dos Clérigos (see p247). There are several sculptures by Spanish sculptor Juan Muñoz at this urban park. Nearby, the winding streets are home to some of the city's quirkiest bars and shops.

Central and Baixa

The civic centre of Porto ranges along the Avenida dos Aliados, or simply Aliados to locals, leading up to the modern Câmara Municipal, or town hall. Along this broad double avenue is a high concentration of the city's banks and offices, and popular outdoor cafés. Look out for the Estação de São Bento; this train station is one of the city's grandest buildings and visitors to the city should pop in to admire its grandeur.

To the east, the Baixa, or "lower level" district, attracts local shoppers, especially to the fashionable jewellery and leather shops in and around the pedestrianized Rua de Santa Catarina and the parallel Rua Sá da Bandeira. Between them lies the two-tier covered Bolhão market. Exuberant and noisy, the market provides an entertaining view of Porto daily life and houses tempting local produce. Everything can be bought here, from fresh fruit and vegetables to flowers, household goods and even pets.

Key

▪ Cathedral District pp244–5

0 metres   300
0 yards   300

VISITORS' CHECKLIST

Practical Information
Map C2. 245,000. Rua Clube dos Fenianos 25 (223 393 472); Sé Cathedral, Calçada de D Pedro Pitões 15 (223 325 174). 2nd half of Jun: Festas da Cidade. w visitporto.travel

Transport
Francisco Sá Carneiro, Pedras Rubras 20 km (12 miles) N (229 432 400). National & International: Campanhã; Regional: São Bento (707 210 220). Praceta Régulo Megoanha; Rua Alexandre Herculano; Rua da Restauração; Interface Casa da Música; Campo 24 de Agosto.

Boavista

Avenida da Boavista is lined with hotels, apartments and shops. In the centre is the Praça de Mouzinho de Albuquerque, a park-cum-roundabout more commonly referred to as Rotunda da Boavista. At the centre stands a great obelisk with a statue of a lion (representing the Luso-British forces) crushing an eagle (the French), marking the victory in the Peninsular War.

Next to the rotunda is the Casa da Música, a striking modern concert hall designed by Rem Koolhaas as part of the city's regeneration project, in 2005. Also nearby is Igreja de São Martinho de Cedofeita (see p249). South of here is some of the best shopping in the city.

Ribeira, the old town of Porto, and the river Douro

Street-by-Street: Porto's Cathedral District

Archaeological excavations show that Penaventosa Hill, now the site of Porto's cathedral, or Sé, was inhabited as early as 3,000 years ago. In its elevated position, the cathedral is a useful landmark and its terrace provides an excellent orientation point. The broad Avenida de Vímara Peres, named after the military hero who expelled the Moors from the city in AD 868, sweeps south past the huddle of steep alleys and stairways of the Barredo. The view to the north is towards the extraordinarily embellished São Bento station and the busy commercial heart of the city.

Rua das Flores
Behind the traditional shopfronts in the Street of Flowers are some of the city's best jewellers and goldsmiths.

RUA DAS F

R. MOUZINHO D. S

RUA ESCURA

CALÇADA DE VAND

Terreiro da Sé
This broad open terrace offers a wonderful panorama of the city. In one corner stands a stone monument, complete with hooks.

TERREIRO
DA SÉ

RUA DE DOM HUGO

Bishop's palace

★ Sé
Although imposing and perhaps a little forbidding, Porto's cathedral contains many small-scale treasures. This 17th-century gilded carving of the Last Supper is in the Capela de São Vicente (see p246).

The Casa-Museu Guerra Junqueiro is a charming museum in a house that once belonged to the 19th-century poet (see p246).

Ponte de
Dom Luis I

Praça de Almeida Garrett
Traffic hurries by oblivious to the architectural diversity of this busy square in the centre of Porto.

★ São Bento Station
Porto's central railway station, on the site of an earlier monastery, was completed in 1916. Inside is a feast of *azulejos* by Jorge Colaço *(see p31)*, depicting early modes of transport, rural festivities and historic scenes.

The Fernandine Wall, named after Dom Fernando, was built in the 14th and 15th centuries; only fragments here and along the Cais da Ribeira *(see p242)* remain.

Santa Clara
The Mannerist church of Santa Clara presents a strong contrast between its simple external façade and the opulent gilded woodwork of its interior.

Praça da Liberdade

PRAÇA DE ALMEIDA GARRETT

São Bento Station

RUA DO LOUREIRO

M AFONSO HENRIQUES

RUA CHÃ

RUA SARAIVA DE CARVALHO

0 metres   50
0 yards   50

Key

— Suggested route

For keys to symbols *see back flap*

Exploring Porto

Throughout Porto there is evidence of the wealth that flowed into the city from the 15th century onwards. Trade in the commodities from Portugal's newly claimed lands *(see pp52–3)* brought Brazilian gold and exotic woods to embellish Porto's churches, and prosperous merchants spent prodigiously on paintings and *azulejos*. Today, this gracious capital of the north is a thriving cultural hub and easily visited on foot, starting in the prime riverside location of the ancient Ribeira district.

The Gothic cloisters on the south side of the Sé

⬆ Sé

Terreiro da Sé. **Tel** 222 059 028. **Open** Oct–Mar: 9am–6pm Mon–Sat (till 7pm Apr–Sep), 9am–12:30pm & 2:30–6pm Sun (till 7pm Apr–Sep). 🚹 11am. Cloisters: **Open** Oct–Mar: 9am–5:30pm Mon–Sat (till 6:30pm Apr–Sep), 2:30–5:30pm Sun (till 6:30pm Apr–Sep).

Built as a fortress church in the 12th and 13th centuries, the cathedral has been modified several times. The beautiful rose window in the west front is from the 13th century. The small chapel to the left of the chancel has a dazzling silver retable, saved from invading French troops in 1809 by a hastily raised plaster wall. The south transept gives access to the 14th-century cloisters and the Capela de São Vicente. An 18th-century staircase leads to the upper levels, where *azulejo* panels depict the life of the Virgin and Ovid's *Metamorphoses*.

🏛 Casa-Museu Guerra Junqueiro

Rua de Dom Hugo 32. **Tel** 222 003 689. **Open** 10am–5:30pm daily. **Closed** public hols.

The home of poet and fiery Republican activist Guerra Junqueiro (1850–1923) is an 18th-century Baroque gem. The poet's private collection ranges from ceramics and Portuguese furniture to Flemish tapestries and a set of English alabaster sculptures. In the Dom João V Room there is a colourful parade of dogs.

⬚ Casa do Infante

Rua da Alfândega 10. **Tel** 222 060 400. **Open** 9:30am–12:30pm & 2–5pm Tue–Sun. **Closed** public hols.

Legend has it that Prince Henry the Navigator was born in this house on Porto's riverfront. Today the building houses Porto's city archives, which include historical documents, among them Prince Henry's christening certificate, photographs and archaeological finds.

⬚ Palácio da Bolsa

Rua Ferreira Borges. **Tel** 223 399 013. **Open** Apr–Oct: 9am–6:30pm daily; Nov–Mar: 9am–12:30pm & 2–5:30pm daily. **Closed** 1 Jan, 25 Dec. compulsory.

Where the monastery of São Francisco once stood, the city's merchants built the stock exchange, or Bolsa, in 1842. The Tribunal do Comércio, where Porto's mercantile law was upheld, is full of historic interest. The glittering highlight is the Arabian Room. This galleried salon, its convoluted blue and gold arabesques inspired by Granada's Alhambra, makes a setting fit for Scheherazade.

🏛 World of Discoveries

Rua de Miagaia 106. **Tel** 220 439 770. **Open** 10am–6pm Mon–Fri (till 7pm Sat & Sun; last adm 30 min before closing). **Closed** 1 Jan, 25 Dec. 🅦 worldofdiscoveries.com

An interactive museum with a small ride, this family adventure is located in the heart of the city centre. The twenty themed areas tell the story of Portugal's history, including the various stages of the Portuguese Discoveries and the country's groundbreaking maritime achievements in the 15th and 16th centuries.

🏛 Museu dos Transportes e Comunicações

Rua Nova da Alfândega, Edifício da Alfândega. **Tel** 223 403 000. **Open** 10am–1pm & 2–6pm Tue–Fri, 3–7pm Sat & Sun. **Closed** 1 Jan, 1 May, 24 Jun, 25 Dec. 🅦 amtc.pt

Housed in a vast Neo-Classical building on the riverfront, this museum includes a permanent exhibition on the automobile and interactive exhibitions on media, science, new technologies and art. The building also houses a coffee shop, various spaces for cultural events and the customs service.

The magnificently gilded Arabian Room in Porto's Palácio da Bolsa

São Francisco's Tree of Jesse

Illustrating biblical episodes, either in stained-glass windows or as elaborate carvings, was a common form of "Bible teaching" before literacy became widespread. A popular subject was Christ's genealogy, showing his descent from the kings of Judah and Israel. This was commonly rendered as an actual tree, tracing the family line back through Joseph to the father of King David, Jesse of Bethlehem.

São Francisco's Tree, in gilded and painted wood, was carved between 1718 and 1721 by Filipe da Silva, António Gomes and Manuel Carneiro Adão. Its sinuous branches and trunk, sprouting from a reclining Jesse, support a dozen expressive figures, culminating in Christ flanked by his mother, Mary, and St Joseph.

Virgin Mary

Jesus Christ

Joseph

Solomon, who succeeded his father, David, was famed for his wisdom and for the building of the Temple in Jerusalem.

Jesse is shown with the roots of the Tree springing from his loins. His youngest son was David, the slayer of Goliath, who became king of Israel and Judah.

King David, identified by his harp

🏛 Igreja da Misericórdia

Rua das Flores 15. **Tel** 222 074 710. **Open** 10am–6pm daily. 🕐 9:30am Tue–Fri & Sun. 📷

This religious hospice, alongside its imposing church, was founded in the 1500s. Its most precious possession is the *Fons Vitae* (Fountain of Life), donated by Manuel I in about 1520. It shows the king and his family kneeling before the crucified Christ. The artist's identity remains unproven, but both Van der Weyden and Holbein have been suggested.

🏛 São Francisco

Rua do Infante D Henrique. **Tel** 222 062 100. **Open** 9am–5:30pm daily (till 7pm Mar–Jun & Oct, till 8pm Jul–Sep). **Closed** 25 Dec. 📷 🎫 Catacombs incl.

This Gothic church was begun in the 1300s, but it is the 18th-century Baroque interior that amazes visitors. Over 200 kg (450 lb) of gold encrust the high altar, columns and pillars, wrought into cherubs and garlands, culminating with the Tree of Jesse on the north

wall. A tour includes the catacombs and treasures from the church's monastery, destroyed in 1832.

🏛 Igreja dos Congregados

Rua da Sá da Bandeira 11. **Tel** 222 002 948. **Open** 8am–6pm Mon–Sat, 8am–1pm & 5–6pm Sun. **Closed** public hols. 🕐 6pm daily.

The modern tiles on the façade of this 17th-century church are by Jorge Colaço (*see p31*). They depict scenes from the life of St Antony, and provide a dignified presence amid the traffic that clogs this part of the city.

🏛 Igreja dos Clérigos

Rua São Filipe de Nery. **Tel** 220 145 489. **Open** 9am–7pm daily. Tower: **Open** 9am–7pm daily. 📷

This unmistakable hilltop landmark was built in the 18th century by the Italian architect Niccolò Nasoni.

The soaring Torre dos Clérigos with which the architect complemented his design is, at 75 m (246 ft), still one of the tallest buildings in Portugal. The dizzying 240-step climb is worth it for the superb views of the river, the coastline and the Douro valley – an excellent photo opportunity.

The Baroque church of Santo Antonio dos Congregados in Almeida Garrett Sqaure

Detail of the *azulejo* panel on the side wall of the Igreja do Carmo

🏛 Igreja do Carmo

Rua do Carmo. **Tel** 222 078 400.
Open 8am–noon & 1–6pm
Mon & Wed, 9am–6pm Tue & Thu,
9am–5:30pm Fri, 9am–1:30pm Sun. ♿

This typically ornate example of Portuguese Baroque was designed by the architect José Figueiredo Seixas. The church was constructed between 1750 and 1768, and one of its most remarkable features is the monumental white-and-blue *azulejo* panel that covers one of the outside walls. This was created by Silvestro Silvestri and depicts the legendary founding of the Carmelite order as a community of hermits on Mount Carmel, in Israel.

The older Igreja das Carmelitas next door, meant for Carmelite nuns, was completed in 1628 in a combination of Classical and Baroque styles. It is now part of a barracks.

🏛 Museu Soares dos Reis

Rua Dom Manuel II. **Tel** 223 393 770.
Open 10am–6pm Tue–Sun (from 2pm Tue). **Closed** public hols. 🅆
W **museusoaresdosreis.pt**

The elegant Carrancas Palace, built in the 18th century, has been a Jewish textile workshop, a royal abode and a military headquarters. In 1809 Porto was in French hands, and Marshal Soult and his troops were quartered here. They were ousted in a surprise attack by Arthur Wellesley, later Duke of Wellington, who then calmly installed himself at the marshal's dinner table.

Today, the palace provides an appropriate setting for an outstanding museum, named after António Soares dos Reis, the country's leading 19th-century sculptor. Pride of place goes to the display of

O Desterrado
Soares dos R...

A River View of Porto

Flowing over 927 km (576 miles) from its source in Spain to the Atlantic, the Douro has been linked with the fortunes of Porto since time immemorial. There is an unsubstantiated story that Henry the Navigator, patron of Portuguese explorers, (*see p53*), was born in the waterfront Casa do Infante. The days are long since gone when ships laden with port or goods from overseas would moor here, but the river continues to be a focal point of the city. A river cruise is a chance to appreciate Porto from a different viewpoint.

Most river-boat operators are based in the shadow of the swooping curve of the splendid two-tier Ponte de Dom Luís I, built in 1886 by an assistant of Gustave Eiffel, to link the city to Vila Nova de Gaia on the southern bank. The city has a largely above-ground metro system, which uses the upper level of the Dom Luís I bridge. Just upriver, the Infante Dom Henrique bridge is for cars. Further views can be enjoyed from the Teleferico de Gaia cable car.

Vila Nova de Gaia is home of the port lodges (*see p253*).

Ponte da Arrábida

Quayside of the Cais da Estiva

Portuguese art. This includes paintings by the 16th-century master, Frey Carlos, and the impressionist, Henrique Pousão. Also hung here are landscapes of Porto by the French artist, Jean Pillement (1728–1808). The star sculpture exhibit, *O Desterrado* (The Exile), is Soares dos Reis's own marvel of pensive tension in marble, completed in 1874. Further sections display Portuguese pottery, Limoges enamels, porcelain and decorative art. Historical exhibits in the museum include an appealing 15th-century silver bust of São Pantaleão, patron saint of Porto.

🚹 Igreja de São Martinho de Cedofeita

Largo do Priorado. **Tel** 222 000 635. **Open** 4–7pm Tue–Fri. 🅰

Constructed in Romanesque style in the 12th century, this plain little church is thought to be the oldest in the city. It is said to have been built on the site where Theodomir, the King of the Suevi (a Germanic tribe who occupied the area), was converted to Christianity in the 6th century by Saint Martin.

🏛 Museu Romântico

Rua de Entre-Quintas 220. **Tel** 226 057 033. **Open** 10am–5pm Mon–Sat, 10am–noon & 2–5pm Sun. **Closed** public hols. 🅰

The Quinta da Macieirinha, a handsome 18th-century mansion, was briefly the residence of the abdicated King Carlo Alberto of Sardinia (1798–1849), who lived here for the final two months of his life. In 1972 the upper floor of the building was converted into a museum. The well-proportioned rooms looking out over the river display French, German and Portuguese furniture, as well as rugs, ceramics and miscellaneous exhibits. Among the oil paintings and watercolours on show here are portraits of Baron Forrester *(see p258)* and Almeida Garrett, the great Portuguese Romantic poet, playwright and author.

🌳 Jardim do Palácio de Cristal

Rua Dom Manuel II. **Open** 8am–9pm daily (Oct–Mar: to 7pm).

Inspired by the Crystal Palace of London's Great Exhibition in 1851, Porto's own crystal palace was begun in 1861. The steel and glass structure of the original was replaced in the 1950s by the Pavilhão Rosa Mota, an ungainly shape dubbed "the half-orange". Concerts are occasionally held here and the leisure gardens are enlivened by a fair at *festa* time. The gardens themselves are the star attraction, with avenues of lime trees and wonderful river views.

Picturesque Jardim do Palácio de Cristal

Cais da Ribeira is one of the quays at which river boats moor.

Bishops' palace

Torre dos Clérigos *(see p247)*

Sé *(see p246)*

Ponte de Dom Luís I

Porto: Further Afield

Away from the city centre, Porto has many additional places of interest. Crossing the Ponte de Dom Luís I brings you to Vila Nova de Gaia, the home of port, and the Mosteiro da Serra do Pilar, with one of the finest views of the old city. In the northern and western suburbs are several fascinating attractions, from the great church of the Hospitallers at Leça do Bailio, north of Porto, to the latest developments in Portuguese art exhibited in the beautifully modern setting of the Museu Serralves.

Along the coast, beyond the river-mouth castle at Foz do Douro, lies Matosinhos, which, despite its industrial port, is renowned for its seafood. The beaches, such as Espinho, are the main draw along the coast south of Porto.

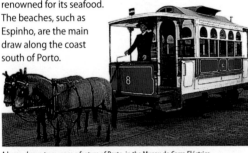

A horse-drawn tram, once a feature of Porto, in the Museu do Carro Eléctrico

⛪ Mosteiro da Serra do Pilar
Serra do Pilar. **Tel** 220 142 425.
Open Tue–Sun. 🖼

From the terrace of this circular 16th-century church, the future Duke of Wellington planned his surprise attack on the French in 1809. The view takes in the port lodges below, the sweep of the River Douro and the old city on the far side.

⛪ Museu do Carro Eléctrico
Alameda Basílio Teles 51.
Tel 226 158 185. **Open** 10am–6pm Tue–Sun; 2–6pm Mon. 🖼
W museudocarroelectrico.pt

Among the trams on show here is No. 22, introduced in 1895 as the first electric tram on the Iberian Peninsula. A ride on No. 1, Porto's last tram, takes a scenic route along the river to Rua Infante Dom Henrique and back.

⛪ Casa da Música
Avenida da Boavista 604. **Tel** 220 120 220. 🕒 9:30am–7pm daily (to 6pm Sun & public hols). **W** casadamusica.com

The Casa da Música is a venue for all types of music, from classical to *fado* and from electronica to jazz. It also promotes research into the origins of Portuguese music.

⛪ Fundação de Serralves Museu de Arte Contemporânea
Rua Dom João de Castro 210. **Tel** 226 156 500. **Open** Apr–Sep: 10am–7pm Mon & Wed–Fri, 10am–8pm Sat & Sun; Oct–Mar: 10am–6pm Mon & Wed–Fri, 10am–7pm Sat & Sun. **Closed** 1 Jan, 25 Dec. 🖼 ♿ **W** serralves.pt

Portugal's main institution for contemporary art is responsible for both the Art Deco Casa de Serralves and the Museu de Arte Contemporânea. Housed in a long, white building, the museum has a permanent collection including works by Christian Boltanski, Bruce Nauman and Julião Sarmento.

⛪ Casa-Museu Fernando de Castro
Rua Costa Cabral 716. **Tel** 223 393 770. **Open** by appt (223 393 770). 🖼

The former residence of poet, businessman and collector Fernando de Castro (1888–1950) houses his collection, which ranges from religious sculpture to works of modern art. Among the highlights are a painting of the infant Jesus attributed to Josefa de Óbidos (*see p55*) and figurines from the 19th and 20th centuries by Teixeira Lopes, father and son.

Environs

Forts around the river mouth, such as the Forte de São João Baptista da Foz at Foz do Douro and Castelo do Queijo just to the north, are reminders that for centuries the coast and ships were under constant threat from the Spanish and pirates.

The church of Bom Jesus, in Matosinhos, was reconstructed by Niccolò Nasoni in the 18th century. Each June, pilgrims come here to honour a wooden statue of Christ allegedly carved by the disciple Nicodemus.

The 14th-century fortified Igreja do Mosteiro at Leça do Bailio, 8 km (5 miles) north of Porto, was Portugal's first headquarters of the Order of Hospitallers. The church has elegant Gothic arches and a splendid rose window.

The Art Deco Casa de Serralves

◀ Attractive, historic houses line the river in the old town of Ribeira, Porto

Vila Nova de Gaia

Afonso III, in dispute with the Bishop of Porto over shipping tolls, established a rival port at Vila Nova de Gaia. In 1253, they reluctantly agreed to share the levies. Today the heart of Vila Nova de Gaia is devoted mostly to the maturation and shipping of port *(see pp258–9)*. Although the regulation that port could be made only in Vila Nova de Gaia was relaxed in 1987, this is still very much the centre of production. Every alley is lined with the lodges or *armazéns* (there are no cellars here) in which port is blended and aged.

Guided tours are a chance to see how port is made *(see pp234–5)* and often end with a tasting to demonstrate the different styles.

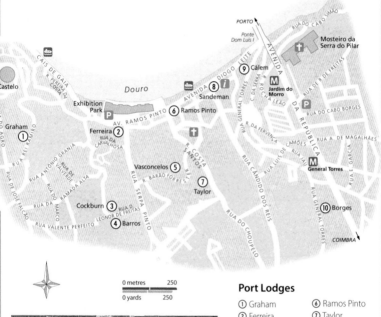

Port Lodges

① Graham	⑥ Ramos Pinto
② Ferreira	⑦ Taylor
③ Cockburn	⑧ Sandeman
④ Barros	⑨ Cálem
⑤ Vasconcelos	⑩ Borges

Visiting the Lodges

Joining a tour: Lodges listed here are among those offering tours. Booking is not usually necessary, but contact a lodge beforehand to confirm times; the tourist office at Avenida Diogo Leite 135 (223 773 089) can supply addresses and telephone numbers.
Opening times: Variable. Usually Mon–Fri; some also at weekends. Most close on public holidays.

The port lodges dominate Vila Nova de Gaia. Over 50 port companies are based in these narrow streets, ageing and blending most of the world's supply of port beneath a sea of red roofs emblazoned with world-famous names.

The former monastery of São Bento at Santo Tirso, now a college

❷ Santo Tirso

Road map C2. 🏘 13,900. 🚊 🚌
🛈 Praça 25 de Abril (252 830 411).
🛒 Mon.

Santo Tirso, a major textile centre, lies beside the River Ave. The town's most notable building is the former monastery of São Bento. Founded by the Benedictines in the 8th century, the monastery was later rebuilt, then modified in the 17th century. The pairs of columns in the 14th-century Gothic cloister are graced with richly carved capitals.

The monastery, now an agricultural college, also houses the **Museu Abade Pedrosa**, featuring local archaeological finds, including stone axes, bronze armlets and ceramics.

🏛 **Museu Abade Pedrosa**
Rua Unisco Godiniz 100.
Tel 252 830 400. **Open** Tue–Sun.
Closed public hols.

The sanctuary of Nossa Senhora da Piedade in Penafiel

Environs
At Roriz, 13 km (8 miles) east of Santo Tirso, the Romanesque church of São Pedro perches above the Vizela valley. A date of 1228 is carved in the porch, although there are claims that a church may have stood here as early as the 8th century. Above the portal is a fine rose window. Set apart from the church are an attractive bell tower and the ruins of the monastic cloister.

Sanfins de Ferreira, 5 km (3 miles) further east, is the hilltop site of a *citânia*, an Iron Age citadel, probably inhabited from around the 6th century BC. Traces remain of a triple ring of defensive walls around about 100 huts, and there is also a small museum on the site. The guard next door will let you in on public holidays.

🏛 **Sanfins de Ferreira**
Sanfins, signposted off N209.
Tel 255 963 643. **Open** Tue–Sun.

❸ Penafiel

Road map C2. 🏘 8,000. 🚌 🛈
Largo Padre Américo (255 710 722).
🛒 10 & 20 of month.

The granite town of Penafiel stands on a hilltop above the River Sousa. Apart from an elegant Renaissance-style Igreja Matriz, there is also a sanctuary, Nossa Senhora da Piedade, built in 1908 in a curious medley of Neo-Gothic and Byzantine styles. Penafiel is chiefly known, however, as

the regional centre for the production of *vinho verde*.

Environs
One of the region's foremost estates producing *vinho verde* is **Quinta da Aveleda**, just north of Penafiel.

Boelhe, around 17 km (11 miles) south of Penafiel, merits a detour for the 12th- century church of São Gens. Only 10 m (33 ft) high, and a mere 7 m (23 ft) in width and length, it is claimed to be the smallest Romanesque church in the country. Its simple design enhances the aesthetic appeal.

In the 13th-century church of São Salvador at Paço de Sousa, 8 km (5 miles) southwest of Penafiel, is the tomb of Egas Moniz. A figure of legendary loyalty, he was counsellor to Afonso Henriques (1139–85), the first king of Portugal.

🏛 **Quinta da Aveleda**
Signposted from N115. **Tel** 255 718 200.
Open Mon–Sat (Apr–Oct: daily).
Closed public hols. 🌐 ♿
🎥 compulsory.

The tiny church of São Gens at Boelhe, south of Penafiel

❹ Amarante

Road map D2. 🏘 70,000. 🚊 🚌
🛈 Largo do Arquinho (255 420 246).
🛒 Wed & Sat.

The pretty, riverside town of Amarante is one of the gems of northern Portugal. Rows of 17th-century mansions with brightly painted wooden balconies line Amarante's narrow streets, and restaurants seat diners on terraces overhanging the river. The origins of the town are uncertain but the first settlement here was probably around 360 BC.

Much of the town was burnt down in 1809, after a two-week siege by the French forces under Marshal Soult. A recurring name in Amarante is that of São Gonçalo, a very popular saint born at the end of the 12th century. There are many stories of the dancing and festivities he organized to keep ladies from temptation by finding them husbands, and he has become associated with matchmaking and fertility. On the first weekend in June, the Festa de São Gonçalo begins with prayers for a marriage partner, followed by dancing, music and the giving of phallic-shaped São Gonçalo cakes.

When the old Roman bridge across the Tâmega collapsed during floods in the 13th century, it was São Gonçalo who was credited with replacing it. The present Ponte de São Gonçalo crosses to the 16th-century **Igreja de São Gonçalo**, where his memory lives on. In the chapel to the left of the chancel, the image on his tomb has been eroded through the embraces of thousands of devotees in search of his intercession.

The **Museu Amadeo de Souza-Cardoso** is housed in the old monastery cloister next to the church. One of the exhibits describes a fertility cult that predates even São Gonçalo. The *diabo* and *diaba* are a pair of bawdy devils

The Ponte de São Gonçalo across the Tâmega at Amarante

carved in black wood, and are 19th-century replacements for a more ancient duo destroyed in the Peninsular War. They gradually became the focus of a type of local fertility rite, and were threatened with burning by an outraged bishop of Braga; the *diabo* was "castrated" instead.

The museum's other prized possession is the collection of Cubist works by the artist after whom the museum is named. Amadeo de Souza-Cardoso (1887–1918), one of Portugal's leading 20th-century artists, was a native of Amarante.

🏠 **Igreja de São Gonçalo**
Praça da República. **Tel** 255 422 050.
Open daily.

🏛 **Museu Amadeo de Souza-Cardoso**
Alameda Teixeira de Pascoães.
Tel 255 420 272. **Open** Tue–Sun.
Closed public hols.

❺ Cinfães

Road map D2. 🚗 4,000. 🚌
ℹ️ Rua Capitão Salgueiro Maia (255 561 230). 🗓 10 & 26 of month.

Cinfães lies just above the Douro, tucked below the foothills of the Serra de Montemuro whose peaks rise over 1,000 m (3,300 ft). The town is a gateway to Lamego and the Upper Douro to the east *(see pp258–9)* and is surrounded by verdant scenery. Cinfães itself is an agricultural centre and local handicrafts include weaving, lacework, basketry, and the production of miniature *rabelos*, the boats that used to ship port down the river to Porto *(see p258)*.

Environs

Around 16 km (10 miles) west of the town, at Tarouquela, is the 12th-century church of Santa Maria Maior. Romanesque columns flank the portal, while later additions include the 14th-century Gothic mausoleum beside the chancel.

In the village of Cárquere, between Cinfães and Lamego, stands another church dedicated to the Virgin Mary. Legend tells how the sickly young Afonso Henriques, future king of Portugal, was healed at Cárquere by his devoted aide, Egas Moniz. In about 1110, guided by a dream, Moniz unearthed a buried statue of the Virgin and built a church for her. Miraculously, his young charge was cured overnight. The present church dates from the 14th or 15th century, but the finest of its treasures is a minute ivory carving of the Virgin, of unknown date.

The 12th-century church of Nossa Senhora de Cárquere, near Cinfães

Painted ceiling panels in São Nicolau, Mesão Frio's Igreja Matriz

❻ Mesão Frio

Road map D2. 🚹 4,900. 🚌
🛈 Avenida Conselheiro José Maria Alpoim (933 911 043). 🛒 Fri.

This scenic gateway to the port-wine-growing region enjoys a fine setting above the River Douro. Around it, the majestic tiers of the Serra do Marão rise to form a natural climatic shield for the vineyards to the east. Mesão Frio itself is known for its wickerwork and a culinary speciality, *falachas* or chestnut cakes.

The Igreja Matriz of São Nicolau was rebuilt in 1877, but has retained its magnificent late 16th-century ceiling panels, each one bearing the portrait of a saint. The tourist office is housed in the pretty 18th-century cloisters of a former Franciscan monastery.

On the western edge of the town, the lavish and Baroque

Casa da Rede can be seen from the roadside. Dating from the 15th century, and occupied until the early 20th century, ths house cannot be visited today.

❼ Peso da Régua

Road map D2. 🚹 21,000. 🚉 🚌
🛈 Av. do Douro (254 312 846).
🛒 Wed & Sat.

Developed from the villages of Peso and Régua in the 18th century, Peso da Régua is the major hub for rail and road connections in the region.

In 1756, Régua, as the town is invariably called, was chosen by the Marquês de Pombal as the centre of the demarcated region for port production. From here, *rabelos*, the traditional wooden sailing ships, transported the barrels of port through hazardous gorges to Vila Nova de Gaia *(see p253)*. They continued to ply the river even after the advent of the Douro railway in the 1880s. Régua suffered frequently in the past from severe floods, and these are still a threat, although they have lessened since dams were built across the Douro in the 1970s and 1980s.

Many visitors to Régua often pause here only briefly on their way to explore the "port country" *(see pp258–9)*, but budding connoisseurs shouldn't overlook Peso da Régua. The **Museu do Douro**, which is set in a beautifully designed contemporary building, portrays the region's rich heritage through paintings,

writings and other forms of local culture is of particular interest.

🏛 Museu do Douro
Rua Marquês de Pombal.
Tel 254 310 190. **Open** 10am–6pm daily. **Closed** public hols.

Environs
In the surrounding countryside are some beautiful *quintas*, country estates producing port. The **Quinta da Pacheca** is at Cambres, 4 km (2 miles) to the southwest. Dating from the 18th century, this winery also produces red and white wines.

🍷 Quinta da Pacheca
Cambres, 5100–424 Lamego. **Tel** 254 313 228. **Open** tours by appt only.

Stained-glass window of the Casa do Douro, Peso da Régua, showing loaded *rabelos*

❽ Lamego

Road map D2. 🚹 11,000. 🚌
🛈 Rua Regimento de Infantária 9 (254 099 000). 🛒 Thu.

An attractive town within the demarcated port area, Lamego also produces wines, including Raposeira, Portugal's premier sparkling wine. This fertile region is also known for its fruit and choice hams.

In its more illustrious past, Lamego claims to have been host in 1143 to the first *cortes*, or national assembly, to recognize Afonso Henriques as first king of Portugal. The town's later economic decline was halted in the 16th century, when it turned to wine and textile production, and handsome Baroque mansions from this prosperous period are still a feature of the town. Today, the main focus of Lamego is as a pilgrimage town.

Vineyards on the slopes of the Serra do Marão around Mesão Frio

to the great 16th-century Portuguese artist, Grão Vasco (see p219). Finely worked 16th-century Flemish tapestries include a vividly detailed life of Oedipus.

Environs

At the foot of the valley 4 km (2 miles) east, the Capela de São Pedro de Balsemão is said to be the oldest church in Portugal. Although much modified, the 7th-century sanctuary, of Visigothic origins, remains. Here, in an ornate tomb, lies Afonso Pires, a 14th-century bishop of Porto. A statue of Nossa Senhora do Ó, the pregnant Virgin, is from the 15th century.

The 12th-century monastery of **São João de Tarouca**, the first Cistercian house in Portugal, lies 16 km (10 miles) south of Lamego. The interior of the church has many fine 18th-century *azulejo* panels, notably those in the chancel depicting the founding of the monastery, and in the sacristy, where none of the 4,709 tiles has the same design. The church also contains a remarkable *St Peter* by Grão Vasco. The Count of Barcelos, bastard son of King Dinis, is buried here, his tomb adorned with vigorous scenes of a boar hunt.

Just to the northeast, Ucanha is famed for its fortified tollgate and bridge, imposing survivals from the 12th century.

⬆ São João de Tarouca
Signposted from N226. **Tel** 254 678 766. **Open** daily. ♿

The grand staircase leading up to Nossa Senhora dos Remédios, Lamego

⬆ Nossa Senhora dos Remédios
Monte de Santo Estêvão. **Open** daily. A small hilltop chapel, originally dedicated in 1391 to St Stephen, became the focus of pilgrims devoted to the Virgin, and in 1761 Nossa Senhora dos Remédios was built on the spectacular site. The church is reached via an awe-inspiring double stairway, similar to Braga's even larger Bom Jesus (see pp284–5). Its 686 steps and nine terraces, embellished with *azulejos* and urns, rise to the Pátio dos Reis, a circle of noble granite figures beneath the twin-towered church. The church itself is of marginal interest, but there is a well-earned view across the town to the Douro and its tributaries.

In early September pilgrims arrive in their thousands for Lamego's Romaria de Nossa Senhora dos Remédios (see p36), many of them climbing the steps on their knees.

⬆ Sé
Largo da Sé. **Tel** 254 612 147. **Open** daily.
Lamego's Gothic cathedral, founded in 1129, retains its original square tower, while the rest of the architecture reflects modifications between the 16th and 18th centuries, including a Renaissance cloister with a dozen arches.

🏛 Museu de Lamego
Largo de Camões. **Tel** 254 600 230. **Open** daily. **Closed** public hols. 📷
One of the country's best local museums is housed in the former bishops' palace. Pride of place goes to the strikingly original *Criação dos Animais* (Creation of the Animals), part of a series of masterly altar panels attributed

The monastery church of São João de Tarouca in its peaceful setting

❾ Port Country Tour

The barrels of port maturing in the port lodges of Vila Nova de Gaia (see p253) begin their life here, on the wine estates (quintas) of the Upper Douro (see pp234–5). Centuries of toil on the poor schist have created thousands of terraces along the steep river banks, many no wider than a person's outstretched arms. Many vineyards have had their terraces widened to allow tractor access, but some of the oldest ones are protected as part of the cultural heritage. Many quintas, including those shown on the map, welcome visitors. Early autumn is the most rewarding time to tour; workers sing as they pick, and celebrate a good vindima or harvest.

The village and vineyards of Vale de Mendiz just before sunset

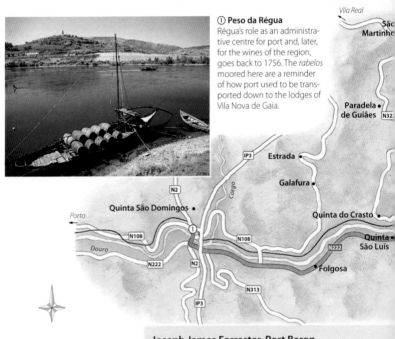

① Peso da Régua
Régua's role as an administrative centre for port and, later, for the wines of the region, goes back to 1756. The rabelos moored here are a reminder of how port used to be transported down to the lodges of Vila Nova de Gaia.

Vila Real

São Martinho

Paradela de Guiães ● N32

Estrada ●

Galafura ●

Quinta do Crasto ●

Quinta São Domingos ●

Quinta ● São Luís

Porto

Folgosa ●

Joseph James Forrester, Port Baron

In 1831, Joseph Forrester arrived from Britain to join his uncle's wine company in Porto, and enthusiastically set about reforming the port trade. In his 1844 treatise, A Word or Two on Port, he waged war on shippers who adulterated the wine. He also studied the vine blight, Oidium tuckeri, drew up remarkably detailed maps of the Douro valley and found time to become a talented watercolourist. His contribution was such that in 1855 Pedro V bestowed on him the title of Barão. In 1862, Forrester's boat capsized at Cachão de Valeira. Dragged down by his moneybelt, he drowned, but the ladies in his company survived, buoyed up by their crinolines.

0 kilometres 5
0 miles 3

Key
▬ Tour route
═ Other roads
— Railway

② Pinhão

Many of the most famous names in port production have *quintas* close to this small town. Its railway station is decorated with 24 dazzling *azulejo* panels depicting local scenes and folk culture.

Tips for Drivers

Tour length: 125 km (78 miles). Beyond Pinhão, steep, narrow roads can make the going slow.
Stopping-off points: The drive beside the Douro has several fine viewpoints. Régua and Sabrosa make good overnight stops *(see pp391–2)* and many of the *quintas* offer tours and port-tasting.

③ Sabrosa

The village of Sabrosa, set among vineyards above the River Pinhão, has a wealth of 15th-century houses. It was in one of these that the explorer Magellan *(see p52)* was born in about 1480.

④ Alijó

Alijó was officially founded in 1226, but a number of *castros* (hill forts) in the area tell of habitation from a much earlier date. The name of the *pousada* here, the Barão de Forrester *(see p406)*, recalls the famous reformer.

⑦ São João da Pesqueira

From São João da Pesqueira's viewpoint, São Salvador do Mundo, there are fine views of the valley and its vineyards. In early spring the landscape foams with almond blossom.

⑤ Tua

Tua, in a region famous for its luscious oranges and figs, has long been a junction on the Douro railway line. Travelling on one of the infrequent trains is an enjoyable way of seeing the valley's terraced vineyards.

⑥ Barragem de Valeira

Until the end of the 18th century the Douro was unnavigable beyond Cachão de Valeira. Even when engineers had bypassed the worst of the rapids, this stretch of water remained treacherous – it was here that Baron Forrester met his death – until the water was tamed by the Valeira dam in 1976.

Map labels: N212, Sanfins do Douro, Cheires, N322, N212, São Mamede de Ribatua, Tua, Quinta do ...ucheiro, Quinta do Casal de Celeirós, Quinta do Portal, N214, Mirandela, Vale de Mendiz, N323, N322-3, Linhares, N214, Duoro, Quinta do Castelinho, ...z, ...e, Pinhão, Valença do Douro, N222, Quinta do Panascal, Cachão de Valeira, N222-3, N222, Vila Nova de Foz Côa, Tavora, ...abuaço

⑩ Casa de Mateus

The splendid manor house, or *solar*, depicted on the labels of Mateus Rosé epitomizes the flamboyance of Baroque architecture in Portugal. It was built in the early 18th century, probably by Niccolò Nasoni, for António José Botelho Mourão, whose descendants still live here. The house, which was declared a national monument in 1911, is also a breeding ground for creativity, offering 11 six-month residencies to budding artists.

The wood-panelled library, repository of many valuable works

The Manor House

Inside and out, the Casa de Mateus was conceived to present carefully created vistas and series of mirror images. A formal pool added in the 1930s continues this spirit of harmonious repetition, reflecting the main façade and its two wings.

Tours start in the first-floor entrance salon, a well-proportioned room graced by a pair of sedan chairs and with a magnificent wooden ceiling featuring family coats of arms. Doorcases and ceilings throughout the house are of richly carved chestnut. The Tea Salon has a 17th-century William and Mary cupboard and matching longcase clock from England, while the

Coat of arms on the entrance hall ceiling

Salon of the Four Seasons gets its name from the large 18th-century paintings on its walls.

Many of the paintings in the house were contributed by the 4th Morgado's uncle, an archdeacon in Rome who was also responsible for the original gardens. The library, remodelled in the mid-20th century, contains volumes dating back to the 16th century, but the rarest book is in the small museum: an 1817 copy of *Os Lusíadas (see p194)*, with engravings by leading artists. It is one of a limited edition produced by the colourful diplomat grandson of the 3rd Morgado (his tomb is in the family

chapel beside the house). Also on display in the museum is family correspondence with famous figures of the era, including Frederick the Great and Wellington.

The Gardens

Beneath the entrance staircase a dark passageway leads between the stables to an inner courtyard and out to the formal gardens on the far side of the house. Little remains of the original gardens planted by the horticultural archdeacon, and the present gardens were laid out in the 1930s and 1940s. The style, however, is of an earlier, romantic era and the complex parterres and formal beds edged with tightly clipped dwarf box hedges form a living tapestry that reflects perfectly the ornate symmetry of the house. In winter

The principal façade of the Casa de Mateus, its pinnacled symmetry reflected in a rectangular pool

VISITORS' CHECKLIST

Practical Information
Road map D2. Mateus, 3 km
(2 miles) E of Vila Real. **Tel** 259 323
121. **Open** May–Oct: 9am–7:30pm
daily (Apr: to 7pm; Nov–Mar: to
5:30pm). **Closed** 25 Dec.
🖼 gardens only.
📷 compulsory in house. 🏠 📖
🌐 casademateus.com

Transport
🚌 to Vila Real. 🚌

mmaculate box-edged flower beds in the
Casa de Mateus gardens

he grand old camellias, relics
rom the 19th century, are a
highlight of the gardens, but
or most visitors the lasting
memory is of the vast cedar
tunnel, greatest among the
many pieces of topiary here.
　Beyond the formal gardens
ie the well-ordered orchards
and fields of the estate.

The Cedar Tunnel

This celebrated feature in the
Casa de Mateus garden was
formed from cedars planted in
1941. It is 35 m (115 ft) long and
7.5 m (25 ft) high, the tight-knit
greenery providing an aromatic walk in summer. To keep
it in shape, gardeners have to
scale specially fashioned
outsize ladders.

⓫ Vila Real

Road map D2. 🚗 20,000. 🚌 🚌
🛈 Avenida Carvalho Araujo 94
(259 308 170). 🕐 Tue & Fri.

Perched over a gorge cut by the
confluence of the Cabril and
Corgo rivers, Vila Real is a busy
commercial centre. As the
communications hub of the
Upper Douro, it makes a
convenient starting point from
which to explore the valley of
the Douro to the south and the
Parque Natural do Alvão to
the northwest. Vila Real also
has a motor-racing circuit,
which hosts major events each
year during June and July.
　Midway along the broad
main street, Avenida Carvalho
Araújo, is the 15th-century Sé.
This fine Gothic cathedral was
originally the church of a
Dominican friary. The other
monastic buildings burnt down
in suspicious circumstances in
the mid-19th century.
　At the southern end of the
avenue, a plaque on the wall at
No. 19 marks the birthplace of
Diogo Cão, the explorer who
discovered the mouth of the
Congo in 1482 (see pp52–3).
　The Igreja dos Clérigos, in
nearby Rua dos Combatentes
da Grande Guerra, is also known
as Capela Nova. It presents a
pleasing Baroque façade
attributed to Niccolò Nasoni
and an interior of fine blue and
white azulejos.

Environs
The small village of Bisalhães,
6 km (4 miles) to the west, is
famed for its boldly designed

black pottery. Examples can
be seen displayed for sale
at the annual Festa de São
Pedro, celebrated in Vila Real
each year on 28–29 June. Also
seen at this time is the fine
linen from nearby Agarez.

The scenic Parque Natural do Alvão

⓬ Parque Natural do Alvão

Road map D1. 🚌 to Ermelo via
Campeã. 🛈 Lago dos Freitas, Parque
Natural do Alvão (259 302 830).

Within the 72 sq km (28 sq
miles) of the nature reserve
between the Corgo and Tâmega
rivers, the scenery ranges from
verdant, cultivated lowlands to
bleak heights that reach 1,339 m
(4,393 ft) at Alto das Caravelas.
Despite hunters and habitat
encroachment, hawks, dippers
and otters can still be spotted.
Between the picturesque
hamlets of Ermelo and Lamas de
Olo, where maize is still kept in
espigueiros (see p277), the Olo
drops in a spectacular cascade,
the Fisgas de Ermelo. From Alto
do Velão, just southwest of the
park, are splendid views west
over the Tâmega valley.

Vila Real, situated on the northern side of the Douro river valley

A farmer and his grazing ox near Carvalhelhos, Serra do Barroso

⓭ Serra do Barroso

Road map D1. ⌷ to Montalegre or Boticas. ℹ Terreiro do Açougue, Montalegre (276 510 205).

Just southeast of the Parque Nacional da Peneda-Gerês *(see pp276–7)* is the wild and remote Serra do Barroso. The landscape of heathery hillsides is split by the immense Barragem do Alto Rabagão, the largest of many reservoirs in the area created by the damming of rivers for hydroelectric power. Water is a mainstay of the local economy: a high rainfall enables farmers to eke out an existence on the poor soil, and the artificial lakes attract fishing and water sports enthusiasts. The source of one of the country's most popular bottled mineral waters is at Carvalhelhos.

The village of Boticas nearby produces a beverage with a more original claim to fame. In 1809, the locals buried their wine rather than have it fall into the hands of the invading French. When the enemy departed, the wine was retrieved and found to have improved. The bottles were colloquially termed *mortos* ("dead"), hence the name of the wine – *vinho dos mortos*. The practice continues and bottles are usually buried for up to two years.

The area's principal town is Montalegre, on a plateau to the north. Its most notable feature is the imposing keep, 27 m (88 ft) high, of the ruined 14th-century castle.

Oxen are bred in the Serra, and inter-village *chegas dos bois* (ox fights) are a popular pastime. The contest is usually decided within half an hour, when the weaker ox takes to its heels.

⓮ Chaves

Road map D1. ⌷ 18,000. ⌷
ℹ Terreiro da Cavalaria (276 348 180).
⌷ Wed.

Beside the upper reaches of the Tâmega stands historic Chaves, attractively sited in the middle of a fertile plain.

Thermal springs and nearby gold deposits encouraged the Romans to establish Aquae Flaviae here in AD 78. Its strategic position led to successive invasion and occupation by the Suevi, Visigoths and Moors, before the Portuguese gained final possession in 1160. The name Chaves ("keys") is often associated with the keys of the north awarded to Nuno Álvares Pereira, hero of Aljubarrota *(see p189)*. A likelier but more pedestrian explanation is that Chaves is simply a corruption of the Latin "Flaviae".

Today Chaves is renowned for its spa and historic centre, and for its smoked hams. A curiosity of the north, the distinctive black pottery is made in nearby Nantes.

The old town focuses on the Praça de Camões. The 14th-century keep overlooking this pleasant medieval square is all that remains of the castle given to Nuno Álvares Pereira by João I. On the south side of the square stands the Igreja Matriz with its fine Romanesque portal. The Baroque Misericórdia church opposite has an exquisite interior lined with 18th-century *azulejos*. Attributed to Policarpo de Oliveira Bernardes *(see p30)*, the huge panels depict scenes from the New Testament.

The 14th-century keep of Chaves castle, set in formal gardens

🏛 Museu Militar and Museu da Região Flaviense

Praça de Camões. **Tel** 276 340 500. **Open** daily. **Closed** public hols. ⌷ joint ticket.

Within the castle keep is a small military museum, where suits of armour, uniforms and associated regalia are on display. Also exhibited are military memorabilia from the city's defence against the attack by Royalists from Spain in 1912. In the flower-filled garden surrounding the keep are a few archaeological finds from Chaves's long history, but most are to be found in the Museu da Região Flaviense behind the keep. Here, in the Paço dos Duques de Bragança, are displayed a variety of local archaeological discoveries. Items of interest include souvenirs of the Roman occupation, such as milestones and coins, alongside an oxcart and a straw mantle of the type worn by shepherds for protection in the rain or the hot sun.

Tiled and gilded Misericórdia church at Chaves

Ponte Romana

The 16-arch Roman bridge across the Tâmega was completed around AD 100, at the time of the Emperor Trajan. Its construction brought added importance to Chaves as a staging post on the route between Braga and Astorga (in northwestern Spain). On the bridge are Roman milestones which record that funds to build it were raised locally.

Thermal springs

Largo da Caldas.
Tel 276 332 445. **Open** daily.

A few minutes on foot from the city centre is one of the hottest springs in Europe. Water here bubbles up at a temperature of 73°C (163°F) and the spa's facilities attract both holiday-makers and patients seeking treatment (see p215). Chaves water is recommended for the treatment of ailments as diverse as rheumatism, kidney dysfunction and hypertension.

The huge cleft Pedra Bolideira near Chaves

Environs

Close to the village of Soutelo, 4 km (2 miles) northwest of Chaves (the route is signposted), is the strange Outeiro Machado Boulder. It measures 50 m (164 ft) in length and is covered with mysterious hieroglyphs and symbols of unknown meaning. These may be Celtic in origin.

Another gigantic boulder, the Pedra Bolideira, lies near Bolideira, 16 km (10 miles) east of Chaves. Split in two, the massive larger section balances lightly, needing only a gentle push to rock it to and fro.

The spa town of Vidago, 17 km (11 miles) southwest of Chaves, is well known for its therapeutic water. The Vidago Palace Hotel (see p392), once the haunt of royalty, has been

renovated but retains the regal charm of its park, lakes and pump room.

Murça's Misericórdia chapel, with its vine-embellished pillars

⑮ Murça

Road map D2. 🚗 7,000. 🚌
ℹ Alameda do Paço (936 548 088).
🍴 13 & 28 of month.

The market town of Murça is famed for its honey, goat's cheese and sausage. Its major attraction, and the focal point of the garden in the main square, is its porca, an Iron Age granite pig with a substantial girth of 2.8 m (9 ft) (see p44). The role of berrões, as beasts such as these are called, is enigmatic, but they may have been linked to fertility cults. Smaller versions survive in Bragança, Chaves and elsewhere. In more recent times the Murça porca has been pressed into service at elections, when the winning political parties would paint her in their colours.

The Misericórdia chapel on the main street is notable for its early Baroque façade, attractively ornamented with designs of vines and grapes.

⑯ Mirandela

Road map D1. 🚗 11,000. 🚌 🚌 ℹ
Rua D Afonso III (278 203 143). 🍴 Thu.

Mirandela, at the end of the Tua narrow-gauge railway line, has pretty gardens running down to the River Tua and an elegant Roman bridge with 20 asymmetrical arches. Built for the deployment of troops and to aid the transport of ore from local mines, it was rebuilt in the 16th century and is now for pedestrians only.

Displayed in the **Museu Municipal Armindo Teixeira Lopes** are sculpture, prints and paintings, including views of Lisbon and Mirandela by the local 20th-century artist after whom the museum is named.

The 17th-century town hall once belonged to the Távoras, but the family was accused of attempted regicide in 1759 and all trace of them was erased.

Museu Municipal Armindo Teixeira Lopes
Rua Coronel Sarmento Pimentel.
Tel 278 201 590. **Open** Mon–Fri; Sat pm. **Closed** public hols.

Environs

In a pretty valley 15 km (9 miles) northeast of Mirandela lies Romeu. Its **Museu das Curiosidades**, as the name implies, is a hotchpotch of exhibits from the turn of the century onwards. The collection of the local Menéres family, it includes Model-T Fords, musical boxes and early photographic equipment. Next door is the famed Maria Rita restaurant (see p408).

Museu das Curiosidades
Jerusalém do Romeu. **Tel** 278 939 133.
Open Tue–Sun. **Closed** pub hols.

The River Tua at Mirandela, with its Roman bridge and waterside parks

⑰ Bragança: the Citadel

This strategic hilltop was the site of a succession of forts before Fernão Mendes, brother-in-law to King Afonso Henriques, built a walled citadel here in 1130. Like several predecessors, it was named Brigantia. Within the walls still stand Sancho I's castle, built in 1187, with its watchtowers and dungeons, and the pentagonal 12th-century Domus Municipalis beside the church of Santa Maria.

The town gave its name to Portugal's final royal dynasty, descended from an illegitimate son of João I who was created first Duke of Bragança in 1442 *(see p305).*

Bragança's walled citadel on its isolated hilltop

Porta da Traiçã

The Museu Militar in the robust Gothic keep includes memorabilia from the Africa campaigns (1895) of a local regiment. The keep is 33 m (108 ft) high.

The medieval pillory has the appearance of skewering a hapless *porca*, an ancient stone pig *(see p44),* to the pedestal.

★ **Castle**
The castle's Torre da Princesa, scene of many tragic tales, was refuge to Dona Sancha, unhappy wife of Fernão Mendes, and prison to other mistreated wives.

Porta da Vila

RUA DOM FERNÃO O BRAVO

Porta de Santo António

To town ←

Santa Maria
The church's elaborately carved portal dates from its 18th-century restoration.

★ **Domus Municipalis**
This, the only surviving example of Romanesque civic architecture in Portugal, served as a hall where the *homens bons* ("good men") settled disputes. Below was the town's cistern.

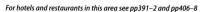

Key

━ Suggested route

0 metres 50
0 yards 50

Porta do Sol

Houses within the Citadel
Bragança had outgrown the
citadel by the 15th century,
but streets of small houses still
cluster within the walls.

Museu Abade de Baçal gardens, where archaeological finds are displayed

Beyond the Citadel

By the 15th century, Bragança
had expanded west along the
banks of the River Fervença.
The Jewish quarter in Rua dos
Fornos survives from this era,
when Jews from North Africa
and Spain settled here and
founded the silk industry.

Despite its royal links, the town
never overcame its isolation, the
Bragança monarchs preferring
Vila Viçosa (see pp304–5). Only
now are the investments of
returning emigrants and the
completion of the Porto-Spain
motorway reviving trade. A
cathedral "for the millennium" was
inaugurated in 1996, another
indicator of the city's rebirth.
Near the modest old cathedral
in the town centre is a lively
covered market where
delicacies such as smoked
hams and alheiras (chicken
sausages) are sold.

🏛 Museu Abade de Baçal

Rua Abílio Beça 27. **Tel** 273 331 595.
Open Tue–Sun. **Closed** public hols.
🎨 (free first Sun of month).

The Abbot of Baçal (1865–1947)
was a prodigious scholar whose
definitive researches into the
region's history and customs,
including its Jewish connections, were published in 11
volumes. Bragança's museum
is named after him.

Highlights among the paintings are The Martyrdom of St
Ignatius, an unsigned triptych
of the 16th century, and watercolours by Aurélia de Sousa
(1865–1922), including A
Sombra (In the Shade). In
another section are colourful
pauliteiros costumes (see p233)

and instruments of torture.
In the garden are a variety of
archaeological discoveries
including porcas and tablets
with Luso-Roman inscriptions.

🏛 São Bento

Rua de São Francisco. **Open** by
appointment. ♿

Founded in 1590 by Bishop
António Pinheiro, São Bento
has two startlingly contrasting
ceilings: a splendid canopy of
Moorish-influenced geometric
carving in the chancel, and a
richly coloured 18th-century
trompe l'oeil over the nave.

🏛 São Vicente

Largo do Principal. **Open** variable hours.

The secret wedding between
Inês de Castro and Dom Pedro is
reputed to have taken place here
in 1354 (see p185). The original
13th-century church was
reconstructed in the 17th century
with the addition of a great deal
of sumptuous gilt work. The
azulejo panel to the right of the
main door depicts General
Sepúlveda exhorting the citizens
of Bragança to free themselves
from French occupation in 1809.

Street in the old Jewish quarter, sloping
steeply down to the river

The sparsely inhabited landscape of the Parque Natural de Montesinho

⓲ Parque Natural de Montesinho

Road map E1. 🚌 to Rio de Onor & Vinhais. 🅘 Parque Florestal, Bragança (273 300 400).

One of the wildest areas in Europe, the reserve covers 700 sq km (270 sq miles) between Bragança and the border with Spain. The region, understandably, is known as Terra Fria (Cold Land). Bleak mountains rise to 1,481 m (4,859 ft) above heather and broom, descending to oak forests and valleys of alder and willow.

Spectacular views of the park can be enjoyed from Vinhais, on its southern fringe, and the wilderness attracts walkers and riders – mountain bikes and horses can be hired locally.

The population clusters in farming communities on the lowlands, leaving much of the Serra an undisturbed habitat for rare species such as wolves and golden eagles, as well as boars, otters and falcons.

Little changed from medieval times, villages such as França and Montesinho are typical in

their stone houses, wooden balconies and cobbled streets. Ancient practices such as herbal cures and reverence for the supernatural linger, and ties are communal rather than national: in Rio de Onor Spanish and Portuguese have been welded into a unique dialect, Rionorês.

⓳ Miranda do Douro

Road map E1. 🅐 3,000. 🚌 🅘 Largo do Menino Jesus da Cartolinha (273 431 132). 🗓 1st day of month.

This medieval outpost stands on top of the Douro gorge, which here forms an abrupt border with Spain. Its key position and the establishment of a bishopric here in 1545 paved the way for the town's development into the cultural and religious centre of Trás-os-Montes. But in 1762, during the Seven Years' War against France and Spain, the powder store exploded, claiming 400 lives and destroying the castle (only the

keep remains). This mishap, compounded by the transfer of the bishopric to Bragança, led the town into a deep economic decline, only halted by trade links with the coast and Spain.

The lovely twin-towered Sé was founded in the 16th century. The graceful woodcarvings of the chancel retable depict, among other themes, the apostles and the Virgin attended by angels. But the cathedral's most original feature is a wooden figure of the Boy Jesus in the south transept. The Menino Jesus da Cartolinha represents a boy who, legend tells, appeared during a Spanish siege in 1711 to rally the demoralized Portuguese to miraculous victory. Devotees dressed the statue in 17th-century costume and later gave him a top hat (*cartolinha*).

The excellent **Museu da Terra de Miranda** houses an eclectic display of archaeological finds, folk costume, a reconstruction of a Mirandês farmhouse parlour and curious rural devices such as an inflated pig's-bladder cosh

Farm parlour, Museu da Terra de Miranda

🏛 **Museu da Terra de Miranda**
Largo Dom João III. **Tel** 273 417 288.
Open Tue pm & Wed–Sun.
Closed public hols. 🅵 (free first Sun of month).

Environs
Just southwest of Miranda, the village of Duas Igrejas is famed for its stick dancers, or *pauliteiros*, who perform at local festivals and overseas (*see p233*). The tradition is in decline, but for the Festa de Santa Bárbara, on the third Sunday in August, the dancers don their distinctive black and white costumes and are accompanied in their energetic display by drums and *gaita de foles* (bagpipes).

A distinctive *pombal* or dovecote still found around Montesinho

The Dovecotes of Montesinho

Doves supply not only food but also droppings, which are highly prized as fertilizer. In this part of Trás-os-Montes the traditional horseshoe-shaped dovecote or *pombal* is still a familiar sight, although many are now disused. The birds nest in rough cells inside the whitewashed schist walls and enter and leave through gaps in the tile or slate roof. They are fed via a small raised door at the front of the *pombal*.

The church and town of Mogadouro, viewed from beside the ruins of its 13th-century castle

⑳ Mogadouro

Road map E2. 🏘 3,000. 🚌
ⓘ Av dos Comandos (279 340 501).
🔄 2 & 16 of month.

Apart from the hilltop tower, little remains of the great castle founded here by King Dinis and presented to the Templars in 1297. From the top there are fine views over the little market town known for its handicrafts, particularly leather goods.

Mogadouro's 16th-century Igreja Matriz features a 17th-century tower, while lavishly gilded retables from the 18th century decorate the altars.

㉑ Torre de Moncorvo

Road map E2. 🏘 3,000. 🚌
ⓘ Rua dos Sapateiros 15 (279 252 289). 🔄 8 & 23 of month.

Famed for the white mantle of almond blossom that fleetingly covers the valleys in early spring (egg-shaped *amêndoas cobertas*, sugared almonds, are an Easter treat), Moncorvo also offers an atmospheric stroll through its maze of medieval streets. Its name is variously attributed to a local nobleman, Mendo Curvo, or perhaps to his raven (*corvo*).

The ponderous 16th-century Igreja Matriz, the largest in Trás-os-Montes, boasts a 17th-century altarpiece depicting scenes from the life of Christ.

Environs
The fate of the Côa valley, south of Moncorvo, was finally decided in 1996 when plans for a dam were dropped to preserve the world's largest collection of open-air Stone Age rock art. Discovered in 1933 and estimated to be 20,000 years old, it features bulls, horses, fish and a naked man, the Homem de Pisco. Vila Nova de Foz Côa, Castelo Melhor and Muxagata offer several guided tours a day into the **Parque Arqueológico do Vale do Côa**, and visits must be booked in advance. The Museu do Côa has interesting art and archaeological exhibits on the Côa Valley.

Rich interior of the Igreja Matriz at Freixo

🏛 **Parque Arqueológico do Vale do Côa/Museu do Côa**
Rua do Museu, Vila Nova de Foz Côa.
Tel 279 768 260. **Open** Tue–Sun.
Closed 1 May, 25 Dec. 🎫 📷
🌐 arte-coa.pt

㉒ Freixo de Espada à Cinta

Road map E2. 🏘 5,000. 🚌
ⓘ Praça Jorge Álvares (279 653 480).
🔄 Second Sat of every month..

Several stories try to explain the curious name of this remote border town. "Ash tree of the girt sword" may derive from the arms of a Spanish nobleman, or a Visigoth called Espadacinta, or from a tale that, when founding the town in the 14th century, King Dinis strapped his sword to an ash.

Dominating the skyline is the heptagonal **Torre do Galo**, a relic from the 14th-century defences. Views from the top are splendid, especially in spring when the almond blossom attracts a great many tourists. The cultivation of silkworms shows a revival of the 18th-century industry. The intricate 16th-century portal of the Igreja Matriz leads into a splendid small-scale version of Belém's Mosteiro dos Jerónimos (see pp108–9). Panels of the altarpiece, attributed to Grão Vasco (see p219), include a fine *Annunciation*.

🏛 **Torre do Galo**
Praça Jorge Álvares. **Open** daily.

MINHO

Known as the birthplace of the nation, the Minho has two of Portugal's most historic cities: its first capital, Guimarães, and Braga, the north's main religious centre. Life in the province is still firmly rooted in tradition. Agriculture thrives thanks to abundant rainfall that makes this the greenest area in Portugal.

The province of Minho occupies land between the River Douro in the south and the River Minho in the north. Fortified hilltop stone forts *(castros)* remain as evidence of the Neolithic history of the region. When Celtic peoples migrated into the area in the first millennium BC, these sites developed into *citânias* (settlements) such as Briteiros.

In the 2nd century BC, advancing Roman legions conquered the land, introduced vine-growing techniques and constructed a network of roads. Roman milestones are still visible in Peneda-Gerês National Park. When Christianity became the official religion of the Roman empire in the 4th century AD, Braga became an important religious centre, a position it holds to this day. The Suevi swept aside the Romans in the 5th century,

followed by the Visigoths, who were ousted in turn by the Moorish invasion of 711. The Minho was won back from the Moors in the 9th century. The region rose to prominence in the 1100s under Afonso Henriques *(see pp46–7)*, who proclaimed himself the first king of Portugal and chose Guimarães as his capital.

The Minho's fertile farms and estates have been handed down within families for centuries, each heir traditionally receiving a share of the land. The economy of the Minho concentrates on medium-scale industry around Braga and Guimarães. Agriculture in the valleys includes production of the area's distinctive *vinhos verdes* or "green wines". Despite the growth of tourism, the Minho has maintained its strong folk traditions. Carnivals and street markets pervade everyday life and ox-drawn carts are still in use.

Cows being herded across a bridge near the Brejoeira Palace, south of Monção

◀ Aerial view of the basilica at Monte de Santa Luzia, near Viana do Castelo

Exploring the Minho

In the south of the Minho lie Braga and Guimarães, the two major cities of the region, both rich in historic sights. From Braga, the Baroque splendour of Bom Jesus or the ruins of Citânia de Briteiros, the country's largest Iron Age site, are within easy reach. Between Braga and the coast lies Barcelos, the ceramics centre of the region, famed for its weekly market. Travelling north, the pretty town of Viana do Castelo is a useful base from which to explore the coast. Turning inland again, the picturesque market town of Ponte de Lima, beside the River Lima, is one of many places in the Minho that provide accommodation in traditional manor houses. In the north of the Minho, the River Minho forms the border with Spain. Along the river, fortified towns offer magnificent views into Spain. To the northeast, walkers and wildlife enthusiasts should not miss the dramatic mountain ranges of the Parque Nacional da Peneda-Gerês.

Foal grazing in the Parque Nacional da Peneda-Gerês

0 kilometres 10

0 miles 5

Manueline portal on the 16th-century parish church, Vila do Conde

Sights at a Glance

1 Caminha
2 Valença do Minho
3 Monção
4 *Parque Nacional da Peneda-Gerês pp276–7*
5 Ponte da Barca
6 Ponte de Lima
7 *Viana do Castelo pp280–81*
8 Vila do Conde
9 Barcelos
10 *Braga pp282–3*
11 *Bom Jesus do Monte pp284–5*
12 Guimarães
13 Citânia de Briteiros
14 Cabeceiras de Basto

Vinho verde vineyards near Monção

Getting Around

The road system is efficient, with motorways joining Porto with Braga, Guimarães, Valença on the Spanish border and Viana do Castelo along the coast. Elsewhere in the region, potholes are a common hazard, and motorists need to allow time for the scenic routes winding through the mountains in the east. Train routes link Porto to Barcelos and Viana do Castelo, en route to the border with Spain; separate lines run to Guimarães and Braga from Porto. A bus network provides frequent service to the main towns, but it is reduced for more isolated destinations, especially those in the east.

Key

━━━ Motorway
━━━ Major road
┈┈┈ Minor road
━━━ Scenic route
╍╍╍ Main railway
─── Minor railway
▬▬▬ National border
━━━ Regional border

Popular cafés in Praça do Conselheiro Silva Torres, Caminha's attractive main square

❶ Caminha

Road map C1. 🚗 2,000. 🚌 🚗 🚈
ℹ️ Praça Conselheiro Silva Torres (258 921 952). 🚌 Wed.

This ancient fortress town perches beside the Minho with fine views across the river to Spain. Occupied in Celtic and Roman times for its strategic position, Caminha developed into a major port until the diversion of its trade to Viana do Castelo in the 16th century. Today it is a small port, with a daily ferry connection to A Guarda in Spain.

On the main square is the 13th-century Torre do Relógio clock tower, once a gateway in the medieval defensive walls, and the 16th-century Paços do Concelho with its attractive loggia supported by pillars. Cross to the other side of the square, past the Renaissance fountain, to admire the seven Manueline windows on the upper storey of the Solar dos Pitas mansion (17th century).

The Rua Ricardo Joaquim de Sousa leads to the Gothic Igreja Matriz. Begun in the late 15th century, it has a superb inlaid ceiling of panels carved in Mudéjar (Moorish) style. Renaissance carvings above the side doors depict the apostles, the Virgin, and several figures in daring poses, including one man with his posterior bared towards Spain.

Environs

Foz do Minho, the mouth of the Minho, lies 5 km (3 miles) southwest of town. From here local fishermen will take groups (by prior arrangement) to the ruined island fortress of Forte da Ínsua.

The small walled town of Vila Nova de Cerveira, 12 km (7 miles) northeast of Caminha on the road to Valença, has a 16th-century castle. The tranquil atmosphere is ideal for a stroll in narrow streets lined with 17th- and 18th-century mansions, or along the riverfront, where a car ferry runs to the Spanish town of Goián.

❷ Valença do Minho

Road map C1. 🚗 3,000. 🚗 🚈
ℹ️ Paiol do Campo de Marte (251 823 329). 🚌 Wed & first Sun of month.

Set in a commanding position on a hilltop overlooking the River Minho, Valença is an attractive border town with an old quarter set in the narrow confines of two double-walled forts, shaped like crowns and linked by a causeway. During the reign of Sancho I (1185–1211), the town was named *Contrasta*, due to its position facing the Spanish town of Tui.

The forts date from the 17th and 18th centuries and were designed according to the prin- ciples of the French architect Vauban. There are fine views from the ramparts across the river into Galicia. Although the town was briefly captured by Napoleonic troops in 1807, its formidable bastions resisted subsequent shelling and attacks from across the rive in 1809.

Lining the cobbled alleys of the old quarter are shops full of linen, wickerwork, pottery and handicrafts to tempt the thousands of Spanish visitors who stroll across the bridge to shop. South of the ramparts is the newer part of town.

In Praça de São Teotónio, Casa do Eirado (1448) boasts a crenellated roof and late Gothic window, adorned with the builder's signature. The 18th-century Casa do Poço presents symmetrical windows and wrought-iron balconies.

A quiet sunlit corner in the old quarter of Valença do Minho

Environs

The Convento de Ganfei, 5 km (3 miles) east of Valença on the N101, was reconstructed in the 11th century by a Norman priest It retains pleasing Romanesque features, including ornamental animal and plant motifs and vestiges of medieval frescoes. To visit the chapel, ask for the key at the house opposite.

Part of the walls and ramparts surrounding Valença do Minho

❸ Monção

Road map C1. 🛆 25,000. 🚌
ℹ️ Praça Deu la Deu, Casa do Curro
(251 649 013). 🛍 Thu.

A remote and charming town,
Monção once formed part of
the string of fortified border
posts standing sentinel on
the River Minho. Both the town's
main squares are lined with
old houses, and decorated
with chestnut trees, flowerbeds
and mosaic paths.

The 13th-century Igreja Matriz
in Rua João de Pinho boasts an
outstanding Romanesque doorway of sculpted acanthus flowers.
Inside, to the right of the transept
is the cenotaph of the valiant
Deu-la-Deu Martins, the town's
heroine, erected in 1679 by a
descendant. A leafy avenue
east of the town leads to the
hot mineral springs used for
the treatment of rheumatism.

A colourful element in the
June Corpus Christi festival
is the Festa da Coca, when
St George engages the dragon
(coca) in comic ritual combat
before giving the final blow.

Environs
The countryside around
Monção produces excellent
vinho verde (see p33); one of
the best-known estates is the
privately owned Neo-Classical
Palácio de Brejoeira, 5 km
(3 miles) south of town.

About 5 km (3 miles) southeast of Monção, the monastery
of São João de Longos Vales

Bridge across the Lima at Ponte da Barca, with the town behind

was built in Romanesque style
in the 12th century. The exterior
capitals and interior apse have
fantastical sculpted figures,
including serpents and monkeys.
Visits are arranged by the tourist
office in Monção.

The town of Melgaço, 24 km
(15 miles) east of Monção provides a useful gateway to the
Peneda-Gerês National Park.

❹ Parque Nacional da Peneda-Gerês

See pp276–7.

❺ Ponte da Barca

Road map C1. 🛆 2,000. 🚌
ℹ️ Rua Conselheiro Rocha Peixoto 9
(258 455 246). 🛍 every other Wed.

The town of Ponte da Barca
derives its name from the
graceful 15th-century bridge

that replaced the boat once
used to ferry pilgrims across
the River Lima (*ponte* means
bridge, and *barca* means boat).
A stroll through the tranquil
town centre leads past the
pillory (crowned with sphere
and pyramid), the graceful
arcades and noble mansions
from the 16th and 17th centuries. The Jardim dos Poetas
(Poets' Garden) and riverside
parks are ideal for picnics, and
the huge open-air market along
the river is well worth a visit.

Environs
Some of Portugal's finest
Romanesque carvings are on
the 13th-century church at
Bravães, 4 km (2 miles) west
of Ponte da Barca. Sculpted
monkeys, oxen and birds of
prey decorate the columns of
its main portal; the tympanum
shows Christ in majesty flanked
by two angels.

The town of Arcos de
Valdevez, 5 km (3 miles) north
of Ponte da Barca, nestles by the
banks of the River Vez and lies
within convenient reach of
Peneda-Gerês National Park.
The impressive church of Nossa
Senhora da Lapa was built in
1767 by André Soares. This
Baroque showpiece has an
oval exterior, yet transforms
the interior into an octagon.

Hiking enthusiasts should
ask the tourist office for directions to follow the circuit of
elevated viewpoints and local
villages from the hamlet of
São Miguel, 11 km (7 miles)
east of Ponte da Barca.

The Heroic Deu-la-Deu Martins

In 1368, when a Spanish army had besieged Monção to the verge
of starvation, Deu-la-Deu Martins used the last of the town's flour
to bake rolls that she flung over the walls to the Spaniards, with

Deu-la-Deu Martins on
Monção's coat of arms

taunts that there were plenty more
to throw at them. Thinking their
time was being wasted in a futile
siege, the troops soon withdrew.
In gratitude for saving the town,
the heroic Deu-la-Deu (the name
means "God gave her") is remembered on the town's coat of arms,
where she is shown holding a
loaf of bread in each hand.
Pãezinhos (bread rolls) *de Deu-la-
Deu* used to be baked to honour
her memory, but the tradition is
no longer followed.

❹ Parque Nacional da Peneda-Gerês

Peneda-Gerês National Park, one of Portugal's greatest natural attractions, stretches from the Gerês Mountains in the south to the Peneda range and the Spanish border in the north. Established in 1971, it extends over about 720 sq km (277 sq miles) of wild, dramatic scenery, with windswept peaks and valleys of oak, pine and yew. It also hosts a rich variety of fauna, including rare wolves and eagles. The park's long-distance footpath is well signposted (in parts); six sections are limited to groups of between 10 and 15 people.

★ **Nossa Senhora da Peneda**
Surrounded by massive rocks, this elaborate sanctuary is a replica of Bom Jesus *(see pp284–5)*. The site is visited in early September by pilgrims from all over the region.

Soajo
The traditional village of Soajo, surrounded by terraced hillsides, is known for its collection of *espigueiros*. The village's local festival takes place in the middle of August.

KEY

① **The 13th-century castle** in the frontier village of Lindoso has been renovated to house an art gallery.

② **Castro Laboreiro** is best known for the breed of sheepdog to which it gives its name. The ruins of a medieval castle can be seen in the village.

③ **Lamas de Mouro**, at the northern entrance to the park, serves as an information centre and offers accommodation.

④ **Caldas do Gerês**, known since Roman times for its spa, now serves as an information centre and base for excursions from the centre of the park.

Melgaço
Nossa Senhora da Peneda
Serra da Pe
Mezio
N202
Arços de Valdevez
Soajo
N304-1
Lima
● **Entre Ambos-os-Rios**
Albufeira Vilarinho das
Campo do Gerês
Braga

0 kilometres — 5
0 miles — 2

Vilarinho das Furnas
Beautifully set in a rocky landscape, the Vilarinho das Furnas reservoir was formed by the damming of the River Homem. There are some good hikes along its shores.

Pitões das Júnias Monastery
Dating to 1147, the picturesque ruins of this monastery lie approximately 3 km (2 miles) south of the road leading into Pitões das Júnias village.

VISITORS' CHECKLIST

Practical Information
Road map C1. 🅸 Caldas do Gerês: on main road (253 390 110); Lamas do Mouro: next to camp site; Arcos de Valdevez: Rua Professor Dr Mário Júlio Almeida Costa (258 520 530). Information on camp sites, hiking & pony trekking is available at these offices at Montalegre *(see p262)* and at Ponte da Barca. Lindoso castle: **Open** daily. **Closed** public hols. 🅿

Transport
🚌 from Braga to Caldas do Gerês; from Arcos de Valdevez to Soajo & Lindoso; from Melgaço to Castro Laboreiro & Lamas de Mouro.

Inverneiras in Seara
Migration during the summer from these solidly built winter houses to *brandas*, stone shelters high in the mountains, is still practised in some villages.

★ Roman Road
Sections of the old Roman road that ran from Braga to Astorga in Spain, can still be seen at points along the Homem river valley.

Granary Designs

The tomb-like architecture of *espigueiros* (granaries) appears in several areas of the park, especially in the villages of Lindoso and Soajo. Constructed either of wood or granite, they are raised on columns and slatted for ventilation. The design keeps grain and maize at the right humidity as well as off the ground, out of reach of hens and rodents. Topped with an ornamental cross or pyramid, the design of *espigueiros* has scarcely changed since the 18th and 19th centuries.

Granite *espigueiro*, Lindoso

Key

= Road
-- Long-distance footpath
- - National boundary

For keys to symbols see back flap

⑥ Ponte de Lima

Road map C1. 🏘 3,200. 🚌
ℹ Passeio 25 de Abril, Torre da
Cadeia Velha (258 240 208).
🗓 every other Mon.

This attractive riverside town takes
its name from the ancient bridge
over the River Lima. During the
Middle Ages, the town played
a pivotal role in the defence of
the Minho against the Moors.

The Roman bridge has only
five of its original stone arches;
the rest were rebuilt or restored
in the 14th and 15th centuries.
The 15th-century church of Santo
António houses the **Museu dos
Terceiros**, a museum of sacred art.
The Museu Rural has antique
farming equipment, an authentic
regional kitchen and gardens.

Ponte de Lima's remaining
medieval fortifications include
the 15th-century Palácio
dos Marqueses de Ponte
de Lima.

The town's market, a
tradition dating back
to 1125, takes place
on the river's wide
and sandy left bank. In
mid-September crowds
gather in the town to
celebrate the Feiras
Novas (new fairs), a
combined religious
festival and
folkloric market.

**Stone carving
of a musician,
Museu dos Terceiros**

🏛 **Museu dos Terceiros**
Avenida 5 de Outubro. **Tel** 258 240
220. **Open** 10am–12:30pm & 2–6pm
Tue–Sun.

⑦ Viana do Castelo

See pp280–81.

Ponte de Lima's Roman bridge, leading to the church of Santo António

Former dormitory of the Mosteiro de Santa Clara, Vila do Conde

⑧ Vila do Conde

Road map C2. 🏘 21,000. 🚉 🚌
ℹ Rua 25 de Abril 103 (252 248 473).
🗓 Fri.

The small town of Vila do
Conde enjoyed its boom
years as a shipbuilding
centre in the Age of
Discovery *(see pp52–3)*;
today it is a quiet
fishing port. By the
river, in the historic
centre, the main
attraction is the Mosteiro
de Santa Clara, founded
in 1318. The principal
dormitory building,
dating from the 18th
century, was used for
some time as a correc-
tional institution for
teenagers. The Gothic church
contains the tombs of the
nunnery's founders, Dom
Afonso Sanches (son of King
Dinis) and his wife Dona Teresa
Martins. The entire building is
now closed for redevelopment.
By the Mosteiro de Santa Clara

are parts of the imposing 5-km
(3-mile) aqueduct, built in
1705–14, with 999 arches.

At the heart of the historic
centre is Praça Vasco da
Gama, with an unusual pillory
in the shape of an arm with
thrusting sword – a vivid
warning to potential wrong-
doers. Bordering the square
by the pillory is the 16th-
century Igreja Matriz, notable
for its wonderfully ornate
Manueline portico, attributed
to João de Castilho.

The town is a centre for lacemaking (bone lace or *rendas
de bilros*). Visitors can buy
samples and see the skills
at the **Escola de Rendas**
(lacemaking school). The same
building also houses the Museu
de Rendas (lace museum).

🏛 **Escola de Rendas**
Rua de São Bento 70. **Tel** 252 248 470.
Open Tue–Fri. **Closed** public hols.

Environs
The town of Póvoa de Varzim,
3 km (2 miles) north of Vila
do Conde, is a resort with
sandy beaches, amusements
and nightlife.

In the village of Rates, 10 km
(6 miles) northeast, the 13th-
century church of São Pedro
de Rates boasts a portal surmounted by gracefully sculpted
statues of saints, and a rose
window. Its nearby counterpart
at Rio Mau, the church of São
Cristóvão de Rio Mau, was
finished in 1151. Above the
door is a bishop (possibly
St Augustine) flanked by helpers.

The Legend of the Barcelos Cock

A Galician pilgrim, as he was leaving Barcelos en route to Santiago de Compostela, was accused of stealing silver from a landowner, and sentenced to death by hanging. As a final plea to save himself, the prisoner requested a meeting with the judge, who was about to tuck into a meal of roast cockerel. The Galician vowed that as proof of his innocence the cockerel would stand up on the plate and crow.

The judge pushed aside his meal and ignored the plea. But as the prisoner was hanged, the cockerel stood up and crowed. The judge, realizing his mistake, hurried to the gallows and found that the Galician had miraculously survived thanks to a loose knot. According to legend, the Galician returned years later to carve the Cruzeiro do Senhor do Galo, now housed in the Museu Arqueológico in Barcelos.

Traditional
Barcelos cock

Anything from clothes to livestock can be bought here. Pottery enthusiasts can browse among bright designs including pagan figurines and the famous clay cockerels.

North of the square stands Nossa Senhora do Terço, the 18th-century church of a former Benedictine nunnery. In contrast to its plain exterior, the interior is beautifully decorated with panels of *azulejos* illustrating St Benedict's life.

In the southwest corner of the square, a graceful cupola crowns the Igreja do Senhor da Cruz, built around 1705 on the site where two centuries earlier João Pires, a cobbler, had a miraculous vision of a cross etched into the ground. The Festa das Cruzes (festival of crosses), the town's most spectacular event, is held at the beginning of May to celebrate the vision. During the celebrations thousands of flowers are laid on the streets to welcome a procession to the church, and events include magnificent displays of local folk costumes, dancing and fireworks.

The other historic attractions in the town are clustered together in a tranquil setting beside the 15th-century granite bridge that crosses over the River Cávado. The privately owned Solar dos Pinheiros is an attractive mansion on Rua Duques de Bragança, built in 1448. The sculpted figure plucking his beard on the south tower is known as Barbadão, the "bearded one". So incensed was this Jew when his daughter bore a child to a gentile (King João I) that he vowed never to shave again, hence his nickname.

A rich Gothic pillory stands in front of the ruined Counts' Palace or Paço dos Condes, destroyed by the earthquake of 1755. The ruins provide an open-air setting for the **Museu Arqueológico**, which displays stone crosses, sculpted blazons, sarcophagi, and its famous exhibit, the Cruzeiro do Senhor do Galo, a cross paying tribute to the Barcelos cock legend. Next to the palace, the Igreja Matriz is Romanesque with Gothic influences, and dates from the 13th century. There are 18th-century *azulejos* inside as well as an impressive rose window. The nearby **Museu de Olaria** illustrates the history of ceramics in the region.

🏛 **Museu Arqueológico**
Paços dos Condes. **Tel** 253 809 600.
Open daily.

🏛 **Museu de Olaria**
Rua Cónego J Gaiolas. **Tel** 253 824 741.
Open Tue–Sun.

Azulejos of St Benedict's miracle of the sickle, Nossa Senhora do Terço

❾ Barcelos

Road map C1. 🏘 10,000. 🚌 🚍
ℹ Largo Dr José Novais 27 (253 811 882). 🛒 Thu.

A pleasant riverside town, Barcelos is famed as the country's leading ceramics and crafts market and the source of the legendary cock that has become Portugal's national symbol. From its origins as a settlement in Roman times, the town of Barcelos developed into a flourishing agricultural centre and achieved political importance during the 15th century as the seat of the First Duke of Bragança. The town's star attraction is the Feira de Barcelos, a huge weekly market held on Campo da República.

16th-century pillory on terrace overlooking the River Cávado at Barcelos

❼ Street-by-Street: Viana do Castelo

Viana do castelo lies in a beautiful setting on the Lima estuary. This 13th-century town gained prominence as a fishing centre in the 1400s; later it provided ships and seafarers for the great maritime discoveries of the 16th century *(see pp52–3)*. From here João Velho set off to explore the Congo, and João Álvares Fagundes charted the rich fishing grounds of Newfoundland. Wealth derived from trade with Europe and Brazil funded the town's many opulent mansions built in Manueline, Renaissance and Baroque styles. Today the main interest lies in the winding streets and intimate squares of the city centre, easily explored on foot.

The fountain, constructed in 1553 by João Lopes the Elder, forms the focal point of the square.

Casa dos Lur
was once
home of
Luna fam

Railway and bus stations

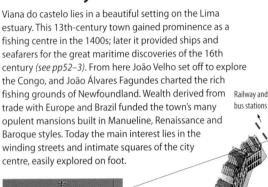

Misericórdia
Built in 1598, this unique Renaissance building features arcades supported by magnificent caryatids.

Palacete Sá Sotto Mayor dates from the Renaissance.

PRAÇA DA REPÚBLICA

Museu Municipal, Nossa Senhora da Agonia

RUA DA PICOTA

VIELA DOS FORNOS

RUA SACADUR

RUA DO POÇO

RUA DO TOURINO

★ Praça da República
The Gothic arches of the restored Paços do Concelho, formerly the town hall, dominate the head of Viana's main square. Manueline motifs include the arms of João III.

PRAÇA DA ERVA

RUA HOSPITAL VELHO

T. DO HOSPITAL VELHO

RUA DA AMÁLIA

The Hospital Velho was originally a pilgrims' hospice. It now houses the Porto e Norte tourist office.

| 0 metres | | 50 |
| 0 yards | | 50 |

Key

━ Suggested route

Practical Information
Road Map C1. 25,000. Viana Welcome Centre, Praça do Eixo-Atlântico (258 098 415). Fri. 2nd Sun in May: Festa das Rosas; 20–23 Aug: Romaria de Nossa Senhora da Agonia. **portoenorte.com**

Transport
Largo da Estação.

Casa da Praça, a magnificent Baroque mansion

Casa de João Velho
is a 15th-century house, said to have belonged to the town's most famous navigator.

RUA GAGO COUTINHO

T. DOS CLÉRIGOS

V. DO SEQUEIRO

The fountain in Praça da República, the centre of daily life in Viana

★ Igreja Matriz
The arch surrounding the west door of Viana's 15th-century, fortress-like parish church is adorned with Gothic reliefs of the apostles.

Exploring Viana do Castelo

Both a busy fishing port and holiday resort, Viana is over-looked by the peak of Monte de Santa Luzia. The town is the capital of Minho folk culture, playing host to lively festivals and supporting a thriving handicrafts industry.

🏛 Museu de Artes Decorativas

Largo de São Domingos. **Tel** 258 809 305. **Open** Tue–Sun. **Closed** public hols. free Sat & Sun.

Set in the 18th-century Palacete dos Barbosas Maciéis, Viana's Museu Municipal has an excellent collection of rare ceramics, furniture, archaeological finds and paintings. In one of the upstairs rooms, walls are tiled with animated allegorical depictions of the continents, while the chapel is lined with tiles signed by 18th-century artist Policarpo de Oliveira Bernardes (see p30). Among the exhibits are a 17th-century Indo-Portuguese cabinet magnificently decorated with inlaid ivory, and pieces of Porto faïence from the Massarelos district, embellished with fine brushwork.

Early 19th-century ceramic, Museu Municipal

🏠 Nossa Senhora da Agonia

Campo de Nossa Senhora da Agonia. **Tel** 258 824 067. **Open** daily.
Northwest of the centre, the mid-18th century Romanesque chapel of Nossa Senhora da Agonia houses a statue of Our Lady of Sorrows *(agonia)*. The chapel, with façade and altar designed by André Soares, draws enormous crowds for the *romaria* of Nossa Senhora da Agonia, a three-day festival held each year in the month of August *(see p233)*. The statue is carried in procession through the town amid much feasting and celebration.

Environs

In order to enjoy exceptional views, take the zigzag road to Monte de Santa Luzia, 5 km (3 miles) north of the town centre. (A funicular runs year-round from the station.) The basilica, completed in 1926 and modelled on the Sacré Coeur in Paris, is a pilgrimage site with little aesthetic appeal. The steep climb, however, is rewarded by the superb views from the top of the dome. Behind the church you can wander along woodland paths or visit the Pousada Monte de Santa Luzia *(see p392)*. From the *pousada*, it is a short walk to the top of the hill, where there are traces of a Celtiberian settlement *(citânia)*.

The excellent beach of Praia do Cabedelo, to the south of the town, is accessible by road via the bridge or by a five-minute ferry crossing from the riverside dock on Avenida dos Combatentes da Grande Guerra. To the north lies Vila Praia de Âncora, another popular beach resort.

⑩ Braga

Churches, grand 18th-century houses and pretty gardens provide the focus for the charm and interest of Braga's centre, once past the urban development on the city outskirts. Known in Roman times as Bracara Augusta, Braga has a long history as a religious and commercial centre. In the 12th century, it became the seat of Portugal's archbishops, and the country's religious capital. The city lost some influence in the 19th century, but today continues as the ecclesiastical capital of Portugal and main city of the Minho.

Not surprisingly, Braga hosts some of Portugal's most colourful religious festivals. Semana Santa (Holy Week) is celebrated with dramatic, solemn processions, while the lively festival of São João in June sees dancing, fairs and fireworks.

The west façade of the Sé, with its 15th-century galilee, or porch

Exploring Braga

The compact historic centre borders Praça da República, the central square. Within the square stands the 14th-century Torre de Menagem, all that remains of the city's original fortifications. A short walk leads to Rua do Souto, a narrow pedestrian street lined with elegant shops and cafés, including the Café Brasileira, furnished in 19th-century salon style. Towards the end of the road stands the impressive Sé, the cathedral of Braga. Other churches worth a visit include the small, 16th-century Capela dos Coimbras, and the 17th-century Baroque Santa Cruz. Many of the finest mansions in Braga also date from the Baroque period, such as the Palácio do Raio and the Câmara Municipal (the town hall). Both buildings are attributed to the 18th-century architect André Soares da Silva. Just north of the city centre is the town mercado (market), where you can buy regional produce and delicacies.

The blue-tiled façade of the Palácio do Raio, also known as the Casa do Mexicano

⛪ Sé

Rua Dom Paio Mendes. **Open** daily. Museu de Arte Sacra: **Tel** 253 263 317. **Open** daily. 🖼

Braga's cathedral was begun in the 11th century, when Henry of Burgundy decided to build on the site of an older church, destroyed in the 6th century.

Since then the building has seen many changes, including the addition of a graceful galilee (porch) in the late 15th century. Outstanding features include the chapel to the right, just inside the west door, housing the ornate 15th-century tomb of the first-born son of João I (see pp50–51), Dom Afonso, who died as a child. The cathedral also houses the Treasury or Museu de Arte Sacra, which contains a rich collection of ecclesiastical treasures as well as statues, carvings and azulejo tiles.

Several chapels can be seen in the courtyard and cloister. The Capela dos Reis houses the tombs of the founders, Henry of Burgundy and his wife Dona Teresa, as well as the preserved body of the 14th-century archbishop Dom Lourenço Vicente.

From Rua de São João you can admire a statue of Nossa Senhora do Leite (Our Lady of the Milk), symbol of the city of Braga, sheltered under an ornate Gothic canopy.

🏛 Antigo Paço Episcopal

Praça Municipal. **Closed** to the public. Near the Sé is the former archbishop's palace. The façades date from the 14th, 17th and 18th centuries, but a major fire destroyed the interior in the 18th century. The palace is now used as a private library and archives. Beside it are the immaculate gardens of the Jardim de Santa Bárbara.

The Jardim de Santa Bárbara by the walls of the Antigo Paço Episcopal

Palácio dos Biscainhos

Rua dos Biscainhos. **Tel** 253 204 650.
Open Tue–Sun.

To the west of the city centre is the Palácio dos Biscainhos. Built in the 16th century and modified over the centuries, this imposing aristocratic mansion now houses the city's Museu Etnográfico e Artístico (Ethnography and Arts Museum), with fascinating displays of foreign and Portuguese furniture. An unusual detail is the ribbed, paved ground floor, which was designed to allow carriages inside the building to deposit guests and drive on to the stables beyond.

Environs

The simple chapel of **São Frutuoso de Montélios**, 3.5 km (2 miles) northwest of Braga, is one of the few remaining examples of pre-Romanesque architecture in Portugal. Built around the 7th century, it was destroyed by the Moors and rebuilt in the 11th century. West of Braga, 4 km (2 miles) from the centre and on the road to Barcelos, is the former Benedictine **Mosteiro de Tibães**. Dating back to the 11th century, this magnificent architectural complex with its gardens and cloisters was rebuilt in the 19th century.

At Falperra, 6 km (4 miles) southeast of Braga, stands the

church of Santa Maria Madalena. Designed by André Soares da Silva in 1750, it is known for its ornate exterior, perhaps the country's finest expression of the Rococo.

The sanctuary at Sameiro, 6 km (4 miles) from Braga, is second only to Fátima (see p190) in the Marian geography of Portugal. It was built in 1863 to honour the dogma of the Immaculate Conception.

São Frutuoso de Montélios
Avenida São Frutuoso. **Tel** 253 622 576. **Open** Tue–Sun.

Mosteiro de Tibães
Rua do Mosteiro 59. **Tel** 253 622 670. **Open** Tue–Sun. **Closed** 1 Jan, Easter, 1 May, 25 Dec. to museum (free 1st Sun of month).

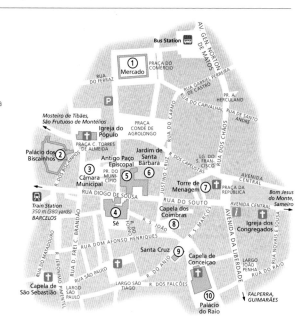
Interior of the old coach stable at the Palácio dos Biscainhos

Braga City Centre

1. Mercado
2. Palácio dos Biscainhos
3. Câmara Municipal
4. Sé
5. Antigo Paço Episcopal
6. Jardim de Santa Bárbara
7. Torre de Menagem
8. Capela dos Coimbras
9. Santa Cruz
10. Palácio do Raio

0 metres 250
0 yards 250

⓫ Bom Jesus do Monte

On a forested slope east of Braga stands Portugal's most spectacular religious sanctuary. In 1722 the Archbishop of Braga devised the giant Baroque Escadaria (stairway) of Bom Jesus as the approach to a small existing shrine. The stairway and the church of Bom Jesus were completed by Carlos Amarante in 1811. The lower section features a steep Sacred Way with chapels showing the 14 Stations of the Cross, the scenes leading up to Christ's crucifixion. The Escadório dos Cinco Sentidos, in the middle section, depicts the five senses with ingenious wall-fountains and statues of biblical, mythological and symbolic figures. This is followed by the similarly allegorical Staircase of the Three Virtues.

At the summit, an esplanade provides superb views and access to the church. Close by are several hotels, a café and a boating lake hidden among the trees. Both a pilgrimage site and tourist attraction, the sanctuary attracts large festive crowds at weekends.

★ Escadórios
The staircase is built of granite accentuated by whitewashed walls. The steps represent an upward spiritual journey.

Entrance Portico
At the foot of the giant stairway stands a portico bearing the coat of arms of Dom Rodrigo de Moura Teles, the archbishop who commissioned the work.

KEY

① Chapel of Darkness

② Chapel of the Kiss of Judas

③ Chapel of the Last Supper

④ Chapel of Christ's Agony in the Garden

⑤ Chapel of the Flagellation

⑥ Chapel of the Road to Calvary

⑦ Chapel of Jesus before Pilate

⑧ Chapel of the Crucifixion

⑨ **The Hotel do Elevador** *(see p392)* stands near the top of the funicular.

⑩ Hotel do Parque

⑪ **The church of Bom Jesus** was built on the site of a 15th-century sanctuary. In front of it stand eight statues of people who condemned Christ, including Herod and Pilate.

⑫ Pelican fountain

⑬ **On the Staircase of the Five Senses** are five fountains, each representing a bodily sense: sight, hearing, smell, taste and touch.

⑭ **Statues, symbols and inscriptions** elaborate on the theme of the senses.

⑮ Chapel of Simon the Cyrenian

⑯ Chapel of the Crown of Thorns

★ Funicular Railway
The funicular *(elevador)* dates back to 1882. Hydraulically operated, it makes the ascent to the terrace beside the church in three minutes.

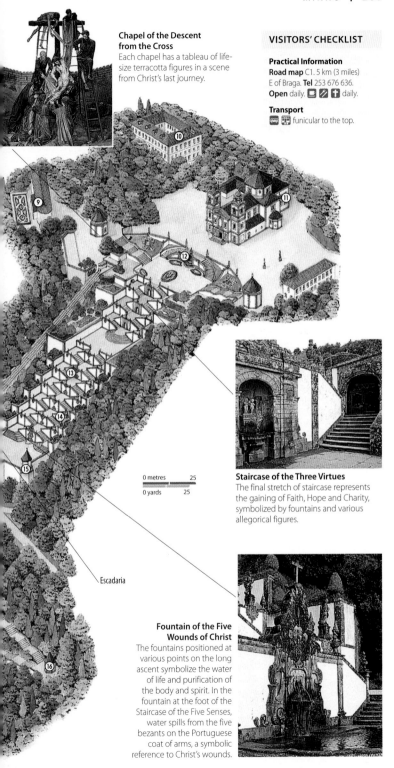

Chapel of the Descent from the Cross
Each chapel has a tableau of life-size terracotta figures in a scene from Christ's last journey.

VISITORS' CHECKLIST

Practical Information
Road map C1. 5 km (3 miles)
E of Braga. **Tel** 253 676 636.
Open daily. 🖥 🚻 🛗 daily.

Transport
🚌 🚋 funicular to the top.

Staircase of the Three Virtues
The final stretch of staircase represents the gaining of Faith, Hope and Charity, symbolized by fountains and various allegorical figures.

Escadaria

0 metres   25
0 yards   25

Fountain of the Five Wounds of Christ
The fountains positioned at various points on the long ascent symbolize the water of life and purification of the body and spirit. In the fountain at the foot of the Staircase of the Five Senses, water spills from the five bezants on the Portuguese coat of arms, a symbolic reference to Christ's wounds.

⑫ Guimarães

A UNESCO World Heritage site, the town of Guimarães is celebrated as the birthplace of the nation. When Afonso Henriques proclaimed himself king of Portugal in 1139 *(see pp46–7)*, he chose Guimarães as his capital, and the distinctive outline of its proud castle appears on the Portuguese coat of arms. In the well-preserved city centre, the narrow streets of the medieval quarter are ideal for exploration on foot. The cobbled Rua de Santa Maria, lined with old town houses embellished with ornate statuary, leads up from the main square, the Largo da Oliveira, past the Paço dos Duques to the castle. To feel the hustle and bustle of the Middle Ages, visit the town in the first week of August for the Festas Gualterianas, a festival of medieval art and costume.

🏰 Castelo de Guimarães

Rua Conde Dom Henrique. **Tel** 253 412 273. **Open** 10am–6pm daily. **Closed** 1 Jan, Easter, 1 May, 25 Dec.

The castle's huge square keep, encircled by eight crenellated towers, dominates the skyline. First built to deter attacks by Moors and Normans in the 10th century, it was extended by Henry of Burgundy two centuries later and, according to tradition, was the birthplace of Portugal's first king, Afonso Henriques. The font where he was reputedly baptized is kept in the tiny Romanesque chapel of São Miguel, situated at the western end of the castle.

🏛 Paço dos Duques

Rua Conde Dom Henrique. **Tel** 253 412 273. **Open** daily. **Closed** 1 Jan, Easter, 1 May, 25 Dec.

Constructed in the 15th century by Dom Afonso (first Duke of Bragança), the Burgundian style of the Paço dos Duques reflects Dom Afonso's taste acquired on his travels through Europe. The palace fell into disuse when the Bragança family moved to Vila Viçosa *(see pp304–5)*. In 1933, under Salazar's dictatorship *(see pp60–61)*, it was renovated as an official presidential residence.

On view in a small museum inside the palace, are lavish displays of Persian rugs, Flemish tapestries and paintings, such as the impressive *O Cordeiro Pascal* (Paschal Lamb) by Josefa de Óbidos *(see p55)*. Paying unusual homage to the nation's maritime exploits, the chestnut ceiling in the banqueting hall imitates the upturned hull of a Portuguese caravel.

🏛 Museu de Alberto Sampaio

Rua Alfredo Guimarães. **Tel** 253 423 910. **Open** 10am–6pm Tue–Sun. **Closed** 1 Jan, Easter, 1 May, 25 Dec.

This museum, housed in the beautiful Romanesque cloister and adjoining rooms of Nossa Senhora da Oliveira, displays some outstanding religious art, *azulejos* and ceramics, all from local churches.

The star exhibits, donated to the church by João I, are his tunic worn at the battle of Aljubarrota in 1385 *(see p189)*, and a 14th-century silver altarpiece, comprising a triptych of the Visitation, Annunciation and Nativity, reportedly taken from the defeated Spanish king. The Santa Clara room contains gilt carving, the work of local craftsmen, taken from the former convent of Santa Clara, now the town hall.

Largo da Oliveira, centre of old Guimarães

🏛 Nossa Senhora da Oliveira

Largo da Oliveira. **Tel** 253 416 144. **Open** daily.

This former monastery lies on the square's east side. Founded by Afonso Henriques, the church was restored by João I in gratitude to Our Lady of the Olive Tree for his victory at Aljubarrota *(see p189)*. The Manueline tower is from 1515.

In front of it is the Padrão do Salado, a 14th-century Gothic shrine housing a cross. It commemorates the legend of how the church and square acquired their name. An olive tree was transplanted here to supply the altar lamp with oil, but it withered. In 1342, the merchant Pedro Esteves placed the cross on it, whereupon the tree flourished. The tree that stands in the square today dates only from 1985.

🏛 Museu Martins Sarmento

Rua Paio Galvão. **Tel** 253 415 969. **Open** Tue–Sun. **Closed** public hols.

Named after the archaeologist who excavated major Iron Age sites in the north, notably Citânia de Briteiros, the museum

The massive battlements surrounding the keep of Castelo de São Miguel

For hotels and restaurants in this area see pp392–3 and pp408–9

s housed in the Gothic cloister of the 14th-century convent of São Domingos. Specializing in finds from these sites, some dating to the Stone Age, the museum contains a wealth of archaeological, ethnological and numismatic exhibits. These include a rare pair of Lusitanian granite warriors, a bronze votive oxcart, and the Pedras Formosas, two stone slabs inscribed with human figures. The most striking exhibit is the Colossus of Pedralva, a stone figure that stands 3 m (10 ft) tall.

São Francisco
Largo de São Francisco. **Tel** 253 439 850.
Open Tue–Sun.

Built in 1400 in Gothic style, the elegant church of São Francisco was reconstructed in the 18th century. The interior of the church boasts a chancel covered in magnificent 18th-century *azulejos* with scenes from the life of St Antony.

Environs
The former monastery of Santa Marinha da Costa is one of Portugal's top *pousadas (see p392)*. It stands 5 km (3 miles) southeast of Guimarães, and was founded in 1154. The gardens and chapel are open to the public.

Renaissance stone fountain at Santa Marinha da Costa monastery

Reconstructed huts at the Iron Age site of Citânia de Briteiros

⑬ Citânia de Briteiros

Road map C1. 15 km (9 miles) N of Guimarães, off N101. **Tel** 253 478 952.
from Guimarães & Braga. **Open** Apr–Sep: 9am–6pm daily; Oct–Mar: 9am–5pm daily.

This Iron Age settlement is one of Portugal's most impressive archaeological sites. Excavated by Martins Sarmento (1833–99), who devoted his life to the study of Iron Age sites, are the foundations of 150 stone dwellings, a number of which have since been reconstructed.

From about the 4th century BC to the 4th century AD, the site was inhabited by Celtiberians, but was most probably under Roman rule from c.20 BC. A network of paths leads visitors past paved streets, subterranean cisterns, sewers and water supply ducts. The Museu Martins Sarmento in Guimarães displays various excavated artifacts.

The *basto* statue of Cabeceiras de Basto

⑭ Cabeceiras de Basto

Road map D1. 17,000. Praça da República (253 669 100). Mon.

The Terras de Basto, once a region of refuge from Moorish invasion, lies east of Guimarães among mountains and forests. Statues known as *bastos*, believed to represent Celtic warriors, are found in various parts of the Terras de Basto where they served as territorial markers. In the main town, Cabeceiras de Basto, the prime attraction is the Baroque Mosteiro de Refojos, with its splendid dome 33 m (108 ft) high, surrounded by statues of the apostles, and topped by a statue of the archangel Michael.

The town also owns the best of the *basto* statues, albeit with a French head; it was changed by troops as a joke during the Napoleonic Wars.

Environs
The fine hiking country of the Terras de Basto, carpeted with flowers in spring, has other villages worth visiting. Mondim de Basto, overlooking the River Tâmega some 25 km (15 miles) south of Cabeceiras, is a convenient base for climbing Monte Farinha which, at 966 m (3,169 ft) is the highest peak in the region. Then climb the steps to the top of the church of Nossa Senhora da Graça on the summit, for splendid views.

Over the Tâmega, the village of Celorico de Basto has a small castle and several manor houses in the surrounding area. Most are private but some, such as the Casa do Campo (*see p392*), are part of the Turismo de Habitação scheme (*see p382*) and take in guests.

SOUTHERN PORTUGAL

Southern Portugal at a Glance

South of the Tagus the vast wheatfields and rolling plains of the Alentejo stretch almost uninterrupted to the horizon. There is a rich legacy of early civilization here, dating back to prehistory, but visitors to Beja and even the World Heritage cities of Évora and Elvas will usually be untroubled by mass tourism – until reaching the southern coast. Many visitors know nothing of Portugal except the tourist play-ground of the Algarve, yet it is least typical of the country. The sandy beaches are a year-round attraction but the historic town centres such as Faro, and the quieter hinterland, are well worth exploring.

Évora, the Alentejo's historic university city, has monuments dating back to the Roman era. Gleaming white arcades and balconies of finely wrought ironwork are reminders that for over 450 years, until 1165, Évora was inhabited by the Moors *(see pp308–11)*.

Beja flourished under the Moors and its museum is housed in a former convent resplendent with Hispano-Arab tiles, such as these in the chapter-house *(see p317)*.

Lagos, principal town of the western Algarve, is flanked by inviting cove beaches, such as Praia de Dona Ana, which make it easy to understand why sunseekers flock here *(see pp326–7)*.

Mora

Arrai

Montemor-o-Novo

Viana do Alentej

A

ALENT
(See pp29

Grândola

Santiago do Cacém

Sines

Vila Nova de Milfontes

Ourique

Zambujeira do Mar

Santa-Clara-a-Velha

Almodôvar

Monchique

Aljezur

ALGARVE
(See pp320–337)

Alte

Silves

Sá de A

Vila do Bispo

Portimão

Lagoa

Loulé

Lagos

Albufeira

Sagres

Faro *(see pp332–4)*

◀ The crystal-clear waters off Praia dos Três Castelos, near Portimão

0 kilometres 25

0 miles 10

Castelo
de Vide

Marvão

o

Portalegre

Alter do
Chão

Camp

Estremoz   Elvas

Évora
Monte

Vila Viçosa

Alandroal

Iondo

Monsaraz

uengos
onsaraz

a

Moura

pa

Mértola

Alcoutim

Odeleite

Vila Real
e S. Antonio

Cacela
Velha

Marvão, within a stone's throw of the Spanish border, sits like a miniature fortress high in the Serra de São Mamede. The granite walls which protect the tiny town merge imperceptibly with the rock and have kept Marvão safe through centuries of dispute *(see p300)*.

Elvas has some of the best-preserved fortifi- cations in Europe *(see p303)*. At the centre of the walled old town lies the Praça da República, where Elvas's former cathedral looks out over the square's striking geometric mosaics.

Vila Viçosa was chosen in the 15th century as the seat of the dukes of Bragança. Here they built their Paço Ducal *(see pp304–5)*, in front of which stands a bronze equestrian statue of the 8th Duke, who became King João IV in 1640.

Faro, the gateway to the Algarve thanks to its international airport, is nevertheless bypassed by many visitors. Much was destroyed by the 1755 earthquake, but the town still has a pleasant historic centre beside the harbour. In spring the streets and squares are scented with the sweetness of orange blossom *(see pp332–4)*.

The Beaches of the Algarve

Facing North Africa to the south, and exposed to the force of the Atlantic in the west, the Algarve has a varied coastline. The Barlavento (windward side) includes the west coast and the south coast almost as far as Faro. Beaches around the promontory of Sagres are backed by cliffs and on the west coast many beaches are deserted. The sea here is colder and rougher than on the south coast, with dangerous currents. Between Sagres and Lagos is the start of a series of beautiful sandy coves, punctuated with grottoes, overlooked by tightly packed holiday resorts. East of Faro, the Sotavento (leeward side) has long, sandy beaches washed by warmer, calmer water.

① Arrifana
The gracefully curving beach of Arrifana is one of the most stunning on the west coast. Sheltered below high cliffs, the approach by road offers dramatic views *(see p324)*.

0 kilometres 10
0 miles 10

Praia de Monte Clérigo

Aljezur

Praia de Arrifana ①

Alfambras

N268

N120

Bordeira

Carrapateira

A22 IC4

Bensafrim

Pedralva

Odiáxere

Portimão

Algoz

Alvor

Lagoa

Ferre

Praia de Castelejo ②

N268

Budens

N125

Lagos ⑥

Ferragudo Alcantarilha

N125

Vila do Bispo

Figueira

Luz

⑤

⑦

⑧

⑨

Albufei

Burgau

Sagres

③ ④

② Castelejo
This long, deserted beach of soft sand can only be reached via a dirt road by bicycle, car or jeep. Its remote location, however, ensures peace and quiet *(see p325)*.

③ Beliche
Despite being at the "world's end", Beliche is sheltered by Ca de São Vicente. The sandy bea is backed by fascinating caves and rock formations *(see p326)*

④ Martinhal
Martinhal is a wide, sheltered expanse of sand east of Sagres. The area is popular for water sports of all kinds, and the beach boasts an aquatic school with parasailing, water-skiing and windsurfing *(see p326)*.

⑤ Dona Ana
A tiny cove on the way to Ponta da Piedade, Dona Ana is one of the prettiest beaches in the Algarve, although crowded during the summer. A boat trip to see nearby caves and grottoes is highly recommended *(see p327)*.

⑥ Meia Praia
A vast expanse of sand stretching for 4 km (2 miles), the sheltered Meia Praia is the longest beach in the Algarve. Easily reached by road, there is also a boat trip from Lagos during the summer months *(see p327)*.

⑦ Praia da Rocha
Framed by ochre cliffs and lapped by calm water, this spacious beach is justifiably famous – and crowded in high season. Water sports can be practised here in a gentler sea than the extreme southwest and visitors are well catered for *(see p328)*.

⑪ Ilha de Tavira

In summer, boats go from Quatro Águas to the sandy Ilha de Tavira. The beach facing the coast has calm water, whereas the beaches on the ocean side, that run the length of the island, offer good swimming and windsurfing *(see p336)*.

⑧ Carvoeiro

Carvoeiro is a fishing village with a diminutive cove. The whole area is great for cove beaches, and a boat trip or a walk along the cliff will take you to spectacular sandy beaches with excellent swimming and snorkelling.

Azinhal

Castro Marim

Vila Real de
Santo António

⑫

Conceição

Cacela
Velha

Loulé

Pereiro

Santo
Estêvão

Tavira

Santa Bárbara
de Nexe

Estói

Luz

⑪
Ilha de
Tavira

⑫ Monte Gordo
The warm water and balmy climate, combined with vast stretches of clean sand backed by pine woods, make Monte Gordo a very popular resort.

Almancil

Quarteira

São João da
Venda

Pechão

Moncarapacho

Fuseta

Olhão

Ilha de
Armona

Faro

Praia de
Faro

Ilha de
Culatra

Cabo de
Santa Maria

⑨ Senhora da Rocha
Senhora da Rocha, named after a small chapel on its eastern promontory, is actually three small, sheltered beaches. Typical of this part of the coast, these half-moons of sand tucked below eroded yellow cliffs are reached via steep steps.

⑩ São Rafael
The small, popular beach of São Rafael offers soft sand and shallow water, with spectacular caves and eroded rock formations to explore. For those without a car, it is a steep walk down from the bus stop on the main road *(see p329)*.

The Flavours of Southern Portugal

Alentejan cuisine is one of the country's most loved. The landscape is a powerful source of culinary inspiration, with its abundant vineyards, silvery olive groves and its wide oaks that provide acorns for pigs, giving an intense flavour to local pork meat. The Portuguese trinity of olive oil, garlic and coriander is at its holiest here, and some of the country's tastiest fish and seafood is caught off the region's rocky western coast. The Algarve boasts a wide variety of fish, a wealth of fruit and vegetables, the *cataplana* (a unique copper pan), and the culinary cosmopolitanism that comes with tourism.

Fresh figs

Algarve chef cooking with a *cataplana* pan

The Alentejo

For a region whose history and identity is bound up with a poor and landless peasantry, the Alentejo has a surprisingly rich culinary heritage. Dishes are varied and use basic ingredients imaginatively, leaving little to waste. One example is Alentejan bread, that famously keeps for a long time. Even when at last it begins to go stale it still has uses. Slices are placed in a broth of hot water, olive oil, garlic and coriander, mashed and topped with a poached egg to make *açorda*.

The ewe's milk cheeses of Serpa, Évora and Nisa are eaten when they are freshly made, soft and even runny, or after prolonged maturing, which hardens them and sharpens their flavour. Shepherds also herd Ibérico pigs, or *porcos pretos* as they are often called. These are fattened up by foraging for acorns, which gives the meat and fat a delicious intensity of flavour to make most other pork seem insipid in comparison.

Olives are a staple of the Alentejo, and the area around Moura is famous for its olive oil.

Oysters   Clams   Crab   Dourada (bream)   Giant prawns
Mussels   Squid
                                           Red mullet

Harvest of fish and seafood from the southern Portuguese coastline

Regional Dishes and Specialities

It might seem strange that one of the great dishes of the Alentejo is a fish soup, but *sopa de cação* masterfully transforms the humble dogfish into a velvety soup with a sweet-and-sour streak. *Ensopado* is a quintessentially Alentejan type of dish, a sort of soupy stew, often served with a slice of bread at the bottom of the bowl. The lamb version, *ensopado de borrego*, is the most popular. *Porco preto* is prepared in any number of ways, from the classic *pézinhos de coentrada* (pig's trotters with coriander), to *lombo de porco em presunto* (tenderloin wrapped in cured ham). The Algarvian *cataplana* pan is often used to cook a rich fish and seafood stew, *cataplana de peixe e mariscos*. Figs feature in many of the region's desserts, including the fudge-like *morgado de figo*.

Olives

Lombo de porco em presunto is often served with baby turnips. The ham keeps the tenderloin moist.

Fresh char-grilled sardines and giant prawns

Small, hot chillies known as *piri-piri* make their way into many local dishes and pickles, while large, sweet red peppers are char-roasted and peeled to add to salads, or mashed into a paste with salt to be preserved as *massa de pimentão*.

The coast yields delicacies such as *sargo* (white bream) and *perceves*, the odd-looking goose barnacle, which is pried off steep cliffsides at low tide. Deep-fried dried eel is popular, and tastes similar to pork crackling.

The Algarve

Portugal's tourist hub is often condescendingly regarded as a culinary cliché of grilled sardines, vinegary salads, grilled chicken and chips, but that misses a few crucial points. In the *cataplana*, a wok-shaped copper pan with a hinged, domed lid, the region has its own cooking utensil and technique as well as a link to its Arabic past. Though many restaurants use it like any other pan, the *cataplana* is above all a steaming device, particularly suited to the coast's many delicious edible shells, such as *ameijoas* and *conquilhas* (types of cockle) and *ostras* (oysters). Tuna is rarer now than it was, but the range at any fish market remains vast.

Oranges ripening in a citrus grove in the Algarve

Inland from its popular beaches, the region is a fertile garden for almost every kind of vegetable – peppers and beefsteak tomatoes are particularly good – and a large variety of fruits including citrus, figs and melons. The *serras*, mostly low mountain ranges forming a natural border with the Alentejo, provide traditional cheeses, herbs, honey and sweets.

REGIONAL WINES

The Alentejo is Portugal's favourite wine region, and accounts for about one-third of the country's vineyards. Parts of it date back to Roman times. It produces wines with styles ranging from traditional, farmyard-scented light reds to deep, berry-flavoured and oaked ones, often made from grapes that are familiar to the region, including Syrah and the Douro variety Touriga Nacional. The leap in quality that the Alentejo has performed over the last couple of decades is perhaps most noticeable in the whites, which are strikingly fresh and fruity for a region of extreme heat. The Algarve has begun a process of renewal and modernization as well, with several individual producers leading the way, and some co-operatives are now making very palatable reds. Wines tend to be soft and aromatic with a high alcohol content.

Ensopado de Borrego uses cheap cuts of lamb marinated with cumin and cloves and simmered until very tender.

Cataplana is named for the pan. Shellfish, squid, prawns and fish are steamed with white wine, garlic and herbs.

Morgado de Figo is a rich, sticky cake of dried figs, almonds, sugar, chocolate, cinnamon and aniseed.

ALENTEJO

The sun-baked Alentejo occupies nearly one-third of Portugal, stretching all the way from the Tagus south to the Algarve. Its vast rolling plains, golden with wheat or silver with olive trees, its whitewashed villages, megaliths and castles, and irresistible Wine Route, are the Alentejo's great attractions for visitors.

Stone circles, dolmens and other relics of Stone Age life pepper the Alentejan plain, particularly around Évora, a historical gem of a city at the region's geographical centre.

Évora, like Beja, Elvas, Alter do Chão and other towns, was founded by the Romans, who valued this land beyond the Tagus – *além Tejo* – for its wheatfields. Introducing irrigation systems to overcome the soil's aridity, they established enormous farms to grow grain for the empire. Worked by peasant farmers, these huge estates, or *latifúndios*, still exist.

Grain apart, the vast plains yield cork from the bark of cork oaks and olives – Elvas is prized for these as well as its candied greengages. Vineyards across the region have long produced powerful wines *(see pp32–3)*, and some areas are classified at the *Denominação de Origem Controlada* (DOC) level. Wine tourism is flourishing. Since 1986, Portugal's membership of the European Union has increased the rate of investment and modernization, although the region is still sparsely populated, supporting only ten per cent of the population. Land tenure has always been a concern here, and communism has a strong appeal – the Alentejans were solid supporters of the 1974 revolution *(see p61)*.

Many towns and villages, especially in the south, carry echoes of the long Moorish occupation in their cube-like white houses, while to the north and east the plains give way to a rocky terrain of fortified villages and scrubland grazed by flocks of sheep. Portuguese from other regions mock the amiable *alentejanos* for their slow ways, but they are widely admired for their singing, handicrafts, gastronomy and wines.

Houses with red-tiled roofs in the historic town of Castelo de Vide *(see p301)*

◄ Marvão castle, dating from the 13th century

Exploring the Alentejo

The ancient city of Évora, with its exceptional historic centre and location in the heart of the Alentejo, is an obvious starting point for exploring this varied and beautiful region.

To the northeast lie the white towns of Estremoz and Vila Viçosa, where local marble has been used in the construction of some fabulous façades, and Alter do Chão, home of Portugal's royal horse, the Alter Real. Nearer the Spanish frontier, towns and villages still shelter within massive fortifications, while travelling south the legacy of the Moors becomes ever more apparent; Beja and Mértola, especially, are full of Moorish history.

On the west coast there are some lovely beaches, with many stretches still relatively untouched by tourism.

The cromlech of Almendres, one of many prehistoric sites around Évora

Sights at a Glance

1. Serra de São Mamede
2. Marvão
3. Portalegre
4. Castelo de Vide
5. Crato
6. Alter do Chão
7. Campo Maior
8. Elvas
9. *Vila Viçosa pp304–5*
10. Alandroal
11. Redondo
12. Estremoz
13. Évoramonte
14. Arraiolos
15. Montemor-o-Novo
16. *Évora pp308–11*
18. Monsaraz
19. Viana do Alentejo
20. Vidigueira
21. Moura
22. Serpa
23. Beja
24. Santiago do Cacém
25. Sines
26. Vila Nova de Milfontes
27. Zambujeira do Mar
28. Mértola

Tours

17. Megaliths Tour

0 kilometres 25
0 miles 10

Noiti
N

Mo

Lavre
N114

Vendas
Novas
MONTEM
O-NO

IP7 A6 N4

Lisboa

A2

IP1
N253

Sar
do Es

Sã
Cr

IC1

Alcácer do Sal

Alc

Torrã

Ribeira de Oditcexa

SETÚBAL

NS

Grândola

O

Melides
IC33

Lagoa de Santo André
Vila Nova de Santo André

Azinheira dos Barros

Ferr
A

SANTIAGO
DO CACÉM 24

Serra de Grândola

N121

IC1

SINES 25

N120

Abela

São Domingos

Al

Porto Covo

Cercal

N262

Messejana

VILA NOVA
DE MILFONTES

26

São Luis

N263

Santa Luz

Almograve

Rio Mira

Ouriqu

ZAMBUJEIRA
DO MAR

27

Odemira

N120

São Teotónio

Santa Clara-a-Velha

N266

Lagos

Albufeira

The fertile farmland and orchards of the northern Alentejo, seen from Estremoz

For keys to symbols *see back flap*

Getting Around

Exploration by road is a more feasible option than by rail, although trains run between the major towns of Évora, Beja and some of the smaller centres. The bus network links most towns and villages, but time and patience are needed to cope with the logistics. For motorists, the tolled A6 (E90) provides fast access from Lisbon right through the Alentejo to the Spanish border, while the tolled IP2 (E802) bisects the region from north to south. Links on to minor roads are generally well marked and roads are mainly in good condition.

Serpa's Nossa Senhora de Guadalupe, startlingly white in the hot sun

Key

▬▬▬ Motorway

▬▬▬ Major road

┈┈┈ Minor road

▬▬▬ Scenic route

╍╍╍ Major railway

──── Minor railway

▨▨▨ National border

▤▤▤ Regional border

A sea of wheat surrounding a farmhouse near Moura

❶ Serra de São Mamede

Road map D4. 🚌 to Portalegre.
ℹ️ Portalegre.

The diverse geology and capricious climate of this remote range, caught between the Atlantic and the Mediterranean, encourage a fascinating range of flora and fauna. In 1989, 320 sq km (120 sq miles) of the Serra were designated a Nature Park classified by the EUROPARC Federation, and griffon vultures and Bonelli's eagles soar overhead. Red deer, wild boar and the cat-like genet live among the sweet chestnut trees and holm oaks, and streams attract otters and amphibians, such as the Iberian midwife toad. The reserve is also home to one of the largest colonies of bats in Europe.

The Serra's apparent emptiness is deceptive: megaliths suggest that it was settled in prehistoric times, and in the south of the reserve, rock paintings survive in the Serra de Cavaleiros and Serra de Louções. Below Marvão is the Roman town of Ammaia (São Salvador de Aramenha), and the Roman network of roads still winds among the trim white villages, offering grand views at every curve.

From Portalegre, the road climbs for 15 km (9 miles) to the Pico de São Mamede at 1,025 m (3,363 ft). A minor road leads south to Alegrete, a fortified village crowned by its ruined 14th-century castle.

Sheep in the summer pastures of the Serra de São Mamede

❷ Marvão

Road map D4. 🏔️ 185. 🚌 🚌
ℹ️ Largo da Silveirinha (245 909 131).
🛒 Thu.

This serene medieval hamlet is dramatically set at 862 m (2,828 ft) on a spectacular escarpment facing Spain. Its 13th- century walls and 17th-century buttresses blend seamlessly into the granite of the mountains, making it an impregnable stronghold. The Romans, who called the outcrop Herminius Minor, were followed by the Moors (the name may have come from Marvan, a Moorish leader) whom the Christians evicted with difficulty only in 1166.

The walls completely enclose the little collection of white-washed houses, a *pousada* (*see p393*) and the 15th-century Igreja Matriz. Rua do Espírito Santo leads past the former governor's house (now a bank)

Looking out over the plain from the heights of Marvão's castle

with its 17th-century iron balcony, and a Baroque fountain, up towards the castle.

Built by King Dinis in about 1299, the castle dominates the village. Its walls enclose two cisterns and a keep. The castle offers spectacular views south and west towards the Serra de São Mamede and east to the Spanish frontier.

The **Museu Municipal**, in the former church of Santa Maria, retains the main altar, and has an exhibition of traditional remedies and local archaeological finds from Palaeolithic to Roman times.

🏛️ **Museu Municipal**
Largo de Santa Maria. **Tel** 245 909 132.
Open Tue–Sun. **Closed** 25 Dec. 🅰️

❸ Portalegre

Road map D4. 🏔️ 12,000. 🚌 🚌
ℹ️ Rua Guilherme Gomes Fernandes 22 (245 307 445). 🛒 Wed & Sat (food); 2nd Wed of month (clothes).
🌐 visitalentejo.com

Strategically positioned on a low plateau of the Serra de São Mamede, Portalegre is of Roman origin. At the end of the 13th century, King Dinis (*see pp48–9*) built a castle on the city's highest point.

Textile, tapestry and silk industries brought prosperity in the 16th and 17th centuries, reflected in the Renaissance and Baroque mansions found along Rua 19 de Junho, the main street of the old town. Close to Praça da República is the only tapestry factory still in use, the Manufactura de Tapeçaria de Portalegre.

Uphill lies the cathedral, or Sé. Built in 1556, it acquired its Baroque façade and twin pinnacles in the 18th century. The late Renaissance interior has a sacristy lined with striking *azulejo* panels. Dating from the first years of the 17th century, these depict scenes from the life of the Virgin Mary and the flight of the Holy Family into Egypt.

The **Museu da Tapeçaria de Portalegre** displays contemporary tapestries and shows the methods, materials and tools used to create them.

The home of the Portuguese poet and dramatist José Régio (1901–69) is near the Praça da República. Now the **Museu José Régio**, it contains some fascinating folk art objects in a variety of media as well as his collection of crucifixes and a recreated Alentejan kitchen. The **Espaço Cultural – Museu Municipal de Portalegre** displays fine examples of 16th-century painting and sculpture, as well as beautifully crafted 18th-century furniture.

Folk crucifix, Museu José Régio, Portalegre

🏛 Museu da Tapeçaria
Rua da Figueira. **Tel** 245 307 530. **Open** 9:30am–1pm & 2:30–6pm Tue–Sun. **Closed** pub hols.

🏛 Museu José Régio
Rua José Régio. **Tel** 245 307 535. **Open** 9:30am–1pm & 2:30–6pm Tue–Sun. **Closed** pub hols.

🏛 Espaço Cultural – Museu Municipal de Portalegre
Rua José Marta da Rosa. **Tel** 245 307 525. **Open** 9am–1pm & 2:30–6pm Tue–Sun. **Closed** pub hols.

❹ Castelo de Vide

Road map D4. 🚗 3,000. 🚌
ℹ Praça Dom Pedro V (245 908 227).
🛒 Fri (clothes).

Sprawled on a green slope of the Serra de São Mamede, this pretty spa town enjoyed by the Romans has worn well. It is fringed by modern development but the lower town, around Praça Dom Pedro V, retains its Baroque church of Santa Maria, the 18th-century town hall and pillory, and handsome mansions from the same era. In the Largo Frederico Laranjo is one of several sources of the town's curative waters: the Fonte da Vila, a carved stone fountain with a pillared canopy. Just above is the maze-like Judiaria, where small white houses sprout vivid pots of geraniums. Its cobbled alleys are lined with fine Gothic doorways and conceal a 13th-century synagogue housing a small museum. The town's oldest chapel, the 13th-century Salvador do Mundo on the Estrada de Circunvalação, has a much admired *Flight into Egypt* by an unknown 18th-century artist.

In the upper town, the tiny Nossa Senhora da Alegria offers a feast of 17th-century polychrome floral tiles. It stands within the walls of the castle that gave the town its name. This was rebuilt in 1310 by King Dinis, who negotiated here to marry Isabel of Aragon. Inside the castle are two small museums, the Megalith Interpretation Centre and the Military Architecture and History Museum.

Red-tiled roofs of Castelo de Vide

❺ Crato

Road map D4. 🚗 2,000. 🚌
ℹ Mosteiro de Santa Maria de Flor da Rosa, inside the *pousada* (245 997 341). 🛒 3rd Thu of month.

Modest houses under outsize chimneys give no hint of Crato's past eminence. Part of a gift from Sancho II to the powerful crusading Order of Hospitallers, Crato was the Order's headquarters by 1350. Its prestige was such that Manuel I and João III were both married here, and João III's nephew was Grand Prior.

In 1662, invading Spanish forces sacked and burned the town, which never recovered. The Hospitallers' castle remains, in ruins, and in Praça do Município the 15th-century Varanda do Grão-Prior marks the entrance to what was the Grand Prior's residence.

Rua de Santa Maria leads, via an avenue of orange trees, to the Igreja Matriz, much altered since its 13th-century origins. In the chancel, 18th-century *azulejos* depict fishing, hunting and travelling scenes.

Environs
Just north of Crato are the imposing monastery and church of Flor da Rosa. Built in 1356 by the Grand Prior of Crato, father of Nuno Álvares Pereira (*see p189*), the monastery was restored and in 1995 opened as a *pousada* (*see p393*). A tapestry in the dining room shows the monastery surrounded by pine forests, as it was until the 20th century.

The crenellated monastery, now a *pousada*, of Flor da Rosa, near Crato

Alter do Chão

Road map D4. ⚠ 3,900. 🚌
ℹ Palácio do Álamo (245 610 004).
🎪 1st Thu of month.

The Romans founded Civitas Abelterium in 204 BC, but razed it under the Emperor Hadrian after the inhabitants were accused of disloyalty. The town was re-established in the 13th century.

Dominating the town centre is the five-towered **castle**. It has a Gothic portal built in 1359 by Pedro I. The flower-filled market square, the Largo Doze Melhores de Alter, lies at its feet.

Several streets northwest of the castle are graced by fine Baroque town houses, many trimmed with Alentejan-style yellow paintwork. The 18th- century Casa do Álamo (open daily) houses an art gallery and library.

🏰 Castle
Largo Barreto Caldeira. **Open** May–Sep: 10am–12:20pm & 3–7pm; Oct–Apr: 9am–12:30pm & 2–5:30pm.

Environs
Alter is best known for the **Coudelaria de Alter**, founded in 1748 to breed the Alter Real. The stud farm extends to 300 ha (740 acres) around attractive stables painted in the royal livery of white and ochre. Accommodation is available here.

Spanning the Seda 12 km (7 miles) west along the N369 is the robust six-arched Ponte de Vila Formosa. This bridge carried the Roman road from Lisbon to Mérida in Spain.

🏇 Coudelaria de Alter
3 km (2 miles) NW of town. **Tel** 245 610 060. **Open** Tue–Sun. **Closed** 1 Jan, 24 & 25 Dec. 🎫 ♿

Campo Maior's macabre but compelling Capela dos Ossos

Campo Maior

Road map E5. ⚠ 8,500. 🚌 ℹ Largo do Barata (268 689 367). 🎪 2nd Sat of month.

According to legend, this town got its name when three families settled in *campo maior*, the "bigger field". King Dinis fortified the town in 1310 and another monumental Porta da Vila was added in 1646.

In 1732 a gunpowder magazine, ignited by lightning, destroyed the citadel and killed 1,500 people. It seems likely that after a decent period, the victims provided the material for the morbid **Capela dos Ossos**, entirely faced in human bones. Dated 1766, it bears an inscription on mortality spelt out in collar bones.

The **Museu do Café** charts the history of this popular beverage with exhibits such as rare antique grinders.

🏛 Capela dos Ossos
Largo Dr Regala 6. **Tel** 268 686 168.
Open daily (if closed, speak to priest).

🏛 Museu do Café
Delta Coffee, Herdade das Argamassas. **Tel** 268 680 000.
Open 9am–1pm & 2:30–6:30pm Mon–Fri; 10am–1pm & 3–6pm Sat.
Closed public hols.

Elvas

Road map D5. ⚠ 20,000. 🚉 🚌
ℹ Praça da República (268 622 236).
🎪 2nd & 4th Mon of the month.

Only 12 km (7 miles) from the Spanish border, Elvas feels like a frontier town. The old town's fortifications are among the best preserved in Europe and a UNESCO World Heritage site. Within the walls a few architectural features and many of the street names are reminders that for 500 years the town was in Moorish hands.

Elvas was liberated from the Moors in 1230, but for another 600 years its fate was to swing between periodic attacks from Spain. Today Elvas is mostly associated with Elvas plums.

Summer roses brightening an Elvas street

Alter Real: Horse of Kings

Most Lusitano horses – Portugal's national breed – are grey, but those called Alter Real ("real" means royal) are purebred bay or brown. King José (1750–77), who yearned for a quality Portuguese horse, imported a stock of Andalusian mares, from which the gracious, nimble Alter Real was bred. The equestrian statue in Lisbon's Praça do Comércio *(see p89)* is of José astride his beloved Alter, Gentil. The stud prospered until the Napoleonic Wars (1807–15), when horse stealing and erratic breeding sent the Alter into decline. By 1930, the royal horse was practically extinct, but years of dedication have ultimately revived this classic breed.

The Fortifications of Elvas

A walk around the top of the battlements gives a fine view of the old town and a vantage point from which to appreciate the ingenious design of the fortifications. Using the principles of the French military architect, the Marquis de Vauban, a series of pentagonal bastions and freestanding angled ravelins form a multifaceted star, protecting the walls from every angle. What survives dates mostly from the 17th century, when the defences held off Spanish troops in the War of Restoration (see pp54–5). Elvas also served as Wellington's base to besiege Badajoz across the Guadiana.

Two surviving satellite forts indicate the strategic importance of Elvas: just to the south-east lies the military fort and museum of **Forte de Santa Luzia** (1641–87; open Tue–Sun), and 2 km (1 mile) to the north is the carefully restored 18th-century **Forte de Graça**, also open to the public.

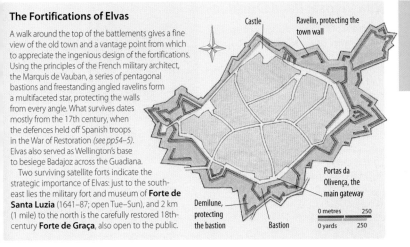

Castle

Ravelin, protecting the town wall

Portas da Olivença, the main gateway

Demilune, protecting the bastion

Bastion

0 metres 250
0 yards 250

🏰 Castle
Parada do Castelo. **Open** Tue–Sun **Closed** 1 & 14 Jan, Easter Sun, 1 May, 25 Dec.

Romano-Moorish in origin, the castle was rebuilt for Sancho II in 1226. It underwent further remodelling over the years, mainly by King Dinis, and in the late 15th century, under João II, whose coat of arms, incorporating a pelican, is seen above the entrance. Until the late 1500s the castle was the residence of the mayors of Elvas.

🏛 Nossa Senhora da Assunção
Praça da República. **Tel** 268 625 997. **Open** Tue pm–Sun. ♿ (via side door).

Until 1882, this was the cathedral of Elvas. Built in the early 16th century, its architect was Francisco de Arruda, who also designed the town's impressive aqueduct. His Manueline south portal survives, but much of the church has been modified. The azulejos in the nave date from the early 17th century.

🏛 Museu Municipal de Fotografia João Carpinteiro
Largo Luís de Camões. **Tel** 268 636 470. **Open** Tue–Sun. **Closed** public hols. 📷

Exhibition space at this fascinating museum is divided into the History of Photography Room, which displays numerous black-and-white images documenting life in the region; and the Collector's Room, which features rare and valuable vintage

cameras and photographic equipment. There is also a library devoted to photography.

🏛 Museu de Arte Contemporânea de Elvas
Rua da Cadeia. **Tel** 268 637 150. **Open** Apr–Sep: 3–6pm Tue, 11am–6pm Wed–Sun; Oct–Mar: 2–5pm Tue, 10am–5pm Wed–Sun.

The only national museum displaying exclusively contemporary Portuguese art occupies a former hospital. The collection includes works by artists such as Adriana Molder, André Gomes and Joana Vasconcelos.

🏛 Nossa Senhora dos Aflitos
Largo do Pelourinho. **Open** Tue–Sun. The plain exterior belies the wealth within the walls of this little 16th-century church. Its appeal is in the fine marble columns and spectacular azulejos added in the 17th century. These line the walls and reach up into the cupola.

Largo do Dr Santa Clara, with its pillory

Just behind the church is the archway of the Arab Porta da Alcáçova, a vestige of Elvas's Moorish fortifications. In the adjacent Largo do Dr Santa Clara is a pillory, carved in Manueline style (see pp28–9) and still armed with its hooks.

The arches of the great aqueduct

🏛 Aqueduto da Amoreira
Until the 16th century the only source of drinking water in Elvas was the Alcalá well in the west of the town. When this began to fail, alarmed citizens conceived the notion of an aqueduct to bring water from the spring at Amoreira, some 8 km (5 miles) away. Work, begun in 1498, was not finished until 1622. The great round buttresses and arches of architect Francisco de Arruda march across the valley and still deliver water to the fountain in the Largo da Misericórdia. The aqueduct has a total of 843 arches in up to five tiers and in places towers to over 30 m (100 ft).

Vila Viçosa: Paço Ducal

The dukes of Bragança owned vast estates, but the lavish palace at Vila Viçosa, begun by Dom Jaime in 1501, became their favoured residence.

When the 8th Duke became king in 1640, many of the furnishings accompanied him to Lisbon, but the long suite of first-floor rooms is still splendid, from the Sala da Cabra-Cega, where royal parties played blind man's buff, to the heroic Sala de Hércules. More intimate are the rooms of King Carlos and his wife, which are much as he left them the day before his assassination in 1908.

Chapel
Despite later additions, the chapel has retained its coffered ceiling and other features from the early 16th century. It was here, on 3 December 1640, that the 8th Duke learnt that he was to become king.

Dining room

First floor

The vast kitchen, which once regularly fed several hundred people, gleams with over 600 copper pots and pans, some large enough to bathe in.

★ **Sala dos Duques**
Lining the ceiling of the Room of the Dukes are portraits of all the dukes of Bragança by the Italian Domenico Dupra (1689–1770), commissioned by João V. On the walls are Brussels tapestries of scenes from the life of Achilles.

Sala da Cabra-Cega

The armouries, in a series of vaulted rooms, display swords, crossbows, halberds and suits of armour.

Ground floor

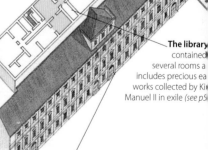

The library contained several rooms a includes precious ea works collected by Kin Manuel II in exile (see p5

Formal Gardens
The Jardim da Duquesa and the Jardim do Bosque are partly enclosed by palace walls, but can be seen from the dining-room windows. Their geometric formality reflects the palace's architectural style.

Entrance

Terreiro do Paço. **Tel** 268 980 659.
Open Apr–Sep: 2:30–5:30pm Tue,
10am–1pm & 2:30–5:30pm Wed–
Fri, 9:30am–1pm & 2:30–6pm Sat
& Sun (Jul & Aug: to 6pm Tue–Sun);
Oct–Mar: 2–5pm Tue, 10am–1pm
& 2–5pm Wed–Fri, 9:30am–1pm &
2–5pm Sat & Sun. **Closed** public
hols, 16 Aug. compulsory.

Key to Floorplan

- Royal rooms
- Library
- Chapel
- Armouries
- Kitchen
- Treasury
- Public areas

Palace Guide

*Guided tours, which last
about an hour, take in the royal
rooms ranged along the first
floor and ground-floor areas
such as the kitchen and the
treasury. Entry to the coach
museum, on the north side of
the palace, and armoury
is by separate tickets. From
time to time areas may
be closed for restora-
tion and rooms
can be shut off
without notice.*

⑨ Vila Viçosa

Road map D5. 8,700.
Praça da República (268 889 317).
Wed.

After the expulsion of the Moors
in 1226, this hillside town was
named Val Viçosa – "fertile
valley". In the 15th century it
became the country seat of the
dukes of Bragança, and when
the 8th Duke became King
João IV, Vila Viçosa was
expanded to meet the needs
of nobles and visiting ministers.
Substantial houses, built from
the local white marble, in streets
lined with orange trees, reflect
its prosperous royal past.

The town is full of reminders
of the Braganças. Dominating
the west side of the Terreiro do
Paço is the long façade of the
Paço Ducal, which stretches for
110 m (360 ft). Visitors to the
palace emerge through the
Porta do Nó, a marble and schist
gateway formed into the knot
symbol of the Braganças.

In the centre of the square a
statue of João IV on horseback
looks across to the Igreja dos
Agostinhos (not open to the
public). Founded in 1267 but
rebuilt in the 17th century, the
church was intended as the last
resting place of the dukes, but
despite their affection for Vila
Viçosa, most Bragança monarchs are buried in Lisbon, at
São Vicente de Fora (see p74).

View from the castle at Vila Viçosa, looking towards the Paço Ducal

In the Renaissance Convento
das Chagas, on the south side
of the square, are the tombs of
the Bragança wives. Founded
by the 4th Duke's second wife
in 1530, the convent has been
converted into a *pousada* hotel.

Alongside the Paço Ducal,
an 18-km (11-mile) wall rings
the tapada real, or royal chase.
Uphill from the Terreiro do
Paço is the castle, where an
exhibition explains the history
of the hunt. The **castle**, built by
King Dinis, was the Braganças'
residence from 1461 until the
Paço Ducal became habitable.

In the nearby 14th-century
church of Nossa Senhora da
Conceição stands a Gothic
image of the Virgin, said to be
from England. During the 1646
cortes João IV crowned her as
patron saint of Portugal, after
which no Portuguese monarch
ever wore a crown.

Castle
Avenida Duques de Bragança.
Tel 268 980 128. **Open** same as
Paço Ducal. **Closed** public hols.

The Royal House of Bragança

Catherine, born at Vila Viçosa in 1638

Afonso, illegitimate son of João I, was
created Duke of Bragança in 1442, first
of an influential but bloodstained
dynasty. Fernando, the 3rd Duke, was
executed in 1483 by his cousin, João II,
who feared his power. Jaime, the
unstable 4th Duke, locked up his wife
in Bragança castle (see p264), then killed
her at Vila Viçosa. It was Dom Jaime who
initiated the building of the palace at Vila
Viçosa, an ambitious work embellished
by later dukes to reflect their aspirations and affluence. The 8th
Duke only reluctantly relinquished a life of music and hunting
here to take up the throne (see p54).

The Braganças ruled Portugal for 270 years, accumulating wealth
and forging alliances (João IV's daughter, Catherine, married Charles II
of England), but inbreeding enfeebled the bloodline. The last
monarch, Manuel II, fled to exile in 1910, two years after his father
and brother were shot by Republicans. The present duke lives in
Sintra, near Lisbon.

The Porta do Nó, its carved knots the symbol of the Braganças

Alandroal, surrounded by groves of cork oaks

⑩ Alandroal

Road map D5. 🚹 2,500. 🚌
ℹ️ Praça da República (268 440
045). 🛒 Wed.

The low-lying town of Alandroal,
wrapped tidily around its castle
ruins, was built by the Knights
of Avis, who settled here from
1220. Little remains inside, but a
surviving inscription shows it
was completed in 1298. The
Igreja Matriz within its walls
dates from the 16th century.
The Misericórdia church near
the castle walls contains beautiful *azulejos* reputed to be the
work of Policarpo de Oliveira
Bernardes (1695–1778).

Environs
Terena, 10 km (6 miles) south
of Alandroal, is well known for
its pottery. The 14th-century
sanctuary of Nossa Senhora de
Boa Nova has frescoes covering
its walls and ceiling; dating from
1706, these depict saints and
Portuguese kings. For access ask
at the house opposite the church.

⑪ Redondo

Road map D5. 🚹 4,000. 🚌 **ℹ️** Praça
da República (266 909 100). 🛒 1st
Sun of month (antiques); 2nd Thu of
month (general).

As with much of the Alentejo
(*see p33*), Redondo is known
for its wines; however, this
medieval town is also famous
for its pottery. Roman-style
water jugs, casseroles and bowls
painted with humorous folk-art
motifs are sold from the tiny
white houses leading up to the
ruins of the castle founded by
King Dinis.

Environs
The Convento de São Paulo
in the Serra de Ossa, 10 km
(6 miles) north, was built in
1376; Catherine of Bragança
stayed here on her return home
in 1692 after the death of her
husband, King Charles II of
England. It is now a luxury
hotel (*see p393*), but retains
its wonderful 16th- to
18th-century *azulejos*.

⑫ Estremoz

Road map D5. 🚹 9,000. 🚌
ℹ️ Rossio Marquês de Pombal
(268 339 227). 🛒 Sat.

A key stronghold in the War of
Restoration (*see p54*) and then
in the War of the Two Brothers
(*see p58*), Estremoz looks out
from its hilltop over groves
of gnarled olive trees.
    The medieval upper town,
set within stout ramparts, is
dominated by a 13th-century
marble keep, rising to 27 m
(89 ft). This is the Torre das
Três Coroas, the Tower of the
Three Crowns, recalling the
kings (Sancho II, Afonso III and
Dinis) in whose reigns it was
built. The adjoining castle and
palace complex, built for
Dona Isabel, is now a *pousada*
(*see p393*). The saintly Isabel (*see
p49*), wife of King Dinis, died
here in 1336 and the **Capela
da Rainha Santa** dedicated to
her is lined with *azulejos*
recording her life.
    Today the bustling weekly
market in the Rossio, the main
square in the lower town, is a

Marble: Alentejo's White Gold

Portugal is the world's second largest exporter of marble, and even
Italy, the biggest producer, buys Portugal's quality stone. Around 90
per cent – over 500,000 tonnes a year – is quarried around Estremoz.
The marble from Estremoz and nearby Borba and Vila Viçosa is white or

Quarrymen near Estremoz, working on elephantine
blocks of prized marble

pink, while the quarries
at Viana do Alentejo
yield green stone. Marble
has been used for con-
struction since Roman
times and in towns such
as Évora (*see pp308–11*)
and Vila Viçosa (*see
pp304–5*), palaces and
humble doorsteps alike
gleam with the stone
often referred to as
"white gold".

reflection of local farming life. Across the square are the remains of King Dinis's once-fine palace and the town's **Museu Municipal**, with a display of archaeological finds, restored living rooms and a parade of *bonecos*, the charming pottery figurines for which Estremoz is famous *(see p417)*.

🏛 Museu Municipal de Estremoz Professor Joaquim Vermelho
Largo Dom Dinis. **Tel** 268 333 608. **Open** 9am–12:30pm & 2–5:30pm Tue–Sun. **Closed** public hols. 🅿

🏛 Capela da Rainha Santa
Largo Dom Dinis. (Access via adjacent Design Gallery.) **Open** Ask at the Igreja de Santa Maria, on Largo Dom Dinis.

⑬ Évoramonte

Road map D5. 🗻 1,000. 🚌 ℹ Rua Santa Maria (268 959 227).

Above the doorway of No. 41, along Évoramonte's single street, is a historic plaque. It records that here, on 26 May 1834, Dom Miguel ceded the throne, ending the conflict with his older brother *(see p58)*.

The eye-catching **castle**, its walls bound by bold stone "ropes", largely replaced an earlier castle that fell in an earthquake in 1531. The 16th-century walls have been restored using a patina technique. An exhibition explains the castle's history.

🏰 Castle
Open Tue pm–Sun. **Closed** last weekend of month. 🅿

⑭ Arraiolos

Road map D5. 🗻 3,500. 🚌 ℹ Praça do Município (266 490 254). 🗓 1st Sat of month.

The foundation of Arraiolos is attributed either to Celts or perhaps to local tribes in about 300 BC. Its 14th-century castle seems overwhelmed by the town walls and looming 16th-century Igreja do Salvador. Typically, houses in Arraiolos are low and white, and are painted with a blue trim to ward off the devil.

The principal sight in Arraiolos, however, is of women stitching at their bright wool rugs in the shadowy rooms behind the main street. Carpets have been woven in Arraiolos since the 13th century and decorate countless manor houses and palaces throughout Portugal. The craft may have begun with the Moors, but floral designs of the 18th century are thought to be the finest. As well as browsing the town's many carpet shops, you can visit the **Centro Interpretativo do Tapete** to discover more about this ancient craft.

🏛 Centro Interpretativo do Tapete
Praça do Município 19. **Tel** 266 490 254. **Open** 10am–1pm & 2–6pm Tue–Sun. 🅆 **tapetedearraiolos.pt**

Environs
At **Pavia**, 18 km (11 miles) to the north, is the startling sight of a tiny chapel built into a dolmen. It is signposted as Anta de São Dinis; if closed, ask at the café nearby.

⑮ Montemor-o-Novo

Road map C5. 🗻 9,000. 🚌 ℹ Largo Calouste Gulbenkian (266 898 103). 🗓 2nd Sat of month.

Montemor was fortified by the Romans and then by the Moors – the Arab warrior Al-Mansur is remembered in the name of the nearby River

The view down the nave of the Igreja Matriz in Montemor-o-Novo

Almançor. The town, regained from the Moors in the reign of Sancho I, was awarded its first charter in 1203. The castle, rebuilt in the late 13th century, is now a ruin crowning the hill.

Montemor's 17th-century Igreja Matriz stands in Largo São João de Deus, named after the saint who was born nearby in 1495. The Order of Brothers Hospitallers that St John of God founded evolved from his care for the sick, especially foundlings and prisoners.

A former convent in the upper town now houses the **Museu de Arqueologia**, where the exhibits include local archaeological finds and antique farming tools.

🏛 Museu de Arqueologia
Convento de São Domingos, Largo Professor Dr Banha de Andrade. **Tel** 266 890 235. **Open** 10am–1pm & 3–5pm Tue–Sun. **Closed** public hols. 🅿 ♿

Arraiolos, crowned by its castle and the Igreja do Salvador

⑯ Street-by-Street: Évora

Rising out of the Alentejan plain is the enchanting walled city of Évora. The town rose to prominence under the Romans and flourished throughout the Middle Ages as a centre of learning and the arts. It was a popular residence of Portuguese kings, but fell out of favour after Spain's annexation of Portugal in 1580. Its influence waned further when the Jesuit university closed in the 18th century. Students once again throng Évora's streets, joined by visitors who come to discover its many historical sites and enjoy the atmosphere of the old town. The city's historic legacy was officially recognized in 1986, when UNESCO declared Évora a World Heritage Site.

★ **Roman Temple**
Popularly believed [to] have been dedicat[ed] to the goddess Dia[na,] this temple was erected in the 2nd [or] 3rd century AD. It w[as] used as armoury, theatre and slaughterhouse before being rescued in 1870.

The Fundação Eugénio de Almeida is a modern art gallery and cultural centre.

Rua 5 de Outubro
The shops along this street sell curios and handicrafts, from painted chairs to carved cork.

RUA DO SALVADOR

RUA DE DONA ISABEL

TRAVESSA DAS CASAS PINT A[…]

PRAÇA DO SERTÓRIO

RUA DE VASCO DA G[…]

RUA JOÃO DE DEUS

RUA NOVA

RUA 5 DE OUTUB[…]

Key

— Suggested route

PRAÇA DO GIRALDO

Tourist information

RUA DA REPÚBLICA

To railwa[y] bus stati[on]

Praça do Giraldo
The fountain in Évora's main square was erected in 1571. Its marble predecessor received the first water delivered by the town's aqueduct (see p311).

| 0 metres | 50 |
| 0 yards | 50 |

For hotels and restaurants in this area see pp393–4 and pp409–11

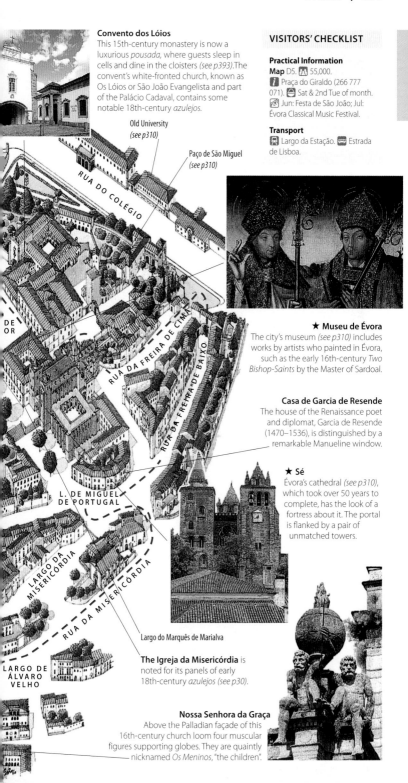

Convento dos Lóios
This 15th-century monastery is now a luxurious *pousada*, where guests sleep in cells and dine in the cloisters *(see p393)*. The convent's white-fronted church, known as Os Lóios or São João Evangelista and part of the Palácio Cadaval, contains some notable 18th-century *azulejos*.

Old University
(see p310)

Paço de São Miguel
(see p310)

RUA DO COLÉGIO

DE
OR

RUA DA FREIRA DE CIMA

RUA DA FREIRA DE BAIXO

L. DE MIGUEL
DE PORTUGAL

LARGO DA
MISERICÓRDIA

RUA DA MISERICÓRDIA

LARGO DE
ÁLVARO
VELHO

Largo do Marquês de Marialva

VISITORS' CHECKLIST

Practical Information
Map D5. 55,000.
Praça do Giraldo (266 777 071). Sat & 2nd Tue of month. Jun: Festa de São João; Jul: Évora Classical Music Festival.

Transport
Largo da Estação. Estrada de Lisboa.

★ **Museu de Évora**
The city's museum *(see p310)* includes works by artists who painted in Évora, such as the early 16th-century *Two Bishop-Saints* by the Master of Sardoal.

Casa de Garcia de Resende
The house of the Renaissance poet and diplomat, Garcia de Resende (1470–1536), is distinguished by a remarkable Manueline window.

★ **Sé**
Évora's cathedral *(see p310)*, which took over 50 years to complete, has the look of a fortress about it. The portal is flanked by a pair of unmatched towers.

The Igreja da Misericórdia is noted for its panels of early 18th-century *azulejos (see p30)*.

Nossa Senhora da Graça
Above the Palladian façade of this 16th-century church loom four muscular figures supporting globes. They are quaintly nicknamed *Os Meninos*, "the children".

Exploring Évora

Squeezed within Roman, medieval and 17th-century walls, Évora's web of streets is an architectural and cultural cornucopia. From the forbidding cathedral, a stroll down past the craft shops of Rua 5 de Outubro leads to Praça do Giraldo, the city's lively main square, whose arcades are a reminder of Moorish influence. Évora's religious dedication is reflected in the number and variety of its churches – over 20 churches and monasteries, including a grisly chapel of bones. On a happier note, Évora's restaurants are excellent and the pleasure of wandering the historic streets is enhanced by evocative names such as Alley of the Unshaven Man and Street of the Countess's Tailor.

Azulejos at the Old University, depicting Aristotle teaching Alexander

🏛 Sé

Largo do Marquês de Marialva.
Tel 266 759 330. **Open** daily (museum Tue–Sun).

Begun in 1186 and consecrated in 1204, the granite cathedral of Santa Maria was completed by 1250. Romanesque melds with Gothic in this castle-like cathedral whose towers, one turreted, one topped by a blue cone, give the façade an odd asymmetry. Flanking the portal between them are superb 14th-century sculpted apostles. The 18th-century high altar and marble chancel are by J F Ludwig, the architect of the monastery at Mafra *(see pp56–7)*. A Renaissance portal in the north transept is by Nicolau Chanterène. In the cloisters, which date from about 1325, statues of the Evangelists stand watch at each corner.

A glittering treasury houses sacred art. The most intriguing exhibit here is a 13th-century ivory Virgin whose body opens out to become a triptych of tiny carved scenes: her life in nine episodes.

🏛 Museu de Évora

Largo do Conde de Vila Flor. **Tel** 266 702 604. **Open** 2–6pm Tue, 10am–6pm Wed–Sun. **Closed** some public hols.

This 16th-century palace, once the residence of governors and bishops, is now the regional museum. Évora's history is all here, from Roman columns to modern sculpture in local marble. Notable upstairs are *The Life of the Virgin*, a 16th-century Flemish polyptych in 13 panels and works by the Portuguese painter the Master of Sardoal, especially his *Two Bishop-Saints* and a *Nativity*.

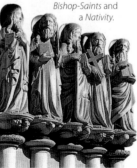

Carved figures of the apostles decorating the Gothic entrance to the Sé

🏛 University

Largo dos Colegiais 2. **Tel** 266 740 875.
Open Mon–Sat. **Closed** public hols.

With the establishment of the Jesuits' Colégio do Espírito Santo, Évora, already noted for its architecture and sacred art, became a seat of learning. The school flourished for 200 years but was closed in 1759 when the reforming Marquês de Pombal banished the Jesuits *(see p57)*.

Today part of the University of Évora, the school still has a graceful cloister and notable *azulejos* – in the classrooms they depict suitably studious themes such as Plato lecturing to disciples (1744–9). The 18th-century Baroque chapel, now the Sala dos Actos, is used for graduation ceremonies.

🏛 Praça do Giraldo

Évora's bustling main square may be named after Geraldo Sem Favour (the Fearless), an outlaw who ousted the Moors for King Afonso Henriques in 1165.

🏛 Paço de São Miguel

Tel 266 748 300. **Open** 9am–12:30pm & 2:30–5:30 Tue–Sun. **Closed** public hols. book in advance.

This grand 15th-century museum was the residence of the influential Counts of Basto and, later, the Eugénio de Almeida family.

🏛 Palácio dos Duques de Cadaval

Tel 266 704 714. **Open** Tue–Sun.
The Palace of the Dukes of Cadaval, on the site of the city's former castle, dates from the 14th century. The façade is noted for its unusual pentagonal tower. Inside, rooms display medieval armour, illuminated 14th-century manuscripts and 18th-century religious art.

🏛 São Francisco

Praça 1° de Maio. **Tel** 266 704 521.
Open daily. to Capela dos Ossos.

The main attraction of this 15th-century church is its Capela dos Ossos, a gruesome chapel of bones created in the 17th century from the remains of 5,000 monks. Two leathery corpses, one of a child, dangle from a chain, and a mordant reminder at the entrance reads: *Nós ossos que aqui estamos pelos vossos esperamos* ("We bones that are here await yours").

Largo da Porta de Moura, with its striking Renaissance fountain

🏛 Largo da Porta de Moura

The western entrance to this square is guarded by the vestiges of a Moorish gateway. Both the domed Casa Soure and the double arches of the belvedere on Casa Cordovil at the opposite end, show the Arab influence on architecture in Évora. The central fountain, looking like some futuristic orb, surprisingly dates back to 1556. Just south of the square, the portal of the Convento do Carmo features the knot symbol, denoting it once belonged to the Braganças *(see p305)*.

🏛 Fundação Eugénio de Almeida

Páteo de São Miguel. **Tel** 266 748 300. Carriage Museum: **Open** Tue–Sun. **Closed** public hols.

This avant-garde modern exhibition space plays host to local and national artists and the occasional international name, such as Marcel Duchamp. It also promotes the performing arts, staging regular concerts and recitals. The building provides access to the Carriage Museum, and tours to the nearby Cartuxa winery can be booked here.

The Romans in the Alentejo

Once the Romans gained dominance over Lusitania *(see pp44–5)*, they turned the Alentejo into a vast wheatfield: their very name for Évora – Ebora Liberalitas Julia – reflects the now-diminished importance of the region's grain supply. *Latifúndios*, large farms instigated by the Romans, survive to this day, as do vestiges of Roman open-cast copper and iron mines. Local marble was used in the construction of the finest villas, and Roman remains can be found scattered throughout the region, especially in Évora and Beja (Pax Julia), the region's principal town *(see p317)* and in more isolated sites such as São Cucufate, near Vidigueira *(see p316)*, and Miróbriga, near Santiago do Cacém *(see p318)*.

Roman bridge over the Odivelas, near Vidigueira

🏛 Walls

The fortifications that have protected Évora down the centuries form two incomplete concentric circles. The inner ring, of which only fragments are discernible, is Roman, from perhaps as early as the 1st century AD, with Moorish and medieval additions – the two stubby towers that give the Largo da Porta de Moura its name mark an Arab gate.

In the 14th century, new walls were built to encompass the growing town. Completed under Fernando I, these had 40 towers and ten gates, including the Porta de Alconchel, which still faces the Lisbon road.

When João IV was defiantly declared king in 1640 *(see p54)*, major fortifications were erected on this outer ring in anticipation of Spanish attack, and it is these 17th-century walls which are most evident today. The fear of attack was not unfounded, and the walls withstood much battering from the besieging Spanish in 1663.

Surviving arches of Évora's 16th-century aqueduct

🏛 Aqueduto da Água de Prata

Évora's aqueduct was built between 1531 and 1537 by the town's own eminent architect, Francisco de Arruda. The construction was regarded with wonder, and is even described in *Os Lusíadas*, the epic by Luís de Camões *(see p194)*. It originally carried water as far as the Praça do Giraldo. Like the walls, it was damaged in the 17th century during the Restoration War with Spain, but a surviving stretch, some 9 km (6 miles) long, can still be seen approaching from the northwest: visitors can follow a well-signposted trail for 8.3 km (5.1 miles).

⑰ Megaliths Tour

Archaeologists date the *pedras talhas,* hewn stones, near Évora to between 4000 and 2000 BC. Their symbolism remains mysterious. Dolmens are thought to be where Neolithic communities buried their dead, together with their possessions – more than 130 have been found in the region. Tall phallic menhirs jutting from olive groves immediately suggest fertility rites, while cromlechs – carved stones standing in regulated groups – probably had religious significance. This tour includes examples of each; more can be found further east, near Monsaraz and Reguengos de Monsaraz, and the museum in Castelo de Vide *(see p301)* has finds related to the area.

② Menhir of Almendres
Standing 2.5 m (8 ft) tall, this solitary stone is located away from the cromlech, in an olive grove behind a row of tall storage bins.

③ Cromlech of Almendres
This oval, made up of 95 ellipitical stones, is believed to have been a temple dedicated to a solar cult. The route to the cromlech is signposted from the N114.

① Évora
In the undulating farmland around the historic city of Évora *(see pp308–11)* at least 150 megalith sites have been found.

⑥ Grutas do Escoural
Discovered in 1963, these caves contain paintings about 15–20,000 years old.

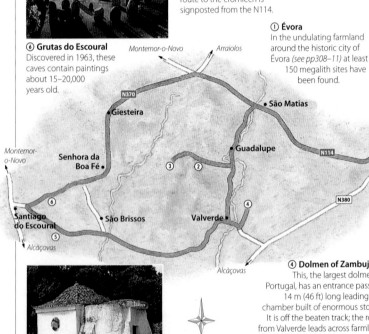

Montemor-o-Novo   Arraiolos

N370

Giesteira

São Matias

Montemor-o-Novo

Senhora da Boa Fé

Guadalupe

N114

③   ②

N380

⑥

Santiago do Escoural

São Brissos

Valverde

④

Alcáçovas

Alcáçovas

④ Dolmen of Zambujeiro
This, the largest dolmen in Portugal, has an entrance passage 14 m (46 ft) long leading to a chamber built of enormous stones. It is off the beaten track; the route from Valverde leads across farmland.

Key
━━ Tour route
══ Other roads

⑤ Dolmen-chapel of São Brissos
Beyond the hamlet of Brissos, this tiny chapel has been created from an *anta* or dolmen. Another is to be found at Pavia *(see p307).*

0 kilometres   5
0 miles   3

Tips for Drivers

Tour length: 80 km (50 miles).
Access to sites: The only guarded site is Escoural. The caves are closed at lunchtime, on Mondays and at some other times. Access roads to the sites are often no more than tracks, and signposting can be erratic. *(See pp444–5.)*

Riding through the narrow streets of Monsaraz on the day of a bullfight

⑱ Monsaraz

Road map D5. 🏘 150. 🚌 ℹ️ Rua Direita (927 597 316).

The tiny medieval walled town of Monsaraz perches above the River Guadiana on the frontier with Spain. Now a pretty backwater, it has known more turbulent times. Regained from the Moors in 1167 by the intrepid adventurer Geraldo Sem-Pavor (the Fearless), the town was handed over to the militant Knights Templar. Its frontier position continued to expose it to Spanish attack, but in 1381 assault came from an unexpected quarter. Troops of the Earl of Cambridge, Portugal's ally, were enraged by lack of pay and the annulment of the earl's betrothal to Fernando I's daughter, and unleashed their wrath on Monsaraz.

Principal access to the town is through the massive Porta da Vila. Rua Direita, the main street, leads up to the castle. Built by Afonso III and Dinis in the 13th century as part of the border defences, it was reinforced in the 17th century. The keep commands glorious views in all directions and at its foot is the garrison courtyard which today serves on occasion as a bullring.

The 16th-century Igreja Matriz in Rua Direita is worth visiting for its tall gilded altars and painted pillars. The 17th- and 18th-century houses along here display coats of arms. In the Gothic Paços da Audiência, now the **Museu de Arte Sacra**, is a collection of vestments, religious books and sculpture. Its earlier role as a law court is reflected in an unusual secular fresco: *O Bom e o Mau Juiz* (The Good and Bad Judge).

🏛 Museu de Arte Sacra
Largo Dom Nuno Álvares Pereira. **Tel** 266 508 040. **Open** Tue–Sun. 🈺

Environs
Surrounded by vineyards, Reguengos de Monsaraz, 16 km (10 miles) west, lies at the heart of one of the region's demarcated wine areas *(see p33)*. São Pedro do Corval, 5 km (3 miles) east of Reguengos de Monsaraz, is one of Portugal's greatest centres for pottery.

A number of striking megaliths is found near Monsaraz. The spectacular Menhir of Outeiro, 5.6 m (18 ft) tall, and the strangely inscribed Menhir of Belhôa are signposted in Telheiro, just north of Monsaraz. About 4 km (2 miles) south is the Cromlech of Xerez, a menhir in a square of lesser stones.

At Mourão, some 8 km (5 miles) further on, the 14th-century castle looks out over Lake Alqueva. Houseboats, canoes and kayaks to explore the lake can be hired at the marina at Amieira, 39 km (24 miles) further south. Sightseeing cruises can also be booked here (Tel: 266 611 173/4).

⑲ Viana do Alentejo

Road map D6. 🏘 3,500. 🚌 ℹ️ Praça da República (266 930 012). 🈺 2nd & last Thu of month.

Viana do Alentejo's castle, begun in 1313, was built to the design of King Dinis, the height of the outer wall exactly calculated to protect soldiers from attacking lancers. The unusual cylindrical towers show a Moorish influence and much of the later remodelling dates from João II, who held a *cortes* here in 1481–2.

Mirroring the castle walls are the crenellations and pinnacles of the adjacent 16th-century Igreja Matriz. The highly carved Manueline entrance to this fortified church leads into a majestic triple-naved interior.

Ten minutes' walk east of the town stands the vast pilgrimage church of Nossa Senhora de Aires, rebuilt in the 1700s. Inside, the chancel's golden canopy contrasts with pilgrims' humble ex votos. Every April, hundreds of people participate in the Moita–Viana do Alentejo Horse Pilgrimage. Originally of a religious nature, the event today has become more of a festival.

Environs
The Moorish-style castle at Alvito, 10 km (6 miles) south of Viana, was built in 1482 for the newly ennobled Barão de Alvito; it now operates as a *pousada*.

The low roofs and distinctive pepperpot chimneys of Mourão, near Monsaraz

Whitewashed houses in the village of Monsaraz ▶

The vineyards around Vidigueira caught in the evening light

⓴ Vidigueira

Road map D6. 🏔 2,800. 🚌 ℹ️ Praça Vasco da Gama 1, inside the Municipal Museum (284 437 260). 🏛 2nd Sat of month. 🌐 **vinhosdoalentejo.pt**

Fine wines make Vidigueira a leading centre of wine production in the Alentejo region. Less well known is the fact that the explorer Vasco da Gama was Conde de Vidigueira. His remains, now in the Mosteiro dos Jerónimos (see pp108–9), lay from 1539 to 1898 in the Convento do Carmo, now private property. A modern statue of the town's most famous son stands in the flowery square named after him. The main features of this little town are a Misericórdia church dated 1620, and a clock tower from Vasco da Gama's time.

Environs
One of Portugal's most notable Roman sites, São Cucufate, named after a later monastery, lies 4 km (2 miles) west. The vaulting belonged to a 4th-century villa, but excavations have revealed the baths of a 2nd-century

house, whose wine presses, reservoir and temple indicate a sumptuous Roman residence. The Cortes de Cima winery is close by and can be visited.

㉑ Moura

Road map D6. 🏔 7,000. 🚌 ℹ️ inside the castle (285 251 375). 🏛 1st Sat of month.

Legend mingles with history in this quiet town among oak and olive trees. Salúquia, daughter of a Moorish governor is said to have thrown herself from the castle tower on learning that her lover had been killed. From this tragedy the town acquired its name – Moura, the Moorish girl. The town's old Moorish quarter is an area of narrow streets and low, whitewashed houses.

Even after the Reconquest in the 12th century, Moura's frontier position left it open to attack. A siege in 1657, during the War of Restoration (see pp54–5), levelled much of it. The 13th-century castle survived, only to be blown up by the Spanish in 1707 – just a skeletal keep and wall remain.

The **Lagar de Varas do Fojo**, a former 19th-century olive press, is now a museum displaying a series of traditional presses, some dating from the 14th century.

🏛 **Lagar de Varas do Fojo**
Tel 285 253 978.
Open Tue–Sun.

View over Moura's quaint Moorish quarter

㉒ Serpa

Road map D6. 🏔 6,000. 🚌 ℹ️ Rua dos Cavalos 19 (284 544 727). 🏛 last Tue of month.

Serpa's stout walls are topped by an arched aqueduct. Beside the monumental Porta de Beja is a *nora*, or Arab water wheel. Won from the Moors in 1232, Serpa successfully resisted foreign control until a brief Spanish occupation in 1707.

Today, Serpa is a quiet agricultural town known for its cheese. Pleasing squares and streets of whitewashed houses are overlooked by a Moorish castle, rebuilt in the late 13th century. The **Watch Museum**, in the Convento do Mosteirinho, boasts some 1,800 timepieces, all of them mechanical and some dating from the 17th century.

🏛 **Watch Museum**
Convento do Mosteirinho. **Tel** 284 543 194. **Open** Tue–Sun.
🌐 **museuregionaldebeja.pt**

Serpa's great Porta de Beja

Environs
Serpa is just 35 km (22 miles) from the Spanish border. The Moors, and later Spain, fought for control of the region, which was finally ceded to Portugal in 1295. Continued disputes have left the legacy of a chain of watchtowers and a peppering of fortresses across these hills. One of the most remote, the deserted fort at Noudar, was built in 1346, but even in this isolated corner, evidence of pre-Roman habitation has been uncovered.

On the border at Barrancos, an incomprehensible mix of Spanish and Portuguese is spoken. A speciality here is the *barrancos* ham made from the local black pigs.

Love Letters of a Heartsick Nun

Lettres Portugaises, published in French in 1669, are celebrated for their lyric beauty. They are the poignant letters of a nun whose French lover deserted her: she was Mariana Alcoforado, born in Beja in 1640; he was the Comte de Saint-Léger, later Marquis de Chamilly, fighting in the Restoration wars with Spain. The true authorship of the five letters may be in doubt, but the story of the lovelorn nun endures – Matisse even

Mariana's window

painted her imaginary portrait. Sentimental visitors to the convent of Nossa Senhora da Conceição (now the Museu Regional) in Beja still sigh over "Mariana's window".

㉓ Beja

Road map D6. 🚉 35,000. 🚌 🚍
ℹ️ Castle (284 311 913). 🛍️ Sat.

Capital of the Baixo (lower) Alentejo, Beja is a city of historic and social importance. It is also a major centre for the production of wines and the harvesting of olives and cork, which are grown on the Bejan plains. The area has a noted wine and rural tourism industry.

The town became a regional capital under Julius Caesar, who called it Pax Julia after the peace made here with the Lusitani (*see p44*). The Praça da República marks the site of the Roman forum. The Moors arrived in AD 711, giving the town its present name and a lively, poetic culture until they were forced out in 1162.

Beja has been the scene of struggles against oppressive regimes. In 1808, occupying French troops massacred inhabitants and sacked the city, and in 1962, during the Salazar regime (*see pp60–61*), General Delgado led an unsuccessful uprising here.

Beja's old town, an area of narrow, often cobbled, streets, stretches from the castle keep southeast to the 13th-century convent of São Francisco, now a superb *pousada (see p393)*.

🏛️ Museu Regional Rainha Dona Leonor
Largo da Conceição. **Tel** 284 323 351. **Open** 9am–12:30pm & 2–5:15pm Tue–Sun. **Closed** public hols. 📷
🌐 **museuregionaldebeja.pt**

In the heart of the old town, the former Convento de Nossa Senhora da Conceição houses the regional museum. A little marble ossuary near the entrance contains the bones of the convent's first abbess. Exhibits are mostly paintings and coats of arms, but the building itself is a remarkable blend of architectural styles, with a Gothic church portal, Manueline windows and a dazzling Baroque chapel. Its *azulejos* are especially beautiful, the most notable being the Hispanic-Arab tiles in the chapterhouse and the early

16th-century examples in the cloister. Upstairs is a section on local archaeology and the romantic "Mariana's window".

🏰 Torre de Menagem
Largo do Lidador. **Tel** 284 311 913. **Open** Tue–Sun. **Closed** 1 Jan, 1 May, 25 Dec. 📷

The unmistakable landmark of the castle keep marks the northwest limit of the old quarter. Built by King Dinis in the late 1200s, it towers 36 m (118 ft) high. The 183-step climb up through its three storeys provides rewarding views from the top.

Beja's landmark castle keep

🏛️ Núcleo Visigótico
Largo de Santo Amaro. **Tel** 284 321 465. **Open** 9am–12:30pm & 2–5:15pm Tue–Sun. **Closed** pub hols. 📷 joint ticket with Museu Regional.

Beyond the castle keep stands Beja's oldest church, Santo Amaro, its columns surviving from its Visigothic origins. The church now houses the Museu Regional's collection of relics from this early period of Portugal's history.

⛪ Igreja Nossa Senhora dos Prazeres & Museu Episcopal
Largo dos Prazeres 4. **Tel** 284 320 918. **Open** 10am–12:30pm & 2:30–6pm Wed–Sun. **Closed** 1 Jan, Easter Sun, 25 Dec. 📷

The sumptuous interior of the 17th-century Baroque Igreja Nossa Senhora dos Prazeres features *azulejo* tiles and carved, gilded and painted woodwork, including a series of extraordinary panels by António de Oliveira Bernardes. The ceiling has a fresco depicting scenes from the life of Our Lady. The adjacent Museu Episcopal is dedicated to sacred art.

Chapterhouse of the former convent, now Beja's Museu Regional

Igreja Matriz, Santiago do Cacém

㉔ Santiago do Cacém

Road map C6. 🚹 7,000. 🚌
🚹 Parque da Quinta do Chafariz
(269 826 696). 🚉 2nd Mon of
month. 🌐 **rotavicentina.com**

Santiago do Cacém's Moorish
castle was rebuilt in 1157 by the
Templars (see pp190–91). Its walls,
which enclose the cemetery of
the adjacent 13th-century Igreja
Matriz, afford great views of the
Serra de Grândola. The church is
the starting point of the 350-km
(217-mile) Rota Vicentina footpath to Cabo de São Vicente
(see p325). The attractive main
square is enhanced by elegant
18th-century mansions.

The **Museu Municipal** still
retains some cells from its days
as a Salazarist prison (see p60).
Exhibits here include Roman
finds from nearby Miróbriga.

🏛 Museu Municipal

Largo do Município. **Tel** 269 827 375.
Open 10am–noon & 2–4:30pm Tue–
Fri, noon–6pm Sat. **Closed** public hols.

Environs

On a hill just to the east of
Santiago do Cacém lies the site
of the Roman city of **Miróbriga**.
Excavations, have uncovered a
forum, two temples, thermal
baths and a circus which had
seating for 25,000 spectators.

🏛 Miróbriga

Signposted off N121. **Tel** 269 818 460.
Open 9am–12:30pm & 2–5:30pm Tue–
Sun. **Closed** public hols. 🖼

㉕ Sines

Road map C6. 🚹 26,000. 🚌 🚉
🚹 inside the castle (269 632 237).
🚉 1st Thu of month.

The birthplace of Vasco da
Gama (see p110) is now a major
industrial port and tanker
terminal ringed with refinery
pipelines. Once past this heavy
industrial zone, visitors reach
the old town with its
popular sandy beach,
but it is not always
possible to escape the
haze of pollution.

A prominent land-
mark above the beach is
the modest medieval
castle, restored in the
16th century by King
Manuel. It was here that
Vasco da Gama, son of
the alcaide-mor, or
mayor, is reputed to have been
born in 1469. A multimedia
museum dedicated to the great
navigator, the **Casa Vasco da
Gama**, is housed in the castle
keep. A modern statue of Vasco
da Gama stands looking out
over the bay.

🏛 Casa Vasco da Gama

Castle of Sines. **Tel** 269 632 237. **Open**
10am–1pm & 2–5pm Tue–Sun (summer:
2:30–6pm). **Closed** public hols.

Environs

North and south of Sines are
attractive beaches. About 10 km
(6 miles) south, Porto Covo is a
picturesque village with an old fort
above a cove beach. A little further
to the south and a short boat ride
offshore is the low hump of Ilha
do Pessegueiro, Peach Tree Island.
Treeless and windswept, with the
ruins of a fort, the little island is
rather less romantic than it sounds.

More appealing are two sea-
blue lagoons, the Lagoa de
Santo André and Lagoa de
Melides nature reserves, set in a
long stretch of sandy coast about
20 km (12 miles) north of Sines.
Camping within the reserves is
prohibited and the area is
patrolled by park rangers.

Whitewashed houses with the traditional blue trim at
Porto Covo, south of Sines

㉖ Vila Nova de Milfontes

Road map C6. 🚹 11,000. 🚌 🚹 Rua
António Mantas (283 996 599). 🚉
2nd & 4th Sat of month in Brunheiras.

One of the loveliest places on
Portugal's west coast is where
the River Mira meets the sea. The
popular resort of Vila Nova de
Milfontes, on the sleepy estuary,
is low key and unassuming, but
offers many places to stay. Its small
castle overlooking the bay once
defended the coast from pirates.
In contrast to the quiet river are
the pretty beaches with their
crashing waves, a major summer
attraction, especially with surfers.

Environs

To the south about 10 km
(6 miles) is the unspoiled
beach of Almograve, backed
by impressive cliffs.

The calm, sunny face of the sandy coast near Vila Nova de Milfontes

㉗ Zambujeira do Mar

Road map C7. 🚗 1,000. 🚌
ℹ️ Rua da Escola (283 961 144).
🌐 sudoeste.meo.pt

A narrow strip of sheltered land divides the Alentejo plains from the bracing Atlantic. Here lies the solitary village of Zambujeira do Mar, the whiteness of its gorgeous beach enhanced by the dark backdrop of high basalt cliffs. The annual Festival Meo Sudoeste, usually held in the second week in August at Herdade da Casa Branca, just outside the village, draws music lovers from all over Europe.

㉘ Mértola

Road map D6. 🚗 1,200. 🚌 ℹ️ Rua da Igreja 1 (286 610 109). **Open** Jul–Sep: 9:30am–12:30pm & 2–6pm Tue–Sun; Sep–Jun: 9am–12:30 & 2–5:30pm Tue–Sun. 🚗 🅿️ 1st Thu of month.

Pretty, whitewashed Mértola is of historical interest as this small town is a *vila museu*, a museum site. It has various discoveries from different eras exhibited in *núcleos*, or areas where a lots of treasures from a particular period can be found. The tourist office has details of each *núcleo*.

Mértola dates back to the Phoenicians, who created a thriving inland port here, later enjoyed by the Romans and the

Mértola's unusual Moorish-style church, high above the River Guadiana

Moors. Roman artifacts can be seen at the Museu de Mértola beneath the exhibition halls.

The post-Roman period is on display in the Núcleo Visigótico and in an early Christian basilica whose ruins adjoin the Roman road to Beja (see p317). The influence bestowed by several centuries of Moorish domination is seen in the museum's Núcleo Islâmico which houses one of the country's best collections of Portuguese Islamic art. The Igreja Matriz below the Moorish walls was formerly a mosque, with a five-nave layout, four horseshoe arches and a *mihrab* or prayer niche.

Overlooking the town is a ruined hilltop castle, with its keep of 1292, offering lovely views of the river valley. The Alcácova do Castelo, the excavated ruins of a Moorish village and earlier Roman cistern are within the grounds.

Environs

The copper mines at Minas de São Domingos, 16 km (10 miles) to the east, were the main employer in the area from 1858 to 1965, when the vein was exhausted. An English company ran the mine under the harshest conditions, with miners' families living in one windowless room. The village's population is about 700, and the ghost-town atmosphere is relieved only by a reservoir and surrounding lush greenery.

Around Mértola, 600 sq km (230 sq miles) of the wild Guadiana valley is a Parque Natural. Birdwatching and nature tour companies include Birdwatch in Alentejo (www.birdwatching alentejo.com) and Birding in Portugal (www.birdingin portugal.com), who can arrange trips to spot species like the rare Spanish imperial eagle.

The Versatility of Cork

Groves of evergreen cork oak *(Quercus suber)* provide the Alentejo with welcome shade and a thriving industry. It was Dom Pérignon, the wine-making monk, who in the 17th century revived the use of cork as a tasteless, odourless seal for wine. Portugal, the world's largest cork producer, has almost 7,000 sq km (2,700 sq miles) under cultivation and turns out some 30 million corks a day. In rural areas, this versatile bark is fashioned into waterproof, heatproof food containers and these decorated boxes are a traditional craft of the Alentejo.

Harvesting cork is a skilled task. Mature trees, stripped in summer every ten years or so, reveal a raw red undercoat until their new bark grows.

The glowing red of a stripped tree in an Alentejan cork grove

ALGARVE

Enclosed by ranges of hills to the north, the Algarve has a climate, culture and scenery very different from the rest of Portugal. Its stunning coastline and year-round mild weather, maintained by warm sea and air currents from nearby North Africa, make it one of the most popular holiday destinations in southern Europe.

The Algarve's fertile soil and strategic headlands and rivers have attracted visitors since the time of the Phoenicians. Five centuries of Arab rule, from AD 711, left a legacy that is still visible in the region's architecture, lattice chimneys, *azulejos*, orange groves and almond trees. Place names beginning with Al are also of Moorish origin; Al-Gharb ("the West") denoted the western edge of the Islamic empire.

When the Algarve was reclaimed by the Christians in 1249, the Portuguese rulers designated themselves kings "of Portugal and of the Algarves", emphasizing the region's separateness from the rest of the country. It was the Algarve, however, that shot Portugal to prominence in the 15th century, when Henry the Navigator *(see p53)* is said to have set up a school of navigation at Sagres, and launched the age of exploration from these southern shores.

The earthquake of 1755 *(see pp66–7)* had its epicentre just south of Lagos, then the region's capital. Virtually all the towns and villages were destroyed or badly damaged, which explains why very few buildings in the region predate this period.

Since the 1960s, when Faro airport was opened, international tourism has replaced agriculture and fishing as the region's main industry. A few stretches of the south-western seashore are now cluttered with high-rise complexes catering for the yearly influx of tourists. However, the whole western seaboard exposed to the Atlantic and the lagoons east of Faro have been less affected by development. Trips inland, to the pretty whitewashed village of Alte or the border town of Alcoutim in the east, provide a welcome reminder that, in places, the Algarve's rural way of life continues virtually uninterrupted.

Beautiful staircase leading up to the Pousada de Faro-Palácio in Estoi *(see p331)*

◄ Sightseeing boats at Ponta da Piedade, near Lagos

Exploring the Algarve

The Algarve is a delight to visit all year round. In summer, the coast between Faro and Lagos attracts thousands of visitors; but even near popular resorts such as Albufeira and Portimão it is possible to escape the crowds. Though often bypassed, Faro itself is well worth a visit. Picturesque Tavira is an ideal centre for the lagoons of the eastern Algarve, while from Lagos you can reach the beaches on the rugged southwest coast. Inland, the hillside villages are peaceful, with lush vegetation, both wild and cultivated. The wooded Serra de Monchique is an area of outstanding beauty offering lovely walks.

Wooded slopes around the vast lake created by the Bravura dam, north of Lagos

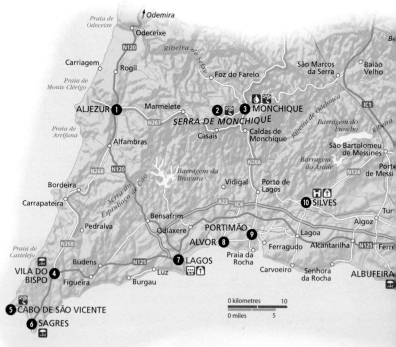

Brightly painted fishing boats in the harbour at Sagres

Key

▬▬ Motorway

▬▬ Major road

═══ Minor road

▬▬ Scenic route

── Minor railway

▬▬ National border

▬▬ Regional border

For keys to symbols *see back flap*

One of the delightful sandy coves near Albufeira

Sights at a Glance

1 Aljezur
2 Serra de Monchique
3 Monchique
4 Vila do Bispo
5 Cabo de São Vicente
6 Sagres
7 Lagos
8 Alvor
9 Portimão
10 Silves
11 Albufeira
12 Alte
13 Vilamoura
14 Almancil

15 Loulé
16 Estoi
17 *Faro pp332–34*
18 Olhão
19 Parque Natural da Ria Formosa
20 Tavira
21 Cacela Velha
22 Vila Real Santo António
23 Castro Marim
24 Alcoutim

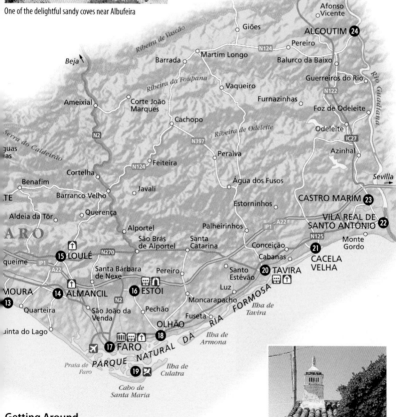

Whitewashed house and lattice-work chimney in Cacela Velha

Getting Around

The tolled A22 (IP1) runs from Lagos to Spain and has relieved the N125, which can become congested in summer. Roads branch off to beaches, coastal towns and inland villages.

A frequent but slow rail service connects the main towns, but stations are sometimes far from the centre. Reliable buses link coastal resorts and inland towns, though progress can be slow.

Commanding view of the countryside from Aljezur's Moorish castle

❶ Aljezur

Road map 7C. 🏔 7,000. 🚌
ℹ 25 de Abril 62 (282 998 229).
🏛 3rd Mon of month.

The small village of Aljezur is overlooked by a 10th-century Moorish castle, reached via the old quarter. Although in ruins, a cistern and towers remain, and there are splendid views towards the Serra de Monchique.

Aljezur's Igreja Matriz, much rebuilt after the earthquake of 1755 (see pp66–7), has a fine Neo-Classical altarpiece. Dating from about 1809, it was probably executed in the workshop of José da Costa of Faro.

Environs

From Aljezur, the wild and deserted beaches of the Algarve's west coast are easily explored, although a car is essential. Open to the strong

currents of the Atlantic, Praia de Arrifana 10 km (6 miles) southwest, and Praia de Monte Clérigo, 8 km (5 miles) north-west, are sandy, sweeping beaches backed by cliffs. On the Alentejo border, Praia de Odeceixe is a sheltered cove that is popular with surfers.

❷ Serra de Monchique

Road map 7C. 🚌 Monchique.
ℹ Monchique (282 911 189).

Providing shelter from the north, this volcanic mountain range helps to ensure the mild southern climate of the Algarve. The highest point is Fóia at 902 m (2,959 ft). This, however, is less pleasantly wooded than Picota, which, at 773 m (2,536 ft), is the second-highest peak. An impressive 4-km (2-mile) walk to this peak from Monchique passes among chestnut trees and fields of wild flowers. A spectacular panorama sweeps down to the Ponta de Sagres (see p326) and there are stunning views of the rest of the range. Whether you explore the Serra on foot or by car, there is a wonderful variety of vegetation to enjoy with rhododendron, mimosa, chestnut, pine, cork oak and patches of terraced fertile land in the valleys. The increased planting of fast-growing eucalyptus trees has given cause

for concern. This highly flammable species is one of the reasons for the serious fires that break out all too often in the Serra.

The 30-km (19-mile) run along the N267 from Nave, just below Monchique, to Aljezur in the west, leads through a beautiful part of the Serra. The landscape is a mixture of woods and moorland, kept fertile by an abundant water supply. Cork oak grows here, home to the nuthatch and lesser-spotted woodpecker.

Manueline portal of the Igreja Matriz in Monchique

❸ Monchique

Road map 7C. 🏔 7,000. 🚌
ℹ Largo de São Sebastião (282 911 189). 🏛 2nd Fri of month.

The small market town of Monchique is primarily famous for its altitude, 458 m (1,500 ft), and consequently spectacular views. It is also known for its wooden handicrafts, particularly the folding chairs the design of which dates back to Roman times.

The 16th-century Igreja Matriz, on the cobbled Rua da Igreja behind the main square, has an impressive Manueline doorway whose knotted columns end in unusual pinnacles. Above the town is the ruined monastery of Nossa Senhora do Desterro. This Franciscan house, founded in 1632 by Dom Pero da Silva, is now only a shell but it is worth visiting for the stunning views across to the peak of Picota.

The mountains of the Serra de Monchique rising above meadows of wild flowers

Environs

A delightful spa, 6 km (4 miles) south, Caldas de Monchique is set in the foothills of the Serra in peaceful wooded surroundings.

The hot, curative waters have attracted the ailing since Roman times, and even though João II died soon after taking them in 1495, their reputation has remained undiminished. In the summer, people come to be treated for skin, digestive and rheumatic complaints. As well as the spring water, bars here offer local firewater, *medronho*.

The shady main square has a large, attractive handicraft centre and there are some pretty walks in the woods.

❹ Vila do Bispo

Road map 7C. 🏘 7,000. 🚌 ℹ️ Sagres (282 624 873). 🎪 1st Thu of month. Nossa Senhora da Guadalupe. **Open** May–Sep: 10:30am–1pm (from 9am Apr–Oct), 2–6:30pm Tue–Sun (till 5:30pm Apr–Oct). 🏛

The grand name of "The Bishop's Town" today refers to a peaceful village, rather remote in feel, which makes the crowds of central Algarve seem very far away. It acquired its name in the 17th century when it was donated to the see of Faro. The town's parish church, Nossa Senhora da Conceição, has a delightful interior decorated with 18th-century *azulejos* from the floor up to the painted ceiling, and an altarpiece dating from 1715.

Environs

The beaches in the area are remote and unspoiled. Praia do

Baroque altarpiece inside Nossa Senhora da Conceição, Vila do Bispo

Promontory of Cabo de São Vicente jutting into the Atlantic Ocean

Castelejo, 5 km (3 miles) to the west, is accessible by a dirt road that winds up from the village over moorland. The intrepid can turn off this track for the 6-km (4-mile) journey to Torre de Aspa, an obelisk at 156 m (512 ft) marking the spot for spectacular views over the ocean. The road is quite rough, so it is advisable to walk the last 2 km (1 mile). The 14th-century Nossa Senhora da Guadalupe near Raposeira is where Henry the Navigator prayed.

❺ Cabo de São Vicente

Road map 7C. 🚌 to Sagres then taxi. ℹ️ Sagres (282 624 873).

In the Middle Ages, this windblown cape at the extreme southwest of Europe was believed to be the end of the world. The Romans called it the Promontorium Sacrum (Sacred Promontory), and today, with its 60-m (200-ft) cliffs fronting the Atlantic, it still presents a most awe-inspiring aspect. The ocean waves have created long, sandy beaches and carved deep caves into the cliffs.

Since the 15th century, Cabo de São Vicente has been an important reference point for shipping, and its present lighthouse has a 95-km (60-mile) range, said to be the most powerful in Europe. For even longer it has had religious associations, and its name arises from the legend that the body of St Vincent was washed ashore here in the 4th century. Prince Henry the Navigator (*see*

p53) was also reputed to have lived here, but, if so, all traces of his Vila do Infante have disappeared. A number of important naval battles have taken place off the Cape, including the defeat of a Spanish fleet in 1797 by the British admirals Jervis and Nelson.

Since 1988 the coast from Sines in the north to Burgau in the east has been made a nature reserve, providing important nesting grounds for Bonelli's eagle, kestrel, white stork, heron and numerous other bird species. There is also a colony of sea otters.

Flowered Narcissus, native to the Algarve region

Flowers of the Western Algarve

The remote headlands of Cabo de São Vicente and Sagres are renowned in botanical circles for their flowers, which put on a strikingly colourful and aromatic display from February to May. The climate, underlying rock and comparative isolation of these headlands have given an intriguing, stunted appearance to the local vegetation. There is a great array of different species, including cistuses, squills, an endemic sea pink, junipers, lavenders, narcissi, milk-vetches and many other magnificent plants.

The enormous Rosa dos Ventos wind compass on Ponta de Sagres

⬤ Sagres

Road map 7C. 🚗 3,500. 🚌 ℹ️ Rua Comandante Matoso (282 624 873). 📅 1st Fri of month.

The small town of Sagres has little to offer except a picturesque harbour. Essentially it is a good base from which to explore the superb beaches *(see p292)* and isolated peninsula west of the town. Henry the Navigator *(see p53)* built a fortress on this windswept promontory and, according to tradition, a school of navigation and a shipyard. From here he realized his dream "to see what lay beyond the Canaries and Cape Bojador… and attempt the discovery of things hidden from men". From 1419–60, he poured his energy and the revenues of the Order of Christ *(see p191)*, of which he was master, into building caravels and sending his fear-stricken sailors into unknown waters.

In 1434 Gil Eanes of Lagos was the first sailor to round the dreaded Cape Bojador, in the region of Western Sahara. With this feat, the west coast of Africa was opened up for exploration *(see pp52–3)* and Portugal poised for expansion.

Little remains of Prince Henry's original fortress: the walls that can be seen today are part of a 17th-century fort. Still visible is the giant pebble wind compass, the Rosa dos Ventos, 43 m (141 ft) in diameter, said to have been used by Henry. The simple chapel of Nossa Senhora da Graça was also built by him. The whole site, looking across to Cabo de São Vicente and out towards the open Atlantic, is exhilarating and atmospheric.

Environs
The town is also within easy reach of many superb beaches. Some, such as Telheiro, 9 km (6 miles) west of Sagres, and Ponta Ruiva 2 km (1 mile) further up the west coast, are only accessible by car. Nearer to Sagres, Beliche is surprisingly sheltered, Tonel, on the tip of the promontory, has wonderful surf and Martinhal, 1 km (half a mile) east, has a water sports school offering water-skiing, surfing and windsurfing.

⬤ Lagos

Road map 7C. 🚗 16,000. 🚉 🚌 ℹ️ Praça Gile Eanes (282 763 031). 📅 1st Sat of month.

Set on one of the largest bays in the Algarve, Lagos is an attractive, bustling town. In the 8th century it was conquered by the Arabs, who left behind fortifications that were

São Gonçalo in Santa Maria, Lagos

extended in the 16th century. A well-preserved section and archway can be seen near Rua do Castelo dos Governadores, where there is a monument to the navigator Gil Eanes.

The discoveries of the 15th century *(see pp52–3)*, pioneered by Henry the Navigator, whose statue gazes scowlingly out to sea, turned Lagos into an important naval centre. At the same time a most deplorable period of history began, with the first slaves brought back from the Sahara in 1441 by Henry's explorer Nuno Tristão. The site of the first slave market in Europe is marked by a plaque under the arcades on Rua da Senhora da Graça. The city was the capital of the Algarve from 1576–1756. Extensive damage was caused by the earthquake of 1755 *(see pp66–7)*, so today the centre consists primarily of pretty 18th- and 19th-century buildings. The citizens of Lagos continue to make their living from fishing, which helps the town to retain a character independent of the tourist trade.

The smart marina on the east side of town provides the first safe anchorage on the south coast for boats coming in from the Atlantic.

🏰 Forte Ponta da Bandeira
Avenida dos Descobrimentos. **Tel** 282 761 410. **Open** 10am–6pm Tue–Sun. **Closed** public hols. ♿

On the seafront stands the 17th-century fortress which defended the entrance to the harbour. Its imposing ramparts afford far-reaching views over the town and the bay.

🏛️ Santa Maria
Praça Infante Dom Henrique. **Tel** 282 762 723. **Open** daily. ♿ 🚻

The parish church of Lagos originated in the 16th century, and still retains a Renaissance doorway. Of local interest is a statue of São Gonçalo of Lagos, a fisherman's son born in 1360 who became an Augustinian monk, preacher and composer of religious music.

Moorish archway leading onto Avenida dos Descobrimentos, Lagos

🏛 Santo António

Rua General Alberto Silveira: entry via the Museu Municipal Dr José Formosinho. **Tel** 282 762 301. **Open** Tue–Sun. **Closed** public hols.

This 18th-century church is an Algarvian jewel. The lower section of the walls is covered in blue and white *azulejos*, the rest in carved, gilded and painted woodwork, an inspirational and riotous example of Baroque carving. Cherubs, beasts, flowers and scenes of hunting and fishing, surround eight panel paintings of miracles performed by St Antony.

A statue of the saint stands above the altar, surrounded by gilded pillars and arches adorned with angels and vines. St Antony was patron and honorary colonel-in-chief of the local regiment and, according to tradition, this statue accompanied it on various campaigns during the Peninsular War (1808–11) *(see p58)*.

Near the altar is the grave of Hugh Beatty, an Irish colonel who commanded the Lagos regiment during the 17th-century wars with Spain. He died here in 1709 and his motto "Non vi sed arte" (Not with force but with skill) adorns the tomb.

🏛 Museu Municipal Dr José Formosinho

Rua General Alberto Silveira. **Tel** 282 762 301. **Open** 10am–5:30pm Tue–Sun. **Closed** public hols. 📷

This eclectic ethnographic museum displays local handicrafts and artifacts, traditional costumes and an impressive Roman mosaic, the Opus Vermiculatum. Also look for the

Ochre sandstone rocks on the sheltered beach of Praia de Dona Ana, Lagos

facsimile of the 1504 town charter. The neighbouring Santo António church forms part of the museum.

Environs
The promontory, called the Ponta da Piedade, sheltering the bay of Lagos to the south has a series of wonderful rock formations, caves and calm, transparent waters. Accessible by road and sea, and most spectacular at sunset, this area is not to be missed. The prettiest beach is Praia de Dona Ana, 25 minutes' walk from the centre of town, but Praia do Camilo, further round to the tip of the promontory, may be less crowded. The long Meia Praia stretches for 4 km (2 miles) east of Lagos; a regular bus service leaves from the centre of town.

A 10-km (6-mile) drive due north of Lagos leads to the huge Barragem de Bravura

reservoir. It is peaceful and especially picturesque seen from a viewpoint high up.

❽ Alvor

Road map 7C. 🏔 5,000. 🚌 🚍 ℹ️
Rua Dr Afonso Costa 51 (282 457 540).

This pretty fishing town of white houses is popular with holidaymakers, but in low season retains its charm. It was a Roman port, and later the Moorish town of Al-Bur. By the 16th century it was again a prosperous town, but it suffered much damage in the earthquake of 1755. The town was rebuilt with stone from the Moorish castle, so little of that fortress remains.

At the top of the town the 16th-century church, Divino Salvador, has a Manueline portal carved with foliage, lions and dragons. The outermost arch is an octopus tentacle.

The attractive, whitewashed fishing town of Alvor

Nossa Senhora da Conceição, Portimão

❾ Portimão

Road map 7C. 🏛 40,000. 🚉 🚌
🛈 Teatro Municipal de Portimão,
Largo 1° de Dezembro (282 402 487).
🚢 1st Mon of month.

The Algarve's second-largest city, Portimão has plenty of character and a long history as a port. The Romans settled here, attracted by the natural harbour on the estuary of the Rio Arade.

Portimão's northern outskirts consist of commercial and residential areas.. Beyond the municipality is the historic 18th-century town centre which has excellent shopping, as well as a large, bustling market. The picturesque riverfront is nearby.

The centre lies around the pedestrianized Rua Vasco da Gama, with shops specializing in leather goods. Along Rua Diogo Tomé, the church of Nossa Senhora da Conceição occupies a low hill. Rebuilt after the earthquake of 1755 (see pp66–7), its

14th-century origins are still visible in the portico with its carved capitals. Inside, there are 17th- and 18th- century *azulejo* panels. The waterfront is lively and restaurants serve fresh fish. The award-winning **Museu de Portimão**, housed in a former canning factory, is located on the southern end of the esplanade.

🏛 **Museu de Portimão**
Rua D Carlos, Zona Ribeirinha.
Tel 282 406 230/265. **Open** Tue–Sun.
🌐 **museudeportimao.pt**

Environs
Just 3 km (2 miles) south lies Portimão's touristic neighbour, Praia da Rocha, a series of sandy coves among protruding red and ochre rocks. At its east end is the 16th-century Fortaleza de Santa Catarina, with superb beach views, and below is Portimão Marina. The Autódromo Internacional do Algarve (www.autodromoalgarve.com) is located 8 km (6 miles) away, north of the city centre.

❿ Silves

Road map 7C. 🏛 10,000. 🚉 🚌
🛈 Parque das Merendas (282 098 927). 🚢 3rd Mon of month.

Silves's commanding position made it the ideal fortified settle-

ment. The Romans built a castle here, but it was under the Arabs that the city flourished, becoming the Moorish capital, Xelb. In the mid-12th century the Arab geographer Idrisi praised its beauty and its "delicious, magnificent" figs. Silves was renowned as a centre of culture in Moorish Al-Gharb until the Knights of Santiago took the city in 1242.

Today, the red walls of the castle stand out against the skyline. The nearby **Casa da Cultura Islâmica e Mediterrânica** houses local exhibitions and events.

🏛 **Casa da Cultura Islâmica e Mediterrânica**
Largo da República. **Tel** 282 442 096.
Open Tue–Fri, Sat pm.
📷 for groups only.

🏰 **Castle**
Castelo de Silves. **Tel** 282 445 624.
Open Jul–Sep: 9am–7pm; Oct–Jun: 9am–5:30pm daily. 📷 ♿ (garden only).

The red sandstone castle dates back mainly to Moorish times, though it has done duty as a Christian fortress and a jail. It was the site of the Palace of the Verandahs, abode of Al-Mu'tamid from 1053 when he was ruler of Seville and Wali of Al-Gharb.

There are superb views of the town and countryside from the massive, polygonal ramparts. Inside, there are gardens and the impressive vaulted Moorish Cisterna da Moura Encantada (Cistern of the Enchanted Moorish Girl).

The castle and town of Silves rising above a fertile valley of orange groves

🏛 Sé

Largo da Sé. **Open** 9am–1pm & 2–6pm Mon–Fri; 9am–1pm Sat. **Closed** public hols. 🅿

Built on the site of a mosque, the cathedral dates from the 13th century. In the chancel, light falls from lovely double windows with stained-glass borders, on a jasper statue of Nossa Senhora da Conceição, believed to date from the 14th century.

Opposite the Sé, the 16th-century Misericórdia church has a Manueline side door and a Renaissance altarpiece.

🏛 Museu Arqueológico

Rua das Portas de Loulé 14. **Tel** 282 444 832. **Open** Jul–Sep: 9am–7pm; Oct–Jun: 9am–5:30pm daily. 🅿

Set downhill from the cathedral, the Municipal Museum was opened in 1990. Its exhibits include Stone and Iron Age tools, sculpted Roman capitals, surgical instruments from the 5th–7th centuries, a 13th-century anchor and items of 18th-century ceramics. The museum is built around a large Arab well-cistern that was uncovered in 1980. The staircase built into the structure descends 15 m (49 ft) to the bottom of the well.

Environs

One kilometre (half a mile) east of Silves is the Cruz de Portugal, an ornate 16th-century granite cross. This may have been given to the city by Manuel I, when João II's body was transferred from Silves Cathedral to Batalha (see pp188–9). The faces are carved with the Crucifixion and the Descent from the Cross.

Silves's Cruz de Portugal

⓭ Albufeira

Road map 7C. 🏛 31,000. 🚋 🚌
ℹ Rua 5 de Outubro (289 585 279). 🗓 1st & 3rd Tue of month.

Once a charming fishing town overlooking a sheltered beach, this is now the tourist capital of the Algarve. The Romans liked it, but it was under Al-Buhar (The Castle on the Sea) that brought prosperity, as Albufeira traded

with North Africa. The Knights of Santiago took it in the 13th century, but the consequent loss of trade almost ruined it. In 1833 it was set on fire by supporters of Dom Miguel during the War of the Two Brothers (see p58).

The **Museu Arqueológico** houses a captivating collection of Stone Age, Roman and Moorish artifacts, with the Islamic-era silo as its highlight. The church of São Sebastião, on Praça Miguel Bombarda, has a Manueline doorway. Rua 5 de Outubro leads through a tunnel to the beach, east of which is the Praia dos Barcos where the fishermen ply their trade. From Praia de São Rafael, 2 km (1 mile) west of Albufeira, to Praia da Oura due east, the area is punctuated by small sandy coves set between eroded ochre rocks.

🏛 Museu Arqueológico

Praca da Republica 1. **Tel** 289 599 508. **Open** Jul–Aug: 9:30am–12:30pm & 1:30–5:30pm Tue, Sat & Sun; 9:30am–5:30pm Wed–Fri, 2–10pm Thur & Fri.

⓬ Alte

Road map 7C. 🏛 500. 🚋 🚌
ℹ Rua Condes de Alte (289 478 060). 🗓 3rd Thu of month.

Perched on a hill, Alte is one of the prettiest villages of the Algarve. The approach from the east along the N124 is the most picturesque, with sweeping views of rolling hills. The focus of this steep, white village is the 16th-century Nossa Senhora da Assunção, which has a Manueline doorway and baptismal fonts, and a fine gilded altarpiece celebrating the Assumption. The chapel of São Sebastião has beautiful, rare 16th-century Sevillian *azulejos*.

About ten minutes' walk from the church, and clearly marked, is the River Alte, overhung with trees, and a water source known as the Fonte Grande. This leafy setting is ideal for picnicking. On the steep slopes, about 700 m (half a mile) from the village is a mill (converted into a restaurant) and a 5-m (16-ft) high waterfall, Queda do Vigário.

Colourful fishing boats on the beach at Albufeira

One of many filigree chimneys that adorn the rooftops of Alte

⑬ Vilamoura

Road map C7. 🏘 9,000. 🚌 ℹ️ Praça do Mar, Quarteira (289 389 209).

The coast between Faro and Lagos has effectively become a strip of villa complexes and high-rise hotels. Vilamoura is a prime example of this kind of development and is set to become Europe's largest leisure complex. Its 16 sq km (6 miles) encompass four golf courses, tennis courts, a riding school, fishing and shooting facilities, and sports complexes. There is even a small landing strip. Its many hotels and apartment blocks are still on the rise, and the already well-established complex is still under construction.

The focal point is the large marina, which bristles with powerboats and is fronted by restaurants, cafés and shops. It makes a diverting excursion, attracting many Portuguese visitors, including Lisbon's jet set. Due east is the crowded Praia da Marina. You can also visit the nearby Roman ruins of **Cerro da Vila**, which date from the 1st century AD and include a bath complex and a house with mosaics depicting fish.

🏛 Cerro da Vila

Avenida Cerro da Vila. **Tel** 289 312 153 (museum). **Open** May–Oct: 10am–1pm & 4–9pm Tue–Sun; Nov–Apr: 9:30am–12:30pm & 2–6pm Tue–Sun.
🅿️ 🌐 **marinadevilamoura.com**

Luxury yachts and powerboats moored at the smart marina at Vilamoura

18th-century tile panels and gilded altar in São Lourenço, Almancil

⑭ Almancil

Road map D7. 🏘 2,000. 🚌 🚏 ℹ️ Rua de Vale (289 400 860). 🛍 1st & 4th Sun of month, antiques 2nd Sun.

Outside the undistinguished town of Almancil lies one of the Algarve's gems, the 18th-century Igreja Matriz de São Lourenço. Its interior is an outstanding masterpiece of decoration in *azulejo* panels. The church was commissioned by local inhabitants in gratitude to St Laurence, who answered their prayers for water.

The copious blue and white tiles were probably designed by master craftsmen in Lisbon and shipped down. They cover the cupola, the walls of the chancel, nave, and nave vault, to stunning effect. The wall panels depict episodes from the life of St Laurence; on one side of the altar the saint is shown healing two blind men, and on the other, giving money to the poor. The nave arches show the saint conversing with Pope Sixtus II; arguing for his Christian belief with the Roman Emperor Valerian; and refusing to give up his faith. The story culminates in his martyrdom. In the last panel on the right, in which the saint is placed on a gridiron to be burned, an angel comforts him. The nave vault depicts the *Coronation of St Laurence*, and the cupola has decorative, trompe-l'oeil effects of exceptional quality. The last tiles were put in place in 1730.

The altarpiece, dated around 1735, was the work of Manuel Martins and was gilded by leading local painters. Astonishingly, the 1755 earthquake *(see pp66–7)* only dislodged five tiles from the vault.

Today, Almancil houses a large community of British expats, and is noted for its property agents and holiday and construction-related shops and services. The town is also within striking distance of some of the best restaurants in the Algarve *(see p411–13)*.

⑮ Loulé

Road map D7. 🏘 20,000. 🚌 🚏 ℹ️ Avenida 25 de Abril (289 463 900). 🛍 Sat.

Loulé is an attractive market town and thriving craft centre. Its Moorish origins are still visible in the bell tower of the church of São Clemente. The castle, on the north side of town, is also Moorish in origin, rebuilt in the 13th century. Remnants of the walls behind the castle afford an overview of the town and the many pretty filigree chimneys, typical of the Algarve.

The heart of the town lies immediately south of Praça da República and encompasses the busy, pink-domed market. On Saturdays the area is particularly lively when gypsies run a simultaneous outdoor market. From Rua 9 de Abril to the Igreja Matriz you can watch handicraft workers carving wood, weaving hats, making lace, decorating horse tackle and painting pottery and tiles.

The 13th-century São Clemente, on Largo da Silva, was badly damaged in three earthquakes, the last in 1969, but its triple nave, defined by Gothic arches, has been conserved. There are two beautiful side chapels dating from the early 16th century. The Capela de Nossa Senhora da Consolação is decorated from floor to vault with superb blue and white *azulejo* panels, while the Capela de São Brás, has a Manueline arch and a blue and gold Baroque altarpiece.

Another religious building of note is the chapel of Nossa Senhora da Conceição, close to Praça da República. Here, the Baroque altarpiece (1745) is complemented by scenes in blue and white *azulejos*. Part of the floor reveals Moorish foundations. The chapel is located near the Banhos Islâmicos, the 13th-century ruins of an Islamic bathhouse known as *hammam de Al-'Ulyà*.

Environs
The 16th-century, hilltop chapel of Nossa Senhora da Piedade, adorned with *azulejo* panels, lies 2 km (1 mile) west of Loulé. Behind it stands a modern white church of the same name built to replace the old chapel but which never became a popular place of worship. The spot also affords spectacular views.

Pink Rococo façade of the Pousada de Faro-Palácio de Estoi

⑯ Estoi

Road map D7. 🏘 4,300. 🚌 ℹ Faro (289 803 604). 🕰 2nd Sun of month.

The quiet village of Estoi has two notable sights, separated by a short distance and about 1,800 years. Just off the main square is the Pousada de Faro-Palácio de Estoi, an unashamedly pretty Rococo pastiche. The palace was the brainchild of a local nobleman, who died soon after work was begun in the mid-1840s. Another wealthy local later acquired the palace, and completed it in 1909. For the vast amount of money and energy he expended on his new home, he was made Viscount of Estoi. The work was supervised by the architect Domingos da Silva Meira, whose interest in sculpture is evident everywhere. The palace underwent restoration of its interior, a feast of pastel and stucco, and is now a *pousada*.

🏛 Palace gardens
Rua do Jardim. **Tel** 289 990 150. **Open** daily. 🚻

The gardens are part of the *pousada* and can be visited. Dotted with orange trees and palms, they continue the joyful Rococo spirit of the palace. The lower terrace has a blue and white tiled pavilion, inside which is a copy of Canova's *Three Graces*. The walled terrace above, the Patamar da Casa do Presépio, has a large pavilion with stained-glass windows, fountains adorned with nymphs and tiled niches.

🏛 Milreu
N2-6. **Tel** 289 997 823. **Open** May–Sep: 10:30am–1pm & 2–6pm Tue–Sun; Oct–Apr: 9:30am–1pm & 2–5pm. **Closed** public hols. 🅿

A 10-minute walk downhill from the other end of the main square leads to the second major sight in Estoi: the Roman ruins of Milreu, a complex that dates from the 1st or 2nd century AD. The buildings probably began as a large farmhouse that was converted in the 3rd century into a luxurious villa, built around a central courtyard.

Ebullient and well-preserved mosaics of fish and other marine creatures still adorn the walls and floor of the baths, located alongside the living quarters; however, most portable archaeological finds from this complex are now housed in the Museu Municipal in Faro *(see p333)*. The importance of the villa is indicated by the remains of a temple overlooking the site.

Roman temple ruins of Milreu in Estoi

⓱ Faro

Capital of the Algarve since 1756, Faro has been reborn several times over the centuries – following invasion, fire and earthquake. A prehistoric fishing village, it became an important port and administrative centre under the Romans, who named it Ossonoba. Captured from the Moors in 1249 by Afonso III, Faro prospered until 1596, when it was sacked and burned by the Earl of Essex, favourite of Elizabeth I of England. A new city rose from the ashes, only to be badly damaged in the earthquake of 1755 *(see pp66–7)*. Although vestiges of the ancient city walls are still standing, the finest buildings date mainly from the late 18th and 19th centuries.

Statue of Dom Francisco Gomes do Avelar in Largo da Sé

Exploring the Old City

The centre of Faro is attractive and easily explored on foot. It fans out from the small harbour to encompass the compact Old City to the southeast. Partly encircled by ancient walls, this is reached via the Arco da Vila. The arch was built on the site of a medieval castle gate in the 19th century for the bishop, Dom Francisco Gomes do Avelar, who had taken it upon himself to redesign the city in decline. The portico is originally Moorish, and a statue of St Thomas Aquinas, patron saint of Faro, surveys the scene. At the heart of the Old City, the Largo da Sé is a peaceful square, lined with orange trees and flanked by the elegant 18th-century seminary and Paço Episcopal (bishop's palace), still in use and closed to the public. Just outside the walls, through another archway of Moorish origin, the Arco do Repouso, is the 18th-century church of São Francisco, impressively decorated with tiled scenes of the life of St Francis. Further north is the 17th-century Nossa Senhora do Pé da Cruz with fanciful oil

Azulejo crucifix in exterior chapel of Nossa Senhora do Pé da Cruz

panels of stories from Genesis, such as the creation of the sun and stars. At the rear is an interesting exterior chapel or *humilhadero*.

🏛 Sé

Largo da Sé. **Open** 10am–6pm (to 5pm Oct–May), 10am–1pm Sat. **Closed** public hols. 🔔 bell tower.

The first Christian church here, built on the site of a mosque, was all but destroyed in the attack by the English in 1596. The base of the bell tower, its medieval doorway and two chapels survived, and long-term reconstruction resulted in a mixture of Renaissance and Baroque styles.

By the 1640s a grander building had emerged, which included a

Orange trees in front of the 18th-century bishops' palace along the Largo da Sé

For hotels and restaurants in this area see pp394–5 and pp411–13

chancel decorated with *azulejos* and the Capela de Nossa Senhora dos Prazeres, decorated with ornate gilded woodcarving. One of the cathedral's most dashing and eccentric features is the large 18th-century organ decorated with Chinese motifs. Its range includes an echoing horn and a nightingale's song, and it has often been used by leading European organists.

🏛 Museu Municipal
Largo Dom Afonso III. **Tel** 289 897 400. **Open** Jun–Sep: 10am–7pm Tue–Fri, 11:30am–6pm Sat & Sun; Oct–May: 10am–6pm Tue–Fri, 10:30am–5pm Sat & Sun. **Closed** public hols. 🖼

Housed in the former convent of Nossa Senhora da Assunção, founded for the Poor Clares by Dona Leonor, sister of Manuel I. Her emblem, a fishing net, adorns the portico.

A variety of local archaeological finds are displayed in the museum, partly in the lovely two-storey Renaissance cloister built by Afonso Pires in 1540.

17th-century chancel of Faro's Sé

The collection contains Roman, medieval and Manueline stone carvings and statuary. However, the most attractive exhibit is a huge, Roman floor mosaic featuring a magnificently executed head of the god Neptune (3rd century AD), found near the railway station.

VISITORS' CHECKLIST

Practical Information
Road map D7. 🗺 55,000.
ℹ Rua da Misericórdia (289 803 604). 🛒 daily.
🎉 7 Sep: Dia da Cidade.

Transport
✈ 5 km (3 miles) SW. 🚉 Largo da Estação. 🚌 Avenida da República.

🏛 Museu Marítimo
Rua da Comunidade Lusiada. **Tel** 289 894 990. **Closed** for renovation. 🖼

This museum is housed in part of the harbour master's building on the waterfront. Its small and curious collection of maritime exhibits centres on models of boats from the Age of Discovery (*see pp50–53*) onwards, including the square-rigged *nau*, prototype of the galleon. One example is Vasco da Gama's *São Gabriel*, the flagship on his voyage to India in 1498. There are also displays of traditional fishing methods from the Algarve.

Faro City Centre
① Igreja do Carmo
② São Pedro
③ Palácio Bivarin
④ Museu Marítimo
⑤ Arco da Vila
⑥ Paço Episcopal
⑦ Sé
⑧ Museu Municipal
⑨ São Francisco
⑩ Museu Etnográfico

For keys to symbols *see back flap*

Exploring Faro

The lively centre of Faro along Rua de Santo António is a stylish, pedestrianized area full of shops, bars and restaurants. Between here and the Largo do Carmo are some fine 18th-century buildings, such as the Palácio Bivarin. The early morning market on Largo de Sá Carneiro, to the north, offers fresh produce, clothing and local crafts. From here, a brisk walk uphill to the Ermida de Santo António do Alto brings a panorama of Faro with the sea and saltpans to the south.

🏛 Museu Regional

Praça da Liberdade 2. **Tel** 289 878 238. **Open** 10am–1:30pm, 2:30–6pm Tue–Fri. **Closed** public hols. 🖭

This ethnographic museum takes a nostalgic look at the Algarve's traditional way of life showing ceramics, looms and decorative horse tackle. Old photographs document peasant farming techniques, with their heavy reliance on manpower, donkeys and oxen. The most charming exhibit is the cart used by the last waterseller in Olhão, in operation until 1974.

Imposing twin-towered façade of the Baroque Igreja do Carmo

🏛 Igreja do Carmo

Largo do Carmo. **Tel** 289 824 490. **Open** Mon–Sat. 🖭 to Capela dos Ossos.

The impressive façade of this church was begun in 1713. Inside, the decoration is Baroque run wild, with every scroll and barley-sugar twist covered in precious Brazilian gold leaf.

In sombre contrast, the Capela dos Ossos (Chapel of Bones), built in 1816, has walls lined with skulls and large bones taken from the friars' cemetery. It is a stark reminder of the transience of human life.

Sumptuous Baroque decoration of the main altarpiece in São Pedro

🏛 São Pedro

Largo de São Pedro.
Tel 289 805 473. **Open** Mon–Sat.

The parish church of Faro is dedicated to St Peter, patron saint of fishermen. Though restored with Italianate columns after the earthquake of 1755, much original Baroque decoration has survived, including the main altarpiece (1689).

Highlights include the chapel of the Santíssimo Sacramento, with a dazzling altarpiece (c.1745) featuring a bas-relief of the Last Supper, and a sculpture of St Anne teaching the young Virgin Mary to read. The altar of the Capela das Almas is surrounded by stunning *azulejos* (c.1730) showing the Virgin and other saints pulling souls out of purgatory.

🕎 Faro Jewish Heritage Centre

Estrada da Penha. **Tel** 289 829 525 or 925 071 509. **Open** 9am–5pm Mon–Fri. **Closed** public hols. 🖭

At the far northeast corner of town is the Jewish cemetery, created for the Jewish community brought here in the 1700s by the Marquês de Pombal (see pp56–7) to revitalize the economy. The cemetery is laid out in the traditional Sephardic way, with children nearest the entrance, women in the centre and men at the back. It served from 1838 until 1932, during which time 60 local families prospered, then moved away. Today there is no Jewish community in Faro.

⑬ Olhão

Road map D7. 🚗 15,000. 🚌 🚏
ℹ Largo Sebastião Martins Mestre 8A (289 713 936). 🛒 daily (fish, fruit and veg).

Olhão has been involved in fishing since the Middle Ages, and today is one of the largest fishing ports and tuna and sardine canning centres in the Algarve. In 1808 the village was elevated to the status of town after 17 of its fishermen crossed the Atlantic Ocean to Rio de Janeiro, without charts, to bring the exiled King João VI the news that Napoleon's troops had been forced out of the country.

Olhão's square, whitewashed houses with their flat roof terraces and box-like chimneys are reminiscent of Moorish architecture. The best view is from the top of the bell tower of the parish church, Nossa Senhora do Rosário, on Praça da Restauração, built between 1681 and 1698 with donations from the local fishermen. The custodian lets visitors through the locked door leading from the nave. In 1758 the parish priest remarked on the fishermen's great devotion to "Our Lady of the Rosary in their grief and danger at sea, especially in summertime when North African pirates often sail off this coast." At the rear of the church is the external chapel of Nossa Senhora dos Aflitos, where women pray for their men's safety in stormy weather. The narrow, pedestrianized streets of the old town wind down from here to the waterfront, the scene of one

Whitewashed chapel of Nossa Senhora dos Aflitos behind the parish church in Olhão

The wide lagoon of the Parque Natural da Ria Formosa

of the region's most lively and picturesque markets. The noisy, covered fish market sells the morning's catch, while on Saturdays outside stalls line the quay, with local farmers selling an array of seasonal produce, including fruit, nuts, honey and live chickens.

Shop selling local basketware in Olhão

Environs

At the eastern end of the quay, beyond the market, boats take you out to the islands of Armona (15 min), Culatra (30 min) and Farol (45 min). These flat, narrow bars of sand provide shelter to the town, and excellent sandy beaches for visitors, particularly on the ocean side. The islands are part of the Parque Natural da Ria Formosa.

⑩ Parque Natural da Ria Formosa

Road map D7. 289 700 210 (Mon–Fri). East of Olhão on N125. from Faro, Olhão & Tavira. **Open** daily.

Stretching from Praia de Faro to Cacela Velha (see p337), this nature reserve follows 60 km (37 miles) of coastline. It was created in 1987 to protect the valuable ecosystem of this area, which was under serious threat from uncontrolled

building, sand extraction and pollution, all by-products of the massive rise in tourism. The lagoon area of marshes, saltpans, islets and channels is sheltered from the open sea by a chain of barrier islands – actually sand dunes. Inlets between the islands allow the tide to ebb and flow into the lagoon.

The lagoon waters are rich in shellfish, such as oysters, cockles and clams: bred here, they make up 80 per cent of the nation's mollusc exports. The fish life and warm climate attract many wildfowl and waders; snakes, toads and chameleons also live here. Apart from fish and shellfish farming and salt panning, all other human activities which might encroach on the park's ecosystem are strictly controlled or forbidden.

Centro de Educação Ambiental de Marim, about 3 km (2 miles) east of Olhão, is an environmental education centre. Its 60 ha (148 acres) of dune and pinewoods are home to various sights, including a restored farmhouse, a tidal mill, a centre for injured birds, as well as exhibitions and aquariums. The web-footed Portuguese water dog, once much used by fishermen, has been bred back from near-extinction here. At the eastern end of the park are Roman tanks where fish was salted before being exported to the empire.

Centro de Educação Quelfes. **Tel** 289 702 071. **Open** Mon– Fri. **Closed** 1 Jan, 25 Dec.

Water Birds of the Ria Formosa

The Ria Formosa is an important area for breeding wetland birds such as cattle egrets, red-crested pochard and purple herons. On drier areas of land, both pratincoles and Kentish plovers can be found. Some northern European species, such as the wigeon and dunlin, winter here, and it is a stopover for migrant birds en route to Africa. Among the resident species is the rare purple gallinule, symbol of the park.

Cattle egrets feed among cattle and are often seen perched on their backs pecking off insects and flies.

The purple gallinule is a dark-coloured relative of the moorhen. It can run fairly fast on its extremely long legs but is a poor flier.

The red-crested pochard is a brightly coloured duck originally from central Europe.

Houses with four-sided roofs, along the river Gilão in Tavira

⑳ Tavira

Road map D7. 🏔 10,000. 🚉 🚌
i Praça da República 5 (281 322
511). 🗓 3rd Sat of month.

The pretty town of Tavira, full
of historic churches and fine
mansions with filigree balconies,
lies along both sides of the
Gilão river, linked by a bridge of
Roman origin. This was part
of the coastal Roman road
between Castro Marim and
Faro *(see pp332–4)*.

Tavira's early ascendancy
began with the Moors, who
saw it as one of their most
important settlements in the
Algarve, along with Silves and
Faro. It was conquered in 1242
by Dom Paio Peres Correia, who
was outraged at the murder of
seven of his knights by the
Moors during a truce.

Tavira flourished until the
16th century, after which a slow
decline set in, aggravated by a
severe plague (1645–6) and
the silting up of the harbour.

Beach on Ilha de Tavira, an island off the
Algarve's eastern coast

The town now accommodates
tourists, without compromising
either its looks or atmosphere.

The best view of the town is
from the walls of the Moorish
castle in the old Arab quarter on
top of the hill. From here the
distinctive four-sided roofs of
the houses that line Rua da
Liberdade are clearly visible.
These pyramid-like roofs possibly
evolved to allow the sudden
torrential rain of the Algarve to
run off easily. From the castle
walls, the nearby clock tower of
the church of Santa Maria do
Castelo also acts as a landmark.
The church itself occupies the
site of what was once the biggest
mosque in the Algarve. Its façade
retains a Gothic doorway and
windows, and its interior, restored
in the 19th century, houses the
tombs of Dom Paio Peres Correia
and his seven knights. Santa
Maria do Castelo and Igreja da
Misericórdia are the only two of
Tavira's 21 churches to be open
outside service hours. Below the
castle, is the 1569 convent of
Nossa Senhora da Graça.

Renaissance architecture
was pioneered in the town by
André Pilarte, and can be seen
on the way up to the castle,
in the Igreja da Misericórdia
(1541–51), with its lovely doorway topped by saints Peter and
Paul, and in the nearby Palácio
da Galeria (open for temporary
exhibitions). The fascinating
Núcleo Islâmico on Praça da
República (Tel: 281 320 570)
showcases Moorish artifacts,
including an 11th-century
figurative vase.

Environs
The sandy, offshore Ilha de
Tavira, provides excellent
swimming. A popular resort in
summer, you can reach it by
ferry from Quatro Águas.

Blue and white houses, Cacela Velha

㉑ Cacela Velha

Road map D7. 🏔 50. *i* Monte
Gordo, Avenida Marginal (281 544
495). 🗓 3rd Sun of month.

This hamlet perches on a cliff
overlooking the sea, reached
via a landscape of fields and
olive trees. It has remained
untouched by mass tourism,
and retains a peaceful
atmosphere. Charming blue
and white fishermen's houses
cluster around a fort (closed to
the public) and a whitewashed
18th-century church.

The beach is sheltered by a
long spit of sand, and fishing
boats are dotted about. The
Phoenicians and Moors used
this protected site until it was
taken over by the Knights of
Santiago in 1240.

ⓒ Vila Real de Santo António

Road map D7. 🚂 10,000. 🅿 🚌
🛈 Avenida Marginal, Monte Gordo
(281 544 495).

Built to a plan by the Marquês
de Pombal in 1774, Vila Real de
Santo António is a little like a
miniature version of Lisbon's
Baixa *(pp82–5)*, rebuilt after the
1755 earthquake also under
the auspices of Pombal. The
symmetrical grid of fairly wide
streets, the equal-sized blocks
with similar façades, the well-
ordered naming system for the
streets, all speak of Pombal's
practical and political ideals.
    Today, the town is one of the
most important fishing ports on
the Algarve coast, as well as a
border town with its markets
geared towards visiting Spaniards.
Its centre now seems too grand
for its size, all of which makes it an
interesting place to drop in on.

Vila Real's Igreja Matriz, famous for its
stained-glass windows

ⓒ Castro Marim

Road map D7. 🚂 4,000. 🚌 🛈 Rua
de São Sebastião (281 531 232).
🛒 2nd Sat of month.

The Phoenicians, Greeks and
Romans all made use of Castro
Marim's commanding location
above the River Guadiana. It was
the gateway to the Moorish
Al-Gharb and for centuries it
was a sanctuary for fugitives
from the Inquisition *(see p55)*.
The castle above the town is
of Moorish origin, the outlying
walls a 13th-century addition.

Environs
The town was also a centre
for salt production, and the

Moorish castle and the abandoned Misericórdia church, Castro Marim

surrounding *salinas* are now
home to the Reserva Natural do
Sapal. Extending for 21 sq km
(8 sq miles) south and east of
town, this is an area of saltpans
and marshes with a large variety
of bird species including
flamingos, avocets and black-
winged stilts, symbol of the
reserve. Individuals don't need
to book, but group tours may
be booked on 281 510 680.

ⓒ Alcoutim

Road map D7. 🚂 400. 🚌
🛈 Rua 1° de Maio (281 546 179).

The tiny, gem-like, unspoilt
village of Alcoutim lies 15 km
(9 miles) from the border with
the Alentejo, and on the natural
border with Spain, the River
Guadiana. The drive there along
the N122-2, a rough, winding
road which sometimes runs
alongside the Guadiana, provides
stunning views of the countryside and across the river to Spain.
    The size of Alcoutim belies its
history. As a strategic location
and river port, it was seized on

by the Phoenicians, Greeks,
Romans and, of course, the
Moors who stayed until the
reconquest in 1240. Here, in
1371, on flower-decked boats
midway between Alcoutim
and its Spanish counterpart,
Sanlúcar de Guadiana, King
Fernando I of Portugal signed
the peace of Alcoutim with
Enrique II of Castile. By the late
17th century, when its political
importance had waned, the
town had acquired a new
reputation – for smuggling
tobacco and snuff from Spain.
    The walls of the 14th-century
castle give an excellent view
over the small village and its
idyllic setting. Alcoutim's unique
visitor attraction is a cross-
border zip line (www.limitezero.
com), set over the river that
divides Spain and Portugal.

Environs
Visitors can reach the village of
Foz de Odeleite by taking a
cruise boat along the Guidana
River. Excursions depart from
Vila Real de Santo António
(www.riosultravel.com).

View from Alcoutim across the Guadiana to Sanlúcar in Spain

PORTUGAL'S ISLANDS

Portugal's Islands at a Glance

Once remote outposts of a maritime empire, today Madeira and the Azores are easily accessible by air from mainland Portugal. The fertile islands of Madeira and Porto Santo, 600 km (375 miles) off the African coast, are popular holiday destinations, with subtropical flora and high mountains. The Azorean archipelago lies further west, close to the Mid-Atlantic Ridge. The climate here is more temperate and the once active volcanoes have created a fascinating scenery of moon-like landscapes and collapsed craters.

THE AZORES

MADEIRA

Terceira is a relatively flat island famous for its bull-running festivals, the *"tourada à corda"*. On the southern coast, the twin-towered church of São Mateus, built at the turn of the century, overlooks the harbour of São Mateus.

Corvo
Vila do Corvo

Santa Cruz das Flores

Flores

THE AZORES
(See pp364–377)

Graciosa
● Luz

São Jorge
Velas ●
Falal   ● Calh
Horta ●   ● Madalena
              ● Piedade
Pico

Pico is the summit of a steep volcano protruding from the sea. On the lower slopes of the mountain that fall towards the sea, the fields are crisscrossed with a patchwork of dry-stone walls made from black volcanic basalt.

◀ The verdant landscape at the Cascada da Ribeira Grande, Flores

Funchal is the capital of Madeira, famous for its flowers. Exotic blooms are sold along Rua do Aljube, which is lined with tall jacaranda trees.

Camacha

Porto Santo

Ponta

Porto Moniz

Madeira

MADEIRA
(See pp346–363)

a do

São Jorge

São Vicente

Ponta Delgada

Porto da Cruz

Curral das Freiras

Caniçal

Machico

Ponta do Sol

Ribeira Brava

Camacha

Funchal

Ilhas Desertas

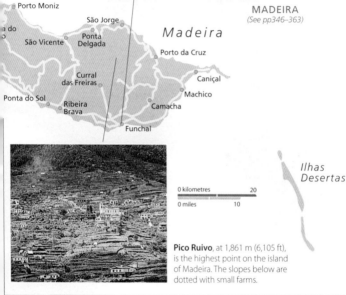

0 kilometres 20

0 miles 10

Pico Ruivo, at 1,861 m (6,105 ft), is the highest point on the island of Madeira. The slopes below are dotted with small farms.

Terceira

Praia da Vitória

Angra do Heroísmo

0 kilometres 50

0 miles 25

São Miguel

Mosteiros

Nordeste

Ponta Delgada

Vila Franca do Campo

São Miguel is popular for its therapeutic spa treatments in hot pools of mineral water. At Caldeira das Furnas, in the east of the island, steaming mud springs bubble from the ground.

Santa Maria

Santo Espírito

The Landscape and Flowers of Madeira

Madeira has a mild, moist climate which promotes a rich cover of vegetation. At first glance, the flowers and foliage appear to harmonize with the environment. The well-travelled botanist, however, will soon become aware of the strange assortment of flowers from around the world. For example, over the past few centuries, many flowers from South Africa's Cape region and exotic blooms from South America have been introduced, which now thrive alongside indigenous plants.

Madeira's Gardens

The subtropical climate and mixture of indigenous and imported plants combine to produce gardens that are the envy of horticulturalists all over the world. Gardens such as the Botanical Gardens in Funchal (see p350) are awash with colour all year. Here are some of the most striking plants that can be found in Madeira's gardens.

Magnolia in bloom

Around the Coast

In many coastal areas the cliffs are spectacular, such as this stretch at Ponta de São Lourenço (see p356). A rich and varied flora, both native and introduced, can be found along Madeira's coast despite the dry and stony habitat.

Hottentot fig is a coastal, ground-cover plant originating from South Africa.

Lampranthus spectabilis is a South African plant which flowers on the coast between May and July.

Canary Island date palms are a familiar sight, especially along the sunny south coast.

Agricultural and Wayside Ground

An irrigation system using man-made channels called *levadas*, such as this one near Curral das Freiras (see p360), allows the islanders to cultivate many otherwise unpromising areas. The margins of agricultural land are often rich with flowers.

Mimosa trees grow especially well in wooded parts of Madeira, where they bloom in winter.

Parrot's beak is a large, striking flower that appears in March and April.

Hibiscus syriacus, from the Far East, flowers between June and October.

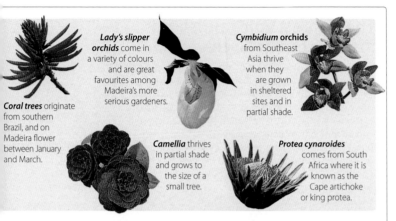

Coral trees originate from southern Brazil, and on Madeira flower between January and March.

Lady's slipper orchids come in a variety of colours and are great favourites among Madeira's more serious gardeners.

Cymbidium orchids from Southeast Asia thrive when they are grown in sheltered sites and in partial shade.

Camellia thrives in partial shade and grows to the size of a small tree.

Protea cynaroides comes from South Africa where it is known as the Cape artichoke or king protea.

High Ground

The views from the summit of Pico Ruivo, the island's highest point (see p360), are spectacular. In upland areas, the vegetation harbours a higher proportion of native species than in the lowlands.

Terraced Plantations

Plantations, such as this one growing bananas near Calheta (see p362), are made by digging terraces into the hillside. A wide range of crops are grown, for home consumption and export.

Isoplexis sceptrum, known as the yellow foxglove, is a flowering shrub native to Madeira.

Broom flowers are colourful and popular with pollinating insects.

Prickly juniper is a hardy, spiny evergreen shrub covered in tough red berries.

Sweet chestnuts grow well in Madeira and produce an abundant autumn harvest.

Pawpaws produce fruit all year round. The plant originates from South America.

Sword aloe has spiky leaves which provide a good physical barrier around plantations.

The Azores: Volcanic Islands Rising from the Ocean Bed

Situated on either side of the Mid-Atlantic Ridge, the Azores are a result of 20 million years of volcanic activity. As the plates of the earth's crust pull apart, volcanic eruptions form a giant ridge of mountains beneath the Atlantic. In places, the ridge is buckled and cut by perpendicular fractures, known as transform faults. Molten rock (magma) has been forced through these faults to form the Azores. These islands, among the youngest on earth, emerged above the waves less than five million years ago. Their striking landscape tells of their volcanic past and is still shaped by volcanic activity today.

The Mid-Atlantic Ridge is a line of submarine volcanoes that runs the whole length of the Atlantic Ocean

Corvo

Terceira lies directly above a major transform fault

Graciosa

Flores

Transform fault

The Mid-Atlantic Ridge marks the join where the African, Eurasian and American plates of the earth's crust are being pulled apart.

Faial

Pico

A mantle plume is a mass of partially molten mantle that has welled upwards, pooling beneath the rocky lithosphere. The magma it produces seeks fissures through which to erupt.

São Jorge

São Miguel has several spectacular water-filled calderas and hot springs.

Santa Maria

Volcanic Resources of the Azores

The dramatic formation of the Azores has left the islands with abundant natural resources. Hot springs, strong building materials and, eventually, fertile soil, are all the result of the ongoing volcanic activity. A wet, temperate climate gradually breaks down the volcanic rocks into fertile soils. Older soils support luxuriant vegetation and are excellent for arable farming, but younger soils, like those found on Pico, support little agriculture yet.

These stone cottages on Pico, like many on the islands, make use of the plentiful basalt rock as a durable building material.

Furnas, on São Miguel, is an area of sulphur and hot mud springs used for bathing and for medicinal purposes.

Rising high above the clouds, the still-active volcanic peak of Pico Alto dominates the island of Pico, which is itself the top of a giant underwater volcano. At 2,350 m (7,700 ft) above sea level, Pico Alto is the highest peak in the whole of Portugal.

The Geology of the Azores

The Azores lie along transform fault lines, cracks in the earth's crust which cross the Mid-Atlantic Ridge. These faults are weak points through which magma can rise. Successive volcanic eruptions have formed hundreds of undersea mountains on either side of the ridge. The highest peaks of these mountains are the nine islands of the Azores. Their emergence above the sea has been aided by the swelling of the mantle plume beneath the ocean crust, which lifts the sea floor closer to the surface of the sea.

Thin ocean crust

Atlantic Ocean

The upper mantle is a layer of dense rock. With the crust above, it forms the lithosphere, a series of semi-rigid moving plates.

The lower mantle, or asthenosphere, is a deep layer of partially molten rock that surrounds the earth's core.

asalt lava blocks used for dry-stone walls provide ٦elter for vines and protect against soil erosion on ٦co. Volcanic soil here is of relatively recent for- ٦ation and suitable for few crops except grapes.

The Formation of a Caldera

A caldera is a large crater that forms during or after a volcanic eruption, when the roof of the magma chamber collapses under the weight of the volcano's cone. Water collecting in the natural bowl of a caldera can form a crater lake.

Caldeira das Sete Cidades on the island of São Miguel

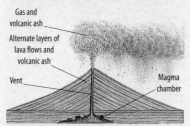

Gas and volcanic ash

Alternate layers of lava flows and volcanic ash

Vent

Magma chamber

In an active volcano, the magma chamber below the cone is full of molten rock. As pressure forces this magma up through the volcano's vent, it is expelled to the surface as a volcanic eruption.

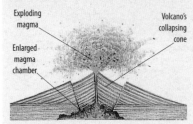

Exploding magma

Volcano's collapsing cone

Enlarged magma chamber

As magma is expelled, the level in the magma chamber drops. This may cause the volcano's cone to collapse under its own weight, leaving behind the characteristic bowl-shaped crater, or caldera.

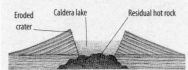

Eroded crater

Caldera lake

Residual hot rock

After the volcano has died down and is eroded, the caldera can fill with water and form a lake. Residual hot rock near the magma chamber may continue to heat the surrounding ground water.

MADEIRA

Madeira is a green, subtropical paradise of volcanic origin, its soils formed from lava and ash, completely different in character from the Portuguese mainland. Blessed with an equable daytime temperature that varies only by a few degrees either side of 20° C (68° F), the island has an all-year-round appeal.

Madeira is a mere dot in the Atlantic Ocean, 608 km (378 miles) from Morocco and nearly 1,000 km (621 miles) from Lisbon. Despite this, Madeira and Porto Santo appear on a Genoese map of 1351. They remained unclaimed, however, until 1418, when João Gonçalves Zarco was blown out into the Atlantic by violent storms while exploring the coast of Africa. Zarco found safe harbour in Porto Santo, returning on a voyage of discovery sponsored by Henry the Navigator (see p53). Early in 1420, after a winter on Porto Santo, he set sail for the mist-shrouded land on the horizon. He found a beautiful, thickly wooded island (madeira means wood), with abundant fresh water. Within seven years the island had attracted a pioneer colony and the early settlers exploited the fertile soil and warm climate to grow sugar cane. The islanders grew rich on this, and slaves were brought in to work the land and create the terraced fields and irrigation channels (levadas) that still cling to the steep hillsides to this day.

Despite the gradients, Madeirans make use of every spare patch of land today, growing bananas, flowers and grapes, although tourism is the main industry. The island's Laurisilva, or laurel forest, is a UNESCO World Heritage site.

Madeira appeals to keen walkers, plant lovers and sun-seekers, water-sports enthusiasts, and those looking for a whale- and dolphin-watching destination. It's also becoming a gastronomic hotspot; two Funchal restaurants are Michelin-starred while several others are Michelin recommended. Madeira's greatest export, wine, is another real draw, with it's famous fortified wine taking the name of the island.

Triangular-shaped houses, typical of the town of Santana on the north coast of Madeira

◀ One of the waterfalls at Vinte e Cinco Fontes (25 Springs), in the west of Madeira

Exploring Madeira

Funchal is the island's capital and the only town of any size. This is where most of the museums and historic buildings are to be found, as well as the best hotels, restaurants and shops. Most of Madeira's agricultural crops are grown along the sunny, prosperous south coast. The cooler, wetter north side has fewer settlements and more cattle. Many parts of the mountainous and volcanic interior remain wild, and some are accessible only on foot. Pico Ruivo, the highest peak on the island, is a favourite destination for walkers.

Terraces near Boa Ventura, on the road from Santana to São Vicente

Getting Around

Cristiano Ronaldo International Airport is at Santa Cruz, 18 km (11 miles) northeast of Funchal. Buses operate to all corners of the island from Funchal but are not geared to tourists. Taxis can be used, but for flexibility car hire is best. From north to south the island is 22 km (14 miles) wide and from east to west just 57 km (35 miles) long. Even so, travelling times are magnified by the mountainous terrain. To reach the nearby island of Porto Santo, you can either fly from Santa Cruz or take the ferry from Funchal to Porto de Abrigo (near Vila Baleira). *(See also pp444–5.)*

The rooftops of Funchal, with the mountainous interior of Madeira beyond

For keys to symbols *see back flap*

19 PORTO SANTO

Ilhéu da Fonte da Areia
Camacha
Ponta do Varadouro
Farrobo
Serra de Dentro
Ilhéu das Cenouras
Serra de Fora
Ponta dos Ferreiros
Ponta da Galé
Campo de Cima
Tanque
Vila Baleira
Ilhéu de Cima
Ilhéu de Ferro
Cabeço da Ponta
Zimbralinho
Ponta
Ponta da Calheta
ATLANTIC OCEAN
Ilhéu de Baixo ou da Cal

THE AZORES
MADEIRA

The wild cliffs of Ponta de São Lourenço,
near Caniçal

Ponta de São Jorge
São Jorge
Ponta de Santana
Ribeira Funda
Achada da Cruz
Ilha
7 SANTANA
achada arques
Queimadas
R101
Faial
mário
R116
Achada do Teixeira
CO RUIVO
Cruzinhas
Referta
Porto da Cruz
Maiata
ico das Torres 851m
Balcões 860m
Portela
Ponta do Espigão Amarelo
Pico da Coroa 738m
Ponta de São Lourenço
9
CO DO RIEIRO
8 RIBEIRO FRIO
Ribeira de Machico
CANIÇAL
R109
6
Prainha
R202
R202
Santo António da Serra
Marocos
Ribeira Seca
R108
R102
5 MACHICO
Passo de Poiso 1400m
João Ferino
Água de Pena
Pico Alto 1129m
Choupana
Águas Mansas
Terça
R203
Sights at a Glance
R103
3 MONTE
Santa Cruz
R102
São João de Latrão
4 CAMACHA
Gaula
io
R101
2 QUINTA DO PALHEIRO FERREIRO
R101
São Gonçalo
Caniço
1
Garajau
Caniço de Baixo
FUNCHAL
Ponta da Oliveira

Sights at a Glance

1 *Funchal pp350–53*
2 Quinta do Palheiro Ferreiro
3 Monte
4 Camacha
5 Machico
6 Caniçal
7 Santana
8 Ribeiro Frio
9 Pico do Arieiro
10 Pico Ruivo
11 Curral das Freiras
12 Paúl da Serra
14 São Vicente
15 Porto Moniz
16 Calheta
17 Ribeira Brava
18 Câmara de Lobos
19 Porto Santo

Walks and Tours

13 Rabaçal Walks

Key

═══ Motorway
─── Major road
∙∙∙∙ Minor road
─── Scenic route
– – Path
△ Summit

❶ Street-by-Street: Funchal

The deep natural harbour of Madeira's capital, Funchal, attracted early settlers in the 15th century. The historic core of the capital still overlooks the harbour and boasts fine government buildings and stately 18th-century houses with shady courtyards, iron balconies and carved black basalt door-ways. Visitors have justly called Funchal a "little Lisbon" because of the town's steep cobbled streets and overall air of grandeur.

The Igreja do Colégio (Collegiate Church) was founded by the Jesuits in 1574. The plain exterior contrasts with the richly decorated high altar, framed by carved, gilded wood (1641–60).

Rua da Carreira and Rua do Surdo have preserved many of their original elegant balconied houses.

São Pedro church

The Museu Municipal houses an aquarium and is a favourite with children.

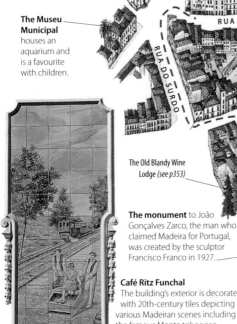

RUA DAS PRETAS

RUA DO SURDO

RUA DA CARREIRA

RUA S. FRANCISCO

The Old Blandy Wine Lodge *(see p353)*

The monument to João Gonçalves Zarco, the man who claimed Madeira for Portugal, was created by the sculptor Francisco Franco in 1927.

Café Ritz Funchal
The building's exterior is decorated with 20th-century tiles depicting various Madeiran scenes including the famous Monte toboggan *(see p354)*.

AVENIDA ARRIAGA

RUA DAS FONTES

The Palácio de São Lourenço is a 16th-century fortress housing Madeira's military headquarters.

Key
— Suggested route

Yacht Marina
Lined with seafood restaurants, the yacht marina on Avenida do Mar is ideal for an evening stroll. The sea wall around the marina offers good views.

Avenida do Mar

Câmara Municipal
Funchal's city hall is an imposing 18th-century mansion with a fountain in its courtyard depicting *Leda and the Swan*. Inside, a small museum traces the history of Funchal in photographs.

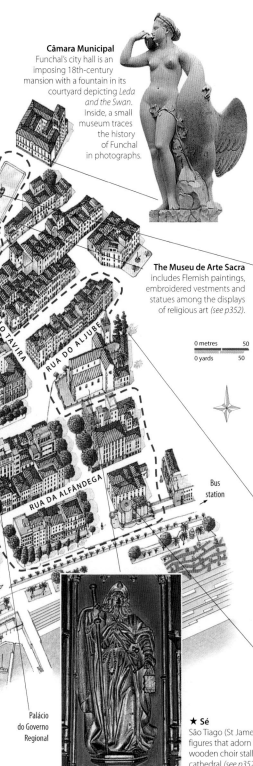

VISITORS' CHECKLIST

Practical Information

📍 111,000.
ℹ️ Avenida Arriaga 16 (291 211 902). 🛒 Mon–Sat. 🎉 Apr/May: Flower Festival; mid-Sep: Wine Festival; 31 Dec: Fireworks. Museu Municipal de História Natural: Rua da Mouraria 31. **Tel** 291 229 761. **Open** 10am–6pm Tue–Fri, noon–6pm Sat, Sun & public hols. 🎫

Transport

✈️ Cristiano Ronaldo International Airport 18 km (11 miles) NE. 🚢 🚌 Avenida do Mar.

The Museu de Arte Sacra
includes Flemish paintings, embroidered vestments and statues among the displays of religious art *(see p352)*.

```
0 metres          50
0 yards           50
```

RUA DO ALJUBE

ÃO TAVIRA

RUA DA ALFÂNDEGA

Bus station

Palácio do Governo Regional

★ Praça do Município
Contrasting black and white stones pave the attractive municipal square. On the northeast side of the square is the Câmara Municipal.

Rua do Aljube
Alongside the Sé, flower sellers in traditional costumes offer a colourful array of exotic flowers.

The Alfândega Velha (Old Customs House) was built in 1477 and is now home to the island's regional parliament.

★ Sé
São Tiago (St James) is one of many gilded figures that adorn the wonderfully carved wooden choir stalls in Funchal's 15th-century cathedral *(see p352)*.

For keys to symbols *see back flap*

Exploring Funchal

Funchal extends in a crescent along the coastline of Funchal Bay, with the Zona Velha or Old Quarter, a warren of former fishermen's houses, at the eastern end and the Hotel or Tourist Zone, dominated by hotels and restaurants, at the western end and beyond. Between is the heart of Funchal, with its attractive historic centre around the gracious Avenida Arriaga. It has a lively marina and working port, where a small fishing fleet is overshadowed by cruise liners. Funchal also has two scenic cable cars. A few blocks inland, the city fans out in a dense web of red-tiled roofs and subtropical greenery.

Sé

Largo da Sé. **Tel** 291 228 155.
Open 7am–noon & 4–6:45pm daily.
The cathedral is one of the few buildings in Madeira to have survived virtually untouched since the early days of the island's colonization. In the 1490s, King Manuel I (see pp50–53) sent the architect Pêro Anes from the mainland to work on the design of the colony's cathedral. The Sé was finally completed in 1514.

The highlights are the ceiling and the choir stalls, though neither is easy to see in the dark interior. The ceiling of inlaid wood is best seen from the south transept, where enough light filters in to illuminate the intricate patterning. The choir stalls depict saints, prophets and apostles in 16th-century costume. Aspects of Madeiran life feature in the decorative details of the armrests and seats: one cherub carries a bunch of bananas, another a goatskin full of wine.

Clock tower of Funchal's Sé

Museu de Arte Sacra

Rua do Bispo 21. **Tel** 291 228 900.
Open 10am–12:30pm & 2:30–6pm Tue–Sat, 10am–1pm Sun.
Closed public hols.
W museuartesacrafunchal.org

Madeiran merchants, who grew rich on the sugar trade, sought to secure their salvation by commissioning paintings, statues, embroidered vestments and illuminated hymn books for their local churches. Hundreds of examples now fill this museum, housed in the former bishop's palace, a building dating from 1600. There are some masterpieces in the collection, such as the late-Gothic processional cross donated by King Manuel I, and religious paintings by major Flemish artists of the 15th and 16th centuries. Some works include portraits of the dignitaries who commissioned them. *Saints Philip and James* is a 16th-century painting showing Simão Gonçalves de Câmara, Zarco's (see p347) grandson.

Quinta das Cruzes

Calçada do Pico 1. **Tel** 291 740 670.
Open 10am–12:30pm & 2–5:30pm Tue–Sun. **Closed** public hols.
W museuquintadascruzes.com

It is said that Zarco, the man who claimed Madeira for Portugal (see p347), built his house where the Quinta das Cruzes now stands. The elegant 19th-century mansion is now the Museum of Decorative Arts, furnished as a wealthy merchant's house with Indian silk wall hangings, Regency sideboards and oriental carpets. On the ground floor is furniture made from mahogany packing cases used in the 17th century for shipping sugar and turned into chests and cupboards when the sugar trade died.

The garden is dotted with ancient tombstones and architectural fragments. These include two window frames from 1507 carved with rope motifs, acrobatic figures and man-eating lions in a Madeiran version of the Manueline style of architecture (see pp28–9).

Convento de Santa Clara

Calçada de Santa Clara. **Tel** 291 742 602. **Open** 10am–noon & 3–5pm Mon–Sat, 10am–noon Sun (church only).

Opposite Quinta das Cruzes is the Convento de Santa Clara, founded in 1496 by João Gonçalves de Câmara, one of Zarco's grandsons. Zarco himself is buried under the high altar, and Martim Mendes Vasconcelos, his son-in-law, has a tomb at the rear of the church. Precious 17th-century *azulejo* tiles cover the walls.

Jardim Botânico

Quinta do Bom Sucesso, Caminho do Meio. **Tel** 291 211 200. **Open** daily. **Closed** 25 Dec.

The Botanical Gardens display plants from all over the world. Desert cacti, rainforest orchids and South African proteas grow here as well as Madeiran dragon trees. There are contrasting sections: formal areas of bedding plants, quiet carp ponds and wild wooded parts.

The intricately patterned formal gardens of the Jardim Botânico

The Old Blandy Wine Lodge

Av Arriaga 28. **Tel** 291 228 978. **Open** 10am–6:30pm Mon–Fri (to 1pm Sat). **Closed** pub hols. compulsory. **W** blandyswinelodge.com

In the cobbled courtyards of the St Francis wine lodge, visitors are greeted by the scents of ancient wood and Madeira. Some of the buildings in this maze of coopers' yards, wine vaults and sampling rooms go back to the 1600s, when the site was part of a Franciscan friary. It is possible to sample wines made here more than 150 years ago as well as more recent (and cheaper) vintages. Included in the guided tour is a visit to the warming rooms where Madeira is "heated" by hot-water pipes *(see p355)*.

The well-stocked tasting room at The Old Blandy Wine Lodge

Mercado dos Lavradores

Largo dos Lavradores. **Tel** 291 214 080. **Open** Mon–Sat. **Closed** public hols.

The Mercado dos Lavradores is where flower growers, basket weavers, farmers and fishermen from all over Madeira bring their products to market. The covered market building, situated on three floors around an open courtyard, is full of the colour and bustle of island life. Stallholders offer slices of mango or custard fruit to prove that theirs are the sweetest and best. On the ground floor, marble tables are draped with great slabs of tuna and black-skinned scabbard fish with huge eyes and razor-sharp teeth.

On Fridays the market spills out into the backstreets of the Zona Velha (Old Quarter), the former

House and gardens of the Quinta do Palheiro Ferreiro

fishermen's quarter. The simple, single-storey dwellings at the pedestrianized eastern end of Rua Dom Carlos I are said to date from the 15th century. The little Corpo Santo chapel was built by 16th-century fishermen in honour of their patron, St Peter, and is said to be the oldest such building in Funchal.

Fortaleza de São Tiago

Rua do Portão de São Tiago. **Tel** 291 213 340. Museum: **Open** 10am–12:30pm, 2–5pm Mon–Sat. Fortress: 10am–11pm. Free. **Closed** public hols.

Along the seafront is the Fortaleza de São Tiago, built in 1614, with additions dating from 1767. The fortress, with its maze of passages and staircases, commands views over Funchal and houses a Museum of Contemporary Art and a restaurant.

Mercado dos Lavradores Market, where one can purchase some of the freshest produce in Funchal

❷ Quinta do Palheiro Ferreiro

Sitio do Balançal, São Gonçalo. **Tel** 291 793 044. **Open** 9am–5:30pm daily. **Closed** 1 Jan, 25 Dec. **W** palheirogardens.com

The Quinta do Palheiro Ferreiro is Madeira's finest garden and a place of pilgrimage for flowerlovers. A French landscape architect laid out the gardens in the 18th century for the wealthy Count of Carvalhal, who built the elegant mansion (not open to visitors) overlooking the garden and the Baroque chapel in the garden itself.

The estate was acquired in 1885 by the long-established Anglo-Madeiran Blandy family, hence its English name: Blandy's Gardens. New species were introduced from South Africa, China and Australia, resulting in a garden that combines the clipped formality of late 18th-century layout with the profusion of English-style herbaceous borders, plus the combination of tropical and temperate climate varieties.

Quite apart from its horticultural interest, the garden is a peaceful wildlife haven, full of beauty and contrast as you pass from the formality of the Ladies' Garden to the tropical wilderness of the ravine ominously signposted "Inferno" (Hell).

The contrasting façade of Nossa Senhora do Monte, created by basalt against whitewash

❸ Monte

🏙 10,000. 🚌 ℹ️ Avenida Arriaga 16, Funchal (291 211 902).

Monte has been a favourite destination for visitors to Madeira since the late 19th century, when a rack-and-pinion railway was built to haul cruise liner passengers up the hillside from Funchal. Coming down they would take the famous Monte Toboggan ride.

An alternative way to get to the Monte is by the cable car that runs from Jardim do Almirante Reis, below the old town, up to the Caminho das Babosas, by the Monte Palace Gardens. The ascent takes 15 minutes, and the car operates between 9am and 5:45pm daily, except for 25 December. The railway closed in 1939, but the station and a viaduct survive, now forming part of the luxuriant Jardim do Monte public gardens. It is a short stroll through the gardens to the church of Nossa Senhora do Monte, whose twin-towered façade looks down on the island's capital. The present church was built in 1818 on the site of a chapel built in 1470 by Adam Gonçalves Ferreira.

The Virgin of Monte is Madeira's patron saint and this church is the focal point of the pilgrimage that takes place annually on 15 August (the Feast of the Assumption) when penitents climb the church's 74 steps on their knees. The object of their worship is a tiny statue of the Virgin on the high altar.

Left of the nave is a chapel housing a mortuary chest, containing the remains of the last Hapsburg Emperor, Karl I, who was deposed in 1918. Exiled in Madeira, he died of pneumonia in 1922, aged only 35.

Toboggan drivers in straw hats wait for passengers every day on the corner of Caminho do Monte, and they run (for a fee) to Livramento and on to Funchal. From the church steps, past the drivers' corner, a left turn signposted "Old Monte Gardens" leads to the **Monte Palace Tropical Gardens**. These landscaped gardens feature areas devoted to Madeiran flora, South African proteas, plants from Japan and China, and azaleas, camellias and orchids. The museum exhibits a collection of contemporary Zimbabwean sculpture and downstairs, minerals and precious stones from around the world.

🏛 **Monte Palace Tropical Gardens**
Tel 291 780 800. **Open** 9:30am–6pm daily (museum: 10am–4:30pm). **Closed** 25 Dec. ♿
🌐 montepalace.com

One of the skilled wicker workers of Camacha constructing a table

❹ Camacha

🏙 9,000. 🚌 ℹ️ O Relógio, Largo Conselheiro Aires de Ornelas 12 (291 922 777). Factory and warehouse 8:45am–6pm.

Most of the wicker products sold in Funchal are made in and around Camacha, and the sole attraction in this otherwise sleepy village is a large shop packed with everything wicker, from picture frames, bedsteads and cradles to peacock-backed armchairs. It is often possible to see weavers at work in the factory, bending the pliant stripped willow round a frame to produce a linen basket or plant-pot container. A Noah's Ark full of paired animals is displayed on the middle floor, along with a full-sailed galleon, as an advertisement of the local wicker weavers' skills.

The Monte Toboggan

Sliding in a wicker basket mounted on wooden runners, it is possible to cover the 2-km (1-mile) descent from Monte to Livramento in 10 minutes. The trip is made by thousands every year, fascinated by the experience of travelling at speed down a public highway on a wooden sled. Ernest Hemingway once described it as "exhilarating". A cushioned seat softens the ride and passengers are in the safe hands of the toboggan drivers, who push and steer from the rear, using their rubber-soled boots as brakes. Madeiran tobogganing was invented as a form of passenger transport around 1850.

The famous Monte Toboggan ride

For hotels and restaurants in this area see p395 and pp413–14

Madeira Wine

In the 16th century, ships stopping at Funchal would take on barrels of local wine. This unfortified Madeira often spoiled during the voyage, so shippers started adding spirit to make it better. The wine now seemed to improve after a long, hot voyage, and quality Madeira began to be sent on round trips as an alternative to maturing it in Funchal's lodges. This expensive method was replaced with the *estufa* system, still very much in use today. Large volumes of wine are heated to between 30 and 50°C for a period of three months to a year. The effect is to hurry up the ageing process: the best wines are "cooked" more gently and slowly. The finest Madeirans are heated by the sun, maturing slowly in the attics of the wine lodges.

Most Madeira is made from the Tinta Negra Mole grape, often blended with one of the four noble varieties listed below.

Making barrels for Madeira, Funchal

The Four Types of Madeira

Sercial is made from white grapes grown at heights up to 1,000 m (3,280 ft). Good-quality Sercial is aged for at least ten years, giving it its amber colour. A dry wine, it is mostly drunk as an aperitif or with soup, and is best served chilled.

Verdelho grapes are grown in cool vineyards at lower heights than the Sercial. This medium-dry tawny wine is also drunk as an aperitif. Sweeter than Sercial, Verdelho goes well with a slice of Madeira cake (invented by the English for just this purpose).

The barrels in the Adegas de São Francisco, where Madeira is warmed, need frequent repair as do the wooden floors that bear their huge weight.

These casks of Verdelho are being aged after the addition of brandy to the wine. Vintage wine must spend at least 20 years in the cask and two in the bottle.

Bual (or Boal) grapes are grown in lower, warmer conditions. Dark, rich and nutty, it is a medium-sweet wine that can be served as an alternative to port. It goes very well with cheeses and dessert, and is best drunk at room temperature.

Malmsey, the most celebrated Madeira, is made from Malvasia grapes grown in sunny vineyards backed by cliffs, where the heat absorbed by the rock by day warms the grapes by night. The result is a rich dark wine drunk as an after-dinner digestive.

Vintage Madeira from every decade as far back as the mid-19th century is still available for sale. The oldest surviving bottle of Madeira dates from 1772.

❺ Machico

🏙 22,000. 🚌 ℹ️ Avenida Arriaga 16, Funchal (291 211 902).

Legend has it that Machico was named after Robert Machim, a merchant from Bristol, who eloped with the aristocratic Anne of Hertford and set sail for Portugal. Caught in a storm and shipwrecked on Madeira, the two lovers died from exposure and were buried. The rest of the crew repaired the boat and sailed to Lisbon, where their story inspired Prince Henry the Navigator *(see p53)* to send João Gonçalves Zarco *(see p347)* in search of this mysterious wooded island.

Machico has been Madeira's second most important town since the first settlements, when the island was divided into two captaincies: Zarco ruled the west from Funchal whilst his fellow navigator, Tristão Vaz Teixeira, ruled the east from Machico. However, Funchal's superior location and harbour soon ensured that it developed as the capital of Madeira while

Main altar in the Capela dos Milagres, Machico

Machico became a sleepy agricultural town.

The Igreja Matriz on Largo do Município, Machico's main square, dates from the 15th century. Above the high altar is a statue of the Virgin Mary, donated by Manuel I *(see pp50–53)*, as were the three marble pillars used in the construction of the Gothic south portal. Inside, there is a fine example of Manueline-style stone masonry in the Capela de São João Baptista, whose arch shows Teixeira's coat of arms, with a phoenix rising from the flames.

Across the River Machico, on Largo dos Milagres, is the Capela dos Milagres (Chapel of the Miracles). The present structure dates from 1815, but it stands on the site of Madeira's first church, where Robert Machim and Anne of Hertford are supposedly buried. The earlier church of 1420 was destroyed in a flood in 1803, but the 15th-century crucifix was found floating out at sea. Machico celebrates the return of its cross with a procession every year on 8 October.

The bell tower of the Igreja Matriz, Machico

View from Ponta de São Lourenço promontory, east of Caniçal

❻ Caniçal

🏙 5,000. 🚌 ℹ️ Avenida Arriaga 16, Funchal (291 211 902).

Caniçal was once the centre of Madeira's whaling industry: the whaling scenes for John Huston's film version of *Moby Dick* (1956) were shot here. Whaling ceased in June 1981, and since then the waters around Madeira have been declared a marine mammal sanctuary – killing whales, dolphins and seals is forbidden. Fishermen who once hunted whales now help marine biologists at the Society for the Protection of Sea Mammals understand whale migrations.

The modern Museu da Baleia (Whaling Museum) illustrates the history of the island's whaling industry through hunting tools, artifacts and vintage photographs. There are also several life-like models of whales.

🏛 **Museu da Baleia**
Rua Garcia Moniz 1. **Tel** 291 961 858. **Open** Tue–Sun. **Closed** 1 Jan, Easter Sun, 24, 25 & 26 Dec. 🅿️ ♿
🌐 madeirawhalemuseum.org

Environs
The easternmost tip of Madeira, the Ponta de São Lourenço, is characterized by dramatic wave-battered cliffs plunging 180 m (590 ft) to the Atlantic. Walkers are attracted by footpaths which meander from one clifftop to another, with wild flowers growing in sheltered hollows. The treeless landscape contrasts totally with the island's wooded interior.

On the road from Caniçal to Ponta de São Lourenço, look out for the signpost to the bay of Prainha, Madeira's only naturally black sandy beach.

❼ Santana

 7,700. 🚌 ℹ️ Rua do Sacristão, Sítio do Serrado (291 575 162).

Named after St Anne, mother of the Virgin, Santana has more than 100 thatched triangular houses, several of which can be visited. The surrounding hillsides are also dotted with thatched byres. The Parque Temático da Madeira has a maze, a water mill and exhibits on various aspects of Madeira.

Santana valley is farmed for fruit and vegetables, and osiers – the willow branches that are the raw material for the wicker workers of Camacha *(see p354)*.

🏛️ **Parque Temático da Madeira**
Fonte da Pedra. **Tel** 291 570 410.
Open Apr–Sep: 10am–7pm daily (till 6pm Oct–Mar). 🎫
🌐 **parquetematicodamadeira.pt**

Bridge across a *levada* on the walk from Ribeiro Frio to Balcões

❽ Ribeiro Frio

 45. 🚌 from Funchal.

Ribeiro Frio is a pretty spot consisting of a couple of restaurants, shops and a trout farm, fed by the "cold stream" after which the place is named.

Surrounding the trout farm is an attractive garden full of native trees and shrubs. This is the starting point for two of the island's best *levada* walks *(see p361)*. The 12-km (7-mile) path signposted to Portela (on the right heading downhill past the restaurants) passes through dramatic mountain scenery but is best left to experienced walkers because of the long tunnels and steep drops in

Sunrise over the mountains, seen from Pico do Arieiro

places. Far easier is the 20-minute walk on the left (going downhill) signposted to Balcões (Balconies). This viewpoint gives panoramic views across the valley of the River Ametade to Penha de Águia (Eagle Rock), the sheer-sided hill that projects from Madeira's northern coast.

❾ Pico do Arieiro

🚌 to Camacha, then taxi.

From Funchal it is about a 30-minute drive up the Pico do Arieiro, Madeira's third highest mountain at 1,810 m (5,938 ft). The route leads through steep

hillsides cloaked in fragrant eucalyptus and bay laurel. At around 900 m (2,950 ft), you will often meet the cloud line and pass for a few minutes through swirling mists and possibly rain, before emerging into a sunlit landscape of volcanic rocks. At the top, the spectacular view is of clouds in the valleys and dramatic mountain ridges with knife-edge peaks. Just visible on a clear day is Pico Ruivo *(see p360)*, connected to Pico do Arieiro by a 10-km (6-mile) path. On especially clear days you may be able to see the neighbouring island of Porto Santo, some 48 km (30 miles) north of Madeira.

The Triangular Houses of Santana

Simply constructed from two A-shaped timber frames, with a wood-panelled interior and thatched roof, these triangular houses are unique to Madeira. They are first mentioned in the 16th century, but most of the surviving examples are no more than 100 years old. Today their doors and windows are often painted a cheerful red, yellow or blue. In the warm year-round climate of Madeira, cooking and eating take place out of doors, and the toilets are placed well away from the house. To the inhabitants, therefore, the triangular houses serve principally as shelter from the rain and for sleeping in. The interior is deceptively spacious, with a living area downstairs and sleeping space up in the loft.

Panoramic view of the mountains from the Pico Ruivo summit

⓾ Pico Ruivo

🚌 to Santana or Faial, then taxi to Achada do Teixeira, then walk.

Madeira's highest mountain at 1,861 m (6,105 ft), Pico Ruivo is only accessible on foot. The easiest way to scale its heights is via a well-signposted footpath which begins at the village of Achada do Teixeira and leads visitors on a 45-minute walk to the top.

Alternatively, follow the walk from the top of Pico do Arieiro (see p357) along one of the island's most spectacular footpaths. Awe-inspiring mountain scenery and glorious views can be enjoyed all along the 10-km (6-mile) walk. This takes two to three hours and is really only suitable for experienced, well-equipped walkers. Vertigo sufferers should not attempt the path, as it involves negotiating narrow ridges with sheer drops on either side.

⓫ Curral das Freiras

⛰ 3,000. 🚌 ℹ️ Avenida Arriga 16, Funchal (291 211 902).

Curral das Freiras means "Nuns' Refuge" and the name refers to the nuns of the Santa Clara convent who fled to this idyllic spot when pirates attacked Funchal in 1566. The nuns have left now, but the village remains. Visitors first glimpse Curral das Freiras from a viewpoint known as the Eira do Serrado, perched some 800 m (2,625 ft) above the village.

The valley is surrounded on all sides by jagged mountain peaks. Until 1959 the only access to the village was by a steep zigzagging path, but road tunnels now make the journey much easier and allow local people to transport their produce to the capital. Television arrived in 1986.

The sweet chestnuts that grow in profusion around the village are turned into sweet chestnut bread, best eaten still warm from the oven, and *licor de castanha*, a chestnut-flavoured liqueur. Both can be sampled in local bars.

Sheep grazing on the wide plateau of Paúl da Serra, east of Rabaçal

⓬ Paúl da Serra

🚌 to Canhas, then taxi.

The Paúl da Serra (literally "high moorland") is a large, boggy plateau, 17 km (11 miles) in length and 6 km (4 miles) in width. The plain contrasts dramatically with the jagged mountains that characterize the rest of Madeira.

Electricity for the north of the island is generated here by wind turbines. Only gorse and grass grow on the thin soil, and the sponge-like volcanic substrata act as a natural reservoir for rainfall. Water filters through the rock to emerge as springs which then feed the island's *levada* system.

The Levadas of Madeira

Madeira possesses a unique irrigation system that enables the plentiful rainfall of the north of the island to be distributed to the drier, sunny south. Rainfall is stored in reservoirs and lakes, or channelled from natural springs, and fed into the network of *levadas* that ring the island. These narrow channels carry water long distances to banana groves, vineyards and market gardens. Altogether there are 1,500 km (932 miles) of canals, some dating back to the 1500s. Maintenance paths run alongside the *levadas*, providing a network of footpaths reaching into remote parts of the island inaccessible by road.

Levada do Risco, one of many walking routes across Madeira

◀ The dramatic landscape of the São Lourenço peninsula

⓭ Rabaçal Walks

Reached down a single-track road near the Paúl da Serra plateau, Rabaçal is the starting point for two, equally magical, *levada* walks. One is a simple 30-minute, there-and-back stroll to the Risco waterfall, while the other is a more demanding two- to three-hour walk to the beauty spot known as Vinte e Cinco Fontes (25 Springs).

Tips for Walkers

Length: These two walks can be combined to create a circular route of 8 km (5 miles), taking around three and a half hours.
Note: The *levadas* can be slippery and sometimes very narrow. In places the path is only 30 cm (1 ft) wide, but the channel runs at waist height and you can hold on. Always check ahead to make sure trails are open (www.visitmadeira.pt).

⑥ **Levada da Rocha Vermelha**
Wild, mountainous terrain forms the backdrop to the steep path down to the lower *levada*.

⑤ **25 Fontes**
A 30-minute walk brings you to a mossy, fern-hung area with a main cascade and many smaller ones.

④ **Ribeira da Janela**
Cross the bridge and then tackle the steep uphill climb on the left.

Levada da Rocha Vermelha
Levada Nova do Rabaçal
Levada Nova do Rabaçal
Levada das 25 Fontes
Ribeira da Janela
Levada do Risco
Levada das 25 Fontes
Paúl Da Serra
Levada do Risco

① **Rabaçal**
Walkers can leave their vehicles at a nearby car park or make use of a shuttle service to reach the starting point, which has a rest house with picnic tables and views of the valley. Follow the signposted path down to meet the Levada do Risco.

③ **Risco Waterfall**
At this magnificent spot, a torrent of water cascades from the rocky heights down into the green depths of the Risco valley far below.

Key

- - Walk route
═ Road
═ River
═ Levada

② **Levada do Risco**
The course of the *levada*, which leads to the waterfall, is shaded by tree heathers draped with hair-like lichens.

0 metres   250
0 yards   250

Simple stone font in the attractively tiled baptistry of the Igreja Matriz in São Vicente

⓮ São Vicente

🗺 5,700. 🚌 ℹ️ Avenida Arriaga 16, Funchal (291 211 902).

This agricultural town has grown prosperous over the years by tempting travellers to break their journeys here as they explore Madeira's northern coast.

To see how the village looked before development began, visit the Igreja Matriz (built in the 17th century), and look at the ceiling painting of St Vincent blessing the town. He appears again over the elaborately carved main altar, blessing a ship.

Around the church, cobbled traffic-free streets are lined with boutiques, bars and shops selling sweet cakes, including the popular Madeiran speciality *bolo de mel*, the so-called "honey cake" (actually made with molasses and fruit).

Nearly 20 m (65 ft) below the ground is a network of caves,

the **Grutas de São Vicente**, that formed 850,000 years ago during a volcanic eruption. Visitors can walk the 1-km (0.6-mile) trail of excavated lava channels dripping with stalactites. By the caves' entrance is the Volcanism Centre.

Around 8 km (4 miles) northeast is Seixal. Despite the storms that batter the coast, this village occupies a remarkably sheltered spot, where vineyards cling to the hillside terraces, producing excellent wine.

🌋 **Grutas e Centro do Vulcanismo de São Vicente**
Sitio do Pé do Passo. **Tel** 291 842 404. **Open** 10am–7pm daily. **Closed** 25 Dec. 🌐 **grutas ecentrodovulcanismo.com**.

⓯ Porto Moniz

🗺 2,700. 🚌 ℹ️ Rua dos Emigrantes, Vila do Porto Moniz (291 853 075).

Although it is only 75 km (47 miles) from Funchal, visitors arriving in Porto Moniz feel a great sense of achievement after the long journey to this remote coastal village, on the northwest tip of Madeira.

Porto Moniz is surrounded by a patchwork pattern of tiny fields. The fields are protected by fences made from tree heather, a necessary precaution against the heavy, salt-laden air that blows in off the Atlantic. Apart from its picturesque charm, the main attraction at Porto Moniz is the series of natural rock pools on the foreshore, where you can swim in sun-warmed water.

The other draw is the Madeira Aquarium (Tel: 291 850 340; open 10am–6pm daily) housed in the old São João Batista fort.

Bananas, a prolific crop in Calheta

⓰ Calheta

🗺 3,500. 🚌 ℹ️ Avenida Arriaga 16, Funchal (291 211 902).

Calheta sits at the centre of what sugar-cane production survives in Madeira. The smell of cane syrup being extracted and turned into rum hangs around the village from the **factory** (the best time is March to April). The **Centro das Artes Casa das Mudas** provides a more contemporary setting. Picasso is among the artists whose work is exhibited here.

The Igreja Matriz looks modern but dates from 1430 and contains a large ebony and silver tabernacle donated by Manuel I (*see pp50–51*). There is also a fine wooden ceiling.

🏭 **Factory**
Avenida D. Manuel 1 29, Vila da Calheta. **Tel** 291 822 264. **Open** 8am–8pm daily.

🏛 **Centro das Artes Casa das Mudas**
Estrada Simão Gonçalves da Câmara 37, Calheta. **Tel** 291 820 900. **Open** 10am–5pm Tue–Sun. **Closed** Mon & public hols. 🌐 **cultura.madeira-edu.pt**

Environs
The 15th-century chapel at Loreto, 2 km (1 mile) east of Calheta, has a Manueline portal and geometrically patterned ceiling. Outside Estreito da Calheta, 3 km (2 miles) northwest of Calheta, is Lombo dos Reis. Here the Capela dos Reis Magos (Chapel of the Three Kings) has a lively 16th-century Flemish altar carving of the *Adoration of the Magi*.

The warm, natural rock pools at Porto Moniz

Part of Porto Santo's splendid sandy beach

⓱ Ribeira Brava

🏠 13,500. 🚌 ℹ️ Forte de São Bento (291 951 675). 🏛️ daily.

Ribeira Brava is a small, attractive resort town, situated on the sunny south coast of Madeira. It has a pebble beach and a fishing harbour, which is reached through a tunnel to the east of the main town.

Overlooking the principal square, São Bento remains one of the most unspoiled churches on Madeira. Despite restoration and reconstruction, several of its 16th-century features are still intact. These include a stone-carved font and ornate pulpit decorated with wild beasts such as wolves, and the Flemish painting of the *Nativity* in the side chapel. The engaging **Museu Etnográfico da Madeira** has a collection of exhibits illustrating Madeiran culture and society.

São Bento's clock tower, Ribeira Brava

🏛️ **Museu Etnográfico da Madeira**
Rua São Francisco 24. **Tel** 291 952 598. **Open** 9:30am–5pm Tue–Fri, 10am–12:30pm & 1:30–5:30pm Sat. **Closed** public hols. 🖥️ **cultura. madeira-edu.pt**

⓲ Câmara de Lobos

🏠 15,000. 🚌 ℹ️ Avenida Arriaga 16, Funchal (291 211 902). 🏛️ Mon–Sat.

This pretty fishing village was several times painted by Winston Churchill, who often visited Madeira in the 1950s. Bars and restaurants are named in his honour and a plaque marks the spot on the main road, east of the

harbour, where the great statesman set up his easels. This is one of Madeira's main centres for catching scabbard fish *(peixe espada)*, which feature on every local menu. Long lines are baited with octopus to catch these fish that dwell at depths of between 800 m (2,600 ft) and 1,600 m (5,250 ft).

The fishermen live in dwellings along the harbour front, and their tiny chapel dates from the 15th century, but was rebuilt in 1723. The chapel is dedicated to St Nicholas, the patron saint of seafarers, and is decorated with scenes from the saint's life, as well as vivid portrayals of drownings and shipwrecks.

Environs
One of the highest sea cliffs in Europe is Cabo Girão, 10 km (6 miles) west of Câmara de Lobos, which peaks at a dramatic 580 m (1,900 ft) above sea level. A transparent viewing platform extends over the cliff edge.

⓳ Porto Santo

🏠 5,000. ✈️🚢 ℹ️ Avenida Dr Manuel Gregório Pestana Júnior (291 985 244).

Porto Santo, the island that lies 37 km (23 miles) northeast of Madeira, is smaller, flatter and drier than its sister island. It possesses something that Madeira lacks: a 9-km (6-mile) beach of golden sand, running the entire length of the island's south coast. There is a daily ferry service between Funchal and Porto Santo, which takes 2 hours and 30 minutes. There are also daily flights, shortening the trip to 15 minutes.

Porto Santo is a popular holiday destination. There are five big, mostly discreet hotels, and several holiday resorts with villas and apartments. Snorkelling is good here and bicycles can be hired.

The one historic site of note on the island is the **Casa de Colombo** (house of Christopher Columbus), located behind Nossa Senhora da Piedade in Vila Baleira. The restored house is built from rough stone, and contains exhibits that tell Columbus's story, including maps, paintings and engravings.

🏛️ **Casa de Colombo**
Travessa da Sacristia 2, Vila Baleira. **Tel** 291 983 405. **Open** Tue–Sat & Sun am. 🖥️ **museucolombo-portosanto.com**

Christopher Columbus on Porto Santo

Historical records vouch for the fact that Christopher Columbus came to Madeira in 1478, probably as an agent for sugar merchants in his native Italian town of Genoa. He went to Porto Santo to meet Bartolomeu Perestrelo, also from Genoa and the island's governor. There he met Filipa Moniz, Perestrelo's daughter. The two were married in 1479, but Filipa died soon after while giving birth to their son. Nothing else is known about Columbus's visit to the island, though this has not prevented local people from identifying his house.

Christopher Colombus by Ridolfo Ghirlandaio (1483–1561)

THE AZORES

Far out in the Atlantic, 1,600 km (1,000 miles) west of Portugal's mainland, the nine islands of the Azores are known for their spectacular volcanic scenery, abundant flora and peaceful way of life. Once wild and remote, they are now a popular destination for travellers who enjoy walking, sailing and getting away from it all.

Santa Maria was the first island discovered by the Portuguese in 1427. The archipelago was named after the buzzards the early explorers saw flying overhead and mistook for goshawks (açores). The islands were settled during the 15th and 16th centuries by colonists from Portugal and Flanders who introduced cattle, maize and vines.

The Azores have profited from their far-flung position in the Atlantic. Between 1580 and 1640, when Portugal came under Spanish rule (see pp54–5), the ports of Angra do Heroísmo on Terceira and Ponta Delgada on São Miguel prospered from the trade with the New World. In the 19th century the islands were a regular port of call for American whaling ships. During the 20th century they have benefited from their use as stations for transatlantic cable companies, meteorological observatories and military air bases. Today the majority of islanders are involved in either dairy farming or fishing,

and close links are maintained with both mainland Portugal and the sizeable communities of emigrant Azoreans in the United States and Canada. Many emigrants return to their native island for the traditional annual festivals, such as the festas of the Holy Spirit, celebrated in the colourful impérios. With few beaches, a capricious, often wet climate and no large-scale resorts, the Azores have escaped mass tourism. Most travellers come here to explore the green mountains embroidered with blue hydrangeas, relax in quiet ports adorned with cobbled streets and elegant Baroque churches, and enjoy the UNESCO World Heritage Sites, such as the fajãs of São Jorge. Once a brave new world of pioneer communities, the Azores are now an autonomous region of Portugal and an exotic corner of the European Union, where life remains refreshingly civil and unhurried.

Small fishing boats on the quayside at Lajes do Pico on the southern coast of Pico

◄ Lush vegetation around the Lagoa das Sete Cidades (Seven Cities Lagoon)

Exploring the Azores

The islands of the Azores are spread 650 km (400 miles) apart and fall into three distinct groups. In the east lie Santa Maria and São Miguel, the largest island and home to the regional capital, Ponta Delgada. The main towns in the central group of five islands are Horta on Faial, a popular stopover port for boats crossing the Atlantic, and Angra do Heroísmo on Terceira, a charming, historic town. From here visitors can travel to the other islands of São Jorge, Graciosa and Pico, the last dominated by a towering volcanic peak 2,350 m (7,700 ft) high. Further west lie the remote, weather-beaten islands of Flores and Corvo.

9 CORVO

Vila do Corvo

Ponta Delgada

Fajã Grande

Santa Cruz das Flores

Fajãzinha

8 FLORES

Lajes

Santa Cruz da Graciosa

GRACIOSA **4**

Praia

Luz

Pico da Velha
495m

Velas

FAIAL **7**

Cedros

R1-2

5 SÃO JORG

Manadas

Calheta

R2-2

Cabeço Gordo
1045m

Capelo

Horta

Madalena

São Roque do Pico

Santo Antão

Candelária

△ Pico Alto
2350m

Piedade

São Mateus

R1-2

R2-2

PICO **6**

Lajes do Pico

Sights at a Glance

1 *São Miguel pp368–9*
2 Santa Maria
3 Terceira
4 Graciosa
5 São Jorge
6 Pico
7 Faial
8 Flores
9 Corvo

Walking among Pico's black volcanic lava rock

For keys to symbols *see back flap*

0 kilometres   25

0 miles   10

Distances between island groups are not shown to

Key

━━ Major road

┅┅ Minor road

━━ Motorway

━━ Scenic route

△ Summit

Getting Around

São Miguel, Santa Maria, Pico, Faial and Terceira have airports, and the local airline, Azores Airlines, flies between all the islands. A year-round car and ferry service runs between Faial and Pico (www.atlanticoline.pt). Between April and September, it also connects with São Jorge to Terceira. Less frequent are sailings between São Miguel and Santa Maria, Graciosa and Flores. However, a regular operation exists between Flores and Corvo. All ferry services are subject to the weather. Bus services on the islands are designed for the locals and therefore not always practical for tourists. Car hire is more convenient and available on all islands except Corvo. *(See also p447.)*

Transatlantic sailing boat moored in Faial's fine marina at Horta

Angra do Heroísmo, capital of Terceira

Biscoitos

e Santa Bárbara
1022m
Praia da Vitória

nta Bárbara

São Mateus — Angra do Heroísmo

3 — **TERCEIRA**

Sete Cidades — Ribeira Grande — Porto Formoso — Nordeste

Capelas

Candelária — Furnas

Ponta Delgada — Lagoa — Povoação

1 — Vila Franca do Campo

SÃO MIGUEL

Ponta Delgada's elegant waterfront, São Miguel

SANTA MARIA **2**

Anjos — Santa Bárbara

Vila do Porto

● São Miguel

With its historic maritime capital, rich green fields and dramatic volcanic scenery, this *ilha verde* (green island) provides a rewarding introduction to the Azores. The largest and most populated of the archipelago's nine islands, São Miguel is 65 km (40 miles) long and was originally two separate islands. The capital, Ponta Delgada, is a good base from which to make day tours of the rugged coast or visit the volcanic crater lakes and steaming thermal springs in the interior of the island.

The 18th-century city gates leading onto Ponta Delgada's central square

Ponta Delgada

Lined with many impressive churches, convents and trim white houses, the cobbled streets of the Azorean capital recall the wealthy days when the port was a crucial staging post between Europe and the New World *(see pp52–3)*. Its hub is the arcaded Praça de Gonçalo Velho Cabral, named after the first captain-donee of the island in 1444, which looks out onto the seafront. It is dominated by three imposing arches, dating from 1783, that once marked the entrance to the city. To the north, in Largo da Matriz, stands the parish church of São Sebastião. Founded in 1533 it has a graceful Manueline portal intricately carved in limestone. The sacristy is decorated with *azulejo* panels and beautiful 17th-century furniture made of jacaranda wood from Brazil.

A short walk west lies the Praça 5 de Outubro, a shaded, tree-lined square overlooked by the Forte de São Brás. This Renaissance fortress, built on a spur overlooking the sea, was greatly restored in the 19th century. Also on the square, the immense Convento da Esperança becomes the focus of intense festivities when the city celebrates the festival of Santo Cristo dos Milagres on the fifth Sunday after Easter. A statue of Christ, wearing a red robe decorated with sumptuous diamond and gold ornaments, leads the procession through the streets. The statue can be seen in the lower church along with other religious treasures, including reliquaries and jewels. Colourful tiles, dating from the 18th century, by António de Oliveira Bernardes *(see p30)* decorate the choir.

The **Museu Carlos Machado**, in the former monastery of Santo André, spotlights the local fishing and farming industries. Of particular interest are the paintings by Domingos Rebelo (1891–1975) showing scenes of Azorean life. The natural history wing is packed with an encyclopedic array of stuffed animals, varnished fish, skeletons and a large relief model of the island. The museum's Núcleo de Arte Sacra is housed in the nearby Igreja do Colégio.

🏛 Museu Carlos Machado
Rua Dr Carlos Machado. Tel 296 202 930. **Open** Apr–Sep: 10am–5:30pm Tue–Sun; Oct–Mar: 9:30am–5pm. **Closed** public hols. 🅿 🆆 **museu-carlosmachado.azores.gov.pt**

West of the Island

The northwest of São Miguel is punctured by a giant volcanic crater, Lagoa das Sete Cidades, with a 12-km (7-mile) circumference. In places its sheer walls drop like green curtains for 300 m (1,000 ft). When not obscured by cloud, the crater is best seen from the viewpoint of Vista do Rei from where a walk leads west around its rim. The crater floor contains the small village of Sete Cidades and four dark green lakes. The crater seen today is believed to have been formed in the 1440s when an eruption destroyed the volcanic peak that had formed the western part of the island. In contrast to the lush vegetation that covers the crater now, the first settlers described the area as a burnt-out shell.

The main town on the north coast, Ribeira Grande has a small **Museu Municipal** housed in the restored 17th-century Solar de São Vicente. *Azulejos* from the 16th to 20th century are on display and in other rooms the crafts and rural lifestyle of the islanders are recorded, including a period barber's shop rescued from Ponta Delgada.

🏛 Museu Municipal
Rua São Vicente Ferreira 10, Ribeira Grande. **Tel** 296 472 118. **Open** 9am–12:30pm & 1:30–5pm Mon–Sat. **Closed** public hols.

Key

═══ Main road

═══ Other road

Turquoise waters of the crater lake, Lagoa do Fogo

VISITORS' CHECKLIST

Practical Information
138,000. Avenida Infante Dom Henrique, Ponta Delgada (296 308 625). 5th Sun after Easter: Santo Cristo dos Milagres (Ponta Delgada); Festas do Espírito Santo *(see p372)*.
W visitazores.com

Transport
3 km (2 miles) W of Ponta Delgada. Avenida Infante Dom Henrique, Ponta Delgada.

East of the Island

The Lagoa do Fogo, "Lake of Fire", was formed in the island's central mountains by a volcanic eruption in 1563. On sunny days its remote sandy beach is a tranquil picnic spot.

Further east, the spa resort area of Furnas is the perfect place to admire the geothermal activity taking place beneath the surface of the Azores *(see pp344–5)*. Scattered around the town are the Caldeiras das Furnas where visitors will see the hot bubbling springs that provide the therapeutic mud and mineral water used for the spa's treatments. In the 18th century, Thomas Hickling, a prosperous merchant from Boston, laid out gardens in Furnas which have now grown into the glorious Parque Terra Nostra. Covering 12 ha (30 acres), the gardens have a rich collection of mature trees and plants, including hibiscus and hydrangeas, as well as a bizarre swimming pool with warm, mustard-coloured water.

The volcanic ground on the northern shores of the Lagoa das Furnas, 4 km (2 miles) south, is so hot the islanders come here to cook *cozido*. The rich meat and vegetable stew is cooked underground for up to six hours.

The far east of São Miguel is a beautiful area of deep valleys. Two immaculately kept viewpoints, Miradouro da Ponta do Sossego and Miradouro da Ponta da Madrugada, have fine gardens – the latter is a popular spot for watching the sunrise.

Caldeiras das Furnas
Off R1-1. *i* Rua Dr Frederico Moniz Pereira 15. **Tel** 296 584 525.

Pristine gardens and picnic area of the Miradouro da Ponta da Madrugada

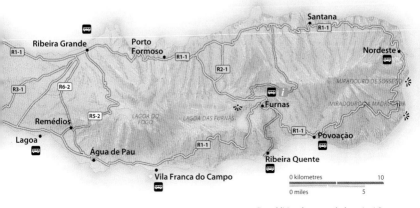

For additional map symbols *see back flap*

The wide bay of São Lourenço on Santa Maria

❷ Santa Maria

🏙 5,500. ✈ 3 km (2 miles) NW of Vila do Porto. 🚢 Vila do Porto. 🚌 Rua Dr Luís Bettencourt, Vila do Porto. 🛈 Aeroporto de Santa Maria, Vila do Porto (296 886 355). 🎉 Festas do Espírito Santo *(see p372)*; 15 Aug: Nossa Senhora da Assunção (Vila do Porto). 🌐 **visitazores.com**

Lying 55 km (34 miles) south of São Miguel, Santa Maria was the first island in the archipelago to be discovered by the Portuguese around 1427. Though only 17 km (11 miles) long, it has great scenic variety and boasts sandy beaches, tranquil countryside and the warmest climate in the Azores. The island's capital, Vila do Porto,

Nossa Senhora da Purificação studded with black basalt in Santo Espírito, Santa Maria

is on the south coast and consists of a long main street that runs down to a small harbour. The west of the island is a dry, flat plateau with a vast airstrip built in World War II. To the north lies the fishing town of Anjos, where a statue commemorates a visit made by Christopher Columbus in 1493 on his return from discovering the New World. Next to it, the small, whitewashed chapel of Nossa Senhora dos Anjos is the oldest in the Azores.

The highest point of Santa Maria is the central Pico Alto, 590 m (1,935 ft) above sea level, which on a clear day offers fine views over the green and hilly east side of the island. Towards the east coast, the village of Santo Espírito is worth visiting for the white Baroque façade of its church of Nossa Senhora da Purificação adorned with black lava decoration, while the vine-covered half-crater of Baía de São Lourenço, north of here, is a delightful summer beach resort.

❸ Terceira

🏙 56,000. ✈ 3 km (2 miles) NW of Praia da Vitória. 🚢 Angra do Heroísmo, Praia da Vitória. 🚌 Avenida 1° de Maio, Angra do Heroísmo. 🛈 Rua Direita 70–74, Angra do Heroísmo (295 213 393) Praia da Vitória Aerogare Civil das Lajes (295 513 140). 🎉 Festas do Espírito Santo *(see p372)*; late Jun: Festas de São João; first week in Aug: Festas da Praia. 🌐 **visitazores.com**

Terceira, meaning "third" in Portuguese, is so named because it was the third island to be discovered, in 1427. It is the most developed of the five central islands – a result in part of the large American-run airbase that has been operating at Lajes since World War II. It is renowned for the brightly painted chapels *(impérios)* devoted to the cult of the Holy Spirit *(see p372)*. Terceira's interior is mainly green pastureland and laurel forest, while the coast has barren areas of black lava.

The brightly coloured Imperio of Sao Sebastiao in Terceira

Angra do Heroísmo

This attractive and historic town was declared a UNESCO World Heritage site in 1983, in recognition of the strategic role the port has played in the Atlantic. For over three centuries the town was a stopover point on the routes between Europe, America and Africa. It was here in 1499 that Vasco da Gama *(see p110)* buried his brother Paulo after their pioneering journey to India, and in the early 17th century its harbour glittered with Spanish fleets returning laden with treasure from the Americas.

The 16th-century Sé (cathedral) at the centre of Terceira's capital, Angra do Heroísmo

Maria II gave the town its name for the bravery *(heroísmo)* it demonstrated during the struggles for Liberalism in the early 19th century *(see pp58–9)*. Despite the severe damage caused by an earthquake in 1980, the city's wealthy past is reflected in the pretty streets lined with monumental churches and balconied houses.

The most spectacular view of the harbour is from Monte Brasil, a volcanic crater on the western side of the bay. Beside this popular picnic spot stands the fort, Fortaleza de São João Baptista, built during Spain's annexation of Portugal *(see pp54–5)* as a treasure store, and still in military use. A second rewarding viewpoint is from the Alto da Memória at the south end of Rua São João de Deus, from where the twin towers of the 16th-century Sé (restored after a fire in 1983) are easily seen. A path leads down into the Jardim Duque da Terceira, the city's restful public gardens. These once formed part of the 15th-century Convento de São Francisco which now houses the **Museu de Angra do Heroísmo**. The museum's exhibits reflect the history of the Azores and the city and include armour, maps, paintings and sculptures.

Wooden John the Baptist, Museu de Angra

Museu de Angra do Heroísmo
Ladeira de São Francisco. **Tel** 295 240 800. **Open** Apr–Sep: 10am–6pm Tue–Sun; Oct–Mar: 9:30am–5pm Tue–Sun. **Closed** pub hols. &

Around the Island

Terceira is a large, oval-shaped island with a gentle green interior of forested hills and farmland. Its centre bears witness to its volcanic origins: the Caldeira de Guilherme Moniz is an eroded crater 3 km (2 miles) wide and one of the largest in the Azores. Nearby, the **Algar do Carvão** is a dramatic volcanic blast-hole, thick with dripping moss where visitors can tour an enormous subterranean cave. West of here, the Furna do Enxofre are hot steaming fumaroles where the heavy sulphur vapours crystallize into brightly coloured formations.

Two viewpoints overlooking the island can be reached by car: in the west, a road bordered with blue hydrangeas winds up through the Serra de Santa Bárbara to a vast lonely crater at 1,022 m (3,353 ft), while the eastern Serra do Cume, at 545 m (1,788 ft), overlooks the airport and Praia da Vitória. This port has a large bay with a sandy beach. Its name pays tribute to a famous victory in 1829 by Liberal forces loyal to Pedro IV over the Absolutists, led by Miguel, during the Portuguese Civil War – the so-called War of the Two Brothers. On the north coast, Biscoitos (which means "biscuits")

takes its name from the rubble of biscuit-like lava spread along the shore. Exhilarating swimming pools, popular in the summer, have been created amongst the rocks. The area is also known for its wine, and the land is covered in a chessboard of stone-walled pens *(curraletas)* built to shelter vines. The friendly **Museu do Vinho dos Biscoitos** explains the simple production methods used to produce the rich *verdelho* wine that was once exported to the Russian court, and provides an opportunity to taste and purchase today's vintages.

Algar do Carvão
Off R5-2. **Tel** 295 212 992. **Open** Apr–May: 3–5:30pm daily; Jun & Sep: 2:30–5:45pm daily; Jul & Aug: 2–6pm daily; Oct–Mar: 3–5pm Mon, Wed & Fri

Museu do Vinho
Canada do Caldeiro 3. **Tel** 965 667 324. **Open** May–Sep: 10–11am, 1–5:30pm Tue–Sun; Oct–Apr: 1:30–4pm Tue–Sat.

Patchwork of stone-walled fields in the northeast of Terceira, near Praia da Vitória

The Holy Spirit Festivals

Festivals are a vibrant feature of life in the Azores and have helped foster the deep sense of community that is a hallmark of the islands' culture. Emigrants and relatives from North America and mainland Portugal often return to their native island to celebrate the most popular *festas*.

The islands' most traditional festivals are associated with the Holy Spirit *(Festas do Espírito Santo)*. Brought to the Azores by the first Portuguese settlers, who called upon the Holy Spirit to protect them against natural disasters, the rituals have remained almost unchanged. An "emperor", often a child, is crowned in the parish church. With a sceptre and a crown on a silver plate and a scarlet flag with a white dove as insignia of the Holy Spirit, the "emperor" presides over the festivities that take place each Sunday for seven weeks after Easter. The seventh Sunday, Whit Sunday, is the day of Pentecost when Christ's disciples were filled with the Holy Spirit, and is the occasion of a great feast.

The distribution of bread for the Festival of the Holy Spirit originates in the donation of food to the poor introduced by saintly Queen Isabel *(see p49)*. On the last day of celebrations, the seventh Sunday after Easter, a Holy Spirit soup is made from beef and vegetables and is handed out along with bread to everyone outside the local *império*.

The Impérios of the Holy Spirit

Império with Gothic windows in Praia da Vitória, Terceira (1941)

Flamboyantly decorated *império* in São Sebastião, Terceira (1918)

Simple *império* in Terra Chã, Terceira (1954)

The focus of the ceremonies is a small chapel or *império* (empire) which is used for the distribution of the Holy Spirit soup on the seventh Sunday. Here, the emperor's crown, sceptre, plate and flag are displayed on the altar on the last day of the festivities. On Terceira, where the cult of the Holy Spirit is particularly strong, many of the 68 *impérios* are painted in bright colours every spring. Up to 500 islanders gather for a village feast accompanied by dancing, brass bands and lavish floral displays. In many places a *tourada à corda* will be held, where a bull, tied to the end of a long rope, is let loose in the street.

An emperor's crown on ceremonial display in an *império* on São Miguel

Traditional ox-drawn cart on the island of Graciosa

❹ Graciosa

🏘 4,500. ✈ 2 km (1 mile) W of Santa Cruz da Graciosa. 🚢 Praia de São Mateus. 🛈 Praça Fontes Pereira de Melo, Santas Cruz (295 712 888). 🎉 Festas do Espírito Santo; Aug: Santo Cristo. 🆆 visitazores.com

Graciosa Island is one of the most peaceful places in the Azores and is classified by UNESCO as a Biosphere reserve. Only 12.5 km (8 miles) long, most of its low-lying land is given over to farms and vineyards where ox-drawn carts and ploughs are still in use. The capital, Santa Cruz da Graciosa, on the northern coast, has a simple quayside backed by rows of stark, two-storey, whitewashed houses with wrought-iron balconies and oval windows. The expanded **Museu da Graciosa** recalls life on this sleepy island with a homely miscellany of toys, sea chests, kitchenware, wine presses, furniture and mementos sent back by emigrants to North America. A building next door houses a whaling boat (*see pp374–5*).

The picturesque Monte da Ajuda that rises behind the town is capped by a 16th-century fortified chapel, Nossa Senhora da Ajuda, decorated with 18th-century tiles. Nearby, a small *vigia* (whalers' lookout) faces the sea.

In the southeast lies the island's principal sight, **Furna do Enxofre**, where visitors can descend flights of steps into the bowels of a volcanic crater. At the bottom is a huge cave with a deep, sulphurous lake and peep-holes where bubbling brews of evil grey liquid can be spied beneath the rocks. The best time to visit is late morning when the sun shines through the small cave mouth and lights the interior.

Above the cave, at Furna Maria Encantada, a natural tunnel leads to the edge of the crater, offering stunning views over the island. Treatments using the island's geothermal waters are available at the coastal resort of Carapacho, at the foot of the volcano.

🏛 Museu da Graciosa
Largo Conde de Simas 17, Santa Cruz. **Tel** 295 712 429. **Open** 9am–12.30pm & 2–5.30pm Mon–Fri. **Closed** pub hols. 🎫

🌋 Furna do Enxofre
2 km (1 mile) E of Luz, follow signs to Caldeira. **Open** Jun–Sep: 10am–6pm daily; Oct–May: 10am–5pm Tue–Fri, 2–5.30pm Sat. 🎫

Santa Cruz da Graciosa overlooking the island

❺ São Jorge

🏘 9,000. ✈ 7 km (4 miles) E of Velas. 🚢 Velas & Calheta. 🛈 Rua Conselheiro Dr José Pereira 1, Velas (295 412 440). 🎉 23 Apr: Festa de São Jorge; Festas do Espírito Santo; Jul: Semana Cultural de Velas (Velas). 🆆 visitazores.com

São Jorge is a mountainous island that stretches for 55 km (34 miles) but is only 8 km (5 miles) wide. On its north coast, sheer cliffs drop 480 m (1,575 ft) to the sea. Over the centuries these cliffs have collapsed in places, creating tongues of land known as *fajãs*-recognized by UNESCO as Biosphere Reserves. It was on these coastal promontories that the island's Flemish colonists first settled in the mid-15th century.

Today many islanders on São Jorge are engaged in the production of a cured cheese, *Queijo de São Jorge*. The pace of life is leisurely, and most visitors come to enjoy the walking along the paths that climb between the *fajãs*. The most popular route is in the northeast of the island from Serra do Topo 10 km (6 miles) down to Fajã dos Cubres.

Most of the settlements lie along the gentler south coast, including the capital, Velas, and Calheta, where the **Museu Francisco de Lacerda** displays objects of local history such as the ornate breads baked for the Holy Spirit festival, a honey press, agricultural utensils and religious sculptures. West of Calheta, in the pretty parish of Manadas, the 18th-century church of Santa Bárbara has an atmospheric carved and painted interior. In Urzelina, 2 km (1 mile) further west, the tower of a church buried by lava in 1808 protrudes defiantly from the ground. In the west of the island there is a pleasant forested picnic area at Sete Fontes, and on a clear day the nearby summit of Pico da Velha offers superb views of the central Azorean islands.

🏛 Museu Francisco de Lacerda
Rua José Azevedo da Cunha, Calheta. **Tel** 295 416 323. **Open** 9am–5.30pm Mon–Fri. **Closed** public hols. 🎫

Dramatic cliffs along the north coast of São Jorge

❻ Pico

🏘 13,000. ✈ 8 km (5 miles) E of Madalena. 🚢 Madalena. 🚌 Avenida Machado Serpa, Madalena. ℹ Gare Marítima, Madalena (292 623 524). 🎉 Festas do Espírito Santo *(see p372)*; 22 Jul: Santa Maria Madalena, Semana dos Baleeiros. 🌐 **visitazores.com**

The majesty of Pico, the highest mountain in Portugal, becomes apparent when it is seen from the neighbouring central islands. Only then does one realize how gracefully this volcanic peak soars out of

Rustic house and well on Pico made from black lava rocks

the Atlantic, shooting up 2,350 m (7,700 ft) to form the summit of the greatest mountain range in the world, the Mid-Atlantic Ridge *(see pp344–5)*.

The island's largest town, Madalena, is a relaxed port that lies opposite Faial's capital, Horta. A regular ferry service crosses the 8 km (5 miles) between the two islands, making a day trip feasible. The entrance to the harbour is guarded by two rocks, Em Pé (standing) and Deitado (lying down) where colonies of birds have made their home.

Many people come to Pico to climb its eponymous peak. It is a strenuous climb, best done alongside a guide, and advance permission is needed. At 1,100 m (3,608 ft), the Casa da Montanha offers refuge and support to hikers and climbers. For further details, contact the tourist offices.

The summit of Pico's volcano

The other main draw to Pico in summer is whale watching. From Lajes do Pico groups are taken out in small boats for three-hour trips organized by companies such as Espaço Talassa. They are guided by radio messages from men who scan the sea for a fluke (tail) from the former *vigias* (lookouts). The history of Azorean whaling is recalled at the **Museu**

In Pursuit of the Whale

Every summer the waters around the Azores are visited by a great variety of whales and dolphins. Until 1984 whaling was a traditional part of Azorean life – in the 18th century American whaling vessels frequently called here to pick up crew for their expeditions, and from the 1870s the Azoreans took up large-scale hunting in their own waters. Flags were waved from clifftop *vigias* (lookouts) giving coded directions so that other villagers would not get to the prize first.

Since whaling was banned in the 1980s, the Azoreans have applied their knowledge gained from hunting to whale watching and conservation.

Scrimshaws are carvings made on the teeth and bones of whales and often depict whaling scenes. This fine example from the Museu do Scrimshau on Faial *(see p376)* shows the long, narrow boats called *canoas* that could hold up to seven men.

Whale watching today takes place in small boats that allow fast and safe access to the whales. As well as trips out to sea, the whales can be observed from the *vigias*. These land-based towers afford spectacular views of the whales in their natural habitat. Expeditions run from Faial, Pico, Graciosa, Terceira and São Miguel *(see p368)*.

dos Baleeiros, also in Lajes, where boats, tackle and whalebone artifacts are displayed. The whales were processed at a vast factory (closed down in 1984) on the north side of the island, at São Roque do Pico. The factory has been preserved as a piece of industrial heritage now housing the **Museu da Indústria Baleeira**.

A coastal road encircles Pico, offering a slow drive that reveals the charm of this island. Minor eruptions have covered parts of its landscape with black mole-hills of lava that the islanders christened *mistérios* (mysteries). The black lava has been used to build houses and grids of stone walls that enclose fields and shelter vines. In some places, notably around **Cachorro** on the north coast, the eroded lava has formed curious arches in the sea.

The island vineyards are a UNESCO World Heritage site. A visitor's centre explains Pico's viniculture, featuring the famous Verdelho wine. There has been a revival of viniculture on the island, with the production of new reds and whites, such as the acclaimed *Arinto dos Açores*. This gives visitors a refined alternative to the ubiquitous *vinho de cheiro* (wine of smell) traditionally drunk by the Azoreans.

Ⅲ Visitor's Centre
Lajido. **Open** Jun–Sep: 10am–6pm daily; Oct–May: 10am–5pm Tue–Fri, 1:30–5pm Sat & Sun.

Espaço Talassa
Rua do Saco, Lajes. **Tel** 292 672 010. Boat trips: Apr–Sep. **w** espacotalassa.com

Ⅲ Museu dos Baleeiros
Rua dos Baleeiros 13, Lajes. **Tel** 292 679 340. **Open** May–Oct: 10am–5:30pm Tue–Sun; Nov–Apr: 9:30am–5pm.

Museu da Indústria Baleeira
Rua do Poço, São Roque do Pico. **Tel** 292 642 096. **Open** May–Oct: 10am–5:30pm Tue–Sun; Nov–Apr: 9:30am–5pm. **Closed** public hols. (free on Sun).

West coast of Pico with Faial in the distance

Marine Life in the Azores

Some 28 species of cetaceans have been sighted in the waters of the Azores. These warm-blooded animals follow the warm currents of the Gulf Stream to feed in the region's abundant, unpolluted waters. Schools of playful and gregarious dolphins are often seen scything through the waves at incredible speeds, but the most impressive sights are sperm whales. These large, sociable animals dive to great depths for giant squid and live in family groups called pods. Like all whales and dolphins they must come to the surface to breathe and this is when whale-watching expeditions make their sightings.

Atlantic spotted dolphins, fast and graceful swimmers

Sperm whales are huge, tear-shaped creatures, the largest of the toothed whales. They can be seen breaching (diving out of the water), spy hopping (raising their head to have a look around) and socializing by rubbing bodies.

Pilot whales belong to the dolphin family and are recognizable from their strong blow of up to 1 m (3 ft).

Risso's dolphins have a squat head and light grey colouring. Older ones are often crisscrossed with white scars.

Bottlenose dolphins are the best known. These playful animals love to ride the waves at the bow of a moving vessel.

Loggerhead turtles, born on Florida's beaches, are frequent visitors to the warm Azorean waters.

Transatlantic yachts moored in the marina at Horta, Faial, with the pointed summit of Pico in the distance

● Faial

🏠 15,000. ✈ 10 km (6 miles) SW of Horta. 🚢 Horta. 🚌 Rua Vasco da Gama, Horta. 🛈 Rua Vasco da Gama, Horta (292 292 237). 🎭 Festas do Espírito Santo *(see p372)*; 1st–2nd Sun in Aug: Semana do Mar (Horta). W **visitazores.com**

Faial was settled by Flemish farmers in the 15th century and prospered with the development of Horta harbour as a stopover for ships and – more recently – flying boats crossing the Atlantic. Today it is a fertile island with an international atmosphere and a mild climate, famous as a yachting destination and for the endless rows of colourful hydrangeas that bloom in June and July.

Horta

Stretching around a wide bay, Faial's capital has been a convenient anchorage for caravels, clippers and sea planes over the centuries. Captain Cook commented on Horta's fine houses and gardens when he called here in 1775. Today, visiting crews crossing between the Caribbean and Mediterranean paint a calling card on the quayside and celebrate their safe passage in **Peter's Café Sport**, which overlooks the harbour. In the upstairs rooms of the café, an engrossing **Museu do Scrimshaw** exhibits engraved whales' bones and teeth dating back to 1884 *(see p374)*. In the **Museu da Horta** displays of antique furniture, portraits, nautical memorabilia and nostalgic photographs of the island's port are upstaged by miniature sculptures of liners and scenes of daily life, painstakingly carved from the white pith of fig trees. These virtuoso examples of a traditional island craft are by the Faial-born Euclides Silveira da Rosa (1910–79).

Ship's calling card on the quayside in Horta, Faial

📷 **Peter's Café Sport**
Rua José Azevedo 9. **Tel** 292 292 327.
W **petercafesport.com**;
W **whalewatchazores.com**

🏛 **Museu de Scrimshaw**
Peter's Café Sport, Rua José Azevedo 9.
Tel 292 292 327. **Open** Mon–Sat. 📷

🏛 **Museu da Horta**
Largo Duque D'Ávila e Bolama. **Tel** 292 392 784. **Open** Jun–Sep: 10am–5:30pm Tue–Sun; Oct–May: 9:30am–5pm Tue–Sun. **Closed** public hols. 📷

Around the Island

Two viewpoints overlook Horta – to its south rises the volcanic peak of Monte da Guia, while the northern Miradouro da Espalamaca is guarded by a huge statue of Nossa Senhora da Conceição. If the cloud cover permits, it is well worth driving 15 km (9 miles) to see Faial's central Caldeira – a vast green crater 2 km (1 mile) wide and 400 m (1,300 ft) deep. The path winding around its rim takes about two hours to walk and has magnificent views.

Faial's other spectacular natural sight is the Vulcão dos Capelinhos in the far west of the island. A volcano erupted here in 1957–8, smothering a lighthouse which can now be seen buried in ash. Around it lies a scorched and barren landscape that has, not surprisingly, been used as the location for a German post-nuclear holocaust film. The story of the eruption is told in the nearby **Centro de Interpretação do Vulcão dos Capelinhos**, where multimedia displays trace the area's geological activity. Also shown are the lava formations created in the eruption.

🏛 **Centro de Interpretação do Vulcão dos Capelinhos**
Farol dos Capelinhos. **Tel** 292 200 470. **Open** Jun–Sep: 10am–6pm daily; Oct–May: 10am–5pm Tue–Fri, 2–5:30pm Sat & Sun. 📷

Barren ash-covered volcanic landscape at Capelinhos, the westernmost point of Faial

❽ Flores

🏔 3,800. ✈ 1km (half a mile) N of
Santa Cruz. 🚢 Lajes. 🚌 Centro de
Saúde, Santa Cruz. ℹ️ Rua Dr Armas
da Silveira 1, Santa Cruz (292 592 369).
🎭 Festas do Espírito Santo *(see p372)*;
24–26 Jun: Festas de São João (hols:
am). 🌐 **visitazores.com**

Often cut off by stormy weather,
the island of "Flowers" is a romantic
outpost that was not permanently
settled until the 16th century. A
notorious hideout for pirates
waiting to raid the treasure-laden
Spanish galleons on their return
to Europe, Flores was the scene of
an epic battle in 1591 between
the ship of the English commander Sir Richard Grenville and a
fleet of Spanish ships. The battle
was immortalized in a poem by
Alfred Tennyson, *The Revenge*
(the name of Grenville's ship).

This westernmost island of the
Azores is a UNESCO listed
Biosphere Reserve. Its name
derives from the abundance of
flowers growing in its ravines. The
capital, Santa Cruz, is enlivened by
the **Museu da Fábrica da Baleia
do Boquerirão**, a museum dedicated to the island's whaling
heritage, and the **Museu das
Flores**, housed in the former
Franciscan convent. Its displays
include shipwreck finds, Azorean
pottery, furniture and agricultural
tools, as well as fishing rods and a
guitar made from whalebone.
The convent church of São
Boaventura, erected in 1641, has a
beautiful carved cedarwood
chancel. The southern half of the
island is the most scenic. The
deep, verdant valleys are

Hydrangeas growing in the mountains of Flores

punctuated with dramatic peaks,
volcanic crater lakes and caves.
Yams and sweet potatoes grow
in the fertile soil. The tranquil
Lagoa Funda, 25 km (16 miles)
southwest of Santa Cruz, is a lake
at the base of a mountain. Visible
from the main road just west of
the lake are the vertical rock formations of the Rocha dos Bordões
formed by solidified basalt.

The winding road continues
northwards over the mountains
and, as the road descends towards
the west coast, there are stunning
views of the green valley and
village of Fajãzinha. The resort of
Fajã Grande, ringed by cliffs, is a
popular base for walkers and
impressive waterfalls plunge into
the sea from the high cliffs. A
short walk north from the town
is the Cascata da Ribeira Grande,
a towering jet of water that

divides into smaller waterfalls
before collecting in a still pool.

🏛 Museu da Fábrica da
Baleia do Boqueirão
Rua do Boqueirão. **Tel** 291 542 932.
Open Jun–Sep: 9am–5:30pm Mon–
Fri, 2–5:30pm Sat & Sun; Oct–May:
9am–12:30pm, 2–5:30 Mon–Fri,
2–5:30pm Sun. 🖼

🏛 Museu das Flores
Edificio do Convento de São
Boaventura. **Tel** 292 592 159. **Open**
9am–12:30pm & 2–5:30pm Mon–Fri.
Closed public hols. 🖼

❾ Corvo

🏔 430. ✈ 🚢 Vila do Corvo. 🚌 Rua
da Matriz, Vila do Corvo. ℹ️ Câmara
Municipal, Rua J da Bola, Vila do Corvo
(292 590 200). 🎭 Festas do Espírito
Santo *(see p372)*. 🌐 **visitazores.com**

Corvo lies 24 km (15 miles) northwest of Flores. The smallest island
in the Azores, it has just one
settlement, Vila do Corvo, and is
blissfully undeveloped, with only
one hotel and a few restaurants.
The entire island is the blown top
of a marine volcano. A green
crater, the Lagoa do Caldeirão,
squats at its northern end. Its rim
can be reached by road, after
which there is a steep descent
down to the crater floor 300 m
(984 ft) below. In its centre, the
crater is dotted with serene lakes
and islands. Corvo has recorded
an large variety of birdlife during
the autumn migration.

A scenic aerial view of the Rasa and Funda lagoons

TRAVELLERS' NEEDS

WHERE TO STAY

Luxury five-star hotels, and many four-star properties, in Portugal often include spas and multi-swimming pools, notable restaurants (some of which are Michelin-starred) and are usually furnished with high tech digital gadgetry. In essence, choosing a place to stay is as much about a lifestyle choice as it is finding a room for the night. Whether it's a chic B&B in

Porto, a boutique hotel in Lisbon or a luxurious all inclusive resort in Funchal, Portugal has a wonderfully eclectic range of options. Advance booking is essential and most rooms are cheaper outside high season. The hotels listed on pages 386–95 have been selected from every price category and represent the best value in each area.

Types of Hotel

Lodgings in Portugal come at all levels of comfort and cost but are classified into two main categories by the Portuguese tourist authority: hotels and *pensões*. Hotels are often purpose-built and take up an entire building. *Pensões* are always housed in shared premises, typically occupying several floors of a residential building.

All hotels and *pensões* are meant to provide meals. If they offer only breakfast, their name must have *residencial* added to it, although not all *residencials* offer breakfast. It is always best to check, since there are many lodgings that operate without classification. Aparthotels are essentially hotels with self-catering apartments, offering most or all of the services that normal hotels do.

Estalagens (*estalagem* in the singular) are usually located outside of city centres and must have a garden. *Albergarias* are the top category of *pensão*,

which means that their facilities are on the same level as those of four- or five-star hotels.

Pousadas

Pousadas are a special type of lodgings – you can find more information on pages 384–5. They come in four categories: historic, historic design, charm and nature. Historic *pousadas* are housed in converted castles, convents or palaces, and they offer excellent service and luxury accommodation, as well as a memorable historical and architectural ambience. The other types of *pousadas* are country inns offering a high level of comfort and are often located in scenic, sometimes remote, areas. With the exception of two mountain inns in Madeira that use the word "*pousada*" in their names, all *pousadas* are state-owned and run as a chain by **Pestana**. Detailed information on these can be found on the **Pousadas de Portugal** website.

The façade of the fashionable Hotel Palácio, Estoril (*see p388*)

Chain Hotels

Portugal has a range of chain hotels in all price categories. International luxury groups such as **Le Meridien** and **Belmond** are well represented in the Algarve and Madeira. Smaller luxury groups include **Tivoli Hotels** – with three hotels in Lisbon, two in Sintra, five in the Algarve and one in Coimbra – and the Pestana group, with ten hotels in Madeira, nine in the Algarve, two in Lisbon and one each in Cascais, Porto and Sintra.

Lower down the scale, **Choice Hotels** operates a number of hotels in its Comfort Inn and Quality Inn categories in the Lisbon area and the north of the country, while **Best Western** and **Sana Hotels** have several hotels countrywide. **Ibis** are also well represented, with properties that are frequently located outside cities and towns, and they offer very good value for money.

Swimming pool in a splendid setting at Tivoli Carvoeiro in Carvoeiro, Algarve (*see p394*)

◀ The interior of the Teatro Nacional Dona Maria II, Lisbon

Gradings

The Portuguese tourist authority rates hotels with one to five stars, five being the top rating. A one-star hotel is known as a *pensaõ*, which in turn is rated in one of four categories: *albergaria* being the top one, followed by First to Third categories. Apart-hotels are also rated from one to five stars. These ratings are based on a fixed set of criteria that covers most aspects of comfort. They do not, however, take into account more subjective factors such as view, atmosphere or the professionalism of the staff.

It is important to remember that hotels and *pensões* are rated separately from top to bottom. In other words, a one- or two-star hotel will always have a lower level of comfort – and lower prices – than an *albergaria* or even a first-category *pensão*. The grading system is quite strict, and all rated establishments should have a sign by the entrance showing their rating.

Prices

In Portugal, establishments are free to decide their own prices, but all tariffs must be clearly displayed at the reception and in the rooms. The cost of the room usually includes all taxes and a continental breakfast. Other meals are charged as

View from the Tivoli Palácio de Seteais, a luxury hotel in Sintra *(see p388)*

extras. It is sometimes possible to bargain for a better rate, especially outside the high season. As a rule, the cost of a single room is around 60 to 75 per cent of the cost of a double room.

Tourist areas, such as the Algarve and Estoril coasts, Madeira and the Azores, can be expensive. However, prices drop substantially outside the peak summer months. Like many European cities, many business-oriented hotels in Lisbon and Porto charge the same rates throughout the year.

Bookings

It is advisable to reserve in advance for all tourist areas, but particularly in high season. Much of the accommodation in the

Algarve and around the Estoril coast is mass-booked by tour operators. For Madeira, Lisbon and Porto, it is best to book ahead regardless of the season, as these are popular tourist cities. Nearly all establishments have a website that accommodation can be booked through, but most receptionists speak English so it is also possible to book by phone.

Pousadas can be booked through Pestana or via the Pousadas de Portugal website. The Portuguese tourist authority, **Turismo de Portugal**, publishes online a comprehensive list of accommodation options rated by the authority, complete with contact details. A number of these establishments can be booked via the **Visit Portugal** website.

Elegantly furnished room in Belmond Reid's Palace in Funchal, Madeira *(see p395)*

Rural Accommodation

Portugal's choices of lodgings is vastly enhanced by the possibility of finding accommodation in private manors, country houses or on farms, usually, but not always situated in the countryside and often with the owners in residence.

This description of rural accommodation choice is known in Portuguese as *Turismo no Espaço Rural* (Tourism in the Country). These fall into four main categories: Turismo de Habitação (TH), which are manors or palatial houses of recognized historical and/or architectural value, including interiors and period furnishings; Turismo Rural (TR), country houses typical of their region located in or near a village; Agroturismo (AG), houses that form part of a working farm; and Casas de Campo (CC), country houses that take in guests, sometimes with the owners in residence.

Most of the grandest Turismos de Habitação are found in Minho, in the north. The **Associação do Turismo de Habitação (TURIHAB)** offers information and booking facilities.

The annual publication *Turismo no Espaço Rural* lists all the houses. Bookings can be made through agents or directly with the owners.

Resort Accommodation

Most of the country's resort accommodation is situated along the Algarve and the Estoril coasts. Hotel prices can drop considerably outside high season, and it is often possible to get a very good deal at less popular times of the year, when these locations are not as packed with visitors.

The *aldeamento turístico* (tourist village) is a unique feature of resort areas such as the Algarve. Graded from three to five stars, these self-contained complexes offer well-furnished and fitted private apartments and usually provide a range of sports facilities, too. They also include beaches, pools, bars restaurants and, sometimes, even a supermarket.

Apartamentos turísticos (tourist apartments) don't have the hotel-style facilities of the tourist villages, but are ideal for those who require flexibility and independence. They are generally purpose-built buildings in resort areas, offering self-catering lodgings with a quality grading between two and five stars.

Budget Accommodation

Pousadas de Juventude (youth hostels) – over 50 in total – are mainly dotted along the coast, and include three each in the Azores and Madeira. They are open all through the year, but advance booking is advisable in the summer. A valid **Hostelling International (HI)** card, which can be obtained from any Youth Hostel Association, is a pre-requisite. Facilities vary greatly and may include the use of a

Casa do Campo de Molares, a manor house in Celorico de Basto *(see p392)*

kitchen, bar and swimming pool. Information is available from **Pousadas de Juventude**, the head office of the Portuguese Youth Hostel Association.

In major cities there is a growing number of luxury hostels that offer stylish, comfortable and clean dormitory accommodation and private rooms, often inclusive of breakfast, as well as free tours and cheap meals. Almost as inexpensive as hostels, but with the advantage of greater privacy, are *quartos* (rooms) in private houses, often rented out in resorts. Lists of *quartos* are available from local tourist offices. Alternatively **Airbnb** offers a number of affordable shared rooms, private rooms and entire homes.

Camping and Caravanning

There are more than 100 official camp sites in Portugal, the majority along the coast. The largest is at Albufeira, in the Algarve, but most are small and quiet. **Orbitur** runs a national chain of camp sites.

Generally the quoted rate is for the tent and per person; extra charges for shower and parking apply. International camping cards that give discounts and provide insurance are available from various organizations. **Camping Portugal** provides a list of camp sites and other relevant information.

Setting up camp outside camping sites in the countryside is severely restricted because of the very real danger of forest fires.

A comfortable room at Hotel do Chiado, Lisbon *(see p387)*

Children

Children are welcome pretty much anywhere in Portugal, and families are well catered for. Some hotels give children under eight years of age a 50 per cent discount on accommodation and meals.

Travellers with Disabilities

Hotels with facilities for the disabled are listed by the Turismo de Portugal office, which also produces a leaflet with useful information. Camp sites and youth hostels that provide special facilities are listed by the relevant organizations and in an online guide published by the **Instituto Nacional Para a Reabilitação**.

Accessible Portugal offers a range of specialized tours for disabled travellers, as well as equipment rental and advice.

Recommended Hotels

The hotels listed by area on pages 386–95 reflect the main types of accommodation in Portugal. **Luxury** options reflect hotels with flawless service and

Entrance to the beautiful Casa da Pérgola, Cascais *(see p388)*

the best facilities in stunning surroundings. **Boutique** properties are high-end and independently run establishments with personable touches. Similarly, hotels listed as **character** offer a unique stay in quirky or unusual surroundings. **Historic** lodgings, often *pousadas*, include restored castles, convents, mansions and palaces and promise a picturesque stay. **Rural retreats** include inns or cottages set in picturesque and

remote settings, while **Pensão / B&B** options are affordable, often providing a hearty breakfast. **Value** and **self-catering** options are self-explanatory.

Throughout the listings, some establishments are highlighted as DK Choice – these offer something particularly special, such as a beautiful location, a building full of character, eco-friendly credentials, outstanding service and amenities or a combination of these.

DIRECTORY

Pousadas

Pestana
Tel 218 442 001.
w pestana.com

Pousadas de Portugal
Tel 218 442 001.
w pousadas.pt

Chain Hotels

Belmond
w belmond.com

Best Western
Tel 0845 776 7676 (UK).
Tel 800 839 361 (Portugal).
w bestwestern.pt

Choice Hotels
Tel 800 277 277.
w choicehotels.eu

Ibis
w ibishotel.com

Le Meridien
w starwoodhotels.
com/lemeridien/index.
html

Sana Hotels
w sanahotels.com

Tivoli Hotels
Tel 218 507 708.
w tivolihotels.com

Booking

Turismo de Portugal
Rua Ivone Silva, Lote 6, 1050-124 Lisbon. Tel 211 140 200. w turismode portugal.pt

Visit Portugal
w visitportugal.com

Rural Accommodation

TURIHAB
Praça de República, 4990-062 Ponte de Lima.
Tel 258 741 672.
w turihab.pt

Budget Accommodation

Airbnb
w airbnb

Hostelling International
w hihostels.com/

Pousadas de Juventude
Tel 707 233 233.
w pousadas juventude.pt

Camping and Caravanning

Camping Portugal
w campingportugal. org

Orbitur
Avenida da Boavista 1681-3°, 4100-132 Porto.
Tel 226 061 360.
w orbitur.com

Travellers with Disabilities

Accessible Portugal
Tel 211 338 693.
w accessibleportugal.com

Instituto Nacional Para a Reabilitação
Conde de Valbom 63, 1069–178 Lisbon.
Tel 215 952 770.

National Tourist Agencies

Associação de Turismo dos Açores
Avenida Infante Dom Henrique 55, Ponta Delgada, 9500–150 São Miguel. Tel 296 288 082.
w visitazores.com

Direcção Regional de Turismo da Madeira
Avenida Arriaga 18, 9004-519 Funchal. Tel 291 211 900. w visitmadeira.pt

The Pousadas of Portugal

The concept of the *pousada* dates from the 1940s, when the Portuguese government decided to establish a national network of state-run country inns, offering "hospitality in keeping with the style and tradition of the region". *Pousadas* are often set in remote, scenic locations, and most have fewer than 30 rooms, so visitors can expect friendly, personalized service and a high degree of comfort. This map does not show all of mainland Portugal's *pousadas*, just the 34 that are particularly recommended.

Pousada da Ria in Torreira, near the port of Aveiro, has 20 bedrooms, most with balconies overlooking the lagoon of Ria de Aveiro *(see p390).*

Pousada Conde de Ourém, located within the medieval walled town of Ourém, offers breathtaking views of the Seica River valley. This *pousada* is the ideal base from which to explore this interesting area of Portugal, including the Shrine of Fátima and the Convento do Cristo at Tomar *(see p389).*

Pousada do Castelo de Óbidos, in the walled town of Óbidos, is situated in a beautifully restored palace inside the 15th-century castle keep. The *pousada* combines a medieval atmosphere with all modern comforts and a highly recommended restaurant *(see p389).*

Pousada Castelo de Palmela boasts an elegant interior, commanding hilltop views over the town of Palmela and the Atlantic Ocean, and an illustrious history. It is a thoughtful conversion of a monastery which was the headquarters of the Portuguese Knights of Santiago in the 13th century.

Pousada de Sagres occupies a spectacular clifftop position in the most southwesterly town of Europe, Sagres. The terrace restaurant of this purpose-built *pousada* has magnificent views over the Atlantic Ocean *(see p394).*

Valença
Minh
Viana do
Castelo
M
B

Porto
Palácio
do Freixo

Aveiro
Ág
Mealha
Figueira   Coi
da Foz
Condeixa-a

Lei
Nazaré
Alcobaça
Peniche   Óbidos
Lourinhã   San
ESTREMADURA
AND RIBATEJO
Vila Franc
de Xira
Queluz
Cascais   Lisbon   THE
                LISBO
Palmela   COAS
                Setúbal
Alcácer do Sal

Grândola
                Sa
Sines   do
        Vila I
        de M

Santa-Cla
        a-Ve
Aljezur   ALG
Portimão
            Al
    Sagres

Pousada Mosteiro Guimarães, housed in a medieval monastery near the city of Guimarães, is one of Portugal's most impressive and historic *pousadas (see p392).*

Pousada de Alijó, named after J J Forrester, an influential figure in 19th-century port production *(see p258)*, enjoys a peaceful setting among vineyards in the small Douro town of Alijó *(see p406).*

Pousada Castelo de Estremoz dominates the town of Estremoz and the surrounding countryside. In the 13th century, the site of the *pousada* was home to King Dinis and his wife Queen Isabel *(see p393).*

Pousada Convento de Évora, also known as the Pousada dos Loios in Évora has been converted from a 15th-century monastery. Adjacent to the remains of a Roman temple of Diana, it features an elegant dining room set in the original monastic cloisters and a Neo-Classical façade that dates from the mid-18th century *(see p393).*

Pousada de Beja is located in the heart of the old Roman town of Beja at the centre of the sun-baked plains of the southern Alentejo. The building incorporates parts of a former Franciscan convent, dating back to the 13th century. It was opened as a *pousada* in 1994 *(see p393).*

Where to Stay

Lisbon

Alcântara

Pestana Palace Hotel €€€
Historic Map 2 F3
Rua Jau 54, 1300-314
Tel *213 615 600*
W pestana.com
Housed in a 19th-century
palace with a modern wing,
this hotel features lavish rooms
and suites.

Alfama

The Keep €€
Pensão / B&B Map 7 C3
Costa do Castelo 74, 1100-179
Tel *218 854 070*
W facebook.com/thekeeplisbon
This homely *pensão* has a rooftop
turret and a garden terrace with
great views of the city.

Solar do Castelo €€€
Historic Map 7 C3
Rua das Cozinhas 2, 1100-181
Tel *218 806 050*
W solardocastelo.com
A hotel with contemporary decor
inside an 18th-century mansion
within the Castelo de São Jorge.

Baixa and Avenida

Shiado Hostel €
Value Map 7 A4
Rua Anchieta 5, 3rd Floor, 1200-023
Tel *213 429 227*
W shiadohostel.com
A hostel with colourful rooms,
shared kitchen and bathrooms,
and a buffet breakfast.

Alegria €€
Pensão / B&B Map 4 F1
Praça da Alegria 12, 1250-004
Tel *213 220 670*
W alegrianet.com
Family-run *residencial* that
offers cheerful rooms with large
windows and fresh flowers.

Avani Avenida
Liberdade Lisbon Hotel €€
Luxury Map 4 F1
Rua J César Machado 7–9, 1250-135
Tel *213 591 001*
W tivolihotels.com
Guests find both luxury and style
at this family-friendly hotel. The
garden has a pool.

Ever Lisboa City Center Hotel €€
Historic Map 5 C5
Avenida da Liberdade 189, 1250-141
Tel *213 522 618*
W everlisboahotel.com
With an ornate staircase, murals,
and a restaurant offering

impressive city views, this hotel
oozes 19th-century charm.

Florescente €€
Pensão / B&B Map 7 A2
*Rua das Portas de Santo Antão 99,
1150-266*
Tel *213 426 609*
W residencialflorescente.com
Located in the heart of downtown
Lisbon's theatre and fine-dining
district, a floral-themed decor
runs throughout this hotel. There
is a gourmet shop and a restau-
rant on site.

Metrópole €€
Historic Map 7 B3
Praça Dom Pedro IV 30, 1100-200
Tel *213 219 030*
W almeidahotels.pt
The Metrópole has elegant rooms
decorated with original 1920s Art
deco furnishings. Some rooms
have a balcony overlooking the
attractive adjoining plaza.

NH Collection
Lisboa Liberdade €€
Boutique Map 4 F1
Avenida da Liberdade 180B, 1250-146
Tel *213 514 060*
W nh-hotels.pt
A rooftop pool and terrace
feature at this minimalist hotel,
situated on a tree-lined avenue,
with cafés and designer shops.

VIP Executive
Éden Aparthotel €€
Self-catering Map 7 A2
*Praça dos Restauradores 24,
1250-187*
Tel *213 216 600*
W viphotels.com
Modern studios and apartments
are housed in this 1930s Art
Deco building with a large
rooftop pool.

Altis Grand Hotel €€€
Luxury Map 4 F1
Rua Castilho 11, 1269-072
Tel *213 106 000*
W altishotels.com
Five-star opulence at this stylish
hotel with soundproof rooms
includes a heated indoor pool.
Prime location in central Lisbon.

Avenida Palace €€€
Luxury Map 7 B3
Rua 1 de Dezembro 123, 1200-359
Tel *213 218 100*
W hotelavenidapalace.pt
A luxurious, romantic hotel full
of old-fashioned charm and all
modern comforts. The impressive
rooms are elegantly furnished
in a classic style.

Britania €€€
Historic Map 5 C5
*Rua Rodrigues Sampaio 17,
1150-278*
Tel *213 155 016*
W heritage.pt
Indulge in 1940s glamour at
this original Art Deco hotel
with large and stylish rooms.

InterContinental
Lisbon €€€
Luxury Map 5 B4
Rua Castilho 149, 1099-034
Tel *213 818 700*
W intercontinental.com/lisbon
The chic, spacious rooms
and suites have contemporary
decor. There is a fine-dining
restaurant and a fitness centre.

DK Choice

Internacional Design
Hotel €€€
Boutique Map 7 B3
Rua da Betesga 3, 1100-090
Tel *213 240 990*
W idesignhotel.com
Each floor of this luxury hotel
is based around a different
theme: urban chic, Zen
philosophy and pop or tribal
culture. Guests choose a
room to suit their personality
and requirements. Special
facilities include a choice of
pillows and the option of a
butler service.

The stylish lobby of the modernist
Britania hotel

View of the grand façade of Bairro Alto Hotel

Lisboa Plaza €€€
Historic   **Map** 4 F1
Travessa do Salitre 7, 1269-066
Tel *213 218 218*
Ⓦ heritage.pt
Located in the heart of the city,
this family-run 1950s hotel has
traditional furnishings, a private
library and a charming terrace.

Mundial €€€
Character   **Map** 7 C2
Praça Martim Moniz 2, 1100-341
Tel *218 842 000*
Ⓦ hotel-mundial.pt
The rooms here are spacious
and some have balconies. There
are splendid city and castle views
plus an excellent bar and
restaurant facilities

Ritz Four Seasons €€€
Historic   **Map** 5 B5
Rua Rodrigo da Fonseca 88,
1099-039
Tel *213 811 400*
Ⓦ fourseasons.com/lisbon
Rooms here are furnished with
antiques. There is a renowned
spa with an indoor pool, and
a rooftop restaurant at this
prestigious hotel.

Sofitel Lisboa €€€
Luxury   **Map** 4 F1
Avenida da Liberdade 127,
1269-038
Tel *213 228 300*
Ⓦ sofitel-lisboa.com
The rooms have soft mattresses
and downy quilts at this luxury
hotel. The restaurant is excellent.

Tivoli Avenida
Liberdade Lisboa €€€
Luxury   **Map** 4 F1
Avenida da Liberdade 185,
1269-050
Tel *213 198 900*
Ⓦ tivolihotels.com
The Tivoli Avenida Liberdade
Lisboa offers luxurious rooms,
a rooftop Skybar, gourmet
restaurants and excellent service.

Bairro Alto and Estrela

Happy@Chiado €
Value   **Map** 4 F3
Rua do Loreto 13, 1200-241
Tel *916 086 246*
Ⓦ happyatchiado.com
A charming guesthouse with
a communal kitchen and clean,
shared bathrooms.

Pensão Londres €
Pensão / B&B   **Map** 4 F2
Rua Dom Pedro V 53, 1250-092
Tel *213 462 203*
Ⓦ pensaolondres.com.pt
Stone's throw away from the
Miradouro de São Pedro de
Alcântara, this clean guesthouse
has simple yet comfortable
rooms, and friendly service.
The fourth-floor rooms have
great panoramic views.

Lisbon Dreams
Guesthouse €€
Character   **Map** 5 B5
Rua Rodrigo da Fonseca 29,
1250-189
Tel *213 872 393*
Ⓦ lisbondreamsguesthouse.com
Bright and cheerful rooms, as
well as self-catering apartments,
are offered at this property.

As Janelas Verdes €€€
Historic   **Map** 4 D3
Rua das Janelas Verdes 47, 1200-690
Tel *213 968 143*
Ⓦ heritage.pt
A restored 18th-century mansion
with Neo-Classical decor and a
romantic, luxurious ambience.
A small courtyard garden and a
top-floor library, overlooking the
Tagus, add to the hotel's charm.

Bairro Alto Hotel €€€
Boutique   **Map** 7 A4
Praça Luis de Camões 2, 1200-243
Tel *213 408 288*
Ⓦ bairroaltohotel.com
This luxury boutique hotel has
a massage room, a gourmet
restaurant and a rooftop bar.

Hotel do Chiado €€€
Boutique   **Map** 7 B4
Rua Nova do Almada 114,
1200-290
Tel *213 256 100*
Ⓦ hoteldochiado.pt
A prestigious boutique hotel
that combines Oriental and
Colonial influences. Modern yet
classic rooms and suites, along
with a rooftop restaurant and bar.

Olissippo Lapa Palace €€€
Historic   **Map** 3 C3
Rua do Pau da Bandeira 4,
1249-021
Tel *213 949 494*
Ⓦ olissippohotels.com
This gracious palace boasts
uniquely decorated rooms in
various styles, from 18th-century
Neo-Classical to Art Deco.

Further Afield

Residencial Roxi €
Pensão / B&B   **Map** 6 E5
Avenida Almirante Reis 31,
1150-009
Tel *218 126 341*
Ⓦ residencialroxi.com
Residencial Roxi features simple,
spacious and traditionally
furnished rooms. Friendly staff.

Real Parque €€
Value   **Map** 5 C3
Avenida Luís Bívar 67, 1069-146
Tel *213 199 000*
Ⓦ realhotelsgroup.com
The rooms here are elegant, with
classical design and decor. Some
have a terrace.

Senhora do Monte €€
Pensão / B&B   **Map** 7 D1
Calçada do Monte 39, 1170-250
Tel *218 866 002*
Ⓦ senhoramonte.blogspot.pt
On a hilltop, this hotel has rooms
with stylish decorative touches and
balconies overlooking the river.

Tivoli Oriente €€
Character   **Map** 5 C3
Avenida Dom João II, 1990-083
Tel *218 915 100*
Ⓦ tivolihotels.com
This hotel offers spacious rooms
with stylish modern decor, an
indoor pool and river views.

Sheraton Lisboa
Hotel & Spa €€€
Luxury   **Map** 5 C3
Rua Latino Coelho 1, 1069-025
Tel *213 120 000*
Ⓦ sheraton.com/lisboa
In addition to chic rooms, the
Sheraton has a great spa and
stylish bars. The award-winning
restaurant offers fine dining and
a panoramic vista.

For more information on types of hotels *see pages 380–83*

The Lisbon Coast

ALCÁCER DO SAL: Pousada
Dom Afonso II
Historic   €€
                     Map C6
Castelo de Alcácer do Sal, 7580-197
Tel 265 613 070
[W] pousadas.pt
Set within a converted castle with
whitewashed walls and floor-to-
ceiling windows, this *pousada*
offers views over the River Sado.

DK Choice

CASCAIS: Casa da Pérgola   €€
Historic   **Map** B5
Avenida Valbom 13, 2750-508
Tel 214 840 040
[W] pergolahouse.pt
Housed in a beautiful 19th-
century Mediterranean-style
mansion with marble floors,
stucco ceilings and ornate
furnishings, this hotel is
decorated with original hand-
painted tiles. The gorgeous
landscaped gardens are filled
with colourful flowers. Dinner
is available on request.

CASCAIS: Farol Hotel   €€€
Luxury   **Map** B5
Avenida Rei Humberto II de Itália 7,
2750-800
Tel 214 823 490
[W] farol.com.pt
This fashionable, chic 19th-
century mansion was given
a 21st-century makeover by
ten international designers.

CASCAIS: Miragem   €€€
Luxury   **Map** B5
Avenida Marginal 8554, 2754-536
Tel 210 060 600
[W] cascaismirage.com
Opulent, stylish hotel overlooking
the bay, with a fantastic gourmet
restaurant and an infinity pool.

COSTA DA CAPARICA:
Residencial Mar e Sol   €€
Pensão / B&B   **Map** B5
Rua dos Pescadores, 42, 2825-325
Tel 212 900 017
[W] residencialmaresol.com
B&B situated near a beach,
offering simple rooms and a
cheerful lounge. Great breakfast.

ERICEIRA: Vila Galé Ericeira   €€
Character   **Map** B5
Largo dos Navegantes, 2655-320
Tel 261 869 900
[W] vilagale.pt
Set on a headland, this lovely
hotel has on-site facilities such
as a health club with a Jacuzzi
sauna and Turkish bath, as well as
a children's club and playground.

ESTORIL: Hotel Alvorada   €€
Value   **Map** B5
Rua de Lisboa 3, 2765-240
Tel 214 649 860
[W] hotelalvorada.com
The large, comfortable rooms
here have sea views; some have
balconies. Popular for conferences.

ESTORIL: Hotel Inglaterra   €€€
Historic   **Map** B5
Rua do Porto 1, 2765-271
Tel 214 684 461
[W] hotelinglaterra.com.pt
Old meets new in this charming
modernized former palace. It has
a pool and massage facilities.

ESTORIL: Hotel Palácio   €€€
Historic   **Map** B5
Rua Particular, 2769-504
Tel 214 648 000
[W] palacioestorilhotel.com
Popular with celebrities, this hotel
has classically styled, elegant
rooms and a gourmet restaurant.

GUINCHO: Senhora da Guia   €€
Character   **Map** B5
Estrada do Guincho, 2750-642
Tel 214 869 239
[W] senhoradaguia.com
Stylish boutique hotel set in
beautiful grounds next to a golf
course. Luxury health club on site.

GUINCHO: Fortaleza
do Guincho   €€€
Historic   **Map** B5
Estrada do Guincho, 2750-642
Tel 214 870 491
[W] guinchotel.pt
A renovated 17th-century fortress
with medieval decor and a
Michelin-starred restaurant with
jaw-dropping Atlantic Ocean views.

PALMELA: Pousada
Castelo Palmela   €€
Historic   **Map** C5
Castelo de Palmela, 2950-317
Tel 212 351 226
[W] pousadas.pt
Surrounded by vineyards and set
in a former convent attached to a

12th-century castle, this luxury
hotel affords fine views of the Sado
estuary and Arrábida mountains.

QUELUZ: Pousada
Palácio de Queluz   €€
Historic   **Map** B5
Largo do Palácio Nacional, 2745-191
Tel 214 356 158
[W] pousadas.pt
This hotel in a renovated 18th-
century clock tower retains many
original stone features.

SESIMBRA: Sana Sesimbra   €€
Character   **Map** C5
Avenida 25 de Abril, 11, 2970-634
Tel 212 289 000
[W] sesimbra.sanahotels.com
Chic rooms have beach and
castle views. There is a sky
lounge with a heated indoor
pool, and an on-site fish and
seafood restaurant .

SETÚBAL: Quinta dos
Moinhos de São Filipe   €€
Character   **Map** C5
Rua de São Filipe, 2900-670
Tel 265 228 278
[W] moinhossaofilipe.com
Located on the slopes of the
Serra da Arrábida, this estate has
lodgings in both the main building
and a restored windmill.

SINTRA: Espaço Edla   €€
Pensão / B&B   **Map** B5
Rua Doutor Alfredo da Costa 52,
2710-523
Tel 925 970 131
[W] espacoedla.pt
Pensão with stylish modern
decor. A gourmet bakery and
teahouse is on site.

SINTRA: Lawrence's Hotel   €€€
Historic   **Map** B5
Rua Consigliéri Pedroso 38–40,
2710-550
Tel 219 105 500
[W] lawrenceshotel.com
The rooms at this renovated manor
with antique furniture are named
after celebrated authors and artists.

The gourmet Grill Four Seasons restaurant in the Hotel Palácio, Estoril

Sun loungers in the pretty garden at the Hotel Lusitano, Golegã

SINTRA: Tivoli Palácio de Seteais
Historic   €€€
                  Map B5
Rua Barbosa du Bocage 8, 2710-517
Tel *219 233 200*
🅆 tivolihotels.com
This opulent, romantic hotel has magnificent 18th-century architecture and furnishings. There is a stylish restaurant, a bar, and a wellness centre and spa within the premises.

Estremadura and Ribatejo

BALEAL: Casa das Marés 2
Pensão / B&B   €€
                      Map B4
Rua Raúl Brandão, Praia de Baleal, Peniche, 2520-009
Tel *262 769 255*
🅆 casadasmares2.com
Set on a spit of land connected to the mainland at specific times of the day, this family-run B&B offers stunning views and cozy interiors.

BARRAGEM DO CASTELO DE BODE: Estalagem Lago Azul
Rural   €€
               Map C4
Ferreira do Zêzere, 2240-132
Tel *249 361 445*
🅆 estalagemlagoazul.com
In a stunning lakefront setting, this hotel has comfortable rooms, some with balconies. The in-house restaurant serves traditional Portuguese cuisine.

CALDAS DA RAINHA: Sana Silver Coast Hotel
Character   €€
                   Map B4
Avenida Dom Manuel Figueira Freire da Câmara, 2500-184
Tel *262 000 600*
🅆 silvercoast.sanahotels.com
A Neo-Classical building with a stylish modern interior. Excellent bar, restaurant and café on site.

CONSTÂNCIA: Quinta de Santa Bárbara
Historic   €€
                  Map C4
Constância, 2250-092
Tel *249 739 214*
🅆 quinta-santabarbara.com
This converted manor house has warm and spacious rustic rooms. It offers beautiful gardens, a rural landscape and a swimming pool with a panoramic setting.

FÁTIMA: Dom Gonçalo Hotel €€
Value   Map C4
Rua Jacinto Marto 100, 2495-450
Tel *249 539 330*
🅆 hoteldg.com
A four-star boutique hotel with modern rooms, set in pretty, manicured gardens. The hotel provides free passes to a wellness and spa centre.

FÁTIMA: Steyler Fátima Hotel €€
Value   Map C4
Praça Luís Kondor 33, 2495-409
Tel *249 533 043*
🅆 steylerfatimahotel.com
Ideal for families, this hotel is close to the shrine, making it popular with pilgrims. It has bright rooms, a children's club, and a restaurant.

GOLEGÃ: Hotel Lusitano €€
Character   Map C4
Rua Gil Vicente 4, 2150-193
Tel *249 979 170*
🅆 hotellusitano.com
The stylish rooms here feature canopied beds. A historic façade with modern interiors, and a fantastic spa.

LEIRIA: Eurosol Residence €€
Self-catering   Map C4
Rua Comissão da Iniciativa 13, 2410-098
Tel *244 860 460*
🅆 eurosol.pt
A complex of apartments and studios, with a sunny terrace, outdoor pool and health club.

NAZARÉ: Mar Bravo €€
Character   Map C4
Praça Sousa Oliveira 71, 2450-159
Tel *262 569 160*
🅆 marbravo.com
Rooms at this small hotel are well appointed and have balconies with town or sea views. It has a good seafood restaurant.

DK Choice

ÓBIDOS: Casa d'Óbidos €€
Historic   Map B4
Quinta de São José, 2510-135
Tel *262 950 924*
🅆 casadobidos.com
This 19th-century manor house features a range of rooms, apartments and cottages with traditional country-style decor. Guests can mingle while enjoying meals around a communal dining table. Explore the lovely garden with fruit trees and hammocks, snuggle by the fireplace or relax on the terrace. Gracious Portuguese host.

ÓBIDOS: Pousada Castelo €€€
Historic   Map B4
Paço Real, 2510-999
Tel *262 955 080*
🅆 pousadas.pt
The rooms in this converted 15th-century castle presiding over the walled city feature four-poster beds and chandeliers.

ÓBIDOS: Praia D'El Rey Marriott
Luxury   €€€
                Map B4
Avenida Dona Inês de Castro 1, 2510-451
Tel *262 905 100*
🅆 praia-del-rey.com
This five-star luxury resort boasts an 18-hole golf course and an acclaimed spa. Rooms are spacious and service is excellent.

OURÉM: Pousada Ourém €€
Historic   Map C4
Largo João Manso, Castelos, 2490-491
Tel *249 540 930*
🅆 pousadas.pt
Consisting of a cluster of restored medieval houses, this family-friendly *pousada* has a pool, sun terrace and all modern comforts.

PENICHE: Casa do Castelo €€
Historic   Map B4
Estrada Nacional 114, Number 16, Atouguia da Baleia, 2525-023
Tel *262 750 647*
🅆 casacastelo.com
This 17th-century manor house has traditional furnishings. a pretty garden and a pool.

Comfortable bed in an apartment at Vintage Lofts, Coimbra

TOMAR: Hotel dos Templários
Value   Map C4   €€
Largo Cândido dos Reis 1, 2304-909
Tel *249 310 100*
🅦 hoteldostemplarios.com
Enjoy four-star comfort and sports facilities within a lush garden setting with river views.

VILA FRANCA DE XIRA: Lezíria Parque
Value   Map C5   €€
Avenida Barranco de Cegos 22, 2600-246
Tel *263 276 670*
🅦 leziriaparquehotel.pai.pt
A functional hotel with 103 tastefully decorated rooms and views over the River Tagus. It has a Portuguese restaurant with outdoor seating as well as a bar.

The Beiras

ALMEIDA: Hotel Fortaleza de Almeida
Character   Map E2   €€
Rua da Muralha, 6350-112
Tel *271 574 283*
🅦 hotelfortalezadealmeida.com
Some of the spacious rooms here have four-poster beds. Guests can unwind in the games room.

AVEIRO: Pousada Ria
Character   Map C3   €€
Bico do Muranzel, Torreira, 3870-301
Tel *234 860 180*
🅦 pousadas.pt
Built on pillars above the water, this *pousada* on the river bank offers bright and comfortable rooms, a tennis court and a pool.

AVEIRO: Veneza Hotel
Character   Map C3   €€
Rua Luís Gomes de Carvalho 23, 3800-211
Tel *234 404 400*
🅦 venezahotel.pt
Stylish rooms and a charming garden with a terrace feature at this hotel in a 1930s house.

BELMONTE: Pousada Convento Belmonte
Historic   Map D3   €€
Serra da Esperança Apartado 76, 6250-073
Tel *275 910 300*
🅦 pousadas.pt
A former convent with fine views of Serra da Estrela, this hotel offers stylish rooms, modern facilities and an old chapel converted into a bar.

BUÇACO: Palace Hotel do Bussaco
Historic   Map C3   €€
Mata do Bussaco, 3050-261
Tel *231 937 970*
🅦 almeidahotels.pt
This 19th-century Manueline-style fairy-tale palace in a forest has period furniture and *azulejos*.

CASTELO BRANCO: Tryp Colina do Castelo Hotel
Value   Map D4   €€
Rua da Piscina s/n, 6000-776
Tel *272 349 280*
🅦 trypcolinacastelo.com
The large balconied rooms offer city views. There is a fitness centre, an indoor pool and a Turkish bath.

CELORICO DA BEIRA: Hotel Mira Serra
Rural   Map D3   €
Rua Calouste Gulbenkian 12, 6360-294
Tel *271 742 604*
🅦 hmiraserra.com.pt
A warm, family-run hotel with a rustic, regional restaurant, the Hotel Mira Serra functions as a good base to explore the Serra da Estrela.

COIMBRA: Casa Pombal
Pensão / B&B   Map C3   €€
Rua das Flores 18, 3000-442
Tel *239 835 175*
🅦 casapombal.com
This Dutch-run guesthouse, located next door to the University of Coimbra, has cosy rooms and a pretty terrace.

COIMBRA: Vintage Lofts
Self-catering   Map C3   €€
Rua Simão de Évora 11, 3000-386
Tel *964 326 556*
🅦 coimbravintagelofts.com
Studios and apartments are to be found in this renovated 18th-century building. A house-keeping service is available.

COIMBRA: Quinta das Lágrimas
Historic   Map C3   €€€
Rua António Augusto Gonçalves, 3041-901
Tel *239 802 380*
🅦 quintadaslagrimas.pt
Choose from three options at this romantic luxury hotel: palace-, garden- or spa-themed rooms.

CONDEIXA-A-NOVA: Pousada Condeixa Coimbra
Historic   Map C3   €€
Rua Francisco Lemos, 3150-142
Tel *239 944 025*
🅦 pousadas.pt
A stately 16th-century palace offering all modern comforts, a garden pool and tennis court.

CURIA: Curia Palace Hotel
Historic   Map C3   €€
Tamengos, 3780-541
Tel *231 510 300*
🅦 almeidahotels.pt
An elegant and glamorous Art Nouveau palace with an Art Deco pool and a golf course.

FIGUEIRA DA FOZ: Hotel Costa de Prata
Value   Map C3   €€
Largo Coronel Galhardo 1, 3080-150
Tel *233 426 620*
🅦 costadeprata.com
In the centre of town, and a short stroll away from Figueira's beach, this brightly decorated, modern hotel affords amazing views. Guests have access to a gym, Jacuzzi, and a number of spa treatments.

GUARDA: Hotel Lusitânia
Character   Map D3   €€€
Urbanização Quinta das Covas Lote 34, 6300-389
Tel *271 238 285*
🅦 hotellusitaniaparque.com
Rooms at Hotel Lusitânia have private balconies. There are indoor and outdoor pools and a health centre.

LUSO: Grande Hotel de Luso
Character   Map C3   €€
Rua Dr Cid de Oliveira 86, 3050-210
Tel *231 937 937*
🅦 hoteluso.com
This large, elegant hillside hotel is set in beautiful grounds. It is family-friendly, with a kids' club.

DK Choice

MANTEIGAS: Casa das Penhas Douradas
Character   €€   **Map** D3
Penhas Douradas, 6260-200
Tel *275 981 045*
🅦 casadaspenhasdouradas.pt
An environmentally friendly hotel built of cork and wood, with spectacular mountain views. There is complimentary tea, coffee and cake, as well as free bike and kayak hire. The spa treatments use local herbs. Service is impeccable.

PENALVA DO CASTELO: Casa da Insua
Historic   €€€   **Map** D3
Penalva do Castelo, 3550-126
Tel *232 640 110*
🅦 casadainsua.pt
Five-star hotel in an 18th-century palace featuring smart rooms and apartments and a lovely garden.

PENHAS DOURADAS: Pousada Serra da Estrela
Rural   €€   **Map** D3
Estrada Nacional 339, 6200-324
Tel *210 407 660*
🅦 pousadas.pt
Mountain-top hotel with on-site facilities such as a playground and a wellness centre with spa.

VISEU: Casa da Sé
Historic   €€   **Map** D3
Rua Augusta Cruz 12, 3500-088
Tel *232 468 032*
🅦 casadase.net
A boutique hotel with views of the cathedral, housed in a restored 18th-century manor full of antiques.

VISEU: Hotel Montebelo
Luxury   €€   **Map** D3
Urbanização Quinta do Bosque, 3510-020
Tel *232 420 000*
🅦 montebeloviseu.pt
Spacious rooms, richly-furnished interior along with a spa and pool feature at this business hotel.

Douro and Trás-os-Montes

AMARANTE: Casa da Calçada
Historic   €€€   **Map** D2
Largo do Paço, 6, 4600-017
Tel *255 410 830*
🅦 casadacalcada.com
Enjoy five-star luxury in this former 16th-century palace. The hotel has its own vineyard as well as a Michelin-starred restaurant. Stylish rooms, two pools and a spa.

BRAGANÇA: Pousada Bragança
Historic   €€   **Map** E1
Estrada do Turismo, 5300-271
Tel *273 331 493*
🅦 pousadas.pt
The interiors of this *pousada* feature stone walls, abstract *azulejo* tiles and wooden furniture.

CHAVES: Hotel Kátia
Modern   €   **Map** D1
Rua do Sol 28, 5400-517
Tel *276 324 446*
A friendly hotel near the town's famous thermal spa, with pleasant rooms and a good breakfast.

CHAVES: Aquae Flaviae
Value   €€   **Map** D1
Praça do Brasil, 5400-123
Tel *276 309 000*
🅦 hoteispremium.com
Comfortable rooms, a pool, a games room and a kids' play area are some of the highlights here.

ESPINHO: Praia Golfe
Value   €€   **Map** C2
Rua 6, 4500-357
Tel *227 331 000*
🅦 praiagolfe.com
This beach hotel with ocean views has 133 large rooms, and features an indoor pool, Turkish bath, and spa.

LAMEGO: Delfim Douro
Rural   €€€   **Map** D2
Quinta do Loureiro, 5100-758
Tel *254 960 000*
🅦 delfimdourohotel.com
The large rooms at this hotel have comfortable seating. A rooftop terrace offers panoramic views.

MESÃO FRIO: Casa de Canilhas
Rural   €€   **Map** D2
Rua do Ervedal 263, 5040-330
Tel *254 891 181*
🅦 canilhas.com
Set in picturesque gardens with breathtaking river and valley views, the rooms have rustic furnishings.

PESO DA RÉGUA: Hotel Régua Douro
Value   €€   **Map** D2
Largo da Estação da CP, 5050-237
Tel *254 320 700*
🅦 hotelreguadouro.pt
This smart and functional Peso da Régua hotel is simply and tastefully furnished, and is particularly popular with business travellers.

PINHÃO: Casa do Visconde de Chanceleiros
Historic   €€   **Map** D2
Largo da Fonte, 5085-201
Tel *254 730 190*
🅦 chanceleiros.com
This imaginatively furnished 18th-century manor house has rustic decor and a lovely garden.

PINHÃO: Quinta de la Rosa
Rural   €€   **Map** D2
Pinhão, 5085-215
Tel *254 732 254*
🅦 quintadelarosa.com
Built on the side of a steep hill, a choice of rooms and cottages is offered at this family-owned, friendly property in a wine estate. Affords stunning views and wine tours.

PORTO: Boa-Vista
Value   €€   **Map** C2
Esplanada do Castelo 58, 4150-196
Tel *225 320 020*
🅦 hotelboavista.com
A comfortable 150-year-old hotel with an attractive terrace pool and panoramic sea views.

PORTO: Gallery Hostel
Character   €€   **Map** C2
Rua Miguel Bombarda 222, 4050-377
Tel *224 964 313*
🅦 gallery-hostel.com
Luxury hostel with some private rooms and an art gallery. Hosts regular concerts and cultural events.

Room service at Praia Golfe, Espinho

For more information on types of hotels *see page 380–83*

PORTO:
Grande Hotel de Paris €€
Historic Map C2
Rua da Fábrica 27–29, 4050-247
Tel *222 073 140*
W hotelparis.pt
Antique furnishings and balconies
feature at this Art Deco-style
hotel with a gorgeous garden.

PORTO: Hotel da Bolsa €€
Character Map C2
Rua Ferreira Borges 101, 4050-253
Tel *222 026 768*
W hoteldabolsa.com
The grand façade of this hotel
hides simple, soundproof rooms
with elegant furnishings.

PORTO: São José €€
Pensão / B&B Map C2
Rua da Alegria 172, 4000-034
Tel *222 080 261*
W saojosehotelporto.com
Traditionally furnished *pensão*
with cosy rooms, helpful staff
and a pleasant atmosphere.

PORTO: Sheraton Porto
Hotel & Spa €€
Luxury Map C2
Rua Tenente Valadim 146, 4100-476
Tel *220 404 000*
W sheratonporto.com
Elegant hotel with steel, wood
and glass design. There is also an
excellent spa. Great cocktails.

PORTO: Infante de Sagres €€€
Historic Map C2
Praça D Filipa de Lencastre 62, 4050-259
Tel *223 398 500*
W hotelinfantesagres.pt
Contemporary decor is combined
with antiques at this boutique
hotel with a Neo-Baroque vibe.

PORTO: Pestana
Vintage Porto €€€
Boutique Map C2
Praça da Ribeira 1, 4050-513
Tel *223 402 300*
W pestanaporto.com
Restored riverfront hotel with
charming modern decor and
engaging views.

DK Choice

PORTO: The Yeatman €€€
Luxury Map C2
Rua do Choupelo, 4400-088
Tel *220 133 100*
W the-yeatman-hotel.com
This award-winning luxury hotel
boasts stylish modern decor and
cutting-edge design features,
such as a decanter-shaped pool,
a world-class spa and an indoor
pool with stunning views over
the River Douro. Attentive service
and exquisite gourmet dining.

Outdoor pool at Casa do Campo de
Molares, Celorico de Basto

VIDAGO:
Vidago Palace €€€
Historic Map D1
Parque de Vidago, 5425-307
Tel *276 990 920*
W vidagopalace.com
Magnificent spa hotel in Vidago
has a grand Neo-Romantic
façade and handsome interiors.
There is also a championship
golf course.

VILA REAL:
Casa Agrícola da Levada €€
Rural Map D2
Timpeira, 5000-419
Tel *259 322 190*
W casadalevada.com
This charming, family-run,
eco-friendly hotel is based in
an Art Deco house with elegant
rooms. There is also a number
of self-catering cottages
and studios.

Minho

BARCELOS: Quinta de
Santa Comba €€
Historic Map C1
Lugar de Crujães, 4755-536
Tel *253 832 101*
W stacomba.com
This handsome 18th-century
country manor house has simply
furnished, elegant rooms full
of rustic charm.

BOM JESUS DO MONTE:
Hotel do Elevador €€
Historic Map C1
Bom Jesus do Monte, 4715-056
Tel *253 603 400*
W hoteisbomjesus.pt
Set in a park, the luxurious, richly
appointed Hotel do Elevador has
comfortable rooms and amazing
park views, as well as a good
Portuguese restaurant.

BRAGA: Dona Sofia €€
Value Map C1
Largo São João do Souto 131, 4700-326
Tel *253 263 160*
W hoteldonasofia.com
The soundproof, simply furnished
rooms here are decorated in
neutral tones. Free Wi-Fi.

BRAGA: Hotel Meliá Braga €€
Modern Map C1
*Avenida General Carrilho da Silva
Pinto, 4715-380*
Tel *253 144 000*
W melia.com
A chic luxury hotel with bright
and spacious rooms, indoor and
outdoor pools and a superb spa.
Apart from single rooms, the hotel
also offers junior and grand suites.

CELORICO DE BASTO: Casa do
Campo de Molares €€
Historic Map D2
Molares, 4890-414
Tel *255 361 231/967 079 075*
W casadocampo.pt
This 18th-century manor house
has a prize-winning garden, an
outdoor pool and a sunny terrace.

GUIMARÃES: Hotel Mestre
de Avis €
Character Map C2
Rua Dom João I 40, 4810-422
Tel *253 422 770*
W hotelmestredeavis.pt
The rooms in this renovated
town house have stylish decor
and ensuite bathrooms.

GUIMARÃES: Casa de Sezim €€
Historic Map C2
*Rua de Sezim s/n, São Tiago de
Candoso, 4835-249*
Tel *253 523 000*
W sezim.pt
A family estate since the 14th
century, this hotel boasts antiques
and hand-painted wallpaper.
There is a tennis court and pool.

GUIMARÃES: Pousada do
Mosteiro €€€
Historic Map C2
*Largo Domingos Leite de Castro,
Ludar da Costa, 4810-011*
Tel *253 511 249*
W pousadas.pt
This *pousada* is inside a 12-century
monastery; rooms are in the
cloisters. It has 18th-century
azulejos and magnificent gardens.

MELGAÇO: Quinta da Calçada €€
Historic Map C1
São Julião, 4960-614
Tel *919 861 459*
W quintadacalcada.com
This 17th-century farmhouse
has cleverly restored rooms
and stunning views. The outdoor
pool is in a pretty garden.

PONTE DE LIMA: Paço de Calheiros €€
Historic Map C1
Calheiros, 4990-575
Tel *258 947 164*
🌐 pacodecalheiros.com
The Count of Calheiros welcomes guests to his 18th-century family palace. Accommodation includes rooms and apartments.

VALENÇA DO MINHO: Pousada de São Teotónio €€
Historic Map C1
Baluarte do Socorro, 4930-619
Tel *251 800 260*
🌐 pousadas.pt
A small *pousada* housed within a fort. Traditionally furnished rooms offer beds with carved headboards.

VIANA DO CASTELO: Hotel Calatrava €€
Pensão / B&B Map C1
Rua Manuel Fiúza Júnior 157, 4900-458
Tel *258 828 911*
Snug and friendly *pensão* with comfortably furnished, spotless rooms, some with balconies.

DK Choice

VIANA DO CASTELO: Pousada Viana do Castelo €€
Historic Map C1
Monte de Santa Luzia, 4901-909
Tel *258 800 370*
🌐 pousadas.pt
From its hilltop position on Mount Santa Luzia, this *pousada* offers incredible views over the Lima estuary, the ocean and the surrounding countryside. Rooms are stylish, well appointed and luxurious, with large windows; some have a balcony. Amenities include a restaurant, bar, tennis court and pool. Excellent service.

VILA DO CONDE: Santana Hotel €€
Value Map C2
Monte Santana, Azurara, 4480-188
Tel *252 640 460*
🌐 santanahotel.net
This simple hotel overlooking the River Ave offers rooms with balconies, as well as a rooftop terrace, hot tub and spa.

Alentejo

BEJA: Bejense €
Rural Map D6
Rua Capitão João Francisco de Sousa 57, 7800-451
Tel *284 311 570*
🌐 hotelbejense.com
This elegantly decorated hotel has a cheerful floral theme, *azulejo* tiles and wall paintings.

BEJA: Pousada Convento Beja €€
Historic Map D6
Largo Dom Nuno Álvares Pereira, 7801-901
Tel *284 313 580*
🌐 pousadas.pt
In a former convent, this *pousada* has bedrooms with arched ceilings. There is an outdoor pool.

CRATO: Pousada Mosteiro Crato €€
Historic Map D4
Mosteiro da Flor da Rosa, 7430-999
Tel *245 997 210*
🌐 pousadas.pt
This impressively renovated 14th-century monastery offers luxury suites with rosewood furniture.

ELVAS: Hotel São João de Deus €€
Historic Map D5
Rua de João de Quintal 1, 7350-000
Tel *268 639 220*
🌐 hotelsaojoaodeus.com
Many original features and furnishings have been retained at this converted convent.

ELVAS: Quinta de Santo António €€
Rural Map D5
Estrada de Barbacena, 7350-903
Tel *268 636 460*
🌐 qsahotel.com
A restored country manor house with a rustic atmosphere and snug guest rooms.

ESTREMOZ: Pousada Castelo Estremoz €€
Historic Map D5
Largo de Dom Diniz, 7100-509
Tel *268 332 075*
🌐 pousadas.pt
Housed in a beautiful 13th-century castle, rooms here have four-poster beds.

ÉVORA: Évora Inn-Chiado €
Character Map D5
Rua da República 11, 7000-656
Tel *266 744 500*
🌐 evorainn.com
Decorated in bright colours and an artistic design, this hotel has comfortable rooms.

DK Choice

ÉVORA: Pousada Convento Évora €€€
Historic Map D5
Largo Conde Vila Flor, 7000-804
Tel *266 730 070*
🌐 pousadas.pt
Set in a 15th-century monastery, this elegant *pousada* has decorative public spaces that contrast with the simple but attractive rooms, converted from the monks' cells. Sculpted Manueline stone windows and arches add to the romantic atmosphere.

MARVÃO: Dom Dinis €
Rural Map D4
Rua Dr Matos Magalhães 7, 7330-121
Tel *245 909 028*
🌐 ter-domdinis.com
Simple and elegant rooms are offered at this charming hotel with medieval-style decor.

MARVÃO: Pousada de Santa Maria de Marvão €€
Historic Map D4
Rua 24 de Janeiro 6–7, 7330-122
Tel *245 993 201*
🌐 pousadas.pt
A cosy town house with colourful rooms that offer panoramic views, and friendly, attentive staff.

REDONDO: Convento de São Paulo €€
Historic Map D5
Aldeia da Serra, 7170-120
Tel *266 989 160*
🌐 hotelconventosaopaulo.com
A beautiful former monastery with *azulejo* panels and the option of overnighting in the monks' cells.

SERPA: Herdade da Retorta €€
Rural Map D6
Monte da Retorta, 7830-305
Tel *284 544 774*
🌐 herdade-da-retorta.pt
This beautifully restored country estate surrounded by olive groves offers simply furnished rooms.

Nineteenth-century furnishings in the Herdade da Retorta, Serpa

For more information on types of hotels *see page 380–83*

VILA VIÇOSA: Casa do Colegio Velho €€
Historic Map D5
Rua Dr Couto Jardim 34, 7160-263
Tel *268 889 430*
W casadocolegiovelho.com
All modern facilities are offered at this hotel in a restored 16th-century mansion, close to the duke's palace.

VILA VIÇOSA: Pousada Convento Vila Viçosa €€
Historic Map D5
Convento das Chagas, Terreiro do Paço, 7160-251
Tel *268 980 742*
W pousadas.pt
In a 17th-century royal convent, this hotel has pretty landscaped gardens and a spacious terrace.

Algarve

ALBUFEIRA: Alfagar €€€
Self-catering Map C7
Aldeamento Turístico, Santa Eulália, 8200-912
Tel *289 540 220*
W alfagar.com
Clifftop apartment complex with three pools, a tennis court and a kids' adventure playground.

ALBUFEIRA: Grande Real Santa Eulália Resort & Hotel Spa €€€
Value Map C7
Praia Santa Eulália, 8200-916
Tel *289 598 000*
W granderealsantaeulaliahotel.com
Modern, well-equipped five-star beach resort with a fantastic Thalasso spa and a stylish bar.

ALTE: Alte Hotel €€
Character Map C7
Estrada de Sta Margarida, 8100-012
Tel *289 478 523*
W altehotel.com
Budget hotel with simple, cosy rooms and a tennis court. Great vistas over the surrounding valley.

DK Choice

CABANAS: Forte de São João da Barra €€€
Historic Map D7
Rua da Fortaleza, 8800-595
Tel *960 375 419*
W fortesaojoaodabarra.com
Overlooking the Ria Formosa, this remarkable boutique B&B is set in a restored 17th-century fort. Enjoy breakfast on the ramparts with scenic views of the lagoon. Amenities include a garden swimming pool and a private water taxi that ferries guests to the outlying islands.

CARVOEIRO: Tivoli Carvoeiro Algarve Resort €€€
Luxury Map C7
Vale do Covo, 8401-843
Tel *282 351 100*
W minorhotels.com
Plush hotel in a gorgeous setting with well-appointed rooms as well as a bespoke spa facility.

ESTOI: Pousada Palácio Estoi €€€
Historic Map D7
Rua São José, 8005-465
Tel *289 990 150*
W pousadas.pt
The sumptuous rooms at this restored 19th-century palace have all modern facilities.

FARO: Hotel Eva €€
Value Map D7
Avenida da República 1, 8000-078
Tel *289 001 000*
W ap-hotelresorts.com
A hotel with well-equipped rooms, a rooftop bar and pool with views over the marina. Helpful staff.

LAGOS: Belavista da Luz €€€
Value Map C7
Praia da Luz, 8600-147
Tel *282 788 655*
W belavistadaluz.com
Ideal for families, with comfortable, well-appointed rooms, two pools and sweeping views of the bay.

LOULÉ: Loulé Jardim Hotel €€
Boutique Map D7
Lg Manuel de Arriaga 25, 8100-665
Tel *289 413 094*
W loulejardimhotel.com
Hotel with pleasant, simple rooms, a terrace and an outdoor pool, close to the historic town centre.

MONTE GORDO: Vasco da Gama €€€
Value Map D7
Rua Infante Dom Henrique, 8900-412
Tel *281 510 900*
W vascodagamahotel.com
Popular with families, this hotel has large rooms with balconies and two outdoor pools.

PORCHES: Vila Vita Parc €€€
Luxury Map C7
Alporchinhos, 8400-450
Tel *282 310 100*
W vilavitaparc.com
Exclusive clifftop spa resort featuring an 18-hole golf course and a Michelin-starred restaurant.

PORTIMÃO: Penina Hotel & Golf Resort €€€
Luxury Map C7
Penina, 8501-952
Tel *282 420 200*
W penina.com
A championship golf course makes this hotel a haven for golfers. Offers stylish rooms and a kids' club.

QUINTA DO LAGO: Hotel Quinta do Lago €€€
Rural Map D7
Quinta do Lago, 8135-024
Tel *289 350 350*
W hotelquintadolago.com
The spacious, elegant rooms at this hotel have views over the Ria Formosa estuary. Private beach.

SAGRES: Navigator €€
Self-catering Map C7
Rua Infante D Henrique, 8650-381
Tel *282 624 354*
W aparthotelnavigator.com
Simple one-bedroom apartments are to be found here. Room service and breakfast are available.

SAGRES: Pousada Sagres €€€
Character Map C7
Ponta da Atalaia, 8650-240
Tel *282 620 240*
W pousadas.pt
Lovely *pousada* overlooking the ocean, with stylish rooms, a terrace bar and a pool.

SILVES: Duas Quintas €€€
Rural Map C7
Santo Estevão, 8300-047
Tel *282 449 311*
W duasquintas.com
This renovated farmhouse retains

Aerial view of the Belavista da Luz against the backdrop of the Praia da Luz bay in Lagos

Alfresco dining on the terrace at Belmond Reid's Palace, Funchal

many original features. It also has a studio apartment.

TAVIRA: Guesthouse Imperial €€
B&B   Map D7
Rua Doutor José Pires Padinha 24,
8800-354
Tel 281 098 005
The rooms at this B&B are elegant
and colourful. There are great river
views from the breakfast room.

TAVIRA:
Quinta do Caracol   €€
Self-catering   Map D7
Rua São Pedro 11, 8800-405
Tel 281 322 475
Ⓦ quintadocaracol.com
These converted farmhouses in
pretty gardens have rooms with
kitchenettes and a sitting area.

VILA REAL DE SANTO ANTÓNIO:
Hotel Apolo   €€
Value   Map D7
Avenida dos Bombeiros Portugueses,
8900-209
Tel 281 510 700
Ⓦ apolo-hotel.com
Located in the heart of the town,
this hotel serves a generous buffet
breakfast. It also has a restaurant.

VILAMOURA: The Lake Spa €€€
Luxury   Map D7
Praia da Falésia, 8126-910
Tel 289 320 700
Ⓦ thelakeresort.com
Stay in style at this luxury resort
with exquisite Mediterranean-
or Oriental-themed rooms.

Madeira

CANIÇO: Quinta Splendida €€€
Self-catering
Estrada Ponte da Oliveira 11, 9125-001
Tel 291 930 400
Ⓦ quintasplendida.com
Villa complex in beautiful
gardens. Accommodation ranges

from studio apartments to
plush suites.

FUNCHAL: Vila Teresinha   €
Pensão / B&B
Rua das Cruzes 21, 9000-025
Tel 291 741 723
Ⓦ vilateresinha.com
A town house with pleasant
rooms, some with great views.
Breakfast is served on the terrace.

FUNCHAL: Hotel Quinta da
Penha de França   €€
Character
Rua Imperatriz Dª Amélia 85, 9000-014
Tel 291 229 261
Ⓦ penafranca.com
Choose between the clifftop
mansion set in tropical gardens or
the modern beachfront hotel,
connected by a footbridge.

FUNCHAL: Quinta Perestrello €€
Historic
Rua Dr Pita 3, 9000-089
Tel 291 706 700
Ⓦ quintaperestrellomadeira.com
Enjoy affordable luxury at this
restored 19th-century mansion
filled with antique furniture.

DK Choice

FUNCHAL: Belmond
Reid's Palace   €€€
Historic
Estrada Monumental 139, 9000-098
Tel 291 717 171
Ⓦ belmond.com
Founded in 1891, Madeira's best-
known hotel boasts a clientele
of wealthy and famous patrons –
former guests Winston Churchill
and George Bernard Shaw have
suites named after them. The
hotel is furnished in the style of a
stately home, with chandeliers in
the Michelin-starred William
restaurant. Take a dip in the
palm-fringed pools or admire
the magnificent clifftop views.

PORTO MONIZ: Hotel Salgueiro €
B&B
Lugar do Tenente, 9270-095
Tel 291 850 080
Ⓦ hotelsalgueiro.com
This residencial offers simple but
comfortable rooms and views of
the town's natural rock pools.

PORTO SANTO: Hotel Torre
Praia   €€€
Value
Rua Goulart Medeiros, 9400-164
Tel 291 980 450
Ⓦ portosantohotels.com
Suites at this hotel have spacious
terraces with sunloungers, while
each room has a balcony and is
comfortably furnished.

The Azores

FAIAL: Quinta das Buganvílias €€
Rural
Castelo Branco, Horta, 9900-330
Tel 292 943 255
Ⓦ quintadasbuganvilias.com
This family-run estate offers
simple, traditional rooms and
apartments. An old mill house
lends authenticity.

FAIAL: Pousada
Forte da Horta   €€€
Historic
Rua Vasco da Gama, Horta, 9900-017
Tel 292 202 200
Ⓦ pousadas.pt
Inside a 16th-century fort, the
stylish rooms here offer views
over the marina and Pico Island.

PICO: Aldeia da Fonte   €€
Rural
Caminho de Baixo 2, Lajes do Pico,
Silveira, 9930-177
Tel 292 679 500
Ⓦ aldeiadafonte.com
This eco- and pet-friendly resort
has six rustic stone houses in lush
gardens. It also has a fitness centre.

PICO: Baía da Barca   €€
Self-catering
Lugar da Barca, 9950-303
Tel 292 628 750
Ⓦ baiadabarca.com
Modern aparthotel with spacious
and comfortable units featuring
all mod cons and fireplaces.

SÃO MIGUEL: Hotel do Colégio €€
Historic
Rua Carvalho Araújo 39,
Ponta Delgada, 9500-040
Tel 296 306 600
Ⓦ hoteldocolegio.com
A converted 19th-century manor
house with large rooms and
classic decor, a pool and sauna.

SÃO MIGUEL: Terra Nostra
Garden Hotel   €€€
Luxury
Rua Padre José Jacinto Botelho,
Furnas, 9675-061
Tel 296 549 090
Ⓦ bensaudehotels.com
Art Deco interiors and rooms in
neutral colours. The hotel has
lush gardens with peacocks, a
pool and wellness centre.

TERCEIRA: Beira Mar   €€
Character
Largo Miguel Corte Real,
Angra do Heroísmo, 9700-182
Tel 295 215 188
Ⓦ hotelbeiramar.com
Overlooking the harbour, this
hotel offers cosy rooms with
basic, simple decor. Attentive staff.

For more information on types of hotels see pages 380–83

WHERE TO EAT AND DRINK

Portugal offers a wealth of fresh fish and seafood to feast on – from clams, lobster and sardines to tuna, swordfish and *bacalhau* (salted cod), the national favourite. However, the Portuguese are also great meat eaters, and they are justifiably proud of such dishes as roast kid and suckling pig. The more popular tourist destinations – such as Lisbon,

Porto and the Algarve – have the entire gamut of eateries, including expensive international gourmet restaurants, but by and large, most eateries are reasonably priced and serve generous portions. This section introduces, and gives tips on, eating places, menus, drinks and ordering to help you make the most of eating out in Portugal.

Restaurant in the historic Pousada Castelo de Palmela *(see p402)*

Types of Restaurants

There is a wide range of options to choose from when eating out in Portugal. Among the most affordable is the local *tasca*, or taverna, often just a room with half-a-dozen tables presided over by a husband-and-wife team. A new wave of tavernas in major cities has turned them into fashionable venues. Restaurants range from small, cosy affairs to large dining rooms with varying degrees of sophistication and formality.

At a *marisqueira* the emphasis is on fresh fish and seafood. The *churrasqueira*, a popular concept imported from Brazil, specializes in charcoal-grilled foods, while a *cervejaria* (beer house) is the place to go for a beer and a snack; many also specialize in seafood or steaks. As a rule, the better hotels also have good eating places, and *pousadas (see pp384–5)* have high-quality restaurants featuring regional specialities.

Sign for Maria Rita's *(see p407)*

Timings

Lunch is usually served between noon and 3pm. During this time many restaurants, especially in the cities, get very crowded. Dinner is served from 7:30 to 10pm in most places, but it can be later in restaurants and *cervejarias* in major cities and resort areas.

Reservations

It is a good idea to book ahead for expensive restaurants and those in popular locations in high season. If you need special assistance, be sure to check on facilities and access in advance. These are generally lacking, but most places will try to be helpful.

The Menu

Some restaurants, especially those in tourist areas, offer an *ementa turística*, a cheap, daily-changing three-course menu served with a drink and coffee. This provides a full meal at a good price with no hidden costs. *Almoço* (lunch) is often a two-course fixed menu, consisting of a fish or meat main course, served with potatoes or rice, and either a starter or a pudding. To sample a local speciality, ask for the *prato do dia* – the dish of the day.

Jantar (dinner) may be two or more courses, perhaps followed by ice cream, fruit, a simple dessert or cheese. Casserole-style dishes, such as fish or meat stews or *carne de porco à alentejana* (pork with clams), are brought to the table in a pot for people to share, as are large fish, which are sold by weight. One serving can easily be shared by two people, and it is fine to ask for a *meia dose* (half-portion). Peculiar to Portugal is the plate of assorted appetizers – olives, cheese and sardine pâté – brought with bread at the start of a meal. These are not included in the menu price, and may add substantially to the bill if you don't send them back.

Tables in the beautiful gardens at Vila Joya, Praia da Galé *(see p412)*

The terrace with wonderful ocean views at Riso, Funchal *(see p414)*

Vegetarians

Vegetarians will not eat as well as fish lovers in Portugal, although local cheeses and breads are excellent. In Lisbon and along the Algarve, vegetarians will benefit from ethnic restaurants. Chefs will usually be happy to provide something meatless, though this will probably be a simple omelette or a salad.

Wine and Drinks

It would be a shame to visit Portugal without sampling its two most famous fortified wines: port *(see pp258–9)* and Madeira *(see p355)*. Irrespective of the location, a bottle or jug of house wine is a perfectly nice option to wash down a meal. Otherwise, choose one of Portugal's many native wines *(see pp32–3)* from the wine list. Sagres and Super Bock are good beers, and the bottled spring water is also recommended. This comes either *com gás* (sparkling) or *sem gás* (still).

Cafés and Cake Shops

Fundamental to Portuguese daily life, cafés vary from plain modern rooms to splendidly decorated, tiled and mirrored places. Many have tables outside. They usually offer a limited range of snacks, cakes and sandwiches. Do not miss the *pastelarias* (cake shops), famed for *pastéis de nata*. The sweet-toothed Portuguese adore cakes, and the selection is usually excellent.

Paying the Bill

It is common practice to add a 5–10 per cent tip to bills if you are satisfied with the service. Note that not all restaurants accept credit cards.

Children

The Portuguese are very fond of children, and most restaurants will serve half- or children's portions of dishes on the menu.

Smoking

Smoking is banned from all restaurants in Portugal including cafés, though on rare occasions a separate room is provided for smokers. Most bars have also imposed the ban. The law is sometimes flouted in rural locations. Look for a blue or red sign near the entrance; blue means that smoking is allowed.

Coffee

Coffee is widely drunk in Portugal and served in many forms. The most popular is a small cup of strong black coffee similar to an espresso. In Lisbon and the south this is called *uma bica*; elsewhere, ask for *um café. Uma meia de leite* is half coffee, half milk.

Recommended Restaurants

The restaurants recommended on pages 398–414 have been selected on the basis of their popularity, quality and value for money. For each area, a range of establishments catering to different tastes – from traditional, home-cooked recipes to Michelin-starred gourmet restaurants – has been included.

Portugal's rich culinary heritage is celebrated throughout the country by restaurants that uphold age-old cooking techniques to prepare food from recipes handed down from generation to generation. Categorized on menus as traditional Portuguese cuisine, this type of gastronomy is complemented by creative chefs who still insist on locally sourced ingredients, but cook using more stylized and contemporary methods to present modern Portuguese cuisine. In major cities and tourist destinations, a variety of other cuisines is also available, including vegetarian options, seafood and international food.

The restaurants that are highlighted as DK Choice have been chosen for one or more exceptional feature. This could be the impeccable service, memorable views, romantic atmosphere or celebrated chefs.

The elegant dining room at Estórias na Casa da Comida, Lisbon *(see p400)*

Where to Eat and Drink

Lisbon

Alfama

Social Mouraria €
International **Map** 7 C3
Beco do Rosendo 8, 1100-460
Tel 927 608 398
This lively restaurant and bar has
a typical back-street Alfama flavour
paired with al fresco dining. An
innovative menu features dishes
from all over the world based on
sustainable ingredients.

Tentações de Goa €
Goan **Map** 7 C3
Rua São Pedro Mártir 23, 1100-555
Tel 218 875 824 **Closed** *Sun;*
Mon lunch
A cheerful establishment with
brightly painted walls and
outstanding Goan cuisine. The
chef tailors the level of spiciness
to guests' tastes. Cash only.

Bica do Sapato €€
International **Map** 8 F3
Avenida Infante Dom Henrique,
Cais da Pedra, 1900-436
Tel 218 810 320 **Closed** *Sun dinner;*
Mon lunch
This trendy restaurant with
minimalist decor in a converted
riverfront warehouse offers a
mouthwatering range of meat
and vegetarian dishes, including
Portuguese and Asian fare.

Casanova €€
Italian **Map** 8 F3
Avenida Infante Dom Henrique
Armazem B, Cais da Pedra, 1900-264
Tel 218 877 532
This trendy riverside restaurant
specializes in pizzas. For dessert,
try the unusual but delicious
chocolate-spread pizza. No
reservations, so try to arrive early.

Via Graça, with panoramic views of Lisbon
from its hilltop location

Chapitô à Mesa €€
International **Map** 7 C3
Costa do Castelo 7, 1149-079
Tel 218 875 077
Choose from several options at
this restaurant in a performing
arts school: bar snacks or grilled
meats on the outdoor terrace or
a more sophisticated à la carte
menu inside the restaurant.

Santo António de
Alfama €€
Traditional Portuguese **Map** 8 E4
Beco de São Miguel 7, 1100-538
Tel 218 881 328
The creative and distinctly
original food at this romantic
restaurant is enduringly popular.
Black-and-white photographs of
film stars adorn the walls.

Casa do Leão €€€
Traditional Portuguese **Map** 8 D3
Castelo de São Jorge,
1100-129
Tel 218 875 962
Enjoy fine dining in a historic
building with stone walls and
azulejo tiles, with spectacular city
views. Smart, attentive waiters
advise guests on food-and-wine
pairings. Reservations in advance.

Faz Figura €€€
Modern Portuguese **Map** 8 F2
Rua do Paraíso 15B, 1100-395
Tel 218 868 981 **Closed** *Mon lunch*
This stylish restaurant draws the
crowds with both its location and
menu. The chef sprinkles an
international touch on traditional
ingredients. The covered terrace
looks out on the River Tagus.

Via Graça €€€
Traditional Portuguese **Map** 8 D1
Rua Damasceno Monteiro 9B,
1170-108
Tel 218 870 830 **Closed** *Sat*
& Sun lunch
Its hilltop position gives Via Graça
panoramic city views. Reserve a
window table and order hearty
Portuguese dishes such as
empada de caça (game pie).
Excellent wine list. Reserve ahead.

Baixa and Avenida

Os Tibetanos €
Vegetarian **Map** 4 F1
Rua do Salitre 117, 1250-198
Tel 213 142 038
With its bright, colourful decor
and leafy garden terrace, this
informal restaurant serves a
selection of hearty Tibetan and
international dishes, including
tofu with pesto. Cash only.

> **Price Guide**
> Prices are based on a three-course meal
> for one, with half a bottle of house wine
> inclusive of tax and service charges.
>
> € up to €20
> €€ €20–€40
> €€€ over €40

Casa do Alentejo €€
Traditional Portuguese **Map** 7 A2
Rua das Portas de Santo Antão 58,
1150-268
Tel 213 405 140
Dine on authentic, hearty
Alentejan fare in the grandeur of
the 19th-century ballroom or the
azulejo-lined dining room in this
wonderful Moorish building.

Chefe Cordeiro €€
Modern Portuguese **Map** 7 B5
Pátio da Galé, Terreiro do Paço,
1400-158
Tel 216 080 090
This stylish gourmet restaurant
with a high, vaulted ceiling and an
open kitchen is the creation of
celebrity chef José Cordeiro. In
addition to the fine dining menu,
traditional Portuguese tapas
(*petiscos*) are served all day.

Fábulas €€
Modern Portuguese **Map** 7 B5
Calçada Nova de São Francisco 14,
1200-300
Tel 216 018 472
Various seating areas to suit mood
and weather are to be found at this
restaurant. The menu features innovative Portuguese dishes with a
modern twist and a great wine list.

Marisqueira Santa Marta €€
Seafood **Map** 5 C5
Travessa do Enviado de Inglaterra 1D,
1150-139
Tel 213 525 638
The good-value fare, such as
seafood rice or stuffed crab,
keeps the local clientele coming

The dining room at Casa do Alentejo, its
walls lined with beautiful *azulejo* tiles

back to this typical, down-to-earth restaurant. Ideal for families. Reserve in advance.

Restaurante 33A €€
Traditional Portuguese Map 5 C5
Rua Alexandre Herculano 33A, 1250-008
Tel *213 546 079* **Closed** *Sat lunch; Sun*
A restaurant with an interior of dark wooden beams and a pretty, shaded garden. The waiters wear smart, formal uniforms, but the ambience is relaxed. There is an excellent wine list and desserts are divine.

Ribadouro €€
Cervejaria Map 4 F1
Rua do Salitre 2–12, 1250-200
Tel *213 549 411*
It is almost obligatory to try the fresh whole fish and seafood priced by the kilo here, although extremely good steaks and *bacalhau* dishes are served too.

Eleven €€€
International Map 5 B4
Rua Marquês de Fronteira, Jardim Amália Rodrigues, 1070-310
Tel *213 862 211* **Closed** *Sun*
At one of Lisbon's top gourmet restaurants, the elegant atmosphere and refined decor contribute to a unique fine-dining experience. There are tasting, à la carte and lobster-themed menus. Reserve ahead.

Gambrinus €€€
Seafood Map 7 B2
Rua das Portas de Santo Antão 23, 1150-264
Tel *213 421 466*
Wooden furniture, stained-glass panels and murals create a sophisticated atmosphere at this well-established favourite. The conch shell filled with seafood is a speciality.

Pabe €€€
International Map 5 C5
Rua Duque de Palmela 27A, 1250-097
Tel *213 537 484*
The mock-Tudor façade, beamed ceilings and wooden walls recreate a traditional English pub atmosphere. The fare includes roasted sea bass, breaded squid and charcoal-grilled baby goat.

Solar dos Presuntos €€€
Traditional Portuguese Map 7 A2
Rua das Portas de Santo Antão 150, 1150-269
Tel *213 424 253* **Closed** *Sun*
A great place to try *presunto* (cured ham), as well as a range of meat and fish dishes. Excellent wine list. Reserve in advance.

The sleek, minimalist interior and neutral colour scheme at Eleven

Bairro Alto and Estrela

Pátio do Bairro €
Modern Portuguese Map 4 F2
Rua da Atalaia 35–37, 1200-037
Tel *914 293 509* **Closed** *lunch*
This popular restaurant and bar specializes in home-made burgers, *petiscos* (Portuguese tapas), *sopa rica do mar* (seafood soup) and *bacalhau à brás* (salt cod with fried potato and onion).

Real Fábrica €
Cervejaria Map 4 E1
Rua da Escola Politécnica 275, 1250-101
Tel *213 852 090* **Closed** *Sun*
Seafood and steaks are served in this former silk factory. Try the *cataplana* (fish stew) along with a variety of well-prepared seafood dishes.

Bota Alta €€
Traditional Portuguese Map 7 A3
Travessa da Queimada 35–37, 1200-364
Tel *213 427 959* **Closed** *Sat lunch; Sun*
The attractive interior here is decorated with ceramics and paintings. Try the *costeletas fumadas à algarvia* (smoked ribs Algarve-style).

Café Buenos Aires €€
Steakhouse Map 7 A3
Calçada Escadinhas do Duque 31B, 1200-155
Tel *213 420 739*
Enjoy succulent and cooked-to-perfection Argentinian steaks in a cosy, unpretentious setting. As an accompaniment, try the flower salad. Reserve ahead. Cash only.

Casanostra €€
Italian Map 7 A3
Travessa do Poço da Cidade 60, 1200-334
Tel *213 425 931* **Closed** *Sat lunch*
This friendly restaurant with simple, bright decor is popular with locals and visitors alike. All of the delicious, home-made

pasta dishes are to be recommended. There is a good wine list too.

A Confraria €€
Modern Portuguese Map 4 D3
York House Hotel, Rua das Janelas Verdes 32, 1200-691
Tel *213 962 435* **Closed** *Mon & Tue lunch*
In a charming historic building, A Confraria offers an inventive menu that reflects the seasonal offerings. Excellent wine list.

Decadente €€
Modern Portuguese Map 7 A3
Rua de São Pedro de Alcântara 81, 1250-238
Tel *213 461 381*
Chic decor, a relaxed atmosphere and creative twists to traditional favourites make this a popular choice. Fabulous cocktails.

Picanha €€
Brazilian Map 4 D4
Rua das Janelas Verdes 96, 1200-692
Tel *213 975 401* **Closed** *Sun dinner; Mon*
This is the perfect place for a top-quality steak grilled on an open fire. Blue-and-white *azulejo* panels decorate the walls. Book ahead.

DK Choice

Taberna da Esperança €€
Modern Portuguese Map 4 E3
Rua Esperança 112, 1120-114
Tel *213 962 744* **Closed** *Mon, Tue–Fri lunch*
This warm and friendly taverna serves traditional Portuguese cuisine with a modern twist. Expect helpful explanations and advice regarding the inventive tapas menu. Eclectic furniture and fading posters create a relaxed, informal ambience. Perfect for all – solo travellers, couples and groups. Reservations highly recommended. Cash only.

Tasca da Esquina €€
Modern Portuguese Map 3 C2
Rua Domingos Sequeira 41C, 1350-119
Tel *210 993 939* **Closed** *Mon lunch;
Sun*
Enjoy a vibrant atmosphere in a
contemporary setting. Signature
dishes include tuna with sweet
potato and skate boiled in olive
oil. Portuguese-style tapas and
tasting menus are also available.

Trivial €€
Traditional Portuguese Map 4 F2
Rua da Palmeira 44A, 1200-314
Tel *213 473 552* **Closed** *lunch; Sun*
Trivial is popular with locals for
reliable, good-quality food served
in a laid-back, intimate setting.
Try the chicken with Elvas plums.

Würst €€
German/Austrian Map 4 E2
*Mercado de São Bento, Rua Nova da
Piedade 1200-297*
Tel *918 905 325* **Closed** *Mon & Tue*
Home-made Austrian-style sausages
are the staple item on the menu
at this organic-based eatery close
to the parliament building.
Vegetarians are also well catered for.

Bistro 100 Maneiras €€€
International Map 7 A3
Largo Trindade 9, 1200-466
Tel *210 990 475* **Closed** *lunch*
A trendy, glamorous bistro with
a creative menu that draws a
fashionable clientele. The upstairs
dining area is quite romantic.

La Brasserie de l'Entrecôte €€€
Steakhouse Map 7 A4
Rua do Alecrim 117, 1200-016
Tel *213 473 616*
This elegant restaurant with an
Art Deco interior offers only one
dish: perfectly tender *entrecôte*
steak with a special sauce made
with herbs and other ingredients.

Estórias na Casa da Comida €€€
Modern Portuguese Map 5 B5
Travessa das Amoreiras 1, 1250-025
Tel *213 860 889* **Closed** *Mon–Sat
lunch; Sun*
A carefully selected wine list
accompanies the mouthwatering
haute cuisine at this restaurant.
For a romantic meal in a
sophisticated setting, ask for a
table in or overlooking the garden.

Kais €€€
**Traditional Portuguese /
International Map** 4 D4
*Cais da Viscondessa, Rua da Cintura,
Santos, 1200-109*
Tel *213 932 930* **Closed** *Sun, Mon,
Tue–Sat lunch*
Housed in a riverside warehouse
and featuring industrial-chic
decor, Kais is two restaurants in

one. Enjoy typical Portuguese
dishes in the downstairs area
or select from the refined
international menu upstairs.

Pap'Açorda €€€
Traditional Portuguese Map 4 F3
Mercado da Ribeira, Av. 24 de Julho 49
Tel *213 464 811* **Closed** *Mon*
Popular for more than 30 years,
this elegant restaurant is named
after its signature dish, *açorda*
(bready stew). Book ahead.

Restaurante Lapa €€€
Portuguese / Italian Map 3 C3
*Olissipo Lapa Palace, Rua do Pau de
Bandeira 4, 1249-021*
Tel *213 949 494*
Housed in a 19th-century palace,
this refined restaurant serves
gourmet dishes such as *leitão de
Bairrada* (Bairrada-style suckling
pig). The wine list is exemplary.

Sea Me €€€
Seafood Map 4 F3
Rua do Loreto 21, 1200-049
Tel *213 461 564*
Specializing in Portuguese and
Japanese cuisines, Sea Me's chef
prepares fresh seafood dishes and
the best sushi in town. Book ahead.

Belém

5 Oceanos €€
Modern Portuguese Map 3 A5
*Doca de Santo Amaro, Armazém 12,
1350-353*
Tel *213 978 015*
This stylish restaurant by the river
focuses largely on fresh fish and
seafood. House favourites include
cataplana (seafood casserole)
and curried lobster with prawns.

Belém 2 a 8 €€
Traditional Portuguese Map 1 C4
Rua de Belém 2, 1300-085
Tel *213 639 055*
This brightly decorated restaurant
is next door to the Palácio de Belém
and is known for its, hearty fare.

Espaço Lisboa €€
Traditional Portuguese Map 3 A4
Rua da Cozinha Económica 16, 1300-149
Tel *213 610 210* **Closed** *lunch; Sun*
Known as "The Grill of Lisbon",
this grand restaurant specializes
in grilled and roasted meats.
It also serves fish dishes,
including an impressive
cataplana (seafood casserole).

Este Oeste €€
Italian/Japanese Map 1 B5
*Centro Cultural de Belém, Praça do
Império, 1449-003*
Tel *215 904 358* **Closed** *Mon*
Este (east) meets Oeste (west)
in the form of freshly prepared
sushi and wood-oven-baked
pizzas at this restaurant. The
river views are magnificent.

Nosolo Italia €€
Italian Map 1 B5
Avenida Brasília 202, 1400-038
Tel *213 015 969*
Excellent pizzas and ice creams,
are served at this glass-walled
restaurant with a terrace that
overhangs the River Tagus.
There is also a children's menu.

Vela Latina €€€
Modern Portuguese Map 1 B5
Doca do Bom Sucesso, 1400-038
Tel *213 017 118* **Closed** *Sun*
Set in lush gardens, this peaceful
and stylish restaurant has views
of the river and the marina.
Menu highlights include lobster-
filled crêpes and hake fillet
with rice.

Further Afield

António €
Traditional Portuguese Map 5 C3
Rua Tomás Ribeiro 63, 1050-226
Tel *213 538 780* **Closed** *Sun*
Popular with locals, this simple
restaurant serves good-value,
large portions of tasty
Portuguese dishes. The lunch
menu changes daily.

The fashionable Bistro 100 Maneiras, Lisbon

For key to prices *see page 398*

Elegant table settings at the Pousada Castelo, Alcácer do Sal

Cervejaria Portugália €€
Cervejaria **Map** 6 E4
Avenida Almirante Reis 117, 1115-014
Tel *213 140 002*
This flagship of a chain of brewery restaurants serves excellent steaks and seafood. Try the bread stew with prawns, and wash it down with the house beer.

Forno d'Oro €€
Italian **Map** 5 A4
Rua Artilharia Um 16, 1250-039
Tel *213 879 944*
Traditional ales and Italian pizzas baked in a large oven dominate the menu at this restaurant. Located in the heart of Lisbon's business district.

La Gondola €€
Portuguese / Italian **Map** 5 B2
Avenida de Berna 64, 1050-043
Tel *217 970 426*
Choose from a range of home-made pasta dishes or traditional Portuguese fare at this bright, spacious restaurant with a pretty garden.

Laurentina €€
Traditional Portuguese **Map** 5 B2
Avenida Conde Valbom 71A, 1050-067
Tel *217 960 260*
Lisbon's self-proclaimed "King of Cod" serves an extensive range of *bacalhau* dishes, as well as tasty meats, such as roast lamb. Live *fado* music on Thursday nights.

O Polícia €€
Traditional Portuguese **Map** 5 B2
Rua Marquês Sá da Bandeira 112A, 1050-158
Tel *217 963 505* **Closed** *Sat dinner; Sun*
This award-winning, family-run restaurant with a non-touristy feel prides itself on its traditional Portuguese cuisine, especially the seafood. Sample the delicious monkfish kebab.

Cenário €€€
Modern Portuguese **Map** 5 C1
Avenida 5 de Outubro 197, 1050-054
Tel *210 435 000*
An innovative menu that changes according to the seasons is offered at this stylish, elegant restaurant in a 5-star hotel. There is also an extensive wine list.

The Lisbon Coast

ALCÁCER DO SAL: Pousada Dom Afonso II €€
International **Map** C6
Castelo de Alcácer do Sal, 7580-197
Tel *265 613 070*
The river-influenced menu here features starters such as clam fish soup. Mains include roast cod and rack of lamb.

CASCAIS: Mayura €
Indian **Map** B5
Rua Freitas Reis 15B, 2750-357
Tel *214 846 540*
An informal and friendly restaurant with a loyal clientele. On the menu are consistently good Indian and Goan dishes.

CASCAIS: Casa Velha €€
Seafood **Map** B5
Avenida Valbom 1, 2750-508
Tel *214 832 586*
Stone walls and a ceiling draped with fishing nets create a rustic, homely ambience. Popular dishes include *caldeirada de peixe* (fish stew), *cherne grelhado* (grilled sea bass) and *paella*.

CASCAIS: Dom Manolo €€
Traditional Portuguese **Map** B5
Avenida Marginal 13, 2750-367
Tel *214 831 126*
A menu highlight at Dom Monola is chicken *piri-piri*, but it is also popular for its grilled sardines and pork ribs with bacon.

The sign outside Laurentina, also known as "The King of Cod"

CASCAIS: O Pescador €€
Seafood **Map** B5
Rua das Flores 10B, 2750-348
Tel *214 832 054* **Closed** *Mon*
This well-established restaurant has a distinctly nautical interior to match the firm emphasis on seafood and fresh fish.

CASCAIS: Taberna da Praça €€
Traditional Portuguese **Map** B5
Cidadela de Cascais, Avenida Dom Carlos I, 2750-310
Tel *214 820 515*
Located inside an old fortress and part of a *pousada*, this restaurant serves traditional food made with local ingredients. House specials include *caldeirada* (fish casserole) and tuna steaks with sautéed onion.

CASCAIS: Gourmet Restaurant €€€
Modern Portuguese **Map** B5
Avenida Marginal 8554, 2775-536
Tel *210 060 600* **Closed** *lunch daily*
The regularly changing gourmet menu and wine list are worth getting dressed up for at this fine-dining restaurant in a romantic setting at the Hotel Miragem, overlooking the marina.

CASCAIS: The Mix €€€
Mediterranean / Sushi **Map** B5
Avenida Rei Humberto de Itália 7, 2750-461
Tel *214 823 490*
Part of the five-star Farol Hotel complex, this modern, elegant restaurant serves beautifully presented and imaginative fusion dishes in three distinct dining areas.

ESTORIL: Pinto's €
International **Map** B5
Avenida Clotilde 52, 2715-311
Tel *214 687 247* **Closed** *Wed*
A restaurant that is good for snacks as well as more substantial meals. The menu ranges from salads and burgers to pizza and shellfish.

ESTORIL: Estoril Mandarin €€€
Chinese **Map** B5
Praça José Teodoro dos Santos, 2765-237
Tel *214 667 270* **Closed** *Mon & Tue*
This plush restaurant situated in the Casino Estoril is considered the best place in Portugal to sample Chinese food. Specialities include Peking duck and dim sum.

ESTORIL: Four Seasons Grill €€€
International **Map** B5
Rua da Particular, 2769-504
Tel *214 648 000* **Closed** *lunch daily*
Located in the Hotel Palácio, this sophisticated fine dining venue features a seasonally changing decor. The superb gourmet dishes are complemented by an inspired wine list and attentive service.

The dining room at Cozinha Velha, in Queluz, dominated by a large stone chimney

GUINCHO: Restaurante Bar do Guincho €€
International **Map** B5
Estrado do Abano 547, 2755-144
Tel 214 871 683 **Closed** Mon (except May–Aug)
This beach restaurant serves a range of salads, sandwiches and burgers, as well as more substantial meat dishes. This is a great place to watch the sunset.

DK Choice

GUINCHO: Porto de Santa Maria €€€
Traditional Portuguese / Seafood **Map** B5
Estrada do Guincho, 2750-642
Tel 214 879 450
Elegant furnishings are complemented by rustic touches at this award-winning beachside restaurant. The menu features a vast range of freshly caught, exquisite fish and seafood dishes, priced by the kilo. Roast sea bream is one of the house specialities. Book ahead.

MONTE ESTORIL: O Sinaleiro €
Traditional Portuguese **Map** B5
Avenida de Sabóia 595, 2765-278
Tel 214 685 439 **Closed** Wed
This simple restaurant and bar serves good-quality fare, with some unusual dishes on the largely traditional menu. Great for full meals, snacks or takeaways.

MONTE ESTORIL: Tertúlia do Monte €
Traditional Portuguese / International **Map** B5
Avenida de Sabóia 515D, 2765-502
Tel 214 681 508 **Closed** Sat lunch; Sun
The menu at this fashionable restaurant features dishes such as risotto with curried prawns and duck cooked in port wine. Save room for the delicious desserts.

PAÇO D'ARCOS: Aquarela do Brasil €
Brazilian **Map** B5
Praça 5 de Outubro 12, 2770-029
Tel 214 415 412 **Closed** Sun dinner, Mon
With a name that means "watercolour of Brazil", expect art on the walls of this restaurant. The menu features superb Brazilian food as well as Portuguese tapas.

PALMELA: Pousada Castelo Palmela €€
International **Map** C5
Castelo de Palmela, 2950-317
Tel 212 351 226
This romantic, luxurious restaurant is located in a former monastery. Specialities include grilled tiger prawns, sautéed pork tenderloin and traditional chicken stew.

PORTINHO DA ARRÁBIDA: O Farol €€
Seafood **Map** C5
Portinho da Arrábida, 2925-378
Tel 212 181 177 **Closed** Mon
This popular seafood restaurant at the water's edge offers good value for money. The rock lobster with rice and clams and sea bass straight off the boat are house favourites.

QUELUZ: Cozinha Velha €€
International **Map** B5
Palácio Nacional de Queluz, 2745-191
Tel 214 356 158
The original stone chimney is the centrepiece of this eatery housed in the palace kitchens. A highlight of the creative menu is the bacalhau grelhado (grilled cod). There is live harp music on Friday evenings.

SESIMBRA: Ribamar €€
Seafood **Map** C5
Avenida dos Náufragos 29, 2970-637
Tel 212 234 853
This colourful restaurant is said to be one of the best in the region. The imaginative chef regularly updates the menu with tasty original concoctions.

SETÚBAL: Poço das Fontainhas €€
Seafood **Map** C5
Rua das Fontainhas 98, 2910-082
Tel 265 534 807 **Closed** Mon
The focus here is firmly on fresh seafood and fish. Try the caldeirada à setúbalense (fish stew). Not easy to find but well worth the effort.

SINTRA: Tulhas €
Traditional Portuguese **Map** B5
Rua Gil Vicente 4–6, 2710-568
Tel 219 232 378
Small, friendly place with a rustic atmosphere. Serves wholesome home-made dishes, as well as delicious cheese and wines, including the house red. Book in advance.

SINTRA: Monserrate €€
International / Traditional Portuguese **Map** B5
Praça da República, 2710-616
Tel 219 237 200
Housed in the chic Tivoli Hotel, this restaurant offers fabulous views of the Sintra Valley. Try the Sintra-style fish soup, followed by the braised salmon fillets. Book ahead.

SINTRA: Lawrence's €€€
Traditional Portuguese **Map** B5
Rua Consigliéri Pedroso 38–40, 2710-550
Tel 219 105 500
Enjoy fine dining in this historic hotel popular with celebrities. Choose from an outstanding à la carte menu and an extensive wine list. Impeccable service.

SINTRA: Restaurante Palácio de Seteais €€€
International **Map** B5
Rua Barbosa do Bocage 8, 2710-517
Tel 219 233 200
The luxurious and elegant decor adds a touch of romance to the fine-dining experience here. Top-class nouvelle cuisine features regional delicacies with French and Italian influences.

Estremadura and Ribatejo

ABRANTES: Cascata €
Traditional Portuguese   Map C4
Rua Manuel Lopes Valente Júnior 19A, 2200-260
Tel *241 361 011*   **Closed** *Sun & Mon dinner*
This award-winning restaurant offers top-quality regional dishes such as *bacalhau ao broa* (baked cod with corn bread) and roast kid.

ABRANTES: Sabores da Cascata €€
Traditional Portuguese   Map C4
Edifício de São Domingos, Rua de São Domingos, 2º Piso, 2200-392
Tel *241 364 453*
Fried shad (in season) headlines the menu at this restaurant, along with other typical, delicious Ribatejan specialities.

ABRANTES: Santa Isabel €€
Traditional Portuguese   Map C4
Rua Santa Isabel 12, 2200-393
Tel *967 893 970*   **Closed** *Sun*
This small restaurant with a rustic ambience has a menu that centres on meat dishes. Try the *migas de alheira* (poultry sausage with breadcrumbs) and the fried eels.

ALCOBAÇA: Trindade €
Traditional Portuguese   Map C4
Praça Dom Afonso Henriques 22
Tel *262 582 397*
The quality of the food makes this well-established restaurant a local favourite. Recommended dishes include *arroz de pato* (duck rice) and *arroz de marisco* (seafood rice).

ALCOBAÇA: Sentidos €€
Modern Portuguese   Map C4
Rua Manuel Rodrigues Serrazina Fervença, 2460-743
Tel *262 505 370*
Relaxed elegance is the setting here in which to enjoy regional dishes from a daily changing menu.

ALMEIRIM: Toucinho €
Traditional Portuguese   Map C4
Rua do Timor 2, 2080-103
Tel *243 592 237*   **Closed** *Thu*
Family-run restaurant best known for its *sopa de pedra* (stone soup). The interiors are decorated with posters of bullfights. Book ahead.

BATALHA: Vintage €€
Traditional Portuguese   Map C4
Largo Mestre Afonso Domingues 6
Tel *244 765 260*
Daily specials at this smart restaurant in the Mestre Afonso Domingues hotel feature regional favourites, including the *bacalhau à Portuguesa* (Portuguese-style cod).

CALDAS DA RAINHA: A Lareira €
Traditional Portuguese / International   Map B4
Rua da Lareira 35, 2500-593
Tel *262 823 432*
With four different dining areas, this huge restaurant caters for events, as well as small groups. It offers a constantly changing *menu do dia* (daily set menu) and a good wine list.

CALDAS DA RAINHA: Adega do Albertino €€
Traditional Portuguese   Map B4
Rua Júlio Sousa 7, 2500-312
Tel *262 835 152*   **Closed** *Sun dinner; Mon*
Traditional decor and checked tablecloths make up the rustic interior of this restaurant. Specialities include pork ribs with wine, honey and almonds, and octopus on roof tile with shrimps.

FÁTIMA: O Convite €€
International   Map C4
Rua Jacinto Marto 100, 2495-000
Tel *249 531 010*
This stylish restaurant is renowned for its attractively presented gourmet cuisine; dishes include braised duck in orange sauce.

DK Choice

FÁTIMA: Tia Alice €€
Traditional Portuguese   Map C4
Rua do Adro 152, 2495-557
Tel *249 531 737*   **Closed** *Sun dinner; Mon; 11–31 Jul*
Chef Tia Alice pours great culinary skills and secret ingredients into her exquisite Estremaduran dishes at this simple, rustic restaurant. Try the veal roasted in a wood oven or the *açorda de camarão* (prawn and bread stew).

LEIRIA: Tromba Rija €€
Traditional Portuguese   Map C4
Rua Professores Portelas 22, 2400-406
Tel *244 855 072*   **Closed** *Sun dinner; Mon*
Take advantage of the huge starter buffet to sample various Portuguese delicacies at this homely restaurant, but leave room for the main course – the pork and bean stew is a must.

NAZARÉ: O Luis €
Traditional Portuguese   Map C4
Rua dos Tanques 7, Sítio, 2450-065
Tel *262 551 826*   **Closed** *Thu*
Take the funicular to this simply decorated restaurant. The speciality is *o barco* (a platter fashioned to look like a boat, filled with seafood of the day), which goes well with *vinho verde*.

NAZARÉ: Mar Bravo €€
Traditional Portuguese   Map C4
Praça Sousa Oliveira 71, 2450-159
Tel *262 569 160*   **Closed** *Tue (Nov–Feb)*
The à la carte menu at Mar Bravo offers seafood dishes such as mussels, *arroz de marisco* (seafood with rice) and *cataplana*. Meat eaters, vegetarians and children are well catered for.

ÓBIDOS: O Alcaide €€
Traditional Portuguese   Map B4
Rua Direita 60, 2510-001
Tel *262 959 220*   **Closed** *Wed*
This small, traditionally furnished restaurant with a cosy ambience serves a range of well-cooked and beautifully presented dishes. The medallions of beef with port wine are delicious.

The elegant interior of Tia Alice, in Fátima, offset by rustic touches

For more information on types of restaurants *see pages 396–7*

ÓBIDOS: Castelo €€€
International Map B4
Paço Real, 2510-999
Tel *262 955 080*
Enjoy gourmet cuisine at this
pousada. Specialities include
monkfish with shrimps and rice
and *trouxas de ovos* (egg pudding).

PENICHE: Estelas €€
Seafood Map B4
*Rua Arquitecto Paulino Montês 21,
2520-294*
Tel *262 782 435*
This award-winning restaurant is
enduringly popular with locals.
Be sure to try the local Berlenga
sea bass. It has an extensive wine
list and a homely atmosphere.

**PENICHE: Marisqueira
Cortiçais**
Seafood €€
 Map B4
Porto d'Areia Sul, 2520-000
Tel *262 787 262* **Closed** *Wed*
A waterfront restaurant that
serves very fresh seafood. The
arroz de marisco (seafood rice)
and the *festival de marisco*
(shellfish platter) are excellent.

**SANTARÉM: Taberna do
Quinzena** €
Traditional Portuguese Map C4
Rua Pedro de Santarém 93–95, 2000-223
Tel *243 322 804* **Closed** *Sun*
Established in 1872, Quinzena
serves great local fare such as
porco preto (Iberian pork) and *ovos
mexidos com farinheira* (scrambled
eggs with flour sausage).

**TOMAR: Casa das Ratas /
Casa Matreno** €
Traditional Portuguese Map C4
*Rua do Doutor Joaquim Jacinto 7,
2300-550*
Tel *249 315 237* **Closed** *Sun dinner;
Mon*
This is two restaurants with a
shared kitchen and menu. The
polvo à lagareiro (baked octopus) is
recommended, and the ratatouille
is a delicious vegetarian option.

TOMAR: Calça Perra €€
Traditional Portuguese Map C4
Rua Pedro Dias 59, 2300-589
Tel *249 321 616* **Closed** *Sun dinner;
Mon (Oct–Apr)*
Beautiful gardens surround this
charming restaurant. Regional
specialities include lamprey, when
in season. Good set lunch menus.

TOMAR: Chico Elias €€
Traditional Portuguese Map C4
Rua Principal 70, Algarvias, 2300-302
Tel *249 311 067* **Closed** *Tue*
An interesting menu of traditional
recipes with imaginative twists
is offered at this family-run
restaurant – such as *feijoada de
caracóis* (snail and bean stew) and
rabbit cooked inside a pumpkin.

**TORRES VEDRAS: O Pátio
do Faustino** €
Traditional Portuguese Map B5
Largo do Choupal, 2560-000
Tel *261 324 346* **Closed** *Mon*
The menu at this rustic restaurant
includes *bacalhau com grão* (cod
with chickpeas) and *porco à
alentejana* (pork, potato and clams).

**VILA FRANCA DE XIRA:
O Forno** €€
Traditional Portuguese Map C5
*Rua Doutor Miguel Bombarda 143,
2600-000*
Tel *263 282 106* **Closed** *Mon*
This traditional restaurant serves
plenty of oven-baked dishes, as
well as meat and seafood kebabs.
There is also a good selection of
wines and desserts.

The Beiras

**ALMEIDA: Hotel Fortaleza
de Almeida** €€
Traditional Portuguese Map E2
Rua da Muralha, Almeida, 6350-112
Tel *271 574 283*
On the menu at this elegant hotel
restaurant are regional delicacies

such as *cabrito grelhado com
migas de batata* (grilled kid with
creamed potato) and *doce de
amêndoa* (almond pudding).

AVEIRO: O Bairro €€
International Map C3
Largo do Praça do Peixe 24, 3800-243
Tel *234 338 567* **Closed** *Wed*
The gourmet dishes here, cooked
by a creative chef, include
pumpkin soup with prawn and
poultry sausage. Be sure to leave
room for the exquisite desserts.

AVEIRO: Mercado do Peixe €€
Seafood Map C3
Largo do Praça do Peixe, 3800-243
Tel *234 351 303* **Closed** *Sun dinner,
Mon*
Ultra-fresh seafood is served here.
The fish soup makes a superb starter,
and the *caldeiradas* are delicious.

**BELMONTE: Pousada do
Convento de Belmonte** €€
International Map D3
Serra da Esperança, 6250-073
Tel *275 910 300*
A beautiful restaurant with original
stone features and wonderful
mountain views. The gourmet
dishes on the tasting menu or
à la carte are equally impressive.

**BUÇACO: Palace Hotel do
Bussaco** €€€
Modern Portuguese Map C3
Mata do Bussaco, 3050-261
Tel *231 937 970*
Arched, lace stonework on the
windows here makes for a
romantic setting in which to enjoy
superb cuisine.

CARAMULO: Montanha €
Traditional Portuguese Map C3
Rua do Clube, 3475-031
Tel *232 862 008* **Closed** *Tue*
Rustic restaurant in the heart of
Serra do Caramulo serving superb
mountain fare. The c*hanfana na
púcara* (meat stew) and *rojões da
aldeia* (chunks of fried pork belly)
are specialities. Sit outdoors in
the garden during summer.

CASTELO BRANCO: O Espeto €€
Traditional Portuguese Map D4
Estrada dos Buenos Aires 23, 6000-069
Tel *272 320 956* **Closed** *Mon*
Bright, spacious eatery with an out-
door patio, featuring an extensive
regional-style buffet with a good
selection of barbecued meats.

**COIMBRA: Fangas
Mercearia Bar** €
Modern Portuguese Map C3
Rua Fernandes Tomás 45–49, 3000-168
Tel *934 093 636*
This small, cheerful restaurant,
bar and grocery store specializes

Refined dining at Castelo, housed in a *pousada* in Óbidos

For key to prices *see page 398*

Classy, opulent interiors of the restaurant at the Palace Hotel do Bussaco in Buçaco

in interesting healthy snacks. Perfect for a light lunch; for a more substantial meal, order several dishes.

DK Choice

COIMBRA: A Taberna €€
Traditional Portuguese Map C3
Rua dos Combatentes da Grande Guerra 86, 3030-181
Tel 239 716 265 **Closed** Sun dinner; Mon lunch
Diners can see their food cooking in the wood-fired oven at this lovely eatery. Waiters serve a selection of vegetables at the table and come back for second helpings. The veal dishes are tender and delicious, as is the octopus. The home-made bread with requeijão (ricotta) is divine.

COIMBRA: O Trovador €€
Traditional Portuguese Map C3
Largo Sé Velha 15–17, 3000-383
Tel 239 825 475 **Closed** Sun; 1–15 Jan
This traditional restaurant with rustic decor serves regional dishes such as chanfana (goat and red wine casserole). Live fado music sometimes accompanies meals on Friday and Saturday evenings.

COIMBRA: Arcadas da Cappella €€€
International Map C3
Rua António Augusto Gonçalves, 3041-901
Tel 239 802 380 **Closed** lunch
The gourmet menu at this luxurious, romantic restaurant in the Quinta das Lágrimas changes with the seasons but never fails to delight, serving great portions of global food.

CONDEIXA-A-NOVA: Santa Cristina €€
Modern Portuguese Map C3
Rua Francisco de Lemos, 3150-142
Tel 239 944 025
The menu at this sophisticated restaurant is packed with regional delicacies. Try the bacalhau assado (roast cod).

FIGUEIRA DA FOZ: Paquette €
Traditional Portuguese Map C3
Avenida Brasil 12, 3080-322
Tel 233 418 488 **Closed** Wed
This simple, traditional restaurant with sea views is good for snacks or full meals. Try the açorda de camarão (prawn and bread stew) or prato do dia (dish of the day).

GOUVEIA: Lá em Casa €
Traditional Portuguese Map D3
Avenida Dom Manuel I 4, 6290-320
Tel 238 491 983 **Closed** Sun dinner; Mon
Mountain fare with an innovative twist. Try the award-winning pork tenderloin stuffed with Serra cheese with black pudding sauce, or the roast kid with chestnuts.

GUARDA: O Ferrinho €
Traditional Portuguese Map D3
Rua Francisco de Passos 21, 6300-558
Tel 271 211 990 **Closed** Thu (Nov–May)
Regional dishes fill the menu in this rustic restaurant. The trout stuffed with presunto ham is delicious, as is the guisado de javali (wild boar stew).

MANTEIGAS: Casa das Penhas Douradas €€
Traditional Portuguese Map D4
Penhas Douradas, Apartado 9, 6260-200
Tel 275 981 045
A wide range of regional-style specialities are served in a gleaming dining room at this

eagle-nest retreat. Diners also enjoy head-spinning views and fresh mountain air.

MEALHADA: Pedro dos Leitões €€
Traditional Portuguese Map C3
Rua Álvaro Pedro 1, 3050-382
Tel 231 209 950
This is just the place to try leitão (spit-roasted suckling pig) – it is outstanding. There are plenty of non-pork options as well.

MONSANTO: Petiscos e Granitos €
Traditional Portuguese Map E3
Rua da Pracinha 16, 6060-091
Tel 964 200 974 **Closed** Mon
Try the baked octopus with cheese and the scrambled eggs with asparagus at this restaurant with granite boulders incorporated into the walls.

SORTELHA: Dom Sancho I €€
Traditional Portuguese Map D3
Largo do Corro, 6320-536
Tel 271 388 267 **Closed** Sun dinner; Mon
The open fireplace here is warm and welcoming, and the menu features substantial dishes such as guisado de javali com batata cozida e castanhas (stewed wild-boar with boiled potatoes) and caldeira de borrego (lamb stew).

VISEU: Casablanca €
Seafood Map D3
Avenida Emídio Navarro 70–72, 3500-124
Tel 232 422 239 **Closed** Tue (Oct–Jun)
This bright, spacious restaurant specializes in seafood. The arroz de polvo com gambas (octopus and prawn rice) is a must. There are plenty of meat dishes too. Reserve in advance.

VISEU: Churrasqueira Santa Eulália €
Traditional Portuguese Map D3
Avenida Luís Martins 86, 3500-719
Tel 232 436 283
This unpretentious restaurant specializes in grilled meats but offers fish and seafood dishes too. The wine list features local Dão wines.

VISEU: Muralhas da Sé €€
Traditional Portuguese Map D3
Adro da Sé 24, 3500-195
Tel 232 437 777 **Closed** Sun dinner; Tue
Granite walls and warm colours at this restaurant create an intimate atmosphere in which to enjoy artistically presented regional dishes, cooked to a high standard. Extensive wine list.

For more information on types of restaurants see pages 396–7

Elegant table setting at Pousada Palacete
Alijó, a *pousada* in a historic building

Douro and Trás-os-Montes

ALIJÓ: Cêpa Torta €€
Modern Portuguese   Map D2
Rua Dr José Bulas Cruz, 5070-047
Tel *259 950 177*   **Closed** *Sun dinner;
Mon*
The modern, sophisticated decor
here matches the gourmet cuisine
of well-presented Portuguese
fare with a modern twist.

ALIJÓ: Pousada Palacete Alijó €€
Modern Portuguese   Map D2
Rua José Rufino, 5070-031
Tel *259 959 215*
The loyal clientele returns for
regional treats such as *alheira*
(poultry sausage) and lamb stew
at this award-winning restaurant
in a historic building.

AMARANTE: Estoril €
Traditional Portuguese   Map D2
Rua 31 de Janeiro 150, 4600-043
Tel *255 431 291*
Tasty, wholesome food, such as
lamb stew with plenty of vegetables,
is served at this restaurant.

DK Choice

**AMARANTE: Largo
do Paço** €€€
International   Map D2
Largo do Paço 6, 4600-017
Tel *255 410 830*
The elegant Largo do Paço
offers a culinary experience to
satisfy the most refined and
demanding of palates. Located
in the historic Casa da Calçada
hotel (*see p391*), this award-
winning restaurant boasts a
Michelin star. Chef André Silva
changes the tasting menus
seasonally to incorporate the
freshest available ingredients.

**BRAGANÇA: Solar
Bragançano** €
Traditional Portuguese   Map E1
Praça da Sé 34, 5300-271
Tel *273 323 875*   **Closed** *Mon (Oct–
Jun)*
Game dishes and chestnuts
feature prominently on the menu
at this family-run restaurant in an
old mansion with an inner patio.

BRAGANÇA: Geadas €€
Traditional Portuguese   Map E1
Rua do Loreto, 5300-189
Tel *273 324 413*   **Closed** *Sun dinner*
This family-friendly restaurant
attracts guests for the peaceful
views of the River Fervença, as
well as the quality of the food.
The partridge with chestnuts
alone makes it worth a visit.

CHAVES: Adega do Faustino €
Traditional Portuguese   Map D1
*Travessa Cândido Reis, Santa Maria
Maior, 5400-423*
Tel *276 322 142*   **Closed** *Sun; 1–20 Jan*
Diners enjoy a good range of
tapas, meat and fish dishes at
this former wine cellar lined
with ancient barrels and jugs.

CHAVES: Carvalho €€
Traditional Portuguese   Map D1
Largo das Caldas 4, 5400-523
Tel *276 321 727*   **Closed** *Sun dinner;
Mon*
The traditional marble and wood
interior at Carvalho complements
the regional fare served. Order the
linguiça assada (flame-grilled
sausage) and enjoy the views.

GIMONDE: Dom Roberto €
Traditional Portuguese   Map E1
*Rua Coronel Álvaro Cepeda 1, N 218,
5300-553*
Tel *273 302 510*
Decor consisting of ancient
farm equipment underlines
Dom Roberto's pastoral heritage.
Be sure to try the award-winning
caldo de cascas (bean-shell soup).

LAMEGO: Vindouro €€€
Mediterranean   Map D2
Rua Macário de Castro 39, 5100-179
Tel *254 401 698*   **Closed** *Sun dinner,
Mon*
Set in a prime location close
to the cathedral, this stylish
eatery offers a choice of à la
carte and executive menus
with the emphasis on
contemporary cuisine.

**LEÇA DA PALMEIRA:
O Chanquinhas** €€
International   Map C2
Rua de Santana 243, 4450-000
Tel *229 951 884*   **Closed** *Sun dinner;
1–15 Aug*
Delicious cuisine is served at
this elegant restaurant in a
former mansion. The wine list
is impressive, as are the desserts.
Try the *pão de ló* (sponge cake).

**MIRANDA DO DOURO:
A Balbina** €
Traditional Portuguese   Map E1
Rua Rainha Dona Catarina 1, 5210-228
Tel *273 432 394*
The home-cooked meals at this
no-frills restaurant include *posta
à mirandesa* (Mirandese steak).
Service is friendly and efficient.
Cash only.

**MIRANDA DO DOURO:
Capa d'Honras** €
Traditional Portuguese   Map E1
Travessa do Castelo 1, 5210-234
Tel *273 432 699*
A memorable steak and excellent
cabrito (kid) can be enjoyed at
this unpretentious restaurant
named after the traditional
capes worn by the local elite.

MIRANDELA: Flor de Sal €€
Modern Portuguese   Map D1
Parque Dr José Gama, 5370-000
Tel *278 203 063*   **Closed** *Sun dinner,
Mon*
This elegant, contemporary
riverside restaurant serves

Geadas in Bragança, with its exposed-brick columns

award-winning cuisine based on fresh local ingredients. A tasting menu is also available.

PESO DA RÉGUA: Douro In €€
Modern Portuguese   Map D2
Avenida João Franco, 5050-264
Tel *254 098 075*
A modern, sophisticated wine bar and restaurant overlooking the Douro. On the menu are creative renditions of traditional Portuguese dishes and a choice of vintage Douro wines.

PESO DA RÉGUA: Varanda da Régua €€
Traditonal Portuguese   Map D2
Lugar da Boavista, 5050-000
Tel *254 336 949*   **Closed** *Mon (Apr)*
There are three dining areas, all offering panoramic river views, at this large, family-run eatery. The adventurous should try *enchidos de região* (regional sausages).

PORTO: Casa das Tortas €
Traditional Portuguese   Map C2
Rua Passos Manuel 181, 400-382
Tel *222 004 338*
Traditional home-made Portuguese fare dominates the menu at this restaurant-cum-pastry shop. Opt for the popular house special, *alheira especial com ovo* (garlic sausage with egg).

PORTO: Solar Moinho de Vento €
Traditional Portuguese   Map C2
Rua de Sá Noronha 81, 4050-527
Tel *222 051 158*   **Closed** *Sun dinner*
The specialities at this restaurant in an old building with wooden beams include fish soup and giblet rice. It has lunchtime set menus which are not to be missed.

PORTO: Ar de Rio €€
Cervejaria   Map C2
Avenida Diogo Leite 5, 4400-123
Tel *223 701 797*
Enjoy great river views from the covered terrace at this restaurant famous for *francesinhas* – stacked, meaty sandwiches covered with cheese and sauce.

PORTO: BB Gourmet €€
Modern Portuguese   Map C2
Rua Fernandes Tomás 764, 4000-213
Tel *222 011 531*
This award-winning restaurant with fashionable decor serves light, refined meals prepared with the freshest ingredients. Tasting menus are available. Reserve in advance.

PORTO: Café Vitória €€
Modern Portuguese   Map C2
Rua José Falcão 156, 4050-315
Tel *220 135 538*   **Closed** *Tue*
There are three seating areas in this bright, cheerful restaurant

The spacious interior of Camafeu in Porto

with vegetarian options. Try the marinated sardines or the mushroom toast.

PORTO: Camafeu €€
Modern Portuguese   Map C2
Praça de Carlos Alberto 83, 4050-158
Tel *937 493 557*   **Closed** *Sun & Mon, lunch Tue–Sat*
Traditional eatery with a varied menu and friendly, personalised service. Try the roast octopus or cod with chick pea purée and crust of corn bread.

PORTO: Casa Aleixo €€
Traditional Portuguese   Map C2
Rua Estação 216, 4300-171
Tel *225 370 462*   **Closed** *Sun*
This family-run restaurant with a warm atmosphere is famous for tripe dishes, but it also serves amazing *filets de polvo* (octopus) and steaks. Superb house wine.

PORTO: Chez Lapin €€
Traditional Portuguese   Map C2
Rua dos Canastreiros 40, 4050-149
Tel *222 006 418*
Three dining areas, each with its unique ambience, make up this restaurant on the waterfront. A menu highlight is the *polvo assado no forno* (roast octopus). Service is excellent.

PORTO: Cometa €€
International   Map C2
Rua Tomás Gonzaga 87, 4050-607
Tel *916 582 608*   **Closed** *lunch; Sun*
The eclectic menu at this small, cosy restaurant features dishes mostly based on the Mediterranean cuisine. Cash only. Reserve in advance.

PORTO: Essência €€
Vegetarian   Map C2
Rua Pedro Hispano 1190, 4150-123
Tel *228 301 813*   **Closed** *Sun*
Creative vegetarian food is the focus at this informal restaurant with stylish 1940s decor and a garden terrace.

PORTO: Oficina €€
International   Map C2
R. Miguel Bombarda 273-282
Tel *220 165 807*   **Closed** *Sun, Mon lunch*
The main focus of this contemporary-style restaurant located in a former automobile shop is the fusion between art and cuisine. Try the fresh scallops with salmon roe.

PORTO: Portucale €€
International   Map C2
Rua da Alegria 598, 4000-037
Tel *225 370 717*
This famous hotel-restaurant with 1970s decor and panoramic city views has a wide-ranging menu and wine list.

PORTO: Restaurante Casa da Música €€
International   Map C2
Avenida da Boavista 604, 4149-071
Tel *220 107 160*   **Closed** *Sun*
The chef here is on a mission to make gourmet food widely accessible. Several show-and-dinner packages, as well as a good-value tasting menu, are available.

PORTO: The Yeatman €€€
Modern Portuguese   Map C2
Rua do Choupelo, 4400-088
Tel *220 133 100*
Housed in one of the city's finest hotels, this luxurious Michelin-starred restaurant offers an inspired gourmet menu and an expertly chosen wine list. There are great views over the historic city centre.

ROMEU: Maria Rita €€
Traditonal Portuguese   Map E1
Rua da Capela, 5370-620
Tel *278 939 134*   **Closed** *Sun dinner; Mon*
Set in a historic town house with a rustic air, this restaurant offers a menu of wholesome favourites, including spicy sausage soup and *feijoada à transmontana* (bean stew).

The plush dining room at The Yeatman, Porto *(see p407)*

SENDIM: Gabriela €€
Traditonal Portuguese   Map E2
Largo da Igreja 27, 5225-106
Tel *273 739 180*
Regional specialities, such as
Mirandese steak in a special
sauce and *sopa de legumes*
(vegetable soup) are served here.

TORRE DE MONCORVO:
O Artur €
Traditonal Portuguese   Map E2
*Lugar de Rentão, Carviçais,
5160-069*
Tel *279 098 000*   **Closed** *Sun dinner*
Decorated with farming
equipment, this restaurant is
renowned locally for Mirandese
steak and *cabrito* (kid).

VILA REAL: Museu dos
Presuntos €€
Traditonal Portuguese   Map D2
*Avenida Cidade Ourense, 43,
5000-690*
Tel *259 327 027*   **Closed** *Mon*
A restaurant offering northern
Portuguese fare, such as
Montalegre-style veal cutlets.
Presunto ham is another speciality,
hence the restaurant's name.

VILA REAL: Terra da
Montanha €€
Traditonal Portuguese   Map D2
Rua 31 de Janeiro 18, 5000-603
Tel *259 372 075*   **Closed** *Sun
dinner*
The rustic decor at this restaurant
includes lots of wine barrels. It
offers hearty local fare and an
excellent wine list.

Minho

ARCOS DE VALDEVEZ:
Costa do Vez €€
Traditonal Portuguese   Map C1
EN 121, Quinta de Silvares, 4970-483
Tel *258 516 122*   **Closed** *Mon*
Mountain views, grilled
meats and baked cod are
what this attractive restaurant

is known for. Finish with the
local cakes, *charutos dos Arcos*
(cigars of Arcos).

BARCELOS: A Vincentina €
Traditonal Portuguese   Map C1
*Rua Dom António Barroso 87,
4750-258*
Tel *253 812 285*
This friendly eatery is very popular
with the locals. The house special
is *francesinha*, a type of steak
sandwich with melted cheese and
a spicy tomato sauce made with
beer and brandy.

BARCELOS: Bagoeira €€
Traditonal Portuguese   Map C1
Avenida Sidónio Pais 495, 4750-333
Tel *253 813 088*
The set menu at this hotel
restaurant offers a selection
of regional fare served in
generous portions.

BRAGA: Anjo Verde €
Vegetarian   Map C1
Largo da Praça Velha 21, 4700-439
Tel *253 264 010*   **Closed** *Sun*
A modern, attractive vegetarian
restaurant. On the menu are
substantial main dishes and
several colourful side dishes,
plus there is a complimentary
herbal tea on arrival.

BRAGA: São Frutuoso €
Traditional Portuguese   Map C1
Rua Costa Gomes 168, 4700-262
Tel *253 623 372*   **Closed** *Sun dinner;
Mon*
Granite and wood dominate
the comfortable interior of this
restaurant. Try the *bacalhau com
castanhas* (cod with onions and
chestnuts) or *bacalhau com broa*
(cod with corn bread).

BRAGA: Arcoense €€
Traditonal Portuguese   Map C1
*Rua Eugenheiro José Justino de
Amorim 96, 4715-023*
Tel *253 278 952*   **Closed** *Sun dinner*
This bright, spacious and
simply decorated restaurant

specializes in regional cuisine.
The menu is heavily biased
towards meat, and there is
an excellent wine list.

BRAGA: Inácio €€
Traditional Portuguese   Map C1
Campo das Hortas 4, 4700-000
Tel *253 613 235*   **Closed** *Tue*
Housed in a historic granite
building with antique decorative
touches, Inácio offers first-class
regional dishes, including
lamprey rice, veal and kid.

CAMINHA: Muralha
da Caminha €
Modern Portuguese   Map C1
Rua Barão de São Roque 69, 4910-340
Tel *258 728 199*
A light, airy hotel restaurant
whose menu offers plenty of
choice within Portuguese food,
including fresh fish.

GUIMARÃES: El Rei
Dom Afonso €
Traditional Portuguese   Map C2
Praça de São Tiago 20, 4810-311
Tel *253 419 096*   **Closed** *Sun*
Named after the first king
of Portugal, this family restaurant
serves regional treats such
as *feijoada à transmontana*
(bean stew) and *bacalhau
mistério* (cod).

> ### DK Choice
>
> **GUIMARÃES:**
> **Cor de Tangerina** €€
> **Vegetarian**   Map C2
> *Largo Martins Sarmento 89,
> 4800-432*
> **Tel** *253 542 009*   **Closed** *Sun
> dinner; Mon*
> Spread across one floor
> and the leafy gardens of
> an old town house, this
> restaurant in a cultural centre
> with funky furnishings and
> frequent art exhibitions
> offers vegetarian daily specials
> made with fresh, locally
> sourced organic produce. An
> extensive range of infusions
> and teas is available.

GUIMARÃES: São Gião €€
Traditional Portuguese   Map C2
*Avenida Comendador Joaquim de
Almeida Freitas 56, Moreira de
Cónegos, 4815-270*
Tel *253 561 853*   **Closed** *Sun dinner;
Mon*
Visit this restaurant for an
intimate fine dining experience;
try the *sopa rica de peixe* (fish
soup) or *robalo grelhado com
molho de camarão* (sea bass in
prawn sauce). Attentive waiters
help with the wine selection.

GUIMARÃES: Solar do Arco
€€
Traditional Portuguese   Map C2
Rua de Santa Maria 48–50, 4810-443
Tel *253 513 072*   **Closed** *Tue*
This restaurant is a good place to sample some unusual regional dishes, such as *cataplana de tamboril, amêijoa e camarão* (monkfish, clam and prawn casserole) and *feijoada de camarão* (prawn and bean stew).

PONTE DA BARCA: O Moinho
€€
Traditional Portuguese   Map C1
Campo do Côrro 1, 4980-614
Tel *258 452 035*   **Closed** *Tue*
A charming restaurant in a beautiful rural setting with river views. Lamprey is the house speciality, when in season, or try the veal steaks. The establishment has a decent wine list which includes locally produced wines.

PONTE DE LIMA: A Carvalheira
€€
Traditional Portuguese   Map C1
Rua do Eido Velho, Fornelos, 4990-620
Tel *258 742 316*   **Closed** *Mon*
Dishes at this restaurant with rustic decor include Portuguese staples such as cod with corn bread and roast kid. There is a good wine list with plenty of *vinhos verdes*.

PONTE DE LIMA: A Tulha
€€
Traditional Portuguese   Map C1
Rua Formosa 4, 4990-117
Tel *258 942 879*   **Closed** *Sun dinner, Mon*
This family-friendly restaurant uses fresh local produce for its weekly changing menu. Must-try delicacies include *bacalhau*, veal steak and the orange pudding.

PÓVOA DE VARZIM: O Marinheiro
€€
Modern Portuguese   Map C2
Rua Gomes de Amorim 1842, 4490-091
Tel *252 682 151*
A trendy, boat-shaped restaurant with a sleek, elegant design. The fresh seafood is the main draw, but meat eaters are well catered for too. There is a children's menu.

VALENÇA DO MINHO: Mané
€€
International   Map C1
Avenida Miguel Dantas 5, 4930-678
Tel *251 823 402*   **Closed** *Mon*
The menu here offers a blend of Portuguese and French influences. Good wine list.

VALENÇA DO MINHO: São Teotónio
€€
Traditional Portuguese   Map C1
Baluarte do Socorro, 4930-619
Tel *251 800 260*
Enjoy lovely country views at this elegant, spacious restaurant in a *pousada*. Try the *arroz de tamboril com camarão* (monkfish with rice and shrimp) or the cabbage soup with Minho sausages. Extensive lunch buffet served on weekends.

VIANA DO CASTELO: O Pescador
€€
Traditional Portuguese   Map C1
Largo São Domingos 35, 4900-330
Tel *258 826 039*   **Closed** *Sun dinner; Mon*
Lamprey is a particular seasonal favourite at this restaurant, with its emphasis on fish and seafood. Another speciliality is the *combinado de mariscos* (seafood platter).

VIANA DO CASTELO: Camelo
€€€
Traditional Portuguese   Map C1
Santa Marta de Portuzelo, 4925-090
Tel *258 839 090*   **Closed** *Mon*
Reputed to be one of the best restaurants serving traditional

The elegant interior of São Teotónio in Valença do Minho

Portuguese cuisine in the country, Camelo has excellent grilled meats and fish dishes and great-value lunch menus.

Alentejo

ALANDROAL: A Maria
€€
Traditional Portuguese   Map D5
Rua João de Deus 12, 7250-142
Tel *268 431 143*   **Closed** *Mon dinner*
The house specialities at this charming, rustic restaurant with blue-and-white walls include delicious *cozido de grão à alentejana* (Alentejan-style chickpea and meat stew).

DK Choice

ALBERNÔA: Herdade dos Grous
€€€
Modern Portuguese   Map D6
Herdade dos Grous, 7800-601
Tel *284 960 000*   **Closed** *Mon–Thu dinner*
This restaurant is housed in a magnificent blue-and-white building on a beautiful country estate. Furnished in warm colours and natural textures, it has a distinct countrified air. Many of the ingredients for the gourmet menu come from the estate itself, including the wine. Try the hare rice with Herdade dos Grous red wine.

ALVITO: Castelo de Alvito
€
Traditional Portuguese   Map D6
Castelo de Alvito, 7920-999
Tel *284 480 700*
The vaulted ceilings of this restaurant, housed in a 15th-century castle, add to the sense of history and grandeur. The food is top-notch and the service is excellent.

The leafy garden at Cor de Tangerina, Guimarães *(see p408)*

BEJA: Adega 25 de Abril €
Traditional Portuguese **Map** D6
Rua da Moeda 23, 7800-000
Tel *284 325 960* **Closed** *Sun dinner; Mon*
Brick walls and giant terracotta urns create a rustic backdrop for typical Alentejan fare, including splendid *sopa de cação* (dogfish soup). For dessert, try the *sericaia* (an incredibly light sponge cake).

BEJA: Espelho d'Água €
Traditional Portuguese **Map** D6
Rua de Lisboa, Parque da Cidade, 7800-292
Tel *284 325 103* **Closed** *Mon*
Beef and pineapple kebabs and *carne de porco à alentejana* (pork and clams) are menu highlights at this modern restaurant with bright colours and park views.

CRATO: Flor da Rosa €€€
Traditional Portuguese **Map** D4
Mosteiro da Flor da Rosa, 7430-099
Tel *245 997 210*
Featuring stylish decor in neutral tones, Flor da Rosa has a menu that favours regional cuisine. Local wines are well represented. There are lovely garden views.

ELVAS: Pompílio €€
Traditional Portuguese **Map** D5
Rua de Elvas 96, São Vicente, 7350-481
Tel *268 611 133* **Closed** *Tue*
The friendly staff will help you select from the excellent regional and extended game menu. Try the *arroz de lebre* (hare rice).

ESTREMOZ: Adega Típico do Isaías €
Traditional Portuguese **Map** D5
Rua do Almeida 21, 7100-537
Tel *268 322 318* **Closed** *Sun dinner*
This restaurant used to be a wine cellar, and it still produces its own house wine. Clay urns line the walls, and the menu features tasty and wholesome home-cooked regional dishes.

ESTREMOZ: Gadanha Mercearia €
Traditional Portuguese **Map** D5
Largo Dragões de Olivença 84A, 7100-457
Tel *268 333 262* **Closed** *Mon*
Brazilian chef Michele Marques heads a kitchen that has received much acclaim for its imaginative take on traditional Portuguese fare, creatively re-inventing regional recipes. The restaurant is also a one-stop grocery store.

ÉVORA: Botequim da Mouraria €€
Traditional Portuguese **Map** D5
Rua da Mouraria 16A 7000-585
Tel *266 746 775* **Closed** *Sat dinner; Sun*
Perch on a stool at the bar and tuck into fine home-cooked Alentejan food at this tiny eatery. Arrive early or expect to wait.

ÉVORA: Fialho €€
Traditional Portuguese **Map** D5
Travessa das Mascarenhas 16, 7000-557
Tel *266 703 079* **Closed** *Mon*
A historic, award-winning restaurant offering inventive cuisine – try the excellent dogfish in coriander sauce. There is a good wine list. Book in advance.

ÉVORA: Tasquinha do Oliveira €€
Traditional Portuguese **Map** D5
Rua Cândido dos Reis 45A, 7000-582
Tel *266 744 841* **Closed** *Sun; early Aug*
Imaginative regional cuisine, including game dishes in season, is served at this restaurant, said to be one of the best in Portugal. The dining area is adorned with decorative plates. Tasquinha do Oliveira has a good wine list.

MARVÃO: Sever €
Traditional Portuguese **Map** D4
Estrada Rio do Sever, Portagem, 7330-347
Tel *245 993 318*
A pretty restaurant with a leafy esplanade overlooking the River Sever. The menu offers carefully prepared and presented regional cuisine, with plenty of game and local produce. Try the chestnut soup or venison stew.

MÉRTOLA: Tamuje €€
Traditional Portuguese **Map** D6
Rua Doutor Serrão Martins 36, 7750-355
Tel *286 611 115* **Closed** *Sun, first week in Sep*
This small family-run restaurant, named after the river it overlooks, serves beautifully prepared regional cuisine and good organic house wine.

MONSARAZ: O Alcaide €
Traditional Portuguese **Map** D5
Rua do Convento, 7200-173
Tel *266 557 168* **Closed** *Thu*
The tempting menu of regional dishes at this attractive restaurant, decorated with farming tools and ceramics, is meat-heavy. There is an impressive wine list. Book ahead.

MONTEMOR-O-NOVO: L'And Vineyards €€€
Modern Mediterranean **Map** C5
Herdade das Valadas, 7050-031
Tel *266 242 400* **Closed** *Mon, Tue*
Using premier grade ingredients, chef Miguel Laffan creates dishes of regionally focused cuisine suffused with distinct flavours at this striking eatery. His contemporary style and attention to detail have garnered the establishment a much deserved Michelin star.

The chic bar area at Flor da Rosa, housed in a former monastery in Crato

The beautiful dining room at Redondo's Convento de São Paulo

PORTALEGRE: Solar do Forcado
Modern Portuguese   **Map** D4   €
Rua Cândido dos Reis 14, 7300-129
Tel *245 330 866*   **Closed** *Sat lunch; Sun*
Imaginative versions of regional recipes are accompanied by good Alentejan wines. The decor makes it evident that the owner is a bullfighting fan.

PORTALEGRE: Tombalobos
Traditional Portuguese   **Map** D4   €€
Bairro da Pedra Basta 16, 7300-529
Tel *245 906 111*   **Closed** *Sun dinner, Mon*
Chef José Júlio Vintém, a native of Portalegre, celebrates local cuisine with a creative menu of delicious cuisine. Expect favourites like *açorda* (see p294).

REDONDO: Convento de São Paulo
Traditional Portuguese   **Map** D5   €€
Aldeia da Serra, 7170-120
Tel *266 989 160*
Azulejo panels line this dining room beneath an arched, painted ceiling. The menu matches the elegant and refined setting and uses top-quality ingredients from the estate.

SANTIAGO DO CACÉM: A Deolinda
Traditional Portuguese   **Map** C6   €
Monte Cruz de Alcaide, 7540-237
Tel *269 822 732*   **Closed** *Mon*
This warm and unpretentious eatery is popular with a local clientele for its hearty game dishes such as *perdíz à casa* (partridge), along with other regional classics.

SERPA: Adega Molhóbico
Traditional Portuguese   **Map** D6   €€
Rua Quente 1, 7830-000
Tel *284 549 264*   **Closed** *Wed; 24 Jun–10 Jul*
The pastoral decor in this popular restaurant is enhanced with paintings by local artists. The dishes are served in generous portions and are excellent value. The wine list favours the region.

TERRUGEM: A Bolota
Modern Portuguese   **Map** B5   €€
Rua Madre Teresa, 7350-491
Tel *268 656 118*   **Closed** *Mon, Tue; early Aug*
Serving inspired gourmet cuisine, the tasting menu at this celebrated restaurant includes such delights as partridge stuffed with mushrooms and chestnuts.

VILA DE FRADES: País das Uvas
Traditional Portuguese   **Map** D6   €
Rua General Humburto Delgado 19, 7960-000
Tel *284 441 023*   **Closed** *Wed*
The menu here celebrates traditional Portuguese gastronomy, with plenty of bias towards hearty Alentejan fare. The rustic interior is lined with massive amphorae or wine pots – *talhas*. This is where *vinho da talha* house wine, produced exactly the way Romans made wine, is stored.

VILA NOVA DE MILFONTES: Marisqueira Dunas Mil
Seafood   **Map** C6   €€
Avenida Marginal, 7645-000
Tel *283 996 420*
Freshly caught fish and seafood make it to the dish of the day or straight to the grill at this popular restaurant overlooking the ocean. Good wines.

Algarve

ALBUFEIRA: Adega do Zé
Traditional Portuguese   **Map** C7   €
Torre da Medronheira, Estrada dos Olhos d'Agua, 8200-635
Tel *289 501 617*   **Closed** *Sun*
Dishes like *Arroz de polvo* (octopus rice) and *espetadas de tamboril* (monkfish kebab) feature on the menu at this lively eatery. A long established institution, it is run by a much-admired local couple.

ALBUFEIRA: Evaristo
Seafood   **Map** C7   €€€
Praia do Evaristo, 8200-903
Tel *289 591 666*
Backed by gardens and overlooking the beach, this bright, spacious restaurant is ideal for grilled fish and seafood.

ALMANCIL: Gourmet Natural
Uruguayan   **Map** D7   €€
Estrada Vale do Lobo, 8135-018
Tel *289 355 271*
Housed in a beautiful 18th-century farmhouse, this restaurant is famous for its top-quality Uruguayan steaks and dishes such as prawn ceviche.

ALMANCIL: A Quinta
International   **Map** D7   €€€
Rua Vale Formoso, 8100-267
Tel *289 393 357*   **Closed** *lunch; Sun*
This warm, elegant restaurant offers fine dining in a romantic setting. The comprehensive menu is based on the freshest seasonal ingredients available.

ALVOR: Ruccala
International   **Map** C7   €€
Rua Poeta João de Deus, 8500-000
Tel *965 839 902*   **Closed** *lunch, Sun*
Enjoy a lively atmosphere and harbour views from the terrace while tucking into lamb shank, steak or sea bass. Book ahead.

ARMAÇÃO DE PÊRA: L'Oasis
Italian   **Map** C7   €
Rua Dom João II, Lj1 r/c, Edifício Atlântico IV, 8365-130
Tel *282 312 869* **Closed** *Tue, Oct–Jun*
Expect a warm welcome and high-quality dishes, such as creative pizzas and home-made pastas, at this cosy restaurant.

CARVOEIRO: Boneca Bar
Seafood   **Map** C7   €
Sitio do Algo Seco, 8401-909
Tel *282 358 391*
Tucked away among rocks and caves above the beach, this family-run restaurant serves great seafood and cocktails. Try the tiger prawns or the catch of the day.

For more information on types of restaurants *see pages 396–7*

Selection of wine bottles lining the walls at Veneza, in Paderne

CARVOEIRO: Bon Bon €€€
International **Map** C7
Urb. Cabeço de Pais, Sesmarias 8400-525
Tel 282 341 496 **Closed** lunch, Wed & Nov–Feb
The unassuming location of this Michelin star restaurant is misleading. Master chef Rui Silvestre delivers highly crafted and wonderfully presented modern cuisine.

CASTRO MARIM: A Tasca Medieval €
Traditional Portuguese **Map** C7
Rua 25 de Abril 65, 8950-122
Tel 281 513 196 **Closed** Tue
The house speciality at this convenient place is açorda de galhina (bread-based chicken stew). Be sure to leave room for one of the sweet almond desserts.

ESTÔMBAR: O Charneco €€
Traditional Portuguese **Map** C7
Rua Joaquim Manuel Charneco 3, 8400-037
Tel 282 431 113 **Closed** lunch, Sun & Jan
Come here for authentic, award-winning Algarvean cooking, including delights such as pernil no forno (oven-baked ham) and borrego guisado com feijão verde (lamb fricassée with green beans).

FARO: A Taska €
Traditional Portuguese **Map** D7
Rua do Alportel 38, 8000-239
Tel 969 441 381 **Closed** Sun
The xarém (thick cornmeal soup with clams or bacon) is a speciality at this typical, rustic restaurant. Look out for the dish of the day or the tasting menu.

FARO: Dois Irmãos €€
Portuguese/International **Map** D7
Praça Ferreira de Almeida 15, 8000-156
Tel 289 823 337
The accent here is on classic Algarvean cuisine. Specialities

include cataplana de peixe (fish casserole) and açorda de marisco (seafood and bread stew).

FARO: O Estaminé €€
Seafood **Map** D7
Ilha Deserta, 8000-138
Tel 917 811 856 **Closed** dinner
Take a water taxi to get to this island restaurant. The trip is well worth the effort for the views, the lovely wooden building and the ultra-fresh seafood.

FERRAGUDO: Sueste €€
Traditional Portuguese / Seafood **Map** C7
Rua Infante Santo 91, 8400-256
Tel 282 461 592 **Closed** Sun & Jan
There are great views over the estuary at this quayside eatery specializing in charcoal-grilled fish. Expect polished service and an excellent wine list.

LAGOS: No Pátio €€
International **Map** C7
Rua Lançarote de Freitas 46, 8600-605
Tel 282 763 777 **Closed** Sun & Mon
Run by a British couple, this charming restaurant with a garden terrace serves perfectly cooked cuisine. The menu changes monthly to incorporate fresh seasonal produce.

LAGOS: Vista Alegre €€
French **Map** C7
Rua Ilha Terceira 19B, 8600-969
Tel 282 792 151 **Closed** Mon
Bookings are essential at this 20-seat French bistro. Service can be a little slow, but the fare is worth waiting for. Try the quail salad or duck in honey sauce.

LOULÉ: Bica Velha €€
Traditional Portuguese **Map** D7
Rua Martin Moniz 17–19, 8100-000
Tel 289 463 376 **Closed** lunch
The food is complemented by the intimate and rustic

atmosphere of the arched ceilings and stone walls of this 17th-century building.

MEXILHOEIRA GRANDE: Adega Vilalisa €€
Traditional Portuguese **Map** C7
Rua Francisco Bivar 52, 8500-132
Tel 282 968 478 **Closed** lunch
Wonderfully understated, and with shared tables, this simple eatery offers a great tasting menu with wines. Reservations recommended.

ODIAXERE: Cacto €€
International **Map** C7
Estrada Nacional 125, 8600-250
Tel 282 798 285 **Closed** lunch, Thu, Wed
Delicious slow-roasted lamb with garlic and herbs is a menu highlight here. Book ahead.

OLHÃO: Horta €€
Traditional Portuguese **Map** D7
Avenida 5 de Outubro 148, 8700-304
Tel 289 714 215 **Closed** Sat
Friendly, no-frills service and huge portions make this restaurant a favourite with locals. Staples include monkfish rice and juicy picanha (beef) kebab.

PADERNE: Veneza €€
Traditional Portuguese **Map** C7
Paderne Albufeira, 8200-488
Tel 289 367 129 **Closed** Tue & Wed lunch; 2 weeks in spring & autumn
The bottles lining the walls here reflect the vast wine list, with over 800 options. There is an impressive menu of home-cooked dishes.

DK Choice

PRAIA DA GALÉ: Vila Joya €€€
International **Map** C7
Estrada da Galé, 8200-416
Tel 289 591 795 **Closed** Dates vary
One of Portugal's finest restaurants, Vila Joya boasts two Michelin stars. With a wine cellar of 12,000 optimally stored bottles, the perfect wine pairing with the gourmet cuisine is guaranteed. Advance reservations are essential, especially for non-hotel guests.

PRAIA DA ROCHA: Vista €€€
Traditional Portuguese **Map** C7
Av Tomas Cabreira, 8500-802
Tel 282 460 280
Headed by young Portuguese chef João Oliveira, this is the in-house restaurant of Bela Vista Hotel & Spa. Vista offers two superb tasting menus, and the maître d' will suggest wine pairings.

QUINTA DO LAGO:
2 Passos €€
International **Map** D7
Praia do Ancão, 8135-905
Tel *289 396 435* **Closed** *dinner (Sep–Jun); Dec–Jan*
Tuck into *lagosta no pote* (lobster in the pot) or T-bone steak at this informal, friendly beachside restaurant with ocean views.

QUINTA DO LAGO:
Casa Velha €€€
French **Map** D7
Rotunda 6, Quinta do Lago, 8135-024
Tel *289 394 983* **Closed** *Sun, mid-Dec–Feb;lunch daily*
A charming restaurant decorated with colourful paintings and sculptures. The rustic interior of the converted old farmhouse features an open fireplace, and there is also a pretty, flower-filled terrace. The dishes are made with fresh Mediterranean produce.

SAGRES: Pousada
de Sagres €€
Modern Portuguese **Map** C7
Ponta da Atalaia, 8650-385
Tel *282 620 240*
This understated restaurant serves regional dishes with a twist, including rack of lamb in muscatel wine and sardines stuffed with tomatoes and herbs. Book ahead.

SAGRES: O Telheiro
do Infante €€
Seafood **Map** C7
Praia da Mareta, 8650-361
Tel *282 624 179* **Closed** *dinner, Tue*
Order the catch of the day, which will arrive grilled to your specification, or try house specialities such as lobster rice at this restaurant with impressive ocean views.

SILVES: Marisqueira
Rui €€
Seafood **Map** C7
Rua Comendador Vilarinho 27, 8300-128
Tel *282 442 682* **Closed** *Wed, Nov*
A lively, informal restaurant, Marisqueira Rui is popular with locals. Try the *sapateria* (crab) or the mixed seafood platter. There is an extensive wine list.

TAVIRA: A Ver Tavira €€
Traditional Portuguese **Map** D7
Calçada da Galeria 13, 8800-303
Tel *281 381 363*
Award-winning chef Samuel Silva serves gourmet fusion cuisine in this special setting with river views. The tasting menu pairs dishes with appropriate wines. There are frequent live *fado* and jazz evenings.

TAVIRA: Brisa do Rio €€
Traditional Portuguese **Map** D7
Rua João Vaz Corte Real 38, 8800-351
Tel *915 434 452* **Closed** *lunch, Wed*
Exuding genuine warmth and hospitality, this is one of Tavira's culinary landmarks. The menu errs towards fresh fish and seafood, though dishes like the rack of lamb are equally appetizing. Book ahead.

VILAMOURA: Oliveira
Dourada €€
International **Map** D7
Rua do Mar 135T, 8125-039
Tel *913 588 099* **Closed** *Mon*
A homely, relaxed restaurant. The eclectic menu, influenced by countries such as India, Mexico, America and Greece, caters for almost every taste.

VILAMOURA: Pepper's
Steakhouse €€€
Steakhouse **Map** D7
Tivoli Marina Vilamoura 8125-401
Tel *289 303 303* **Closed** *lunch*
A sophisticated restaurant situated in the Tivoli Marina hotel. The menu features impressive steaks as well as plenty of other options. There is a superb wine list. Book ahead.

Madeira

CAMACHA: Abrigo do Pastor €€
Regional Portuguese
Estrada das Carreiras 209, 9135-350
Tel *291 922 060* **Closed** *Tue, 25 Dec*
Enjoy dishes like succulent mixed grills, oven-roast octopus or weekend treats like *favada de javali* (wild boar and bean stew) at this suitably rustic and homely eatery.

CÂMARA DE LOBOS:
Adega da Quinta €€
Traditional Portuguese
Quinta do Estreito, Rua José Joaquim da Costa, 9325-039
Tel *291 910 530*
This lovely restaurant with garden and ocean views has a rustic interior featuring beamed ceilings. It serves fine regional cuisine and the wine cellar is stocked with vintage Madeiras.

FUNCHAL: O Tapassol €
Traditional Portuguese
Rua Dom Carlos I, 62, 9050-041
Tel *291 225 023*
Reserve a table on the upstairs terrace of this restaurant for lovely city views. There are typical Madeiran dishes as well as many other options.

DK Choice

FUNCHAL: Armazem
do Sal €€
Modern Portuguese
Rua da Alfândega 135, 9000-000
Tel *291 241 285* **Closed** *Sat lunch; Sun*
The stone walls and thick wooden beams of this sophisticated restaurant are offset with stylish furnishings. The *haute cuisine*, a blend of regional and international recipes, is on a par with Michelin standards. An equally impressive wine list features staff choices and vintage labels.

FUNCHAL: Barqueiro €€
Seafood
Centro Commercial Centromar Loja 21, 9000-113
Tel *291 765 226*
Enjoy some of the city's best seafood, including *lapas* (limpets) and *ovas de espada* (swordfish roe), in a relaxed, informal ambience.

The dining room of the Pousada do Sagres, Sagres

For more information on types of restaurants *see pages 396–7*

FUNCHAL: O Celeiro　€€
Seafood
Rua Aranhas 22, 9000-044
Tel *291 230 622*　　**Closed** *Sun*
One of the oldest restaurants in
the region, O Celeiro is furnished
with dark wood and *azulejo* tiles.
The reasonably priced menu is
dominated by fish and seafood.

FUNCHAL: O Jango　€€
Traditional Portuguese
Rua de Santa Maria 166,
9060-291
Tel *291 221 280*
Dishes are carefully prepared
and presented at this restaurant
with an African-themed decor
and a varied menu. Try the
house steak or *gambas à*
Indiana (prawns).

FUNCHAL: Riso　€€
International
Rua de Santa Maria 274, 9050-040
Tel *291 280 360*　　**Closed** *Mon*
The menu here is devoted to rice.
In addition to *paella*, there are
all kinds of imaginative risottos
and other rice-based dishes.
The views of the ocean are
spectacular too.

FUNCHAL: Dona Amélia　€€€
International
Rua Imperatriz Dona Amélia 83,
9000-018
Tel *291 225 784*
A pretty restaurant overlooking
tiled rooftops. Dishes such as
gnocchi with lobster and tuna
steak with fettuccini grace the
menu, along with flambéed pork
and fish. Book ahead.

FUNCHAL: Il Gallo d'Oro　€€€
Modern Portuguese
Cliff Bay Hotel, Estrada Monumental
147, 9004-532
Tel *291 707 700*
Two Michelin stars shine
above this acclaimed gourmet
restaurant. French chef Benoît

Riso in Funchal, which specializes in risotto dishes

Sinthon surprises with his
creativity, using regional
produce whenever possible.
The wine list is extensive and
features local as well as
international labels.

FUNCHAL: Ristorante
Villa Cipriani　€€€
Italian
Estrada Monumental 139,
9000-098
Tel *291 717 171*　　**Closed** *lunch*
The checked tablecloths lend an
informal air to this gourmet
Italian restaurant. Sweeping
ocean views from the terrace
add to the dining experience.

FUNCHAL: Uva　€€€
International
Rua dos Aranhas 27A, 9000-044
Tel *291 009 000*
Within the Vine Hotel, this
contemporary dining spot
serves delicious gourmet fare.
The rooftop views are splendid.

PORTO SANTO: Hotel Quinta
do Serrado　€€
Traditional Portuguese
Sítio do Pedregal, 9400-010
Tel *291 980 270*
The restaurant at Hotel
Quinta do Serrado specializes
in traditional Portuguese
dishes with a local Algarvean
twist. Try the *pudim de*
maracujá (passion fruit
pudding) for dessert.

PORTO SANTO: Ponta da
Calheta　€€
Seafood
Sítio de Calheta, Calheta,
9400-001
Tel *291 985 322*　　**Closed** *Jan & Feb*
This is a great place to watch
the sun set and enjoy
incredibly fresh fish and seafood dishes, such as bean and
prawn stew. For an entirely
relaxed evening ,call to arrange
a hotel pick-up.

RIBEIRA BRAVA: Fajã
dos Padres　€€
Seafood
Estrada Padre António Dinis
Henriques I, 9300-261
Tel *291 944 538*　　**Closed** *dinner*
Reached by cable car, this
restaurant, offering a vast
selection of fresh seafood and
regional dishes, can accommodate
dinner bookings for large
groups and visits to the
vineyards by appointment.

SANTANA: Cantinho
da Serra　€€
Traditional Portuguese
Estrada do Pico das Pedras,
9230-107
Tel *291 573 727*
Warm colours and a huge
fireplace give this restaurant a
cosy, welcoming atmosphere.
Hearty regional dishes and
interesting home-made liqueurs
are on the menu.

SANTANA: Quinta do Furão　€€
International
Achada do Gramacho, 9230-082
Tel *291 570 100*
The high-ceilinged dining area
features two huge fireplaces,
while the sheltered terrace offers
stunning views. Organic and
local produce is used almost
exclusively. Vegetarian options
are available.

The Azores

CORVO: Traineira　€
Traditional Portuguese
Rua Matriz, 9980-020
Tel *292 596 088*　　**Closed** *Sun*
The dishes offered at this
simple restaurant vary
according to what is available.
Starters usually include
enchidos (sausages) and *queijo*
da ilha (local cheese). Servings
are substantial.

The modern interior of Uva in Funchal,
with ocean views

FAIAL: Medalhas €
Traditional Portuguese
Rua Serpa Pinto 22, Horta, 9900-095
Tel *292 391 026* **Closed** *Mon*
This restaurant retains its
original *taberna* atmosphere and
is equally popular for snacks
and full meals. The menu varies
depending on availability
but includes both meat and
fish dishes.

FAIAL: Sal & Pico €€
Modern Portuguese
Rua Vasco da Gama, Horta, 9900-017
Tel *292 202 200* **Closed** *Dec & Jan*
Set in the historic Pousada Forte
da Horta overlooking Horta Bay,
this pleasant restaurant is one of
the best on Faial Island. House
specialities include fried pork
with pineapple and roast tuna.

FLORES: Sereia €
Seafood
*Rua Doutor Armas da Silveira 30,
Santa Cruz das Flores, 9970-331*
Tel *292 592 220* **Closed** *Sun*
This small, friendly restaurant has
been popular with locals and
visitors for many years. Try the
catch of the day or the *caldeirada
de peixe* (fish and potato casserole).

GRACIOSA: Quinta das Grotas €€
Traditional Portuguese
*Caminho das Grotas 28, Ribeirinha
9880-020*
Tel *295 712 334* **Closed** *Mon (winter)*
Set in a beautiful stone-clad
farmhouse in the middle of the
countryside, the hearty rustic fare
served here is enhanced in
winter by a roaring log fire.

PICO: Ancoradouro €€
Traditional Portuguese
Areia Larga, Madalena, 9950-302
Tel *292 623 490* **Closed** *Mon*
A modest restaurant with an
attractive veranda and glorious
views of Faial Island. The *morcela
com laranja* (black pudding with
orange) is delicious.

Sal & Pico restaurant, in a historic *pousada*
in Faial

PICO: Cella Bar €€
Modern Regional
Lugar da Barca, 9950-303
Tel *292 623 654* **Closed** *Hours vary*
Located just outside Madalena,
this chic bistro wine bar-
restaurant has won awards for its
striking architectural design.
Seafood is the speciality (try the
roasted octopus).

PICO: Fonte Cuisine €€
International
*Caminho de Baixo, Lajes do Pico,
9930-177*
Tel *292 679 504*
Both vegetarians and meat eaters
will find good options at this
hotel restaurant. Regular buffets
feature Portuguese and
international dishes as well as
Azorean fare.

SANTA MARIA: Mesa d'Oito €
Modern Portuguese
*Rua Teófilo de Braga 31, Vila do Porto
9580-535*
Tel *296 882 107*
Setting new culinary standards is
this stylish eatery, the in-house
restaurant of the Charming Blue
Hotel. A menu of contemporary

Portuguese cuisine replete with
an excellent wine choice
complements the chic décor.

SÃO JORGE: Fornos da Lava €€
Traditional Portuguese
*Travessa de São Tiago 46, 9800-347
Santo Amaro, Velas*
Tel *295 432 415* **Closed** *22 Dec–1 Jan*
The vegetables and herbs used
in dishes such as sea bass with
avocado are grown in the garden
of this charming, rustic eatery. The
kitchen uses wood-fired ovens to
bake delicious bread.There are
wonderful views across Velas.

SÃO MIGUEL: Monte Verde €
Seafood
Rua da Areia 4, Ribeira Grande, 9600-000
Tel *296 472 975* **Closed** *Mon*
Choose fish from the display
counter and have it grilled or fried
to perfection. The house speciality
is *tigelada de chicharro*, a stew
made with thin, sardine-like fish.

SÃO MIGUEL: Alcides €€
Traditional Portuguese
*Rua Hintze Ribeiro 67–77,
Ponta Delgada, 9504-000*
Tel *296 629 884* **Closed** *Sun*
This unpretentious restaurant is
renowned for its steaks, especially
the house speciality, *bife à Alcides*.
The stylish interior features brightly
painted walls and stone arches.

SÃO MIGUEL: O Miroma €€
Traditional Portuguese
*Rua Dr Frederico Moniz Pereira 15,
Furnas 9675-055*
Tel *296 584 422*
Some of the house specialities
here are baked underground,
using heat generated by the
volcanic springs. This is what
makes the unique *cozido* (stew)
so delicious and popular.

**TERCEIRA: Quinta do
Martelo** €
Traditional Portuguese
*Canada do Martelo 24, Cantinho,
São Mateus, 9700-576*
Tel *295 642 842* **Closed** *Wed*
A quaint, rural restaurant that
serves authentic Azorean dishes
such as *alcatra* (meat stew)
and *Sopa do Espírito Santo*, a
soup of meat and vegetables in
white wine.

TERCEIRA: O Pescador €€
Traditional Portuguese
*Avenida Beira Mar, Bloco C, Praia da
Vitória, 9760-441*
Tel *295 513 495* **Closed** *Sun*
This popular restaurant exudes a
friendly and informal ambience
and is renowned for its delicious
grilled swordfish with sautéed
vegetables. Book ahead.

The well-stocked bar area at Fonte Cuisine, Pico

SHOPPING IN PORTUGAL

Portugal offers a wealth of tempting goods at reasonable prices for shoppers. The best buys include handmade leather goods and shoes, handcrafted gold and silver jewellery, fine porcelain and crystal, glassware, and high-quality clothes from hand-knitted sweaters to the latest fashion garments and designer labels. The appearance of shopping malls has brought a range of recognised brands onto the market. Fortunately, traditional arts and crafts have not been lost as a result of this modernization. Pottery and ceramics, embroidery and lace, woodcarving and cork, copper artifacts, tapestries, carpets and fresh produce are of a high standard. The regional tourism office shops are some of the best places to buy genuine Portuguese handicrafts and souvenirs.

Lisbon's enormous Centro Colombo shopping mall

Opening Hours

Normal shopping hours are 9am–1pm and 3–7pm Monday to Friday and 9 or 10am–1pm on Saturdays. However, many shops in the bigger towns and cities remain open during the lunch hour and on Saturday afternoons. The big shopping centres are open every day, including Sundays, from 10am to 11pm or midnight.

Tax-Free Goods

On most goods a 23 per cent value-added tax (IVA – Imposto sobre o Valor Acrescentado) is charged in mainland Portugal. In Madeira the tax is 22 per cent and in the Azores it's 18 per cent.
   Portugal has more than 1,600 shops affiliated with the "Tax Free for Tourists System"' which can be identified by the logo of that name. Non-European Union visitors are exempt from IVA, provided that they stay in Portugal no longer than 180 days.
   Obtaining a rebate in smaller shops may be complicated; it is simpler to buy in a shop with a 'tax free' sign outside. Ask the shop assistant for an Isencão na Exportação form, which must be presented to a customs official on your departure from Portugal. For more details consult **Global Blue**.

How to Pay

Most shops accept credit and debit cards, though you may need to pay with cash in some of the smaller shops outside the big cities. You may be asked to show a passport when purchasing expensive items by credit card.
   Under EU regulations on consumer goods, you have a two-year guarantee on products. Faulty goods must be returned with the original receipt for exchange or repair.

Shopping Malls

Springing up in ever increasing numbers, large shopping malls have exerted a big influence on shopping habits in Portugal. Lisbon's huge **Centro Colombo** boasts nearly 400 stores. Opened in 1997, it is the Iberian Peninsula's largest shopping mall. It also houses a leisure complex, multiplex cinema, health club, driving range, chapel and bowling alley.

Markets

A social and commercial occasion, the street market is integral to Portuguese life. It is usually held in the town's main square; ask for the mercado or feira if in doubt. Most markets sell a wide range of goods from food to household items and clothes, but you will also see sites devoted to antiques and local crafts. Roadside stalls offer produce from smallholdings, including delicious home-made liqueurs, pastries and cakes. Most markets are held in the mornings only, but in tourist areas they may go on until late afternoon.

Ceramics for sale at the open-air market in Barcelos

Colourful handmade ceramics from the Alentejo region

Portugal's most famous market is the one in Barcelos *(see p279)*, held Thursday in the main square. Here you can buy a vast range of household goods and local produce, and handicrafts such as pottery, lace, rugs and clothes.

Lisbon's Feira da Ladra (Thieves' Market) *(see p75)* is probably the best-known flea market and attracts large crowds. The **Feira de Antigui-dades** at Estação Oriente in the city is another good hunting ground, and the **Feira de Carcavelos**, **Feira de Cascais** and **Feira de São Pedro** in Sintra attract bargain hunters by the thousands.

A traditional clay *boneco* (doll)

renowned for its regional pottery, especially figures based on everyday rustic life and religious themes. The best can be seen in the local museum and **Centro de Artesanato** in the city, and finely made replicas are on sale in shops and markets. The village of São Pedro do Corval in the Alentejo region is known for its colourful hand-painted plates and pots depicting flower motifs or rural scenes, such as the harvest or the pig-slaughter. **Porches Pottery** in the Algarve is famous for its plates and pots decorated with revivalist designs of ancient Iberian forms and motifs.

Ceramics

Antique hand-painted glazed tiles *(azulejos)* are highly sought after and expensive *(see p419)*, but excellent repro-ductions are available in museum shops such as Lisbon's Museu Nacional do Azulejos *(see pp124–5)*. **Azulejos Sant' Anna** also produces excellent replicas of early tiles. Portugal's oldest established ceramics company is **Vista Alegre Atlantis**, which produces high-quality porcelain.

If you are visiting Viseu *(see p219)*, look out for the beautiful black earthenware pottery made by a handful of master potters. Viseu is one of the last few places where ceramics of this type are made. Barcelos is

Handicrafts

Portugal is well known for its delicate embroidery and fine lace, and the best-known source is the island of Madeira. On the mainland, the best lace and embroidery comes from towns in the Minho such as Viana do Castelo, also famous for its brightly printed shawls. Embroidered bedspreads are sold in Castelo Branco in the Beira Baixa, and colourful carpets, such as those from Arraiolos, are sold throughout the Alentejo.

Popular regional items are embroidered lovers' handker-chiefs *(lenços dos namorados)* in the Minho region and the typical local costume which is notable for its brilliant colours,

rich ornaments and variety. The Minho is famous for its filigree gold and silver work, from traditional necklaces, heart-shaped pendants, earrings and rings to religious votives and trinkets.

Also unique to the Minho is the ancient floral art of *palmito*, a type of bouquet made with metallic coloured paper by young girls and women for religious ceremonies and as souvenirs. These are available in the workshops on the **Alto Minho Handicrafts Route**.

Arraiolos in the Alentejo has been famous since the late 16th century for its hand-embroidered carpets, which are sewn in wool on a canvas frame. Originally, they followed traditional Persian and Indian designs, but from the 18th century, more modern designs became popular. Fine examples are on sale in many shops in the town, especially at **Tapetes de Arraiolos**, and elsewhere in Portugal.

The Alentejo is also the best region for buying handmade rugs and bed-spreads in brightly coloured materials. In the town of Estremoz you will find the unique traditional clay figures known as *bonecos* (dolls). The making of these gaily painted pieces depicting religious and rustic themes dates back more than two centuries.

Ornately embroidered clothing from Viana do Castelo in the Minho

Preparing to sample the wine at a stall in the Minho region

Wine and Spirits

While it may be best known for fortified wines such as port and Madeira, Portugal also has a wide and varied range of excellent table wines *(see pp32–3)*, which are well represented in shops, supermarkets and wine merchants. Some of the most characterful wines, particularly reds, are made in the Douro region, where port is also made. More approachable reds (and increasingly, whites) are made in the Alentejo, whose wines are much loved by the Portuguese themselves. Wines are widely available, but for a good selection try **Garrafeira Nacional** in Baixa, or the **Coisas do Arco do Vinho** or **Solar do Vinho do Porto** in Lisbon.

The wines in Portugal are inexpensive compared to other European countries, and include the whole range, from young green wines *(vinho verdes)* through popular rosés, fruity whites and robust reds to Madeira wine and ports. It is often cheaper to shop direct from the winemaking co-operatives.

Home distilling is also a favourite pastime in Portugal. Apart from distilled wine *(aguardente)* and a spirit made from grape skins *(bagaço)*, various liqueurs are made with cherries *(gingjinha)*, almonds *(amêndoa)* and figs *(figo)*.

A speciality in the Algarve is *medronho*, a local firewater made from the fruit of the wild strawberry tree. Another Algarve regional product is *brandymel*, a mixture of honey, herbs and *medronho* – once a traditional home-made remedy for coughs and influenza, but now produced commercially and much loved by the Portuguese.

Clothing and Shoes

Portugal has a thriving textile industry, despite fierce competition from China and India, though much of the country's production in clothes and shoes goes to supply well-known designer brands abroad. With the advent of large clothing stores and shopping malls, however, there is no shortage of quality designer clothes. The Portuguese brand **Parfois** has a network of over 550 stores.

Some excellent-value seconds are on sale at local markets everywhere; a particularly well-known one is at Carcavelos between Lisbon and Estoril.

Shoemaking is a vital part of Portugal's economy. Hundreds of factories produce a range of different styles of shoes and sandals, which are exported all over the world. They also make good souvenirs.

Leather goods, such as bags, purses, wallets, gloves and belts, are consistently good. Variations in price reflect the quality of the products.

Quality leather boots from Madeira – a popular gift

Ornately embroidered women's linen blouses, fashioned in the regional style, are available in many craft shops. Prices are also reasonable for knitwear and woollen fishermen's sweaters from Nazaré *(see p186)*.

Size Chart

Women's dresses, coats and skirts

Portuguese	34	36	38	40	42	44	46
British	8	10	12	14	16	18	20
American	6	8	10	12	14	16	18

Women's shoes

Portuguese	36	37	38	39	40	41
British	3	4	5	6	7	8
American	5	6	7	8	9	10

Men's suits

Portuguese	44	46	48	50	52	54	56	58 (size)
British	34	36	38	40	42	44	46	48 (inches)
American	34	36	38	40	42	44	46	48 (inches)

Men's shirts

Portuguese	36	38	39	41	42	43	44	45 (size)
British	14	15	15½	16	16½	17	17½	18 (inches)
American	14	15	15½	16	16½	17	17½	18 (inches)

Men's shoes

Portuguese	39	40	41	42	43	44	45	46
British	6	7	7½	8	9	10	11	12
American	7	7½	8	8½	9½	10½	11	11½

Antiques

Whether you are a connoisseur or casual collector, Portugal's antique shops and markets are bound to have something to catch your eye. Antique markets (*feiras de velharias*) take place in many regions, usually on Saturday or Sunday.

There is a steady demand for rare and unusual antiques, especially those connected with Portugal's trading links with the Orient over past centuries: Japanese lacquer work and mother of pearl, carvings in wood and ivory, and religious icons. Hand-painted tiles, introduced by the Moors in

An antique shop full of wares in Lisbon

medieval times, now attract buyers from all over the world.

The best hunting grounds in Lisbon are in the Rua São Bento, Largo de S Martinho, Rua Augusto Rosa, and Rua D Pedro V. **Antique Tiles** has great tiles, and **Arca de São José** is good for antiques.

Regional Produce

Every region in Portugal offers its own specialities and it is best to buy fresh items in the

Serra cheese from the Serra da Estrela

region where they are made, though most of the better-known regional produce can be found throughout the country. Cured ham (*presunto*) from the north of Portugal is particularly good in Chaves (*see pp262–3*). Monchique (*see pp324–5*) in the Algarve also has a reputation for cured ham. Spicy pork sausages (*linguiça*) are a speciality of Porto. The Minho region is known for its tasty garlic sausage made with turkey and chicken meat (*alheira de Mirandela*) and a sumptuous black sausage (*morcela*) made from pork.

A wide variety of cheese is made in Portugal. The best is reputed to be from the town of Serpa (*see p316*) and the surrounding region of the lower Alentejo. Serpa cheese finds its way into many shops throughout the country. It is rivalled in taste and quality perhaps only by cheese made in the Serra da Estrela region (*see p221, pp224–5*).

DIRECTORY

Tax-Free Goods

Global Blue
w globalblue.com

Shopping Malls

Centro Colombo
Avenida General Norton de Matos, Benfica, Lisbon.
Tel 217 113 600.
w colombo.pt

Markets

Feira de Antiguidades
Estação Oriente, Lisbon.

Feira de Carcavelos
Largo Mercado, Carcavelos.

Feira de Cascais
Placa Mercado Municipal, Cascais.

Feira de São Pedro
São Pedro Sintra, Sintra.

Ceramics

Azulejos Sant'Anna
Rua do Alecrim 95, Chiado, Lisboa.
Map 7 A5.
Tel 213 422 537.
w santanna.com.pt

Centro de Artesanato
Largo Dr José Novais 27.
Tel 253 811 882.

Porches Pottery
EN 125 Porches, Algarve.
Tel 282 352 858.
w porchespottery.com

Vista Alegre Atlantis
Largo do Chiado 22–23, Chiado, Lisbon.
Map 7 A4.
Tel 213 461 401.
w vistaalegre atlantis.com

Handicrafts

Alto Minho Handicrafts Route
w visitportugal.com

Tapetes de Arraiolos
Rua Lima e Brito 8, Arraiolos. Tel 266 419 526.
w casatapetes arraiolos.com

Wine and Spirits

Coisas do Arco do Vinho
Centro Cultural de Belém, Lisbon. Map 1 B5.
Tel 213 642 031.

Clothing and Shoes

Parfois
Rua Augusta 146, Baixa
Map 7 B4.
Tel 932 264 398.

Garrafeira Nacional
Rua de Santa Justa 18, Baixa.
Map 7 B3.
Tel 218 887 9080.

Solar do Vinho do Porto
Rua S Pedro de Alcântara, 45 Bairro Alto, Lisbon.
Map 7 A3.
Tel 213 475 707.
w ivdp.pt

Antiques

Antique Tiles
Solar Rua D Pedro V 68-70, Bairro Alto, Lisbon.
Map 4 F2.
Tel 213 465 522.

Arca de São José
Rua de São José 188, Lisbon.
Tel 213 548 462.

ENTERTAINMENT IN PORTUGAL

The traditional love of music, dance and singing in Portugal is reflected in a vast range of cultural activities and folk festivals that are celebrated in every corner of the country. Lisbon is considered to be one of the liveliest places in Europe after hours, hosting a major parties at night plus a large number of entertainment and cultural activities throughout the year. For specific information on Entertainment in Lisbon, see pp130–131. Theatre, classical and contemporary music, opera, dance, film festivals, pop, rock and jazz festivals and variety shows featuring internationally renowned performers are also held in other cities and regions of the country.

Lisbon's Teatro Nacional Dona Maria II

Information

The tourism boards issue a free monthly calendar of programmes, events and venues. All Portuguese newspapers have a "what's on" section. The best guides in English are *Follow Me*, which can be found in Lisbon, *Portugal News* (www.the-news.net), which is available in the Algarve with some outlets in Lisbon.

Theatre and Dance

A wide range of professional and amateur productions can be seen in many cities and towns. Lisbon and Porto offer the widest choice, with many established theatres and cultural centres staging world-class productions.

Lisbon's Teatro Nacional Dona Maria II (*p131*) is the principal theatre venue and Porto's **Teatro Rivoli** presents a prestigious two-week International Festival of Iberian theatre.

The Algarve is well served by municipal theatres. One of the biggest regional events is the **Algarve Folk Music and Contemporary Dance Festival** that takes place at different venues with dancers from all over the world.

The Sintra Festival of classical music and dance is the pinnacle of cultural events in Portugal. It takes place in various stunning fairy-tale venues, including the romantic Palácio de Pena (*pp166–7*), Palácio Nacional de Queluz (*pp170–71*) and Palácio de Seteais (*p161*).

Film

All of the latest releases, usually with subtitles, are screened in cinemas in shopping malls all over the country, while fringe cinema can be seen at a number of cultural centres and theatres.

The **Doclisboa** is the only festival dedicated exclusively to documentary films; it attracts entries from all over the world. The **Porto Film Festival** screens sci-fi, fantasy and thrillers.

The **Lisbon & Sintra Film Festival** is international in scope and features masterclasses, workshops, debates, performances, exhibitions and other events.

Classical Music, Opera and Ballet

Some of the world's most famous orchestras and artists perform at the major venues. The most prestigious is the Funcação Calouste Gulbenkian (*p131*), with its own orchestra and ballet company. The **Casa da Musica** in Porto has an extensive programme of dance and music.

Rock, Jazz and Performing Arts

The biggest open-air rock festivals are **Rock in Rio Lisboa** (held every two years), **Super Bock Rock Festival** and **NOS Alive**. Another big international event is the **Festival MED** featuring some of the leading World Music singers and musicians.

Some of the biggest names in world jazz and blues appear at the major concert halls in the big cities and at the jazz festivals in Lisbon, Porto, Guimarães, Viana do Castelo, and the Algarve.

Major venues in Lisbon for world-class performances of jazz and other modern music include the Centro Cultural de Belém (*p131*), Coliseu dos

The Rock in Rio Lisboa festival attracts huge crowds

Women sporting colourful costumes during the Festas de Lisboa

Recreios *(p131)*, **Culturgest**, and the MEO Arena *(p131)*.

One of the highlights of the year is the **Festival Porta-Jazz**, with some of the legendary names in jazz and blues participating. The **Centro Cultural Vila Flor** in Guimarães hosts one of Portugal's most important jazz festivals.

Carnivals

Celebrated mostly in honour of the Saints or Our Lady, Portuguese festivals and carnivals are colourful events with costumed dancers, decorated floats and papier-mâché models. Two of the most famous are the **Loulé Carnival** in Algarve and **Funchal Carnival** in Madeira. Thousands of visitors come to join in the three days of parades and merrymaking. One of the most exuberant religious festivals is the Romaria de Nossa Senhora d'Agonia *(see p35)*.

Another major festival is **Festas de Lisboa**, which takes place in Lisbon throughout June. Cinema, theatre and music events are held, as well as street festivities and parades, including the big St Anthony's folk parade (known as Marchas Populares).

Nightlife

There is no shortage of places to enjoy a drink, listen to music and dance until the early hours of the morning in a nightclub or late-night bar. Irish bars are in vogue for a lively night out and gay bars have sprung up in many regions. For nightlife, Lisbon reigns supreme and the choice is almost endless. The main districts are Cais do Sodré near the riverfront, and the Bairro Alto, known for its *(fado)* houses *(see pp68–9)*. Lux *(see p131)* is one of the more sophisticated club venues, and attracts a fashionable crowd. The jet-set in Algarve flock to **T-Clube** in Quinta do Lago.

Bullfighting

The Ribatejo region northeast of Lisbon is bullfighting country *(see pp150–51)* and the principal arena in this region is **Praça de Touros** in Santarem. Lisbon's major arena is the Campo Pequeno *(see p122)*.

The colourful Romaria de Nossa Senhora d'Agonia religious festival

DIRECTORY

Theatre and Dance

Algarve Folk Music and Contemporary Dance Festival
W visitalgarve.pt

Teatro Rivoli
Praça D João, Porto.
Tel 223 392 201.
W rivoli.bilheteira
online.pt

Film

Lisbon & Sintra Film Festival
Tel 213 255 835.
W leffest.com

Doclisboa
Rua da Rosa 277, Lisbon.
Map 4 F2.

Tel 213 470 816.
W doclisboa.org

Porto Film Festival
Rua Aníbal Cunha 84,
Porto. Tel 222 058 819.
W fantasporto.com

Classical Music, Opera and Ballet

Casa da Musica
Av de Boavista 604-610,
Porto. Tel 220 120 220.
W casadamusica.com

Rock, Jazz and Performing Arts

Centro Cultural Vila Flor
Avenida D Afonso
Henriques, Guimarães. Tel
253 424 700. W ccvf.pt

Culturgest
Rua do Arco do Cego 50,
Lisbon. Map 6 D2.
Tel 217 905 155.
W culturgest.pt

Festival Porta-Jazz
Tel 223 392 201.
W teatromunicipal-
doporto.pt

Festival MED
W festivalmed.pt

NOS Alive
W nosalive.com

Rock in Rio Lisboa
W rockinriolisboa.
sapo.pt

Super Bock Rock Festival
W superbock.pt

Carnivals

Festas de Lisboa
W festasdelisboa.com

Funchal Carnival
W visitmadeira.pt

Loulé Carnival
Tel 289 800 400.
W visitalgarve.pt

Nightlife

T-Clube
Quinta do Lago, Almancil,
Algarve. Tel 289 356 213.
W tclube.com

Bullfighting

Praça de Touros
Santarém. Tel 243 304
437 (tourist office).

OUTDOOR ACTIVITIES AND SPECIALIST HOLIDAYS

Portugal offers an amazing variety of terrain with sports and leisure activities to match. The mild climate in the Algarve, Madeira and the Azores means that many outdoor leisure pursuits can be enjoyed throughout the year. Specialist holidays are available for a variety of activities, including microlight flying, whale watching, big game fishing, surfing and horse riding. Water-skiing, jet-skiing, canoeing and kayaking can also be enjoyed, as can mountaineering and rock-climbing. The unspoiled landscape invites leisurely walking. Golf *(see pp426–7)* and tennis facilities are well established.

Information

Regional tourist offices can provide information on sport and outdoor activities. In addition, the following English language/bilingual publications provide informa-tion: *Essential Algarve*, *Essential Madeira* and the weekly newspapers *The Resident* and *Portugal News*.

Water Sports

Surfing, windsurfing, diving, water-skiing and jet-skiing are popular along the coast and around the Atlantic islands. Vilamoura Lda and **Algarvexcite**, operating out of **Vilamoura Marina**, are leading Algarve companies offering specialist holidays. Jet-skis, water-skis and wakeboards (along with powerboats) can be hired with the services of expert instructors.

The best beaches for surfing are on the Lisbon coast at Guincho and Ericeira. In the Algarve the long, sandy Praia de Arrifana *(see pp292–294)* on the west coast is a major destination.

Equipment can be hired or bought from **Algarve Surf School Camp**, which offers lessons for beginners.

The Azores islands catch huge swells, though access can be difficult, and waves up to 2 m (6 ft) in summer and 4.5 m (15 ft) in winter are for professionals only. The most popular spots are Ribeira Grande and Rabo de Peixe on the north coast of São Miguel.

Madeira's coastline boasts exceptional conditions – expecially near the village of Jardim do Mar, Paul do Mar, the Ponta Pequena and the renowned Ponta do Jardim. Excellent but difficult surfing waters to access front the villages of Contreira, Ponta Delgada and São Vicente.

For windsurfers, Praia do Martinhal, near Sagres in west Algarve, is one of the most popular spots, a location served by water sports operator **Windsurf Point**.

Scuba divers are drawn to Portugal's clear, mild waters and wealth of marine life. The best diving is in the Algarve,

Surfing – a popular pastime along the mainland coast and islands

the Berlengas Islands near Peniche on the Silver Coast, and Madeira and the Azores, where divers may see tropical species such as barracuda, monkfish, dolphins, rays and giant mantas. Diving centres include **Dive Time** in Lagos, **Algarve Dive Experience** in Carvoeiro, **Torpedo Diving** in Vilamoura and **Espírito Azul Diving** on São Miguel, Azores.

Sailing and Canoeing

The marinas at Lagos and Vilamoura in the Algarve are important sailing and yachting centres where international regattas are staged. The **Portimão Marina** and **Lagos Marina** cater for the growing interest in yachting in southern Europe. The marina on the island of Faial in the Azores is a stopping-off point for trans-Atlantic yachtsmen. Madeira is an excellent destination for boating and yachting, with many marinas.

Water sports operator **Bork**, runs sea kayaking excursions out of Oeiras Marina, on the Lisbon Coast.

Windsurfing near Martinhal in the Algarve

Walking along one of Madeira's *levadas* (irrigation channels)

Boating

Tour operators in the Algarve, Madeira and the Azores offer sightseeing cruises. Specialist holidays designed especially for wine buffs are offered by **Douro Azul** in the famous wine-growing region in northern Portugal. The itinerary combines river trips with journeys on the old steam engines along riverside routes that once transported the wines to the city of Porto, and include overnight stays at traditional wine-growing farms *(quintas)*.

Walking and Cycling

Madeira is ideal as a walking destination, with picturesque villages, amazing mountain landscapes, rugged coastlines and golden beaches. The favourite routes follow the island's extensive network of irrigation channels *(levadas)*.

The Azores are a paradise for walkers and hikers, with flowered roads, volcanic moun-tainous terrain and verdant countryside. **Sherpa Expedi-tions** specializes in walking holidays here and in Madeira.

The Silver Coast (western central Portugal) has undulating terrain, forested hills and long, sandy beaches, almost deserted for most of the year.

The Algarve offers exhilarating clifftop walks, especially along the west coast. **Portugal Walks** specializes in walking holidays in this region. In the east of the Ria Formosa Natural Park *(p335)*

and the Sapal Nature Reserve near Castro Marim *(p337)* are popular locations for nature lovers and bird-watchers.

Inland, the 300-km (186-mile) **Via Algarviana** snakes through the Algarve hinterland, from Alcoutim in the east to Cabo de São Vicente in the west. Another long distance footpath, **Rota Vincentina** runs along the Alentejo coast.

Verdant and more densely forested North Portugal is a joy to explore on foot. Here, you can follow the ancient paths of the pilgrims to the holy shrine of Santiago de Compostela in Spain.

Also well worth exploring are the Peneda-Gerês National Park *(pp276–7)* and further east Montesinho Natural Park *(p266)*, which offers scenic mountain routes.

The Alentejo has vast tracts of open plains, and near the bigger towns and cities – such

as Évora, Elvas, and Serpa – the landscape and monuments are inspirational.

The Lisbon coastline stretching north has enjoyable coastal and countryside routes. The areas around Cascais and Sintra, with its mountainous terrain and lush forestation, is pleasant for walks.

Mountain bikes can be hired in many areas of the country to search out the most scenic trails. **Mountain Bike Adventures** is a good source of information.

Flying, Paragliding and Skydiving

Microlight flying is available at the **Algarve Air Sports Centre**. The centre was established by ex-world champion Gerry Breen, who is the chief instructor here.

You can take lessons leading to a pilot's qualification recognized by the **Federação Portuguesa de Voo Livre** (National Association for Free Flight), or occasional pleasure flights along the rugged west Algarve coastline.

The weather conditions and terrain in parts of Portugal are also ideal for paragliding. Most students bring their own gear.

Adrenalin seekers can indulge in the exhilarating sport of skydiving at the **Aerodrome Municipal de Portimão** in the Algarve.

Fishing

The coastline, waterways and rivers of Portugal offer plenty of opportunities for fishing, from angling for trout in the rivers to

Microlight flying over Lagos Bay in the Algarve

Whale-watching expedition up close to a whale

big game fishing off the shores of the Algarve, the Lisbon Coast, the Silver Coast, Madeira and the Azores. Many of the rivers and lakes yield abundant trout, carp and eels.

A licence obtained locally from the **Instituto Florestal** is required to fish the rivers, but not for line fishing from the shore or from a boat at sea. Contact **Federação Portuguesa de Pesca Desportivo** for further information.

Among the companies offering big game fishing are **Pescamar** and **Cruzeiros da Oura** in the Algarve; **Madeira Game Fishing**, **Nautisantos Big Game Fishing**, **Turipesca** and **Madeira Marlin** in Madeira; and **Sports Fishing Azores** in the Azores.

Tennis player at the Vale de Lobo resort in the Algarve

Tennis

Tennis courts are found almost everywhere in Portugal and are an integral part of the facilities in most tourist resorts. Many resorts also have squash courts. The larger Algarve resorts, such as **Vale do Lobo**, offer tennis coaching holidays,

or you can book a specialist tennis holiday in the western Algarve through **Tennis in the Sun**.

Whale Watching

The Azores is a prime spot to see whales and other cetaceans, such as dolphins, that are attracted to the warm waters and abundant food. As many as 20 different species have been seen. The whale-watching season lasts from May to October due to weather conditions, though whales inhabit the waters throughout the year.

Whale-watching holidays as well as daily expeditions are offered by **Whale Watch Azores**, **Futurismo Azores Whale Watching**, **Espaçotalassa** and **Ocean Emotion**.

Horse Riding

Portugal's proud riding tradition stems mainly from the country's handsome Lusitano horses and the sturdy Garrano breed that roams free in the Peneda-Gêres National Park (see pp276–7).

One of the most renowned equestrian centres for training Lusitano and Garrano horses is **Centro Equestre Vale do Lima**, where equestrian holidays with lessons and tuition in horse care, riding and dressage are provided.

In the Algarve, **Gois Valley Riding Holidays**, **Pinetrees Riding Centre** and **Quinta do Paraiso Alto** are well-known riding centres.

Caving

The Algarve has more than 100 subterranean caves scattered across the central and eastern region, some dating from the Jurassic period. For more information, browse the **Visit Algarve** website.

Many of the caves have stalagmites and stalactites but visitors should explore only with a recommended guide.

On the Azores island of Terceira the Algar do Carvão is one of the volcanic wonders of the world. It is a giant cave that spirals down-wards nearly 100 m (300 ft) from the opening of its conduit, ending at a crystal-clear lake. Milky white stalactites and stalagmites cover large areas of the roof and walls.

On Pico, the Gruta das Torres is the largest lava tube in the Azores and a Regional Natural Monument. For more information, visit the **Montanheiros** website.

Climbing and Mountaineering

Madeira's volcanic origins and rugged mountain terrain, with cliff faces rising from the sea, offer exciting conquests for experienced climbers. The favourite areas are the central mountain range, the sea cliffs and some of the northern cliffs. The Azores offers a similar landscape, and the island of Pico provides the ultimate challenge to scale its 2,341-m (7,680-ft) mountain – the highest in Portugal.

Rock climbing in the rugged, volcanic terrain of Madeira

DIRECTORY

Water Sports

Algarve Dive Experience
Tivoli Carvoeiro Algarve Resort, Vale Covo, Algarve.
Tel 282 351 194.
W algarve-scuba-diving.com

Algarve Surf School
Sagres, Algarve.
Tel 963 133 009.
W algarvesurf school.com

Algarvexcite
Vilamoura Marina, Algarve.
Tel 937 777 913.
W algarvexcite.com

Dive Time
Marina de Lagos, Lagos, Algarve. Tel 282 099 774.
W dive-time.net

Espírito Azul Diving
Marina de Vila Franca do Campo, São Miguel, Azores. Tel 914 898 352.
W espiritoazul.com

Torpedo Diving
Vilamoura, Algarve.
Tel 289 314 098.
W visitalgarve.pt

Vilamoura Marina
8125-409 Vilamoura.
Tel 289 310 560.
W marinade vilamoura.com

Windsurf Point
Meia Praia, Lagos.
Tel 282 792 315.
W windsurfpoint.com

Sailing and Canoeing

Bork
Oeiras Marina, Lisbon Coast.
Tel 919 506 136/916 097 744.
W borkyou.com

Lagos Marina
Lagos, Algarve.
Tel 282 770 210.
W marlagos.pt

Portimão Marina
Edifício Admin Ponta da Areia, Portimão. Tel 282 400 680. W marinade portimao.com.pt

Boating

Douro Azul
Rua de Miragaia 103, 4050-387, Porto.
Tel 223 402 500.
W douroazul.com

Walking and Cycling

Mountain Bike Adventures
Tel 918 502 663.
W themountainbike adventure.com

Portugal Walks
Vila do Bispo, Algarve.
Tel 393 479 489.
W portugalwalks.com

Rota Vincentina
Estrada da Circunvalação Odemira, Alentejo.
W rotavincentina.com

Sherpa Expeditions
W sherpaexpeditions.com

Via Algarviana
Rua de S. Domingos 65, Loulé, Algarve.
Tel 289 412 959.
W viaalgarviana.org

Flying, Paragliding and Skydiving

Aerodrome Municipal de Portimão
Montes de Alvor.
Tel 282 480 360.
W cm-portimao.pt

Algarve Air Sports Centre
Aerodróme de Lagos, Lagos 8601-903, Algarve.
Tel 914 903 384.
W gerrybreen.com

Federação Portuguesa de Voo Livre
Av Cidade de Lourenso Marques, Modulo 2 Praceta B, Lisbon.
Tel 218 522 885.
W fpvl.pt

Fishing

Cruzeiros da Oura
Cais Q Escritório no 3, Marina de Vilamoura,

Algarve.
Tel 289 301 900.
W cruzeiros-da-oura.com

Federação Portuguesa de Pesca Desportiva
Rua Eça de Queirós 3 1º, 1050-095 Lisbon.
Tel 213 140 177.
W fppd.pt

Instituto Florestal
Avenida da República 16, 1050-191 Lisbon.
Tel 213 124 800.
W icnf.pt

Madeira Game Fishing
Tel 291 227 169.
W madeiragamefish.com

Madeira Marlin
Rua da Estalagem 23, São Gonçalo 9060-415 Funchal, Madeira.
Tel 291 790 350.
W madeira-marlin.com

Nautisantos Big Game Fishing
Funchal Marina, Funchal, Madeira. Tel 291 231 312.
W nautisantosfishing.com

Pescamar
Marina de Lagos, Algarve.
Tel 966 193 431.
W pescamar.info

Sport Fishing Azores
Ponta Delgada, São Miguel, Azores.
Tel 296 636 592.
W sportfishing azores.com

Turipesca
Marina do Funchal, Madeira.
Tel 291 231 063.
W madeirafishing centre.com

Tennis

Tennis In The Sun
Tel 0333 566 0045.
W tennisinthesun.com

Vale do Lobo
Estrada Vale do Lobo, Almancil, Algarve.
Tel 289 353 333.
W valedolobo.com

Whale Watching

Espaçotalassa
Lajes do Pico, Pico, Azores.
Tel 292 672 010.
W espacotalassa.com

Futurismo Azores Whale Watching
Portas do Mar, Loja 24, Ponta Delgada.
Tel 296 628 522.
W futurismo.pt

Ocean Emotion
Marina de Angra do Heroísmo, Terceira, Azores.
Tel 967 806 944.
W oceanemotion.pt

Whale Watch Azores
Marina da Horta, 9900-017 Horta, Faial Island. Tel 292 293 891.
W whalewatchazores.com

Horse Riding

Centro Equestre Vale do Lima
Quinta da Sobreira, Sernados, Ponte de Lima.
Tel 258 943 873.
W grupojpimenta.com

Gois Valley Riding Holidays
Cada do Linteiro 3330-421, Vila Nova do Ceira, Gois. Tel 235 778 689.
W ridingportugal.com

Pinetrees Riding Centre
Casa dos Pinheiros, Corgo da Zorra, Almancil.
Tel 289 394 369.
W pinetrees.pt

Quinta do Paraiso Alto
Bensafrim, 8600 Lagos.
Tel 282 687 596.
W qpahorseriding.com

Caving

Associação Os Montanheiros
Rua da Rocha 8, Angra do Heroísmo, Terceira, Azores.
Tel 295 212 992.
W montanheiros.com

Visit Algarve
W visitalgarve.pt

Golfing Holidays in Portugal

Portugal is well established as a golfing destination, and specialist golfing holidays have become a very popular way of visiting the country. The Algarve in particular has emerged as one of Europe's premier golfing regions. Its mild winters and large number of quality courses make it attractive to the serious as well as the recreational golfer. The other main golfing region is the area around Lisbon, but there are courses in central and northern Portugal as well. The Porto Golf Club has the distinction of being one of the oldest courses in Europe. Madeira and the Azores also cater for the golfer.

The scenic Penha Longa Golf Club, Central Portugal

General Information

The majority of Portugal's nearly 60 golf courses are by the sea, with spectacular scenery. Along the mainland west coast and in exposed areas of western Algarve, the wind increases as the day progresses, so golfers wishing to avoid it should opt for an early start. The main season runs from mid-autumn to late spring, but summer can also be busy. Always book ahead. Rates vary from just over €30 to over €150 for a round of 18 holes, but discounts are available through tour operators, hotels and booking services.

Major Tournaments

Portugal currently hosts three PGA tournaments: the Madeira Island Open, held at the Santo da Serra (March); the Open de Portugal, held in the Algarve or Lisbon area (March or April); and the Portugal Masters, first held at Victoria Vilamoura in October

2007. Visit www.pga.com for more details on tournaments.

Northern Portugal

The north is the least developed in terms of golf courses, though it was here that golf began in Portugal when Scottish and English port shippers founded the **Oporto Golf Club** in 1890. The course is the oldest in the Iberian peninsula; the par-71 circuit is laid out on sand dunes by the Atlantic. The **Amarante Golf Club** offers a varied par-68 mountain course.

Lisbon and Central Portugal

Near Óbidos, the **Praia d'El Rey Golf Club** is one of Portugal's most highly regarded. Laid out by American golf architect Cabell Robinson, the long par-72 course is set in a coastal resort and extends across sand dunes, cliffs and pine woods. The course is accessible to

players of all levels. **Oitavos Dunes** is part of the Quinta da Marinha resort near Cascais. The par-71 course, designed by Arthur Hills, offers great views of the Atlantic and of the Sintra hills. It is set in the Sintra-Cascais Natural Park and runs in a loop among reforested sand dunes, pine woods and open coastal terrain. There is another 18-hole course located within the resort, the **Quinta da Marinha Golf Club**. Nearby is the **Penha Longa Golf Club** with a par-72 course set in a landscape similar to that of the Oitavos course. This is comple-mented by a 9-hole course. Sections of **Tróia Golf**, a challen-ging par-72 course of small greens and narrow fairways, run alongside Tróia beach, with a view of the Arrábida hills, which offer the course and beach pro-tection from the northerly winds.

Southern Portugal

The Algarve is one of Europe's top golfing destinations. Across the region there are no fewer than 40 golf courses, including many designed by the sport's greatest names, such as Jack Nicklaus, Nick Faldo and Sir Henry Cotton. The choice of layouts is inspiring, with the Algarve's varied coastline providing the setting for some truly spectacular and challenging courses. Inland, there is a more rustic backdrop, but the game is no less demanding. The number and density of golf courses in the Algarve means that a visitor to any part of the region can reach a golf course in a couple of hours at most.

Putting at historic Porto Golf Club, Northern Portugal

One of the scenic golf courses at Vilamoura resort in central Algarve

Madeira and the Azores

Palheiro Golf is a beautiful mountain course. **Santo da Serra Golf** hosts the Madeira Island Open. **Porto Santo Golf** features two 18-hole courses, designed by Severiano Ballesteros. Dramatic clifftop ocean holes are combined with long holes along the island's famous beach. São Miguel, the main island in the Azores archipelago, has two golf courses: **Furnas** and **Batalha**. The former overlooks the stunning Furnas valley and the latter is by the ocean, on the island's north coast.

The oldest course along this coast is Penina, part of the Penina Hotel & Golf Resort (see p394). The par-73 parkland course is complemented by two 9-hole courses. Farther east, **Vale da Pinta** is a highly regarded par-71 course.

The vast Vilamoura resort in central Algarve is home to five golf courses, all of the highest standard. **Victoria Vilamoura** was acclaimed as one of the best courses in Europe within a year of opening. Slightly farther east is **Vale do Lobo**, the first golf resort in the Algarve, opened in 1962. Its Royal course is a demanding par-72 course overlooking the beach and the Atlantic. The resort's other course, Ocean, is equally challenging.

Neighbouring **Quinta do Lago**, has two excellent golf courses, South and North. Also within the resort, but not owned by it, are two other top par-72 courses, **San Lorenzo** and **Pinheiros Altos**.

Over in the east, par-72 **Monte Rei** lies amid rolling hills peppered with olive trees.

Winner at Santo da Serra, Madeira

Porto Santo Golf on the island of Porto Santo, northeast of Madeira

DIRECTORY

Northern Portugal

Amarante Golf Club
Quinta da Deveza, Fregim.
Tel 255 446 060.
w golfedeamarante.com

Oporto Golf Club
Paramos, Espinho.
Tel 227 342 008.
w oportogolfclub.com

Lisbon and Central Portugal

Oitavos Dunes
Quinta da Marinha.
Tel 214 860 600.
w oitavosdunes.com

Penha Longa Golf Club
Estrada da Lagoa Azul, Linhó.
Tel 219 249 011.
w penhalonga.com

Praia d'El Rey
Vale de Janelas (near Óbidos). **Tel** 262 905 100.
w praia-del-rey.com

Quinta da Marinha Golf Club
Quinta da Marinha. **Tel** 214 860 100. w quintada marinha.com

Tróia Golf
Complexo Turístico de Tróia, Carvalhal.
Tel 265 499 400.
w troiagolf.com

Southern Portugal

Monte Rei
Sesmarias, Algarve.
Tel 281 950 960.
w monte-rei.com

Pinheiros Altos
Quinta do Lago, Almancil.
Tel 289 359 910.
w pinheirosaltos.pt

Quinta do Lago
Nr Almancil.
Tel 289 390 700.
w quintadolago.com

San Lorenzo
Quinta do Lago, Nr Almancil.
Tel 289 396 522.
w sanlorenzogolf course.com

Vale do Lobo
Nr Almancil.
Tel 289 353 465.
w valedolobo.com

Vale da Pinta
Carvoeiro, Nr Lagoa.
Tel 282 340 900.
w pestanagolf.com

Victoria Vilamoura
Vilamoura, EN 125.
Tel 289 320 100.
w dompedrogolf.com

Madeira and the Azores

Batalha
Fenais da Luz.
Tel 296 498 559.
w azoresgolfislands.com

Furnas
Achada das Furnas.
Tel 296 584 651.
w azoresgolfislands.com

Palheiro Golf
Rua do Balançal, São Gonçalo. **Tel** 291 790 120.
w palheirogolf.com

Porto Santo Golf
Sítio das Marinhas, Porto Santo. **Tel** 291 983 778.
w portosantogolfe.com

Santo da Serra Golf
Santo da Serra, Nr Machico.
Tel 291 550 100.
w santodaserragolf.com

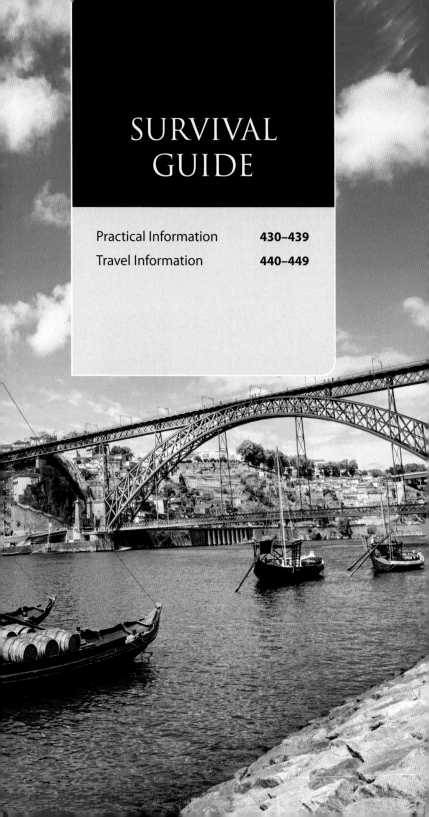

SURVIVAL
GUIDE

PRACTICAL INFORMATION

Portugal manages to pack a great deal for a small country. Its north is remote and mountainous, while the flat central plains give way to a coastline fringed with golden beaches. Spanning this geographically diverse nation is an excellent network of roads and rail services. Nationwide tourist offices provide up-to-date information on attractions and accomodation, while the country has reliable Wi-Fi coverage. Easily reached by air from the rest of Europe and beyond, Portugal is easy to explore.

When to Go

The country's long Atlantic coast is the single most important factor in Portugal's climate. Coastal regions can be very rainy in winter, and although temperatures don't drop that low, it often feels very cold. In the mountainous north it's not uncommon for snow to fall on higher ground.

The Algarve, then, is the only year-round destination, with hot summers and mild winters. Other coastal areas generally have warm to hot summers, with either balmy or windy evenings. Inland areas throughout the country are subject to more extreme conditions, with colder winters even in the Alentejo and hotter summers even in Trás-os-Montes. Madeira enjoys a more temperate climate, but the Azores are susceptible to winter storms. Spring and autumn are good times to visit because the weather is mild, but spring in particular may be wet (see pp38–9).

Visas and Passports

EU nationals need only a valid passport to enter Portugal, which is a signatory to the Schengen Agreement. If they stay for more than six months, they should apply for a residence permit. There is currently no visa requirement for Americans, Canadians, New Zealanders or Australians entering Portugal. Nationals of those countries may stay for up to 90 days and then apply for an extension (usually another 90 days). However, travellers from outside the EU should check with the nearest Portuguese embassy or consulate before going, as visa regulations are subject to change.

Travel Safety Advice

Visitors can get up-to-date travel safety information from the **Foreign and Commonwealth Office** in the UK, the **State Department** in the US and the **Department of Foreign Affairs and Trade** in Australia.

Customs Information

Restrictions apply to liquids carried on board aircraft.

Consulates can generally provide up-to-date information on particular customs regulations and prohibited goods. For more details on customs and other tax-related matters, see pages 416–17.

Tourist Information

The Portuguese Ministry of Tourism divides the country into a number of touristic regions, which are separate from its adminis-trative districts.

Bottles of port

All major cities or large towns within each touristic region have a municipal tourist office (Posto de Turismo), as do the larger towns on Madeira and the Azores. This guide gives details of the relevant tourist information office for each sight. Here, visitors can obtain information about the region, town plans, maps and details on regional events. In some cases they will also sell tickets for local shows and concerts. Information about local hotels will be available from the tourist office, though they will not usually book the accommodation.

Opening hours vary, but they generally follow the same opening hours as local shops. There are tourist offices at all the major airports, as well as in all cities and large towns. In more rural areas, offices are often closed at weekends, and may not offer the same services that can be found in larger towns. Visitors can also obtain information prior to travelling, from Portuguese tourist offices

High season on a beach in the resort of Carvoeiro, in the Algarve

◀ Boats on the Duoro river, in Porto

Signpost in the village of Marvão

abroad. These offices will normally provide visitors planning a trip with a wide range of useful maps, fact sheets and tourist brochures.

Etiquette

Although English is more widely spoken in Portugal than in neighbouring Spain, the Portuguese appreciate visitors' efforts, however small, to communicate in their language. A simple *bom dia* (good morning) or *boa tarde* (good afternoon) can work wonders. For any attempts at more advanced communication, be prepared to repeat yourself several times, allowing your listener to adjust to the peculiarities of your pronunciation. Portuguese retains some old-fashioned modes of address that are seen as polite rather than formal, including *o senhor* and *a senhora* where English uses "you". This contrasts with the informality of cheek kisses, used between men and women, as well as between women, in most situations except formal and business introductions. Men tend to shake hands.

Although dress is generally relaxed these days, arms should be covered up and shorts should not be worn when visiting churches.

Language

Written Portuguese is fairly similar to Spanish, so if you know Spanish you should have little difficulty understanding Portuguese text. However, spoken Portuguese sounds nothing like spoken Spanish. The Portuguese are proud of their language, which is widely spoken throughout the world as a result of former colonial ties with Brazil and a number of countries in Africa, and they may take offence at being addressed in Spanish. A phrase book containing the most useful words and phrases, along with their phonetic pronunciations, can be found on pages 479–80.

Museums and Admission Prices

Most of Portugal's museums are run by the state, although there are also some private ones. In addition to the main national museums and galleries, there are many regional ones scattered around the country. These cover a range of topics, from the history of a region to the works of local artists. Most museums charge a small fee, which varies from €1 to €3. These charges are sometimes reduced or waived altogether on Sundays and public holidays. People under 14 and pensioners (with proof of age) may obtain a 40 per cent discount. Those under 26 with a *Cartão Jovem* (youth card) or ISIC card (International Student Identity Card) are entitled to half-price entrance.

Tourists to Lisbon may also buy a Lisboa Card, available from the airport, tourist offices, travel agents and the askmelisboa.com website. It allows free entry to 25 of the city's museums and reduced entry to many others, including a number of historic monuments, as well as free public transport for a fixed period. Lisboa Cards are valid for one, two or three days.

Opening Hours

Museums are usually open 10am–5pm from Tuesday to Sunday, with many closing for lunch either noon–2pm or 12:30–2:30pm. Smaller and private museums may have different opening times. Most museums and some sights close on Mondays and public holidays. Major churches are open during the day without a fixed timetable, although some may close between noon and 4pm. Smaller churches and those in rural areas may only be open for religious services, and in some cases you may need to find the keyholder for admittance.

Public Conveniences

The Portuguese for toilets is *casa de banho*. If the usual figures of a man or woman are not shown, look for *homens*, *senhores* or *cavalheiros* (men), and *senhoras* or *damas* (ladies).

Toilet facilities are provided at motorway service areas approximately every 40 km (25 miles) and at coach and railway stations. They can also be found in shopping malls.

National Museum Soares dos Reis at the Carrancas Palace in Porto

Family fun at the Slide & Splash park near Estombar, in the Algarve

Travellers with Disabilities

Facilities for the disabled in Portugal have improved greatly, with wheelchairs and adapted toilets available at airports and the main stations, and reserved car parking increasingly evident. Ramps and lifts are installed in many public places. Some buses can accommodate wheelchair-bound passengers (identified by the blue-and-white wheelchair emblem at the front of the vehicle).

Portugal-based specialist tour companies **Accessible Portugal** and **Ourico do Mar** design holidays for people who have reduced mobility or are in wheelchairs.

Travelling with Children

Portugal is a family-friendly destination, and children from 4 to 12 years old enjoy a number of travel and sightseeing discounts, sometimes as much as 75 per cent; for those under 4, it's very often free. Most restaurants have half-price kids' menus, and hotels and some guesthouses offer reduced tariffs for children under the age of 8 if they share their parents' room. Many of the larger establishments provide a supervised crèche and playground facilities.

Senior Travellers

Travellers aged 60 and over can take advantage of a range of benefits – including discounted rail travel and reduced admission fees to many sightseeing attractions such as museums, national monuments and theatres – simply by showing some ID. Buses and metro trains have designated seating areas reserved for the elderly and the infirm, but you'll find that passengers are usually more than willing to give up their own seat if necessary.

Student Travellers

Young people aged 12–25 may buy a *Cartão Jovem* (youth card), which costs about €10 and is valid for a year. It offers travel insurance and discounts for shops, restaurants, museums, travel and youth hostels *(see p382)*. This card is supplied by the **Instituto Português da Juventude** (Portuguese Youth Institute). The International Student Identity Card (ISIC) provides the same benefits as the *Cartão Jovem* and can be bought in your own country. Backpackers have a good choice of budget accommodation in Portugal, including several award-winning hostels in Lisbon and other large cities.

Student card

Women Travellers

Travelling alone in Portugal is fairly safe for women, although common principles, such as keeping to well-lit, public areas after dark, still apply. Some areas of Lisbon, such as the Baixa, Cais do Sodrá, and Porto's Ribeira (riverfront) are probably best avoided at bar closing time. Resorts on the Algarve and Lisbon coasts tend to be the worst for unwanted attention. Hitching alone is not safe; use registered taxis or take public transport.

Religion

Roman Catholicism is the dominant religion in Portugal. Church services are held most evenings and every Sunday morning, as well as on religious holidays. Sightseeing in churches may sometimes be difficult (and is certainly not encouraged) while services are in progress.

Churches of other denominations, including Church of England, Baptist and Evangelical, can be found in larger towns and cities. **St Vincent's Anglican Church**, which travels from place to place, holds a number of religious services in the Algarve.

Time

Portugal and Madeira follow Britain in adopting Greenwich Mean Time (GMT) in winter and moving the clocks forward one hour from March to October (as in British Summer Time). In the Azores, clocks are one hour behind GMT in winter and the same as GMT in summer. The 24-hour clock is more commonly used throughout Portugal.

Electricity

Voltage in Portugal is 220 volts, and plugs have two round pins. Most hotel bathrooms offer built-in adaptors for electric razors.

Responsible Travel

Portugal's green credentials are impressive, and they are exemplified by the proliferation of ecotourism organizations such as **Center**, which promotes cultural and environmental awareness through its partnership with Solares de Portugal, a nationwide network of historic private properties that are open to the public. At Zambujeira do Mar, in the Alentejo, is **Zmar**, the country's first sustainable and eco-friendly camp site, which harnesses solar energy to power its chalets.

Marina at Vilamoura resort, Algarve

Nearly 300 beaches and 17 marinas in Portugal have been honoured with a **Blue Flag** award, an initiative that works towards sustainable development through water quality, environmental education and safety. Many of these beaches are in the Algarve, where the Vilamoura resort has also won a Green Globe award, an accolade that recognizes businesses that strive to protect and conserve resources, reduce waste and prevent pollution.

Visitors to Portugal can make their own eco-friendly contribution by purchasing organic produce at local markets and opting for souvenirs made from cork, a totally sustainable product.

Conversion Chart

Imperial to Metric
1 inch = 2.54 centimetres
1 foot = 30.5 centimetres
1 mile = 1.6 kilometres
1 ounce = 28 grams
1 pound = 454 grams
1 pint = 0.6 litres
1 gallon = 4.6 litres

Metric to Imperial
1 millimetre = 0.04 inches
1 centimetre = 0.4 inches
1 metre = 3 feet 3 inches
1 kilometre = 0.6 miles
1 gram = 0.04 ounces
1 kilogram = 2.2 pounds
1 litre = 1.8 pints

DIRECTORY

Embassies and Consulates

Australia
Avenida da Liberdade 200, 2°, 1250-147, Lisbon. **Map** 5 C5.
Tel 213 101 500.

Canada
Avenida da Liberdade 196–200, 3°, 1269-121, Lisbon. **Map** 5 C5.
Tel 213 164 600.

Republic of Ireland
Avenida da Liberdade 200-4°,1250-147, Lisbon.
Map 4 F1.
Tel 213 308 200.

United Kingdom
Rua de São Bernardo 33, 1249-082, Lisbon.
Map 4 D2.
Tel 213 924 000.

British Consulates
Azores **Tel** 296 628 175.
Funchal **Tel** 291 212 860
Portimão **Tel** 282 490 750.

USA
Avenida das Forças Armadas, 1600, Lisbon.
Tel 217 273 300.

Travel Safety Advice

Australia Department of Foreign Affairs and Trade
w smartraveller.gov.au

UK Foreign and Commonwealth Office
w gov.uk/foreign-travel-advice

US Department of State
w travel.state.gov/

Tourist Offices

Coimbra
Praça da República 3000–343 Coimbra.
Tel 939 010 034.
w turismodecoimbra.pt

Faro
Rua da Misericórdia 8-12, 8000-296, Faro.
Tel 289 803 604.
w visitalgarve.pt

Lisbon
Lisboa Welcome Center, Rua do Arsenal 29, 1100-038, Lisbon. **Map** 7 B5.
Tel 210 312 700.
w visitlisboa.com

Porto
Rua Clube dos Fenianos 25, 4000–172, Porto.
Tel 223 393 472.
w visitporto.travel

In the UK:
11 Belgrave Square, London SW1X 8PP.
Tel 020 7201 6666.
w portugaloffice.org.uk

In the USA:
590 Fifth Ave, 4th floor, New York.
Tel 212 220 5772.

Travellers with Disabilities

Accessible Portugal
Tel 211 338 693.
w accessible portugal.com

Ourico do Mar
w ouricodomar.com

Student Information

Instituto Português da Juventude
Avenida da Liberdade 194, 1250 Lisbon.
Tel 707 203 030.
w juventude.gov.pt/portal

Places of Worship

St George's Church
Rua de São Jorge à Estrela 6, Lisbon.
Tel 214 692 303.

St James's Church
Largo da Maternidade de Júlio Dinis, Porto.
Tel 226 064 989.

Lisbon Synagogue
Rua A Herculano 59, Lisbon.
Tel 213 881 592.

St Vincent's Anglican Church (Algarve)
Apartado 135, Boliqueime.
Tel 289 366 720.

Responsible Travel

Blue Flag
w blueflag.org

Center
w center.pt

Zmar Eco Camping Resort
w zmar.eu

Personal Health and Security

Portugal does not have a serious crime problem, but simple precautions should always be taken. Watch out for pickpockets in crowded areas and on public transport, avoid carrying large amounts of cash and never leave valuables in parked cars. The police are helpful, although bureaucratic and reporting a crime can be slow but is necessary. For minor health complaints, consult a pharmacist.

Police station at Bragança in the Trás-os-Montes region

Portuguese Police

In all main cities and towns, the police force is the Polícia de Segurança Pública (PSP). A special unit patrols the rail and metro systems. Law and order in rural areas is kept by the Guarda Nacional Republicana (GNR). The Brigada de Trânsito (traffic police) division of the GNR, recognizable by its red armbands, is responsible for patrolling the roads.

Motorway SOS telephone

Reporting a Crime

If you have any property stolen, contact the nearest police station immediately. Theft of documents, such as a passport, should also be reported to your consulate. Many insurance companies insist that policy holders report any theft within 24 hours. The police will file a report, which you will need in order to claim from your insurance company on your return home. Contact the PSP in towns or cities, or the GNR in rural areas. In all situations, keep calm and be polite to the authorities to avoid delays. The same applies should you be involved in a car accident. In rural areas you may be asked to accompany the other driver to the nearest police station to complete the necessary paperwork. Ask for an interpreter if no one there speaks English.

Personal Security

Violent crime is rare in Portugal; however, it is worth taking a few sensible precautions. In Lisbon, avoid quiet areas such as the Baixa after dark, and don't stroll alone through Bairro Alto, Alfama or around Cais do Sodré after bars' closing time. Always be aware of pickpockets and bag-snatchers. Similar precautions apply to some of the resorts in the Algarve and to the Ribeira district of Porto.

It is a good idea to ignore any jeers and heckles – they are usually not as serious as they sound. Other precautions include not carrying large amounts of cash, and holding on to mobile phones and cameras. If you are robbed, do not try to resist.

What to Do in an Emergency

The number to call in an emergency is 112. Dial the number and ask for the service you require – police (polícia), ambulance (ambulância) or fire brigade (bombeiros). If you need medical treatment, the casualty department (serviço de urgência) of the closest main hospital will treat you. On motorways and main roads, use the orange SOS telephone to call for help if you have a car accident. The service is in Portuguese; press the button and then wait for the operator, who will connect you.

Health Precautions

No vaccinations are needed for visitors, although doctors recommend being up-to-date with tetanus, diptheria and measles jabs. Tap water is safe to drink throughout the country. If you are visiting during the summer it is advisable to bring insect

Traffic policeman

PSP officer

GNR officer

Fire engine

Ambulance

Police car

repellent, as mosquitoes, while they do not present any serious health problems, can be a nuisance.

Medical Treatment

Social security coverage is available for all EU nationals, although you may have to pay first and reclaim later. To reclaim, you must obtain a European Health Insurance Card (EHIC) before you travel. Apply for this at post offices throughout the UK or from the Department of Health; it comes with a booklet called *Health Advice for Travellers*, which explains entitlements and how to claim them. The card covers emergencies only, so medical insurance is strongly advised. Bear in mind that private health care is expensive in Portugal, and get an itemized bill for your insurance carrier. The **British Hospital** in Lisbon has English-speaking doctors, as do health centres on the Lisbon coast and throughout the Algarve. For details, look in the local English-language press.

Pharmacies

In the event of minor ailments, head to the nearest pharmacy *(farmácia)*, where they can diagnose simple health problems and suggest treatment. Pharmacists can dispense a range of drugs that are available on prescription in many other countries. The sign for a *farmácia* is a green cross on a white background. They are open from 9am to 1pm and 3pm to 7pm on weekdays, and from 9am to 1pm on Saturdays. Each pharmacy displays a card showing the address of the nearest all-night pharmacy and a list of those with late closing (10pm).

Travel and Health Insurance

While specific health risks are rare in Portugal, accidents can happen, so you should always take out comprehensive travel and health insurance before travelling. Make sure the policy covers you for medical and health costs for an injury or a

sudden illness abroad, medical repatriation and personal liability. Always check any exclusions, and ensure that your policy covers you for all the activities you wish to undertake while away. It's also a good idea to make several photocopies of the policy, leaving one copy at home for reference.

An insurance policy that covers the costs of legal advice, issued by companies such as Europ Assistance or Mondial Assistance, will help with the legal aspects of your insurance claim should you have an accident.

If you have not arranged this cover and need legal assistance, call your nearest consulate or the **Ordem dos Advogados** (lawyers' association), which can give you the names of English-speaking lawyers and help you with obtaining representation.

Lists of interpreters, if you require one, are given in the local Yellow Pages *(Páginas Amarelas)* under *Tradutores e Intérpretes*, or you can contact the **AP Portugal**, which is based in Lisbon, for information.

Banking and Local Currency

As a member state of the European Union, Portugal falls within the eurozone, and its unit of currency is the euro. Traveller's cheques are the safest way to carry money, but cashing them can be quite expensive and time-consuming, plus they are seldom accepted as payment. Credit and debit cards are often a more convenient option, and funds can be readily obtained from ATMs. Still, it is always a good idea to arrive with enough euros in cash to cover one or two days' expenditure. Bank exchange rates can vary and bureaux de change may be more convenient.

A Multibanco machine (ATM)

Banks and Bureaux de Change

In Portugal, banks are open between 8:30am and 3pm, Monday to Friday. Some branches stay open for longer, usually until 6pm – enquire at individual banks to find out which these are, since they sometimes change. Banks are closed at weekends and on public holidays.

Money can be changed at banks, bureaux de change (agências de câmbios) and at many hotels. Bank branches are everywhere, but be aware that their rates of exchange and commissions vary. Waiting times and bureaucratic practices can make banks a time-consuming option. Bureaux de change charge higher commissions than many banks but offer a more expedient service, as well as longer opening hours (including weekends). As a rule, hotels have the highest rates of exchange. At banks and bureaux de change you may be asked to show your passport or some other form of identification for exchange transactions. Alternatively, there are financial service companies, like Western Union, based in Portugal that can arrange person-to-person money transfers and money orders.

Traveller's Cheques and Cards

Traveller's cheques are a safe but not very convenient way of carrying money. It is very rare for shops or hotels to accept them as payment, and cashing them may be quite expensive. In general, bureaux de change are better for this than banks, where commissions may be high.

Most visitors, however, find it most practical and convenient to withdraw cash from an ATM (Multibanco, or MB) using their credit/debit card. Multibanco machines are typically found inside and outside bank branches, at public transport hubs and in shopping centres. Most accept Visa, MasterCard, American Express, Maestro and Cirrus cards. Bear in mind that transaction fees are always charged when withdrawing cash on a card, and that these are sometimes irrespective of the amount withdrawn. Fewer and larger withdrawals are therefore preferable to many small ones.

Larger denomination banknotes, such as the €200 and €500 notes, have a limited circulation in Portugal, and some establishments may refuse to accept them, preferring instead to work with smaller, more manageable denominations.

Regional Cost Variations

Costs in Portugal can vary considerably depending on which part of the country you are visiting. For example, hotel prices in Lisbon and P orto at some of the larger holiday resorts in the Algarve are generally higher than in similar establishments located inland and in the north of the country. Likewise, in these locations, you should expect to pay more for meals and drinks. In Madeira and the Azores, taxi hire is pricier than on the mainland.

DIRECTORY

Major Banks

Banco Bilbao Vizcaya Argentária
Avenida da Liberdade 222, Lisbon. **Tel** 213 117 200.

Banco Português de Investimento (BPI)
Rua de Passos Manuel 103, Porto. **Tel** 222 046 160.

Banco Santander Totta
Avenida dos Aliados 37, Porto. **Tel** 222 046 410.

Banco Português de Investimento (BPI)
Avenida da Liberdade 249, Lisbon. **Tel** 213 531 170.

Caixa Geral de Depósitos
Rua Dom Francisco Gomes 2, Faro. **Tel** 289 810 590.

Lost Cards or Traveller's Cheques

American Express
Tel 180 052 284 800 (USA).

MasterCard
Tel 080 096 4767 (UK).

Travelex
Tel 800 880 508 (Portugal).

Visa
Tel 800 811 824 (Portugal).

The Euro

The euro (€) is the common currency of the European Union. It went into general circulation on 1 January 2002, initially for 12 countries. Portugal was one of those 12 countries, and its original currency, the escudo, was phased out by March 2002. EU members using the euro as sole currency are known as the eurozone. Several EU members have opted out of joining this common currency.

Euro notes are identical throughout the eurozone countries, each one including designs of fictional architectural structures. The coins, however, have one side identical (the value side), and one side with an image unique to each country. Both notes and coins are exchangeable in each of the eurozone countries.

Banknotes

Euro banknotes have seven denominations. The €5 note (grey in colour) is the smallest, followed by the €10 note (pink), €20 note (blue), €50 note (orange), €100 note (green), €200 note (yellow) and €500 note (purple). All notes show the stars of the European Union.

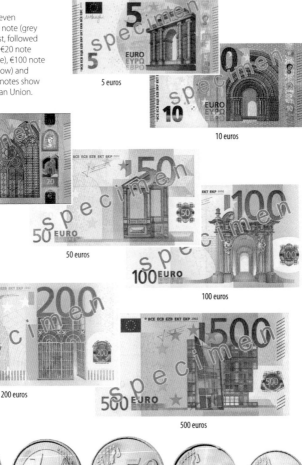

5 euros

10 euros

20 euros

50 euros

100 euros

200 euros

500 euros

2 euros

1 euro

50 cents

20 cents

10 cents

Coins

The euro has eight coin denominations: €1 and €2; 50 cents, 20 cents, 10 cents, 5 cents, 2 cents and 1 cent. The €1 and €2 coins are both silver and gold in colour. The 50-, 20- and 10-cent coins are gold. The 5-, 2- and 1-cent coins are bronze.

5 cents

2 cents

1 cent

Media and Communication

Information and telecommunications technology in Portugal has advanced at a remarkable rate. Visitors should have few problems using public telephones, whether coin-operated or those that accept phone cards. The country's three main mobile phone operators, Vodafone, TMN and Optimus, all have excellent coverage across the entire country, including Madeira and the Azores. Internet cafés can be found in all urban areas and some post offices also offer online facilities. English-language newspapers and magazines are readily available in major cities.

Public Telephones

Public pay phones in Portugal are mostly card operated; it is rare to find one that accepts coins. They are found in booths in the streets as well as in bars, cafés and shopping centres. Card operated phones are more common and more convenient, accepting a variety of phone cards available from post offices, newsagents, tobacconists and Telecom company outlets. They also tend to be cheaper, with an average of about 3 Euro cents for a local call. Some also accept credit cards, although that incurs a small extra charge.

International calls and calls to mobile phones are more expensive, but there are always special cards and deals to be found. An alternative is to make a call from a post office, if you have neither change or a card. You simply step into a free booth, make your call, and pay the cashier afterwards. The cost per unit is relatively low. Some cafés and bars still have a units meter connected to their phone and calculate the cost of your call. They tend to charge more than the post office but less than many hotels.

When making international calls and – in particular – calls to mobile phones, it pays to bear in mind that rates are lower off-peak between 9pm and 9am and at weekends and on public holidays.

Mobile Phones

In 2017, the EU ended roaming charges meaning European

A public phone booth

visitors travelling within the continent (including Iceland, Norway and Liechtenstein) can use their mobile data abroad without incurring charges, making it cheaper and easier to use your phone abroad than ever before.

There are four main GSM frequencies (Global System for Mobile Communications) in use around the world, so if you want to guarantee that your phone will work, make sure you have a quad-band phone. Tri-band phones from outside the US are also usually compatible but, because the US uses two frequency bands itself, a US tri-band phone may only have limited global coverage. Contact your service provider for clarification.

To use your mobile phone in Portugal, it will need to be equipped for GSM network frequencies 900 and 1800 MHz. Note that you may need to get permission from your network operator as you often have to

pay a substantial premium for the international leg of the call.

Another popular option is to purchase a local SIM card – the electronic chip that links your phone to a particular network – that can be topped up with credit and uses the local mobile phone networks. You can only do this if your handset is "unlocked" – some operators lock their phones to specific networks. In Portugal hiring or even purchasing a mobile phone is a good idea if you intend to remain in the country for an extended period. The cost of calling both nationally and internationally will be significantly cheaper and you will not be charged for calls to a Portuguese phone unlike a phone from another country.

It is worth checking your insurance policy in case your phone gets stolen and keeping your network operator's helpline number handy for emergencies. Remember to bring an electrical adaptor for the charger if necessary.

Internet and Email

Wi-Fi Internet is widely available in Portugal. There are still some internet cafés found in cities, towns and at coastal resorts. Facilities can be also found at larger coach and rail terminals

---

Making a Telephone Call

- To make a call within a town or region, or from one town or region to another, dial the nine-digit number that you require.
- To phone Portugal from abroad dial the Portugal country code (+ 351), and then the nine-digit local number that you require.
- To call abroad from Portugal, dial 00 then the country code and local number. The country code for US and Canada is 1; Ireland is 353; UK is 44; Australia is 61; and New Zealand is 64.
- Portugal's directory enquiries number is 118 (Portugal enquiries only).

Internet cafés, popular in Portuguese cities

and most large hotels provide complimentary Wi-Fi.

Post office customers can use NetPost, an Internet facility payable per hour using a special card. Wi-Fi hotspots, found in airports and some shopping malls, enable users to log in on the go, but this facility is not always free. Those using mobile phones or laptops should check with their Internet service provider (ISP) before departure.

Postal Services

The postal service in Portugal is known as the "ctt Correios". It is reasonably efficient: a letter sent to a country within the EU should take five to seven days, and a letter sent to the USA or further afield should take about seven to ten days. The "Correios" sign depicts a horse and rider in red.

Post offices are usually open from 9am until 6pm from Monday to Friday. Central post offices in major cities have different opening times. These are 8am–10pm from Monday to Friday and 9am–6pm on Saturdays.

Sending a Letter

First-class mail is known as *correio azul* and second-class mail is called *normal*. First-class letters are posted in blue postboxes and second-class post in red ones. At post offices there may be separate slots for national and international mail. There are also express mail services called Correio Verde and EMS and for valuable letters, a recorded delivery service *(correio registado)* is available. Stamps *(selos)* can be bought from post offices or from any shop displaying the red and white "Correios" sign, and also from vending machines. These are found in airport terminals and in railway stations, as well as on the streets of large towns. If mailing larger items, using an international courier company such as FedEx or DHL may be a better option. Both have offices in Lisbon.

ctt correios

Correios (postal service) logo

Portuguese Addresses

Portuguese addresses often include both the storey of a building and the location within that floor. The ground floor is the *rás-do-chão* (r/c), first floor *primeiro andar* (1°), the second floor is expressed as 2°, and so on. Furthermore, each floor is divided into left, *esquerdo* (E or Esq^do), right, *direito* (D or D^to).

Newspapers and Magazines

English-language newspapers printed in Europe are easily available at large newsagents on the day of publication, including the American *International New York Times*. Several other European newspapers and periodicals are also generally on sale the same day of home publication, except following a bank holiday. UK papers and magazines purchased abroad are more expensive, and some sections, notably weekend supplements, are not included. Portuguese daily newspapers include *Diário de Notícias* and *Público*, and the leading weekly newspaper is *Expresso*. The weekly *Portugal News*, published on Friday, is the country's main English-language publication. Catering to the expat population, it provides a range of news and information about local events. Listings magazines available include the weekly *Time Out Lisbon*, published in Portuguese. A special edition, *Lisbon for Visitors*, is printed in English. The *Algarve Resident* is a widely distributed English language magazine that carries news and details of upcoming events.

Radio and Television

In Portugal there are two state-owned television channels – RTP1 and RTP2 – and two privately owned channels – SIC and TVI. Most foreign-language programmes are broadcast in the original language, with Portuguese subtitles. Other European and international broadcasts are available via satellite and cable, and include the usual 24-hour news, music, sports and feature channels.

The Algarve-based Kiss FM is the only station that broadcasts year-round in the English language.

Information on collection times

First-class postbox

Correio Azul

última hora .30

Portugal's Postboxes
First-class letters should be posted in blue ("Correio Azul") boxes and second-class letters in red boxes.

Second-class postbox

CORREIO

TRAVEL INFORMATION

Portugal, Madeira and Porto Santo, as well as the major Azorean islands, have airports served by TAP, the national airline, and Azores Airlines (SATA). European and other airlines fly to the international airports of Lisbon, Porto, Faro and Funchal, which all get busier during the holiday season. Charter flights are often the cheapest alternative. Portugal's mainland rail network is fast and modern on busy lines such as Lisbon–Porto and Lisbon–Faro, but slow on provincial lines. Trains are inexpensive, especially if you are eligible for any of the discounts. Buses are sometimes faster and generally offer a wider choice of departures than the rail network. Car rental is not cheap (pre-arranged package deals are often the best value), but it does offer the greatest flexibility. Diesel costs less than petrol, while motorway tolls can be expensive.

Green Travel

Portugal's provincial rail system is not very extensive, and many railway stations are located some distance away from the towns and villages they serve. A private vehicle is therefore necessary to explore much of the country beyond major cities and main tourist zones. Likewise, without your own transport, it is difficult to travel around Madeira properly; in the Azores it is almost impossible. Buses and coaches are the alternatives, but off the beaten track they can be slow and infrequent.

Cycle tourism is gaining popularity. A designated cycle route, the 240-km (150-mile) **Ecovia** in the Algarve, connects Vila Real de Santo António in the east with Sagres in the west. Hikers fare better, since Portugal enjoys an extensive network of tracks, trails and footpaths. The **Instituto Geográfico do Exército** sells good large-scale maps. The country's leading environmental organization, **Quercus**, arranges guided walks in parts of the country and is involved in a number of ongoing eco projects.

Fuel-efficient houseboats can be hired to explore the Alqueva reservoir in the Alentejo, the largest man-made lake in Europe. This option does away with the need for a vehicle, and passengers can travel around the lake's 1,200-km (745-mile) shoreline with minimal disruption to the environment.

Arriving by Air

Lisbon and, to a lesser extent, Porto have regular scheduled flights from European capitals and major cities, including London, Paris, Madrid, Rome, Munich, Frankfurt, Zurich and Milan. Most of these are daily, and in many cases there are several daily connections. **TAP**, Portugal's national carrier, currently operates daily flights from London (four from Heathrow depending on your departure day; two from Gatwick; three from London City Airport) to Lisbon, and two to Oporto (from Gatwick), plus several weekly ones. Faro is the usual Portuguese destination for charter flights and low-cost airlines, particularly during the holiday season. Many companies also fly to Lisbon.

Madeira and Porto Santo are important package-holiday destinations, and charter flights are available to Funchal. The Azores are becoming a more accessible holiday destination, in terms of flights and prices (*see opposite*).

Air Fares

Charter flights are available to Lisbon, Porto, Funchal, Ponta Delgada and Faro, in the Algarve, particularly during the summer months. Tickets have

Lisbon airport terminal

Airport	ⓘ Information	Distance to City Centre	Taxi Fare to City Centre	Public Transport to City Centre
Lisbon	218 413 500	7 km (4 miles)	€12–15	🚌 20 minutes
Porto	229 432 400	20 km (12 miles)	€18–20	🚌 30 minutes
Faro	289 800 800	6 km (4 miles)	€10–12	🚌 15 minutes
Funchal	291 520 700	18 km (11 miles)	€20–24	🚌 30 minutes
Ponta Delgada	296 205 400	3 km (2 miles)	€7–8	🚌 10 minutes
Horta	292 943 511	10 km (6 miles)	€8–10	🚌 15 minutes

fixed outward and return dates, but as they are often cheaper than regular one-way tickets, many people only use the outward flight.

Major low-cost airlines also fly to Faro: **Ryanair** from Liverpool, East Midlands, Dublin and Shannon; **easyJet** from Gatwick, Luton, Bristol, Liverpool, Glasgow and Belfast; and **British Airways** from London Gatwick, London Heathrow, London Stansted and London City.

The best way to get a cheap ticket is to check websites such as www.cheapflights.com, which offer an overview of currently available deals.

Long-Haul Flights

Travellers from North America will usually have to change at a European hub. TAP's only direct flights are from Newark, Boston and Miami to Lisbon. **United Airlines** also runs a daily direct service between Newark and Lisbon. **Delta** flies to Lisbon via Paris (using a partner airline) daily. South America is better served, thanks to Portugal's ties with Brazil: TAP has direct flights to and from several Brazilian destinations, as well as Caracas in Venezuela.

There are no direct flights to mainland Portugal from Canada, Australia or New Zealand; travellers from these countries usually change in London. North Americans visiting the Azores and Madeira will find a greater choice of direct connections, due to the large Azorean and Madeiran communities in the US and Canada.

TAP Air Portugal aircraft on the tarmac at Lisbon Airport

Internal Flights

TAP also flies between major domestic destinations, including Lisbon, Porto, Faro, Funchal and Porto Santo Island, and from Lisbon to São Miguel, Terceira and Faial in the Azores. TAP also code-shares these destinations with **Azores Airlines (SATA)**.

Package Deals

Specialist holidays are a popular option in Portugal. These include stays in manor houses and *pousadas (see pp384–5)*, short breaks to Lisbon and Porto, tennis and golfing holidays in the Algarve, and walking holidays in the Minho. These, together with package deals including hotel, villa or apartment accommodation, will often include bus transfer to your destination from the airport. Fly-drive deals are also available, to the Algarve especially, allowing you to spend less time at the airport dealing with paperwork. Car hire, when booked as part of a package deal, may be very reasonable. A list of companies specializing in these holidays is available from the **Portuguese National Tourist Office** (Turismo de Portugal).

Signs at the airport for visitors' facilities

DIRECTORY

Green Travel

Ecovia (cycle routes)
W ciclovia.pt

Houseboats
W amieiramarina.com

Instituto Geográfico do Exército
Tel 218 505 300.
W igeoe.pt

Quercus
W quercus.pt

Arriving by Air

British Airways
London Tel 0844 4930 787.
W britishairways.com

easyJet
W easyjet.com

Ryanair
W ryanair.com

TAP Air Portugal
London Tel 218 431 100.
Lisbon Tel 707 205 700.

Long-Haul Flights

Delta
W delta.com

United Airlines
W united.com

Internal Flights

Azores Airlines (SATA)
Ponta Delgada
Tel 707 227 282.
W sata.pt

TAP
Lisbon
Tel 707 205 700.
W flytap.com

Package Deals

Portuguese National Tourist Office
11 Belgrave Square, London.
Tel 020 7201 6666.

The spacious check-in area at Porto's Sá Carneiro Airport

Travelling by Rail

The Portuguese state railway, Comboios de Portugal (CP), provides an inexpensive, country-wide network. Quality of service can vary considerably, however, and while modernization to the system continues, progress is slow. The Alfa Pendular trains between Lisbon and Porto, via Coimbra, and Lisbon and Faro, via Tunes, are fast and efficient, but for longer journeys, such as Lisbon to Évora, it may be quicker to take the bus.

High-speed Alfa Pendular train at Oriente station in Lisbon

Carved arch over entrance to Lisbon's Rossio station *(see p86)*

Arriving by Train

There are two main routes into Portugal by train. The first is to travel overnight from Austerlitz station in Paris, changing at Irún on the French-Spanish border, then continuing on to the Portuguese border town of Vilar Formoso in the north. The train splits near Coimbra, heading north for Porto and south for Lisbon, coming into Santa Apolónia station. The entire journey from London to Lisbon, using the Eurostar to reach Paris, takes 30 hours.

An alternative is to travel on the overnight train from Madrid, passing through Marvão and Santarám, then on to Lisbon. Travel from Madrid to Lisbon takes ten hours. The Rail Europe website provides more details on trains and facilities.

Travelling by Train

Most areas of Portugal are served by rail, although the more remote lines, such as Tua to Mirandela, have sadly been made obsolete due to new road links. A bus service covers any gaps in the system, although it is wise to confirm that the service you require exists before setting off.

There are several categories of train in Portugal. The most comfortable and quickest is the modern Alfa Pendular, which travels between Lisbon, Coimbra and Porto, and Lisbon, Tunes and Faro. The Rápido Inter-Cidades (IC) is only marginally slower, although less luxurious, and connects most important towns and cities. Most smaller towns and villages throughout the country are served by the Regional and Inter-Regional lines. These local lines are slower than the Rápido and Alfa Pendular, with fewer facilities, but they stop at many more stations.

Logo for Comboios de Portugal

City Stations

Lisbon has four rail termini. **Santa Apolónia** station, on Avenida Infante Dom Henrique, serves the north and all international destinations. **Oriente**, by the former Expo site, Parque das Nações, is on the same line as Santa Apolónia and serves the south. **Entre-campos**, in the city centre, also serves the south. For more routes south and east, cross the river (taking a ferry from Terreiro do Paço) to catch a train from **Barreiro**. Trains for Estoril and Cascais (a 30-minute trip) leave from **Cais do Sodré** station. The suburban Fertagus line runs south across the river to stations along the Lisbon coast.

Rossio station, near Praça dos Restauradores, serves Sintra and stations along the coast as far north as Figueira da Foz. Care should be taken on the Lisbon to Sintra line at night.

Coimbra has two mainline stations: trains from Lisbon and Porto stop at **Coimbra B**, a five-minute shuttle ride from the central **Coimbra**.

Porto has two mainline stations: international and long-distance trains come into **Campanhã**, to the east of the city; regional and suburban trains come into **São Bento** in the centre. From here there is a shuttle service to **Campanhã** station. The former rail station at Trindade is now a metro station.

Exterior of station at Santiago do Cacém with *azulejo* decoration

Time　　Destination　　Platform　　Type of train　　Other remarks

Departures board in Santa Apolónia station, Lisbon

Fares

Fares within Portugal are fairly cheap in comparison with other European countries and there are numerous discounts available. Children under the age of four travel free, and

Portugal's Principal Railway Lines

those from four to twelve pay half-fare. There are also discounts for groups, students and pensioners.

Visitors are advised to check the CP website for changing information regarding fares and also for information on discounted tickets for selected groups. First-class travel on Portugal's trains is 40 per cent more expensive than second class, and second-class travel, while fairly basic on some lines, is usually sufficiently comfortable. Families can save money by using the *bilhete família*, which is available in two different types. The long-distance travel option gives a 50 per cent discount for between three and nine family members on two networks on Saturdays. The city option offers discounts for travel in Lisbon and Porto on Saturdays, Sundays and public holidays. There are also two types of Interrail pass available to European Union residents under 30 (although there are also adult and senior rates). The Global Pass is valid for 30 different countries, including Portugal, and prices for second-class travel start at €305 (2nd Class) for 5 days of travel over a 10-day period. The Portugal Pass costs from €49 for 3 days' travel in Portugal only over a 1-month period.

Buying Tickets

Tickets for Alfa and Rápido (IC) trains can usually be booked up to 30 days ahead, although some services only offer 10-day advance bookings, so it is important to check first. Reservations can be made at stations or travel agents. If you want to buy a ticket the day you travel, arrive early as queues at the ticket office are normal, especially during peak hours and holiday periods. It is important that you buy a ticket before boarding, otherwise you are liable to be fined on the spot by the conductor. If buying your ticket online via CP's website (in English and Portuguese), note that you'll have to print out the ticket in colour to present it with your passport.

Sign at ticket office showing where to buy advance tickets

Sign at ticket office showing where to buy tickets on day of travel

Timetables

Main stations in Portugal provide a complete rail timetable, the Guia do Horário Oficial, which details all routes for Alfa Pendular, IC, Inter-Regional and Regional trains. A section in Portuguese only has details of the tickets and discounts that are available. The CP website displays all travel information including a countrywide timetable.

DIRECTORY

Railway Stations

Comboios de Portugal
Tel 707 210 220 or +351 707 210 220 (outside Portugal).
🔲 cp.pt

Coimbra/Faro/Lisbon/Porto
All stations served by:
Tel 707 210 220 or +351 707 210 220 (outside Portugal).

Driving in Portugal

Portugal's road network includes an expanding motorway system, but some older main roads may be in need of repair, while minor roads can be very rough and tortuous. Traffic jams are a problem in and near cities. Never attempt driving in the rush hour, and be wary of reckless Portuguese drivers. Always carry your passport, licence, logbook or rental contract, and car insurance. Failure to produce these *documentos* if the police stop you will incur a fine. It's obligatory for drivers and passengers to don green fluorescent vests following a breakdown or an accident. In addition, drivers must carry a collapsible warning triangle in the trunk to be used in the event of such an emergency.

A steep road near Gouveia in the Serra da Estrela *(see pp224–5)*

Arriving by Car

The quickest route is to cross the French–Spanish border at Irún and then take the E80 via Valladolid to Vilar Formoso in Portugal. To go to Lisbon or the Algarve, turn off at Burgos, head for Cáceres and then on to Badajoz.

Taking the car ferry to northern Spain from the UK reduces time on the road, but crossings are extremely long: 24 hours to Santander and 35 hours to Bilbao. **Brittany Ferries** travels to Santander, leaving from Plymouth once a week and Portsmouth twice a week throughout the year. Brittany Ferries also operates a route from Portsmouth to Bilbao twice a week. There are currently no car ferry services operating between Madeira and mainland Portugal. Similarly, there are no ferry services from the mainland to the Azores.

Driving time may also be reduced by using the Motorail link from Paris Gare d'Austerlitz to Lisbon, a twice-weekly service. Drivers load their cars one day, travel by passenger train the next, and pick up their cars on the third day. Check the **Autotrain** website for more information.

Travelling Around by Car

Major roads include EN (Estrada Nacional) roads, many of which have been upgraded to either IP (Itinerário Principal) or IC (Itinerário Complementar) roads. IP roads are much used by heavy goods lorries and avoiding motorway tolls, and they can be slow as a result.

Always fill up with petrol in town before setting off, because petrol stations can be scarce in remote areas.

The best road maps are those published by Michelin or the Portuguese motoring organization, the **ACP** (Automóvel Clube de Portugal).

Rules of the Road

Traffic drives on the right-hand side, continental rules of the road apply and the international sign system is used. Unless there are signs to the contrary, traffic from the right has priority at squares, crossroads and junctions. Cars on roundabouts travel anticlockwise, and have priority over waiting traffic. There is very little advance warning of pedestrian crossings.

It is compulsory to use a seatbelt, and the blood-alcohol limit is 0.05 per cent. Speed limits are 50 kph (31 mph) in towns and 90 kph (55 mph) on other roads, and 120 kph (74 mph) on motorways. Breaking the speed limit incurs an on-the-spot fine, as does talking on a mobile phone while driving.

Motorways and Tolls

Portugal's expanding motorway network *(see map on back endpaper)* links Lisbon with Braga and Guimarães in the north, and Porto with Amarante and the Algarve in the south. Another section goes from Lisbon to Leiria, and a cross-country stretch runs east to the Spanish border at Elvas.

Traffic queueing to pass over the Ponte 25 de Abril, Lisbon

Apart from some sections near Lisbon and Porto, all motorways have two lanes. Tolls are payable on motorways and on Lisbon's bridges – the Ponte 25 de Abril and the Ponte Vasco da Gama. Do not use the Via Verde (green lane) at tolls; this is only for drivers who subscribe to an electronic system allowing them to pay automatically. Visit www.portugaltolls.com for more information.

Parking

Finding a parking space in cities can be difficult. Most parking spaces in Lisbon and Porto are now pay-and-display during the working week. A simpler and safer, if more expensive, alternative is one of the many underground car parks. Follow the blue signs with a white P.

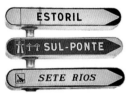

Signs in Lisbon for the coast, south via the Ponte 25 de Abril, and zoo

Petrol (gasoline)

Petrol is relatively expensive, and generally the same price countrywide. Diesel *(gasóleo)* is cheaper than petrol. Some pumps are self-service and colour-coded: green for unleaded and black for diesel.

Breakdown Services

There is a reciprocal breakdown service between the ACP and other organizations. To qualify, drivers should take out European cover with their own organization. On the motorway, use the SOS phones and state that you are entitled to ACP cover. For drivers without cover, most towns have a garage with breakdown lorry.

The Guadiana International Bridge on the Portugal-Spain border

Car Hire

Car hire agencies may be found at Lisbon, Faro and Porto airports and in main towns. Local firms usually offer better rates than international ones, but check the condition of the car and the insurance coverage carefully. You must have a valid driving licence, be over the age of 21 and have held a licence for at least one year.

Great Drives

A particularly scenic drive is the EN1063 from Foz de Odeleite in the eastern Algarve, which hugs the banks of the River Guadiana all the way to the pretty riverside village of Alcoutim. The N255 from Reguengos de Monsaraz to Moura skirts the Alentejo's Barragem de Alqueva lake. To explore port wine country, take the N222 from Peso do Régua to Pinhão in the Douro.

For breathtaking mountain scenery in Madeira, head northwest out of Funchal, and follow the narrow hairpin ER107 to Curral das Freiras, in the heart of the island.

The R1-1 coastal road encircling Pico, in the Azores, allows you to take in both a stark, majestic landscape and the Atlantic Ocean.

Road Numbers

Roads in Portugal may have up to three different numbers. Thanks to a building and upgrading programme, former EN or Estrada Nacional roads can also be IP (Itinerário Principal) roads. A road with an E (Estrada Europeia) number indicates that it is also a direct international route.

The Bragança-Porto road is now the IP4, part motorway (A4) and part dual carriageway.

IP 4

210

The road's original EN number (**Estrada Nacional**).

E 82

The E82 is an international route, ending in Spain near Valladolid.

Travelling by Coach

Since the privatization of Portugal's bus network, the Rodoviária Nacional (RN), coach companies have multiplied, and some routes are now even run by foreign companies. Regional operators compete with each other to offer better services to more destinations, and as a result, many coach journeys, such as Lisbon to the Algarve, are quicker and often more comfortable than the equivalent train journeys. Coaches also cover the increasing number of defunct sections of railway, such as Mirandela–Bragança and Beja–Moura.

A Rodonorte coach, which covers the far north of the country

Getting to Portugal by Coach

Travelling to Portugal by coach is cheap but very time-consuming. **Eurolines** runs a weekly summer service from Victoria Coach Station in London to Porto. Passengers change in Area Suco in central Spain, and the journey takes 34 hours in total. The London-to-Lisbon service, which runs all year, takes even longer. Passengers change in Paris and spend two nights on the coach.

Travelling Around by Coach

Coach operators in Portugal include **Renex**, which links Faro, Lisbon, Porto and Braga, and **EVA**, which focuses on the Algarve. **Rodoviária de Lisboa** connects Lisbon with Estremadura. In Vila Real, **Rodonorte** covers the extreme north, and **Rede Expressos**, based in Porto, covers the inland areas of Portugal.

The Terminal Rodoviária de Sete Rios, located in Lisbon's Sete Rios district, is the city's main bus station and the hub for the main intercity coach routes of Portugal. In Porto, the main departure and arrival points is at Rodoviário no Porto Campo 24 de Agosto.

Information on routes and prices is available from tourist offices and travel agencies.

Coach Tours

Bus, coach and minibus tours around Lisbon and Porto are plentiful. **Cityrama** runs sightseeing tours of Lisbon and its coast, and day trips to sights such as Batalha, Sintra and Mafra. It also offers a night-time tour of the city, taking in the Jerónimos monastery and then dinner with a *fado* show. From Porto, it runs tours of the Minho and Douro valleys, and a six-day trip to Lisbon. **Gray Line**, part of Cityrama, also offers day trips

A Cityrama hop-on hop-off sightseeing tour bus in Lisbon

from Lisbon to Évora, a cruise on the Tagus and a trip lasting three days to the Algarve. Pick-up points are at the main hotels or central locations. It is also possible to arrange longer trips to areas of historical or scenic interest.

In the Algarve, there are frequent coach trips to places of interest such as Loulé, Silves and Monchique, the southwest and the River Guadiana, and further afield to Évora and Lisbon. Tourist offices, hotels and travel agencies can help with these, and pick-up points are the main coastal hotels.

Travelling Around the Islands

On the rocky, mountainous islands of Madeira and the Azores, the pace of transport is necessarily slow, and some places are only accessible on foot. Driving needs care and patience, and you may find organized trips by coach or taxi are more relaxing and rewarding.

On the smaller islands it is usually easy to hitch a lift.

To enjoy the Azores on foot, ask your taxi driver to drop you off at the start of a route and pick you up further on. Try to obtain a detailed map of the Azores before arrival. Some routes are listed in specialist guidebooks sold locally.

The Porto Santo Line ferry in Funchal harbour

Island Hopping

Aero VIP flies several times a day between Funchal and Porto Santo in the Madeira group; on the Azores, flights are operated by SATA *(see p441)*. Flights to Flores and Corvo are often disrupted by bad weather, so for extensive island hopping it is a good idea to insure against delays. SATA flights should be confirmed at least 72 hours before take-off.

Porto Santo Line runs a daily car ferry service between Madeira and Porto Santo. Regular car ferry services connect all the islands of the Azores except Corvo, which is served by passenger ferry, and are run by **Atlanticoline**. It's also possible to explore the waters surrounding Madeira's Ilhas Desertas by boat, then join a guided tour on land. **Madeira Wind Birds** offers day-trips and cruises to Ilha Desertas.

Around Madeira

Companies such as **Intertours** and **Blandy** organize coach trips. Taxis can be hired, but car rental is far more flexible *(see p445)*. Book ahead and allow plenty of time for travel: roads are steep and tortuous. Motorway extensions along the south coast have cut journey times considerably, but many places are still accessible only on foot.

Around the Azores

Cars can be hired on all the Azores except Corvo, from firms such as **Ilha Verde Rent-A-Car**. Charges are reasonable, and the roads are precipitous, so it may be more economical to explore the smaller islands by taxi. For day trips, agree a price, itinerary and return time before setting off. You should also pay for the driver's lunch. Check the weather first: if clouds conceal the mountains, there is no point setting out.

Tourist offices can supply information on coach trips by **Agência Açoreana de Viagens** and others, and on boat trips along the coast. Bicycles can be hired, but the mountainous terrain makes cycling difficult.

DIRECTORY

Madeira

Blandy
Avenida Zarco 2, Funchal.
Tel 291 200 660.
🅦 blandytravel.com

Intertours
Avenida Arriaga 30, Funchal.
Tel 291 208 900.
🅦 intertours.com.pt

Azores

Agência Açoreana de Viagens
Rua de Lisboa, Edifício Varela, Ponta Delgada, São Miguel. **Tel** 296 301 840. 🅦 agenciaacoreanade viagens.pt

Ilha Verde Rent-A-Car
Campo São Francisco 19, Ponta Delgada. **Tel** 296 304 800.
🅦 ilhaverde.com

Ferry Services

Atlanticoline
Tel 707 201 572/296 304 311.
🅦 atlanticoline.pt

Madeira Wind Birds
Tel 917 777 441.
🅦 madeirawindbirds.com

Porto Santo Line
Tel 291 210 300.
🅦 portosantoline.pt

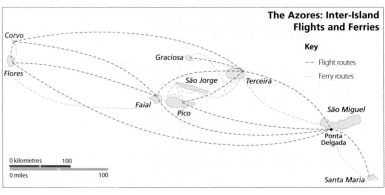

The Azores: Inter-Island Flights and Ferries

Corvo

Flores

Graciosa

São Jorge

Terceira

Faial

Pico

São Miguel

Ponta Delgada

Santa Maria

Key

-- Flight routes

-- Ferry routes

0 kilometres 100

0 miles 100

Travelling in Lisbon and Porto

The interesting parts of most towns and cities in Portugal – generally the *centró histórico* – are small and eminently walkable, if you have both the time and inclination. In hilly cities such as Porto and, particularly, Lisbon, the steep climbs can be avoided by using a choice of options such as centenarian tram, funicular or lift. Other cities are well served by buses, trolleybuses and taxis. Transport of any kind is best avoided during rush hour (8–10am and 5:30–7:30pm).

Buses

Buses are a practical way to travel round and see the main cities, and Lisbon has an extensive network. When boarding the bus, enter at the front door and exit by the central door.

Tickets may be bought from the driver on boarding and must be clipped by the *(obliterador)* machine near the driver. However, it is much cheaper to buy tickets beforehand, usually for two journeys. Travelling without a valid ticket, if discovered by roaming inspectors, will incur a hefty fine.

Every bus *(autocarro)* must display its destination *(destino)* on a sign located at the front and most bus stops *(paragens)* have information for passengers about the route the bus will take.

Bus Tours

In Porto, **Cityrama** runs city tours at least twice a week, and more often in summer. They include a visit to a port lodge with tasting *(see p253)*. Tickets are sold at the Cityrama office, and the tourist office in Praça Dom João I, where the buses depart. Cityrama also operates sightseeing tours in Lisbon, Madeira and the Azores, however, they have no office, but the tourist office can take bookings and enquiries.

Trams and Funiculars

Fun ways of exploring Lisbon are by tram *(eléctrico)*, funicular or lift (both *elevador*). Porto has two short tram routes along and near the waterfront, and a funicular, the Elevador dos Guindais. In Lisbon, **Carris** runs a "hill tour" (Linha das Colinas) by antique tramcar.

Antique red tram operating the Linha do Tejo tour in Lisbon

No.15, Lisbon's long, streamlined tram

A variety of funiculars offer wonderful views over Lisbon and ascend from river level up to the Bairro Alto: the Elevador da Bica starts near Cais do Sodré station and the Elevador da Glória goes from Praça dos Restauradores. The lifts in the Elevador de Santa Justa take visitors to a café at the top of the Bairro Alto *(see p88)*. The Elevador da Lavra, can be taken from Rua das Portas de Santo Antão, which climbs to the Hospital São José.

Lisbon Metro

Lisbon's Metro network has four lines, mainly on the north–south axis, and is divided into zones. It is the most efficient way to get around, especially during rush hour (8–10am and 5:30–7:30pm). The Metro operates between 6:30am and 1am.

Tickets are bought from machines or ticket offices at the station and are sold as reusable Viva Viagem cards. Each card will expire after one year and has an initial cost of €0.50. Cards must be validated on entering the platform area by passing them over an electronic scanner to open

Viva Viagem card

Tickets in Lisbon

Bus, tram, metro and funicular tickets are all the same and can be bought from any Carris kiosk. The basic multitrip Carris ticket is for two journeys and valid for an unlimited number of days. The other option is a ticket valid for 24 hours. The Metro has its own system, and tickets cost €1.45 for one journey on the whole network. There are also passes known as Viva Viagem cards, as well as combined Carris/Metro 1-day tickets for €6.15 (includes €0.50 cost of Viva Viagem card). This card can be recharged at ticket machines.

Lisbon's Elevador da Glória ascending to the Bairro Alto

the gate, indicated by a green light. Exiting the station requires the same procedure.

When purchasing your cards you should always keep the receipt as you may need to present it when changing the card, or if it is damaged. Fines for travelling without a valid card are severe, so make sure it is in a safe and accessible place.

Porto Metro

Porto's Metro network is in fact a light railway system with five lines that extend well beyond the city centre, through several zones. The hub is Trindade station, which is linked to the airport. The Metro operates between 6am and 1am.

Smart tickets (Andante Cards) can be bought from stations and at Andante shops and kiosks for an initial cost of €0.65.

The reusable Andante Gold Card is a straightforward and convenient choice for visitors. In addition to the initial cost of €6, the card can then be charged according to how many zones will be crossed. The Porto Card for 1, 2 or 3 days gives access to the entire public transport network and entrance to many top attractions. Cards are validated by scanning machines.

Taxis

Taxis are relatively inexpensive, and if you share the cost, it sometimes works out cheaper than a bus. A green light indicates that the taxi is available; two green lights mean that the higher rate is being charged (10pm–6am daily, weekends and public holidays), one that the normal rate applies. From behind, the lights glow counter-intuitively red. Occupied taxis have their rooftop "taxi" signs switched on. A flat rate of €1.60 is charged for any luggage placed in the trunk. The starting rate for a taxi hailed in the street or at a taxi

rank is €2.50. A telephone callout from a firm such as **Autocoope** costs an extra €0.80. The meter should always be used, although the driver might agree on a price beforehand for long trips.

DIRECTORY

Bus and Tram Tours

Carris, Lisbon
Rua 1° de Maio 93,
Santo Amaro, Lisbon.
Tel 213 613 000 (9am–5pm Mon–Fri). **W** carris.pt

Radio Taxis

Autocoope (Lisbon)
Tel 217 932 756.
W cooptaxis.pt

Raditáxis (Porto)
Tel 225 073 900.
W raditaxis.pt

Metro

Lisbon call centre
Tel 213 500 115 (Mon–Fri).
W metrolisboa.pt

Porto head office
Tel 225 081 000.
W metrodPorto.pt

Lisbon's Metro System

Key
- Linha azul
- Linha amarela
- Linha verde
- Linha vermelha
- Linha azul extension
- O Interchange station

General Index

Acknowledgments

Dorling Kindersley would like to thank the following people whose contributions and assistance have made the preparation of this book possible.

Consultant
Martin Symington was born and brought up in Portugal. A freelance travel writer, he is the author of *New Essential Portugal* (AA), and has contributed to *Eyewitness Great Britain* and *Eyewitness Seville and Andalusia*. He writes extensively on Portugal and is a regular contributor to the *Daily Telegraph, Sunday Telegraph* and other British national newspapers.

Contributors
Susie Boulton studied history of art at Cambridge. She is a freelance travel writer and author of *Eyewitness Venice and the Veneto*.

Christopher Catling is a freelance travel writer and author of *Madeira* (AA) and *Eyewitness Florence & Tuscany*. He also contributed to *Eyewitness Italy* and *Eyewitness Great Britain*.

Marion Kaplan has written for a wide range of magazines and newspapers. She has lived in Portugal and wrote *The Portuguese* (Viking/Penguin 1992). She also contributed to the *Berlitz Travellers Guide to Portugal*.

Sarah Mcalister is a freelance editor and writer for *Time Out* guides and has spent much time in Lisbon and the surrounding area.

Alice Peebles is a freelance editor and writer and has worked on several *Eyewitness Travel Guides*.

Carol Rankin was born in Portugal. As an art historian, she has lectured extensively on Portuguese art and architecture and has acted as consultant for various cultural projects.

Joe Staines is a freelance writer and co-author of *Exploring Rural Portugal* (Helm).

Robert Strauss is a travel writer and publisher. He worked for the Luso-British Institute in Porto and has written several titles for Lonely Planet and Bradt Publications.

Nigel Tisdall is a freelance journalist who has written many articles on the Azores. He also contributed to *France, Spain* and *California* in the Eyewitness Travel Guide series.

Edite Vieira has written many books on Portuguese food including *The Taste of Portugal* (Grub Street). She is a member of the Guild of Food Writers and broadcasts regularly for the BBC World Service.

Additional Contributors
Dr Giray Ablay, Paul Bernhardt, Julie Dawn Fox, Mihaela Rogalski, Gerry Stanbury, Paul Sterry, Paul Vernon.

Additional Illustrations
Richard Bonson, Chris Forsey, Chris Orr, Mel Pickering, Nicola Rodway.

Revisions Team
Gillian Allan, Douglas Amrine, Emma Anacootee, Gillian Andrews, Avanika, Claire Baranowski, Paul Bernhardt, Uma Bhattacharya, Tessa Bindloss, Julie Bond, Neha Chander, Vivien Crump, Alyse Dar, Surya Deogan, Joy FitzSimmons, Anna Freiberger, Camilla Gersh, Roger Green, Swati Gupta, Mark Harding, Vinod Harish, Mohammad Hassan, Paul Hines, Jasneet Kaur, Zafar ul Islam Khan, Sumita Khatwani, Priya Kukadia, Vincent Kurien, Esther Labi, Kathryn Lane, Michelle de Larrabeiti, Felicity Laughton, Jason Little, Carly Madden, Hayley Maher, Nicola Malone, Helen Markham, Caroline Mead, Rebecca Mills, Robert Mitchell, Adam Moore, Helena Nogueira, David Noonan, Rakesh Kumar Pal, Garima Pandey, Susie Peachey, Alice Peebles, Helen Peters, Marianne Petrou, Adrian Potts, Andrea Powell, Tom Prentice, Rada Radojicic, Mani Ramaswamy, Andrew Ribeiro-Hargreave, Akshay Rana, Lucy Richards, Ellen Root, Azeem Siddiqui, Sands Publishing Solutions, Sadie Smith, Alison Stace, Roseen Teare, Amanda Tomeh, Helen Townsend, Tomas Tranaeus, Vinita Venugopal, Fiona Wild.

Index
Hilary Bird, Helen Peters.

Additional Photography
Paul Bernhardt, Steve Gorton/DK Studio, John Heseltine, Dave King, Martin Norris, Ian O'Leary, Jorge Morgado, Roger Phillips, Rough Guides/Eddie Gerald, Rough Guide/ Natascha Sturny, Clive Streeter, Matthew Ward.

Photographic and Artwork Reference
Steven Evans, Nigel Tisdall.

Special Assistance
Emília Tavares, Arquivo Nacional de Fotografia, Lisboa; Luísa Cardia, Biblioteca Nacional e do Livro, Lisboa; Marina Gonçalves and Aida Pereira, Câmara Municipal de Lisboa; Caminhos de Ferro Portugueses; Carris, Lisboa; Enatur, Lisboa; Karen Ollier-Spry, John E Fells and Sons Ltd; Maria Fátima Moreira, Fundação Bissaya-Barreto, Coimbra; Maria Helena Soares da Costa, Fundação Calouste Gulbenkian, Lisboa; João Campilho, Fundação da Casa de Bragança, Lisboa; Pilar Serras and José Aragão, ICEP, London; Instituto do Vinho de Porto, Porto; Simoneta Afonso, IPM, Lisboa; Mário Abreu, Dulce Ferraz, IPPAR, Lisboa; Pedro Moura Bessa and Eduardo Corte-Real, Livraria Civilização Editora, Porto; Metropolitano de Lisboa; Raquel Florentino and Cristina Leite, Museu da Cidade, Lisboa; João Castel Branco G Pereira, Museu Nacional do Azulejo, Lisboa; Turihab, Ponte de Lima; Ilídio Barbosa, Universidade de Coimbra, Coimbra; Teresa Chicau at the tourist office in Évora, Conceição Estudante at the tourist office in Funchal and the staff at all the other tourist offices and town halls in Portugal.

Photography Permissions
Dorling Kindersley would like to thank the following for their assistance and kind permission to photograph at their

establishments: Instituto Português do Património Arquitectónico e Arqueológico (IPPAR), Lisboa; Fundação da Casa de Alorna, Lisboa; Instituto Português dos Museus (IPM), Lisboa; Museu da Marinha, Lisboa; Museu do Mar, Cascais; Igreja de Santa Maria dos Olivais, Tomar and all the other churches, museums, hotels, restaurants, shops, galleries and sights too numerous to thank individually.

Picture Credits

a = above; b = bottom; c = centre; f = far; l = left; r = right; t = top.

The work illustrated on page 119b, *Terreiro do Paço* by Dirk Stoop, is reproduced by kind permission of the Museu da Cidade, Lisboa.

The publisher would like to thank the following individuals, companies and picture libraries for permission to reproduce their photographs:

123RF.com: Juliane Jacobs 102; Brenda Kean 161tl; Carlos Edgar Soares Neto 331bl; Moura Pereira 175cl.

Maurício Abreu: 151tr, 344bc/br, 367cla, 370cr/bl, 372ca, 374tr/ca/cb, 376t, 377tr, 399b; **Alamy Images:** paul abbitt rml 128cl; age fotostock 169br; The Art Archive 8-9; Art Collection 3 42tr; Jose Atunes 421cr; B.A.E. Inc. 151cr; Buzz Pictures 422cra; Cephas Picture Library/Peter Stowell 418tl; Chronicle 59br; Cro Magnon 200, 294cla; Jean Dominique Dallet 419cla; Paul Gapper 92cl; Goncalo Diniz 128br; Michele Falzone 193tl; John Ferro Sims 1, 417c; Peter Forsberg 152cla; Chris Hellier 43cb; Michael Howard 422bl; Iain Davidson Photographic 295tl; imageBROKER 209tc; Imagebroker/Günter Lenz 424tl, Imagebroker/Martin Moxter 441bl; Marion Kaplan 232bc, 417br; Hideo Kurihara 268; Yahdid Levy 153c, 423tl; Mediacolor's 295cb; PACIFIC PRESS 233c; Panther Media GmbH 151cl, 373c; Photobliss 129tl; 237tl; photolocation 2 155b; PM Photos 405tl; Alex Ramsay 114; Robert Harding Picture Library Ltd 321b; H. Souto 417tl; Stockfolio/Gaboria 418crb; Travel Pictures 37cr; Travelshots.com 153tl; Damien Tully 237cb; Mikael Utterstrom 424br; Ken Walsh 109tl; Ken Welsh 73ca; John Warburton-Lee Photography/Ian Aitken 236cla; David Wingate 447cla; Z1 Collection 42bc; **Aldeia da Fonte Hotel:** 415bl; **Arquivo Nacional De Fotografia-Instituto Português De Museus,** Lisboa: Museu Nacional De Arte Antiga/Pedro Ferreira 100tr, 101t (all); Francisco Matias 53tl; Carlos Monteiro 50cla; Luís Pavão 43tl, 56clb, 57ca, 64tr, 98bl/br, 99bc, 101c; José Pessoa 28bl, 29tr, 49ca, 53cra, 54tr, 55tc/clb, 98tr, 99ca/cr, 100bl, 101br; Museu Nacional Do Azulejo *Painel De Azulejos Composição Geométrica,* 1970, Raul Lino-Fábrica Cerâmica Constância 31tr; Francisco Matias 30b; José Pessoa 30cra/31cb/bl; Colecções Arquivo Nacional De Fotografia/San Payo 43tr; Igreja De São Vicente De Fora/Carlos Monteiro 43bl; Museu Nacional Dos Coches/José Pessoa 43bc, 103bl, 105bl, 150br, 151b (all); Henrique Ruas 106bl; Museu Nacional De Arqueologia/José Pessoa 45ca/cb, 107c; Museu Monográfico De Conimbriga 45tl; Museu De Mértola/Paulo Cintra 46cl; Igreja Matriz Santiago Do Cacém/José Rubio 47tl; José Pessoa 49tl; Biblioteca Da Ajuda/José Pessoa 48cla; Museu De São Roque/Abreu Nunes 51tl; Museu Grão Vasco/José Pessoa 52bl; Universidade De Coimbra, Gabinete De Física/José Pessoa 56tr; Museu De Cerâmica Das Caldas Da Rainha/José Pessoa 58cla; Museu Do Chiado 59tl; Col. Jorge De Brito/José Pessoa 66-7t; Col.

António Chainho/José Pessoa 68bl; Arnaldo Soares 68tr, 69tl; Museu Nacional Do Teatro/Arnaldo Soares 68cl; Luisa Oliveira 69tr; Museu De Évora/José Pessoa 309cra; 42c, 48bl, *Portrait Of Fernando Pessoa* by Almada Negreiros © DACS 2011 60ca, 61br, 66-7c.

Barrio Alto Hotel: 387tl; **Jorge Barros S.p.a.:** 232cr; **Instituto Da Biblioteca Nacional E Do Livro,** Lisboa: 41b, 50cb/bc, 51crb, 54cb, 55br, 57br, 171bl, 189br; **Bistro 100 Maneiras:** Constantino Leite 400br; **Gabriele Boiselle:** 150bl; **Boutinot Prince Wine Shippers,** Stockport: 234br; By Permission of **The British Library, London:** *João I of Portugal Being Entertained by John of Gaunt* (D), From De Wavrin's *Chronicle D'Angleterre* (Roy 14E lv 244V) 50–1c; © **Trustees Of The British Museum, London:** 47cla, 52br, 58clb.

Câmara Municipal De Lisboa: 55crb, António Rafael 66cl; **Câmara Municipal De Oeiras:** 56clb; **Caminhos De Ferro Portugueses:** 442c; **Casa Da Comida:** 397br; **Casa do Campo de Molares:** 392tc; **Casa da Pergola:** 383tr; **Centro De Arte Moderna:** José Manuel Costa Alves 122tl; **Centro Europeu Jean Monnet:** 61tl; **Cephas:** Mick Rock 32crb; **Cockburn Smithes & Cia, S.A.** (An Allied Domecq Company): 234crb; **Cor De Tangerina:** 409bl; **Corbis:** Tony Arruza 36c; Atlantide Phototravel/Stefano Amantini 288-9; Marco Cristofari 420cla; Richard Cummins 84clb; JAI/Mauricio Abreu 15br; Jose Fuste Raga 320; Reuters/Mike Finn-Kelcey 61cra; Robert Harding World Imagery/Stuart Forster 70; Hans Georg Roth 338-9; Sylvain Sonnet 78-9; Peter Wilson 242bl; **CTT,** Correios: 439c.

Diário De Notícias: 59cla; **Michael Diggin:** 340bl, 365b, 366bl, 367cra, 371t, 375cra; Dow's Port 235cr; **Dorling Kindersley:** Rob Reichenfeld 31br; Tony Souter 92bc; Linda Whitwam 30cla; 30clb, 30cb; Peter Wilson 31cr; **Dreamstime.com:** Steve Allen 353bc; Anitasstudio 22t, 34clb; Helena Bilková 445tr; Yuriy Brykaylo 292tr; Olena Buyskykh 367bl; Chrupka 72tr; Wessel Cirkel 27ca; Daniel M. Cisilino 59cr; Jacek Cudak 192bc; Henner Damke 90, 369tl; Devy 327b; Dinozzaver 2-3; Drimi 17bc; Peter Etchells 293bl; Europhotos 4crb; Armando Frazão 297b; G0r3cki 24t; William Giannelli 82; Iliuta Goean 335br; Goncaloferreira 116b; José Goulão 73tl; Gvictoria 17tr, 104bc; Hieronymusukkel 20; Iralis 146-7; Inge Hogenbijl 25t; Juliane Jacobs 154; Wieslaw Jarek 35tr; Wangkun Jia 131tl; Jorisvo 210cl; Joyfull 37t; Keantian 343crb; Sergey Kelin 64cl; Denis Kelly 65bl; Kvintet 343bl; Brian Lasenby 335crb; Martin Lehmann 23b, 85br, 104tr; Peter Lovás 73bc, 440crb; Lsantilli 182-3; Luisafonso 364; Dariusz Majgier 64br; Rui Matos 22bl; Mikelane45 175br; Miragik 342br; Moedas1 293c; Carol R Montoya 342crb; Naturefriend 342bl; Neirfy 25bl; Orxystock 358–9; Photogolfer 427tl; Inacio Pires 10c, 16br, 314-5; Rui Pires 228-9; Pp1 342clb; Pstedrak 343cb (1); Luca Quadrio 377bl; Vítor Ribeiro 14br, 246cl, 274-5; Stewart Rigby 435ca; Mauro Rodrigues 37br; Saiko3p 206b, 245br, 246br, 249cr, 428-429, 431br; Sam74100 96b; Rui G. Santos 435c; Miyuki Satake 342bc; Schlenger86 89br; Richard Semik 5tc, 296; Luis Lopes Silva 325cr; Sohadiszno 93crb; Jose I. Soto 176; TasFoto 243tl, 245cr; Anibal Trejo 340cr, 370cr; Ferenc Ungor 117tl; Vallefrias 177; Vanessak 346; Véronique Lestoy 356bl; Whiskybottle 343cb; Xantana 243br, 250-251, Zhykharievavlada 126tr, Zts 31cl, 130br, 247br.

Espaço Talassa: Gerard Soury 374bl; **ET Archive:** Naval Museum, Genoa 363br; Wellington Museum 199bc; **European**

Commission: 437; Greg Evans International: Greg Balfour Evans 293br; Mary Evans Picture Library: 55bl, 67tr, 167bl, 217br; Expo '98: 61ca.

Fotolia: Carson Liu 14tr; ruigsantos 11tr; Mario Savoia 13tl; Jose Ignacio Soto 62-3; Fototeca Internacional, Lisboa: Luís Elvas 37cl, 150tr/cr; César Soares 421tl; Luíz O Franquinho/António Da Costa: 343clb; Fundaçao Da Casa De Bragança: 304t/c/b, 305bl; Fundaçao Da Casa De Mateus: Nicholas Sapieha 260b; Fundação Ricardo Do Espírito Santo Silva, Museu-Escola De Artes Decorativas Portuguesas: 74c.

Jorge Galvaõ: 61clb; Geadas Restaurant: 406br; Gerry and Manuela Breen's Algarve Airsports Centre: 423br; Getty Images: AFP/Francisco Leong 434bc; Allsport: Mike Powell 61crb; Paulo Amorim 261br; DEA / G. DAGLI ORTI 43tl, 50clb, 108br; DEA / S. VANNINI 167tl; Pedro Gomes 130cr; John Harper 185tl; Richard Heathcote 427c; Lonely Planet Images/Holger Leue 353cl; Print Collector 47bl; STRINGER / Stringer 60br; Giraudon: 52cla; Warren Little 36tl; Guarda Nacional Republicana: 434br.

Robert Harding Picture Library: 21b; Jose Antonio Moreno 87bl; Herdade da Retorta: 393br; Hotel Britania: 386bl; Hotel Convento de Sao Paulo: 411tl; Hotel Do Chiado: 382bl; Hotel Lusitano: 389tr; Kit Houghton: 36b.

Images Colour Library: 232bc; IMAGES OF PORTUGAL: 426cl; iStockphoto.com: zulufriend 421tl; José Maria da Fonseca – Vinhos SA: 32tr; Marion Kaplan: 150cla, 233tr/cr; Laurentina Restaurante: 401bc; Lusa: António Cotrim 69ca; André Kosters 95tl; Manuel Moura 60cb, 363tl; Luís Vasconcelos 94br.

José Manuel: 67br; António Marques: 302clb, 303b; Metropolitano De Lisboa: 448cr; John Miller: 29b; Museu Calouste Gulbenkian, Lisboa: Enamelled Silver Gilt Corsage Ornament, René Lalique © ADAGP, Paris and DACS, London 2011 118ca, 118tr/cb/b, 119tl/ca/cb/bl, 120tr/c/bl, 121tr/clb/br; Museu Da Cidade, Lisboa: António Rafael 66bl/br; 67cr/bl; Museu Da Marinha, Lisboa: 42br, 60cl, 110b.

National Maritime Museum, London: 54cla; Nationalmuseet, Copenhagen: 52tr; Naturepress: Juan Hidalgo-Candy Lopesino 36tl; NHPA: Michael Leach 375crb; Jean-Louis Le Moigne 335cr.

Oceanario De Lisboa: Mafalda Frade 12br; Oporto Golf Club: 426br; Orient-Express Services Ltd: 381b, 395tl.

Palácio Nacional de Sintra: PSML_MJS 166clb; PSML_Wilson_ Pereira 171tl, 171br; PSML-AngeloHornak 165tl; Palacio De

Pena: 166cla; Palacio Estoril Hotel Golf & Spa: 380cr, 388br; Fotografia Cedida Y Autorizada Por El Patrimonio Nacional: 46cb; Pictures Colour Library: 416cl; Porto Santo Golfe: Filipe Pacheco 427cr; Pousadas De Portugal/Grupo Pestana: 384–5 all, 396cla, 401tl, 402t, 404bl, 406tl, 409tr, 410b, 413br, 415tc; PraiaGolfe Hotel: 391br.

Radio Televisão Portuguesa (RTP): 58tr, 59clb, 60tr; RCL, Parede: Rui Cunha 35cl, 131t, 342cr, 343cr, 345cra, 371c, 372br, 383; Dias Dos Reis: 123tl; Norman Renouf: 380bl, 385b; Relais & Chateaux: 399tr; Restaurant Camafeu: 407tr; Reuters: Marcos Borga 420br; Rex Features: Sipa Press/Michel Ginies 61bl; Manuel Ribeiro: 30t; Riso Restaurant: 397tl, 414tr; Rodonorte: 446cla.

Harry Smith Horticultural Photographic Collection: 343cla; Solar do Vinho do Porto: 258b; Spectrum Colour Library: 242tr; Tony Stone Images: Tony Arruza 34ca; Shaun Egan 292b; Graham Finlayson 45crb; Simeone Huber 290bl; John Lawrence 35br; Ulli Seer 323tl; SuperStock: Album / Oronoz / Album 46-47c; age fotostock/André Gonçalves 16tr, /Igor Gonzalo Sanz 378-9, /João Almeida 238; Design Pics 331tr; Prisma/Pepper 15tl; Symington Port and Madeira Shippers: Claudio Capone 33cl, 235t/cla/bc.

TAP Air Portugal:441tr; Tia Alice Restaurant: 403br; Nigel Tisdall: 345tl, 368, 369crb, 370tl, 373tl/br, 376c/b; Topham Picture Source: 60cra; Arquivos Nacionais/Torre Do Tombo: 40, 48clb, 273bl; Turihab: Roger Day 382tl.

Uva Restaurant at Hotel The Vine: 414bl; Veneza Restauarant: 412tl; Villa Joya/XN Brand Dynamics: 396bl; Vintage Lofts: 390tl; Peter Wilson: 34br, 35tr, 60bl, 86tl, 95tl, 232tr/cl; Wyse Travel Confederation: 432b; The Yeatman Restaurant: 408tl.

Jacket
Front and Spine – AWL Images: Sabine Lubenow; Back – Dreamstime.com: Sean Pavone.

Front Endpaper: Juliane Jacobs lcr; Alamy Images: Cro Magnon rcr; Hideo Kurihara ltr; Wilmar Photography lcr; Corbis: Jose Fuste Raga rbr; Robert Harding World Imagery/ Stuart Forster lbr; Dreamstime.com: Luisafonso lc; Richard Semik rbc.; Jose I. Soto rc; Vanessak lcl; SuperStock: age fotostock/João Almeida Rtr.

All other images © Dorling Kindersley. For further information see www.DKimages.com.